HUMAN RESOURCE
DEVELOPMENT

Sara Miller McCune founded SAGE Publishing in 1965 to support the dissemination of usable knowledge and educate a global community. SAGE publishes more than 1000 journals and over 800 new books each year, spanning a wide range of subject areas. Our growing selection of library products includes archives, data, case studies and video. SAGE remains majority owned by our founder and after her lifetime will become owned by a charitable trust that secures the company's continued independence.

Los Angeles | London | New Delhi | Singapore | Washington DC | Melbourne

EUGENE SADLER-SMITH

HUMAN RESOURCE DEVELOPMENT

FROM THEORY INTO PRACTICE

Los Angeles | London | New Delhi
Singapore | Washington DC | Melbourne

Los Angeles | London | New Delhi
Singapore | Washington DC | Melbourne

SAGE Publications Ltd
1 Oliver's Yard
55 City Road
London EC1Y 1SP

SAGE Publications Inc.
2455 Teller Road
Thousand Oaks, California 91320

SAGE Publications India Pvt Ltd
B 1/I 1 Mohan Cooperative Industrial Area
Mathura Road
New Delhi 110 044

SAGE Publications Asia-Pacific Pte Ltd
3 Church Street
#10-04 Samsung Hub
Singapore 049483

Editor: Ruth Stitt
Assistant editor: Jessica Moran
Production editor: Martin Fox
Copyeditor: Martin Noble
Proofreader: Christine Bitten
Indexer: Elske Janssen
Marketing manager: Lucia Sweet
Cover design: Naomi Robinson
Typeset by: C&M Digitals (P) Ltd, Chennai, India

Library of Congress Control Number: 2021935491

British Library Cataloguing in Publication data

A catalogue record for this book is available from the British Library

ISBN 978-1-5297-3213-9
ISBN 978-1-5297-3212-2 (pbk)

CONTENTS

EXTENDED CONTENTS

ABOUT THE AUTHOR

Professor Eugene Sadler-Smith, BSc, PhD, FCIPD, FRSA, FAcSS is Professor of Organizational Behaviour, Surrey Business School, University of Surrey, UK. His main research interests are hubris (in leadership) and intuition (in organizational decision-making). His work has been published in international peer-reviewed journals, such as *Academy of Management Executive, Academy of Management Learning and Education, Academy of Management Perspectives, British Journal of Management, British Journal of Psychology, British Journal of Educational Psychology, Business Ethics Quarterly, Creativity Research Journal, Human Relations, International Journal of Management Reviews, Journal of Occupational & Organizational Psychology, Leadership, Journal of Organizational Behaviour, Long Range Planning, Management Learning, Organization Studies, Organizational Dynamics, Organizational Research Methods, Strategic Entrepreneurship Journal*, etc., and professional journals, such as *People Management* and *Work*. His research has featured in *The Times* as well as on BBC Radio 4 and Insight TV's *Secrets of the Brain*. He is the author of several books including *Learning and Development for Managers* (Blackwell, 2006), *Inside Intuition* (Routledge, 2008), *The Intuitive Mind* (John Wiley & Sons, 2010, shortlisted for CMI Management Book of the Year in 2011, published in four foreign language editions – Japanese, Korean, Portuguese, Russian) and *Hubristic Leadership* (SAGE, 2019, and also published in Korean). He has worked with organizations such as AcademiWales, CIPD, *Forbes* (Korea), Home Office, ICSA, Medact, Metropolitan Police, Surrey Police, Scottish Government, Tesco, The Mind Gym, etc. He was educated at Wade Deacon Grammar School for Boys in Widnes, has a BSc in geography from the University of Leeds and a PhD from the University of Birmingham. Before becoming an academic he worked in HRD for British Gas plc from 1987 to 1994 during which time he completed his PhD on a part-time basis (1988–1992).

PREFACE

Introduction

Welcome to *Human Resource Development: From Theory into Practice*. HRD is a multidisciplinary, applied body of academic knowledge and an important area of professional practice in human resource management, occupational and organizational psychology, organization development (OD), leadership development, coaching and mentoring, e-learning, consulting practice, general management, and related areas. HRD seeks to help employees to acquire the knowledge and skills required so that they can achieve their full potential and their organization can achieve its strategic goals in ways that maximize stakeholder value, respect justice and fairness, and maintain the integrity of the natural environment.

This book explores how. It does so by offering readers a comprehensive and detailed introduction to HRD that is theory-based, evidence-driven and practically oriented. The ethos of the book is the author's firm belief that learning is one of the most important sources, if not *the* most important source of competitive advantage, resilience and sustainability for organizations in the twenty-first century. If organizations are to survive and thrive in volatile, uncertain, complex and ambiguous environments then they and their employees need to increase their capacity for effective action through learning,[1] and they need to do so with meaning and purpose in ways that both transform and transcend the self.

Structure and content

Physicists study the universe both at the grand scale of planets, solar systems and galaxies and the minute scale of atoms and sub-atomic particles. Economists study both how the overall economy works in terms of bigger-picture macroeconomics as well as how individual markets function at the smaller microeconomic scale.[2] Likewise, HRD can be studied at different levels by zooming-out to look at the bigger picture and zooming-in to look at the fine detail. This book splits the field of HRD into two sub-fields:

- 'Micro-HRD', which is concerned mostly with the detailed study of the micro-processes of learning and development in organizations at the individual and group levels; as such it seeks to give readers tools that will help them to describe and explain, as well as make predictions about the efficacy of, learning and development in organizations using concepts, models and theories from the behavioural sciences and related scientific disciplines;

- 'Macro-HRD', which is concerned mostly with the describing, analysing and making predictions about learning and development in organizations at the operational, strategic and organizational levels and in relation to broader contextual factors at the national, international and global levels using concepts, models and theories from economics, systems theory, strategy, organizational learning, organizational knowledge, etc.

The book's two parts are 'Micro-HRD' (Chapters 1–7) and 'Macro-HRD' (Chapters 8–14) as listed below.

Micro-HRD is covered in the following chapters:

- Chapter 1, 'Setting the scene for HRD': this chapter covers the history, identity and purposes of HRD;
- Chapter 2, 'Inside the black box': this chapter explores behaviourist and cognitive theories of learning;
- Chapter 3, 'Learning from and with others': this chapter covers social and situated theories of learning;
- Chapter 4, 'Experience-based modalities of learning': this chapter discusses experiential learning theory, action learning and andragogy;
- Chapter 5, 'Neurolearning and HRD': this chapter explores implications of neuroscience and learning and development in organizations;
- Chapter 6, 'Formal and informal learning': this chapter compares and contrasts formal methods such as training with informal and incidental learning processes;
- Chapter 7, 'Maximizing employees potential': this chapter looks at coaching, mentoring, career and talent development and leader development.

Macro-HRD is covered in the following chapters:

- Chapter 8, 'The bigger picture': this chapter looks at HRD's macro environment in terms of megatrends and grand challenges;
- Chapter 9, 'HRD as a strategic partner': this chapter covers the relationships between HRD and strategy and strategic human resource management, and strategic HRD (SHRD);
- Chapter 10, 'The HRD system': this chapter covers systematic and systemic approaches to HRD and the related idea of a 'learning ecosystem';
- Chapter 11, 'Hybrid HRD': this chapter explores how HRD methods, including digital and e-learning, can be blended to produce the optimum mix;
- Chapter 12, 'Does HRD cost or pay?': this chapter discusses methods for evaluating HRD's 'bottom line' contribution;

- Chapter 13, 'The only sustainable source of competitive advantage': this chapter discusses theories of organizational learning;
- Chapter 14, 'Knowledge and the new learning organization': this chapter discusses theories and models of organizational knowledge and the learning organization.

The book's content is aligned with the CIPD Professional Standards and the CIPD's Level 7 Advanced Diploma in Strategic Learning and Development. This book will support you in developing the necessary specialist knowledge, expertise and skills that can be applied in learning and development practice so as to make a positive impact and add value for organizations and their stakeholders. The book will help you to do this through the application of concepts, models and theories from the behavioural sciences and related fields and by the use of systematic and systemic approaches to drive individual and organizational performance and maximize employees' potential.[3]

Pedagogical and support features

The book uses various pedagogical and support features that make it suitable both for self-study and classroom-based study:

- 'Chapter check-in': these are the objectives for each chapter and state what readers should be able to do on completion of the chapter;
- 'Research insight': these are short summaries of relevant research (including systematic reviews and meta-analyses) from scientific fields related to HRD as well as from HRD research itself. They build on and illustrate key points in the adjoining text;
- 'Perspectives from practice': these are short vignettes, case studies, examples, etc. from the professional practice of HRD; they illustrate how relevant concepts, models and theories apply to the world of learning and development in organizations;
- 'In their own words': these are commentaries and quotations from seminal figures whose work is foundational to HRD research and practice;
- 'Reflective questions': these are interactive devices to enable readers to consider and critically evaluate issues raised in the text (for example as a 'what would you say to...?' based on the principle of 'devils' advocacy'). They are intended both for self-study use and as a basis for classroom debate and discussion;
- 'Delve deeper': this is additional content in the form of journal articles, chapters, books, websites, etc., that has been collated and curated to enable readers to explore specific topics in greater depth;
- 'Chapter checkout': numbered list of key concepts to be used as self-checks of knowledge and understanding;

- 'Skills development': each chapter ends with an exercise, usually based on a specific business skill (such as creating a PowerPoint presentation, designing a job aid, writing an email response to a boss, etc.), which enables readers to apply the knowledge and skill to a specific work-related problem or task. These skills development exercises are designed both for self-study and for use as group or individual activities in classrooms.

It is the author's intention and anticipation that by studying the contents of this book its readers will be equipped with the professional knowledge and skills that will enable them to plan, implement and evaluate learning and development processes in organizations in ways that create value, meaning and purpose in people's working lives, based on the conviction that learning is at the heart of organization.[4]

ONLINE RESOURCES

Visit https://study.sagepub.com/sadlersmith to access the following lecturer resources to support teaching:

For lecturers

- A **Teaching Guide** providing tutor's notes and answers to key questions in the book.
- **PowerPoint slides** accompany each chapter that can be downloaded and edited to suit your own teaching needs.

PART I
MICRO-HRD

1

SETTING THE SCENE FOR HUMAN RESOURCE DEVELOPMENT (HRD)

Contents

On completion of this chapter you should be able to:

- Define human resource development (HRD);
- Explain the origins, development, identity and purposes of HRD;
- Explain the significance and role of theory, research philosophy and ethics in HRD;
- Critically evaluate the purposes of HRD.

Introduction

Human resource development (HRD) is an 'area of professional practice and an inter-disciplinary body of academic knowledge'[1] that seeks to empower and enable individuals to achieve their full potential and organizations to achieve their strategic goals. History matters, and it's believed widely that the term 'human resource development'[2] was first proposed in 1964 by two labour economists, Frederick Harbison and Charles A. Myers in their book *Education, Manpower and Economic Growth: Strategies for Human Resource Development*. Their research was based on the economic concept of 'capital' taken from the writings of the Scottish Enlightenment philosopher Adam Smith (1723–1790) and the related concept of 'human capital' which achieved prominence in the work of the Nobel Prize laureate Gary Becker, author of *Human Capital* (1964):

- Capital: wealth in the form of money or other assets owned by an organization;[3]
- Human capital: stock of knowledge and skills that a workforce possesses and is regarded as a resource or asset.

Harbison and Myers' research wasn't focused on human resource development (HRD) as we know it. They studied education's role in economic development and ways of integrating 'human capital formation' into general economic development and planning in 75 different countries. However, the conclusions they arrived at in the early 1960s are still relevant and resonant in the twenty-first century. They said (their words are shown in 'single quotation' marks):

- Economic growth is often diminished by shortages of human resources, particularly of 'high-level' human resources, such as managers, engineers, scientists, technicians, supervisors, and skilled workers (what might be referred to in today's knowledge economy as a shortage of knowledge workers);
- Formal education is only one way to develop 'high-level human resources'; such resources also can be developed, 'as every personnel manager knows', on-the-job through 'adult education', 're-training' and 'incentives for self-development' (what we might, as you will discover in later chapters, refer to today as informal and incidental learning, hybrid learning, 70:20:10 learning, etc.);

- Continual re-training will be necessary for skilled workers and professionals, and mid-career training will become more common because the idea that a job or a profession will last unchanged for a lifetime is fast-disappearing (what we might refer to as experiential learning, on-job learning, lifelong learning, retraining and reskilling, lifelong employability[4], etc. as a result of demographic, technical and structural changes in the economy);
- Every organization should have its own strategy of human resource development, and that developing such a strategy is one of the central tasks of effective 'personnel administration' (what we might refer to as strategic human resource management, strategic HRD, talent development, etc.) (p. 69).[5]

In Harbison and Myers' view, classical economics had developed a 'tunnel vision' for Gross National Product (GNP) as the only worthwhile measure of the wealth of a nation. They proposed an alternative view: the development of 'human resources as the wealth of nations'. Harbison and Myers' critique of 1960s economic orthodoxy has a very familiar ring and highlights the importance of current 'who-where-how-when-why' questions of contemporary HRD, Figure 1.1.

Who?

- HRD emphasizes the importance of learning and development for all employees in order that they can realize their potential and add value to the organization and wider society

Where and how?

- Learning takes place through informal and incidental learning as well as formal and intentional learning; also online/offline, face-to-face/distant, synchronous/asynchronous, etc.

When?

- Learning and development isn't a one-off, it's a lifelong project; in a 'digitized' world learning is available on-demand and 'always-on'

Why?

- Organizations need to be strategic in developing their human resources in order to deliver value for their stakeholders (not just shareholders)

Figure 1.1 Some 'who-where-how-when-why' questions of contemporary HRD

There is a saying that 'history doesn't repeat itself, but it often rhymes', attributed to the nineteenth century American author Mark Twain. Harbison and Myers' study (1964) represents the beginning of the history, and heritage, of HRD as we know it. Subsequently, the mantra 'people are our most important asset' has become one of the management orthodoxies of our time. Harbison and Myers' work is prescient and it resonates strongly with on-going and current challenges that managers in general face and that HR practitioners in particular must respond to as a result of 'mega-trends' such as globalization, digitization and demographic change.

Adam Smith, the originator of 'human capital'; Frederick Harbison, an originator of 'human resource development'

As noted above, even though the history of HRD is generally agreed to have begun in the 1960s, its 'ancient history' dates back to Adam Smith, as exemplified in this quote from Smith's *An Inquiry into the Nature and Causes of the Wealth of Nations, Book 2* (1776) on the nature of 'human capital':

The acquired useful abilities of all the inhabitants or members of society. The acquisition of such talents, by the maintenance of the acquirer during his [her] education, study, or apprenticeship, always costs a real expense, which is capital fixed and realized, as it were, in his person. Those talents, as they make a part of his fortune, so do they likewise of the society to which he belongs.

The HRD-relevance and implications of Smith's point, especially in the knowledge economy and information age, are that:

- Capital in the form of knowledge and skill is both 'embrained' in the heads and 'embodied' in the hands of employees;
- The creation and maintenance of such capital is both a cost and an opportunity which ideally should, in the longer term, pay-off both for the individual and the organization.

Frederick Harbison described human resources as 'the energies, skills, and knowledge of people which are, or which potentially can or should be, applied to the production of goods or the rendering of services'. And, although he was discussing economic development, his comments resonate with the aims of HRD, namely that one way of expressing the 'wealth' of an organization is in terms of the 'level of development and the effectiveness of utilisation of human energies, skills, and knowledge for useful purposes' (p. 426). Read Harbison's critique of the economic orthodoxy of the 1960s and his plea for human resource development as an alternative to GNP in: Harbison, F. H. (1964). Human resources as the wealth of nations. *Proceedings of the American Philosophical Society, 115*(6), 426–431.

The human capital view can be criticized for taking an 'instrumental' (ends-focused, treating people as a means to an end rather than as ends in themselves), 'functional' (serving a tightly defined purpose), 'managerialist' (privileging managerial aims and values), and short-term perspective (for example in 'maximizing shareholder value', MSV). Critics have argued that a more 'humanistic' approach entails HRD practitioners and academics having the 'the courage to challenge existing assumptions about the scope and purpose of HRD' so that the field might 'enable individuals and organizations to flourish in more equitable, responsible and sustainable ways'.[9] But this critique itself is not unproblematic since 'humanistic' approaches may be incompatible with the realities of organizational life, and demands to deliver shareholder value that may conflict with other stakeholder values where budgets are tight and when economic and market-based approaches are embedded structurally.[10] As you'll discover in later chapters of this book, human capital theory is one of the building blocks of HRD but it's also a contested idea, especially in 'critical HRD' (CHRD) circles.

Reflective question 1.1

To what extent do you agree with the assertion that a 'humanistic' approach in HRD is incompatible with the realities of organizational life if, as some people might argue, employees' prime responsibility is to deliver shareholder value?

Growth and consolidation of HRD

Shortly after Harbison and Myers' work, the growth of HRD as we now know it began to gather pace in the late 1960s, for example in the foundational work of a number of HRD pioneers including Leonard Nadler (1922–2017) at George Washington University (GWU), author of the seminal book *Developing Human Resources* (1970). HRD gained traction and established its existence and identity through the 1970s and 1980s, with the establishment of the American Society for Training and Development (ASTD, now the Association for Talent Development or ATD), and the Institute for Training and Development (ITD), which was the UK's professional body for trainers and developers (later incorporated into the Chartered Institute of Personnel and Development, CIPD). The 1990s saw the establishment of the Academy for Human Resource Development (AHRD) and the publication of several new academic journals in the field (see below). The term gained in popularity in terms of the number of academic journal articles published on the topic over this period as shown in Figure 1.2.

Newcomers to the field of HRD are sometimes perplexed by the different terminologies such as 'training and development', 'employee development', 'learning and development', 'talent development', etc. They are all linked together by the three cornerstone terms 'education', 'training' and 'development' (as summarized in Figure 1.3 from the work of Thomas Garavan). Underpinning them all is the concept of 'learning' which is taken to be the acquisition of knowledge, skills or attitudes (KSAs) through study or experience.

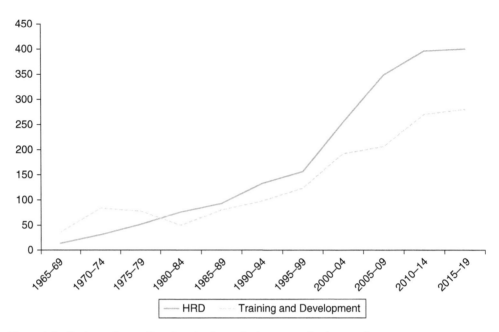

Figure 1.2 Business Source Complete database citation counts for the term 'human resource development' or 'HRD' in the title of peer reviewed journal articles from 1965 to 2019, with 'training and development' for comparison purposes

Domain	Training	Development	Education
Learning in order to...	Perform job/task	Maximize/job career potential	Live happy, responsible. successful life
Focus is on...	Task/Job	Job/Career	Career/Life
Timescale is over..	Shorter term	Medium term	Longer term
Payback is...	Immediate	Career-long	Lifelong

Figure 1.3 Relationships between the domains of education, development and training

Not unsurprisingly, different HRD researchers have offered their own definitions of 'human resource development'. The outcome is that there are many different definitions of HRD. For example, as far back as 1998 one review identified 18 different definitions, and since that time it's unlikely that the number of definitions has reduced. For the purposes of this book the practice of HRD is defined as:

> The practice of human resource development (HRD) is the management of individual and collective learning and development processes in organizations in such a way as to enable individual employees to achieve their full potential and organizations to achieve their strategic goals in ways that maximize stakeholder value, respect justice and fairness, and maintain the integrity of the natural environment.

'Management' in this definition does not indicate a managerialist agenda, instead it is intended to capture the processes of planning, organizing, administrating, and evaluating learning and development in organizations. Alternative definitions of HRD, including Monica Lee's refusal to define it, are presented in Figure 1.4.

Nadler and Wiggs (1986: 5)

- HRD is a comprehensive learning system for the release of the organization's human potentials – a system that includes both vicarious (classroom, mediated, simulated) learning experiences and experiential, on-the-job experiences that are keyed to the organization's reason for survival.

Chalofsky (1992: 179)

- HRD is the study and practice of increasing the learning capacity of individuals, groups, collectives and organizations through the development and application of learning-based interventions for the purpose of optimizing human and organizational growth and effectiveness.

McClean and McLean (2001)

- Any process or activity that, either initially or over the long-term, has the potential to develop adult's work-based knowledge, expertise productivity and satisfaction, whether for personal or group/team gain or for the benefit of an organizational community, a nation or ultimately the whole of humanity.

Swanson (2001: 304)

- A process of developing and/or unleashing human expertise through organizational development (OD) and personnel training and development (T&D) for the purposes of improving performance.

Lee (2004: 38)

- I will not define HRD because it is indefinable, and to attempt to define it is only to serve [the] political or social needs of the minute, [and] to give the appearance of being in control.

Figure 1.4 Selected definitions of human resource development (HRD) in chronological sequence

Sources: Nadler, L., & Wiggs, G. D. (1986). *Managing human resource development*. San Francisco: Jossey-Bass; Chalofsky, N. (1992). A unifying definition for human resource development. *Human Resource Development Quarterly*, 3(2), 175–182; McLean, G. N., & McLean, L. (2001). If we can't define HRD in one country, how can we define it in an international context? *Human Resource Development International*, 4(3), 313–326; Swanson, R. A. (2001). Human resource development and its underlying theory. *Human Resource Development International*, 4(3), 299–312; Lee, M. (2001). A refusal to define HRD. *Human Resource Development International*, 4(3), 327–341.

This book's definition of HRD is a definition of the *practice* of HRD, which is assumed to be a proactive process even when this entails, for example, informal and incidental learning (since these need to be recognized, understood and managed if they're to be efficient and effective). It's not a definition of HRD as an area of academic inquiry, a discipline, or as a field of research.

So much for history and definitions; HRD is an area of practice and an applied field, so what does it look like 'in practice' and 'in action'?

Perspective from practice 1.1

How do 'Googlers' learn?

Google is a US multinational technology company founded in 1998 by Larry Page and Sergey Brin while they were PhD students at Stanford University in California. Google's products include Google Search, Google Images, Google Books, Google Scholar and YouTube. It's headquartered in Mountain View, California, at the time of writing had over 100,000 employees, and its revenue in 2019 was $162 billion. Google is a knowledge-based company and therefore learning and development is vital to its success. Learning by Google employees ('Googlers') is driven by a number of principles or 'learning beliefs' which inform how the business designs and delivers learning[11]:

- Learning is an on-going process, not a one-off event;
- Learning requires motivation, practice and feedback;
- Learning happens in real life, on-the-job and every day;
- Learning should accommodate personal preferences about how, when and what is learned;
- Learning is a social process involving other people, communities and networks.

HRD at Google is a good example of how far learning and development has evolved from traditional training and development (T&D) models. Even though Google still uses external learning and development providers and some internal HRD professionals to deliver 'classes', it does so only where it's appropriate, for example in highly specialized topics and executive development. In fact, 'formal learning' is used quite sparingly at Google. Google estimates that 80 per cent of all learning and development is run through an employee-to-employee network called 'g2g' (Googler-to-Googler). g2g is a 6000-strong volunteer network of learning facilitators (g2g'ers) who dedicate a portion of their time to helping other Googlers learn and develop. The g2g'ers participate in a wide range of learning and development delivery methods including teaching 'courses', providing 1:1 mentoring, and designing and curating learning materials. Topics that are covered include general professional soft skills such as negotiating and leadership, as well as role-related technical skills such as sales training and high-level programming language coding. For example, when mobile computing on smartphones took off, a large number of Googlers went through an Android training bootcamp which was delivered by the Googlers who worked on the Android system itself.

Google is keen to stress that this approach isn't about 'doing more with less' or having HRD delivered 'on-the-cheap' by resentful employee 'teachers' to employees who are forced to participate. Instead two key ingredients in the success of g2g learning are that it's voluntary on both sides and it's embedded in a 'learning culture'.[12]

─Reflective question 1.2─

Analyse Google's approach to HRD in terms of the 'who, where, how, when and whys' of HRD as discussed above.

HRD's identity

Like any relatively new field of study, HRD is faced with questions of intellectual identity, legitimacy and status. The sorts of questions that have arisen include those listed below. Provisional answers are given in brackets but it's by no means an exhaustive list, and needless to say the answers are contestable:

- Is there a single over-arching 'theory of HRD'? (short answer, 'No');
- Is HRD an 'applied field'? ('Yes');
- Can HRD claim to be an academic 'discipline'? ('Debatable');
- How does HRD relate to other substantive academic disciplines such as psychology and economics, or more recently neuroscience? ('It applies and further develops its own theories from them');
- Where does HRD sit in relation to human resource management (HRM)? ('They're very close relatives').

Geography, like history, matters. In the USA, unlike in the UK (see below), HRD has strong links to adult education and vocational education as well as business management,[13] and several American scholars working in this area have used adult education and instructional design theories (for example, Malcolm Knowles' theory of adult learning, also known as 'andragogy', see Chapter 4).[14] The ground-breaking work referred to earlier that established HRD in the US took place at a number of pioneering institutions including George Washington University (led by Leonard Nadler) and Bowling Green State University (for example, by Richard Swanson and others). In Europe, especially the UK and Ireland, the emergence of HRD was associated with the rise of human resource management (HRM) and strategic HRM in the 1980s and 1990s, with fewer if any explicit ties to the field of education or adult education in comparison with the US. In the UK and Ireland HRD tends to be located in business schools and is typically affiliated to departments of human resource management, linked to sub-fields of management such as organizational behaviour (OB) and organizational studies, and with strong ties to professional training and accreditation programmes such as that of the Chartered Institute of Personnel and Development (CIPD).

Research insight 1.1

Management and HRD as 'design sciences'

HRD is a practical subject and a multidisciplinary applied field which seeks to 'enhance learning, human potential and high performance in work-related systems'[15] such as business organizations. A systematic way of understanding what applied fields, such as medicine, engineering, management and HRD, are and what they seek to achieve is to be found in the concept of 'design science'. Herbert A. Simon (1916–2001, Nobel Laureate, author of *Administrative Behaviour* first published in 1947, and one of the most important figures in management research) proposed that management is a 'design science' (in his book *The Sciences of the Artificial* 1969/1996). The role of a design science is to develop valid knowledge which can be used by thoughtful practitioners to solve organizational problems in the 'field' (that is, in real world settings).[16] The 'classical' design sciences, such as medicine and engineering, have the mission to develop actionable knowledge that doctors and engineers can use to design solutions for their field problems (such as curing patients, building bridges, etc.). Design sciences stand in contrast to 'explanatory sciences', such as sociology, psychology, physics, chemistry, biology, etc., whose mission is to develop discipline-specific theories which can be used to describe, explain and predict phenomena in the natural or social world. Concepts, models, and theories from the explanatory sciences can be borrowed and applied by the design sciences. The purpose of a design science is to produce 'artefacts' (something that is the product of human invention, such as an iPhone or an aircraft) or interventions (such as a surgical procedure or a training course) which change situations from how they are now to how they ought to be in order to attain a particular goal or state of affairs,[17] for example to change a patient's condition from being ill to being well, to move an object (such as a passenger) from London to Boston safely and quickly. HRD can be considered a design science because it uses concepts, models and theories from explanatory sciences such as psychology and economics to solve field problems related to the acquisition of the knowledge and skills required in order to realize human potential and enhance performance in work-related systems. Read more about HRD as a design science in: Sadler-Smith, E. (2014). HRD research and design science: Recasting interventions as artefacts. *Human Resource Development International*, *17*(2), 129–144.

Whilst many would agree that HRD is a multidisciplinary applied field of academic study as well as a practical subject and a profession, there have been debates about whether or not it can be considered to be a 'discipline' in its own right. An academic discipline is an area of scholarship which has accumulated its own body of specialist knowledge (in the form of concepts and theories) which is specific to that discipline and not generally overlapping with that of other disciplines. Disciplines tend to have a 'local' language and repertoire of research methods which are tailored to their area of study and which have to be mastered as a condition of entry to the field or 'community of practice' (see Chapter 3).[18] Disciplines also tend to be built around several well-articulated theories and designed to address a set of highly-related questions.[19] This begs the question of does HRD pass the 'theory test' of having:

- An accumulated body of specialist knowledge;
- Concepts and theories specific to it, and not generally shared with another discipline;
- Language and research methods tailored to its area of study;
- A set of highly-related research questions?

HRD scholar Peter Kuchinke argued that HRD is not a discipline in the same way that economics, psychology or philosophy are disciplines, nor will it ever be one. Other HRD scholars would agree. Kuchinke sees HRD as an applied field with multiple 'source' or 'core' disciplines at its roots and as the foundations which nourish and sustain a diverse, multidisciplinary and highly pragmatic intellectual programme.[20] Kuchinke also sees little justification for restricting the number or type of source disciplines (as some have suggested, see below) since each discipline provides a potentially useful 'lens' through which to view the 'field (that is, real world) problems' that HRD seeks to solve (see 'Research insight' above). Indeed, one of the strengths of a multidisciplinary applied field such as HRD is that it can mobilize insights from across the spectrum of social sciences, philosophy, arts and humanities. This makes HRD a challenging as well as invigorating place to be as a scholar, researcher, student or practitioner. Although consensus has not been, and is unlikely ever to be, arrived at regarding HRD's research philosophy, theory or methods, for an applied field such as HRD this needn't be a problem and could even be considered a strength.[21]

History and geography matter, and so does language. As noted above, the term 'human resource development' appears to have been first coined in the early 1960s by labour economists Harbison and Myers working within a human capital paradigm. The term took hold in the US in 1970s and 1980s in the pioneering work of Nadler[22] referred to above and colleagues who followed in his wake. HRD supplanted, or at least complemented, more traditional terminologies such as 'training and development' (T&D) and latterly 'employee development'. In the 1990s the field began to flourish in academia through the work of organizations such as the Academy for Human Resource Development (AHRD), University Forum for HRD (UFHRD) and others. The journal *Human Resource Development Quarterly* was first published in 1990, and this was later supplemented with other HRD-specific journals including *Human Resource Development International* in 1998, *Advances in Developing Human Resources* in 1999 and *Human Resource Development Review* in 2002. These new publications complemented existing journals such as the *European Journal of Training and Development* and *Industrial and Commercial Training*.

The term HRD has flourished in academic research with regular international HRD conferences as well as journal publications and university teaching programmes (with post-graduate programmes in HRD and strong HRD presence in HRM programmes). However, in the professional world various terminologies are used, such as 'employee development', 'training and development', 'learning and development', 'learning and talent development', etc. For clarity on terminology you may find the ATD's glossary to be informative and useful.[23] Also Figure 1.5 shows how a selection of national and international professional bodies describes the area of practice that corresponds broadly to HRD.

Delve deeper 1.1

Read more about the history of HRD in:

Lee, M. (2015). The history, status and future of HRD. In Poell, R., Rocco, T. S., & Roth, G. L. (eds) *The Routledge companion to human resource development* (pp. 41–50). Abingdon: Routledge.

McGuire, D., & Cseh, M. (2006). The development of the field of HRD: A Delphi study. *Journal of European Industrial Training*, 30(8), 653–667.

Swanson, R. F., & Holton, E. F. (2001). *Foundations of human resource development*. San Francisco: Berrett-Koehler (specifically Chapter 3, 'History of HRD').

Theory in HRD

As far as the importance of theory in social science is concerned, Kurt Lewin's famous saying, 'nothing is quite so practical as a good theory' is often cited. The strategic management researcher Andrew van de Ven expanded on this when he remarked that:

> A central mission of scholars and educators in professional schools of management [business schools] is to conduct research that contributes knowledge ... and to apply that knowledge to the practice of management as a profession. (p. 4)[24]

Being competent in HRD requires a grounding in the profession's body of knowledge, and the mastery of its practice rests on becoming acquainted with the concepts, models and theories of the field and developing the ability to apply them to solving problems

Chartered Institute of Personnel and Development (CIPD)	• 'Learning and Development' (L&D) one of ten 'professional areas' in CIPD's 'Profession Map' • Competence in L&D: 'build individual and organisational capability and knowledge to meet current and strategic requirements and create a learning culture to embed capability development'
Society for Human Resource Management (SHRM)	• 'Learning and Development' is HR functional area within the 'People' technical competency of SHRM's Body of Competency and Knowledge (BoCK) • Activities to enhance the knowledge, skills, abilities and other characteristics (KSAOs) and competencies of workforce in order to meet organization's business needs
Academy for Human Resource Development (AHRD)	• AHRD's vision to lead human resource development through research • HRD profession is interdisciplinary field; focuses on systematic training and development, career development, and organization development to improve processes and enhance learning and performance of individuals, organizations, communities, and society
Association for Talent Development (ATD)*	• Vision to 'create a world that works better' by 'empowering professionals to develop talent in the workplace' • ATD professionals include talent development managers, trainers, instructional designers, performance consultants, frontline managers, workplace learning professionals

Figure 1.5 Perspectives on HRD from selected HRD-relevant professional bodies

*formerly American Society for Training and Development (ASTD)

Sources: CIPD Profession Map: How it all fits together. London: CIPD. Available online https://www.cipd.co.uk/cipd-hr-profession/cipd-hr-profession-map/default.html; SHRM Body of Competency and Knowledge. Available online https://www.shrm.org/certification/recertification/Documents/18-1534%202019%20BoCK_WEB.pdf; Academy of Human Resource Development (AHRD) https://www.ahrd.org/page/about_ahrd_2; Association for Talent Development (ATD) https://www.td.org/ (accessed 24-12-20)

and taking decisions in organizational settings.[25] Whilst 'best practice' is both informative and important, it is theory that is the best guide towards finding answers to interesting and important questions that:

- Enlighten and enliven HRD as a field of intellectual and academic inquiry;
- Extend HRD as a body of knowledge;
- Inform and improve the practice and profession of HRD in the field.

Theory has a central role to play for a number of reasons. In management and organization studies a theory is a systematically organized set of relationships between concepts that enable us to:

- Construct a coherent description and explanation of observed or experienced organizational phenomenon (for example, the relationship between motivation and performance);
- Make logically justifiable predictions that can be used to improve management practice and individual and organizational performance (for example, how certain types of goals can improve performance).[26]

Most HRD researchers agree that it's important to specify HRD's underlying theories (plural) and that a minimalist approach to theory (i.e. using none or only a few) will not do. Theory is vital because HRD, and related and topical areas such as executive education, coaching and mentoring, and leadership development, are vulnerable to the vagaries of off-the-shelf, pre-packaged, fashionable solutions. This is a potential problem because managers who lack relevant and in-depth professional HRD knowledge may become vulnerable to fads and fashions in the employee training and development market which, by their nature, wax and wane. The risk is that organizations invest time and resources in shallow solutions to problems or products that aren't needed ('solutions looking for problems', rather than the other way around).[27] At its worse this situation can fuel the emergence of short-term solutions which fall short of the necessary standards of professional practice and scientific rigour. This may satiate an immediate need but may do little to address underlying systemic issues in ways that are credible and sustainable. This challenge is not unique to HRD, it is an issue which management and organization studies in general has grappled with. The 'double hurdle' of rigour and relevance was captured in a two-by-two matrix developed by Neil Anderson and colleagues, which can be used as typology and for debating the value and worth of HRD research and practice; see Figure 1.6.

It goes without saying that the aspiration for any field of management and organization research, including HRD, is to be in the 'high-rigour and high-relevance' quadrant. It can only do so by grounding itself resolutely in a theoretically rigorous and empirically verified set of principles and practically relevant propositions, recommendations and HRD solutions.

---Reflective question 1.3---

What would you say to someone who said that HRD research that doesn't produce *actionable* knowledge that can be *applied* to the management of individual and organization learning processes in an organization is of doubtful worth and should cease forthwith?

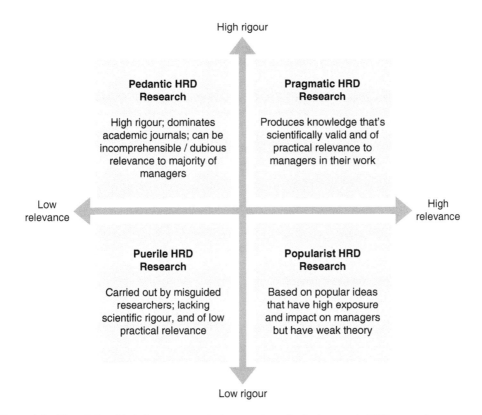

High rigour

Pedantic HRD Research

High rigour; dominates academic journals; can be incomprehensible / dubious relevance to majority of managers

Pragmatic HRD Research

Produces knowledge that's scientifically valid and of practical relevance to managers in their work

Low relevance

High relevance

Puerile HRD Research

Carried out by misguided researchers; lacking scientific rigour, and of low practical relevance

Popularist HRD Research

Based on popular ideas that have high exposure and impact on managers but have weak theory

Low rigour

Figure 1.6   The relationship between research rigour and practical relevance in HRD research

Source: adapted from Anderson, V., Garavan, T. and Sadler-Smith, E. (2014) Corporate social responsibility, sustainability, ethics and international human resource development. *Human Resource Development International*, 17, 497–498, p. 498. Reprinted by permission of the publisher (Taylor & Francis Ltd, http://www.tandfonline.com).

A question that HRD researchers have debated at length is not 'is theory important?' (it is) but 'which theory or theories are important?'. This debate manifested most noticeably in proposals that were made several decades ago by one of HRD's foundational figures – Richard Swanson of the University of Minnesota – that there are three 'core' theories for HRD. Swanson argued that HRD, as a process or system within a larger organizational and environmental system, relies on three 'core disciplines';[28] see Figure 1.7.

Based on the view that HRD must be both clear about its theoretical foundations and make moves towards theoretical unification, Swanson used the metaphor of a 'three-legged stool'[29] in which the legs are the three 'core disciplines' and the seat is their 'full integration into a unique theory of HRD' (p. 305). Some have taken issue with these proposals, not least Swanson's friend and colleague at the University of Minnesota, Gary McLean. Other metaphors were suggested playfully by McLean in his repost to Swanson: a '100-legged centipede' might better represent the complexity of HRD, or an 'eight-legged octopus' might be more manageable. In a similar vein it's been suggested that HRD, being a multidisciplinary field, could be thought of as a river system with many tributaries feeding into the main channel.[30]

Psychology

- Human learning and development and socio-technical systems, includes behaviourism, cognitivism; transfer of learning theory; social learning; experiential learning; action learning and andragogy

Economics

- Efficient and effective use of resources to meet organizational goals in competitive environments and aligning with an HRD 'performance paradigm'; includes human capital theory

Systems

- Interactions between individual and group variables, work processes, organizations and environments in 'input–process–output' terms; acommodates complexity

Organizational learning and knowledge

- Learning is a collective and social process; error detection and correction; learning as the 'only sustainable source of competitive advantage'

Learning organization

- Sustainable vision for development of organizations; learning organization facilitates learning of its members and continuously transforms itself

Strategic management and strategic HRM

- Aligns HRD vertically to business strategy via resource based view of the firm and strategic HRD (SHRD) models; integrates HRD horizontally with human resource management (HRM)

Neuroscience and organizational neuroscience

- Biological, genetic, evolutionary; aims to map neural mechanisms as prime causes of organizational behaviour, including learning and development; 'brain-based' learning principles

Figure 1.7 Swanson's 'core theories' of HRD (psychology, economic, systems) with selected additional 'candidate' theories

Source: adapted from Weinberger, L. A. (1998) Commonly held theories of human resource development. *Human Resource Development International*, 1(1), 75–93. Reprinted by permission of the publisher (Taylor & Francis Ltd, http://www.tandfonline.com).

HRD is an applied field that draws on many source, or core, disciplines.[31] Like management and organization studies more generally it's a 'borrower'[32] (in the best sense) from other disciplines in the sciences and social sciences and the humanities (for example, neuroscience, psychology, economics, philosophy, history, etc.) as well as from sub-disciplines (for example, cognitive psychology, social psychology, etc.) and from related multidisciplinary fields (such as organizational behaviour). It also 'borrows' theories developed by other fields and sub-fields of management, such as human resource management (for example, the 'contingency and fit models' of HRM), strategic management (for example, the resource-based view of the firm), etc.

The source disciplines of HRD are a combination of sciences, social sciences and humanities and include, but are by no means confined to, psychology, sociology, economics, anthropology, organizational behaviour and organizational theory, adult education, and instructional design. As HRD develops so new source disciplines are co-opted. For example, in the light of the critical turn in HRD (see below) HRD researchers turned to philosophy and the theories of the post-structuralists such as

Derrida and Foucault, whilst HRD researchers who are positivistically-inclined are intrigued by the potential insights that neuroscience can bring to HRD research and practice.

The question of *which* disciplines HRD borrows from is less important than *why* HRD borrows from them. Two guiding principles for why HRD should use robust and relevant theories from intellectually rigorous source disciplines are in order that:

- HRD solutions are based on sound concepts, robust theory and solid empirical evidence;
- Faddish solutions in the mode of the puerile and popularist sciences (see Figure 1.6) which only serve to undermine HRD's credibility and utility are avoided.

The question of which disciplines are more assistive in solving the applied, or 'field', problems that HRD seeks to address are likely to vary both with the nature of the problem and as the disciplines in the sciences and humanities themselves change and evolve. For example, a couple of decades ago HRD did not concern itself with brain science in any significant way because the scientific discipline of neuroscience was not evolved enough to be able to offer useful concepts, models and theories. That has now changed, and we have seen the development of relevant sub-fields of neuroscience such as social cognitive neuroscience and organizational neuroscience (ONS) which HRD can usefully apply (see Chapter 5). We can try to predict, but nobody can know, what the new disciplines that HRD will borrow from in the years ahead. All we can do is keep our ear to the ground and look outside the HRD 'box' for scientifically rigorous and practically relevant knowledge from the natural and social sciences and intellectual insights from the humanities and related fields.

Delve deeper 1.2

Extend your knowledge of the professional importance of theory building in HRD and the challenges that scholars have faced by reading Susan Lynham's classic article from the early 2000s:

Lynham, S. A. (2000). Theory building in the human resource development profession. *Human Resource Development Quarterly*, *11*(2), 159-178.

For a typology of different types of HRD practitioners in terms of their level of theoretical sophistication and which culminates at the level of 'scholar practitioner' read:

Ruona, W. E., and Gilley, J. W. (2009). Practitioners in applied professions: A model applied to human resource development. *Advances in Developing Human Resources*, *11*(4), 438-453.

Finally, for an appreciation of some of the barriers in applying theory and research to HRD, and the need for collaborations between scholars and practitioners of HRD read Carol Packard's article:

Packard, C. B. (2017). Next steps: Valuing, supporting, and promoting the intersection of HRD theory and practice. *Advances in Developing Human Resources*, *19*(3), 262-278.

Research philosophy and HRD

Philosophy (from the Greek 'philosophia' meaning the 'love of wisdom') helps us to understand, reflect on and critique the fundamental assumptions that are the basis of our thoughts and behaviours, and also what we consider to be morally 'good' and proper. Philosophy in HRD can help us to understand, reflect on and critique how we think about HRD, how we put HRD into practice, and how we make choices when faced with ethical dilemmas. Philosophy is a vast and complex field and what follows is only the briefest of introductions to a few of these issues as they relate to HRD research.

There are three branches of philosophy that are relevant to the meaning, understanding and purposes we attach to HRD research: 'ontology', 'epistemology' and 'axiology'.

Ontology means 'the study of being' and is concerned with how we fundamentally see the social world and what the essential nature of social reality is for us as individuals.

- For example, for someone who's a realist there's an objective social reality that exists externally 'out there' that's waiting to be discovered by the application of rigorous, objective scientific methods;
- On the other hand, for a relativist there are multiple social realities which are socially constructed, and the meanings attached to 'reality' are created rather than discovered.[33]

An HRD realist would believe, for example, that there's an objective relationship waiting to be discovered between investment in HRD and firm performance, whereas an HRD relativist would assume that managers construct their own subjective 'reality' of the relationship between HRD and 'outcomes' and how this relationship works inside their particular organization.

Epistemology, meaning 'the study of knowledge', is concerned with how we think about the world and what 'counts', or can be considered, as acceptable knowledge.

- A positivist will be inclined towards the methods of natural and physical sciences and prefer using scientific methods involving the collection of objective data to look for plausible cause-and-effect relationships;
- An interpretivist would incline more towards the view that in studying a social reality it's inappropriate to try to reduce observed phenomena to simple cause-and-effect relationships and that the particular aspects of the world you're interested in trying to understand can only be interpreted subjectively rather than discovered objectively.

An interpretivist HRD researcher would, for example, be more likely to enter into the research participants' world and try to see it from their point of view. On the other hand, a positivist HRD researcher would be more likely to see organizations and the entities within them as measurable objects.[34] A positivist might conduct a survey to measure the relationship between HRD and performance whilst an interpretivist might talk to managers and other employees to explore their 'lived experiences' of HRD in their organization.

Axiology, literally the study of value or worth, is concerned with the value system we adopt in practice when we interact with the world:

- A positivist is likely to undertake research in a way that aims to be 'value-free' with claims to be able to see the world objectively;
- An interpretivist is more likely to undertake research in ways that acknowledge research as value-laden and with the acknowledgement that the researcher is part of what's being researched and that 'you' and 'it' (the object of your study) can't be separated.[35]

In HRD, for example, the realist-positivist would likely operate in a way that sees the relationship between HRD and performance as value-free, whereas the relativist-interpretivist might look for underlying beliefs and values that affect how research participants talk about HRD in their organization and what values and beliefs the researcher brings to the study of the phenomenon of interest.

Unlike the traditional physical sciences and some sub-disciplines of social science (for example, experimental psychology) which tend to have dominant research paradigms that are realist and positivist, there's no dominant paradigm in HRD that's either realist or relativist. In common with management and organization studies more generally, HRD research spans the continuum from realism to relativism, and positivism to interpretivism. Many HRD researchers consider this to be a healthy position; it means that HRD doesn't look at the world through one lens at the expense of another, listen to a single voice, or silence other views or voices.[36]

HRD is an applied field and as such it should endeavour to produce knowledge that is actionable by managers to solve field problems. But what does this mean for HRD researchers who are keen for their work to have real-world impact? Claire Gubbins and Denise Rousseau, in developing the concept of evidence-based HRD (EBHRD), offered five suggestions for how HRD research can be made more actionable:[37]

- Conduct research that's relevant to real-world problems;
- Undertake scientifically rigorous, high-quality research;
- Provide summaries and syntheses in the form of meta-analyses and systematic reviews that identify what has been discovered and what needs to be discovered;
- Translate and disseminate the results of research into a form that's readable and accessible by practitioners;
- Show how research findings can be transformed into actionable knowledge in the form of recommendations, tools, decision rubrics, and action guidelines.

Evidence-based HRD (EBHRD) translates principles based on best evidence into HRD practices. As a result of being evidence-based in their work, HRD practitioners (that is, trainers, consultants, etc.) develop into 'experts' who take decisions/offer advice based on the best available scientific evidence rather than purely personal preferences or fads and fashions. By doing so HRD practitioners continually expand their evidence/research base for 'what works in HRD and why', and in so doing add to the development of HRD as an applied field. Gubbins and Rousseau argue convincingly that achieving these goals requires HRD researchers to conduct research that has both a 'descriptive' and a 'prescriptive' remit:

- Descriptive: For example, in academic articles the research is often framed in terms of descriptions of phenomena and explanations of the relationships between variables (in positivistic research) or interpretations of participants lived experiences (in interpretative research);
- Prescriptive: On the other hand, articles published in practitioner publications (such as the periodicals produced by HR professional bodies and commercial training publications) emphasize prescription by offering guidelines for how managers should take decisions and act in the real world.

In bridging 'description' and 'prescription' HRD researchers can produce summaries of their work for practitioner audiences in professional publications and trade magazines. They can also be bolder in their recommendations for practice when they publish in academic journals and by making such articles more freely and easily available to curious practitioners. Students of HRD should be open to ideas from all of the above and from a range of credible sources, for example specialist HRD practitioner journals such as *HR Magazine* (from the Society of HRM), *Work* and *People Management* (from the Chartered Institute of Personnel and Development), *Training Journal*, *HRD Connect*, general HR publications such as *HR Director*, *Personnel Today*, etc. as well as general management publications aimed at practitioner audiences such as *Forbes*, *Harvard Business Review*, *Management Today*, etc. This is a list of UK- and US-centric publications but it is by no means an exhaustive list, and other nations likely have similar publications that are just as useful to students and practitioners.

Delve deeper 1.3

Read more about the research-practice and academic-practitioner divide and how to bridge it in:

Brown, T. C., & Latham, G. P. (2018). Maintaining relevance and rigor: How we bridge the practitioner–scholar divide within human resource development. *Human Resource Development Quarterly*, 29(2), 99–105.

Ross, C., Nichol, L., Elliott, C., Sambrook, S., & Stewart, J. (2020). The role of HRD in bridging the research-practice gap: The case of learning and development. *Human Resource Development International*, 23(2), 108–124.

Tkachenko, O., Hahn, H. J., & Peterson, S. L. (2017). Research–practice gap in applied fields: An integrative literature review. *Human Resource Development Review*, 16(3), 235–262.

Wang, J. (2017). Integrating research and practice: Looking forward. *Advances in Developing Human Resources*, 19(3), 331–343.

Extend your knowledge of research philosophy and research methods in HRD by reading:

McGoldrick, J., Stewart, J., & Watson, S. (2004). Philosophy and theory in HRD. In J. Woodall, M. Lee and J. Stewart (eds) *New frontiers in HRD* (pp. 27–40). Abingdon: Routledge.

Saunders, M. K. N. & Tosey, P. (2016). *Handbook of research methods on human resource development*. Cheltenham: Edward Elgar.

Ethics and purpose in HRD

A philosophical perspective on HRD also involves considerations of 'moral philosophy'. Moral philosophy is a branch of philosophy that's concerned with questions of what constitutes 'right' and 'wrong' behaviour and how we should fundamentally live our lives, for example, in Aristotelian terms, the pursuit of a life 'well-lived' in the community ('eudaimonia'). In relation to HRD, moral philosophy leads us to ask questions about the ethics of HRD research and practice, for example:

- What constitutes 'right' and 'wrong' in the dilemmas of everyday HRD practice;
- How HRD should be conducted in relation to its deeper, wider and longer-lasting effects on its stakeholders, organizations and the wider community and environment.

As noted earlier, Richard Swanson in his discussion of the underlying theories of HRD used the metaphor of the three-legged stool (the 'seat' is HRD and the 'legs' are the theories that HRD stands on, and the legs don't need to be prescribed, and there are likely more than three legs). Swanson also developed the metaphor further with the idea that there is an 'ethical rug' which acts as a filter between HRD and the 'floor' which represents the organization, this is shown in Figure 1.8.

In order to explore the role of ethics in HRD and the idea of ethics as mediating between HRD and the organization of which it is a part we need an appreciation of some fundamentals of business ethics. Ethics is a vast and complex field and what follows is brief overview of some of the most basic principles as they apply to HRD.

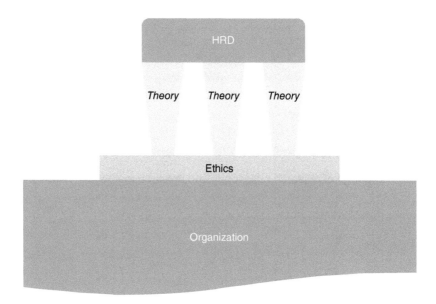

Figure 1.8   Relationships between ethics (the 'rug'), HRD (the 'stool') and the organization (the 'floor')

Source: adapted from Swanson, R. A. (2001) Human resource development and its underlying theory. *Human Resource Development International*, 4(3): 299–312. Reprinted by permission of the publisher (Taylor & Francis Ltd, http://www. tandfonline.com).

Business ethicists Andrew Crane and Dirk Matten distinguish between two types of ethical theories which differ in terms of the relationship between principles (or motivations), actions and outcomes:

- Consequentialist ethical theories: if the outcome of an action is desirable then the action is morally right, if not it is morally wrong. Utilitarianism is an example of a consequentialist ethical theory. An example in HRD could be as follows: of the several investments that a business could make in HRD, the morally right one is that which has the best overall consequences for the organization. Because moral goodness depends on consequences, the more 'good' consequences that an act produces the 'better'. This example is 'utilitarian' because the manager's actions seek to maximize welfare or utility (greatest good for greatest number) from investing in HRD. Taking the decision to invest in HRD in a way that is likely to produce the best overall consequences can be seen therefore as morally 'good';
- Non-consequentialist ethical theories: an action is morally right or wrong because the underlying principles and motivation guiding the action are always absolutely right. The focus here is on what people do rather than on the consequences of their actions. Non-consequentialist ethics are duty-based or rule-based and sometimes referred to as 'deontological'. Kant's 'categorical imperative' is an example of an ethic of duty that should be applied to every moral issue.[38] An example in HRD could be a refusal to train employees in

the manufacture of lethal weapons because killing people is wrong. Because some acts, such as killing another person, are intrinsically wrong in themselves refusing to train employees in lethal weapon manufacture can be seen, in the terms set out above, morally good.

However, according to Crane and Matten, these ethical theories can be criticized for being too abstract, reductionist, elitist, impersonal, rational and codified. In response to the limitations of utilitarian and deontological approaches in business, several alternative ethical frameworks have been proposed, including:

- Virtue ethics: founded in the writings of Aristotle, morally correct actions are undertaken by persons with virtuous characters (for example, courageous, temperate, honest, wise, etc. which are examples of virtues or character strengths);
- Feminist ethics: prioritizes empathy and harmony in interpersonal and social relationships and the avoidance of harm;
- Post-modern ethics: locates morality in a supra-rational realm of moral impulses, emotions, and gut feelings about what's right and wrong.

In considering the fundamentals of ethics and HRD, Jim Stewart argued that there are three core aspects that must be considered; see Figure 1.9.

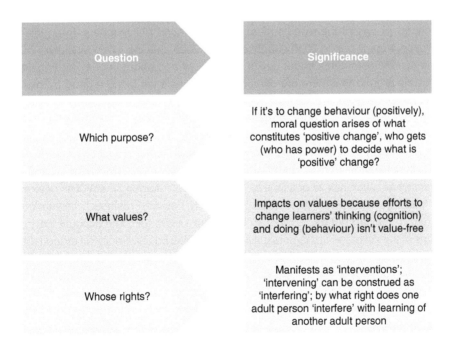

Figure 1.9 Core aspects of ethics in HRD

Source: adapted from Stewart, J. (2007) The future of HRD research: Strengths, weaknesses, opportunities, threats and actions. *Human Resource Development International*, *10*(1), 93–97. Reprinted by permission of the publisher (Taylor & Francis Ltd, http://www.tandfonline.com).

Ethics is important and integral to HRD because if forces us to ask the essential questions of meaning and purpose about 'what, as an HRD practitioner, should one *do?*'[39] As such it provides us with a system for critical self-reflection and inquiry.

Virtue ethics deserves a special mention as it has become prominent in business ethics in recent decades. Virtue ethics is an alternative to utilitarian (utility-based) and deontological (duty- or rule-based) ethical theories. Virtue ethics was first presented systematically in Aristotle's (385–323 BC) *Nicomachean Ethics* over two millennia ago. Modern virtue ethicists (such as Alastair MacIntyre in his seminal book *Before Virtue* published in 1984) and business ethicists such as Robert Solomon updated and applied Aristotelian principles in ethics generally (MacIntyre) and business ethics in particular (Solomon and others). In the field of HRD, Peter Kuchinke argues that virtue ethics provides an ethical theory which focuses on the development of practical wisdom (*phronesis*) and that the development of this virtue should be a priority of learning and development.

---In their own words 1.2---

Alasdair MacIntyre on virtue in business

Alasdair MacIntyre (b. 1929) is a Scottish moral and political philosopher and has been described as one of the world's most influential moral philosophers. In an interview in *Prospect* magazine in 2010 shortly after the 2008 financial crisis MacIntyre offered some acerbic comments about ethics in business and about 'money trading' in particular. He argued that there are certain skills, for instance being a good burglar, that are fundamentally against being virtuous and those engaged in finance – particularly money trading – are like good burglars: 'MacIntyre appeals to the classical (Aristotelian) golden mean: "The courageous human being…strikes a mean between rashness and cowardice… and if things go wrong she or he will be among those who lose out", that is they have "skin in the game". But skilful "money-men", MacIntyre argues, want to transfer as much risk as possible to others without informing them of its nature, and this leads to a failure to "distinguish adequately between rashness, cowardice and courage". They do not and cannot, in MacIntyre's view, take into account the human victims of the collateral damage resulting from market crises. Hence he argued that the financial sector is in essence an environment of "bad character" despite the fact that it appears to many a benevolent engine of growth. One symptom of this, MacIntyre contends, is gross inequality. In 2009, for instance, the chief executives of Britain's 100 largest companies earned on average 81 times more than the average pay of a full-time worker.'

Source: Cornwell, J. (2010). MacIntyre on money. *Prospect Magazine*, October. www.prospectmagazine.co.uk/magazine/alasdair-macintyre-on-money

Taking an ethical stance is one way of being reflexive and critical of one's own and other's current practices. Tim Hatcher researches at the intersection of HRD, ethics and critical perspectives. He argues more needs to be accomplished in developing HRD's ethical foundations. In Hatcher's view, one reason why HRD faces moral questions and ethical challenges is because of an adherence to its human capital heritage (see above) and the 'commodification' of learning and development in pursuit of shareholder interests (that is, treating learning as a 'commodity' to be used instrumently in pursuit of managerialist agendas and shareholders' interests and maximizing shareholder value). On the positive side however he argued that HRD can take the lead in ethics and social and environmental moral responsibility because HRD is well-positioned to be able to:

- Question the economic, shareholder value-based approach that is integral to the 'performance paradigm';
- Take on the role of being a 'conscience' of business organizations in a way that cuts across and transcends traditional functional boundaries or silos.[10]

In Hatcher's view, HRD is well-positioned for ethical inquiry and debate because it has a breadth and depth of reach that gives it a unique vantage point from which to scrutinize and critique as well as develop and disseminate more ethical business practices.[11]

In the mid-1990s the Academy of Human Resource Development (AHRD) debated whether HRD needed a code of ethics and if so what the content of such a code should be. In the intervening years the AHRD has provided guidance on ethics and integrity for HRD professionals engaged in practice, research, consulting and teaching. The first edition of this ethical code was published in 1999 and a new edition was published in 2018.

Perspective from practice 1.2

Standards of ethics and integrity in HRD

The AHRD *Standards on Ethics and Integrity* identifies a common set of values and is an important 'educational vehicle' for the articulation of the 'values to which HRD professionals should aspire in their work' and lists standards for professional practice in six areas:

- Competence: behaviour demonstrating high standards of competence; recognizing the limits of one's competence and expertise; only engaging in activities for which one is qualified by education, training or experience.
- Integrity: being honest, fair, and respectful of others; not making statements that are false, misleading, or deceptive; being reflexive of one's belief systems, values, needs, and limitations and the effects these might have on one's work.

(Continued)

- Professional responsibility: upholding professional standards of conduct; acting appropriately and accepting responsibility for one's actions; serving the best interests of one's clients.
- Respect for people's rights and dignity: honouring the dignity and worth of others; respecting privacy, confidentiality, self-determination, and autonomy; exercising awareness of differences and diversity (including age, gender identity, race, ethnicity, national origin, religion, sexual orientation, disability, language, and socioeconomic status).
- Concern for others' welfare: contributing to the welfare of clients and others; exercising sensitivity to power differentials between themselves and others.
- Social responsibility: exercising awareness of and behaving in ways that reflect professional responsibilities to one's community, wider society, and the planet.

Since their publication the HRD standards have been subject to on-going development. Engaging with questions of what constitutes ethics standards and moral behaviour may be better thought of as a journey rather than a final destination.

Sources: AHRD Standards on Ethics and Integrity. Academy of Human Resource Development. www.ahrd.org/page/standards (accessed 24-12-20); Russ-Eft, D. (2018). Second time around: AHRD standards on ethics and integrity. *Human Resource Development Review, 17*(2), 123–127.

Acknowledging the applied nature of HRD begs the question of 'applied for the *purpose of what?*'. For example, should employers' and shareholders' interests and organizational performance be paramount in HRD's purpose, or should employees' learning and development needs take priority?

In the past HRD researchers have juxtaposed an 'HRD learning paradigm' versus an 'HRD performance paradigm'. A learning paradigm emphasizes an individual-level, employee education and development-led approach. On the other hand, a performance paradigm emphasizes HRD's purpose as 'advancing the mission of the organizational system which sponsors the HRD efforts by improving the capabilities of individuals working in the organization and improving the organizational systems in which they perform their work'.[42] Which purpose individual HRD practitioners or researchers incline towards will depend on a range of personal (for example, individual beliefs and values) and contextual factors (for example, their role, the organizational context, etc.).

Such arguments often tend to polarize into 'either A or B', win–lose, 'zero–sum' debates which end up depicting learning and performance as incommensurable and as though opting for 'performance' robs us of 'learning' and vice versa. An alternative stance is '*both* a learning *and* performance' paradigm rather than an '*either* learning *or* performance' paradigm that:

- Leverages 'both/and' solutions, rather than 'either/or' incompatibilities;
- Maximizes the learning of individuals whilst simultaneously assisting the organization in achieving its strategic goals.

Viewed in this way, the learning paradigm and the performance paradigm become compatible, for example by aligning employees' learning and development needs and career aspirations with organizational mission and goals in the HR planning and performance management process.

That said we should always be mindful of the tensions that can polarize learning and performance and the different interests they may serve, such as employer versus employee, manager versus worker, long-term versus short-term, industry versus natural environment, etc. It's all too easy to sweep critical issues and tensions under the carpet. For instance, the performance paradigm often glosses over the issue of power and the privileges that power confers on certain groups, the power asymmetries this creates, the effects this can have on groups that don't hold power, creating the potential for injustices, and how this relates to and affects learning. The difficulties of de-problematizing the HRD performance paradigm resonate with critical HRD (see below) and debates about 'performance' are central to the identity and purposes of HRD. Bob Hamlin and Jim Stewart echoed and expanded the notions of learning and performance when they identified core purposes of HRD based on a detailed analysis of how HRD is defined in the literature:

- Improving individual, group and organizational effectiveness and performance;
- Developing individuals' knowledge, skills and competencies and enhancing human potential and personal growth.[43]

In spite of the problems and criticisms of the 'performance paradigm' or 'performance-based HRD',[44] as Hamlin and Stewart's research shows, performance in one form or another pervades much of HRD research and practice:

- Many HRD researchers are interested in describing, explaining and predicting the HRD-performance link;
- Managers and other stakeholders are interested in improving individual and organizational learning and performance, and HRD is one way of achieving this goal.

In his 'defence' of the performance paradigm HRD researcher Ed Holton[45] identified a number of core assumptions of performance-based HRD:

- The ultimate purpose of HRD is to improve the performance of the system in which it's embedded, and which provides the resources to support it;
- The primary outcome of HRD is not only learning, but both learning and performance (that is, it's 'both/and' not 'either/or');
- HRD practitioners have a moral obligation to ensure that attaining organizational performance goals is not conducted in a way that treats employees in unethical ways;

● Effective performance systems should be productive and rewarding for the organization and for individual employees.

The debates relate to wider issues such as stakeholder capitalism, ESG (environment, social and governance) issues, and corporate social responsibility (CSR). As already noted, in HRD a 'learning purpose' and a 'performance purpose' are sometimes juxtaposed as if they were opposites, but this need not be the case. The idea of a paradox (the juxtaposition of two seemingly contradictory ideas, such as 'exploration' and 'exploitation'), and the related area of paradox theory, can help us to make sense of how it might be possible to hold a 'both performance and learning' (rather than an 'either learning or performance') view of the purpose of HRD in which the tensions between learning and performance can be reconciled even if they can't be resolved (see Delve Deeper below). A 'paradox mindset' is an important intellectual tool in any manager's (or student's or researcher's for that matter) cognitive toolkit.

----Delve deeper 1.4----

Read more about ethics in HRD in:

Ardichvili, A. (2013). The role of HRD in CSR, sustainability, and ethics: A relational model. *Human Resource Development Review, 12*(4), 456–473.

Kuchinke, K. P. (2017). The ethics of HRD practice. *Human Resource Development International, 20*(5), 361–370.

Russ-Eft, D. (2014). Morality and ethics in HRD. In Chalofsky, N. E., Rocco, T. S., & Morris, M. L. (eds) *Handbook of human resource development*. Hoboken, NJ: John Wiley and Sons, pp. 510–526.

Get to grips with paradox, paradox theory, the 'paradox mindset', and how tensions in paradoxes can be reconciled by reading:

Lewis, M. W., & Smith, W. K. (2014). Paradox as a metatheoretical perspective: Sharpening the focus and widening the scope. *The Journal of Applied Behavioral Science, 50*(2), 127–149.

Papachroni, A., & Heracleous, L. (2020). Ambidexterity as Practice: Individual Ambidexterity through Paradoxical Practices. *The Journal of Applied Behavioral Science, 56*(2), 143–165.

Critical HRD

Asking questions about HRD's deeper, and perhaps ultimate, purpose are one way in which we can be critical and critically reflective about what HRD is and what it seeks to achieve. Before embarking on a discussion of critical perspectives in HRD, it's worth pausing to consider what it means to be 'critical'.

As students of HRD, or any other subject for that matter, it's important to be able to critically evaluate ideas and their underlying assumptions and come to an informed opinion rather than simply accept them on face value. For example, we should not necessarily take it for granted that any particular theory is 'true', nor should we accept a particular 'best practice' without weighing-up the evidence. When we 'critically evaluate' something (as students are often asked to do) we gather evidence, analyse the evidence, consider both sides of an arguments and decide on the quality, relevance and currency of the ideas being presented in order to arrive at a balanced, logical and rational conclusion. Critically evaluating is an essential academic skill and is likely to involve intellectual activities such as: appraising; arguing; assessing; balancing; concluding; criticizing; critiquing; defending; debating; deciding; evaluating; gauging; judging; justifying; reviewing; vindicating; and weighing-up. Students sometimes approach the task of critically evaluating with anxiety and trepidation, but if you're doing some or all of the above (or other related cognitive activities) you're likely to be 'critically evaluating' (but bearing in mind that this is not an exhaustive list).

'Critical' in the context of 'critical HRD' (CHRD) and 'critical management studies' has a somewhat different meaning; they ask deeper questions about issues such as power, politics, social injustice, etc. CHRD developed in the wake of the critical management studies (CMS) movement that rose to prominence in management and organization studies in the early 1990s. It was framed as a critical response and radical alternative to mainstream management theory. CMS has its intellectual roots in various traditions and schools of thought, including the works of French philosophers such as Derrida, Foucault and Deleuze. CMS exists in many guises but amongst its foundational features are a scepticism towards the 'moral defensibility' of the 'social injustices and ecological destructiveness' that are attributable to prevailing conceptions, forms and practices of management and organization.[46] In so doing critical management seeks to provide a 'voice' for marginalized and repressed groups in organizations and wider society, it also exposes the manipulation of power and repression in organizations in pursuit of shareholder value.[47] Ultimately CMS seeks to reformulate and transform management practice radically and progressively so as to alleviate the negative social and environmental consequences of traditional, predominant and 'hegemonic' management practices.

Reflective question 1.4

What would you say to a sceptical colleague who was of the view that critical perspectives are a purely intellectual endeavour and have no place in an applied field such as HRD which seeks to empower and enable individuals to achieve their full potential and assist organizations in achieving their strategic goals?

Following a CMS ethos, the goal of CHRD is likely to encompass radically reformulating HRD research and practice in order to progressively transform its predominant practices in ways that contribute to greater social justice and environmental sustainability. In so doing CHRD draws on philosophical theories such as those of the post-structuralists referred to above thereby further broadening HRD's theoretical foundations even further. HRD has taken a 'critical turn'. It did so in the early 2000s by challenging the assumptions, values and methods of 'traditional' HRD. CHRD has gained a significant foothold in HRD scholarship.[48] As a critical approach CHRD faces particular challenges because it's a sub-field located in a relatively newly-emerged and strongly applied and highly practitioner-relevant field (HRD) whose predominant practices are configured towards working with managers who are frequently looking for efficient and effective ways to enhance individual and organizational performance and stakeholder deliver value.[49] In an attempt to take CHRD forward constructively, educational researcher Tara Fenwick offered a number of political, epistemological and methodological principles which provide a guide for the important and neglected endeavour of critiquing HRD research and HRD practice; see Figure 1.10.

Political

- Critical HRD should have political purpose to reform learning and development practices in ways that are aligned with principles of equality, fairness, justice and participation

Epistemological

- Learning and development in organizations should recognize workplaces as 'contested terrain', criss-crossed by different genders, sexes, ethnicities, generations, histories, cultures; through critical inquiry CHRD unearths/exposes unitarist illusions that underpin traditional assumptions about knowledge and learning

Methodological

- Critical HRD should challenge assumptions about how knowledge is created and constructed, what counts as knowledge and who gets to decide and how these assumptions influence HRD practices

Figure 1.10 Principles for taking a critical stance in HRD

Source: adapted from Fenwick, 2004.

An independent study was published in 2017 of the views of leading CHRD researcher scholars from the United States and the United Kingdom. It concluded that:

- The HRD curriculum in higher education has tended to neglect issues of emotion, power and politics;
- The study of HRD should take a more critical stance and do more to 'problematize' HRD practice by embracing questions about uncertainty and ambiguity in HRD theory and practice;
- HRD ultimately should endeavour to be a political and identity-shaping project,[50] by inspiring critique, and hence continuous learning, amongst students of the subject.

As CHRD scholar Carole Elliott noted we are perhaps as much 'human becomings' as 'human beings' that is 'a human who is constantly becoming is also one who is subject to many influential processes, whether these be – to name but a few – social, political, historical, or economic. Consequently, a human becoming is a fragile entity'.[51]

Delve deeper 1.5

Read more about Critical Management Studies (CMS) in general in:

Adler, P. S., Forbes, L. C., & Willmott, H. (2007). Critical management studies. *The Academy of Management Annals*, *1*(1), 119–179.

For an overview and conceptual analysis of how CMS has been applied in the field of CHRD and an in-depth account of 'critical thinking' in HRD read:

Sambrook, S. (2014). Critical HRD. In N. E. Chalofsky, T.S. Rocco, M.L. Morris (eds) *Handbook of human resource development*. Hoboken, NJ: Wiley (pp. 145–163).

Elliott, C., & Turnbull, S. (eds) (2004). *Critical thinking in human resource development*. Abingdon: Routledge.

Conclusion: Meanings and purposes

The practice of HRD is defined in this book as the management of individual and collective learning and development processes in organizations so that individual employees can realize their potential and organizations can achieve their strategic goals in ways that maximize stakeholder value, respect justice and fairness, and maintain the integrity of the natural environment. This definition reflects HRD's core pragmatic purposes of improving individual, group and organizational effectiveness and performance and developing individuals' knowledge, skills and competencies and enhancing their potential and personal growth.[52] On this basis HRD is an applied field and can be considered as a design science.

HRD research, as compared to HRD practice, seeks to understand individual and collective learning and development processes in organizations and to theorize them both in terms of established theories drawn from HRD's core or base disciplines but also by developing theories of its own. Even though theory is vital to HRD practice and research, there isn't, and there is unlikely ever to be, a 'grand theory of HRD'. But this isn't a problem, so long as HRD has a meaning and a purpose. In fact any aspiration to HRD having its own theories in the sense that traditional explanatory sciences and academic disciplines have their own theories is, it could be argued, a fruitless endeavour. HRD isn't an explanatory science (like physics or biology), but it can be thought of as an applied multidisciplinary field or 'design science' (in the tradition of the design sciences of engineering, medicine, education, etc). In developing itself as such and in maturing and growing as a field it can learn lessons from the ways in which these established design sciences have created their own unique bodies of knowledge and identities and demonstrated their credibility in solving real world (i.e. field) problems.

The challenge for HRD is to take theories from various sources that enable researchers and practitioners to describe, explain and make predictions about the world and turn these into viable and useful actions that can deliver on HRD's core purposes of improving performance, enhancing potential and promoting personal growth whilst respecting the values of competence, diversity, inclusion integrity, justice, professionalism and responsibility.

Organizations have moral obligations to contribute to the advancement of fair, equitable and responsible workplaces and societies by exercising their corporate social and environmental responsibility remit seriously. This means that there is more to doing 'good business' than simply maximizing shareholder value (MSV). By balancing the tensions between the learning and performance paradigms and different stakeholder interests HRD can:

- Enable individual employees to maximize their potential through the acquisition and development of the knowledge and skills that are necessary for a rewarding occupation, opportunities to succeed and realize one's aspirations, and maintain a healthy work-life balance;
- Be the strategic partner who enables organizations to develop their workforce's knowledge and capabilities to enable them to achieve their long-term goals and generate sustainable, long-term value for stakeholders in a world that appears to be increasingly volatile, uncertain, complex and ambiguous;
- Contribute to equity, justice, fairness and responsibility and support the integrity and sustainability of individuals and their communities and of the natural environment.

As HRD researcher Neil Chalofsky observed HRD creates opportunities for the jobs which make up a good proportion of our waking lives to reflect who we are by leveraging the 'fit' between the 'self' and the work that we do, and in so doing HRD has the potential to make both work and life purposeful and meaningful and thereby contribute not just to a 'good living' but to a 'good life'.[53]

Chapter checkout

Use this list to check your understanding of the key points of this chapter.

1   **HRD's history**   The term 'human resource development' (HRD) originated in the 1960s, is traceable back to Adam Smith's notion of 'human capital', and gained traction as an academic field in the 1990s

2   **HRD definition**   The practice of human resource development (HRD) is the management of individual and collective learning and development processes in organizations in such a way as to enable individual employees to achieve their full potential and organizations to achieve their strategic goals in ways that maximize stakeholder value, respect justice and fairness, and maintain the integrity of the natural environment

3   **HRD identity**   HRD is not generally considered to be an academic 'discipline' as such; it's a multidisciplinary applied field ('design science')

4   **HRD and theory**   Theories (plural) are important in HRD because theories enable researchers and practitioners to describe and explain learning and development processes, and also make predictions about the likely efficacy of HRD solutions

5   **Rigour and relevance**   HRD should endeavour to become a high rigour and high relevance 'pragmatic science' (sometimes referred to as 'Mode 2', that is 'theory-sensitive' and 'practice-led')

6   **Research philosophy and HRD**   HRD research is ontologically and epistemologically eclectic, spanning the continua of relativism to realism and interpretivism to positivism, and is methodologically rich and varied

7   **Ethics in HRD**   Ethics is at the interface of HRD theory and practice and the social context in which HRD is situated; guides what constitutes 'right' and 'wrong' in dilemmas of practice and in relation to its deeper, wider and longer-lasting effects on stakeholders and organizations

8   **Critical HRD**   One of the goals of critical HRD (CHRD) is to reformulate HRD research and practice radically and transform its predominant practices in ways that maximize human potential whilst minimizing harm

SKILLS DEVELOPMENT 1
PREPARING FOR AND GETTING A JOB IN HRD

Imagine if as part of the selection process for the entry-level HR job of HRD adviser you've been asked to put together a PowerPoint presentation that lasts no longer than 15 minutes and includes only two slides, one on 'What is human resource development' and the other one on 'Why does human resource development matter?'. Prepare two slides that present your answers to the questions. You should follow established guidelines for good PowerPoint practice.[54]

It's been claimed that we don't really understand something unless we can explain it to someone who has no knowledge whatsoever of the topic ('you don't really understand something unless you can explain it to your grandfather/grandmother'). Now imagine that you've been successful in the selection process, and been offered and accepted the job, how would you explain how you'll be earning your living to a member of your family who has absolutely no knowledge of HRD, HR, or business for that matter?

2
INSIDE THE 'BLACK BOX'

Contents

On completion of this chapter you should be able to:

- Describe and explain behaviourist and cognitive theories of learning;
- Critically evaluate behaviourist and cognitive theories of learning;
- Use your knowledge and understanding of behaviourist and cognitive theories of learning to advise on the design and delivery of HRD.

Introduction

This chapter is about behaviourist and cognitive theories of learning. It is the first of four chapters (Chapters 2–5) on the important topic of 'theories of learning'. The chapters group theories together, for example Chapter 3 discusses social and situated theories of learning, Chapter 4 considers the 'experience-based modalities' of experiential learning theory, action learning and andragogy, whilst Chapter 5 explores insights that neuroscience provides about learning and HRD. Together, these theories are micro-foundations for HRD. Behavioural and cognitive theories are grouped together both for historical reasons and because cognitive theory can be seen as a response to and a reaction against behaviourist theory. The behaviourists treated the mental (cognitive) processes between stimulus and response as a 'black box'; cognitivism went inside the black box, hence the title of this chapter. Cognitive theory also connects strongly to other theories of learning such as social cognitive theory, situated cognition and neuroscience. However, before we explore theories in any detail we'll pause to consider in more detail why theories of learning are relevant for HRD.

A theory describes and explains what a phenomenon (for example, 'gravity') is and how it works. Theories are based typically on evidence and observation (for example, 'large objects attract smaller objects'). A theory enables us to make useful predictions about the world (for example, 'the force of gravity can cause apples to fall out of trees'), and good theories are testable – they allow us to check the validity of our predictions and, by extension, the theory on which the predictions were based. From theories we can formulate hypotheses, and hypotheses can be tested (and falsified). This is how scientific progress is achieved.

In applied fields, such as HRD, good theories are also highly practical. Take Edwin Locke and Gary Latham's goal-setting theory as an example.[1] It's one of the most widely-cited, robust and useful theories in management and from it it's been possible to develop 'actionable knowledge', such as:

- The value of setting clear (specific, measurable, achievable, realistic and time bound) and challenging ('stretch') goals;
- The importance of securing commitment, gaining feedback, and hitting the right level of complexity in a task.

Goal-setting theory is a very good theory, not least because it provides guidelines for action based on scientific evidence,[2] that is it provides 'actionable knowledge'. In applied fields, such as management and HRD (which are concerned fundamentally with taking action) theories are invaluable because:

- Without theory we'd lack coherent and credible concepts and established principles that enable managers and other professionals to solve problems, take decisions, and make plans;
- Without theory and an empirical evidence base we'd have to solve every problem from scratch, we'd end-up constantly 'reinventing the wheel';
- Without theory, applied fields such as HRD become not only inefficient and ineffective, they also become intellectually impoverished.[3]

Also, it's worth noting (and as alluded to in Chapter 1) there isn't, nor is there ever likely to be, any 'grand theory' of learning for HRD. Instead HRD deploys a diverse range of concepts, models and theories from across the behavioural and brain sciences, for example psychology and neuroscience, as well as other fields such as economics, sociology, etc. HRD takes the best and most appropriate theories from these source disciplines and applies them to real world learning and development problems (in design science terms, HRD's 'field problems').[4] Finally, it's worth noting that not only did one of the founders of social psychology, Kurt Lewin (1890–1947), remark that 'nothing is as practical as a good theory'[5], but also the great management thinker and scholar Sumantra Ghoshal (1948–2004) remarked as well that 'nothing is as dangerous as a bad theory'.[6]

Reflective question 2.1

What would you say to a sceptical manager who offered the opinion that 'Theories are all very well for academics in their "ivory towers", but we're in the real world and we've got a job to do; take my advice and forget all about theory; management is all about *doing* not *theorizing*'?

HRD is a practical field; however, students of HRD and those involved closely in HRD (such as HRD specialists and HR generalists) stand to benefit from understanding theories of learning and knowing how to apply them. From the perspective of the UK's professional body for human resources, the Chartered Institute of Personnel and Development (CIPD), theories of learning matter because HR practitioners 'need to have a working knowledge on emerging insights into how people learn'.[7] Insights into how people learn are derived from scientific theory and practical experience. Theories also equip HRD students and practitioners with the 'intellectual toolkit' that's required in order to take an evidence- and science-based approach. Evidence-based HRD (EBHRD) is theory-driven and, as noted by Claire Gubbins and colleagues, based on 'use of the "best" available scientific evidence' (such as meta-analyses and systematic reviews) which form the basis for 'actionable knowledge'.[8]

Learning

As noted in Chapter 1, one of the aims of HRD practice is the management of learning processes in organizations so that employees can achieve their full potential and organizations can achieve their strategic goals. But in order to understand, and ultimately be able to manage, learning processes, it's necessary to explore the meaning of the term 'learning' itself. Figure 2.1 lists some definitions of learning from a number of HRD-relevant fields.

Behaviourist

- The shaping (conditioning) of behaviour through positive reinforcement or negative reinforcement

Cognitivist

- Change in learner's mental models (or schemas); transfers and flows of information from the sensory register, through short-term (working) memory to long-term storage through processes of encoding, retrieval and storage

Constructivist

- 'The process whereby knowledge is created through the transformation of experience' – David Kolb

Humanist

- 'It has the quality of personal involvement (both of feelings and cognitive aspects), of being self-initiated (the impetus comes from within), of being pervasive (making a difference in the behaviour, attitudes and even personality of the learner), of being evaluated by the learner (who knows if it is meeting a need) and of having the essence of meaning' – Carl Rogers

Instructionalist

- 'A change in human disposition or capability that persists over a period of time and is not simply ascribable to processes of growth' – Robert Gagné

Figure 2.1 Some definitions of learning by seminal figures in fields related to HRD

For the purposes of this book individual learning is defined as 'a longer term change in the knowledge possessed by an individual, their type and level of skill, or their assumptions, attitudes or values'. It's possible to unpack the elements of this definition further, for example knowledge can involve 'knowing', 'comprehending', 'applying', 'analysing', 'synthesizing', and 'evaluating', and it can be 'explicit', 'tacit', 'declarative', 'procedural', etc. Likewise skills can be broken down into 'psychomotor', 'intellectual', 'social', etc. These topics will be explored later in this book.

In the remainder of this chapter we'll look at two related theories of learning: behaviourist theory and cognitive theory. These two theories are related historically (behaviourism provided the practice of training and development with one of the first systematic theories of learning, whilst cognitivism can be seen as a reaction against behaviourism) and have proven to be influential and useful in HRD research and practice. These two theories are mostly at the 'individual level of analysis'. In later chapters we'll meet models and theories of learning that are at the organizational (macro) level of analysis.

Reflective question 2.2

Reflect on your experiences of learning at school, college, university, the workplace or in life generally. Identify an experience in which learning was effective, that is where you experienced a longer term change in the knowledge you possess, your type and level of skill, or your assumptions, attitudes or values. What was it about this experience that made it effective, what were the things that *enabled* learning for you? Then identify an experience in which learning was ineffective, that is you failed to acquire knowledge or skills even though you intended to do so. What was it that made this experience ineffective, what were the things that *constrained* learning for you? As you work through this and the other theories of learning chapters try to be mindful of how a knowledge of them could help to explain your personal 'enablers' and 'constrainers' of learning. Also be mindful of how a knowledge of these theories can help to improve learning and development processes and practices in organizations.

Behaviourist theories of learning

Having considered the role and significance of theories of learning in general we can now turn our attention to the first of our theories of learning. Behaviourism is a theory of learning that's concerned with observable behaviours rather than internal ('black box') phenomena such as thinking (cognition) or feelings (emotion). One of behaviourism's main assumptions is that learning takes place through an organism's interactions with environmental stimuli and the processes of conditioning by rewarding and reinforcing behaviours. In its most 'radical form', behaviourism explains behaviour (b) in terms of a 'black box' with sensory input (s) entering from the left and behaviour exiting from the right as a function (f) of the input, i.e. $b = f(s)$; see Figure 2.2. As the leading cognitive scientist Gerd Gigerenzer has noted, in behaviourism there was a 'time honoured' tradition of keeping the black box firmly shut: the focus is on 'observations only, without any speculations'.[9]

Figure 2.2 The mind as a 'black box'

The leading figures in the behaviourist school of thought were the Russian physiologist Ivan Pavlov (1849–1936) and the Americans B. F. Skinner (1904–2001), E. L. Thorndike (1874–1949) and J. B. Watson (1878–1958). A clear statement of the precepts of behaviourism are to be found in Watson's 1913 *Psychological Review* article 'Psychology as the behaviourist views it'. Watson's theory was a reaction against the subjectivism of 'introspection' in the psychology of that time. It rejected unobservable mental states such as 'expecting', 'remembering', and 'deciding', and instead it was a 'manifesto' for a 'proper' scientific focus on the study of objective and tangible entities such as the relationships between observable stimuli and observable responses (that is, behaviours). Behaviourism dominated academic psychology until well into the twentieth century prior to the 'cognitive revolution'.[10]

The general principles of behaviourist learning theory are based on the idea that learning and behaviour can be understood scientifically without consideration of cognitive states, and that learning is influenced predominantly by 'hard' physical variables such as environment and reinforcement. For example, reinforcement theory in behaviourism can be used in behaviour modification through the mechanisms shown in Figure 2.3.[11]

Positive reinforcement

- Behaviour is strengthened by providing a consequence an individual finds rewarding, for example a monetary reward for doing a household chore means that this behaviour is more likely to be repeated in the future

Negative reinforcement

- Behaviour is strengthened by the removal of an unpleasant reinforcement, for example failure to complete a household chore requires you to make a payment thus strengthening motivation to undertake the task

Punishment and extinction

- Decrease the frequency of a behaviour through the use of an adverse consequence (punishment) or the removal of a reinforcer (extinction)

Figure 2.3 Reinforcement theory in behaviourism

These types of reinforcement mechanisms have informed the design of learning materials (such as the 'drill and practice' routines that instructional design theory often recommends) in which information is presented in small 'chunks' with questions to test learning and feedback and remediation based on the learners' response. Even though the basic discoveries were made over a century ago, this approach is alive-and-well in some e-learning programmes, especially those which are essentially 'electronic page turning' with links to assessment of responses, feedback and remediation.[12]

The behaviourists downplayed the influence of cognition, emotion and free will,[13] and as a theory of human learning behaviourism has many problems and limitations. For example, it failed to pay sufficient regard to learners' intentions, feelings, motives and desires even though common sense tells us that the reality of human learning is that people are:

- Purposeful participants, rather than passive recipients, in the process of learning and the creation of knowledge;
- Social beings whose learning is influenced by what they see, how they see the situation they're in, and how they relate and respond to other people.

The renowned Harvard cognitive psychologist Stephen Pinker argued that behaviourism turned out to be flawed because it failed to take into account desires and beliefs and how human beings use their beliefs and desires to predict – and for the most part pretty well – the behaviour of others:[14]

> In our daily lives we all predict and explain other people's behaviour from what we think they know and what we think they want. Beliefs and desires are the explanatory tools of our own intuitive psychology, and intuitive psychology is still the most useful and complete science of behaviour there is. (p. 63)

Behaviourism has relevance to HRD, albeit limited. Two areas where behaviourism has found applications are 'reinforcement' (see above) and 'objectives' (as in the 'Check-in' to each chapter of this book).

Research insight 2.1

Pavlov's dogs and Skinner's pigeons

The roots of behaviourism are to be found in the 1870s with Pavlov's research into the physiology of digestion and the reflex action of salivation. It was sparked by incidental observations of what was referred to as 'psychic salivation' where a dog would salivate not by being fed but simply by the presence of the food container or of the laboratory attendant who usually carried out the feeding. In his famous experiments Pavlov showed that after experiencing a number of pairings of a 'stimulus' (for example, a bell tone) and a 'reinforcer' (that is, food) the dogs salivated to the bell just as they did to the food. This is called 'classical conditioning'. However, classical conditioning is limited because it only explains passive (reflexive) learning. Skinner on the other hand had the idea

(Continued)

that an animal could operate on the environment to generate an outcome, for example, by learning to press a lever to obtain food. This is called 'operant conditioning'. In his operant conditioning experiments Skinner taught pigeons to press a lever to obtain food. He also taught them to play with a ping pong ball (the video clip is available on YouTube).

Many of the most significant advances in behaviourism occurred in North America whilst in Europe a number of important psychologists were pursuing a different path, for example:

- 'Gestalt' psychologists, including Max Wertheimer (1880–1943) and Wolfgang Kohler (1887–1967) studied mental phenomena such as insight ('Eureka!' moments) and problem-solving;
- In Swiss psychologist Jean Piaget's (1896–1980) studies of the development of the mind the learner is seen as an active explorer of the world (we'll meet the Piagetian concepts of 'assimilation' and 'accommodation' in connection with 'mental models' in the chapter on 'organizational learning').

Two further problems with behaviourism are that learning can occur without there necessarily being a change in behaviour, and complex skills, such learning a language (which humans beings appear to do 'naturally', see Chomsky's genetically encoded 'universal grammar'), cannot be explained by conditioning. Although classical and operant conditioning were successful in shaping and predicting animal behaviour in laboratory settings, as Gigerenzer notes, behaviourism was eventually overthrown by the 'cognitive revolution' of the 1950s and '60s which opened the lid of the behaviourists' black box.[15] 'Behaviourism' as discussed in this section shouldn't be confused with 'behavioural science' which seeks to 'understand how people react psychologically and respond behaviourally to interventions, environments and stimuli'.[16] Behavioural science draws on many aspects of psychology and related fields and informs various aspects of HR management including recruitment, reward, and learning and development.

Perspective from practice 2.1

Behaviours and learning objectives in HRD

Observed behaviours are important in learning theory, learning design and HRD practice. Behavioural objectives are statements of the outcomes of learning expressed in terms that can be observed and hence measured (note they are not referred to as 'behaviourist' objectives). They are used widely in the design of learning and the assessment of learning. You may have noticed that each chapter of this book begins with the statement 'On completion of this chapter you should be able to...'. An important HRD skill is to be able to write 'learning outcomes' (as 'behavioural learning objectives') since they specify how:

- A learning solution (such as a training course) will meet an identified learning need;
- The learning that has taken place (for example, during a training course) will be measured (to see if the objective has been met).

A common temptation, and shortcoming, is to specify learning outcomes in broad, unspecific terms such as 'by the end of this course the learners will be able to *understand* the principles of time management', or 'upon completion of this workshop learners will *appreciate* the challenges associated with chairing a meeting'. But the question then arises of how would we know if the learner 'understood' or 'appreciated' and how could we produce some form of objective evidence to show that learning had taken place? What outcomes or behaviours would we look for?

A better way of expressing these outcomes might be: 'by the end of this course you will be able to *manage* your time effectively' and then to detail the various sub-tasks or sub-objectives involved in 'managing time'. Similarly, 'by the end of this workshop you will be able to *organize* a meeting' effectively, again with the various sub-tasks and sub-objectives specified.

In designing certain types of HRD precise performance terms such as 'manage' and 'organize' are to be preferred over vaguer and more abstract words like 'understand' or 'appreciate'. The key difference is that 'manage' and 'organize' are 'doing words' (verbs). And since we could actually observe someone 'managing' or 'organizing' we'd know whether they can 'manage' time or 'organize' a meeting or not. Also, this would help with the assessment and evaluation of learning.

Reflective question 2.3

How will you be able to tell if you've achieved the learning objectives/learning outcomes that were set for this chapter in the Check-in for Chapter 2?

A useful test with learning objectives is to ask yourself 'does the objective I have written specify a general state of being (such as 'understand' or 'appreciate') or an actual performance (doing something concrete)?' The acid test is 'could I observe someone doing it?'. It would be relatively easy to tell if someone could 'time manage' by giving them a time management task to do or by watching them do it in real life, but how would you know if they 'understood' it? If your response is 'by giving them a time management task to do' then that proves the point. Behavioural objectives are a useful bridge between behaviourism and cognitivism, as they are about both observable behaviour and internal mental (that is, cognitive) states.

Cognitive theories of learning

Cognitive psychology is the scientific study of the mind. It developed in the 1950s out of a dissatisfaction with behaviourism; it was an attempt to understand internal mental processes by delving inside the behaviourist's 'black box' rather than simply studying stimulus-response relationships as in behaviourism. Key thinkers in cognitive learning theory include the Canadians John Anderson (b. 1947) and Endel Tulving (b. 1927), British psychologists Alan Baddeley (b. 1934) and Donald Broadbent (1926–1983), American George Miller (1920–2012), and the German-born American Ulric Neisser (1928–2012). The cognitive revolution brought mental states and mental representations into the realm of scientific psychological investigation and to the forefront of the study of human learning.

A metaphor that the cognitivists used was of the mind as an 'information processing' system, analogous to a computer in that it receives inputs (via the senses), processes and stores information in its cognitive systems (for example, memory systems), and delivers an 'output'. They built models of human cognition that sought to describe, explain and make predictions about processes such as attention, consciousness, creativity, language, memory, perception, problem-solving, thinking, and learning.

In their own words 2.1

Ulric ('Dick') Neisser

The Association for Psychological Science described Ulric (Dick) Neisser as the 'father of cognitive psychology'. His 1967 book *Cognitive Psychology* brought together ideas on internal mental processes such as perception, pattern recognition, attention, problem-solving, and remembering which the behaviourists had consigned to their 'black box'. Neisser described his book, *Cognitive Psychology*, as an 'assault on behaviourism'. He was highly uncomfortable with behaviourism because he considered the behaviourists' assumptions wrong and limiting for psychology.[17] In *Cognitive Psychology*, cognition is described as 'all the processes by which the sensory input is transformed, reduced, elaborated, stored, recovered, and used' which manifest as 'sensation, perception, imagery, retention, recall, problem-solving and thinking' and as such 'cognition is involved in everything a human being might possibly do; that every psychological phenomenon is a cognitive phenomenon' (p. 4).

The cognitivists' information processing theories modelled human cognition as a number of sequential stages:

- Input processing involving attention to incoming information in the 'sensory registers' (visual, auditory, smell, etc.);
- Recognition, temporary storage and active processing in 'short-term' or 'working' memory (STM or WM);
- Encoding and storage of information in long-term memory (LTM) where it could be recoded, reorganized and manipulated, and retrieved;
- Output responses manifested in problem-solving, reasoning, etc.

A typical information processing model is shown in Figure 2.4a. An alternative cognitive model to the information processing approach is 'connectionism', sometimes referred to as 'neural networks' model (Figure 2.4b). Each mental unit is connected to other units and processing is parallel and distributed across the network, rather than serial as in the information processing approach.[18]

In the simple example in Figure 2.4b the central nodes in the network are the cars (A, B and C) and activation of this node leads to other activations such as ownership, colour,

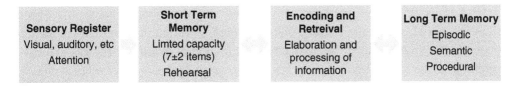

Figure 2.4a   Information processing model

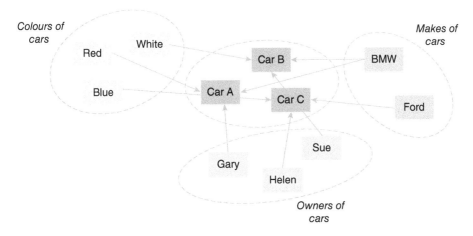

Figure 2.4b   Connectionist model

make and model and further connections (not illustrated) through a 'spread of activa-tion' to other nodes in the network. Knowledge is stored as connections between units and learning occurs when new units (nodes) and connections (links) are added and made, new knowledge is built on and linked to existing knowledge.[19] These intercon-nected networks are related to the concept of a 'mental model' or 'schema'. We'll return to the concept of mental models (schemas or schemata) below and in the later chapter on organizational learning. The concept of connectionism illustrates why prior learning is important when learning new material: for learning to be 'meaningful' links should be made between information already known and new information.

In terms of how information processing works, the German experimental psychologist Hermann Ebbinghaus (1850–1909) was one of the first scientists to attempt to formulate fundamental laws about the processes of human memory (and prior to behaviourism). Ebbinghaus found that most of the loss of information in a rote learning and memoriza-tion task occurred within the first few minutes after training (that is, when the information was acquired). Once the information got through a crucial early period in temporary stor-age it appeared to have much more stability, having been transferred to a long-term storage system. This is often presented as Ebbinghaus' famous 'forgetting curve', where memory for new material declines very rapidly unless it's reinforced 'little and often', and also sub-ject to 'spaced review'. Spaced review actively processes new information, reinforces learning and consolidates long-term storage. In the learning of new material (for example a class taking place over several weeks with reviews), spaced learning and review have been shown to have benefits over 'massed practice' (training without intermittent pauses and opportunities for consolidations), to enhance the transfer of training to the job, and have beneficial longer term effects on performance.[20] Incidentally, spaced review is a good revi-sion technique when preparing for examinations.

Memory's role in learning

Research by Harvard psychologist George Miller in the 1950s revealed the capacity of the brain's temporary storage system to be restricted to approximately seven items (plus or minus two), giving rise to the classic '7±2 rule' of short-term memory. Short term memory (STM) is the most transient component of memory; as well as being limited to 7±2 items, the duration of STM is between about 15 and 30 seconds, after which information fades and can be lost unless it is processed, encoded and stored.

In the 1970s the British psychologist Alan Baddeley further developed the idea of short-term memory (a temporary storage system) into the idea of an active 'working memory' (analogous to a mental 'workspace'). In Baddeley's model working memory has:

● A central executive that controls and integrates information from verbal and visual subsystems;

- A 'phonological loop' for verbal information;
- A 'visuo-spatial sketchpad' for visual information.

Working memory can be thought of as a 'portal' to long-term memory. One of the most important ways of maximizing the chances of information transitioning from working into long term memory is by 'staying on task', that is by maintaining the task goal in one's mind and exercising vigilance in searching actively for connections, meaning and relevance in the new material that's being presented.[21]

The concepts of 'limited capacity' and 'staying on task' highlight the importance of another cognitive concept that's relevant to learning: 'cognitive load'. The concept of cognitive load (the amount of information in working memory at any one time) helps to explain why it's important not to overburden learners' working memory and exceed cognitive load capacity.

George Miller, in addition to his 'seven plus or minus two rule', also researched the importance of 'chunks' or units of information. A chunk is a coherent piece of information that's meaningful to the learners. Miller found that by 'chunking' information the limits of working memory capacity can be overcome to some extent and associated problems with cognitive load ameliorated. For example, the seemingly non-sensical letter string FBICIAUSA can be remembered without much difficulty if it is split into these three familiar and meaningful chunks: FBI CIA USA. Many of us use, probably without realizing it, a similar approach in order to learn telephone numbers which have more than seven digits.[22]

After information has been processed in working memory it's encoded and passes into long-term storage (long-term memory, LTM). In the 1970s the cognitive psychologist Endel Tulving suggested that there are a number of types of long-term memory according to the type of knowledge stored:[23]

- Declarative knowledge ('knowing that') which is subdivided into semantic LTM (for example, knowing that the capital of China is Beijing) and episodic LTM (for example, knowing where you were on 25 December last year);
- 'Procedural' knowledge ('knowing how') such as how to ride a bicycle, play a musical instrument, operate a piece of machinery, etc.

These components and sub-components of LTM are shown in Figure 2.5.

These different types of long-term memory require different types of learning strategies, for example:

- Use of stories that trigger an emotional, personal or experiential connection with new material to be learned activates episodic LTM;
- Repeated practice with coaching and feedback, either real or simulated, develops procedural LTM;
- Sematic LTM can be built up by presenting information in bite-sized chunks, presenting information in multiple ways and prompting learners to actively engage with material rather than passively reading it.[24]

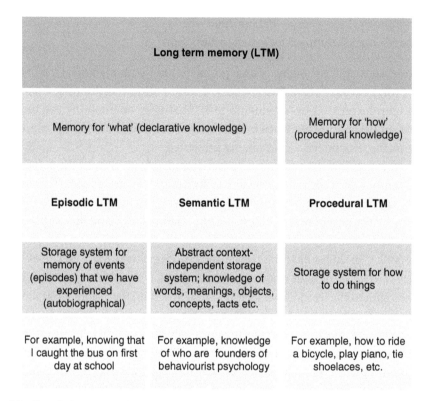

Figure 2.5 Knowledge types and long-term memory (LTM)

Unlike the processes involved in declarative memory, procedural long-term memory does not necessarily involve conscious processing. For example, someone who has knowledge of how to ride a bicycle does so automatically and are unlikely to be able to explain effectively how it's done; nonetheless they could show you the procedure involved.[25] Also, we normally think about knowledge as explicit; however the implicit (i.e. non-declarative) memory for a skill is an example of 'tacit knowledge'. If we stop and think for a moment there are many routine things that we do every day that rely on tacit knowledge, such as tying shoe laces, forming and speaking a sentence, etc. Tacit knowledge is discussed in more detail in later chapters.

As well as having implicit memories (i.e. memories that aren't part of our conscious awareness) and knowing how to do things tacitly or non-consciously, it's also possible to learn non-consciously or implicitly even though we normally think of learning as a deliberate, that is explicit, process. Implicit learning is the acquisition of knowledge that takes place:

- Independently of conscious attempts to learn;
- Without awareness of how learning took place;
- In the absence of explicit knowledge about what knowledge or skill was acquired.[26]

Even though learners may have acquired new knowledge or skill, they may not necessarily be conscious of or able to articulate what they've learned, even though they may be able to perform the skill (for example, non-consciously imitating observed behaviours). A significant proportion of our knowledge is acquired implicitly, as well as incidentally and informally ('informal and incidental learning' are topics we'll return to a Chapter 6).

—Delve deeper 2.1—

Demographic changes, such as people living longer, is one of a number of important 'megatrends' that are affecting the economy and society (see Chapter 8). Aging has a number of physical effects on the brain which influence learning processes (see Chapter 5). Extend your knowledge of the cognitive implications of demographic changes by reading the article by Mary Ann Taylor and Jenifer Bailey Bisson of Clemson University's 'Institute for Engaged Aging'. They explore the practical implications for HRD (many of which apply to learners of all ages) from the scientific literature on age-related changes in cognitive and intellectual functioning and information processing abilities, for example: allowing older learners more time to work through training tasks, allowing the opportunity for self-paced learning, allowing the learner the time and materials to take notes and develop memory aids, allowing time for repetition and practice, using multiple short sessions instead of all-day events, and encouraging questioning.

Source: Taylor, M. A., & Bisson, J. B. (2020). Changes in cognitive function: Practical and theoretical considerations for training the aging workforce. Human Resource Management Review, 30(2). https://doi.org/10.1016/j.hrmr.2019.02.001

Cognitive learning theory and HRD

An important insight for HRD from cognitive learning theory is that in order for new material to be learned, i.e. transferred from short-term memory to long-term memory (and from where it can be retrieved) it has to be 'processed' and 'encoded'. The concepts of cognitive load and schemas are important in learning because of the implications they have for how to increase the chances of information passing from working memory into longer term storage, being integrated meaningfully with what the learner already knows, and be retrievable and useable on some future occasion:

- Cognitive load: Because working memory has limited storage capacity, it's important not to overload working memory and therefore efforts should be made to reduce cognitive load during learning;

- Cognitive schemas: Because new material has to be integrated with previously learned material (the 'nodes' in the 'neural network'), it's important to activate material that is already in long-term memory, and then, by actively processing the new information, link the new material to the old, for example by giving an overview of the new information in the form of an 'advance organizer' (as in the chapter contents that begin each chapter of this book).

There are a number of ways in which cognitive load can be reduced, for example by managing the modes in which new information is presented (as text, speech, and pictures) and 'chunking' information into digestible pieces. Cognitive overload in the verbal and visual 'channels' can be managed by for example 'off-loading' textual information into visual images (a diagram or 'infographic') or recorded speech (such as a podcast) and signalling the importance of key concepts by typographical cues such as *italics*, **bold**, <u>underline</u>, 'single quotes', etc.[27] These strategies don't just apply to textual materials such as worksheets, books, manuals, etc; they also apply to other media PowerPoint presentations, on-screen information, etc. The use of technology makes it much more feasible than it used to be for managing the mode, size and sequencing of the presentation of material to be learned.

   Committing new material to memory is sometimes frowned upon, but in some situations it can be essential, such as when interacting face-to-face with customers, giving a talk, being interviewed, etc. and where looking something up on script or in a manual or referring to notes could look bad or isn't an option. A tried-and-tested method for remembering and recalling (by in effect managing the flow of information between long-term and working memory) is the use of 'memory tricks' such as mnemonics and other devices. These work by putting labels, hooks (often in a visual mode), etc. on knowledge in order to enable its recall at a later time without recourse to written material. Some of the most common ones are the following:

- Acronyms are a way of forming a word from the initial letters of the list of words to be remembered. The word can be real or made up, but the important thing is that is it memorable to the individual. For example, a simple acronym for three types of learning is MUD (i.e.<u>m</u>emorizing, <u>u</u>nderstanding, and <u>d</u>oing);
- Acrostics are words that make some grammatical sense when formed from the initial letters of the word sequence or list to be remembered. For example, in the UK, children are sometimes taught to remember the colours of the rainbow with the acrostic '<u>R</u>ichard <u>of</u> <u>Y</u>ork <u>g</u>ave <u>b</u>attle <u>in</u> <u>v</u>ain' (red, orange, yellow, green, blue, indigo, violet);
- The 'method of loci' (plural of 'locus' meaning 'place' or 'location') has been used by skilled speechmakers since ancient times to remember their script. For example, if you need to make a speech without notes then associate the items to be remembered with objects in the room and use the sequence of locations (loci) of the objects to recall the items and their correct order in an imaginary journey

around the room. World memory champions use this method to remember thousands of meaningless items, and one of them advised that the more colourful, exciting and unusual the images are, the better.[28]

Acronyms are a part of everyday life, they aid memory and recall and speed-up communication (for example, ASAP, ATM, FYI, KISS, LOL, PS, etc.), and they're particularly common in the language of business and management.

Reflective question 2.4

Common management and HR acronyms include SMART, SMARTER, P2P, C2C, B2B, PESTLE, SWOT, CSR, FIFO, DIF, KISS, BRIC, LEAR, BBB, MOOC, JIT, STEM, VLE, USP, TNA, ROI, TBL/3BL, 4P, 7S,[29] etc. How many can you name? For the ones which you know (and probably use), would you be able to remember their meaning or significance, and use them to communicate quickly and easily without the acronym? Could the use of this memory trick aid your learning of HRD? Where might you apply it? Would it be a desirable way to learn?

The principles of cognitive load and managing the flow of information between stores are related to the concept of 'cognitive schemas'. One reason schemas are important is because they help to reduce the load placed upon the system by enabling us to ignore irrelevant material that could swamp our senses and overload working memory[30]; also they help build links between old information (that is, information already in LTM) and new information. A schema (sometimes used interchangeably with 'mental model') is a mental (cognitive) representation of some aspect of experience that's structured in such a way as to facilitate its use in reasoning, problem-solving and decision making. Schemata (schemas) are personal assemblages of declarative and procedural knowledge derived from prior experiences stored in LTM, for example social schemas are frameworks for how to interpret and act in social settings (be respectful, pay attention, etc.). There are also 'person schemas', 'event schemas' and 'self-schemas'. Schemata direct attention towards particular stimuli in the environment (selecting and making sense of relevant information and screening-out irrelevant information), assist in making sense of the world and provide heuristics ('rules of thumb') for how to take decisions and solve problems.

Activating schemata or mental models that are already in LTM is one way of linking new material to be learned with old material that's already been learned. For this reason it's often recommended that relevant prior learning and experience should be evoked from long-term storage in order that the new information can be processed in relation to existing knowledge and connected with it to make a more elaborate mental model. In this way learning becomes 'meaningful'.[31] Pre-learning activities or pre-reading material introduced before learning takes place ('pre-learning interventions') can improve the efficiency and effectiveness of the time spent on learning.

Research insight 2.2

Using pre-learning interventions to make HRD more efficient and effective

Researchers in the US undertook a meta-analysis of the effectiveness of five common types of pre-learning intervention. Based on an analysis of the results from 128 different research articles they found strong support for the idea that pre-learning preparation (for example, advance organizers, preparatory information, goal orientation through objectives, etc.) enhances learning processes and outcomes for cognitive (knowledge-based) skills and affective learning. These pre-learning interventions work by:

- Focusing learners attention on appropriate stimuli (for example, with typographical cues such as *italics*);
- Highlighting learning objectives (as in the Check-ins to the chapters in this book);
- Showing the relationships between new material and existing knowledge (as in a 'concept map');
- Facilitating effective sematic (i.e. verbal) encoding of information (by explaining the meaning of new terminology using definitions);
- Alerting learners to facilitating and inhibiting factors in the learning process (for example, common misconceptions);
- Self-monitoring progress towards learning goals (for example, by regular reflections and self-checks at the end).

The research also shows that these positive effects work across a wide range of types of learning and development, including typing and proofreading skills, computer programming, diversity and sexual harassment seminars, team-building programmes, and police operations and military combat training. Moreover, the methods used as pre-learning interventions are in the main flexible, simple and easy-to-implement.

Source: Mesmer-Magnus, J., & Viswesvaran, C. (2010). The role of pre-training interventions in learning: A meta-analysis and integrative review. *Human Resource Management Review*, 20(4), 261–282.

The principles of cognitive learning theory are generalizable and can be translated readily into guidelines for designing, developing and implementing more effective face-to-face learning experiences as well as improving the design of learning materials in print (such as books, workbooks, infographics, etc.) and electronic form (such as web pages, PowerPoint slides, e-learning, etc.).

Reflective question 2.5

What have you learned from studying cognitive theory about how you could improve your own learning processes? What are some of the 'enablers' (see Reflective Question 2.2, these are the things that help to maximize learning, for example having a clear target or goal to guide achievement) of learning that you could 'takeaway' from cognitive learning theory? Have you learned anything from cognitive learning theory about things that constrain your personal learning?

Cognitive theory and motivation

The processes of cognition are closely connected to the psychology of motivation, and motivation is one of the most important factors in whether or not people engage with learning in the first place and also in how they learn. Cognitive theories recognize this fact and argue that motivation is important in learning because for learning to occur it must be 'energized' in some way. Expectancy theory and goal-setting theory are cognitive process theories that are relevant to HRD.

Victor Vroom's 'expectancy theory' from the 1960s states that in order for an individual to make an effort at a task he or she must believe that exerting the effort will increase the probability of getting the desired reward. Vroom's theory has three elements:

- Expectancy: the belief that effort and performance are linked;
- Instrumentality: the perceived likelihood that performance will achieve an outcome;
- Valence: the value (positive, negative or neutral) that an individual attaches to the outcome.

Vroom argued that learners will engage in learning because they think it's important to acquire knowledge and skills (valence); they believe that the more effort they put into learning the more knowledge and skills they'll acquire (expectancy); and they believe that the more knowledge and skill they acquire the more their performance will be enhanced (instrumentality).

Other practical implications of expectancy theory for HRD include the fact that the attitudes and values that an individual brings with them to the learning situation are crucial in deciding the extent to which they will engage in learning. It may, therefore, be necessary to try to explain the value of learning in order for learners to engage in learning and make explicit the anticipated links between learning performance, effort and reward. It's also important to recognize that attitudes towards learning are likely to vary between individuals depending on a wide variety of personal factors such as background, education, age, etc.[32]

In Edwin Locke and Gary Latham's 'goal-setting theory' a goal is defined as a desirable level of achievement and the theory is based on the assumptions that:

- Individuals who are given complex and challenging goals (that is, specific targets to be reached) perform better than those given no goals or simple and unchallenging ones;
- Goals are more effective in eliciting enhanced performance when they are specific rather than vague;
- To maintain or enhance individual's self-efficacy the goal should be commensurate with the individual's ability to successfully accomplish the goal;
- Participation in goal setting can enhance performance: the individual has to accept the goal that has been set;
- For goal-setting to be effective individuals need to be aware of the extent to which they are achieving the goal.[33]

Goal-setting theory has implications for HRD; for example, learning targets should be clear, challenging and achievable, goals should be negotiated and agreed in advance between learners and instructors, coaches, line managers, etc., and learners should be given feedback on the extent to which learning goals are being, or are likely to be, met.

In their own words 2.2

Gary P. Latham on the birth of goal-setting theory

In this interview based on an *Annual Review of Organizational Psychology and Organizational Behaviour* article in 2019 Gary P. Latham reflects on how he teamed up with Ed Locke in their seminal work on goal-setting theory. As Latham observes, 'The laboratory experiments show that if you tell someone a specific high goal [such as] for a number of simple additional problems to solve or anagrams to make words out of those with specific high goals do better than those who are urged to do their best.' In a separate study Latham found 'that loggers who set a specific high goal for the week harvest[ed] more trees than those who don't...What are the chances! I'll be darned!' You can listen to the rest of this fascinating interview with Professor Latham at: www.youtube.com/watch?v=fAHD7LN4CbU

Delve deeper 2.2

Increase your knowledge of goal-setting theory by reading Edwin Locke and Gary Latham's reflections on the past and future of goal-setting theory in:

Locke, E. A., & Latham, G. P. (2006). New directions in goal-setting theory. *Current Directions in Psychological Science, 15*(5), 265–268.

Having HRD goals that are driven by the principles of goal-setting theory (for example, 'achieve a score of 90 per cent' or 'beat your previous best time') is likely to mobilize goal-specific efforts on the part of the learner, direct their attention, increase persistence, and affect the strategies that learners use to accomplish complex tasks. On the other hand, simply asking someone to 'do their best' or 'try harder next time' is less likely to have the same beneficial effects on motivation or achievement. Likewise, HRD is likely to be enhanced when employees are provided with learning and development opportunities which they believe are important for the acquisition of job- and career-relevant knowledge and skills, where they can see a clear link to the enhancement of their potential and performance, and where there's a connection between effort and personal growth, performance and reward.

Perspective from practice 2.2

'Gamification' and learning

The learning and development company 'Growth Engineering' offers a checklist on its website for how to maximize employees' motivation to learn; they also suggest that 'gamification' (that is, taking something that's not a game, such as HRD, and applying 'game mechanics' to leverage participation and motivation) is a useful strategy for engaging and motivating employees to get involved in learning. They suggest using techniques such as 'game mechanics' or 'leader-boards' to encourage healthy competition, badges to give recognition and 'exploit the collector urge', and levels to give the intrinsic reward of progress to keep people going and to stretch learners. The method has been found to be especially suited to online learning where it's applied to the design of digital 'experiences' that will engage and motivate people to achieve a goal. However, it may also be the case that people who prefer online learning to face-to-face also enjoy 'gaming' in general.

Source: www.growthengineering.co.uk/motivate-employees-training/ (accessed 24-12-20).

Criticisms of the cognitive approach

One of the advantages of the cognitive approach over the behaviourist approach was that it looked inside the 'black box' of human cognition. It modelled learning as 'information processing' with various stores, different types of memory systems, and flows between them. However, one of the strengths of the cognitive approach is also one of its drawbacks, that is it tends to focus mainly on the individual mind and its internal mental processes (based on the assumption that human mental processes, such as learning, could be likened to the operations of a computer's information processing system).

This stance makes cognitive theory particularly useful in areas such as instructional design (which is concerned with optimizing the presentation, sequencing, etc. of information) and study skills (for example, by knowing some of the principles of cognitive learning we might be better paced to manage our own learning processes more effectively).

However, taking a purely cognitive approach runs the risk of overlooking the fact that learning in workplaces, or any other human context for that matter, arises out of the interactions between human beings and their social and physical environments (the people and things with which they interact). These criticisms can be summed up in the 'three-Es' of situated cognition:

* Cognition depends on the body as well as the brain ('embodiment');
* Cognitive activity is linked intimately with its physical and social environment ('embeddedness');
* The boundary of cognition extends beyond the boundary of the individual human organism ('extension').[34]

It was this observation that led some psychologists in the 1980s (such as John Seely Brown whose work we'll meet in the chapters on organizational learning and knowledge, and Edwin Hutchins, see below) to react against models of the human mind and human learning as 'computational' and take instead a 'situated' perspective on cognition and learning. The central argument of the situated cognition school of thought is that knowledge emerges out of the interaction between human learners and their environment. Proponents of this view have suggested that this shift is 'at least as profound as was the cognitive revolution that led to the over-turning of the then-dominant behaviourist paradigm'.[35]

These criticisms of the cognitive approach provide a useful bridge from cognitive theory to the social and situated learning theories that are the subject of the next chapter. In summary, the social and situated cognition perspectives move debates about learning and development in organizations forward by acknowledging that:

* Cognition is embodied (connected to the material body of the learner) and situated (in the learners' social setting, such as the workplace);
* Cognition arises out of the interaction between the individual and the context and is enacted for some purpose i.e. in order to do something.

The boundaries within which learning takes place are therefore expanded outside of the behaviourist's black box into which the cognitivists delved and into the world in which the learner is located. This also creates interesting connections to related concepts such as Edwin Hutchins' ideas about 'distributed cognition (DCog)' (cognition and knowledge aren't confined to an individual but are distributed across people, objects etc. in the environment, the 'mind is in the world' rather than 'the world is in the mind'[36]) and the idea of 'extended mind' (concerned with questions of where the mind stops and the rest of the world 'out there' begins).[37] As we'll discover in the next chapter, Bandura's social learning theory and Lave and Wenger's situated learning theory offer a somewhat different view in that both of them frame the psychology of human learning essentially as a social and relational process in which learning processes in social spaces, such as workplaces, are influenced profoundly by being around other people.

Delve deeper 2.3

Read more about criticisms of cognitivism and the responses from embodied and situated cognition, and the idea of the extended mind, in:

Clark, A., & Chalmers, D. (1998). The extended mind. *Analysis, 58*(1), 7–19.

Dawson, M. (2014). Embedded and situated cognition. *The Routledge handbook of embodied cognition.* Abingdon: Routledge.

Hutchins, E. (2000). Distributed cognition. *International encyclopaedia of the social and behavioral sciences.* Elsevier Science, p. 138.

Roth, W. M., & Jornet, A. (2013). Situated cognition. *Wiley Interdisciplinary Reviews: Cognitive Science, 4*(5), 463–478.

Conclusion: Meta-learning

Having completed this chapter on behaviourist and cognitive learning theories you will have gained knowledge and understanding about these two theories of learning, but in addition you may also have, incidentally, arrived at some insights into your own learning processes. You might have gained a personal understanding of how reinforcement has supported (or impeded) your learning (behaviourism), how your memory operates and what has made successful learning experiences meaningful for you (cognitivism); you might also be able to develop study skills and strategies to enhance the effectiveness of your own learning. Therefore, a supplementary outcome from reading the theories of learning chapters and understanding and applying their content might be that you will learn more about how to learn ('learning-how-to-learn'). As a result of this you will hopefully become a better learner. If you've learned about your own learning practices, preferences and processes then 'meta-learning' will have taken place.

'Meta' is from Greek, and it means 'after', 'higher-order' or 'self-referential'. This chapter is, in a sense, 'meta' in that one of its implicit aims is to help you to learn about (your own) learning from the perspective of behaviourist and cognitive learning theories. Meta-learning refers to processes such as how individuals monitor, assess and regulate their learning and thinking processes, and makes use of explicit tools and techniques such as study skills and time management. Developing personal meta-learning strategies will help you to overcome many of the challenges associated with acquiring new knowledge and skills, and hence help you to be able to learn, and think, more effectively and efficiently. Although there are some generic 'meta-learning strategies',[38] every individual has to develop their own custom-built approach based on what works best for them but learning how to learn is also a vital strategy for being an effective lifelong learner.

Chapter checkout

Use this list to check your understanding of the key points of this chapter.

1 **Learning**   Longer-term change in the knowledge possessed by an individual, their type and level of skill, or their assumptions, attitudes or values (KSAs)

2 **Theory**   Describes and explains a phenomenon based on evidence and observation; theories enable predictions to be made and are testable through falsification

3 **Behaviourist learning theory**   Describes/explains learning in terms of shaping (conditioning) of behaviour through positive reinforcement or negative reinforcement; focuses on observable behaviours rather than internal phenomena such as thoughts or feelings

4 **Cognitivist learning theory**   Describes/explains learning in terms of transfers and flows of information from sensory register, through short-term (working) memory to long-term storage; mechanisms operate through processes of encoding, retrieval and storage of information in mental models (schemas)

5 **Meaningful**   Cognitive theory suggests that to be effective, learning should be 'meaningful' for example by linking new information to information already in LTM

6 **Motivation**   Motivation as an essential prerequisite and component of the learning process; in the design of HRD motivational factors should be acknowledged and accommodated, for example in managing expectations, and the process of goal setting

7 **Criticisms**   Cognitive information processing models focus on individual brains and may overlook the significance of social and environmental factors (situated cognition was one response to this shortcoming)

8 **Meta-learning**   Understanding concepts/theories of learning offer insights into one's own learning processes; through such insights we can monitor and control, and improve, our own learning, and thinking processes

SKILLS DEVELOPMENT 2
USING BEHAVIOURIST AND COGNITIVE LEARNING THEORY TO ENHANCE ON-JOB TRAINING

On-job training is one of the commonest methods of training. It involves training at the learner's place of work (desk, workstation, machine, etc.), and can be by means of self-study using digital learning, coaching from a co-worker or line manager, etc.[39] Imagine that you are the HRD advisor to a company which will delegate much of the training that is currently undertaken off-job (for example, in training rooms) by specialized instructors to line managers and delivered as on-job training. Amongst the reasons for using this method are:

- Line managers are closer to the job and understand not only how the job should be done but also what knowledge and skills each employee needs;
- Involving line managers in the delivery of training will be more effective and efficient, for example it is likely to enhance the transfer of training (see Chapter 6) and result in cost savings;
- Delivering training on the job will result in reduced down time and therefore save on training costs.

You have been given the task of helping the line managers (none of whom are educated to degree level) to become more effective as on-job trainers by sharing with them the basics of behaviourist and cognitive learning theories and giving them 'actionable knowledge' of when, why and how behaviourist and cognitive principles can be used in on-job training. Prepare a list of 'handy hints' for line managers that they could use when delivering on-job training to their staff.

Your 'handy hints' should be in the form of a credit card-sized 'job aid' that can fit into the manager's purse, wallet or pocket and which has 'Do's' on one side, and 'Don'ts' on the other. A job aid is 'any material that provides simple information about how to perform a task', for example, a checklist, prompts, protocols, flowcharts, handy hints, etc. They can be a very efficient way to present new information and getting employees up-to-speed in applying new learning to the job. If a job aid does its job it should eventually become redundant as the information on it becomes second nature to the employee. If you're not sure what one looks like follow the link in the endnote to a commercial website with examples.[40]

3
LEARNING FROM AND WITH OTHERS

Contents

On completion of this chapter you should be able to:

* Describe and explain social and situated theories of learning;
* Critically evaluate social and situated theories of learning;
* Use your knowledge and understanding of social and situated theories of learning to advise on the design and delivery of HRD.

Introduction

In the previous chapter emphasis was placed on individual learners' cognitive processes, but as we discovered the focus on the individual can be seen as a drawback of cognitive learning theory. In this chapter the emphasis switches from individuals' behaviours and cognitions to learning through social processes situated in the workplace and other social contexts. It's about learning from and with others. The chapter explores two theories of learning that offer complementary perspectives on how individuals learn from and in relation to others: 'social learning theory' (sometimes referred as 'social cognitive learning theory') and 'situated learning theory'. One of these (social learning theory) is a mainstream psychological learning theory (as were behavioural and cognitive learning theories), whilst the other (situated learning theory) is more of a sociological and anthropological theory.

The underlying theme in both of these theories is that human learning is essentially a social and relational process and as such it is influenced profoundly by being around and interacting with other people. This not only fits with common sense and experience, it also makes sense from an evolutionary perspective given that *Homo sapiens* is amongst the most social of all species. It also makes sense that without social learning human beings, all the way back to our earliest ancestors, would not have been able to develop the technologies that enabled our species not only to survive and thrive but to dominate the planet. Our learning is not only 'embrained' and 'embodied',[1] it is also 'encultured' in that it occurs in a process of cultural and social immersion.[2] Social and situated learning theories put these common sense observations onto a theoretical footing. Social and situated learning theories provide HRD research and practice with good scientific reasons for why methods such as role modelling and apprenticeships are highly effective means of developing knowledge and skills. Like cognitive theory from the previous chapter and the experienced-based modalities in the next chapter, social and situated learning theories help us as students, researchers and practitioners to describe, explain and make predictions about learning and development in the social and situated setting of the workplace.

Social learning theory

This section provides a brief introduction to social learning theory and discusses some of its applications in HRD. The pioneer of social learning theory was the Canadian-American psychologist Albert Bandura (1925–2021) of Stanford University. Bandura proposed that humans learn through observation, imitation and modelling of others. Modelling relies on 'identification', that is a process in which a 'person patterns [her] his thoughts, feelings or actions after another person who serves as a model'.[3] Bandura's comment that 'the provision of social models is an indispensable means of transmitting and modifying behaviour' summarized one of the most actionable ideas behind his theory.[4]

Much of Bandura's research focused on child development but his discoveries have been extended and can be applied more widely. It was in the early 1960s that Bandura set out to explore how simply watching how another person behaved, in this case an adult, could influence a child's behaviour. He studied a controversial and important topic – aggression. A view at the time, which seems extraordinary now, was that watching aggression for example in a movie, or on the new and increasingly popular medium of TV, would somehow act cathartically as a release valve and lead to lower levels of aggression. Bandura's research overturned this idea radically. In a famous series of experiments Bandura and his team of researchers were able to raise and lower the levels of aggression in young children by manipulating the levels of aggression in the behaviour of an adult role model who was being observed by the children. The children could be induced to act more aggressively by watching an adult (referred to in the theory as the 'model') being aggressive: the children acted in an aggressive and violent way as a result of observing an adult model's behaviour.

Bandura's most famous experiments involved studying how children learned from observing adults' behaviour towards a 'Bobo' doll. Bandura put a child and an adult in a room with a large inflatable Bobo doll (a popular toy in the 1960s a metre or so high made of plastic and featuring an image of a clown, designed to self-right when pushed over). Seventy-two children were involved in the experiments in which there were two conditions ('aggressive adult role model' and 'non-aggressive adult role model') and a 'no model' control group. There were 24 children in each group. In the 'aggressive' experimental condition the adult assaulted the Bobo doll in a violent manner for several minutes by kicking and hitting it with a hammer and shouting. The researchers were interested in what a child would then do when they were left in the room alone with the Bobo doll? The results were, at the time, surprising as well as shocking:

- The children assaulted the doll in much the same ways as they had observed the aggressive adult role model behaving towards the doll;
- A parallel group who'd watched an adult role model play gently didn't show aggressive behaviour towards the doll.

In later studies Bandura and colleagues found that even when a child merely saw a film in which another person was being rewarded for hitting the doll they were also more likely to be aggressive themselves. The closest match in behaviours was when the child had observed an adult of the same sex.

The major insight from this research was that behaviour is learned from social stimuli in the environment through the processes of observational learning. The conclusion was that human behaviour could be readily influenced, and potentially manipulated, socially both directly and indirectly. The findings had significant implications, not least for the new medium of TV and how it might be able to influence human behaviour on a large scale. The social process of learning from a human model is called 'observational learning' and Bandura's Bobo doll research laid the foundations for social learning theory. Bandura is keen to point out that observational learning is not merely mimicry, because once learners learn the underlying principles of behaviour they can use them to generate or improvise new instances of behaviour in contexts other than those in which the observational learning took place.[5] It should also be noted that Bandura's studies were criticized on a number of grounds, for example, the sample was biased in that the children were nursery school age and all attended the Stanford University nursery. Questions were also asked about how generalizable and long-term the effects were likely to be.

In their own words 3.1

Albert Bandura on social learning theory

Albert Bandura (1925–2021), see above, was a Canadian-American Stanford University social psychology professor, and one of the most influential psychologists of the twentieth century. He was presented with the National Medal of Science by President Barack Obama in 2016. Bandura summed up the principles and the value of social learning theory in these words for his 1977 book *Social Learning Theory*: 'Learning would be exceedingly laborious, not to mention hazardous, if people had to rely solely on the effects of their own actions to inform them what to do. Fortunately, most human behaviour is learned observationally through modelling: from observing others one forms an idea of how new behaviours are performed, and on later occasions, this coded information serves as a guide for action.' Although Bandura's work uses behaviourist-type terms such as 'conditioning' and 'reinforcement' the vital difference is that, as Bandura himself explained 'I conceptualized these phenomena as operating through cognitive processes…[some] continue to mischaracterize my approach as rooted in behaviourism'; he himself would characterize it as 'social cognitivism'.[6]

You can listen to Albert Bandura explaining the background and principles of social learning theory in this video: www.youtube.com/watch?v=KOMkZbQauOA and a more in-depth interview at www.youtube.com/watch?v=-_U-pSZwHy8 exploring Bandura's remarkable career and seminal contribution to social psychology.

Social learning theory describes, explains and predicts how social influences can alter individuals' thoughts, feelings and actions through cognitive, vicarious (that is, through the experiences of others), self-regulative and self-reflective processes. Social learning theory argues that as well as learning through direct experiences, individuals can learn vicariously by observing another individual making a particular action or response and by witnessing the outcomes of that action or response. Through observation and interpretation we can profit from the successes and mistakes of others, and we can learn good as well as bad habits from merely watching what they do. The process of social learning involves four stages; see Figure 3.1.

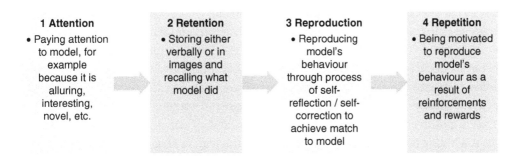

Figure 3.1 The process of social learning

As mentioned above, Bandura's original research happened to be conducted at the time, the 1960s, when television was taking-off as a mass medium of entertainment, and it soon became clear that the processes of social learning via mass media created the possibility of influencing the behaviour of large numbers of people. Advancements in technology amplify observational learning's power for both good and bad.[7] For example in the post-TV digital age, social media use combined with anonymity facilitates the social learning processes in ways that can foster negative behaviours such as cyberbullying.[8]

── Reflective question 3.2 ──

In the light of what you already know about your own experiences of learning, what role has observational learning and role modelling played in significant learning episodes in your life? What would you say to Bandura's claim that 'Virtually *all* learning resulting from direct experience can also occur on a vicarious basis by observing the behaviour of others and its consequences' (emphasis added).[9] What are the positive behaviours and qualities that you would expect a role model manager or leader to display?

Social cognitive learning theory

Bandura's theory came to be known as 'social cognitive theory' on the basis that learning is an outcome of interactions between behavioural, cognitive and environmental factors. The relationships between the individual and their environment is bi-directional in that the environment influences the individual's learning but the individual also influences the environment. This three-way relationship between behaviour (B), cognitive and other personal factors (P) and environment (E) is called 'triadic reciprocal determinism' ('reciprocal' meaning that the three events, P, B and E, operate interactively, and 'determinism' meaning that events produce effects).[10] It's based on the assumption that learners' personal characteristics, thoughts, feelings and behaviours play an active and interactive role in the learning process (unlike in behaviourism where learning simply involves learning of associations and reinforcements). For example, a trainee who is not motivated to learn (personal factor) and is uncooperative (behavioural factor) may have an effect on the training environment such that demotivation is socially contagious; the trainer may have to change the training environment to accommodate these effects as a consequence, and these changes may reciprocally create a positive change in the trainee and the rest of the group.[11] Bandura's theory forms a bridge between behaviourism and cognitivism; see Figure 3.2.

Bandura's theory has stood the test of time, and more recently neuroscience is also offering a biological perspective into the processes of social cognition and learning. Researchers in the early 2000s discovered 'mirror neurons' in the brains of macaque monkeys which 'fired' not only when the monkey executed grasping actions itself (for example, grabbing a grape), but also when it observed an experimenter or another monkey doing the same thing. Mirror neurons aren't easy to fool either: they fire only in response to the observation of a real hand not a mechanical grabbing device such as pliers. Mirror neurons may offer a biological explanation for how human actions can be influenced unconsciously by merely observing the actions of another person and for empathy.[12]

Behavioural factors

- Receiving reinforcement through encouragement or approbation; can be direct or indirect (for example, watching someone else being rewarded for a particular behaviour)

Cognitive factors

- Thinking about mechanisms that link causes and effects; takes place prior to imitation; mediates between the observed stimulus (such as the role model behaviour) and the behavioural response

Environmental factors

- Social context such as learned social norms for what is acceptable in a given situation; learning on the basis of relationships in a social setting such as perception of role model behaviour, behavioural response to role model

Figure 3.2 Social learning theory links behaviour, cognition and environment

---

Delve deeper 3.1

Find out more about the history and fundamentals of Bandura's social learning theory by reading the original studies from the early 1960s. Also a film of the original experiments is widely available on the internet:

Bandura, A., Ross, D. & Ross, S. A. (1961). Transmission of aggression through imitation of aggressive models. *The Journal of Abnormal and Social Psychology, 63*, 575–582.

Bandura, A., Ross, D., & Ross, S. A. (1963). Imitation of film-mediated aggressive models. *The Journal of Abnormal and Social Psychology, 66*(1), 3–11.

Bandura, A. (1977). *Social learning theory*. Englewood Cliffs, NJ: Prentice Hall.

These are the classic social learning studies from over half a century ago. For a more recent summary of social learning theory and observational learning go to:

Bandura, A. (2008). Observational learning. In *The international encyclopaedia of communication*. Wiley online library.

Social learning theory and HRD

Social learning theory later became known as 'social cognitive theory' in order to reflect its emphasis on cognition. It links behaviourism (for example, the concept of rewards, punishments and reinforcements) with cognitivism (for example, internal mental states, attention, motivation and memory). The theory is behavioural in that it involves, amongst other things, reinforcement, but it's also cognitive in that it recognizes, unlike the radical behaviourists who weren't interested in internal states, human beings' ability to intuitively work-out and predict cause-and-effect relationships and the role of contingent environmental and social factors.

Applications of social learning are to be found in a number of HRD methods and activities wherever one person learns from another, this can be learning from a trainer in a training room, from a supervisor in on-the-job learning, or from a coach or mentor in management and leader development. Research suggests that managers learn from both positive and negative role models. Exemplars of positive managerial behaviours observed in role models included supporting colleagues, empathy, feedback, work ethic, results-focus, honesty and coping. Exemplars of negative managerial behaviours observed in role models included insensitivity, bullying, lack of engagement, prioritizing process over people, and ineffectiveness. Researchers have concluded that HRD practitioners should 'recognise and enhance the everyday process of role modelling to ensure managers learn the crucial facets of management and leadership practice which cannot be taught through [formal] management education'.[13]

Perspective from practice 3.1

Making a difference through role models

Effective role models from whom employees can learn can make a significant difference to individual performance and well-being as well as organizational climate and culture. Practical tips for getting the best out of role modelling are set out in Figure 3.3.

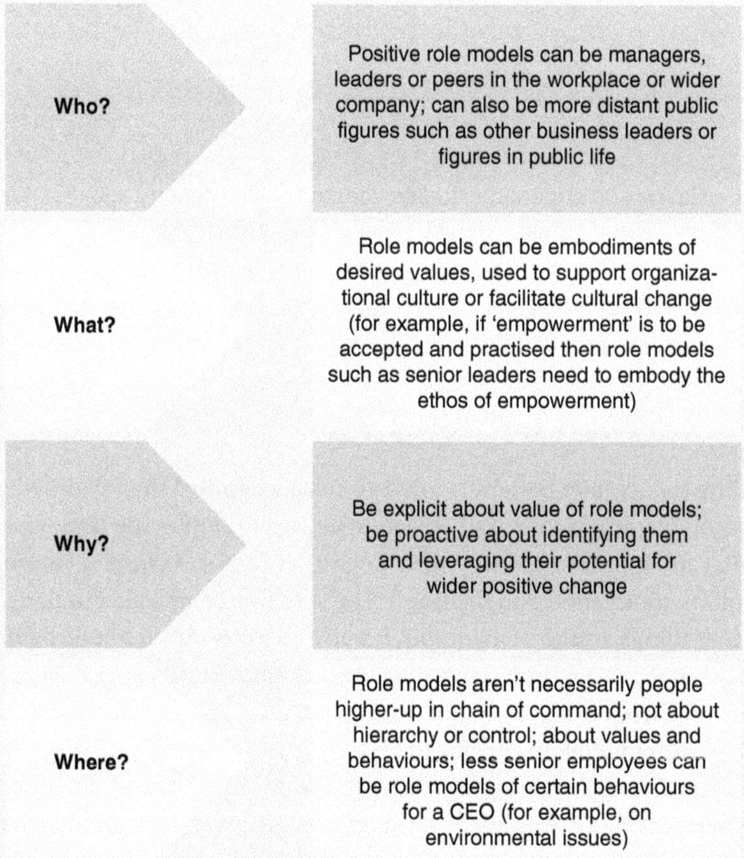

Who?	Positive role models can be managers, leaders or peers in the workplace or wider company; can also be more distant public figures such as other business leaders or figures in public life
What?	Role models can be embodiments of desired values, used to support organizational culture or facilitate cultural change (for example, if 'empowerment' is to be accepted and practised then role models such as senior leaders need to embody the ethos of empowerment)
Why?	Be explicit about value of role models; be proactive about identifying them and leveraging their potential for wider positive change
Where?	Role models aren't necessarily people higher-up in chain of command; not about hierarchy or control; about values and behaviours; less senior employees can be role models of certain behaviours for a CEO (for example, on environmental issues)

Figure 3.3   Who, what, why and wheres of role modelling

It's important to acknowledge that role models can be negative as well as positive, therefore anyone who is a potential role model (and perhaps we all are) is vigilant and self-reflective about how they are behaving and how their behaviour can influence, inform and impact upon those who might be looking to them as examples even if this may not be immediately apparent.

Sources: Cook, S. and McCauley, S. (2014). Making a difference. Training Journal. www.trainingjournal.com/articles/feature/making-difference (accessed 03-01-21); Warhurst, R. (2011). Role modelling in manager development: Learning that which cannot be taught. Journal of European Industrial Training, 35(9), 874–891.

Another important idea that came out of Bandura's research was 'self-efficacy', defined as 'judgement of one's capability to accomplish a certain level of performance'.[14] Social learning theory exerts an important influence on learning and workplace behaviours through the development of individuals' beliefs in their capability to perform effectively in a given situation. When self-efficacy is high an individual is more likely to set higher goals and have a firmer commitment to those goals. As we know from goal-setting theory,[15] goals in many aspects of work (and personal life) including learning and development provide a sense of purpose and direction, and individuals seek self-satisfaction by fulfilling those goals.

In the HRD context if individuals 'believe in themselves' it's more likely that they'll make the extra effort required to acquire new knowledge and skills. Additionally, encouragement from peers, leaders and managers functions as a form of social persuasion and can also be important in helping individuals to overcome self-doubts. In practical terms, learners can be given the opportunity to achieve success by having 'quick wins' which encourages them to strive harder; this also means that they'll be less likely to be put off by failure. Allied to this, setting challenging ('stretch') goals is important: meeting a stiff challenge or overcoming failure boosts self-efficacy, gives a sense of achievement and motivates learning.[16]

Work engagement (positive, fulfilling, work-related state of mind that is characterized by vigour, dedication and absorption)[17] has been shown to have significant effects on employee performance and well-being. Higher work engagement is a 'win–win': being more engaged means that employees are more likely not only to do a better job but also feel good about it and about themselves. In HRD settings social learning operates through the processes of observation, practice, feedback and correction and have applications in a wide range of tasks and roles including customer service training, leadership development, new employee induction and on-boarding, on-job training (OJT) and executive coaching. In the field of mentoring (see Chapter 7) research has found that mentees tend to select mentors who they see as role models on the presumption that they might 'assimilate aspects of the role model's attitudes, behaviours and values, and ultimately occupy the role model's life situation'.[18]

Moreover, because learning from role models and model behaviour can operate indirectly and at a distance (that is, vicariously) it isn't just confined to face-to-face learning in the classroom, factory or office, it can be used in video and other technology-based methods. For example, the CIPD leverages digital tools (for example, online communities, webinars and learning resources) to enable virtual mentoring relationships across geographically dispersed locations.[19] Not surprisingly, social media has significant implications for social learning processes in organizations given how social media has fundamentally changed how social interactions occur in society. The popularity of social media platforms such as Facebook, LinkedIn, Twitter, etc. confirms that we crave human interaction, even though it may be virtual, and underlines the potential of such media for learning from others vicariously in distributed social learning communities in negative as well as positive ways. Even though we are fundamentally 'human beings' and not 'virtual or cyber beings' social media can be a cost-effective and efficient way to place leaders in visible and accessible positions as role models for learning.[20]

Delve deeper 3.2

Extend your knowledge of the relevance of Bandura's theory for HRD by reading:

Gibson, S. K. (2004). Social learning (cognitive) theory and implications for human resource development. *Advances in Developing Human Resources*, 6(2), 193–210.

Read about role modelling in mentee-mentor relationships in:

Weinberg, F. J. (2019). How and when is role modelling effective? The influence of mentee professional identity on mentoring dynamics and personal learning outcomes. *Group & Organization Management*, 44(2), 425–477.

Read Bandura's classic article on his theory of self-efficacy in:

Bandura, A. (1977). Self-efficacy: Toward a unifying theory of behavioral change. *Psychological Review, 84*, 191–215.

Situated learning theory

Situated learning theory describes and explains how learning takes place informally, and often unintentionally, through activities in authentic, real-world contexts (such as the workplace). Like Bandura's theory, it links social processes to cognitive processes. Situated learning theory explains learning as a 'social' and 'relational' process in which knowledge and skill are produced and reproduced in situ rather than being transmitted in a classroom.[21] Learning takes place within a social setting (for example the relationships between a master and an apprentice or mentor and protégé) and individuals construct meaning through collaboration and interaction with others.

The origins of situated learning theory can be traced back to the work of the Russian psychologist Lev Vygotsky (1896–1934) who studied the role of social interaction in cognitive development. Vygotsky's work was mainly with children. It studied how learning takes place by the learner being steered by those who are more knowledgeable and skilled from where they are now to where they want or need to be. The process takes place through guidance, practice and feedback that steer the learner through their 'zone of proximal development' (ZPD); see Figure 3.4.

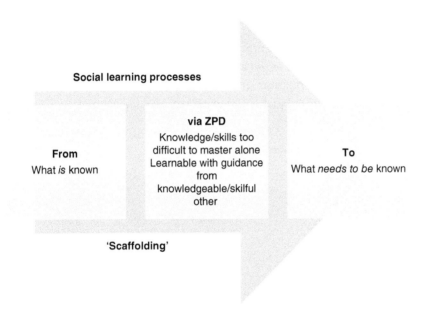

Figure 3.4 Zone of proximal development (ZPD) between what is known and what is not known

The ZPD occupies the space between what the learner knows/can do and what they don't know/can't do. In Vygotsky's theory learning should provide experiences that are within (that is neither beyond nor below) the ZPD, in his words: the 'distance between the actual developmental level determined by individual problem-solving and the level of development as determined through problem-solving under guidance or in collaboration with more capable peers'.[22] Related to this is the notion of 'scaffolding' (an addition by others to Vygotsky's original theory), which is the process whereby a more capable person (sometime referred to as a 'more knowledgeable other', MKO) guides the learner through the ZPD and tapers-off help as it becomes no longer required, analogous to the scaffolding being removed from a building once the required height has been reached and its support is no longer needed.

The 'authentic' real-world contexts in which socially-situated learning processes occur were labelled 'communities of practice' by the two researchers who are most closely associated with situated learning theory: the social anthropologist Jean Lave, and social learning theorist Etienne Wenger.[23] In the 1970s and 1980s Lave and Wenger conducted anthropological studies of forms of apprenticeships in different parts of the world, including midwives, tailors, navy quartermasters, meat cutters, insurance claims processors and several other domains of practice (though not all these involved a 'master–apprentice' relationship).

The theory of situated learning and the related concepts of 'community of practice' (CoP) and 'legitimate peripheral participation' (LPP) have central place in the knowledge, organizational learning and HRD literatures.[24] Jean Lave's original 1991 work expressed the key idea succinctly: 'Such a view invites a rethinking of the notion of learning, treating it as an emerging property of whole persons' legitimate peripheral participation in communities of practice' (p. 63). Lave describes situated learning as a 'cognition plus' view because it describes and explains how people process, represent, remember and recall information (that is, they cognitively process it) 'in relation to each other and while located in a social world' (p. 66); see Figure 3.5.

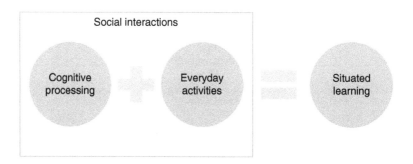

Figure 3.5　Situated learning as 'cognition plus' everyday activity in the context of social interactions

In this view learning and knowing cannot be separated from everyday activity and social interaction. The process and activity itself is referred to as 'situated learning'. One of the main implications of this theory is that human cognition is embedded in and inseparable from the sociocultural context in which it's placed.

In their own words 3.2

Jean Lave and Etienne Wenger on communities of practice and everyday life and learning

For a brief general introduction to what communities of practice are and why researchers and practitioners in so many different contexts find them useful as an approach to knowing and learning go to the website of Etienne and Beverley Wenger-Trayner: https://wenger-trayner.com/introduction-to-communities-of-practice/. By following this link you can watch Jean Lave talk about 'everyday life and learning' in this University of California video: www.youtube.com/watch?v=FAYs46icCFs

---

Learning, legitimacy and participation

Some of the original research that was used in developing situated learning theory was conducted amongst apprentices (in domains such as midwifery, tailoring and butchery). In situated learning theory the term 'master–apprentice' is often used but it should not be thought of as 'teacher–pupil' in disguise. The more knowledgeable others in situated learning can be 'capable peers' or 'masters' (such as a master craftsperson) in a 'community of practice' but they do not engage typically in direct 'didactic' learning (or teaching) methods. The capable peer, more knowledgeable other or master, as well as being sources of knowledge and skill, also provide newcomers with legitimate (that is, 'authenticated') access to the community and its practices.[25] In apprenticeships, the apprentice becomes a member of the master's professional community by spending a significant amount of time in that community carrying out tasks that are within the community's domain of practice. As a result they are absorbed into the community and the profession gradually and naturally.[26] Through transformations of knowledge, understanding, skill and identity 'newcomers' become 'old timers'.[27] The new old-timers constitute the community of practice for the next newcomers and so the process continues. In Lave and Wenger's theory of situated learning a community of practice has three components: domain, community and practice; see Figure 3.6.

Domain

- A community of practice isn't just a network of people or a club
  (for example, bird watching doesn't qualify, for 'why' see text)
- Its identity is defined by a shared domain of interest (e.g. radiologists, teachers, street gang members, artists, etc.)
- Membership implies a commitment to the domain of interest

Community

- Members interact and engage in mutual activities by sharing information, helping each other out, and building relationships
- Processes enable them to practise in their domain of interest and learn from each other
- Doesn't require that they work together on a daily basis
  (e.g. the Impressionist painters were a community of practice even though they worked alone)

Practice

- Members need to be practitioners of a recognized practice
  (e.g. delivering babies, performing surgical procedures, educating children, painting impressionist pictures, etc.)

Figure 3.6 Components of a community of practice

—Research insight 3.1—

Medicine as a community of practice

Researchers from McGill University in Montreal explored the relevance of situated learning theory as a framework and 'foundational theory' for medical education. They described medical practice in terms of the three elements as follows:

- Domain: the domain of medicine is 'the prevention of disease and the promotion of the public good';
- Community: medicine consists of many communities of practice and physicians, for example, generally belong to more than one including the global and local medicine communities, their medical speciality, their professional institution, etc.;
- Practice: this is the set of 'frameworks, ideas, tools, information, styles, language, stories and documents' that members share and practice consists of 'clinical care, educational practices, and research'.

Engaging medical students in joining their community of practice supports their professional identity formation and 'the development of their own identities helps them to better understand their personal journeys from laypersons to professionals'. The researchers conclude with a quote about the nature of medical expertise: 'Expertise is not simply a property that passes from teacher to learner, but a dynamic commodity that resides within communities of practice; learning, according to the theory, is a process of absorbing and being absorbed into the culture of such a community' (p. 190). Try this out for HRD in Reflective Question 3.3 (p. 79).

Source: Cruess, R. L., Cruess, S. R., & Steinert, Y. (2018). Medicine as a community of practice: Implications for medical education. *Academic Medicine*, *93*(2), 185–191.

The community of practice concept can be extended well beyond the idea of apprenticeships and is a useful tool for theorizing learning in workplace settings more generally. The apprenticeship is a formalized relationship, but Lave notes that communities of practices in workplaces are mostly ad hoc, for example as in the 'shop floor' culture of workplaces. Lave and Wenger's foundational ideas about situated learning in communities of practice have been applied widely across domains as diverse as management, law, health, and education. It's hard to know what it's like to be in a specific community of practice without being in one. Nonetheless, from the outside looking in there are some signs to look out for; see Figure 3.7.

A community of practice is a building block of a social learning system. The members of the community are legitimately 'practitioners', not just people who meet and talk

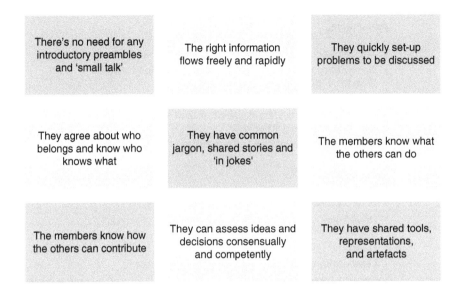

Figure 3.7 What does a community of practice look or feel like?

Source: adapted from Amin, A., & Roberts, J. (2008). Knowing in action: Beyond communities of practice. *Research Policy, 37*(2), 353–369.

about something they like to do for fun (for example, like friends who meet in a birdwatching club). They have a consequential shared practical endeavour (usually in an organizational or work system context), repertoire of resources such as language, tools, experiences, stories, etc., they engage in joint activities and discussions, they learn and interact together, and help each other and share information. The community's identity is defined by a shared domain of interest, and they are not limited by formal structures: they create connections among people across organizational and geographic boundaries.[28] Examples of communities of practice include such diverse groups as actors, teachers, surgical teams, footballers, flute-makers, orchestral players, street gangs, students, university professors, and HRD practitioners.

Situated learning processes

Newcomers to the community learn and are admitted and absorbed into them through the process of legitimate peripheral participation. Newcomers become included in a community of practice through engaging in the practices of the community legitimately (permitted by the community) and at first peripherally ('on the edge' as a precursor to full participation); see Figure 3.8.

Peripherality

- Approximation and precursor to full inclusion in the community
- Gives newcomers access and exposure to real world practice 'from the edge'
- Affords them a sense of how the community operates
- Content of the community members' shared endeavour is not an explicit written-down scheme
- Shared endeavour integral to the practices of the community itself

Legitimacy

- Potential members are selected by the community
- Newcomers who are selected to participate are potential full members of the community
- Newcomers on the edge at first
- Lessons newcomers are 'given' aren't about practice
- Lessons are part of practice
- Learning takes place within practice

Figure 3.8 Components of 'legitimate peripheral participation'

New members also learn through a process of 'enculturation' that draws on the community's anecdotes, jokes and stories and which constitute an important part of its collective memory.[29] Membership also comes with a collective responsibility for creating and managing knowledge, and in their practices members attend to the tacit and dynamic aspects of knowledge creation and knowledge sharing. The fact that knowledge is 'situated' (that is, in context), 'provisional' (in flux), and 'pragmatic' (in use) is illustrated by a Julian Orr's classic study of Xerox photocopying machine maintenance technicians *Talking about machines: An ethnography of a modern job* (1996). Xerox's own research into organizational learning by John Seely Brown and Paul Duguid found that the ways people actually work differ substantially from the ways in which their work is formally described in manuals, job descriptions, etc. ('canonical practice'), i.e. the actual practice was 'non-canonical' (not 'by-the-book'). In the case of technicians, the stories shared by technicians about the complex technical problems they encountered served three learning functions:

- Informational function: circulating and preserving new knowledge about problems encountered and solutions found in doing their work;
- Educational function: further developing technicians' diagnostic and trouble shooting skills;
- Identity function: enabling members to establish and maintain their identity within the community, newcomers demonstrating their identity as members of the community by participating in storytelling and contributing to the collective knowledge of the community.[30]

Orr described the practice of experienced technicians maintaining Xerox photo-copiers as a 'continuous highly skilled improvisation within a triangular relationship of technician, customer and machine' (p. 1) in which the primary element of the practice is 'narrative', technicians shared discourses about their experiences. The 'circulation of stories' (p. 2) within the community of practice constitutes the social distribution of learnings not from formal classes (even though the technicians were highly skilled and formally well-trained) but from their lived experience of their practice.[31]

Reflective question 3.3

What would be the 'domain', 'community' and 'practice' for HRD? Given that communities of practice aren't formally constituted departments, or project teams or task forces and aren't organizationally bounded but are in Lave's words 'mostly ad hoc' (p. 79),[32] do you think that a community of practice can ever be a legitimate HRD intervention or solution (that is, something that's deliberately created and managed)? Or could trying to capture the knowledge and skills that are enacted in the community's practices be a futile endeavour because once they're extracted and formalized they lose their meaning? Explain your reasoning.

On the face of it the answer to this question ought to be 'no', given what has already been said about autonomy, emergence, freedom, independence, tacitness, informality, and organicism and the structuring of spontaneity in learning. But there have been efforts at managing communities of practice and also intentionally creating them. Such efforts rely on strategies for developing trust, encouraging collaboration, and creating shared meaning (for example, developing shared mental models) as well as managing the power dynamics within the group.[33] Even though knowledge creation and exchange within a community is organic and emergent, it can be facilitated if managers are able to create a psychologically safe environment. Such an environment recognizes knowledge sharing, encourages fairness and reciprocity, rewards helping behaviours, and satisfies basic requirements for affiliation by creating spaces in which members can interact both professionally and socially.[34] Supporting naturally occur-ring, or even deliberately creating, communities of practice can be justified in terms of the benefits they bring for managing change, enabling easier access to knowledge and giving quicker response times to problems. Communities of practice have been shown to have more efficient 'learning curves' and are able to generate ideas for new products and services more quickly and develop organizational memory faster. Communities of practice can also be constructive disruptors of the organizational status quo.[35]

──Delve deeper 3.3──

Read about the classic Xerox research and its wider implications in:

Brown, J. S., & Duguid, P. (1991). Organizational learning and communities-of-practice: Toward a unified view of working, learning, and innovation. *Organization Science*, 2(1), 40–57.

Orr, J. E. (2006). Ten years of talking about machines. *Organization Studies*, 27(12), 1805–1820.

Yanow, D. (2006). Talking about practices: On Julian Orr's talking about machines. *Organization Studies*, 27(12), 1743–1756.

Read more about evolutionary explanations for the pervasiveness and power of storytelling in human social groups in:

Yang, C. (2013). Telling tales at work: An evolutionary explanation. *Business Communication Quarterly*, 76(2), 132–154.

Apprenticeships

As noted above, Lave and Wenger's original research included anthropological studies of different types of apprenticeship learning (including midwives, butchers and tailors) in which novices learn not only from 'masters', that is experts, but also from other novices in the social setting of their practice (for example, the workplace of the supermarket for the butchers). The concept of an 'apprenticeship' can be traced back as far as the Middle Ages in Europe whilst in China apprenticeships had been the major approach to training handicraft workers for thousands of year through the processes of 言传身教 ('hands-on learning') and 现场传授 ('on-site teaching').[36] In Europe's medieval craft guilds apprentices were employed and craft proficiency was certified by completion of an apprenticeship 'indenture' (an agreement).[37] An apprentice is a 'learner of a craft, bound to serve, and entitled to instruction from, her or his employer for a specified period'.[38] It's a term that's also used to describe a beginner or novice. A 'journeyman' is at an intermediate stage between an apprentice and a master.

The idea of apprenticeship has been more popular in some cultures than others. In countries such as the UK it suffered a decline in popularity in recent decades and became seen as something of an anachronism in the knowledge economy and with the expansion of university education. However, there have been encouraging moves towards reclaiming apprenticeships. In the UK there has been government support for initiatives that combine on-the-job training with a programme of study and the introduction of degree apprenticeships that enable learners to gain a bachelor's or master's degree by combining working with studying part-time at a university. These developments confirm that the master–apprentice relationship is alive-and-well as one of the most enduring and powerful learning and development 'tools' because it:

- Affords learners a unique supportive structuring for knowledge acquisition and skills' development;
- Gives a graduated approach to learners' formation as experts (as in 'scaffolding', see above);
- Builds not only individual but also collective expertise though mutual learning between peers as well as through the expert/novice relationship;
- Is highly consistent with relevant learning concepts and theories (such as role modelling, situated learning, experiential learning, etc.).

In an apprenticeship, consistent with situated learning theory, learners are introduced to the periphery of a legitimate community of practitioners (for example, an occupational group such as pastry chefs, potters or plumbers). As such they become immersed increasingly in the activities of their 'trade', they see and feel the community from the earliest stages of their learning journey. By being absorbed into the community apprentices also attain a broader perspective on what their trade is about over-and-above the minutiae of the tasks they're involved in.[39] Learning by apprenticing is arguably the ultimate in 'learner-centredness'. The goal is an attainment of a level of craft (whether it be a plumber, musician or a lawyer) at which the apprentice can work without supervision and be accepted as a full member of the occupational community of practitioners.[40]

Perspective from practice 3.2

Making apprenticeships work

Apprenticeships are a distinct asset to learners, managers, organizations and wider society. However, to fulfil their potential both government and employers have to take responsibility for ensuring that they work as effectively as possible. The CIPD has set out its views on what employers need to do if apprenticeships are to fulfil their potential:

- Apprenticeships need to be part of regular workforce planning;
- Apprenticeships need to be aligned with business need and growth strategies;
- They should be targeted at areas where there are current or anticipated skills gaps and shortages;
- Apprenticeships must be high quality and offer a training route into a skilled role;
- Recruitment to apprenticeship programmes should maximize equality and diversity;
- Employers need to exercise due diligence in choosing providers of high quality off-job training;
- Employers need to be committed to providing the necessary practical support and guidance to make the scheme work.

(Continued)

When properly resourced and effectively implemented, apprenticeships present invaluable learning and development opportunities for individuals, and for organizations and society to build job relevant knowledge and vocational skills to a high level. They provide a structured route into the labour market for young people and enable them to progress their careers whilst at the same time supplying employers a motivated and engaged part of the workforce who will sustain and develop the higher level skills needed in a globally competitive environment. Apprenticeships are an important long-term, capacity-building investment in human capital.

Source: www.cipd.co.uk/news-views/viewpoint/apprenticeships-investment-training (accessed 23-02-2020)

In terms of how learning takes place in an apprenticeship, and also in communities of practice in general, knowledge and skills are conveyed explicitly from the expert (master) to novice (apprentice) in the forms of words or images, but tacit (that is, 'unspoken') knowledge also grows through the observing and mirroring of behaviours. One of the originators of the term 'tacit knowledge' and author of the famous quote 'we can know more than we can tell', Michael Polanyi, observed that 'by watching the master and emulating his efforts in the presence of his example, the apprentice unconsciously picks up the rules of the art, including those which are not explicitly known to the master himself'.[41] To be effective, apprenticeship learning[42] should have both breadth and depth:

- Breadth of exposure to authentic tasks gives learners an appreciation of the scope of the domain of their knowledge and skill and builds social capital;
- Depth of learning requires a productive relationship to be forged between theory and practice and whereby knowledge and skill, and theory and practice are dualistic rather than detached from each other.

A practical implication of this is that the combination of on-job and off-job learning that apprenticeships provide gives learners opportunities to develop and apply theoretical and conceptual knowledge in the work situation, and also to think and reflect on their learning and working practices in the formal learning setting of the classroom. This highlights the importance of the social aspects of apprenticing and the fact that, in the words of cognitive psychologist Robert Sternberg, 'getting connected to people in the know' is a wise strategy for the acquisition not only of tacit knowledge but also the 'practical intelligence' (or 'nous') that's needed in order to navigate successfully though volatile, uncertain, complex and ambiguous learning and working environments.[43]

Criticisms of situated learning

'Community' is often interpreted as a 'friendly' word, with positive connotations; however, communities of practice like all human institutions have their downsides. Etienne Wenger himself points to a number of these, including the effects of cliques, disconnectedness, dogmatism, dysfunctionality, exclusivity, factionalism, imperialism, localism, mediocrity, and narcissism.[44] Some of these drawbacks are paradoxical in that they are over-extensions of the community's strengths (that is, its strengths can become its weaknesses). Other researchers have identified problematic issues with communities of practice relating specifically to:

- The influence of power from within and outside on learning processes;
- How trust can enable or constrain learning in communities of practice;
- The limits that habits and predispositions place on learning.

Power is the ability to achieve some end by control, force or influence, and even though communities of practice ideally should be places that are free from the negative effects of power, inevitably there will be individuals within a community of practice who have more power. Pressures from internal and external sources of power (for example, organizational structures, cultures and hierarchies, government policy, etc.) may inhibit learning, knowledge creation and knowledge sharing. A challenge is to constrain, inhibit or eliminate negative effects of power (and of organizational politics) whilst utilizing power relations in ways that enable learning. Trust is a prerequisite for the cooperation and openness which are necessary for effective learning, however dysfunctional power dynamics and adversarial relationships between colleagues allied to stringent hierarchical controls can reduce trust and undermine the process. Finally, with regard to 'predispositions', if the community's own codes, habits and predispositions become static and rigidified they may actually undermine the processes of learning and knowledge creation, especially in the case of radical innovations that challenge the status quo of the community and its members.[45] An effective community of practice acknowledges its own weaknesses and is prepared to act, learn and change, accordingly.[46]

Delve deeper 3.4

Consolidate and extend your knowledge of situated learning theory and communities of practice by reading this review of the field in which the works of several of the key theorists (including Lave, Wenger and others) are summarized succinctly:

Cox, A. (2005). What are communities of practice? A comparative review of four seminal works. *Journal of Information Science, 31*(6), 527–540.

(Continued)

Read about how learning processes happen at the heart of communities of practice in this study of situated learning in the UK National Health Service in:

Pyrko, I., Dörfler, V., & Eden, C. (2017). Thinking together: What makes communities of practice work? *Human Relations*, *70*(4), 389–409.

And read about journalism as a community of practice in:

Meltzer, K., & Martik, E. (2017). Journalists as communities of practice: Advancing a theoretical framework for understanding journalism. *Journal of Communication Inquiry*, *41*(3), 207–226.

Conclusion: Human nature

Human learning is profoundly influenced by observations of and interactions with other persons. This observation fits with the fact that human beings are intensely social creatures therefore it makes intuitive sense that much of the knowledge and many of the skills that we acquire are learned from other people. As rational, social beings we are more likely to do things that we have seen others succeed with and being rewarded for and avoid those actions that we have seen them fail in or being punished for. It would also make sense that *Homo sapiens* – as the most social of all the primates, sometimes referred to as 'the ultra-social animal' – evolved sophisticated skills of social cognition for maintaining social relationships and learning from others in the group.[47] Social learning theory puts this common-sense observation onto a scientific footing. Situated learning is a social phenomenon that occurs through newcomers' legitimate peripheral participation in ongoing social practice in a community of practitioners and in which the cognitive processes of representation, encoding, memory, retention and recall, as well as problem-solving, decision-making and creativity, occur in situ and in relation to others located in the social world.[48] Social learning processes are not confined to humans, for example other primates learn complex skills from observation and interaction with others of their species.[49] In evolutionary terms, opportunities for social learning and situated learning that present themselves in group living species, such as humans, allow an individual to acquire many learned skills that it couldn't acquire on its own. As Bandura argued, social and situated learning are more efficient and effective than learning on one's own. Social and situated learning theories provide HRD with good behavioural, cognitive, evolutionary and social reasons for why informal and incidental learning methods including apprenticeships as well as other socially-mediated learning methods such as job-instruction training, job rotation, coaching, mentoring and various aspects of leadership development are highly efficient and effective ways for individuals to acquire important new knowledge, develop necessary skills and undergo significant attitudinal and personal change and development. One of the many things that the pandemic of 2020 has taught or reminded us of is that as a species we're not 'virtual beings' able to exist in isolated, impoverished screen-based lives; we are, and always will, be by our nature 'human beings' who survive and thrive on social proximity and the fullness of face-to-face interactions.

Chapter checkout

Use this list to check your understanding of the key points of this chapter.

1 **Social learning principles**   If people had to only rely solely on effects of their own actions to inform them what to do then learning would be laborious and potentially hazardous

2 **Social learning mechanisms**   Humans learn through observation, imitation and modelling of others; learning is an outcome of bi-directional interactions between behavioural, cognitive and environmental factors (three-way, or triadic, reciprocal determinism)

3 **Social learning process**   Social leaning can be modelled as a four-stage process of: attention, retention, practice, repetition

4 **Mirror neurons**   Offer biological explanations for how human behaviour can be influenced unconsciously by observing actions of another person and for empathy

5 **Social learning applications**   Social learning occurs wherever one person learns from another, including from trainers, peers, supervisors, coaches, mentors, leaders etc., and learning can be direct or vicarious

6 **Self-efficacy**   Learning is enhanced when individuals believe in their capability to perform and are set appropriate expectations and goals

7 **Situated learning principles**   Describes and explains how learning takes place informally, sometimes unintentionally, through activities in authentic, real-world contexts

8 **Situated learning theory**   Learning is an emergent property of a persons' legitimate peripheral participation in informally constituted communities of practice in a relevant work domain

9 **Situated learning process**   Through transformations of knowledge, understanding, skill and identity 'newcomers' become 'old timers'; new old-timers become the community of practice for the next wave of newcomers

10 **Situated learning applications**   Apprenticeships ('master' and apprentice) are archetypal; situated learning applies also to other real-world contexts where there are relationships between the learners and a capable peer, more knowledgeable other, a coach or mentor

SKILLS DEVELOPMENT 3
WRITE A LEARNING AUTOBIOGRAPHY

A learning autobiography is a personal narrative of a consequential learning event or events in one's life. Learning autobiographies help us to make sense of the significant changes in our knowledge or skills, and in the shaping of our attitudes and values.

(Continued)

In this chapter it's been argued that situated learning involves cognitive and social processes and that theories of social and situated learning provide us with concepts and models that can be used as tools with which we can articulate our personal learning journey and make sense of our learning experiences. For this task write a short learning biography as follows: select a consequential learning event or episode (for example, being an undergraduate, being a member of a work group, etc.) and frame your learning biography around your responses to some or all of these questions:

- What was the 'domain'?
- What was the 'community'?
- What were the practice(s)?
- How did being a member of a community of practice enable the process of 'situated learning' to take place for you?

What role did 'capable peers', 'more knowledgeable others', 'masters', 'role models', etc. play in this process?

Finally, what have you 'learned about learning' from reading this chapter, and how can you personally use the knowledge and understanding that you've gained to learn more efficiently and effectively in the future?

4

EXPERIENCE-BASED MODALITIES OF LEARNING

Contents

On completion of this chapter you should be able to:

- Describe and explain experience-based modalities of learning (experiential learning theory, action learning and andragogy);
- Critically evaluate experiential learning theory, action learning and andragogy;
- Use your knowledge and understanding of experience-based modalities to advise on the design and delivery of HRD.

Introduction

The theory, methods and models of learning that we'll explore in this chapter are vitally important in understanding the role that learners' experiences play in the processes of learning and development in occupational and professional contexts. They are a mixed bag of descriptive, formal theory and prescriptive, practical methods. 'Experiential learning theory' is associated with the field of organizational behaviour; the method of 'action learning' is most often associated with the practice of management and organization development; 'andragogy' is a model of adult learning. They are grouped together here as 'experience-based modalities':

- In experiential learning new 'knowledge is created through the transformation of experience', hence experience is foundational and fundamental in the learning process;[1]
- In action learning the most valuable learning asset that managers have at their disposal is their 'lived experience' but this is sometimes 'deep and difficult to discover'; action learning is one way for managers to surface and share their experiences and become 'personally involved in offering [their experiences] to others';[2]
- In andragogy adults' experiences impact learning and development, they are a source of individual difference, a rich resource for learning, can be an inhibitor or enabler of learning, and a grounding for self-identity.[3]

Experiential learning, action learning and andragogy can also be seen as reactions against – in their different ways – the application of educational and pedagogical assumptions and practices to learning and development in the workplace. These experience-based modalities are the work of three important and original thinkers in the fields of management learning, HRD and adult learning: David Kolb (experiential learning), an American business school professor of organizational behaviour; Reg Revans (action learning), a British management and organizational development consultant; and Malcolm S. Knowles (andragogy), an American professor of adult education.

In understanding their work, history and philosophy are important. The significance of experience in learning was explored by the great American pragmatist philosopher John Dewey (1859–1952). The main principle of pragmatism is that the value of an idea lies in its practical application.[4] For Dewey it was not merely experience, but the quality of experience that was important for learning. In his 1938 book *Experience and Education* Dewey remarked that we cannot learn from experiences 'unless we go over past experiences in our mind...unless we *reflect* on them'.[5] Subsequently, researchers such as David Boud in Australia and David Kolb in the United States utilized ideas from Dewey and others in developing a practical theory of experiential learning that can be applied in understanding and enabling learning in workplaces.

The idea of learning from experience has been one of the 'main sources of inspiration' for researchers and practitioners in HRD.[6] Experience-based modalities are important in HRD because learning in organizations is intimately and inextricably linked with 'doing' and therefore it can be argued that it is 'meaningless to talk about learning in isolation from experience' because learning in workplaces 'builds on and flows inevitably from' experience.[7] At a more mundane level in the popular '70:20:10' model of learning,[8] learning from experiences makes up a notional '70 per cent' of learning in workplaces (the remaining proportions are '20 per cent' learning from others and '10 per cent' learning from formal training). 70:20:10 is discussed in more detail in Chapter 11.

Revans innovated his experience-based modality, action learning, in the 1940s based on his practical observation that managers could come together in small groups of 'comrades in adversity' (as members of action learning 'sets'), share ideas and problems with each other and in so doing, and without the need of an 'expert', co-create practical solutions to their 'pressing problems'.

Malcolm Knowles' andragogical model of learning sought to answer the question 'how do you tailor education to the learning needs of adults?'. Knowles innovated this idea in the United States in the 1970s. Andragogy was ground-breaking because it sought to clarify the differences between how adults learn and how children learn on the basis that applying principles of learning as they apply to children, that is 'pedagogy', was not appropriate for adults. Andragogy provides a useful set of adult learning general principles that apply across personal, professional and educational contexts.

Experiential learning theory

In management and HRD the concept of 'learning though, or from, experience' – experiential learning – is most often associated with the work of the American psychologist David Kolb. Kolb's 'experiential learning model' (ELM) is one of the most influential theories in training and development, HRD and management learning and education. The model's fundamental idea is summed up powerfully and succinctly in this quote from Kolb's seminal book first published in 1984 *Experiential Learning:*

Experience as the Source of Learning and Development: learning is a process whereby 'knowledge is created through the transformation of experience. Knowledge results from the combination of grasping and transforming experience' (p. 41). Kolb's theory can be thought of as a 'constructivist' theory of learning because of the emphasis it gives to the subjective, 'personal knowledge' of the learner which is created through a holistic 'thinking–feeling–perceiving–behaving' interaction between the individual and their environment. As such experiential learning theory attaches as much importance to the learning process as it does to learning outcomes.

Kolb's ELM stands in stark contrast to instructionalist 'transmission' models of learning in which pre-existing knowledge is transmitted from someone who knows (the teacher or trainer) to someone who doesn't know (the learner). For example, theories of 'instructional design' (as in the influential work of scholars such as Robert Gagne and Leslie J. Briggs in the 1960s) are more focused on transmission of knowledge rather than the personal and subjective construction of knowledge out of one's unique experiences. This contrasts with the core principle Kolb expressed in *Experiential Learning*:

> Learners, if they are to be effective must be able to involve themselves fully, openly and without bias in new experiences. They must be able to reflect on and observe their experiences from many perspectives. They must be able to create concepts that integrate their observations into logically sound *theories*, and they must be able to use these *theories* to make decisions and solve problems. (emphases added, p. 30)

The above extract not only captures the essence of Kolb's position on knowledge and learning, it also draws attention to an important point about the use of the word 'theory' in experiential learning. By 'theory' in the above Kolb doesn't mean a 'scientific theory' as such (as in Newton's theory of gravity or Bandura's social learning theory for example); rather, in the context of experiential learning, by 'theory' Kolb means:

- That a 'theory' is another word for the 'rules' (that is, our 'personal theories') that we establish for ourselves by reflecting on our experiences of how the world works (as a result of having been through an experiential learning process or cycle);
- That these 'theories', if they are valid and useful, will help us to navigate through the real world in taking decisions, solving problems, making sense of situations, etc.;
- These personal theories are also 'provisional' in the sense that they are constantly being refined and revised, as well as refuted.

History and context matter. As alluded to above, the experiential learning model (referred to from now on as 'Experiential Learning Theory' or ELT), is rooted in the work of several major figures in the history of philosophy, education, psychology and social science. The 'foremost intellectual ancestors'[9] of experiential learning are summarized in Figure 4.1.

John Dewey (1859–1952) American pragmatist philosopher/educator

- Dewey's writings on education from 1930s influenced Kolb's theory not only with regard to the importance of the practice of reflection but also on a philosophical level, for example by helping to position Kolb's theory as a 'progressive' rather than 'traditional' approach to learning

Kurt Lewin (1890–1947) German-American social psychologist

- Lewin's work was the source of the idea of a 'dialectical' tension between subjective experience ('here-and-now' concrete experiences) and objective analysis ('there-and-then' theoretical detachment). Lewin's most famous quote is that 'there's nothing so practical as a good theory'

Jean Piaget (1896–1980) Swiss developmental/cognitive psychologist

- Piaget's ideas about learning and development as a 'lifelong process'; how intelligence is shaped by experience; how 'institutions' (including business organizations, although Piaget was concerned mainly with child development) have enormous power to nurture/enable or inhibit/constrain learning; concepts of assimilation/accommodation in learning

Figure 4.1 Some of the 'intellectual ancestors' of experiential learning

Other influences on Kolb were the American humanistic psychologist Carl Rogers (whose definition of learning is reproduced in Chapter 2) and the Brazilian educator and revolutionary Paolo Freire.

In their own words 4.1

David Kolb on 'What is experiential learning theory?'

Here are some observations that David Kolb gave in an interview entitled 'What is experiential learning?': 'Experiential learning is a concept which I took from the works of John Dewey, Jean Piaget and Carl Jung and Kurt Lewin and William James and what experiential learning says is that the centre of learning is experience your own subjective experience.' He also referred especially to the idea in the work of the American philosopher and psychologist William James, that 'as human beings all we have is our experience and all knowledge begins in our experience. As a learner it's my experience that guides how I learned and says when I have learned something, and the exciting thing about this idea is that when experience is the centre of the learning process you are in control of it and you are able then to take initiative and create the kinds of experiences for yourself that you want.' Kolb was keen to emphasize the centrality of the role of the learner and her experience in the process, that is 'it's not the teacher who is the centre but it's the learner who is at the centre'.[10]

As far as the 'nuts-and-bolts' of the theory are concerned, there are four stages in the experiential learning process. In recent renditions of the theory Kolb has altered terminology slightly (for example concrete experience is simply 'experiencing'), and it's the more recent usage that is given here (notice the use of the '-ing'[11] form of the verb for each of the steps emphasizing the strong 'processual'[12] nature of what happens):

- 'Experiencing': immediate real-life, here-and-now experiencing initiates learning (Kolb originally called this 'concrete experience', abbreviated to 'CE');
- 'Reflecting': stepping-back and observing and reflecting upon these experiences ('reflective observation', RO);
- 'Thinking': assimilating one's reflections and observations into general (abstract) concepts or rules ('abstract conceptualization', AC);
- 'Acting': active testing of these general concepts or rules and using them as guides for creating or testing out new experiences ('active experimentation', AE).

Alice Kolb and David Kolb explain the significance of the model's different stages and their respective functions with the analogy, from William James, of a pair of scissors: 'in the same way we need both blades [of the scissors] to cut, we need both concrete experience and abstract thinking to make sense of the world' (p. 11),[13] and likewise with reflecting and acting they're opposing ways of transforming understanding but both, like the blades of a pair of scissors, are needed. The process, which is called the experiential learning cycle (ELC), and the other elements of Kolb's model are shown in Figure 4.2.

The process of experiential learning involves a balanced integration of all four stages in the cycle. One of the challenges for learning in busy workplaces is that speed is often seen to be of the essence and the temptation is to move from problem-to-problem (if not crisis-to-crisis) without taking the time to reflect and 'theorize' (in Kolb's sense of the word, see above). This can be short-sighted and ineffective ultimately because time needs to be allowed for reflecting and thinking before acting. Researchers have suggested a number of ways in which this process can be facilitated and managed proactively.[14] For example, in 'debriefings' reflecting should be open and honest and elicit constructive critiques; negative messages shouldn't be glossed-over, and the lessons learned should be captured and stored in an accessible and flexible knowledge management system. Likewise conducting after-action interviews with the key players in critical events and incidents enables them to reflect and interpret what happened and captures the lessons learned as soon as possible in 'experiential learning histories' and helps participants work out what went well and why and what went badly and why. These are in a sense 'post mortems' on learning, but other researchers such as the decision researcher Gary Klein have suggested that project 'pre-mortems', as a form of anticipatory thinking, can help with planning and avoid things going wrong in the first place.[15]

The experiential learning cycle involves 'dialogical' processes. Management researchers Ann Cunliffe and Mark Easterby-Smith argued that a reflective approach to experience-based learning can be enhanced through 'practical reflexivity', which, rather than being a purely cognitive activity, is dialogical and relational, that is it involves talk (dialogue)

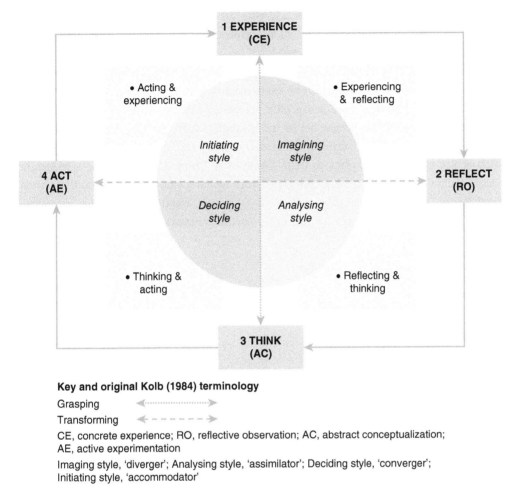

Key and original Kolb (1984) terminology

Grasping   ◁·····················▷

Transforming   ◁ – – – – – – ▷

CE, concrete experience; RO, reflective observation; AC, abstract conceptualization; AE, active experimentation

Imaging style, 'diverger'; Analysing style, 'assimilator'; Deciding style, 'converger'; Initiating style, 'accommodator'

Figure 4.2   The experiential learning model

and others (social interactions).[16] At the level of the organization, the failure to learn from experiences reflectively and collectively may lead to 'corporate amnesia' which can lead to mistakes being repeated ('Those who fail to learn from history are doomed to repeat it'). These ideas are returned to in Chapter 13 (organizational learning).

Reflective question 4.1

Experiential learning is sometimes equated (simplistically and inaccurately) to 'learning by doing' or 'learning from mistakes'. What would you say to a sceptic who said that using experiential learning in HRD is potentially dangerous because it legitimizes making mistakes and excuses them as 'learnings'?

Finally, experiential learning theory also addresses the important, and sometimes neglected, issue of power in learning and development in organizations. Management learning researcher Michael Reynolds, in observing that experiential learning theory has had a 'profound influence', argued that it raises the issue of power in learning which, as critical HRD (CHRD) researchers have noted, has tended to be overlooked in HRD. As such experiential learning presents a challenge to traditional pedagogical practices of education because it questions 'the assumptions as to where authority lies in the learning process' (p. 388) and the 'dominant hierarchical arrangement' in learning processes, systems and structures.[17] Russ Vince and Michael Reynolds in the preface to their *Handbook of Experiential Learning in Management Education* draw attention to the fact that experiential learning, and the act of reflection which it entails can be a critical process because it 'can discourage and disrupt our tendency to produce prescriptions for learning, [and] attempts to define "best practice"' (p. 3).[18]

Delve deeper 4.1

Read more about the theory and practice of ELT in these two articles by Alice and David Kolb:

Kolb, A. Y., and Kolb, D. A. (2005). Learning styles and learning spaces: Enhancing experiential learning in higher education. *Academy of Management Learning & Education*, 4(2), 193–212.

Kolb, A. Y. & Kolb, D. A. (2018). Eight important things to know about the experiential learning cycle. *Australian Educational Leader*, 40(3), 8–14.

Extend your knowledge of the 'business' of experiential learning by visiting the company website of Alice and David Kolb's 'Experience Based Learning Systems'. It contains a wealth of information on the ELC and how the Kolb's have applied it in their consulting business. For an authoritative overview of ELT take a look at the video:

https://learningfromexperience.com/themes/experiential-learning-theory-videos/.

ELT and learning styles

An aspect of Kolb's model that sometimes gets obscured or overlooked is that the cycle – the ELC – isn't simply four stages. As alluded to above, there are also two underlying dimensions that are at right angles (that is, orthogonal) to each other. These dimensions represent contrasting ways in which people 'receive' information and how they 'transform' information in the experiential learning process:

- Receiving information (also known as 'grasping'): in the ELC there are two ways of receiving information or 'grasping experience', this is either by 'experiencing' the world or 'thinking' about the world. They are opposite ends of 'experiencing-thinking' dimension and as such are in 'tension';

- Transforming information: in the ELC there are two ways of transforming information, this is either by 'reflecting' on new information or 'applying' it in action. These are also are opposite ends of the 'reflecting-acting' dimension and as such they too are in a state of tension.

You might recall that the relationship between the poles of each dimension were explained using the analogy of a pair of scissors (we need both experiencing and thinking, and reflecting and acting). Kolb refers to the relationship between the opposing poles of each dimension (experiencing versus thinking and reflecting versus acting) as a 'dialectic'. This means they are an exchange that is seeking or requires resolution (this idea can be traced back to Lewin, see above). In moving effectively through the different stages of the learning cycle a dialectic process is established in which the tensions between opposites is 'reconciled' (which means that it is acknowledged, accepted and accommodated – not the same thing as being 'resolved').

Kolb used the concept of tensions between the poles of the receiving and transforming dimensions to develop the idea of 'learning styles' based on the assumption that we each have our personal preferences for how we:

- Receive information, either through 'experiencing' or through 'thinking' (that is, we prefer either experiencing or thinking);
- Transform information, either through 'reflecting' or through 'acting' (that is, we prefer either reflecting or acting).

Combining together the poles of the dimensions gives four preferred learning styles (again Kolb's recent terminology differs slightly from the original usage, see below):

- 'Imagining style': people with this style prefer to learn through a combination of experiencing and reflecting (Kolb originally referred to this group as 'divergers');
- 'Analysing style': people with this style prefer to learn through a combination of reflecting and thinking (originally 'assimilators');
- 'Deciding style': people with this style prefer to learn through a combination of reflecting and acting ('convergers');
- 'Initiating style': people with this style prefer to learn through a combination of acting and experiencing ('accommodators').[19]

Kolb also devised a psychometric instrument, called the *Learning Styles Inventory* (*LSI*), which measures self-reported preferences for each of the four dimensions and then combines these to give a preferred learning style. The *LSI* diagnosis helps individuals to see where their strengths in the experiential learning process are, but also where they need to develop given that many activities in the real world, including most jobs, require engagement with all four stages of the cycle. The characteristics of the four styles are summarized in Figure 4.3.

Imagining style ('Diverger')

- 'Experiencing' and 'Reflecting'
- Imagination; meaning and values; view situations from multiple perspectives
- Observation rather than action
- Works best in idea generation. Socio-emotional experiences not task accomplishment

Analysing style ('Assimilator')

- 'Reflecting' and 'Thinking'
- Reasoning, creating theoretical models, integrative explanations
- Less socio-emotional more theoretical/conceptual
- Ideas valued for logic/precision rather than practicality/utility

Deciding style ('Converger')

- 'Thinking' and 'Acting'
- Strength in problem solving, decision-making, practical application
- Works best where there is a single solution
- Task accomplishment/productivity focused, not socio-emotional

Initiating style ('Accommodator')

- 'Acting' and 'Experiencing'
- Doing things; carrying out plans/tasks; getting involved in new experiences
- Opportunity seeking, risk taking and action
- Suited to situations where need to adapt to change. If theory/plan doesn't fit situation discard it

Figure 4.3   Four ELT learning styles

As far as HRD is concerned it would be useful to know if individuals have learning preferences based on their learning styles because this information could then be used to maximize the value each person gets from their learning. Research suggests that experiential learning styles do tell us something about what individuals are likely to prefer in formal learning situations:

- Imagining style: prefer to work in groups, listen with an open mind, and receive personalized feedback;
- Analysing style: prefer readings, lectures, exploring analytical models, and being given the time to think things through;
- Deciding style: prefer to experiment with new ideas, use simulations, and practical assignments and applications;
- Initiating style: prefer work with others to get assignments done, set goals, to do field work, and to test out different approaches to completing a project.[20]

However, it's unlikely that one single style will suit all learning situations or job types, therefore it's important that learners use a knowledge of their style as a starting point in order to move outside of their learning 'comfort zone' and into other parts of the cycle which they might be less familiar or less comfortable with. It's not enough to simply match learning to the style, in fact to do so might be against learners' long-term interests. Only by being exposed to each stage in the cycle can an individual become 'rounded' and versatile as a learner and hence learn how to learn effectively from the wide range of experiences they're likely to encounter both in their professional and personal lives. Kolb refers to this versatility as being able to 'touch all the bases' in the experiential learning process.[21]

Reflective question 4.2

In ELT what are the differences between: (1) 'dialogic' and 'dialectic'; (2) 'grasping' and 'transforming'; (3) 'reconciling' and 'resolving'? There are various online and print resources that are available to help you identify your preferred learning style (not only ELT styles), for example https://vark-learn.com/the-vark-questionnaire/; others may be available through your college, university or employer. Try out one of them (such as VARK, that is 'visual-auditory-read-kinaesthetic' styles; see above). How accurately do you feel your style has been diagnosed? How useful do you think this information is likely to be for you personally? How useful is it likely to be in HRD?

Various learning style inventories are also available commercially. The popular Honey and Mumford *Learning Styles Questionnaire* (LSQ) (based on a version of experiential learning theory) is available from the Pearson 'TalentLens' Group website.[22] The Kolb LSI is available through the management consultancy Hay Group (now Korn Ferry) website.[23]

More broadly the topic of learning styles is contentious amongst psychologists and educationalists, and therefore needs to be approached with caution. For example, the 'visual-auditory-read-kinaesthetic' (VARK) model of learning styles (see above, and which is quite popular in schools) has been criticized. Research has found that learners who self-reported that they preferred learning 'visually' judged that they would remember pictures better and vice versa; however, self-reported learning styles (for example, visual or verbal) showed no relationship with what was actually learned and recalled in words or in pictures.

The general message from this research is that self-reported learning styles seem to capture peoples' 'learning preferences' (what they like, and if they like a particular mode of learning the chances are they think they'll learn better from it) rather than actual styles of information processing (which are difficult to assess using self-report questionnaires). Learning from materials that are presented in a mode you prefer (for example, pictures rather than words) might have a positive effect on motivation and some indirect effect on learning outcomes, but the effects may be somewhat tenuous.[24] A practical strategy might be to try to present information in a dual mode where a synergy is created between words and pictures and which gives the learner control over which one to focus on or the option to use both. 'Self-adapting' packages customize modes of presentation to the learning style of the trainee on the basis of learning styles' assessment.[25]

Delve deeper 4.2

Read more about learning styles and the related concept of cognitive (thinking) styles in business, management and HRD in:

Armstrong, S. J., Cools, E., & Sadler-Smith, E. (2012). Role of cognitive styles in business and management: Reviewing 40 years of research. *International Journal of Management Reviews*, *14*(3), 238–262.

Sadler-Smith, E. (2014). Learning styles and cognitive styles in human resource development. In Walton, J. and Valentin, C. (eds) *Human resource development: Practices and orthodoxies*. Abingdon: Routledge, pp. 85–106.

Waters, R. J. (2012). Learning style instruments: Reasons why research evidence might have a weak influence on practitioner choice. *Human Resource Development International*, *15*(1), 119–129.

Criticisms of experiential learning theory

Looking more broadly at the application of ELT to learning in the workplace, there are challenges, in the form of inefficiencies and risks, in learning from experience. For example, relying on unmanaged or ad hoc experiences as a way of learning is likely to be somewhat 'hit-and-miss' not to say hazardous.[26] For experiential learning to be effective and efficient each of the four stages need to be recognized explicitly and managed systematically. Whilst many experiences are sure to contain mistakes and wrong turnings, simply assuming that it's 'ok' to make mistakes (based on a shallow reading of ELT) and that we can learn from them is far-fetched and risky (since some mistakes can be much more expensive than others, for example would we want an airline pilot to learn from her mistakes – clearly 'no' – that's why simulators are used). Moreover too many hard knocks can have demotivating and damaging psychological effects on learners and their learning.[27] As well as these pragmatic objections, there have been a number of challenges to and criticisms of ELT from researchers, including the following:

- Not every learning situation demands a balanced integration of the four stages, some situations are more likely to require reflecting and thinking (for example, learning a theory in an academic context) whilst others (for example, learning how to ride a bike) are more likely to require acting and experiencing with very little theoretical input required;

- ELT doesn't give enough attention to emotional factors such as anxiety, fear and doubt (especially given that direct experiences can sometimes be unsettling and even threatening), or social factors (for example, the first and the final stages of the cycle, experiencing and acting, are likely to involve and implicate others in learning) and how these can affect the process of learning;[28]

- Criticisms have been levelled at the psychometric properties of the Kolb *Learning Styles Inventory* (LSI) and alternatives have been suggested.[29] Also, it could be argued that the LSI measures individuals' self-reported preferences for the different stages of the learning cycle rather than actual learning behaviours.

It's also been suggested that ELT is not as clear as it might have been on what constitutes an 'experience'. For example, taking on a new project at work or chairing a meeting for the first time certainly would seem to count as experiences, but what about simply sitting and reading a book, what about a casual corridor conversation, what about any number of different encounters, or the constant stream of experiences that our life is adorned with and that knowledge is created from?

Annette Clancy and Russ Vince argue that experiential learning has a 'shadow side' (where shadow, suggesting 'dark' or 'unseen', is a common metaphor in psychodynamics) noting that emotions are a complex part of any experience and there are aspects in the emotional experience of learning that are 'noticeable but often ignored' (p. 175).[30] They argue that in learning more generally it is important to recognize how unacknowledged emotions can subvert the learning processes but that the act of acknowledging emotions can be difficult because learners, managers and leaders are embedded in power relations within organizations which they may be seeking to transform. Hence, learning is a political, as well as a cognitive and behavioural, process.

In spite of these criticisms, Kolb's ELT remains the 'clearest expression' and one of the most influential and widely cited theories of how people in organizations learn through their work.[31] The theory can also accommodate ideas of learning that go beyond the cognitive into the physical and embodied aspects of learning. For example, cognitive theories have been criticized for privileging the role of the 'brain' over the 'body' in learning, but actually when learners are immersed with their bodies in experiences information becomes 'embodied' (rather than just 'embrained'), for example acquiring psychomotor skills, 'know how', tacit knowledge, intuition and expertise; hence, experiential learning can be interpreted as a process in which the body and the mind are intimately 'intertwined'.[32]

---Delve deeper 4.3---

Read more about the criticisms and 'shadow side' of ELT in:

Clancy, A., & Vince, R. (2019). 'If I want to feel my feelings, I'll see a bloody shrink': Learning from the shadow side of experiential learning. *Journal of Management Education, 43*(2), 174–184.

Kayes, D. C. (2002). Experiential learning and its critics: Preserving the role of experience in management learning and education. *Academy of Management Learning & Education, 1*(2), 137–149.

Reynolds, M. (2009). Wild frontiers – reflections on experiential learning. *Management Learning, 40*(4), 387–392.

Sanderson, K. (2020). Instilling Competence: Emotional preparation for experiential learning. *Journal of Management Education*, doi.org/10.1177/1052562920965637.

Read more about the theory and practice of experiential learning more generally in:

Reynolds, M., & Vince, R. (eds) (2007). *Handbook of experiential learning and management education*. Oxford: Oxford University Press.

Action learning

Action learning is not an 'academic theory' as such, it is a practical method of learning and development in which managers work in groups or 'sets' of peers (typically four to eight people) to tackle important organizational problems. In doing so they undergo significant personal learning and development as a result of their reflections which impact on them personally and their organizations.[33] Michael Marquardt describes action learning as being about resolving real problems in real time and a 'powerful experiential learning methodology that builds leaders, teams and organizations' (p. 95):[34]

- The starting point is the 'pressing' (that is, 'here-and-now') problem;
- Learning takes place between managers in a 'set' (whom Revans referred to as 'comrades in adversity');
- The set, not outside 'experts', produces actions for tackling the problem.

The method was innovated by Reg Revans in the UK in the second half of the twentieth century whilst he was working for the UK's National Coal Board. Revans (1907–2003) was an Olympic long-jumper (1928, Amsterdam) who studied physics at Cambridge and worked in the Cavendish laboratory under Lord Rutherford (the 'father of nuclear physics') and J. J. Thompson (physics Nobel Prize, 1906). Action learning is based on the principle that in a turbulent, fast-moving and uncertain business environment the rate of learning must exceed the rate of change if an organization is to stay ahead and remain competitive and effective. The approach uses a novel technique for facilitating learning through sets consisting of mixed groups of managers all of whom are facing their own practical management problems and uncertainties.

Revans' scientific background came out in the way he expressed the principles of action learning as two 'equations'. The first equation relates learning (L) to the rate of change in the environment (C):

$$L \geq C \text{ (Equation 4.1)}$$

The second equation expresses the relationship between learning (L) and pre-exiting knowledge (p), such as in text books, and the managers' ability to pose relavant, challenging and insightful questions (Q).

$$L = p + Q \text{ (Equation 4.2)}$$

Revans deliberately called pre-programmed (that is, 'textbook') learning 'little p' (p) and the questions that need to be asked 'big Q' (Q) because 'big Q' is more important than 'little p' in action learning, even though both little p and big Q are needed.

Figure 4.4 Relationship between 'little p' and 'big Q' in action learning

By working together jointly on problems in action learning sets (see below) managers are better able to ask insightful questions relating to the specific problem and also to develop the general ability or skill of being able to ask insightful questions (Equation 4.2) in order to keep up with or stay ahead of change (Equation 4.1).

Revans developed a clear set of guiding principles for facilitating action learning. Like experiential learning (and as we shall see andragogy also), action learning can be seen as a reaction against the prevailing educational model of the day which tended to produce 'clever' managers (technical specialists with convergent thinking styles) rather than 'wise' managers (those with the right kind of thinking and problem-solving styles, for example 'divergent' thinkers, who are able to see a bigger picture and ask penetrating questions). Revans reacted against educational and pedagogical principles that relied on pre-programmed knowledge (p) that was by definition in the past and which, once it had been written down, may not be as useful for solving 'here-and-now' problems. As he saw it, what's likely to be much more effective is the ability to ask penetrating, meaningful and insightful questions (Q) about one's assumptions, beliefs and behaviours (see Equation 4.2 above).

Management and organization development researcher Joseph Raelin observed similarities between action learning and 'action research' (derived from the work of Kurt Lewin) and 'action science' (as exemplified in the work of Chris Argyris and Donald Schön, whose work will be discussed in Chapter 13). Raelin described action learning, which involves set members who are not 'experts' but instead are learning 'peers', as a highly dialogical process that involves talking, discussing, listening, posing insightful and penetrating questions, offering suggestions, brainstorming ideas, experimenting with alternatives, giving constructive feedback, etc.[35]

In their own words 4.2

Reg Revans on action learning

Revans' primary motivation was to work with managers and organizations in order to help them learn how to respond effectively to the challenges of change in order that they might not only survive but also thrive in the face of dynamism and uncertainty in their environments. He came up with the idea in what must have been a time of great turbulence and uncertainty as well as opportunity at the end of World War II. His thoughts about how managers can deal with change are as relevant today as they were in the 1940s when he first had the idea for action learning:

'When, in an epoch of change, tomorrow is necessarily different from yesterday, and so new things need to be done, what are the questions to be asked before the solutions are sought? Action learning differs from normal training (education, development) in that its primary objective is to learn how to ask questions in conditions of risk, rather than to find the answers to questions that have already been precisely defined by others' (p. 65).[36]

In his varied career Revans visited India and was struck by the similarity between Buddhism and action learning. He is also quoted as saying that 'intuition, the unremembered urges of the past, must always be the first weapon of the manager, he [or she] must be able to grasp the underlying structures of situations that challenge him [or her]' (p. 10).[37]

Action learning in practice

In terms of the 'nuts-and-bolts' of the process, as noted above, action learning is organized on the principle of learners working together in groups known as 'action learning sets'. A set usually comprises between four and eight participants and is facilitated by a skilled set adviser. In the spirit of skilled enquiry and a focus upon practice it is important that the adviser is not seen to be, or indeed acts as, an expert. The experts are the participating managers themselves both individually and collectively; they are 'comrades in adversity' (to use Revans' phrase). The 'content' is 'live' (that is real world) projects that are complex and challenging organizational problems that cannot be answered using solely p (in Equation 4.2). Pre-existing knowledge that's written down in books and was invented in the past is not enough in an uncertain present and for an unknown future. The live projects are ones that each individual participant is confronted with in their job role. The advantages of working on real problems may be self-evident. Not only do participants have to find workable solutions, leadership, learning-to-learn and other facilitative skills are also developed incidentally in the process. The learning transfers to the work context immediately (transfer of learning isn't an issue) and learning of process skills are likely to be more widely applicable beyond the immediate project (general inquiry skills are developed).[38] Moreover, action learning has applications across organizations in all sectors and of all sizes and may be particularly suited to the learning requirements of small and medium sized enterprises (SMEs) which are unlikely to have the dedicated HRD function that is usually found in larger firms.

Perspective from practice 4.1

Action learning in SMEs

Engaging UK SMEs in HRD has been beset with problems. Reasons include lack of resources and lack of expertise in the relevant aspects of HRD practice within smaller firms. Whilst SMEs may take advantage of government and externally funded HRD projects, embedding learning and development over the longer term into SMEs has proven to be a challenge. Jean Clarke and colleagues researched action learning as a method for developing SMEs. In a study of 19 learning sets involving over 100 SMEs in the north west of England, the researchers gathered longitudinal data through embedding 'learning historians' in the firms who recorded data from an insider's perspective over a period of 12 months. These learning histories were supplemented by interviews with set members and data from 'learning diaries'. They found that:

- The discursive and critical reflection aspects of discussions within the sets helped managers to see the limits of their current perspectives and mindsets and open them to new ideas;
- The sets gave diverse types of managers 'common ground' for learning especially when the sets were comprised of a mixture of experienced and less experienced managers; however if the sets were too diverse finding common ground became a barrier to learning;
- Networking and forming alliances was an important outcome in that the sets catalysed the formation of networks which were engaged with outside and beyond the project thereby facilitating the creation of 'social capital' with the added value of the learnings that accrue from this.

(Continued)

The final and unanticipated positive outcome from the action learning was the opportunity to disengage from the day-to-day running of a small business, take a structured and purposeful time-out, think beyond the operational and look towards strategy. The researchers concluded that action learning's 'emphasis on relational and conversational practices' whilst also retaining a naturalistic and socially embedded context 'has proven highly beneficial to the owner-managers involved in the project' (p. 450).

Source: Clarke, J., Thorpe, R., Anderson, L., & Gold, J. (2006). It's all action, it's all learning: Action learning in SMEs. Journal of European Industrial Training, 30(6), 441–455.

Action learning has been applied widely and works effectively as a means for significant personal and organizational development; however as Raelin noted, in order to be successful:

- Action learning sets should not operate in a strategic or organizational vacuum;
- Action learning projects should have organizational sponsorship;
- The set's recommendations should be listened to by senior managers;
- Action learning should not be seen as a one-off individual learning exercise;
- Problems must be followed through and treated as organizational learning opportunities.[39]

Action learning projects work best in organizational cultures that tolerate risk taking and experimentation and when they are successful action learning projects they may take on a life of their own and have the potential to catalyse organizational development, learning and renewal.

Delve deeper 4.4

Read about the practice of action learning in:

Pedler, M. (ed.) (2011). *Action learning in practice*. Aldershot: Gower Publishing, Ltd.

Pedler, M., & Burgoyne, J. (2008). Action learning. In Bradbury, H. (ed.) *The SAGE handbook of action research*. London: SAGE, 319–332.

Raelin, J. A. (2009). Action learning and related modalities. In Armstrong S. & Fukami, C. (eds) *The SAGE handbook of management learning, education and development*. Thousand Oaks: SAGE, 419–438.

Andragogy

Malcolm Knowles (1913–1997) used the term 'andragogy', derived from the Greek *aner* meaning 'of the man [adult]' and *agogus* meaning to 'lead or accompany' and signifying adult learning, in order to differentiate the theory and practice of adult learning from that of pedagogy (from the Greek *paid* meaning 'of the child' and signifying 'youth learning'). It's believed widely that the term was coined in the 1800s by a German educator, Alexander Knapp, to refer to the methods or techniques used to teach adults (*andragogik*) on the basis that methods used to teach children do not translate to the education of adults. The idea appears to have 'disappeared' for a while, but re-appeared in the 1920s, again in Germany, and became popularized in the 1960s following the publication of an article entitled 'Androgogy [sic], Not Pedagogy' by Knowles in the journal *Adult Leadership* in 1968.[40]

Knowles' model of adult learning is based on the view that pedagogical (child-centred) assumptions about learning (which tend to be more teacher-, topic-, curriculum- and policy-centred) become less valid, whilst andragogical assumptions (which are more self-determined by the learner in terms of purpose, process and product) become more valid, as a person grows older and matures. Knowles' most influential book on the subject, *The Adult Learner: A Neglected Species*, was first published in 1968. A later edition of this book, co-authored with Ed Holton and Richard Swanson, is re-subtitled: *The Adult Learner: The Definitive Classic in Adult Education and Human Resource Development* (8e, 2015).

Andragogy, which some have argued is not a psychological or behavioural learning theory as such,[41] provides a useful set of assumptions and guidelines for HRD practice that are aligned with a humanist philosophy of learning (that is, individualism, choice, development, self-esteem and self-actualization). It aligns particularly well with Carl Rogers' definition of learning, that is 'personal involvement (both of feelings and cognitive aspects), self-initiated (the impetus comes from within), of being pervasive (making a difference in the behaviour, attitudes and even personality of the learner), of being evaluated by the learner (who knows if it is meeting a need) and of having the essence of meaning'[42] (pp. 121–122).

Andragogy's assumptions are shown in Figure 4.5, and the model is applicable to a wide spectrum of learning contexts, ranging from adult education and community education projects to human resource development in organizations.

Andragogy's assumptions (self-directed by the learner rather than other-directed by the teacher; responsive rather than rigid; informal rather than formal; intrinsically-motivated rather than extrinsically-motivated; collaborative rather than controlled) translate into learning and development practices such as:[43]

- Creating a climate for collaborative learning: attention to the physical and social aspects of the learning environment (for example, removing barriers and hierarchies with circular seating arrangements and the course leader inviting student inputs into the planning and the process);
- Providing a structure for collaborative/peer learning: the course leaders give up being the only 'expert' in the room and the idea that students are there to be

'instructed'; instead the course leader's role is to facilitate conversations, provide new ideas, etc.;

● Operationalizing abstractions: the course leader or facilitator should enable and empower students to turn 'knowing that' (abstract declarative knowledge gained in classes) into 'knowing how' (concrete procedural knowledge for application in the real world), for example through methods such as role play, simulations and case studies.

Assumption	Andragogy	Pedagogy
Learner's need to know	Adults need to know why they need to learn something before undertaking it	Learners learn what the curriculum/teacher determines; limited choice
Learner's self-concept	Responsible for their own decisions (including why, what and how to learn)	Greater dependency; less well-developed self-concept; less capability / opportunity to be self-directing
Role of experience	Greater volume and variety of life experience than younger learners	Children have less experience; teachers' experience 'counts' more
Readiness to learn	Ready to learn things that they need to know to cope with their real-life situations	External factors determine what is learned and when learning takes place
Orientation to learning	Life-centred; some form of 'pay-off' from learning for work or personal life	More subject-matter oriented
Motivation to learn	Internal pressures such as job satisfaction, career progression, self-esteem and quality of life	External drivers more important than internal drivers

Figure 4.5 Six assumptions of andragogy

Source: based on descriptions of andragogy versus pedagogy from Knowles et al., 2015: 41–47

Although andragogy has an 'intuitive appeal' and has been influential in HRD circles, especially in the USA, there have been a number of criticisms of Knowles' model, including:

- The division of learning into two discrete stages, of child learning and adult learning when in fact it may be a continuum;
- The fact that adult learners themselves are highly heterogeneous with different needs, styles, degrees of autonomy, confidence to be self-directed, preferences, etc.;
- A reluctance to criticize andragogy because it presents a socially desirable view of adult learners;
- A number of the attributes of so-called andragogy are similar to developments in school-based learning that have taken place in recent decades (for example, self-direction, problem based learning, etc.).[11]

A further aspect of the problematic status of the model may be found in its principal aim of 'how to tailor *education* to the learning needs of adults' (emphasis added). Knowles and colleagues address this issue in their opening remarks in *The Adult Learner* (8e) when they state that care should be taken to avoid confusing the core principles of the adult learning (andragogical) model with the 'goals and purposes for which the learning event is being conducted'. They go on to say that 'human resource development in organizations has a different set of goals and purposes, which andragogy does not embrace'; however the core principles of Knowles' model are useful guidelines in designing and implementing learning experiences, both formal and informal, in workplaces.

Reflective question 4.3

Reflecting on your own recent 'learning history', for example as a college or university student or later as an employee, to what extent has the experience been andragogical (rather than pedagogical) and how has this enabled or constrained your learning?

Delve deeper 4.5

Read more about andragogy in the classic text by Knowles and two leading HRD researchers:

Knowles, M. S., Holton E. F., & Swanson, R. A. (2015). *The Adult Learner: The Definitive Classic in Adult Education and Human Resource Development* (8e). Abingdon: Routledge.

Explore why 'andragogy' is to be preferred over 'pedagogy', links between andragogy and neuroscience, and the pre-history of andragogy in:

Forrest III, S. P., & Peterson, T. O. (2006). It's called andragogy. *Academy of Management Learning & Education, 5*(1), 113–122.

(Continued)

Hagen, M., & Park, S. (2016). We knew it all along! Using cognitive science to explain how andragogy works. *European Journal of Training and Development, 40*(3), 171–190.

Loeng, S. (2017). Alexander Kapp – the first known user of the andragogy concept. *International Journal of Lifelong Education, 36*(6), 629–643.

Finally, read about the links between action learning and experiential learning in:

Yeo, R. K., & Marquardt, M. J. (2015). (Re) Interpreting action, learning, and experience: Integrating action learning and experiential learning for HRD. *Human Resource Development Quarterly, 26*(1), 81–107.

Conclusion: Learning to think

Experiential learning, action learning and andragogy are grouped together here as a broad family of 'experienced-based modalities' of learning that:

- Acknowledge the importance of experience and context in the learning process;
- Draw on John Dewey's pragmatist philosophy and his championing of the role of experience in learning;
- Emphasize that learning is a highly individual process linked to a range of personal factors including learning styles, motivation to learn, identity, autonomy and learners' experiences;
- Put the learner and her experiences at the focal point of the learning process;
- Recognize that learning is both experiential and relational (an idea that will be explored in more detail in subsequent chapters).

Kolb's theory and Revans' and Knowles' models emphasize the internal subjective frame of reference of the individual learner and the need to give them the knowledge and skills, as well as learning-to-learn skills, to find the solutions for themselves albeit with the guidance of and in interaction with peers, supervisors, managers, coaches and mentors, as well as trainers. Each of these modalities in their different ways pose challenges to the normal power relationships in learning and development in organizations. The difference between traditional pedagogical practices (which both ELT, action learning and andragogy can be seen as responses to and reactions against) and learning in occupational and organizational domains entails a shift in mind-set from seeing learners as 'passive recipients' of generalized knowledge to 'active participants' in the process of acquiring and co-creating job-related and job-relevant knowledge, skills and attitudes. Experience-based modalities shed light on how learning actually occurs in the real world and in real time. In the experience-based modalities of experiential, action and adult learning the promise and potential exists for the devolution of power in the learning relationship from an expert 'sage-on-the-stage' to the learner whose potential learning and development organizations seeks to realize. As will be apparent, learning by adults in the workplace tends to be in the main informal, situated, self-directed, dialogical, relational, collaborative, practical, experiential, and outcomes-focused; it reaches 'out of the mind' and is ultimately active (rather than passive) and pragmatic (rather than theoretic). The last words must go to the inspiration behind many of the experience-based and action-based modalities that are so important in learning and development, and adult education, in the words of John Dewey: 'Learning is active. It involves reaching out of the mind. Learning is learning to think.'[45]

Chapter checkout

Use this list to check your understanding of the key points of this chapter.

1 **Experiential learning**   Knowledge created through transformation of experience, complementary processes of grasping and transforming experience; Kolb

2 **Experiential learning theory (ELT) process**   Learning is a four-stage cycle of 'experiencing' (concrete experience, CE), 'reflecting' (reflective observation, RO), 'thinking' (abstract conceptualization, AC) and 'acting' (active experimentation, AE)

3 **ELT dialectics**   Two ways of receiving (grasping) information (by experiencing or thinking, CE or AC) and two ways of transforming information (by reflecting or acting, RO or AE)

4 **ELT learning styles**   Four experiential learning styles, an imagining style (experiencing and reflecting, also known as divergers), analysing style (reflecting and thinking, assimilators), deciding style (thinking and acting, convergers) and initiating style (acting and experiencing, accommodators)

5 **Action learning principles**   Approach for facilitating dialogue, reflection and learning in 'sets' made up of mixed groups of managers all of whom face problems and uncertainties; Revans

6 **Action learning practice**   Members of action learning sets work together collaboratively to ask insightful questions, share experiences and develop creative, flexible and successful strategies to pressing problems

7 **Andragogy assumptions**   Pedagogical assumptions about learning become less valid and andragogical assumptions become more valid as a person matures; Knowles

8 **Andragogy principles**   Six principles of andragogy are learners' needs, learners' self-concept, role of experience, learners' readiness to learn, and learners' motivation to learn

9 **Andragogy implications**   Learning should be learner-(self-)directed, responsive to learners' needs and preferences, informal, be intrinsically-motivated, and collaborative

SKILLS DEVELOPMENT 4
ANALYSING AN EXPERIENCE OF LEARNING IN THE WORKPLACE

You are undertaking an internship in a large city centre hotel as an HR advisor whilst also studying part-time for a qualification in HRM. As part of the internship you attend employee induction sessions led by the HR manager, her animated talk energizes new employees and they leave the room motivated and inspired. You debrief with the HR manager and as part of the HRM course you keep a personal journal in which you write about how the experience of the employee induction session affected you.

You have recently studied the topic of social learning and you see a connection between the concept of role modelling in social learning theory (see Chapter 3 for more detailed discussion of this concept and theory) and think that the concept of 'role modelling' could be a very effective method for learning new behaviours.

When you're tasked by the HR manager with planning a new induction programme for newcomers (which includes an 'Introduction to customer service skills') you use videos of ideal, that is 'model', good and bad customer service encounters with the trainees. You get them to role model a good customer service encounter and give them feedback on their performance. You then ask them to debrief on the learning process and get them to summarize what, for them, the main learning points were and how relevant they were and how they could be applied to their jobs.[46]

Through this process you will have constructed your own personal knowledge (in Kolb's terms 'theories') of how to conduct an induction programme without any formal instruction as such in how to conduct induction training. You use the lessons that you've learned (your 'theories') on a subsequent project in which you are tasked with a training session on unconscious biases in recruitment and selection.

(1) Analyse the learning process in terms of the four stages of the experiential learning cycle.; (2) What features of andragogy are you able to recognize in the process and its outcomes both for yourself and the trainees?; (3) How could you develop your learning and development further in this situation through an action learning approach?

5
'NEUROLEARNING' AND HRD

Contents

On completion of this chapter you should be able to:

- Explain why neuroscience is important to HRD;
- Describe some basics of brain structure and function;
- Explain the effects of neuroplasticity, neurodiversity, ageing and emotions on learning;
- use your knowledge and understanding of the neuroscience of learning to advise on the design and delivery of HRD.

Introduction

The neurosciences are one of the most exciting and fastest-moving areas of biology. Neuroscience emerged as a field of academic study in the 1960s. It aims to describe and explain how the nervous system enables and controls behaviour. Findings from neuroscience have found applications in many areas of business management including marketing ('neuromarketing'), strategic management ('neuro-strategy') and leadership ('neuro-leadership'). In marketing for example, eye-tracking has been used to assess how much attention customers pay to product placement in order to better understand how the brain's unconscious processes influence consumers' buying behaviour. In leadership development the newly-established field of 'neuro-leadership' claims to 'develop brain-friendly talent strategies, and, educate learners at all levels about the brain – improving decision-making, conversations, and outcomes' (https://neuroleadership.com/). In business strategy, researchers are applying neuroscience to shed new light on long-standing strategic management issues such as executive judgement and decision-making.[1] A report in the *Financial Times* summarized the situation when it quoted a dean of a major US business school who remarked: 'we've reached a point where we understand so much about the human brain-how it processes information-that we can use neuroscience to do business better'. In echoing this view, this chapter is about using neuroscience to improve the theories and practice of HRD.

In a report for UK's The Royal Society (the world's oldest independent scientific academy) entitled *Neuroscience: Implications for education and lifelong learning* a number of the UK's leading neuroscientists argued that educational practices can be transformed by brain science just as medical science was transformed by biological science a century or so ago.[2] Several of the report's insights show how learning and development in organizations could be enhanced by embracing the principles of neuroscience. However, if this is going to happen HRD researchers and practitioners need a basic knowledge and understanding of some of the fundamentals of neuroscience in order to be able to apply them. Also, we shouldn't get carried away; even though there's a lot of public and professional interest in brain science we should be cautious about applying brain-based methods without an understanding of the science behind the findings. One of the Report's key recommendations was that the training and continuing professional development (CPD) of practitioners 'should include a component of neuroscience' (p. 20).

Neuroscience also offers a bridge between HRD and the biological sciences. Leading neuroscientists Sarah Jayne Blakemore and Uta Frith, in their book *The Learning Brain*[3] gave several convincing reasons why the time is right for neuroscience to be applied to learning and development across contexts from the classroom to the boardroom:

- Understanding the brain mechanisms that underlie learning could enable us to design and implement learning and development in ways that meet the needs of people of all ages, needs and backgrounds;
- Contrary to what was previously thought, new understandings about brain 'plasticity' (see below) show that the adult brain is flexible in a number of ways and that age needn't be a barrier for learning, development and change;
- Studies of brain development show that environmental influences can be as important as genetics, that the brain constantly adapts to its environment, and that the richness of the learning environment can have a significant effect on learning;
- A number of simple, natural and cost-effective measures, such as healthy diet, adequate exercise and sufficient sleep, can produce significant improvements in brain functioning and learning.

Encouragingly, the promise of neuroscience has been recognized and embraced by HR professional bodies such as Society for HRD (SHRM)[4] in the USA and Chartered Institute of Personnel and Development (CIPD)[5] in the UK. In his research for the CIPD, leading neuroscientist Paul Howard-Jones remarked that learning and the brain could not be more closely intertwined: the win–win is that 'our brains build our learning and learning builds our brains'. Moreover if our brains do not impose strictly defined biological limits on our learning potential, and HRD is about enabling employees to achieve their full potential, then brain science offers a powerful way for HRD to realize this ambition. Finally, neuroscience is important in the on-going development of HRD as a scientifically grounded, multidisciplinary, evidence-based field.

Reflective question 5.1

What would you say to a colleague who's sceptical about the hype that sometimes surrounds neuroscience; she's doubtful about whether neuroscience will ever have any useful applications in HRD and remarked sardonically to you that 'the potential applications for neuroscience in HRD are just around the corner, and always will be'?

Neuroscience and HRD: 'Caveat emptor'[6]

There can be little doubt that neuroscience is a topic that deserves to be firmly on the HRD agenda.[7] The CIPD's research reports *Neuroscience and Learning* (2012) and *Neuroscience in Action* (2014) concluded that concepts from neuroscience will impact increasingly on HRD and that HR practitioners who don't engage with neuroscience are

Myth	Debunking
'We only use 10 per cent of our brain power'	A healthy person uses 100 per cent of their brain
'Intuition is in the right brain'	Intuitive processing is distributed across a number of neural systems that traverse left and right hemispheres
'Listening to classical music increases children's reasoning ability'	There's little consistent evidence to support the so-called 'Mozart effect'
'The brain learns better when it's presented with material in its preferred style'	The brain does not have a learning style; learners may have preferences but evidence that matching makes for better learning is not strong
'The brain stops developing in adulthood'	Brain development continues well into adulthood and some brain processes and structures improve and grow with learning, age and experience
'Some people are left-brainers and some are right-brainers'	Hemispheres work together in healthy cognitive functioning; 'left-brain'-/'right brain' are metaphors for different types of cognitive processing (e.g. 'convergent/divergent')

Figure 5.1 Some common neuromyths

Sources: https://www.psychologytoday.com/gb/blog/the-athletes-way/201708/debunking-neuromyths-eight-common-brain-myths-set-straight; https://ibe-infocus.org/articles/the-neuroscience-of-learning/ (accessed 13-01-21).

likely to miss out in terms of enhancing the effectiveness and the credibility of HR. But as well as being optimistic we also need to exercise caution when buying into neuroscience and be a little circumspect about applying neuroscience indiscriminately in HRD. The CIPD, for instance, alongside its endorsement of brain science's potential to enhance learning and development in organizations, also recommended that engagement with neuroscience needs to be balanced by being wary of unwarranted faith, lack of scepticism and the potential for the spread of inaccuracies and 'neuromyths'. Some of these well-known myths, such as 'we use only 10 per cent of our brains' or 'intuition is in the right brain', are summarized in Figure 5.1.

The remainder of this chapter outlines why we can be optimistic about the insights and applications that HRD stands to gain from the application of neuroscience. But also, as mentioned in the introduction, there are good reasons to be cautious in this highly complex, technical and fast-moving field:

- Images that are used to show brain activations associated with certain mental processes can be seductive and convincing. However, as non-specialists we need to be careful when interpreting neuroimaging studies carried out in laboratory settings when these are extrapolated as neural correlates of real-world cognitive processes such as reasoning, problem-solving, decision-making and learning;[8]
- Because neuroscience is so seductively scientific it can cause us to lapse into reductionism (overemphasizing the role of the brain at the expense of other factors) and determinism (mistakenly thinking we're at the mercy of the way our brain is configured). See the section 'Beware of neuro-bunk' below.[9]

There's great interest in, and consequently a market for, 'brain-based' learning techniques and technologies. There are risks consequently of jumping-in prematurely with 'first-to-market' and sometimes over-hyped applications in business and management; as a writer in the *Financial Times* remarked we need to be wary of the inevitable charlatans and 'snake-oil salesmen'.[10]

Research insight 5.1

Beware of 'neuro-bunk'

In a 2012 TED Talk called 'Beware neuro-bunk' Yale University neuroscientist Molly Crockett discussed how brain science is ubiquitous in several areas of business but there are also instances of where it has been misused. For instance, in marketing many of the claims of so-called 'neuro-enhancements' aren't proven scientifically. Crockett shows how 'brains sell', explains the limits of interpreting neuroscientific data, and demonstrates why we need to be aware of them. She pointed out how pictures of brains seem to have some very 'special properties'. In one study researchers asked

(Continued)

a sample of people to read a scientific article, half of them had the article with a brain image in it, and for the other half it was the same article without the brain image. Readers of the article were then asked whether they agreed with its conclusions. Predictably but somewhat worryingly, more people agreed with the findings when there was a brain image to back it up. Her conclusion was if you want to sell something 'put a brain on it'. This unfortunately creates opportunities not only for misinformation but also for unscrupulous individuals to exploit over-enthusiastic but under-informed consumers of brain science.

Source: www.ted.com/talks/molly_crockett_beware_neuro_bunk?language=en (accessed 13-01-21).

Having acknowledged some of the 'health warnings' around neuroscience, we'll now move on and consider some 'brain science basics' (brain structures, functions and processes involved in learning) that are foundational for understanding if and how brain science can inform the practice of HRD.

Brain science basics

The human brain weighs-in at about 1.4 kilograms and compared to those of other mammals, including great apes, our brains are outsized;[11] your brain is about twenty times that of your pet cat if you have one, four times that of one of your closest relatives the gorilla, the same as a dolphin, half that of an elephant, and about a fifth of one of nature's largest creatures, the sperm whale. In appearance and texture the human brain has been described as about the 'size of a coconut, the shape of a walnut and the consistency of firm jelly'.[12] The majority of the brain's mass is made of glial cells (from the Greek meaning 'glue') which hold the brain's structure together and support and protect neurons.

Neurons are the cells 'where the action is': they carry electrical signals from one to another through structures known as:

- Axons: these are tube-like structures which conduct electrical signals away from the cell nucleus;
- Dendrites: these are branching structures which receive incoming information and conduct it to the cell body.

The gap between where the axon of one cell meets the dendrite of another is called the synapse. Neurotransmitters enable electrical signals to cross the synapse. There are many different types of neurotransmitters, for example dopamine (associated, amongst other things, with pleasure, reward and reinforcement) and serotonin (sometimes called the 'feel-good' chemical and associated with, amongst other things, mood, anxiety, digestion[13] and sleep). Neurotransmitters have a variety of functions, for example:

- Neurological and psychiatric disorders: too little or too much of a neurotransmitter can result in disorders such as Alzheimer's disease or schizophrenia respectively;[14]
- Sleep: neurotransmitters are important during sleep, especially because they help to consolidate the previous day's experiences and learnings.

Each neuron can connect to up to 10,000 others and the brain itself is estimated to contain around 100 billion neurons, making it the most interconnected and complex structure known to exist (for comparison there are approximately 7.7 billion people on the Earth and its age is 4.6 billion years).[15] There's a saying in neuroscience that 'neurons that fire together wire together' and recent research at MIT suggests that this phenomenon affects whole groups of neurons that lie in close proximity to each other analogous to how 'a massive shoal of fish can suddenly change direction, en masse, so long as the lead fish turns, and every other fish obeys the simple rule of following the fish right in front of it'.[16] These networks are important for learning because the acquisition of new knowledge and skills involves modifications to the brain's neural connections and circuits, for example encoding in memory involves changes in synaptic connections and neural circuitry.[17] This is one reason why learning is sometimes described, metaphorically, in terms of a 'mesh' of neurons all interacting with each other and the 'rewiring of the brain' that happens whenever something new is learned. This idea of connectivity was illustrated by the great theoretical physicist Stephen Hawking's (1942–2018) remark that 'We are all now connected by the Internet, like neurons in a giant brain.'[18]

If we 'zoom-out' to look at the bigger picture of brain structure, the brain has two hemispheres, a right and a left, separated by the midline and connected together by a bundle of nerves called the corpus callosum. Incidentally, a study published in the journal *Brain* in 2014 reported that Einstein's corpus callosum was especially thick suggesting that his extraordinary mental capacities (his 'genius') might be attributable at least in part to greater connectivity between the two hemispheres of his brain.[19] Almost all sensory information crosses from one side of the body to the opposite side of the brain (so a stroke on the left side of the brain affects functioning on the right side of the body). The brain's lobes, of which there are four, are covered in a wrinkled grey tissue called the cerebral cortex (less than a quarter of an inch thick) which has in-folds (sulci) and bulges (gyri). The four lobes are shown schematically in Figure 5.2, and their functions are summarized in Figure 5.3. Other brain regions and structures that are relevant to the topics covered in this chapter include:

- Amygdala (from the Greek word meaning almond): part of the memory system for emotionally salient events, produces autonomic unconscious responses (for example, fear, disgust, etc.); there are two of them, one on each side (plural amygdalae) located in the frontal part of the temporal lobe;

- Hippocampus (so named because it is said to resemble the shape of a sea horse): involved in the formation, organization and storage of new memories and connecting emotions to memories; humans have two hippocampi, one in each hemisphere located just above each ear;
- Striatum (a sub-cortical cluster of neurons): part of the brain's reward and reinforcement system, associated with feelings of reward and pleasure and aversion behaviours.

The amygdala and hippocampus are considered to be part of the limbic system (involved in emotional processing and memory formation) located between the brain-stem (which is continuous with the spinal cord) and the cerebral hemispheres.

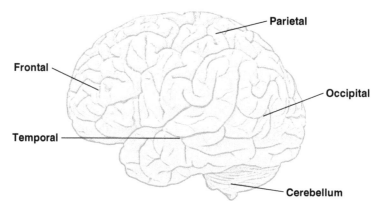

Figure 5.2 Simplified schematic structure of human brain
Source: from MS Word online pictures Creative Commons.

The study of the brain has come on in leaps and bounds in recent decades, as a result we live in what's been described as a 'golden age' of discovery brain science.[20] Many of the advances in brain science have been enabled by developments in the range and power of techniques that are available to study the brain structure and function. For example:

- Electroencephalography (EEG): which involves the placing of electrodes on the face and scalp; is used to measure brain activity associated with particular psychological states reflecting over- or under-activity in certain parts of the brain.
- Functional Magnetic Resonance Imaging (fMRI): measures fluctuations in neural activity during mental tasks as a result of changes in blood flow ('haemodynamics'); see Figure 5.4;

- Positron emission tomography (PET): measures the levels of the sugar glucose in the brain so as to locate where neural 'firing' is taking place.[21]

Frontal ('front')

- Higher-level 'executive' functions
- Planning, decision making, judgement
- Controlling impulsive and acceptable/unacceptable behaviours

Temporal ('side')

- Short- and long-term memory function
- Processing sensory input (inc. language in Wernicke's speech comprehension and Broca's speech production areas)
- Formation of emotional memories based in inputs from the amygdala

Occipital ('back')

- Visual cortex
- Receives sensory information from the eyes
- Processes visual information including space, colour and motion

Parietal ('top')

- Processing sensory information from different parts of the body including touch (the somatosensory cortex)
- Spatial processing and navigation (right parietal lobe)
- Symbolic processing such as language and mathematics (left parietal lobe)

Figure 5.3   Selected and simplified functions of the brain's four 'lobes'

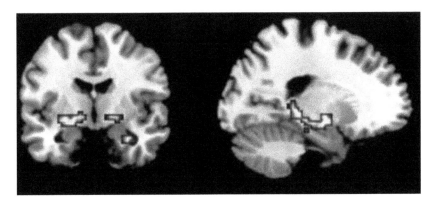

Figure 5.4   Example of fMRI scan images showing positions of amygdalae (left) and hippocampus (right)

Source: from MS Word Online images Creative Commons.

However, as Paul Howard-Jones noted in his research for the CIPD, we should always bear in mind that tools such as functional magnetic resonance imaging (fMRI), electro-encephalography (EEG) and positron emission tomography (PET) are highly sophisticated and specialized ways of constructing images of brain activity. Neuroscientists use these imaging techniques in conjunction with complex statistical methods, consequently 'brain scans' need to be interpreted in an informed way with care, caution and precision. In business management the relatively newly established field of 'organizational neuroscience' (ONS) applies brain science, including the use of brain scanning technologies, to the understanding of behaviour in organizations.[22]

Delve deeper 5.1

Read more about ONS in:

Becker, W. J., Cropanzano, R., & Sanfey, A. G. (2011). Organizational neuroscience: Taking organizational theory inside the neural black box. *Journal of Management*, *37*(4), 933–961.

Read more about the criticisms of the application of neuroscience to leadership by reading:

Lindebaum, D., & Zundel, M. (2013). Not quite a revolution: Scrutinizing organizational neuroscience in leadership studies. *Human Relations*, *66*(6), 857–877.

As far as HRD is concerned it's worth bearing in mind that management, leadership and behaviours in organizations in general involve complex tasks that are likely to entail functions in multiple brain areas. We should be wary, therefore, of research that attributes specific organizational behaviours, such as decision-making, planning, etc., to small numbers of highly localized brain areas. We should also bear in mind that management is a social activity, therefore we need to be cautious in extrapolating from results of studies of individual behaviours in neuroscience labs to group behaviours in organizational settings.

Plasticity

In this section we'll focus on one of the most important and HRD-relevant aspects of brain function: 'plasticity'. The term 'plastic' is from the Greek word meaning 'to mould'. So when we talk about 'brain plasticity', or 'neuroplasticity', we mean the brain's capacity to change in response to stimuli. Such stimuli can include experience, environment and learning. Up until the 1960s it was thought, mistakenly, that the human brain didn't change much after childhood and that by the time human beings got to adolescence the brain was pretty much fixed, and that beyond the age of 20 years or so decline starts to set in. The concept of plasticity changed this view significantly.

Modern brain science has shown that experience, environment and learning are able to alter the human brain in quite significant, and even remarkable, ways for example by compensating for brain injury or enhancing its structural components through learning.[23] Plasticity manifests in two ways, structurally and functionally:

- Structural plasticity: changes the brain's physical structure in response to external stimuli such as learning;
- Functional plasticity: migration of a specific brain function from one area of the brain to another in response, for example, to damage; see Figure 5.5.[24]

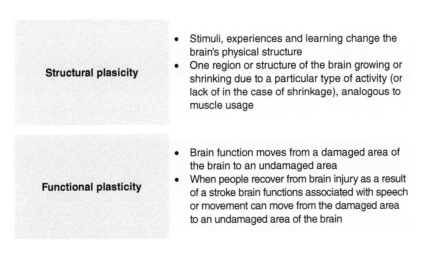

Figure 5.5 Structural and functional plasticity

Source: adapted from Peters, R. (2006). Ageing and the brain. *Postgraduate Medical Journal*, 82(964), 84–88. doi:10.1136/pgmj.2005.036665/

In this section we'll focus mainly on structural plasticity and its relationship to learning in areas such as skill development and the acquisition of expertise.

What does the phenomenon of plasticity mean for learning? In terms of synaptic connections it's straightforward enough: those that are used grow stronger, whilst those that are not used 'wither and die'. This makes sense because it would be inefficient for the brain to devote precious resources to parts of the system that weren't serving any useful function. The system needs to be as efficient as possible because the brain is a voracious consumer of energy compared to some other parts of the body (the brain burns calories by consuming around 20 per cent of the body's energy use according to eminent neurologist Marcus Raichle).[25] Perhaps the most famous illustration of structural plasticity and learning are the studies of London taxi drivers' brains which gave strong support to the age-old HRD saying of 'use it or lose it'.

Research insight 5.2

Taxi drivers' brains 'grow' stronger on the job

One of London taxi drivers' most remarkable capabilities[26] is how they're able to navigate the city's intricate warren of streets. Taxi drivers can be hailed in the street and be expected to know how to get anywhere in the city; this means that to become a taxi driver requires a thorough knowledge of London. This is why Transport for London (TfL) requires London taxi drivers to pass the world-famous 'Knowledge' test. The Knowledge was introduced in 1865 and, according to TfL, mastering it takes three to four years and is one of the 'toughest exam processes around' involving 320 routes (or 'runs', listed in the 'Blue Book') and various points of interest within a six-mile radius of Charing Cross. The process to becoming a London taxi driver involves seven arduous stages.[27]

Human beings', including London taxi drivers', remarkable spatial navigation skills are associated with a brain structure called the hippocampus.[28] The hippocampus is a curved structure located in the temporal lobe and responsible for forming, organizing and storing long-term memory; we have one in each hemisphere, hence 'hippocampi'. The firing of neurons in the hippocampus is location-specific and thus helps us to learn the layout of an environment. As a result of this process a complex cognitive 'map' is built-up. In studying the role of the hippocampus in how London taxi drivers develop their extraordinary navigation skills researchers have found that the:

- Hippocampus is activated (i.e. it 'lights up' in brain scans) when taxi drivers navigate around a complex environment in laboratory simulations;
- Volume of the posterior hippocampus (its 'grey matter volume') in taxi drivers is greater than that of non-taxi drivers (including London bus drivers) and retired London taxi drivers.

The implications are that the hippocampus (specifically the posterior part of it) is vital in navigating large-scale and highly complex environments, that it grows in response to experience and learning, and that it shrinks when it's not being used (the neuroplasticity in the hippocampus, and likely other parts of the brain, works both ways). Importantly from the perspective of learning, it also shows that environment is vitally important in structural neuroplasticity and related changes in memory.

Source: Woollett, K., Spiers, H. J., & Maguire, E. A. (2009). Talent in the taxi: A model system for exploring expertise. *Philosophical Transactions of the Royal Society B: Biological Sciences, 364*(1522), 1407–1416.

There's an important implication from this research for the relationship between the brain, genes and environment: as Paul Howard-Jones remarked, the brain's plasticity shows clearly that our genes determine our learning only partially and that the environment that we're in, that we create or is created for us, can influence strongly 'how our brains are constructed'.[29] This is important because the opportunities that the environment offers for learning appear to be able to influence brain structure itself.

There are also implications from this and related research for how we think about and understand expertise and expert performance. London taxi drivers are experts, but their expertise isn't innate (they're not born with a map of London inside their heads) nor is it related to intelligence, instead:

- Developing expertise is possible with extensive effort and intensive learning;
- There are particular brain regions that are associated with particular types of expertise (for example, in the hippocampus for spatial location);
- If experts, or anyone else for that matter, don't continually use or update their knowledge and skills there's a good chance that their expertise will lapse and lose its edge.

Neuroplasticity isn't just confined to spatial memory nor does it take a lifetime to develop; for example research has shown that the auditory cortex of skilled musicians is 25 per cent larger than in non-musicians and even a non-musician learning a simple five-finger exercise on the piano for two hours a day for five days can enlarge the relevant sensory and motor areas of the brain.

Although it's indisputable that there are people who have exceptional innate abilities (for example, geniuses such as W. A. Mozart in music, or Marie Curie in science), it's also beyond doubt that the high levels of knowledge and skill that are the hallmarks of expertise can be developed through extensive experience, practice, coaching and feedback. The processes which 'sculpt' our plastic brains can be remarkably quick in response to regular and systematic experience, learning and practice. Once they become experts, even highly skilled people need to continuously learn and practice in order to keep their brains in 'shape'. Expertise is analogous to physical fitness – it needs to be constantly honed and exercised to prevent it from declining or decaying.[30]

Delve deeper 5.2

The scientific evidence for the effects of brain plasticity and other aspects of neuroscience can be highly technical and complex to interpret. The HR professional bodies are aware of the importance of neuroscience for HR and of the need to translate neuroscience for a 'lay' audience. A cover article in the SHRM's professional magazine *HR Magazine* entitled 'The brain at work' explored questions such as why people only retain a fraction of what they learn, get a boost of energy when their bosses meaningfully praise their work, and tire when focusing on one activity. Read more in:

(Continued)

Fox, A. (2008). The brain at work. *HR Magazine*. www.shrm.org/hr-today/news/hr-magazine/pages/3fox-your%20brain%20on%20the%20job.aspx (accessed 13-01-21).

The Jacobs Foundation, which seeks to 'provide children and youth with effective knowledge, skills, attitudes, tools and equitable opportunities to reach their full learning potential and thrive together' published a highly readable 'white paper' in 2018 on brain plasticity and its implications for human learning and development. Read more in:

McLaughlin, K.A., Mackey, A., Bunge, S. A. , Fernandes, G. F., Brown, K., & Buhler, J. C. (2018). *Human brain plasticity: Future directions and implications for children's learning and development.* Zurich: Jacobs Foundation.

Neurodiversity and learning

The term 'neurodiversity' is thought to have been coined by Australian social scientist Judy Singer in the 1990s. It came to wider public attention in late 1998 in an article in *The Atlantic* magazine by Harvey Blume entitled 'Neurodiversity: On the neurological underpinnings of geekdom' in which he argued that in any human population there are bound to be inevitable departures from the neurological norm and that 'neurodiversity may be every bit as crucial for the human race as biodiversity is for life in general'.[31]

There are a number of well-known dimensions of neurodiversity that are common in the human population, for example, the occurrence of autism is estimated at 1 in 42 amongst males and 1 in 189 amongst females in the United States. Leading neuroscientist, Simon Baron-Cohen, in writing about autism, commented that when we examine the biological, neurological and cognitive bases of autism (for example, larger amygdala and smaller posterior corpus callosum) we do not see evidence of 'dysfunction' (and hence the labelling of autism as a disorder) but instead we see evidence of 'difference'. He describes autism is one example of 'diversity in the set of all possible brains' none of which are 'normal' and all of which are simply 'different'[32] and which are expressions of variability in the human genome.

Research insight 5.3

Evolution, autism and the systematizing mechanism

Simon Baron-Cohen argued that *Homo sapiens* diverged from other animals as a result of the evolution of a unique mental tool which he refers to as the 'Systematizing Mechanism' between 70,000 and 100,000 years ago. It is this mental system that enables humans to analyse and construct all types of systems including collectible systems (such as postage stamps), mechanical systems (such as an engine), numerical systems (such as train timetables), natural systems (such as weather patterns), etc. The systematizing mechanism works by asking questions about the world and working out 'if-and-then' patterns in the regularities and rules by which the system operates (such as, 'if we multiply 3 by 12 then we get 36', 'if we turn the switch then the light becomes dimmer'). This mechanism not only can be used to build testable theories about the world it may also be the 'engine' of invention.[33] Baron-Cohen argued that this mechanism helps to explain: (1) the social and communication difficulties that are to be found in autism; (2) the 'intact', and often superior, skills in systemizing (he describes people who are autistic as 'hyper-systematizers').

Source: Baron-Cohen, S. (2009). Autism: The empathizing-systemizing (ES) theory. *Annals of the New York Academy of Sciences*, *1156*(1), 68–80; Baron-Cohen, S. (2020). *The pattern seekers: How autism drives human invention*. London: Allen Lane.

The term neurodiversity has been applied to a range of neurodevelopmental phenomena and conditions including not only autism spectrum conditions (ASC), but also ADHD, dyslexia, dyspraxia, OCD etc. that arise as a result of interactions between both genetic and environmental factors. As a form of human diversity neurodiversity is subject to the same social dynamics, including forms of discrimination, that affect other forms of diversity in society.[34] In recognizing these issues, the CIPD observed that the occurrence of neurodiversity – as a manifestation of natural variability in the population – means that 'neurominorities' represent a significant and important proportion of existing employees, job applicants and customers. As a result positive steps should be taken to acknowledge and accommodate this aspect of diversity as a way of utilizing, developing and attracting new and different talents that may be at risk of being overlooked in the labour market. This is an important issue of equality of opportunity given that levels of unemployment may be especially high amongst neurodiverse groups.

Robert Austin and Gary Pisano, writing in the *Harvard Business Review*,[35] frame neurodiversity as a source of competitive advantage since many neurodiverse individuals have higher-than-average abilities in areas such as pattern recognition, memory, mathematical skill, etc. but they may be impaired in other ways and also struggle to fit into conventional job profiles. They also noted that a growing number of well-known and forward-thinking companies are reforming their HR policies and procedures to accommodate neurodiverse individuals, including Ernst and Young, Dell, Ford, JP Morgan Chase, Microsoft, SAP, etc. (part of the 'Autism Round Table').

Perspective from practice 5.1

Neurodiversity at Microsoft

In 2015 the Director of Inclusive Hiring and Accessibility at Microsoft announced the Autism Hiring Program to coincide with World Autism Day.[36] Microsoft started the programme because the company's traditional hiring process, 'the front door to Microsoft', could be a major barrier of entry for many talented candidates. By 'adjusting the shape of the door' they were able to help talented candidates 'showcase and demonstrate' their capabilities. Microsoft sees this diversity as a strength and a recognition that the cognitive differences that exist in the human population can be of significant value and a sustainable source of competitive advantage. In the first wave Microsoft recruited 50 full-time employees. The engineers recruited are writing code for products and services used by millions of customers daily. As far as HRD was concerned, the learning needs of the new hires were accommodated by 'providing feedback more often, sharing recaps of meetings in writing, and giving clear expectations'. A video which explains Microsoft's approach and gives voice to employees with autism can be found at: https://blogs.microsoft.com/accessibility/autismawareness2018/.

Microsoft's commitment is aligned with Austin and Pisano's observation that neurodiverse hiring is especially pertinent at a time when many economies are facing severe shortages of IT workers. The abilities of neurodiverse people can be a good match for data analytics and IT services roles. Other aspects of neurodiversity also offer untapped opportunities for organizations to make use of a unique talent pool and redress issues of inequality. In the UK there are legal implications for organizations who discriminate against neurodiverse employees in recruitment and selection, for example if they are put at a disadvantage in relation to 'neurotypical' candidates in recruitment processes.[37]

If HRD seeks to manage learning processes in such a way as to enable all employees to maximize their potential then it must acknowledge and accommodate the challenges and opportunities of a neurodiverse workforce. As the CIPD notes, HR can respond by recognizing that neurodiversity not only creates challenges for specific individuals it also presents opportunities. They give the example of dyslexia which is a dimension of neurodiversity which, like other aspects, is accompanied by impairments. Dyslexia affects literacy and language-related skills, difficulties with phonological processing, working memory and processing speed but also confers advantages in areas such as creativity, insight and atypical problem-solving.

Perspective from practice 5.2

Practical steps for accommodating neurodiversity in HRD

Remploy is a government-owned business in the UK that delivers employment and skills support for disabled people and for people with particular health conditions. Remploy's guidelines can be adapted for HRD purposes, for example for Autism Spectrum Condition (ASC) the implications include:

- Such employees may be unable to pick-up on team dynamics;
- Training needs to be delivered in a highly systematic and routine fashion;
- Job coaching should be used to help individuals complete tasks;
- Use of visual prompts can aid comprehension;
- Clarity of language helps to avoid ambiguity;
- Training sessions should have a clear structure and allow adequate time.

For a detailed discussion of managing learning and development issues created by some of the common aspects of neurodiversity consult: Remploy (2017) *Disability Guide*. Leicester: Remploy Maximus. Available online: www.remploy.co.uk/employers/resources/disability-guide (accessed 29-12-20).

Acknowledging and accommodating neurodiversity entails providing suitable learning and development opportunities for neurodiverse colleagues, avoiding treating neurodiverse colleagues at a disadvantage in accordance with codes of practice and equality legislation,[38] training neurotypical co-workers and managers to develop their awareness of neurodiversity[39] and recognizing the challenges and opportunities that a neurodiverse workforce presents.[40]

Delve deeper 5.3

In addition to the work of Simon Baron-Cohen discussed above, you can extend your knowledge of autism and the future of neurodiversity by reading:

Wired reporter Steve Silberman's best-selling book *NeuroTribes* (2015) which 'casts light on the growing movement of "neurodiversity" activists seeking respect, support, technological innovation, accommodations in the workplace and in education, and the right to self-determination for those with cognitive differences'.[41]

Thomas Armstrong's *The Power of Neurodiversity* (2011) counters traditional pathologizings of neurodiversity.[42] The neurodiversity perspective has not been universally accepted and has been criticized from within the medical profession.

(Continued)

Read a response to some of these criticisms of neurodiversity from an autistic autism researcher in Jacquiline den Houting's article:

den Houting, J. (2019). Neurodiversity: An insider's perspective. *Autism: The International Journal of Research and Practice*, 23(2), 271.

For practical resources on the theme of 'neurodiversity creates opportunity' and case studies of organizations that have embraced the opportunities as well as the challenges of neurodiversity visit the 'Neurodiversity Hub' website:

www.neurodiversityhub.org/

Emotions and learning

Much of our conscious and unconscious cognitive activity appears to be driven 'from below' by basic emotional processes and their underlying biological and neurological mechanisms. Consequently emotion has the potential to modulate virtually every aspect of cognition, including learning.[43] Learning can involve a wide range of positively and negatively valenced emotions such as enthusiasm, exhilaration and excitement, as well as fear, frustration and boredom. In any learning situation some topics and approaches can elicit passion and motivation whilst others can elicit distaste and aversion. Emotion influences learning through its effects on attention, motivation, memory, reasoning and problem-solving which can both enable and constrain learning. For example:

- The brain has limited processing capacity hence emotions help to guide sensory perception and resolve tensions between competing choices (in this respect the emotional salience of material modulates how well or badly learners attend to it);[44]
- Emotions can increase cognitive load and impede processing through their constraining effects on working memory, cognitive processing and performance.[45]

As for the brain structures that are implicated in emotion, one of the most important is the amygdala. The amygdalae are part of the limbic system and often considered to be the emotion centre of the brain. There's one amygdala in each hemisphere and their role is to evaluate the emotional valence of a stimulus (for example, fear). The amygdala has been referred to metaphorically as a brain-based 'smoke detector' because it helps us to respond, for example with fight-or-flight reactions by increasing heart and breathing rate. Daniel Goleman, the author of the best-selling book *Emotional Intelligence – Why It Can Matter More than IQ*, referred to a process of 'amygdala hijacking' where, in the face of a perceived threat, attention narrows and neural pathways to our prefrontal cortex become 'closed-off', and complex decision-making 'disappears'.[46] The amygdala is also involved in emotional memory and learning on the basis of reward (positively valenced emotions) and punishment (negatively valenced emotions).[47] The 'affect heuristic' is a mental shortcut whereby positive emotions make us more likely to take risks and try new things, and negative emotions curb our risk-taking and adventurousness which works through emotion modulating our perception of the balance between risk and benefits.[48]

Reflective question 5.2

You can gain a deeper understanding of your own emotional intelligence (EI) by taking one of the many EI tests that are currently available, for example on the *Harvard Business Review* website: https://hbr.org/2015/06/quiz-yourself-do-you-lead-with-emotional-intelligence. Follow the instructions. How informative are the results for how you experience and interpret your own emotions? Could the results be of any potential use in your understanding and interpretation of emotions in others? Can you envisage any potential uses for such tests in HRD?

To single-out one brain region or structure or a particular function, such as the amygdala and emotions, as being the main influencer of learning is an over simplification. Human cognition is a highly complex process driven by various processing systems distributed across many different brain regions. For example, there is the 'hot', intuitive (experiential) system (System 1) of which the amygdala is a part and the 'cold', analytical (rational) system (System 2) of which the prefrontal cortex (PFC) is a part. Note this is not equivalent to the idea of left brain and right brain, or the 'neuromyth' of experiential processes such as intuition being in the 'right brain'. Effective cognitive functioning involves the integration and balancing of cognitive and affective processes – sometimes referred to metaphorically as balancing 'head' and 'heart' – emanating from brain structures and regions such as:

- The amygdala which enhances the processing of emotionally arousing stimuli and the consolidation in memory of emotionally-salient material;
- The PFC which enhances higher-order, analytical cognitive functions that affect working memory and promote the encoding and establishment of long-term memory traces.[49]

Both are vital and many decades of evidence from brain science show that emotional processes emanating from the limbic system (which includes the amygdala and the hippocampus) exert a significant influence over cognitive processes such as attention, learning, perception, memory, problem-solving, reasoning and decision-making.

As far as the implications for HRD are concerned, the effects of emotion on learning can be both positive and negative, and complex for example:

- Emotionally salient material is attended to and remembered more clearly, accurately and for longer periods of time than emotionally neutral material, therefore, to engage attention material should be made emotionally salient for example, by using vivid images and 'stories';

- Stress is a negative emotional state; mild and acute stress can facilitate learning and cognitive performance, whilst excess and chronic stress can significantly impair learning and is detrimental to overall memory performance,[50] hence stress levels in the learning environment need to be monitored and managed sensitively;
- Curiosity is a positive emotional state which is associated with heightened interest in novel activities and prepares the brain to learn and remember,[51] therefore the use of techniques that arouse curiosity can be used to elicit and sustain interest.[52]

Brain science shows clearly that it is a mistake to think of the role of emotion and cognition ('heart' and 'head') in learning as separate processes. An extensive body of research shows that emotions and rational thought must work together, for example by applying emotional intelligence to our reasoning processes and making rational sense of our emotional experiences.[53] HRD has an important role to play in developing employees' knowledge and understanding of the neuroscience of learning and thereby enhancing their ability to learn-how-to-learn more effectively.

Perspective from practice 5.3

Five brain-based characteristics of effective learning

The Lego Foundation commissioned a report into the relationships between play and learning, and whilst much of the report focused on children's learning there are a number of general implications regarding 'playful' learning experiences that are of interest and relevance to HRD, namely that effective learning entails five brain-based attributes; see Figure 5.6.

Joy
- Associated with increased dopamine (the so-called 'feel-good' neurotransmitter) levels in the brain's reward system; supports enhanced attention, creativity, memory and motivation

Meaningful
- Making connections between unfamiliar material and familiar material builds stronger connections; enhancing connections makes learning easier and more rewarding

Engaged
- Being actively engaged in learning enhances the encoding and retrieval of new material, strengthens connections, and gives an enhanced sense of control over learning

Iterative
- Repetition, persistence and achievement are linked to the building of expertise, reward systems, support learning over the longer term; iterative thinking through trail and error builds resilience

Interactive
- Positive social interactions promote positive emotions; buffer stresses and setbacks which can impede learning; social interaction builds the skills needed for detecting mental states of others; 'mirror neurons' are a potential mechanism

Figure 5.6 Five brain-based attributes of effective learning

These observations resonate with cognitive and social theories of learning and draw attention to the fact that learning theories should not be thought of as existing in separate 'silos'. The reality is that different theories of learning are mutually supportive thus enhancing their validity, credibility and utility.

Source: Liu, C., Solis, S. L., Jensen, H., Hopkins, E. J., Neale, D., Zosh, J. M., Hirsh-Pasek, K., & Whitebread, D. (2017). *Neuroscience and learning through play: A review of the evidence*. The LEGO Foundation, DK. Available online: neuroscience-review_web.pdf (legofoundation.com) (accessed 29-12-2020).

Mindfulness and learning

Given the power that emotions have over our perceptions, motivations, reasoning, decision-making and problem-solving, mastering techniques for emotion regulation, such as 'mindfulness meditation', can enhance learning processes and HRD outcomes significantly. Mindfulness meditation has a long history and is associated with a variety of religious, spiritual and philosophical practices, such as Buddhism. It involves the conscious and deliberate monitoring and controlling of one's attention, and the regulation of emotions and self-awareness. There are variety of meditation traditions and techniques including 'Zen', 'mantra', 'transcendental', 'yoga', 'vipassana', etc.

Dan Seigel of the UCLA Mindful Awareness Research Centre explains the mechanisms of mindfulness in terms of functional plasticity: 'new patterns of repeated neural circuit activation strengthen the synaptic connections' associated with mindful states leading to synaptic strengthening and synaptic growth. In relation to the specific brain regions involved, researchers have investigated the role and function of the medial prefrontal cortex (mPFC) which is part of the brain's frontal lobe and has a central role in a number of aspects of cognitive control, including planning, attention, problem-solving, error-monitoring, decision-making, social cognition and working memory.[54] As far as mindfulness is concerned, the mPFC is:

- Thought to be the brain region responsible for the unconstrained 'mind chatter' that reinforces established ways of thinking and fuels anxieties;
- One of the brain regions that mindfulness mediation helps to 'quiet' and thereby promoting mental well-being by reducing preoccupations, worries and anxieties.

A number of big corporates, including Adobe, Ford, General Mills, and Google have followed the evidence from neuroscience and psychology in instigating their own mindfulness and meditation programmes.[55] Researchers have explored the use of mindfulness in management development and identified benefits, including a better sense of perspective, improved self-confidence, enhanced inter- and intra-personal sensitivity and 'meta-cognition' (ability to think about their own thinking).[56] The popularity of mindfulness meditation is evident from the number of popular psychology and self-help books on the subject (for example, the works of John Kabat-Zinn), websites (such as, www.mindful.org/) and apps (such as, 'Headspace').

In their own words 5.1

Steve Jobs on mindfulness meditation

Perhaps the most famous corporate practitioner of mindfulness meditation was Apple's founder and former chief executive, Steve Jobs. Jobs spent time in India, was strongly influenced by Zen Buddhism and was a meditator himself.[57] Jobs told his biographer Walter Isaacson that: 'If you just sit and observe, you will see how restless your mind is [and] If you try to calm it, it only makes it worse, but over time it does calm, and when it does, there's room to hear more subtle things – that's when your intuition starts to blossom, and you start to see things more clearly and be in the present more. Your mind just slows down, and you see a tremendous expanse in the moment. You see so much more than you could see before. It's a discipline; you have to practise it.'

It's been suggested that mindfulness meditation can assist in emotion regulation in some specific and important HRD practices such as coaching and mentoring. Leading coaching researcher and practitioner Jonathan Passmore argues that mindfulness can help coachees/mentees to:

- Observe their behaviour, thoughts and feelings and in doing so, encouraging them to become more self-aware;
- 'Step outside' of their thought stream of rumination about past events;
- Take a more objective perspective on situations and events;
- Observe their own thoughts and feelings, and make choices about thoughts, feelings and behaviours which may be more productive and helpful.[58]

Mindfulness meditation costs little to implement or participate in and has been shown to have positive effects on the human brain and cognitive functioning and has been used successfully in developing self-awareness and for stress management. In common with exercise, sleep and diet, it's a tried-and-tested method for mobilizing sustainable improvements in employees' performance, well-being and their ability and motivation to learn. Research into the effects of mindfulness and mediation practices on brain structure and cognitive functioning present good evidence for mediation as a learning and development practice which could not only improve emotion regulation and thereby have beneficial effects on HRD outcomes, but can also enhance a range of work-relevant skills and abilities.

—Reflective question 5.3—

Experience mindfulness for yourself with the classic 'Raisin meditation' developed by mindfulness pioneer Jon Kabat-Zinn from the University of Massachusetts Medical School: https://ggia.berkeley.edu/practice/raisin_meditation. For additional mindfulness resource there are various websites, for example 'Mindful: Healthy Mind, Healthy Life' www.mindful.org/meditation/mindfulness-getting-started/.

The UK government, under ex-Prime Minister David Cameron, showed an interest in mindfulness meditation with the establishment in 2015 of a 'UK Mindfulness All-Parliamentary Group'. The group published a report that sought to address physical and mental health concerns in the workplace through the application of mindfulness-based solutions. The report recognized that there is strong interest in mindfulness in the workplace as a means for tackling rising costs of both absence and presenteeism, work-related stress and depression, and the need to boost productivity in workplaces that are being transformed radically by new information technologies. The report's authors remarked that 'Many organisations are well aware of the importance of encouraging employee wellbeing, creativity and commitment to achieve success in what are often challenging circumstances but are unsure how to prevent mental health problems developing' (p. 40).[59]

—Delve deeper 5.4—

Read more about the scientific evidence for the benefits of mindfulness in the workplace in:

Aikens, K. A., Astin, J., Pelletier, K. R., Levanovich, K., Baase, C. M., Park, Y. Y., & Bodnar, C. M. (2014). Mindfulness goes to work: Impact of an online workplace intervention. *Journal of Occupational and Environmental Medicine, 56*(7), 721–731.

Killingsworth, M. A., & Gilbert, D. T. (2010). A wandering mind is an unhappy mind. *Science, 330*(6006), 932.

Zeidan, F., Johnson, S. K., Diamond, B. J., David, Z., & Goolkasian, P. (2010). Mindfulness meditation improves cognition: Evidence of brief mental training. *Consciousness and Cognition, 19*(2), 597–605.

Read more about how to use mindfulness-based practices in leadership development and HRD in:

Brendel, W., & Bennett, C. (2016). Learning to embody leadership through mindfulness and somatics practice. *Advances in Developing Human Resources, 18*(3), 409–425.

Ageing and learning

An important factor that shapes the human brain, and which none of us can escape, is time and hence age. The United Nations estimated in 2019 that:

- There were 703 million people over the age of 65 years and this is projected to double by 2050 so that one in every six of humanity will be 65 or over;
- Older people (65 years or older) account for more than one-fifth of the population in 17 countries;
- By 2100 this will be the case for 155 countries, covering a majority (61 per cent) of the world's population.[60]

The ageing population is a global 'megatrend' (see Chapter 8) and it is a demographic inevitability that age-related brain changes will become increasingly relevant as the profile of workforces across the globe become more skewed towards older workers. This has significant implications for organizations and has been identified as one of the leading shifts in 'talent trends' for HRD[61] simply because the brain loses some of its capacities due to the passage of time. However, it doesn't appear to be a simple matter of neuronal 'fall outs'. Research suggests that:

- Cortical neuron numbers may not decrease by as much as first thought;
- Intellectual decline may be due to localized changes in some quite specific brain areas, such as the PFC and hippocampus, and specific brain function such as episodic memory;[62]
- Other, cognitive manifestations of age-related brain changes include reduced reasoning ability and working memory capacity, simultaneous processing and retention of information.[63]

However, a reason to be cheerful about age-related brain changes is that as we grow older and more experienced the brain can become more 'efficient'. It does this through the process of reducing the number of synaptic connections that are needed by about half. In this process of 'synaptic pruning' the remaining synaptic connections are strengthened. Environment is also an important shaper of the brain through its influence on processes such as pruning. Figure 5.7 summarizes some of the changes that take place in the human brain as a result of ageing and also lists some of the steps that can be taken to maintain cognitive function as much as possible or slow its decline.

Although there are inevitable changes in brain structure and functioning with age – the so-called 'ageing brain' – contrary to what was previously thought, older adults can be highly adept in learning new skills under the right conditions. Moreover, even though some mental abilities decline (such as short term memory), the brain also becomes more powerful in its abilities to recognize patterns and make complex judgements; as a result the important qualities of expertise, intuition and 'wisdom' improve with practice, exposure and experience.[64]

Some of the specific implications of age-related changes for learning include:

- Loss of cortical cells, and pruning unused networks;
- Increasing connectivity throughout what remains;

Ageing effects

- Prefrontal cortex and hippocampus are most affected by age-related reductions; occipital cortex least (fits with observed cognitive changes)
- Most widely seen cognitive change is in memory; most affected is episodic memory (decline from middle age)
- 'Synaptic pruning' makes some brain functions more efficient
- Biological age of brain not necessarily same as chronological age

Protective measures

- Diet higher in energy and lower in antioxidants is a risk factor
- Increased consumption of fish and seafood may be protective and reduce the risk of stroke
- Low to moderate alcohol intake may reduce cardiovascular risk and stimulate hippocampus
- Exercise associated with increased executive functioning and reduction in age-related decline

Figure 5.7 Ageing effects and protective measures

Source: Peters, R. (2006). Ageing and the brain. *Postgraduate Medical Journal*, *82*(964), 84–88.

- More integration across hemispheres, and less hemispheric specialization;
- Slower cognitive processing but more parts of the brain are activated simultaneously;
- Loss of processing speed and focus, but expanded capacity for seeing the big picture;
- Becoming more adept at solving complex problems required for 'navigating' in the real world. [65]

Finally, an improved comprehension of meaning and a preference for storytelling may go towards making older adults better at teaching than learning and adept at transmitting cultural wisdom and the ongoing shaping of culture. [66] The world-renowned neuroscientist Elkhonon Goldberg refers to this phenomenon of 'the mind becoming stronger as the brain grows older' as 'the wisdom paradox'. [67]

Reflective question 5.4

What would you say to an ill-informed colleague who is of the view that providing learning and development opportunities for older workers isn't a good use of scarce HRD resources because, in his words, 'you can't teach an old dog new tricks, and anyway the future of the organization is in the hands of the younger generation of employees so that's where we should be focusing our efforts'?

---Delve deeper 5.5---

Read more about how neuroscience can be used to enhance HRD practice by reading:

Collins, S. (2015). *Neuroscience for learning and development: How to apply neuroscience and psychology for improved learning and training*. London: Kogan Page.

For a bibliography of suggested readings on neuroscience and its applications in HR consult:

Londhe, A. (2018). Suggested readings on neuroscience and its application in HR. *NHRD Network Journal*, *11*(4), 100–103.

For those readers interested in their own neurological future I suggest reading Elkhonon Goldberg's authoritative and optimistic book:

Goldberg, E. (2007). *The wisdom paradox: How your mind can grow stronger as your brain grows older*. London: Penguin Random House.

Conclusion: HRD at the 'cutting edge'

This chapter has explored ways in which HRD practice could be enhanced by engaging with neuroscience. HRD researchers and practitioners need a firm grasp of some of the fundamentals of neuroscience so that they might, where appropriate, apply neuroscience concepts and principles to HRD theory, research and practice. Any discussion of neuroscience comes with the caveat that we shouldn't get carried away and rush to apply brain-based methods without appreciating some of the scientific evidence behind the findings. In its report into the promise and potential of neuroscience for HRD practice, *Neuroscience in action: Applying insights to L&D practice*, the CIPD highlighted a number of HRD-relevant benefits, including:

- An evidence base for practice which could offer a science-based case for learning and development and investment in HRD;
- As a tool for reflection that can validate commonly-used HRD methods or catalyse critical reflection of existing practices;
- Breaking down barriers and overcoming prejudices and discrimination based on knowledge of brain structure and function (for example, in neurodiversity).[68]

A further advantage of integrating neuroscience into HRD is the bridging of disciplinary boundaries between business and management, education, behavioural sciences and biology given the fact that HRD aspires to be an evidence-based, inter-disciplinary, applied field.

Confirming our intuitions about how people learn and validating personal experiences of learning by being able to understand and apply neuroscience to learning and development can increase levels of confidence in and enhance the credibility of HRD in organizations. Moreover, just as a knowledge of anatomy and physiology is fundamental to medical practitioners' professional knowledge and practice, so knowing about the neuroscientific bases of how people learn is a fundamental aspect of HR practitioners' professional knowledge. The challenge to HRD researchers and practitioners is to be able to 'make sense' of neuroscience without being encumbered in the technicalities and to be able to apply it in ways that add value for individual employees and business organizations and enhance science- and evidence-based HRD practice.[69] Adding neuroscience to the theoretical foundations of HRD's professional and practitioner knowledge base contributes to making HRD an evidence-based, interdisciplinary, applied field of research and practice that is at the 'cutting edge'.

Chapter checkout

Use this list to check your understanding of the key points of this chapter.

1 **Neurons and synapses** Neurons carry electrical signals through axons and dendrites; gap between an axon and a dendrite is a called a synapse; neurotransmitters enable electrical signals to cross the synapse

2 **Hemispheres** The brain has two hemispheres (right and left), separated by a midline, connected together by bundle of nerves called the corpus callosum)

3 **Lobes** The brain has four lobes (frontal, occipital (back), temporal (side) and parietal (top)) covered by cerebral cortex in which there are in-folds (sulci) and bulges (gyri)

4 **Amygdala and hippocampus** The amygdalae are involved in emotional processing, the hippocampus is involved in the formation and storage of long-term memories

5 **Neuro-methods** Advances in neuroscience have been enabled by brain imaging methods such as fMRI and PET and related techniques such as EEG

6 **Neuroplasticity** The brain has a capacity to change structurally in response to stimuli from sources such as experience, environment and learning (as in enlarged posterior hippocampus in London taxi drivers)

7 **Expertise** Expertise is gained through extensive practice, coaching and feedback and declines without constant upkeep and upgrading, hence 'use it or lose it'

8 **Neurodiversity** Neurodiversity recognizes the range of neurological differences that exist in any population; acknowledging and accommodating the challenges and opportunities of a neurodiverse workforce is part of HRD practice

9 **Emotions and the brain** Emotions can have both negative (for example, as a result of stress) and positive effects on learning (for example, motivation) and these potential effects need to be accommodated in the design and delivery of HRD

10 **Ageing and the brain** Age is associated with loss of cortical cells, pruning unused networks, increased connectivity/integration across hemispheres, slower processing/simultaneous activation, lower processing speed/focus, expanded capacity for seeing bigger picture/navigating real world, and wisdom

SKILLS DEVELOPMENT 5
CREATING GUIDELINES FOR BRAIN-BASED HRD

You are the HR Adviser in an organization with several thousand employees which develops software solutions for large corporate clients and has office locations in various parts of the country. Your boss, the HR Manager has asked you to take responsibility for a workstream which aims to accommodate neurodiversity in the organization's HRD policy as one part of the organization's strategy for enhancing diversity and inclusion. She would like you to create a set of guidelines for the delivery and support of a 'brain-based' approach to HRD which does not discriminate against employees on the basis of brain-related factors. The guidelines should be based on the knowledge that you've gained of a brain-based approach to HRD. Assume that the organization has a balance of ages from college leavers to those approaching retirement, and there is the normal range of neurodivergence amongst the workforce. The guidelines should be formulated in such a way as to be able to be understood and applied by trainers, coaches, mentors, line managers as well as outside providers in the design, delivery and support of learning and development. Use an appropriate and easy to use format such as a checklist, infographic, etc.

6

FORMAL AND INFORMAL LEARNING

Contents

On completion of this chapter you should be able to:

- Distinguish between informal/formal and planned/incidental learning;
- Explain the concept of transfer of learning and how learning transfer can be maximized;
- Use your knowledge and understanding of formal and informal learning to advise on the design and delivery of HRD.

Introduction

This chapter explores why there can be as much value in informal, unplanned, incidental learning as there is in formal, planned, deliberate learning. The variety and interconnectedness of HRD methods, both formal and informal, makes the learning system of the modern organization a diverse and complex entity. For example, the UK's Chartered Institute of Personnel and Development (CIPD) in its *Learning Methods Factsheet* identified multiple methods of learning delivery including internal versus external provision of learning, team versus individual learning, formal versus informal techniques, digital versus face-to-face delivery, created versus curated content, learning at the workplace versus away from the workplace, etc. Likewise, the US Society for Human Resource Management (SHRM) has identified a 'menu' of HRD tools and resources which includes coaching and mentoring, cross-training and 'stretch' assignments, job enlargement and job enrichment, job shadowing and job rotation, corporate universities and online employee development, and so forth.[1] In its *State of the Industry Report* for 2019 the Association for Talent Development (ATD) reported that nearly all participants reported that employees frequently use desktops or laptops to access e-learning, and another rapidly growing delivery method is 'virtual classrooms' to reach dispersed workforces in real time while reducing or eliminating travel costs and time. As far as the choice about how to deliver HRD is concerned there's no shortage of methods and there is a significant 'uptick' in the use of digital and web-based learning; see Figure 6.1.

The richness and variety of learning and development methods that are available for HRD can sometimes be perplexing to newcomers and non-specialists. In practical terms it's less likely to be a question of whether to use one method or another (each has its place), it's more likely to be a question of how to choose and combine learning delivery methods together to give the right HRD 'blend' that addresses the learning need, at the right time, in the right place, and in the right way. An important practical skill and professional judgement in HRD practice is how to strike the right balance between various methods of delivering HRD. In this chapter we will look at various micro-theoretical

UK's Chartered Institute of Personnel and Development (CIPD)

- Internal versus external provision of training
- Team versus individual
- Formal versus informal
- Digital versus face-to-face
- 'Created' versus 'curated' content
- Learning at workplace versus away from workplace, etc.

US Society for HRM (SHRM)

- Coaching and mentoring
- Cross-training
- 'Stretch' assignments
- Job enlargement, enrichment and rotation
- Work shadowing
- Corporate universities
- Online employee development, etc.

Association for Talent Development (ATD)*

- Live (synchronous) 'traditional' instructor-led face-to-face classroom (40%)
- Self-paced (asynchronous) e-learning (26%)
- Live (synchronous) 'virtual' instructor-led classroom (19%)

Figure 6.1   The range of HRD methods as identified by three HR/HRD professional bodies

*ATD (2019) *State of the Industry Report* (SOIR; per cent reported use, N =283)[1]

[1]Association for Talent Development (ATD) (2019) *State of the Industry Report*. Available online: https://www.td.org/soir2019 (accessed 30-12-20).

aspects of formal and informal learning whilst in Chapter 11 we'll look at the macro-operational and strategic aspects of how they can be combined together into hybrid HRD systems and ecosystems.

A fundamental aspect of HRD practice is managing the relationship between the available learning and development options, for example, the relationship between formal/off-job methods versus informal/on-job methods:

- Well-designed formal learning can be an efficient way of delivering consistent content to groups of employees at a scheduled time, place and pace but it can be ineffective and an inefficient use of resources if the learning doesn't transfer to the job;
- Informal learning can often be highly effective when it's integrated in the everyday activity of working so that learning and working become one, that is in the 'flow of work' (think of 'situated learning' from a previous chapter), but it can be inefficient, disruptive and even wasteful if it isn't managed well.

If 'effectiveness' in HRD is 'doing the right thing' (and 'ineffectiveness' is the opposite), and 'efficiency' is 'doing the thing right' (and 'inefficiency' is the opposite), then the relationships between efficiency and effectiveness in HRD can be mapped in a 'two-by-two' relationship (see Figure 6.2). Take the simple example of a training course. The value that it can add will vary greatly depending on how efficient and effective it is:

- Type 1, 'value-adding training': effective and efficient;
- Type 2, 'added-value missed': effective but inefficient;
- Type 3, 'added-value misguided': efficient but ineffective;
- Type 4, 'value-diminishing training': ineffective and inefficient.

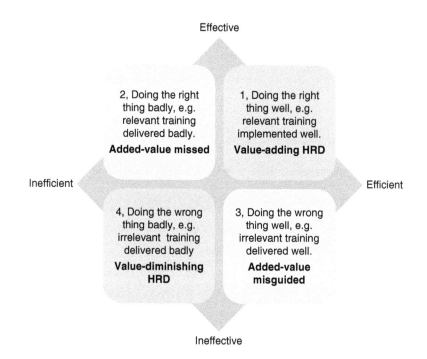

Figure 6.2 Relationships between effectiveness and efficiency in HRD

The challenge for HRD is to configure the delivery and implementation of learning and development generally (not just training courses as in the example above) such that it's both effective and efficient (that is, it does the right sorts of things well). This is most likely to be achieved through an approach that leverages the strengths of the different approaches, such as those shown in Figure 6.1. Getting the balance right:

- Makes the difference between successful and unsuccessful HRD;
- Adds value for stakeholders;
- Improves the chances of employees engaging enthusiastically in HRD;

- Increases the likelihood of a return on HRD investment;
- Enhances HRD's professional credibility and esteem.

Getting the balance right is theory-driven and evidence-based whilst at the same time needing to be realistic and pragmatic and, moreover, is vitally important because the methods used are the most 'client-facing' aspects of HRD practice.

The range of available methods is growing quickly as learning technologies develop through rapid advances in digital and communications technology and as HRD practices themselves evolve as a result of the accumulation of knowledge about which methods work well and why along with insights from newer areas such as neuroscience. Moreover greater agility in how HRD is delivered is being demanded by stakeholders in volatile, uncertain, complex and ambiguous organizational environments. The aim of this chapter is to equip you with relevant knowledge so that you can make informed choices about which HRD methods to use and why so as to maximize HRD's impact on individual, team and organizational performance. These are some of the reasons why HRD methods matter.

Formal learning and employee training

A simple conceptual distinction that will be used in this chapter is between 'formal' learning (for example, a traditional classroom based training course) and 'informal' learning (for example, on-job learning). Both informal learning and formal learning have important roles to play in enabling employees to realize their full potential and organizations to attain their strategic goals.

Much of education uses formalized learning and it's the approach that we are most familiar with from our experiences of school, college, and university, as well as training courses at work. Formal learning includes activities that:

- Take place within a designated learning context, for example in a learning 'space' including the lecture hall, training room, workshop, etc.;
- Are organizationally-sanctioned, for example, as part of formal training policy or educational curriculum;
- Have external direction, for example, from the HR or relevant business function or policy-making body;
- Are led by instructor and/or a syllabus rather than by an individual's self-direction or curiosity;
- Have formalized learning objectives towards which the learning process proceeds in linear fashion with a discrete beginning, middle and end.

Formal learning in an organizational context manifests most typically as the familiar traditional 'training course'. Psychologists Ed Salas and Julia Cannon-Bowers offered a succinct definition of training as a set of 'planned and systematic activities' that are 'designed to promote the acquisition of knowledge and skills and to influence and inform attitudes' based on 'pedagogically sound' methods of delivery 'through instruction, demonstration, practice, and timely diagnostic feedback'.[4] The differences between training and development from a practical and professional perspective (the CIPD's) are shown in Figure 6.3.

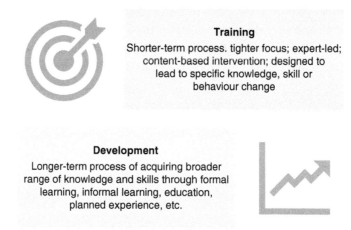

Figure 6.3 Differences between training and development from the CIPD perspective[1]

[1]CIPD (2020). *Learning Methods*. Available online: www.cipd.co.uk/knowledge/fundamentals/people/development/learning-methods-factsheet (accessed 27-01-21).

Organizations spend billions every year on training and developing their workforces, and whilst it's hard to be definitive about what counts as 'training spend', here are some estimates for annual investments in training:

- In the United States the 2018 Training Industry Report found that training expenditure by US businesses amounted to $87.6 billion[5] (by comparison the US government is reported to have budgeted for $20 billion for 'infrastructure' in the same year);[6]
- A survey by the UK Commission for Employment and Skills found that employers invested £21.3 billion on training (excluding the wages of those being trained), and of this £3.3 billion was spent on 'external provision' of training[7] (by comparison the UK transport budget in 2018 is reported to have been £37 billion).[8]

There can be little doubt that formal training can be highly effective; it's considered by some to be a 'strategic weapon in the battle for competitive advantage'.[9] This view is justified by a substantial body of evidence pointing to positive relationships between investment in training and a variety of firm-level outcomes. 'Meta-analyses' provide a useful overview of published research studies by abstracting general patterns and conclusions on which recommendations for practice can be based. Meta-analysis is considered to be a 'gold' standard of research evidence.[10] The effectiveness of formal training programmes has been well documented through a number of meta-analyses over several decades. Evidence from selected studies of the relationship between training and firm-level outcomes is summarized in Figure 6.4.

Birdi et al. (2008)

- Longitudinal study of the productivity of 308 companies over 22 years
- Extensive training has a significant positive main effect (6 per cent added value per employee) on productivity even when operational practices (e.g. lean production) and other HR practices (e.g. selection, appraisal and reward) are taken into account.

Kim and Ployhart (2014)

- Financial performance (profit) growth under different environmental (economic) conditions using 359 firms with over 12 years of longitudinal firm-level profit data
- Training directly and interactively (with staffing) influences firm profit growth through effects on firm labour productivity.

Sung and Choi (2014)

- Effects of training and development investments on innovative performance. Time-lagged, multi-source data collected from 260 Korean companies representing diverse industries
- Expenditure for internal training predicts interpersonal and organizational learning practices, which, in turn, increase innovative performance. Relationship stronger within organizations that have stronger innovation climates.

Figure 6.4 Summary of selected studies of relationship between training and firm-level outcomes

Sources: Birdi, K., Clegg, C., Patterson, M., Robinson, A., Stride, C. B., Wall, T. D., & Wood, S. J. (2008). The impact of human resource and operational management practices on company productivity: A longitudinal study. *Personnel Psychology*, *61*(3), 467–501; Kim, Y., & Ployhart, R. E. (2014). The effects of staffing and training on firm productivity and profit growth before, during, and after the Great Recession. *Journal of Applied Psychology*, *99*(3), 361; Sung, S. Y., & Choi, J. N. (2014). Do organizations spend wisely on employees? Effects of training and development investments on learning and innovation in organizations. *Journal of Organizational Behavior*, *35*(3), 393–412.

However not all training spend produces the desired results hence questions can be asked legitimately about why some formal training doesn't have the impact that was intended. This is in a context in which HRD researchers David McGuire and Claire Gubbins observed that HRD practices have become 'more informal, situated, outcome focused and experiential'; as a result of these changes formal learning 'now plays a greatly diminished role' which has led to it being branded (unjustifiably in McGuire and Gubbins' view) as an 'outdated delivery mode' based on an 'old-fashioned anti-quated pedagogy' (p. 249).[11] An important question and a significant factor in determining the contribution, reputation, standing of formal learning methods, such as traditional training, is why some of the knowledge and skills acquired through traditional training approaches sometimes do and sometimes don't transfer to the workplace and have the intended effects on job performance and organizational effectiveness.

Perspective from practice 6.1

The failings of 'fire-hosing'

In an article in the general business magazine *Forbes* the writer told the story of a company sales training programme in which a world-class sales trainer 'blasted a fire hose of selling concepts at a sales team seated classroom-style in a hotel conference room'.[12] The writer approached the trainer a couple of days later to ask what'll happen a month from now. The response was depressing, but unsurprising: 'They're going to forget everything I taught them…I tell my customers that they're wasting their money if they don't either bring me back or follow-up themselves to revisit the core concepts.' When asked how often he gets invited back the response was: 'Rarely. They say they blew the budget on the event.' The writer used this story to extract three general points about traditional 'classroom' training:

- People may forget much of what they've learned if follow up isn't a routine part of the process because in work-related learning it's definitely a case of 'use it or lose it' (and there are good neuroscientific reasons for this);
- Timing is vitally important because trainees must be able to apply new knowledge and skills immediately to their work;
- People aren't always disciplined enough to do the kind of deliberate practice that'll make the new learning 'stick' (that is, transfer to the job), so organizations have to do everything possible to make sure that happens;
- Managers sometimes don't even realize that they have a role in supporting trainees to help the all-essential follow-up happen.

Even if much-needed training delivered by an inspirational instructor gets highly favour-able reactions from trainees, the crux of the matter is whether or not the results from the training experience add value by transferring to the job and lead to meaningful and productive changes in job performance.[13] In this situation it sounds like they were trying to do the right thing but the training course was not being used in the right way, it was a missed opportunity because the new knowledge and skills didn't transfer to the job.

We need some clarity on if, when, why and how formal training has an impact on job performance and organization-level outcomes. The concept of 'transfer' (of learning or training) is at the heart of the matter and we turn to this important topic in the next section. Before that however, you can explore the research that has looked at the bigger picture of the relationships between training and performance by delving deeper into the meta-analyses summarized below.

Delve deeper 6.1

Read some of the debates about the relevance of traditional training in:

McGuire, D., & Gubbins, C. (2010). The slow death of formal learning: A polemic. *Human Resource Development Review*, 9(3), 249–265.

Read about if, when, and how formal training is effective in these meta-analyses:

Arthur, W., Jr., Bennett, W., Jr., Edens, P. S., & Bell, S. T. (2003). Effectiveness of training in organizations: A meta-analysis of design and evaluation features. *Journal of Applied Psychology*, 88, 234–245.

Bell, B. S., Tannenbaum, S. I., Ford, J. K., Noe, R. A., & Kraiger, K. (2017). 100 years of training and development research: What we know and where we should go. *Journal of Applied Psychology*, 102(3), 305–323.

Colquitt, J. A., LePine, J. A., & Noe, R. A. (2000). Toward an integrative theory of training motivation: A meta-analytic path analysis of 20 years of research. *Journal of Applied Psychology*, 85(5), 678.

Salas, E., DiazGranados, D., Klein, C., Burke, C. S., Stagl, K. C., Goodwin, G. F., & Halpin, S. M. (2008). Does team training improve team performance? A meta-analysis. *Human Factors*, 50(6), 903–933.

For introductory advice and guidance on how to conduct systematic reviews and meta-analyses (the 'gold standard' of evidence in social sciences) consult:

Crocetti, E. (2016). Systematic reviews with meta-analysis: Why, when, and how? *Emerging Adulthood*, 44(1), 3–18.

For a more detailed and technical treatment consult:

Cooper, H. (2016). *Research synthesis and meta-analysis* (5e). London: SAGE.

Hunter, J. E., & Schmidt, F. L. (2014). *Methods of meta-analysis: Correcting error and bias in research findings* (3e). London: SAGE.

Reflective question 6.1

Identify a skill that you use regularly in your work, academic study or personal life and in which you are highly proficient, that is you can apply it with little effort and maximum results. How did you acquire this skill, and what was it about the way in which you acquired this skill that has led you to become so proficient in it?

Transfer of learning

'Transfer of learning', also referred to as 'transfer of training', is one of the most critical concepts in HRD.[14] The study of the transfer of learning has a long history in psychology,

reaching back well over 100 years.[15] The crux of the matter is that formal, off-job training, even though it can be an efficient way to expose employees to relevant and new
knowledge and skills, is likely to be a waste of resources (time, money and effort) if it
doesn't have a positive impact on (that is 'adds value' to) learners' job performance and
subsequent organization-level outcomes. The situation can be made worse if the training ends up demotivating employees to undertake further training and incurs significant
reputational harm for HRD. The root of this issue is often referred to as the 'transfer
problem'[16] and the extent to which new learning transfers from the learning situation
(for example, a classroom) to a new or different situation (an actual task in
the workplace).

Learning transfer/transfer of training is defined by organizational psychologists
Timothy Baldwin and J. Kevin Ford as: the degree to which learners are able to apply
knowledge, skills and attitudes gained during training in a generalized manner ('generalization') to the job context over a period of time ('maintenance').[17] Take the example
of flight simulator training for aircraft pilots in which it's assumed that:

- Learning how to perform a task in one situation (the simulator) can be generalized
  to the performance of that same task in another (in a real aircraft);
- Performance improvement as a result of training can be maintained over a period
  of time (it would not be helpful if the learning was not maintained especially
  because some difficult and important tasks are rarely if ever used, such as an
  emergency landing).

The difficulty, importance and frequency with which a task is performed (in the form
of a 'DIF' analysis) can help to assign a 'training priority', for example:

- Difficult tasks that are important but infrequently carried out are likely to have a
  high priority for training (since employees probably don't have frequent, if any,
  opportunities to apply them on the job);
- Tasks that are not difficult, are important and are carried out frequently are likely
  to have a low priority for training (since employees are likely to be practising these
  skills day-in day-out).[18]

This is useful way in which to decide between training that's a 'nice to have' versus
training that's a 'need to have'.

The assumption in designing training is that if transfer of learning occurs the learner
will be able to apply what she or he has learnt in the training context to performing the
same task effectively in a 'real world' situation. The extent to which transfer occurs is
likely to be a function of three factors: the learner, the training and the task environment; see Figure 6.5. In this framework effectiveness and efficiency determine the value
added (as shown earlier in Figure 6.2) and for HRD to add value, it must clear the double
hurdle of being both effective and efficient.

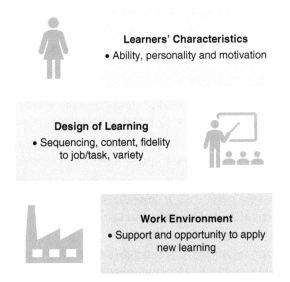

Figure 6.5   Factors affecting transfer of training

Source: adapted from Baldwin, T. T., & Ford, J. K. (1988). Transfer of training: A review and directions for future research. *Personnel Psychology*, *41*(1), 63–105, pp. 64–65. Reprinted by permission of John Wiley and Sons.

As noted above, psychologists have long-studied the conditions that are necessary for transfer to occur efficiently and effectively. Transfer of learning research goes back to the early years of the last century, for example in the work of the behaviourist E. L. Thorndike (1847–1949).[19] The problem of how to maximize transfer was taken-up by the cognitivists, for example in Ausubel's theory of 'meaningful learning' (1963).[20] Transfer of learning research has identified at least two possible mechanisms that can increase the probability of transfer of learning:

- Transfer through 'identical elements' (derived originally from Thorndike's work): transfer will occur so long as there are identical elements in the learning and the work situations, for example in control room training for nuclear power operatives the control board in a display in the training environment should be as close as possible to the control board in the real environment.[21]
- Transfer through 'principles' (a cognitivist model): learning should focus upon acquiring general principles so that the learner can abstract and apply them and generalize problem solutions across a range of tasks and contexts which are by no means identical to the training situation. In cognitive terms, learning should support the acquisition of mental models (that is, 'schemas', see Chapter 2) that are capable of being applied in novel situations.[22]

Two related concepts are 'near transfer' and 'far transfer'. Near transfer occurs when the trained behaviour and training context and the work task and application context are highly similar (for example, you don't have to re-learn how to operate a new laptop every time you upgrade). Far transfer occurs when the trained behaviour has to be applied in different or changing contexts, which requires the application of principles and judgement.[23]

A simple example of near transfer involving identical elements would be the skill of being able to drive any make and model of right-hand drive vehicle having learned to drive in a particular make and model of right-hand drive vehicle. If I get a new car I don't have to re-learn how to drive. Near and far exist on a continuum. A bit further away would be the skill of being able to drive a left-hand drive car having learned to drive in a right-hand drive car. Whether near or far transfer is required depends on the particular skill that's being trained for and the context in which that skill will be applied; moreover even with training that seeks to achieve near-transfer only there's often likely to be spill-over into related contexts.[24] Further away again and towards the far end of the spectrum would be the possibility that with some effort, practice and caution I might be able to apply some of the principles I had learned for driving a right-hand drive car to a left-handed truck even though this wasn't explicitly trained for (although clearly I would be by no means proficient or safe in this new task).

Simulation training

The use of simulation provides a helpful illustration of the concept of transfer. Simulation is a technique which replaces real experiences with artificial experiences that are highly structured, and can be 'immersive' (for example, with background noise and other simulated workplace effects), and aim to evoke and/or replicate salient and

Figure 6.6   Flight simulator

Credit: Keena ithar/Shutterstock.com

substantial aspects of the real world in a 'fully interactive fashion'.[25] Simulators (such as flight simulators and simulation-based medical education, and increasingly virtual reality, VR) can be used for the acquisition of skills that might be difficult or dangerous to acquire in the real setting (such as flying a passenger aircraft or performing a surgical procedure) with immediate feedback, no risks and multiple usage thereby reducing costs and time; see Figure 6.6.

Research insight 6.1

Startle-and-surprise in flight simulator training

Much of the initial and recurrent training for pilots involves high-skill, but nonetheless standardized and relatively predictable scenarios. However, the skills acquired in this way can sometimes be 'brittle' rather than 'adaptive', meaning that they transfer better to predictable situations rather than novel and unexpected situations. Dutch researchers tested whether making simulator training more unpredictable and variable (U&V) improves pilot performance in 'startle and surprise' tests (for example, the challenging scenario both of losses in engine power and decreased rudder control).[26] In the experiments:

- The control group was told when the engine failure would occur and whether the take-off was to be aborted or continued;
- The U&V group was only instructed to respond to the scenario as they 'saw fit' as it emerged in the course of the simulation.

The researchers found that, compared with the control group, the U&V group was more stimulated to perform 'sensemaking' activities during the training, which helped them to develop better schemas (mental models) of the effects of variables such as asymmetric thrust, control inputs, and airspeed on aircraft behaviour. Sensemaking in this context refers to how people make sense of data through 'frames' (frames define what counts as data but also shape what counts as data; for example, an engine failure on an aircraft will be perceived differently by a pilot, air traffic controller or passenger).[27] The researchers concluded that:

- Including unpredictable and variable (U&V) events in pilot training improves the generalization of skills and the ability to respond to unexpected in-flight situations that are not explicitly trained for;
- One-sided and predictable training is not sufficient in preparing pilots for unexpected and novel situations;
- Acquiring knowledge about principles that overarch and transcend specific training experiences is essential for building resilient, complex and adaptable skills.

(Continued)

Aviation safety organizations have recognized the benefits of such an approach, and for aviation companies this is one way of continually improving airline pilot safety training and adding value for airlines and their passengers.

Source: Landman, A., van Oorschot, P., van Paassen, M. M., Groen, E. L., Bronkhorst, A. W., & Mulder, M. (2018). Training pilots for unexpected events: A simulator study on the advantage of unpredictable and variable scenarios. Human Factors, 60(6), 793–805.

Learning transfer by principles is an example of a 'constructivist' approach; this means that learners 'create' their own knowledge actively by making sense out of information they're presented with or experiences that they have or are exposed to deliberately. For example, in simulations learners build mental models of cause-and-effect relationships, as did the trainee pilots in the unpredictable and variable simulations.[28] It aligns with the principles of 'meaningful' (cognitive), as opposed to 'drill-and-practice' (behaviourist), learning.

The learning transfer environment

As far as the environment or context in which the learning will be applied, both the specific task environment and the general work environment should support the transfer of learning. Practical suggestions for how this can happen include:[29]

- Guaranteeing that learners have the opportunity to apply their newly-acquired skills in the work environment;
- Ensuring equipment in the learning situation is as similar as possible to that in the work environment;
- Assigning an experienced co-worker to give feedback on the application of new skills in the job environment;
- Easing job pressure to enable learners to get up-to-speed;
- Practising beyond the minimum level of competence (this is sometimes referred to as 'over-learning' a skill).

These factors are part of the 'transfer climate' and the general 'learning climate' in an organization and include issues such as responsibility and accountability on the part of both learners and managers. The organization's transfer climate should be supportive of the new learning, and research shows that a positive transfer climate can have a significant impact on learning. HRD researcher Ed Holton and colleagues have developed a theoretical model of what constitutes a 'good transfer climate' and a questionnaire (the Learning Transfer System Inventory, LTSI) which captures many of the learner- and learning-related, social, and contextual factors that support the transfer of learning; see Figure 6.7.

Learner Factors

- *Readiness*: learners need to be prepared to engage positively with learning
- *Motivation*: learners should have the motivation to transfer their learning
- *Reward*: learning must have anticipated benefits for the learner
- *Self-efficacy*: learners should be confident in new skills and their ability to apply them
- *Capacity*: learners should have the time and space to transfer learning to job

Social Factors

- *Peers*: reinforce and support the new learning on the job
- *Supervisors and managers*: reinforce, support and reward application of learning

Contextual Factors

- *Opportunity*: learners should have opportunity/resources to apply new learning
- *Norms*: group is open to change and encourage application/practising of new skills
- *Feedback*: learner should get feedback on how well they're applying new learning

Design of Learning Factors

- *Validity*: learning should be valid and relevant to the job
- *Design*: learning should be designed to enable transfer to happen

Figure 6.7 Holton's dimensions and elements of an effective learning transfer climate

Source: Holton III, E. F. (2005). Holton's evaluation model: New evidence and construct elaborations. *Advances in Developing Human Resources*, 7(1), 37–54.

Research insight 6.2

Accountability mechanisms for promoting learning transfer

Rebecca Grossman and Lisa Burke-Smalley contend that organizations can improve learning transfer by deliberately targeting variables that promote accountability, where accountability is defined as: being responsible, and answerable, for fulfilling one's obligations, duties, and expectations. Accountability also extends to the work environment itself which should promote transfer by making relevant resources available, having systems and procedures for monitoring transfer-relevant goals and putting rewards and consequences in place for appropriate use of newly acquired skills in the workplace. Accountability factors that promote the transfer of learning include:

(Continued)

- Ensuring that reward systems align with transfer goals so as to motivate learners to transfer what they have learned to their jobs (this is an example of the integration between HRD and HRM);
- Communicating transfer expectations following formal training and signalling that transfer is important to and valued by the organization, for example through 'after action reviews' (AARs);
- Managing other job responsibilities so as to give trainees sufficient space to apply their new skills at work, for example by modifying trainees' workloads;
- Cultivating favourable attitudes towards the transfer of learning in the organization because when trainees feel positive about learning and perceive it to be useful they are more likely to incorporate new knowledge and skills into their working practices;
- Providing post-training support, for example by setting specific goals which communicate to the learner what they are expected to be able to do with their new skills.

Properly managing accountabilities post-training is one way of reducing the likelihood that investment in training isn't wasted.

Source: Grossman, R., & Burke-Smalley, L. A. (2018). Context-dependent accountability strategies to improve the transfer of training: A proposed theoretical model and research propositions. *Human Resource Management Review*, 28(2), 234–247.

The place of training transfer in the wider HR and organizational system shouldn't be overlooked. For example, transfer can be leveraged through peer and supervisor support and by horizontally integrating learning and development into HR performance and reward systems. Transfer can be aided by aligning training with the employees' aspirations and potential and the business' strategy,[30] so that trainees learn what matters both to them and their jobs and to their organization.

─Reflective question 6.2─

Critically evaluate the following statement: without taking steps to ensure the efficient and effective transfer of training any investment in training is likely to be value-diminishing rather than value-adding both for HRD and for the organization.

Maximizing the impact of training

In spite of the problems of transfer that can impede the effectiveness of training, organizations should not lose sight of the significant value that formal training can add if it's designed and implemented efficiently and effectively. Formal training remains one of the most important HRD solutions, and there's little doubt that businesses will continue to use formal training and development programmes to develop employees' knowledge and skills. This is because they:

- Represent an investment not only in employees' capabilities to perform their current job, they also prepare them for future positions and career opportunities;
- Help to ensure a planned, consistent and company-wide approach to workforce knowledge and skills development;
- By being systematic and linked both to organizations' goals and HR practices, planned training and development can ensure vertical alignment and horizontal integration with business and HR strategies respectively.[31]

That said, there's no shortage of evidence to suggest that investment in training could be wasted if it's not strategically aligned and horizontally integrated and if the right conditions aren't put in place to support learning transfer.[32] Transfer of training researcher J. Kevin Ford and colleagues drew on several meta-analytical studies to delve more deeply into the empirical evidence and they concluded that transfer can be a significant problem, and offered the following insights and recommendations:[33]

- Transfer is stubborn and this 'highlights the folly of organizations investing their time and money almost exclusively on training' (p. 220) whilst at the same time viewing transfer itself as 'free', therefore effort should be expended on ensuring transfer as well as delivering training;
- Too little is known about what types of transfer support are needed and when and where it should be made available, therefore organizations should determine how transfer can be supported and enabled, and managers should put the necessary systems and processes in place.

The nub of the problem is that training can, all-too-often, be treated as a one-off 'event', rather than an episode in a longer-term process. More broadly, formal training is only one item on the 'HRD menu' of options and an element – albeit an important one – of an effective and efficient learning 'ecosystem'. Hence, HRD practitioners need to be alert to and mindful of ways in which the linkage between learning, however it occurs, and performance can be managed and strengthened in whatever way is appropriate and necessary for a particular type of training and the context in which it is to be applied.

This broader view prompts us to think critically about the relationship between learning and working somewhat differently than a traditional 'training and development' mindset would suggest. As we know from social and situated learning theories, being engaged 'in the flow' of work activities, mindfully watching and listening, and by simply being in the rich physical and social environment of the workplace[34] affords invaluable opportunities for informal and incidental learning and development to take place. Moreover such experiences add a unique value that cannot be replicated or replaced by formal training; hence the place of informal and incidental learning in HRD is at least as important as that of formal training.

Delve deeper 6.2

Read more about transfer of training in:

Baldwin, T. T., Ford, J. K., & Blume, B. D. (2009). Transfer of training 1988–2008: An updated review and agenda for future research. *International Review of Industrial and Organizational Psychology, 24*(1), 41–70.

Blume, B. D., Ford, J. K., Baldwin, T. T., & Huang, J. L. (2010). Transfer of training: A meta-analytic review. *Journal of Management, 36*(4), 1065–1105.

Burke, L. A., & Baldwin, T. T. (1999). Workforce training transfer: A study of the effect of relapse prevention training and transfer climate. *Human Resource Management, 38*(3), 227–242.

Ford, J. K., Baldwin, T. T., & Prasad, J. (2018). Transfer of training: The known and the unknown. *Annual Review of Organizational Psychology and Organizational Behaviour, 5*, 201–225.

Informal and incidental learning

The concept of 'informal and incidental learning' was formalized theoretically by Victoria Marsick and Karen Watkins in the 1990s.[35] They did so by distinguishing between formal and informal learning in terms of the processes involved and the outcomes achieved:

- Formal learning: normally classroom-based and highly structured; often institutionally sponsored (for example, by one's company); outcomes of the process may be intentional (as in pre-specified learning outcomes or objectives) or unintentional (as in something that was picked-up incidentally along the way);
- Informal learning: not normally classroom-based, or highly structured, control of learning lies mainly in the hands of the learner; not normally institutionally sponsored; the outcomes of the process may be intentional (as in the outcomes of an informal coaching session) or unintentional (as in the case of the acquisition of 'tacit knowledge' through 'implicit learning' processes).[36]

It's been argued by John Cross in his book *Informal Learning: Rediscovering the Natural Pathways that Inspire Innovation and Performance* that informal learning is the 'workhorse' (p. xiii) of the economy; he estimated that it accounts for between 70 and 80 per cent of workplace learning and observed that it's highly integrated into everyday work activities.[37] But what does informal learning look like in practice? By way of illustration, let's take the example of the essential service of hairdressing.

Research insight 6.3

Informal learning in practice

Employment studies researchers in the UK as part of a Government initiative studied the impact of informal learning at work on business productivity, and one of their case studies was a very modest single-owner hairdressing salon with eight staff.[38] Employees' motivation to learn in the salon was stimulated first-and-foremost by the desire to earn money and to ensure that the salon achieved maximum capacity, but also boosted by the fact that if stylists continually reached their targets they could be promoted and eventually end-up as profit-sharing partners in the business. Employees learned informally and incidentally in the workplace by simply observing the best techniques, coaching each other to improve their skills and reading trade magazines. The success of informal learning in the salon was embedded in a performance measurement and productivity system that was transparent; everyone was aware of how the salon was performing at any one time and the organizational culture and career structure encouraged staff to learn from each other and to share ideas throughout the working day in their community of practice.

Source: Fuller, A., Ashton, D. N., Felstead, A., Unwin, L., Walters, S., & Quinn, M. (2003). *The impact of informal learning at work on business productivity*. London: Department for Trade and Industry.

As this example illustrates, there are a number of person- and non-person-related ways in which informal learning in the workplace can occur, including:

- Intra-personally: Learning from oneself, for example by self-reflecting, trial-and-error, experimenting, improvising, etc.;
- Inter-personally: Learning from others, for example coaching, feedback, dialogue, discussion, debate with peers, supervisors, managers, clients, etc.;
- Impersonally: Learning from 'inanimate' sources such as books and manuals, digital and non-digital sources, etc.[39]

The skill of designing and delivering effective learning in the workplace depends, at least in part, on the application of insights from mutually reinforcing theories (for example, the 'experienced-based modalities' discussed in Chapter 4). Informal learning theories recognize the significance of learning from other people (see social and situated learning theories), but as educationalist Michael Eraut has noted they imply 'greater scope for individual agency than [mere] socialization' and can be considered as a 'partner to learning from experience' which is usually construed as intrapersonal (as in Kolb's theory) rather than interpersonal.[40] Eraut links informal learning theory to a variety of workplace activities; see Figure 6.8.

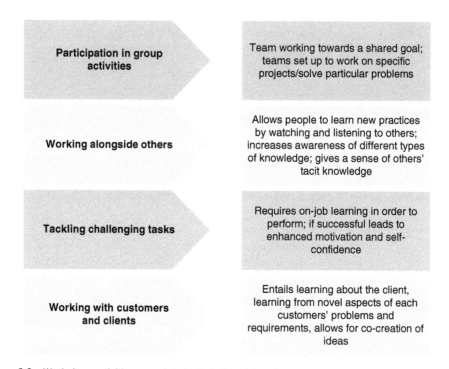

Figure 6.8 Workplace activities associated with informal learning

Source: adapted from Eraut, M. (2004). Informal learning in the workplace. *Studies in Continuing Education*, 26(2), 247–273, pp. 266–267.

Informal and incidental learning is a broad term, and there are a variety of concepts that occupy the same 'conceptual space' for example, 'workplace learning' overlaps with informal and incidental learning, as well as with theories that can help to explain how such learning occurs (for example, experiential, social, situated, etc.). Workplace learning has been defined as:

- Learners' participation in situated work activities where the 'affordances' (that is, the things that the work environment provides for the learner) and constraints of the workplace setting interact with 'agency' (that is, an individual's ability to act independently) and their backgrounds (sometimes referred to as the 'biography') of the learner;[41]
- A natural and largely autonomous learning process derived from the characteristics of the workplace and its work processes and their inherent social interactions; these are often implicit and sometimes hard to differentiate from work itself.[42]

Management and organization development researcher Joseph Raelin describes a model of 'work-based learning', based on the principles of action learning (see Chapter 4), as a way to develop leader*ship* rather than lead*ers* where:

- Meaningful, relevant and useful learning 'is acquired in the midst of action and dedicated to the task at hand';
- The creation, sharing and application of new knowledge is a collective activity and learning, therefore, is part of everybody's job.

Over-and-above these specifics, Raelin also notes that work-based learning builds a capacity for 'meta-learning', that is learning-how-to-learn (both individually and collectively), whereby individuals, teams and organizations question the underlying assumptions that guide, but which can also constrain, practice, and especially innovation (this links individual and informal learning to the related concept of organizational learning, see also Chapter 13).[43]

In terms of the language and terminology of informal and incidental learning, it's worth bearing in mind that there are various terms that are related or can be equated with informal and incidental learning, workplace and work-based learning, etc.; see Figure 6.9.

In summary, it's impossible to estimate but there can be little doubt that a large proportion of the learning that takes place in organizations occurs informally and incidentally and on an on-going basis in the flow of working and socially interacting.[45] Informal learning is related directly to relevant concepts and theories from Chapters 3 and 4, and its efficacy stems from the fact that it offers employees opportunities for:

- Engaging in high-fidelity practice and on-going updating of skills (transfer of learning);
- Interactions with colleagues in real time and in situ (experience-based modalities, and social and situated learning);
- Demonstrating personal initiative, self-direction, intent to learn, and showing commitment by going beyond formal training requirements (andragogy, expectancy, goal setting and motivation).[46]

Having now defined and circumscribed the field of informal and incidental learning, the next section explores theories of informal and incidental learning.

Formal learning behaviours (FLBs)

- Activities pursued for knowledge and skill acquisition that take place within formally-designated learning contexts; organizationally sanctioned; externally directed; classroom- and/or course-based
- Driven by instructor/syllabus rather than by self/ curiosity
- Clearly articulated learning objectives; proceed in linear fashion; discrete beginning and end

Informal learning

- Wide range of behaviours and activities such as knowledge exchanges, feedback giving and seeking, experimenting, self- and public-reflection; learning from interpersonal and non-interpersonal sources

Informal learning behaviours (ILBs)

- Activities pursued for knowledge and skill acquisition that take place outside formally-designated learning contexts
- Predominantly self-directed/initiated, experiential, social and workplace-based
- Not driven by instructor/syllabus-based; no discrete beginning or end

Self-development

- All deliberate learning and development activities not formally required by the organization

Self-directed learning

- Learners take the initiative in identifying their learning needs and goals, choose learning resources and strategies

Voluntary employee development

- Employee participation in non-mandatory, discretionary learning related to current job and longer term effectiveness and career development

Workplace learning

- Processes by which employees acquire new, or develop further, knowledge and skills through engaging in activities and interaction that are presented by naturally occurring opportunities in the workplace

Figure 6.9 Terms related to informal and incidental learning

—In their own words 6.1—

Marsick and Watkins on the roots of informal and incidental learning theory

Marsick and Watkins observed that when they developed their model in the 1980s and 1990s learning and training were dominated by 'instructional design' approaches (as in the work of Leslie J. Briggs, Robert M. Gagne, Robert F. Mager and others, see the 'instructionalist' definition of learning in Chapter 1). They acknowledge the work of the economist Tony Carnevale who was amongst the first to recognize that '80 per cent' (notionally) of workplace learning is informal: 'With one foot in the world of human resource development (HRD) and organization development (OD) and the other foot in the world of adult learning, Marsick and Watkins teamed up to shed light on the 80% of learning that happens outside of training...By emphasizing learning rather than training, we do not intend to devalue the importance of appropriate structured learning activities. However, we believe that an overriding interest in how best to organize learning through training has taken attention away from the natural opportunities for learning that occur every day in a person's working life.' They also acknowledge inspiration from American pragmatist philosopher John Dewey (1859–1952) who 'emphasized the centrality of reflective thought' in dealing with the 'felt difficulty' that comes with ambiguous situations, and 'those who drew upon him' including Chris Argyris and Donald Schön (action science), Kurt Lewin, and David Kolb.

Source: Marsick, V. J., & Watkins, K. E. (2018). Introduction to the special issue: An update on informal and incidental learning theory. *New Directions for Adult and Continuing Education*, (159), 9–19.

Processes of informal learning

There are clear links between the informal and incidental learning model and various learning theories discussed in previous chapters, such as experiential, social and situated learning, and related organizational-level concepts such as knowledge management and organizational learning which are covered later. Marsick and Watkins' theoretical model of the process shares some of its intellectual roots with those of Kolb's experiential learning model, including the pragmatist philosopher/educator John Dewey and social psychologist Kurt Lewin. Marsick and Watkins' model was based on a synthesis of 'cognitivist' and 'constructivist' assumptions about learning, namely that it:

- Occurs under non-routine circumstances (e.g. where there is a trigger or 'jolt');
- Calls for heightened attention in order to determine the nature of the problem;
- Requires critical reflection to search for underlying causes;
- Results in a 'reframing' of the situation and finding a solution in order to take action.[47]

Learning emerges out a process of 'meaning-making' as individuals – but it can also involve a group of employees collectively making meaning – make sense of the situation that caused the 'jolt' in the first place (with similarities to the catalysing effect of a 'disorienting dilemma' in Jack Mezirow's (1923–2014) theory of 'transformative learning'[48]). The process also entails:

- Intent to learn: recognition of the need to acquire knowledge in order to perform successfully or solve a pressing problem (as is the case with action learning);
- Experience and action: based on their 'intent', employees engage in relevant activities to acquire requisite knowledge and skills through experiencing, acting, experimenting, practising, improvising, etc.;
- Feedback: employee receives feedback from the task, seeks feedback, or is provided with feedback by others;
- Discretion and control: informal learning is largely self-initiated and controlled by the individual.

This last point has led some to speculate that engagement in informal learning might also be related to learners' personal characteristics. A study of managers in the US hospitality sector didn't find any relationship between personality type and informal learning but did find a relationship with 'zest' (approaching life with eagerness, energy and anticipation). It was this zest that appeared to give informal learners the intellectual and emotional resources (such as 'emotional energy' and 'cognitive liveliness') to seek new information and new experiences.[49] Marsick and Watkins offer a number of suggestions for how informal and incidental learning can be encouraged, enabled and enhanced:

- Task: by the learner deliberately attending to goals and outcomes (that is, what they need to achieve);
- Context: by the learner consciously scanning the environment for changes and being alert to the need to respond and adapt;
- Cognition: by the learner adopting an 'inductive mindset'[50] (that is, learners 'iteratively' discover solutions that meet their needs in relation to the problem they are investigating);
- Self-regulation: by learners deliberately making time and creating space for learning (and may arrive at a better understanding of their own learning processes through meta-learning and meta-cognition);
- Relationships: by learners collaborating and cooperating, trusting and sharing in exchanges of knowledge and skills.

Marsick and Watkins also point out that although such learning processes are informal they should not be left to chance. For example, one way in which informal learning processes can be 'managed' is through the use of 'learning contracts'.

Perspective from practice 6.2

Learning contracts in nursing education

Learning contracts are formal agreements between learners and someone, or something, that has an interest in helping them to learn (for example, their manager or employer) that help to structure self-directed and informal learning. They have been used in a variety of workplace and educational settings. Researchers in South Korea studied the effects of learning contracts on student nurses' problem-solving skills, self-directed learning capability and communication self-efficacy by comparing these outcomes for experimental (learning contract) and control (no learning contract) groups (25 students in each group). They found statistically significant differences between the two groups on all measures (higher for learning contract than non-learning contract group) and concluded that:

- Learning contracts support the development of problem-solving skills;
- These skills can be developed through self-directed learning;
- Learners who are well-versed in self-direction are able to evaluate critically their current levels of knowledge and performance;
- Self-direction enhances motivation and communication self-efficacy.[51]

Learning contracts help learners to attain a 'voice' and give them some responsibility in the planning of their own learning by specifying what's going to be learned, how it's going to be learned, and how learning will be assessed or verified, and be used in a 'personal development plan' (PDP) agreed with a line manager.[52]

The concept of informal learning in the workplace has significant commercial applications. For example, Josh Bersin's idea of 'Learning in the Flow of Work' focuses on the process of learning 'in the moment', without any disruption to work activity. Based on the observation that employees need knowledge and skills in the moment to solve their pressing problems, Bersin differentiates between two types of need:

- 'I need help now' micro-learning based on useful, accurate and timely content using videos, articles, tools and techniques, etc.;
- 'I want to learn something new' based on authoritative and educational resources such as courses, classes, MOOCs, etc.[53]

One of the drawbacks of traditional approaches, especially those that rely on face-to-face contact and 'synchronous' interactions are that they are not well-suited to employees getting the right skills, in the right place, at the right time. Informal learning overcomes this by offering learning opportunities that are 'on-demand' and 'always-on' and one way in which this is achieved is through the use of 'hybrid HRD' (see Chapter 11).

─── Delve deeper 6.3 ───────────────────────────────

Read more about the processes and practices of informal and work-based learning in:

Cross, J. (2007). *Informal learning: Rediscovering the natural pathways that inspire innovation and performance*. San Francisco, CA: Pfeiffer.

Raelin, J. A. (2008). *Work-based learning: Bridging knowledge and action in the workplace*. San Francisco: Jossey-Bass.

Read about informal learning and HRD research in:

Jeong, S., Han, S. J., Lee, J., Sunalai, S., & Yoon, S. W. (2018). Integrative literature review on informal learning: Antecedents, conceptualizations, and future directions. *Human Resource Development Review, 17*(2), 128–152.

You can read more about Jack Mezirow's work on 'transformative learning theory' in:

Mezirow, J. (1991). *Transformative dimensions in adult learning*. San Francisco: Jossey-Bass.

Mezirow, J. (2009). An overview on transformative learning. In Illeris, K. (ed.) *Contemporary theories of learning*. Abingdon: Routledge, pp. 90–105.

Kitchenham, A. (2008). The evolution of John [Jack] Mezirow's transformative learning theory. *Journal of Transformative Education, 6*(2), 104–123.

Conclusion: Learning and working

The success of formal learning depends on using the right methods, at the right time, in the right way, in the right place and for the right purpose. As we shall discover in Chapter 10 being systematic in the operationalization of these requirements goes a long way towards ensuring the success of formal HRD. The success of informal and incidental HRD depends to a large extent on learners themselves being proactive, confident and engaged, setting their own appropriate learning goals and monitoring progress, as well as on the quality of the social relationships in the workplace and the creation and sustaining of a climate that supports workplace learning.[54] A psychological climate that is conducive to and safe for informal learning in the workplace shares a number of the features of 'psychological safety' identified by Amy Edmondson in her work on learning behaviours in work teams. A psychologically safe place for learning, both formal and informal, is one where:

- There's a learning climate that's characterized by interpersonal trust, mutual respect and where people are comfortable in 'being themselves';
- Learning behaviours are valued, respected and rewarded, and concerns are alleviated about behaviours that could be seen as uncomfortable, embarrassing or threatening;

- There's a shared belief that the workplace is a safe place for risk taking and learning, and tolerance of errors by openly discussing mistakes.[55]

To this we can add the need to make sufficient resources available for employees to develop new knowledge and skills in the workplace, for example easy access to digital sources, time for learning, spaces where learning can take place, etc.[56] It also relates to the wider HR system: the creation and sustaining of a learning climate can be enhanced by setting learning goals in HR performance appraisals, carving-out time for on-going team meetings to discuss past errors, providing sufficient room for employees to both experiment and reflect in-action/on-action, and allowing them sufficient job autonomy to try out new methods of working.[57]

Just-in-time (JIT) learning (for example, learning delivered from a mobile device) has become an expectation of many employees, and especially so with millennials and others who have grown up as 'digital natives', for example in healthcare, clinical guidelines and policies are widely available in the flow of work for employees to access from hospital intranets or on the internet and are quickly accessible using QR codes.[58] As the CIPD rightly point-out, the world of HRD has changed from one in which learning is a separate 'intervention' – something that you go away and do away from the 'day job' – to learning being about continual engagement and integrated into the flow of working and performing. They suggest that as a result the role and contribution of the HRD practitioner has shifted:

- From the 'sage on the stage' model of formal, off-job training with experts producing and presenting learning to passive consumers;
- To a 'curator-concierge' model which directs actively-involved learners to current, convenient and credible content.

A practical implication of informal learning theory and the above changes in the learning environment is that in seeking to manage and maximize knowledge and skill acquisition through informal learning behaviours (ILBs) organizations should:

- Take steps to include ILB in their learning needs analysis;
- Help employees in developing their ILB capabilities (such as learning to learn);
- Put in place structures, systems, infrastructure and resources to support ILBs and motivate and reward ILBs;
- Remove obstacles and obstructions to ILBs.[59]

It's sometimes convenient to think of formal and informal learning behaviours as separate entities, however the reality is that effective HRD entails a carefully crafted combination of formal and informal learning using the full range of delivery methods and platforms in ways that optimize efficiency and effectiveness and add value for individual learners and for organizations, for example by embedding hybrid HRD in a learning ecosystem (see Chapters 10 and 11).

Use this list to check your understanding of the key points of this chapter.

1 **Formal learning**   Takes place within a designated learning context that has formalized learning objectives towards which the process proceeds in a linear fashion

2 **Training**   Planned and systematic activities designed for acquiring knowledge, developing skills and informing attitudes based on theoretically sound delivery methods

3 **Training transfer**   Extent to which learners can apply knowledge, skills and attitudes gained during training to the job context

4 **Transfer mechanisms**   Learning transfer occurs through 'transfer by identical elements' (more behavioural) and 'transfer through principles' (more cognitive/constructivist)

5 **Transfer climate**   Organization's transfer climate should be supportive of new learning; positive transfer climate impacts on efficiency and effectiveness of HRD

6 **Informal (workplace) learning**   Not normally classroom-based/highly-structured; learner-controlled; sources may be intrapersonal, interpersonal or impersonal; outcomes of the process may be intentional or unintentional

7 **Informal learning process**   Involves critical reflection, sometimes triggered by unexpected event/'jolt', search for underlying cause and effect mechanisms; results in a reframing of the situation, finding a solution and taking action

8 **Managing informal learning**   Incorporate informal learning (IL) in learning design process, develop employees' IL capabilities, have structures/systems to support IL, motivate/reward IL behaviours, removing obstacles/obstructions to IL behaviours (ILBs)

SKILLS DEVELOPMENT 6

CHALLENGING TRADITION

Imagine that you are the HR advisor ('Richard Davis') with special responsibility for learning and development in your organization and therefore you are the 'go to' person for professional advice and recommendations on anything learning-related. Here's an email you've received from your boss, the chief HR officer Ms. Smith. She is a very traditional 'old school' HR manager with pedagogy that's entrenched in the 'sage on the stage' model of instruction and is absolutely convinced of the value of formal learning. Write an email offering your views based on what you've learned from this and earlier chapters in response to your boss's concern. Your response should be theory-driven and evidence-based without being explicitly so (as this might cause Ms. Smith to 'switch off').

To: Richard Davis, HR Advisor (Learning and Development)

From: Ms. Smith, Chief HR Officer

Dear Richard,

I've just received line managers' evaluation reports for all of our in-house learning and development courses this year. As you know, our menu of training courses is the cornerstone of our contribution to this business; it's where we add value. Regrettably however, the report doesn't make happy reading for us. The constant complaint, which makes me think there must be something in it is that our training courses get good reports on the end-of-course 'happy sheets' (most people really enjoy the sessions) but then they just don't seem to have much impact on job performance. I think we need to formulate a response to the CEO as soon as possible. I'm sure when the CEO sees this she's not going to be very happy and will start to question whether the training budget should be reduced and our excellent menu of courses cut-back. This is something that we need to guard against at all costs. I look forward to hearing from you at your earliest convenience.

Regards,

Ms. Smith

7

MAXIMIZING EMPLOYEES' POTENTIAL

Contents

Chapter check-in

On completion of this chapter you should be able to:

- Explain the similarities and differences between coaching and mentoring;
- Explain when and why coaching and mentoring should be used in HRD;
- Describe what is meant by the terms career and talent development, explain how they should be applied in developing individuals and organizations;
- Describe what is meant by the terms 'leader development' and 'leadership development', and explain how they should be applied in developing individuals and organizations;
- Use your knowledge of coaching, mentoring, and career, talent and leadership development to advise on the design and delivery of HRD.

Introduction

This chapter discusses how HRD can contribute to maximizing employees' potential and talents, how it can help them to develop their careers and live fulfilled working lives, and how leaders and leadership can be cultivated and nurtured. The focus switches more towards some of the key practices of HRD, such as coaching and mentoring and leader development, rather than theories as such. Nonetheless the chapter is in Part 1 of the book because it is concerned with specific micro-processes of learning and development as they pertain to the maximizing of employees' potential. The chapter begins by exploring coaching and mentoring and it does so for two reasons: first, they're important because they consume a considerable amount of resources, both human and financial, in HRD practice; second, they have grown significantly in their popularity as HRD methods in recent decades and are used widely in leader development, it's therefore logical and convenient to group them together, for example, *Forbes* magazine valued the leadership training and development industry at $360bn globally,[1] the International Coach Federation (ICF) 2016 Global Coaching Study judged the global revenue from coaching to be $2.4bn,[2] and it's been estimated that over 70 per cent of Fortune 500 companies have some kind of mentorship programme.[3] The chapter then moves on to a discussion of the related topics of career and talent development and leader and leadership development. The chapter's general theme is how to maximize employees' potential in ways that add value for both the individual and the organization.

When coaching, mentoring and leadership development are designed and implemented effectively and efficiently they can work to deliver significant added value for individuals and organizations that is hard to achieve by other means. On the other hand, according to some critics, if they're designed and delivered ineffectively and inefficiently they can be value diminishing and the results can be worse than never having 'not tried at all'.[4] Clearly, coaching, mentoring and leadership training and development are big business and the stakes are high. Therefore the questions should be asked about when and how should they be used, are they value for money, and do they deliver the desired results?

Coaching and mentoring are terms that are often used – as indeed they are in this chapter – in conjunction, but as we'll discover there are important differences between them. Leader development is important in organizations because it's senior leaders who set direction, make strategic choices and navigate organizations through organizational change and turbulent business environments. Hence having the right leaders in place with the right knowledge and skills at the right time is a vitally important way in which HRD can add value to organizations. Just as important though is leadership development—as distinct from leader development—which aims to build leadership capacity at all levels within an organization. Leadership can make the organization itself more agile and adaptable in the face of volatility, uncertainty, complexity and ambiguity. As with coaching and mentoring, leader development is a significant consumer of resources, and the same questions arise as for coaching and mentoring: how is it best used and does it deliver value for stakeholders?

Coaching and mentoring

Coaching and mentoring are widely-used, well-established methods of learning and development in the corporate and public sectors alike. In terms of value-added, a survey by the International Coach Federation (ICF) estimated that 80 per cent of people who receive coaching report increased self-confidence, and 70 per cent reported benefit in improved work performance, relationships and communication skills. Even though the financial impact is not easy to assess, the same ICF survey reported that 86 per cent of companies reported a recouping of the original investment, and a survey by PriceWaterhouseCoopers (PWC) estimated that the return on coaching can be up to seven times the original investment. People development expert John McGurk observed that it's not 'if' but 'why' and 'how' coaching and mentoring are used: companies that are using coaching and mentoring to best effect are those that are 'aligning it with the business', on the other hand 'when it's just a "cosy conversation", it's divorced from [the] issues, [and] so it won't be as effective'.

Although coaching and mentoring are distinct concepts and practices in their own right (see separate sections below), they both:

- Use a process that is typically one-to-one, face-to-face communication and interaction, that said they can also be delivered remotely and in group sessions (and increasingly so);
- Make use of experience and expertise on the part of the coach or mentor, which may be 'domain' or 'content' knowledge (for example, in marketing, HR, etc.),

or interpersonal or 'process' skills (for example, conflict management, problem-solving, etc.);

- Are based on a relationship of mutual respect, confidence and trust between the mentor and the mentee, and the coach and the coachee;
- Have an agreed and definitive purpose that present learners with productive challenges which help them to improve performance and realize their full potential.

Coaching expert David Gray and his colleagues tracked the 'rise and rise' of coaching and mentoring and found that, for example:

- In the UK's National Health Service (NHS) up to 20 per cent of all staff are engaged in some kind of mentoring activity;
- 70 per cent of Fortune 500 companies have mentoring arrangements in place;
- There are around 45,000 business coaches operating worldwide;
- 75 per cent of organizations surveyed by the CIPD used some form of coaching and mentoring.

Coaching and mentoring are complementary approaches to workplace/work-based learning that have the potential to develop highly job-specific skills in ways that can minimize or even eliminate transfer of learning problems, offer individuals professional, career and personal development opportunities whilst simultaneously providing organizations with a flexible talent development tool, and are a way of 'doing more with less' of the HRD budget.[8]

Perspective from practice 7.1

Professionalization of coaching and mentoring

Coaching and mentoring have become increasingly organized, regulated and structured. There are a number of coaching and mentoring professional bodies, including the Association of Coaches (AC), European Mentoring and Coaching Council (EMCC, www.emccuk.org/) and International Coach Federation (ICF, www.coachfederation.org.uk/), which seek to set standards, ensure ethicality, promote best practice, and develop excellence in the coaching profession. Other professions and disciplines have developed links with coaching, for example The British Psychological Society has a Special Group in Coaching Psychology (SGCP) www.bps.org.uk/member-microsites/special-group-coaching-psychology. For a discussion of the relationship between the professional practice of coaching and the related fields of HRD and organizational development (OD) read: Hamlin, R. G., Ellinger, A. D., & Beattie, R. (2009). Toward a profession of coaching? A definitional examination of 'coaching', 'organization development' and 'human resource development'. *International Journal of Evidence Based Coaching and Mentoring, 7*(1), 13–38.

One of the challenges for students of, and newcomers to, HRD is that there are long-standing, and on-going, debates about differences between coaching and mentoring. Figure 7.1 summarizes some of the differences and similarities between coaching and mentoring.

Aspect	Dimension	Coaching	Mentoring
Differences	Object	Specific skills; performance enhancement	General; career development
	Time Frame	Shorter; fixed	Longer; more open-ended
	Focus	Goal-setting, practical application, feedback, instruction; needs of individual and organization	Modelling, counselling, supporting, advocating, introducing, sheltering (as exhibited behaviours); needs of individual
	Role and Remit	Often a paid professional activity; limited sector knowledge	Often a voluntary activity within an organization; in-depth sector knowledge
Similarities	Span	Dyadic usually (one to one; but see 'team' versions)	
	Direction	Downward (from supervisor, senior colleagues, expert, etc. to coached/mentored; see 'peer' versions)	
	Locus	Tends to be internal (but often external inputs especially at executive levels)	
	Process	Coaches can mentor and mentors can coach	
Sample Modes		Brief/solution-focused coaching; expert coaching; leadership coaching; life coaching; executive team coaching, etc.	Co-mentoring; developmental mentoring; e-mentoring; executive mentoring; peer mentoring; sponsorship mentoring; traditional mentoring; etc.
Functions		Performance focus; specific agenda; task-orientation within the workplace; coach can be subject expert skilled in questioning / listening	Safe place for reflection; listening and support; explore strengths and weaknesses; whole person; facilitation without tight agenda; self-directed with facilitation

Figure 7.1   Differences and similarities between coaching and mentoring[1]

[1]Based on: D'Abate, C. P., Eddy, E. R., & Tannenbaum, S. I. (2003). What's in a name? A literature-based approach to understanding mentoring, coaching, and other constructs that describe developmental interactions. *Human Resource Development Review*, 2(4), 360–384; Macafee, D., & Garvey, B. (2010). Mentoring and coaching: What's the difference? *BMJ*, 341, c3518

As far as the practicalities are concerned, there's no 'one-size-fits-all' model of coaching or mentoring, but in choosing the right coach or mentor, potential users ('clients') might be well-advised to consider a number of basic questions:[9]

- How much effort, money and time are you prepared to commit to coaching/mentoring?
- What outcomes are you seeking from coaching/mentoring?
- How will you manage the process?
- How will you balance the demands of coaching/mentoring with other commitments, both personal and professional?
- What will be the optimum delivery method (for example, face-to-face or virtual)?
- What is the experience, track record and credentials of the potential coach/mentor?
- How will you set-out the agreement/contract with the coach/mentor?

Potential users/clients should also ask whether a coach or mentor is the right solution or are other roles/functions such as advisor, consultant, counsellor, therapist, or even just a conversation with a trusted peer, a better option? There are tensions between these uses, for example David Gray and colleagues found that in SMEs managers tended to choose coaches with psychotherapeutic rather than non-psychotherapeutic backgrounds and concluded that even in the highly competitive SME environment 'coaching was used as a largely personal, therapeutic intervention rather than to build business-oriented competencies'.[10]

Delve deeper 7.1

Read about the theory and practice of coaching and mentoring and the psychology behind them in:

Garvey, R., Garvey, B., Stokes, P., & Megginson, D. (2017). *Coaching and mentoring: Theory and practice.* London: SAGE.

Passmore, J., Peterson, D., & Freire, T. (2013). The psychology of coaching and mentoring. In *The Wiley-Blackwell Handbook of the Psychology of Coaching & Mentoring*, pp. 3–11.

The rise and practice of coaching

The rise of coaching in recent decades has been 'meteoric'.[11] It's been estimated that the coaching industry generates about $2bn a year in revenue.[12] It's a widely used HRD method for personal and professional learning development and spans domains from business-related fields such as management, leadership and executive coaching to non-work and general domains such as sports, health and life coaching. Developments in technology (for example, Skype, Zoom, etc.) now mean that remote coaching can be used to extend its applications and benefits to much more geographically-dispersed groups. These benefits have become recognized increasingly by businesses as they turn more toward remote working practices and distributed workforces. This is illustrated in a quote from the head of executive development at the British multinational financial services company Standard Chartered: 'Remote coaching enables us to increase the scope and consistency of our approach across 71 countries and is a flexible way to offer global quality coaching to a diverse community of leaders who would otherwise not have access to it'.[13]

As noted earlier, the work of coaches has become much more professionalized in recent decades. The International Coach Federation (ICF), which describes coaching as 'partnering with clients in a thought-provoking and creative process that inspires them to maximize their personal and professional potential', was established in 1995 and its membership has grown to over 30,000 members.[14] In the UK coaching regularly comes near the top of the list of 'most-used' and 'most effective' methods in the CIPD 'Learning and Development' surveys.[15] But exactly what is coaching? Who counts as a 'coach'? How does the process work in practice?

There's no agreed definition of coaching, but leading scholars of the subject define it as a collaborative solution-focused, results-orientated and systematic process in which the coach facilitates the enhancement of performance, life experience, self-directed learning and personal growth of individuals and organizations through practically focused, robust support and challenge marked by clear, strong feedback and which helps the client ('coachee') to realize more of their potential.[16]

Coaches can be specialist coaching practitioners (internal or external to the coachee's organization) or managers, leaders or HR practitioners who coach as part of their line management, leadership or HR brief. Each of these different approaches has its advantages and disadvantages, for example an external coach can provide confidentiality, fresh ideas and knowledge and an experienced coaching skill set, but on the other hand they're unlikely to have the 'insider' knowledge of the business that an internal coach can bring to the process.[17]

One of the most well-known models of the coaching process is the GROW model, which is a framework for how to structure the coaching process. It was developed in the 1980s and is a simple and memorable format that can be applied to a wide variety of coaching interactions. According to one of the pioneers of executive coaching in Europe, Graham Alexander,[18] GROW has become the 'industry standard', whilst Sir John Whitmore (1937–2017) describes it as the 'worlds' most popular coaching model'.[19] The process begins with deciding on a subject for discussion, and proceeds from goal (G), through reality (R) and options (O) to wrap-up or will (W) depending on which version is being used. Sample questions that might be asked in a GROW session include those listed in Figure 7.2.

Goal (targets, aspirations, outcomes)

- 'What are you seeking to achieve?' 'What do you want to get out of this process?'

Reality (Current context, internal/external enablers/ and inhibitors

- 'What's your current situation' 'What are the enablers/inhibitors to achieving the change you're seeking?'

Options (possibilities and constraints)

- 'What are your options?' 'Which option do you find most appealing or most workable?'

Wrap-up/Will (actions, timeframe and accountability)

- 'What will you do and when will you do it by?' 'How will you know if it's been successful?'

Figure 7.2 Sample questions for a GROW coaching sessionl

Other models of coaching have been developed, these often have several more steps and equally memorable acronyms, for example 'ACHIEVE', 'PRACTICE', AND 'OUTCOMES'. The proliferation of models – sometimes trademarked for professional practice and commercial consulting purposes – can be bewildering to the outsider, so much so that leading coaching psychologist Alan M. Grant of the University of Sydney made a passionate plea for 'keeping it [coaching] simple!' because in a world where one size can't fit all, simplicity gives greater flexibility in accommodating and responding to individual circumstances and situations. The situation is compounded by the fact that there are so many different types of coaching (executive, life, business, systemic, performance, leadership, etc.). A straightforward and often-used distinction is between coaching that has a 'task function' and coaching that has a 'developmental function'; see Figure 7.3.

Task Function

- Improve employee's proficiency in specific task
- Informal help or instruction from more experienced / skilled colleague
- Goes on much of the time in organizations
- Informal, ad hoc, often short term
- Includes 'on-job training' (OJT)

Developmental Function

- Longer-term and growth focus especially when applied to manager, leader or executive development (includes executive coaching)
- Often involves coach external to organization
- Process is more organized, lasts over a period of months or even longer
- Often a paid professional activity

Figure 7.3 Task and development functions of coaching

Developmental coaching goes beyond the 'instruction' of task coaching; it can help coachees to define their needs and values ('what's important to them?') and if executed well, can produce a synergy between an individual's professional and personal lives. It can bring about significant changes in goal attainment, solution-focused thinking, ability to deal with change, self-efficacy, and resilience, and can enhance health and well-being outcomes. Over the longer-term coaching can be instrumental in the achievement of personal and career goals and if designed and implemented properly it can be flexible enough to fit in with work schedules thus minimizing down-time. A further advantage is that it can result in tangible 'quick wins' thereby improving individuals' self-efficacy, continuance motivation and commitment to the process.[20] However, pitfalls are likely to be encountered if:

- The process isn't managed properly;
- Coach and coachee aren't well-matched;
- The wrong type of coaching is being provided (for example when coaching is being used when counselling or psychotherapy might have better);
- The coach is inexperienced or unskilled or if one or more of the parties aren't committed fully.

Leading coaching researcher and practitioner Peter Hawkins argued that if coaching is to deliver value to organizations, and if coaching itself is to develop further as profession, then coaches need to simultaneously ensure that their coaching is mutually beneficial both for the coachee and for their sponsoring organization. Hawkins argues that this requires the acknowledgement that coaching isn't an end in itself, it is a means to an end (see the 'G' in GROW). The related method of 'strengths-based coaching' is a person-centred approach for enhancing optimal functioning by bringing out and developing a person's strengths and guiding them towards possibilities for 'self-actualization'.[21] In the words of consultant, speaker and author Sally Bibb you can never reach your full potential by trying to fix your weaknesses (a 'negativity bias'), 'knowing your strengths changes your life. If you keep trying to be someone you're not, you'll always be frustrated' (p. xi).[22] Well-executed, strengths-based coaching can be a potent way of helping someone to 'find their true calling' in a way that goes beyond just serving their fragmented or 'egoistic self' or instrumental ends.[23]

Reflective question 7.2

In the words of Sally Bibb, author of *The Strengths Book*, a strength is 'something that someone is naturally good at, loves doing and is energized by' (p. 10). She argues that we all have strengths and that they are the route to excellence and fulfilment, but a

(Continued)

problem can be that many people don't realize what their strengths are, take them for granted and undervalue them, or don't know how to use them to their best advantage. She also points out the paradox that sometimes when we overdo a strength it can become a weakness (for example, if 'being analytical' is a strength over-analysis can lead to 'paralysis-by-analysis'). What are your strengths? If you're not sure, talk it through with someone trusted who knows you well. Are you using your strengths to their best advantage? Are you overdoing any of your strengths to the extent that they become a weakness? Read more about this approach in: Bibb, S. (2017). *The strengths book*. London: LID Publishing Limited.

Given that coaching is one of the most popular HRD methods and represents significant investment of time and money by individuals and organizations, a legitimate and important question for HR practitioners to ask is 'does coaching have an effect on practically-relevant outcomes?'. This relates to some of the identified weaknesses of the coaching literature in general which:

- Has tended to be descriptive rather than analytical, is all-too-often based on anecdotes or single case studies (for examples go to the endnote[24]);
- Is faced with the challenge of achieving the right balance between offering recommendations and prescriptions for practitioners and building and testing models and theories.

Meta-analyses of prior research, systematic reviews of the research evidence and experimental studies can help to shed light on this important question.

Research insight 7.1

Does coaching work?

A meta-analysis of 18 coaching studies by Tim Theeboom and colleagues identified and categorized the various outcomes of coaching and suggested that it can have significant positive effects on performance and skills, well-being, coping, and work attitudes, and goal-directed self-regulation. The researchers concluded that coaching is an effective tool for improving the functioning of individuals in organizations, but suggested that the questions about coaching now need to shift from 'does it work?' to 'how and why does it work?'

More recently, Erik de Haan and colleagues, in what is believed to be the largest randomized controlled trial in executive coaching, found that 'coaching effectiveness scores' for an experimental group were significantly better than for a control group and that the coaching relationship (measured using Horvath and Greenberg's 'Working Alliance Inventory') mediated between antecedents (such as coaching behaviours) and outcomes (coaching effectiveness, and resilience to derailment). Overall the 'study demonstrates the effectiveness of coaching in an organizational setting, the importance of the working alliance, and that coaching may mitigate the risks of leaders derailing in large organizations' (p. 1).

Sources: De Haan, E., Gray, D. E., & Bonneywell, S. (2019). Executive coaching outcome research in a field setting: A near-randomized controlled trial study in a global healthcare corporation. *Academy of Management Learning & Education, 18*(4), 581–605; Theeboom, T., Beersma, B., & van Vianen, A. E. (2014). Does coaching work? A meta-analysis on the effects of coaching on individual level outcomes in an organizational context. *The Journal of Positive Psychology, 9*(1), 1–18.

An in-depth, critical review by Simmy Grover and Adrian Furnham (see below) concluded that there isn't enough data to come to a definitive judgement about the effectiveness of coaching because of methodological limitations such as 'questionable experimental rigour', over-reliance on self-report, not having large enough sample sizes, too few longitudinal studies, and insufficient contextual information (given that coaching is likely to be highly individualized and client-focused and therefore hard to make comparisons). That said, Grover and Furnham leaned towards a positive evaluation of coaching as a potentially effective intervention for enhancing employees' self-efficacy, career satisfaction, goal-attainment and leadership skills and potential. They noted that coaching also benefits organizations indirectly through its effects on individual employees and their job performance. Moreover, Grover and Furnham found encouraging signs that in the welter of publications appearing year-on-year on the subject of coaching there appears to be discernible improvements in the quality of the research that's being conducted. But in the words of David Gray, 'in final analysis the style and paradigm adopted by coaches needs to be linked to the goals of the client (the organizational sponsor) and to the needs of the coachee…but it is acknowledged that the coaching process is a complex journey where the actual final destination is often unknown, the road is dark and there are no maps' (p. 493).[25]

Delve deeper 7.2

Read more about coaching research and practice in:

Blackman, A., Moscardo, G., & Gray, D. E. (2016). Challenges for the theory and practice of business coaching: A systematic review of empirical evidence. *Human Resource Development Review, 15*(4), 459–486.

Feldman, D. C., & Lankau, M. J. (2005). Executive coaching: A review and agenda for future research. *Journal of Management*, 31, 829–848.

(Continued)

Grant, A. M., Passmore, J., Cavanagh, M., & Parker, H. (2010). The state of play in coaching. *International Review of Industrial & Organizational Psychology*, 25, 125–168.

Grover, S., & Furnham, A. (2016). Coaching as a developmental intervention in organisations: A systematic review of its effectiveness and the mechanisms underlying it. *PloS one*, *11*(7).

Passmore, J., & Fillery-Travis, A. (2011). A critical review of executive coaching research: A decade of progress and what's to come. *Coaching: An International Journal of Theory, Practice & Research*, 4, 70–88.

Mentoring

As has been acknowledged on several occasions in this book, history matters. Mentoring has a long tradition in Western culture. The word 'mentor' comes from a character in Homer's *Odyssey*. The story goes that as a result of Odysseus' travels to and from the Trojan wars, Telemachus (son of Odysseus and Penelope) had been deprived of a 'father figure' to serve as a role model. The goddess Athena intervened in Telemachus' life as part of her obligation to Odysseus and set out in the guise of Mentor – a fusion of the human and the divine – to educate, support and develop Telemachus. Telemachus developed physically and mentally, and by giving him new challenges of increasing complexity, Mentor's role transformed from instructor and trainer to supporter and enabler. Moreover, as Telemachus' development continued, Mentor's support was reduced, and he was eventually left to carry on without Mentor's sustenance making the transformation from a 'timid youth' to a self-confident and resourceful adult.

The concept of a mentor has been part of culture and society for a long time and in various guises (for example, it's found in the apprentice system which can be traced back to the craft guilds in the Middle Ages, see also Chapter 3).[26] The idea is very much alive-and-well in popular culture as well as professional circles: the talk show host Oprah Winfrey, in recognizing that she serves as a role model and unofficial mentor to many women, described a mentor as 'someone who allows you to see the hope inside yourself...to know that no matter how dark the night, in the morning joy will come... to see the higher part of yourself when sometimes it becomes hidden to your own view'.[27] As far as mentoring research is concerned, two of the most significant developments in mentoring's emergence as a topic of academic study and as a professional field in the latter years of the last century are to be found in the work of Kathy Kram in the USA and David Clutterbuck in the UK.

The Boston-based academic Kathy Kram did much to establish the concept of mentoring in the management literature with her pioneering research first published in the early 1980s of paired mentoring relationships between older and younger workers.[28] Her 1985 book *Mentoring at Work* offered one of the most widely-accepted definitions of mentoring and provided a solid theoretical framework for understanding the different types of mentoring relationships at work: 'relationship between an older more experienced mentor and a younger less experienced protégé for the purposes of helping and developing the protégé's career'. In Kram's formulation the relationship is dyadic, and there are two principal functions of mentoring: career and psychosocial (also referred to as 'transactional' or 'sponsorship' mentoring and 'relational' or 'developmental' mentoring); see Figure 7.4.

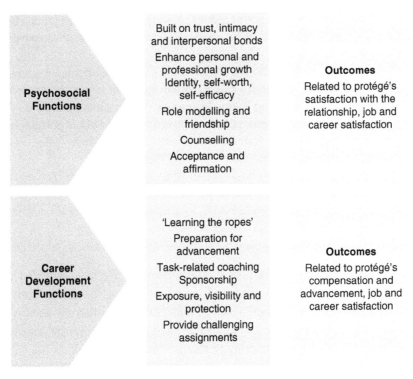

Figure 7.4 Kram's functions of mentoring

Source: Ragins and Kram, p. 5.

In the UK, at around the same time, the publication of David Clutterbuck's best-selling and highly influential practical book *Everyone Needs a Mentor* in 1985 established mentoring firmly as part of the learning and development landscape in UK business. Mentoring was taken up enthusiastically by executives, leaders, managers, trainers, HR practitioners and professional bodies such as the CIPD.

In their own words 7.1

Kathy Kram and David Clutterbuck on mentoring

In an interview with Dawn Chandler in the *Journal of Management Inquiry*, Kathy Kram was asked a question about mentoring which prompted her to comment on its relation to issues of diversity, equality and inclusion: 'Mentoring had been going on in companies

(Continued)

for decades, and yet no one in academia explored it because it seemed that the process was working just fine. People only started to pay attention to mentoring because it became clear that only some people – namely White men – were being targeted for promotion…[The] questions companies face are how can we keep our best talent and how can we get our newcomers up to speed quickly? How do managers lead groups across gender and racial boundaries? Part of the response is in developmental relationships and mentoring' (p. 31).[29]

In an interview with Australia's ABC Radio in 2017 David Clutterbuck commented on the differences between American and European style mentoring: 'American mentoring is about sponsoring, doing things for people, telling them what to do…very directive. Whereas in the European tradition which is much more about philosophy, it's much more about helping somebody with the quality of their "wisdom". So, use your wisdom to help somebody develop their wisdom of their own'.[30]

The Kathy Kram interview can be found at: Chandler, D. E. (2011). The maven of mentoring speaks: Kathy E. Kram reflects on her career and the field. *Journal of Management Inquiry*, 20(1), 24–33. Follow this link for Clutterbuck's interview in full: https://radio.abc.net.au/programitem/pgQ7eMqgL7?play=true

Also, and related to the latter point, new types of mentoring have emerged recently including peer mentoring, e-mentoring, and virtual mentoring using telephony as well as the use of AI algorithms to deliver a basic level of mentoring thereby leaving professional mentors, in the words of David Clutterbuck, to focus on the 'messy, more transformational issues that clients bring to them'.[31] In commenting on the challenges that coaching and mentoring are likely to face in the 2020s Clutterbuck points to 'complexity' (most current practice employs 'linear thinking'), 'diversity' (coachees and mentees tend to choose coaches/mentors who are like themselves), 'rise of AI' (algorithms can conduct a basic GROW conversation), need for 'democratization' (making coaching and mentoring more widely available) and 'decolonization' (the model is primarily 'western'), and 'over-supply' (is the bubble about to burst?), and 'relevance' (the need to address society's 'grand challenges' such as poverty, climate change, etc.).[32]

Perspective from practice 7.2

Mentoring in the creative industries

Nesta is an 'innovation foundation' based in the UK which seeks to promote innovation across a broad range of sectors (www.nesta.org.uk/). Nesta's Creative Business Mentor Network (CBNM) was set up to support owner–managers of creative industry SMEs (film, advertising, digital media, TV and games) in growing their businesses. In the NESTA creative industries programme mentors offered ten, two-hour sessions over a 12–month period. In one of the Nesta case studies a games business (involved in producing commissioned games for broadcasters, brands, entertainment and learning companies) was looking to make the difficult transition from a developer of commissioned games to original games that the business itself would own. One of the main challenges it faced was not having the contacts to get the company in front of the right publishers and funders and other important industry figures. The firm's mentor was a renowned video games expert who personally facilitated eight high-level business meetings, from which the firm made a number of important new contacts and helped them to get a stand at a major games showcase in San Francisco, none of which would have happened without the mentor's industry contacts and knowledge. Another firm (a specialist software company involved in strategy, design and development of mobile, social and interactive applications) came to the mentoring process on the back of a difficult period during a recession. Their mentor worked with them to increase their confidence, in parallel with helping structure a proper business plan and set viable targets for growing the business. In a third example, a marketing firm benefitted because before being mentored 'they knew what they wanted' but didn't know how to achieve it or even if it was the right thing to do. Their mentor affirmed and supported the existing company strategy.

Source: Nesta (2014). *Impact of Mentoring: How Creative Businesses Have Benefitted.* https://media.nesta.org.uk/documents/creative_business_mentor_network_impact_report_10.pdf (accessed 27-01-21).

As with coaching, a crucial question about mentoring – over and above case studies of successful programmes and companies' testimonials – is: does it work? The best place to go for a sense of the bigger picture around important evidence-related questions such as these is meta-analysis. A meta-analysis of research studies of mentoring shed a positive light on the benefits of mentoring, but it was also found that the observed effects on career outcomes were small, more specifically the researchers found that:[33]

- Career success indicators, for example compensation and promotion, are more strongly related to career mentoring than to psychosocial mentoring;
- Psychosocial mentoring behaviours, such as role modelling, affirmation, counselling and friendship were more highly related to satisfaction with the mentor than was career mentoring;
- Career and psychosocial mentoring had comparable relationships with job and career satisfaction.

The main conclusion of the research was that mentoring is more strongly related to subjective indicators of career success, for example career and job satisfaction, than it is to objective career success indicators such as promotion and remuneration. Critics have commented that mentoring can work well, but it comes as no surprise to learn that this is only if it's executed properly. It has also been pointed out that the landscape of mentoring, like that of HRD in general, is undergoing radical changes (see also Clutterbuck's comments above):

● The more traditional approaches to mentoring were developed in a world where it was the norm to stay in full-time occupation with the same company for long periods and sometimes for a working lifetime.
● They need to accommodate approaches which can work when the mentors and mentees aren't in close proximity, for example using e-mentoring in remote working where in some global companies employees and their managers live and work in different countries.[34]

Other developments include the development of new models of mentoring in which the relationship is 'flipped'. For example, contrary to the traditional model, the mentor–mentee relationship can be reversed as described by Audrey Murrell and colleagues in their book *Intelligent Mentoring: How IBM Creates Value through People Knowledge and Relationships*. They discuss the example of Jack Welch at GE who in the late 1990s required 500 top managers to find and be mentored by workers. In 'reverse mentoring' programmes the key resource to be exchanged is knowledge and expertise which is not necessarily related to hierarchy or status. The success of the approach meant that its use spread to other organizations including Proctor & Gamble.[35]

There are inevitably ethical issues associated with mentoring especially if the mentoring relationship deteriorates, becomes dysfunctional or is corrupted by power. The ethical issues are as important as practical and commercial issues when choosing and using mentoring. Researchers have identified a number of ethical issues in mentoring, including:

● Cultural replication thus reinforcing unquestioning acceptance of cultural norms and values;
● Access to mentoring, for example, difficulties of women and under-represented groups in accessing mentoring, white middle-class male mentors choosing proteges with similar backgrounds to themselves, etc.;
● Power and discrimination, for example, in cross-gender and cross-race mentoring.[36]

Clearly there are significant ethical issues to be taken into account when using mentoring (or coaching for that matter) in HRD given that ethical practice requires that HRD has both the authority and the will to influence mentoring policy in ways that prevent or remediate potential ethical problems.[37]

Delve deeper 7.3

Read more about the theory and practice of mentoring in:

Ragins, B. R., & Kram, K. E. (2007). *The handbook of mentoring at work: Theory, research, and practice*. Thousand Oaks: SAGE.

Clutterbuck, D. A., Kochan, F. K., Lunsford, L., Domínguez, N., & Haddock-Millar, J. (eds) (2017). *The SAGE handbook of mentoring*. London: SAGE.

Career and talent development

The word 'career' (which comes from the Latin word 'carrus' meaning 'wheeled vehicle') refers to the combination and sequence of work activities as they unfold over a person's working lifetime. The term 'career dynamics' is used to describe how work activities progress over time and is as relevant as ever given that in all but a few occupations the idea of a 'job for life' is a thing of the past. As a consequence of these major structural and related societal changes, career and talent development matter more than ever.[38] In the 1980s and 1990s the business and management writer and 'guru' Charles Handy, in books such as *The Empty Raincoat* (1994), predicted that the number of contractors and casual staff working in organizations would increase and that a 'portfolio career' was likely to become the norm. In a portfolio career people change their jobs several times during their working lives as a result of being forced to leave or choosing to leave a job to pursue new opportunities. Other researchers have investigated similar career models to describe and explain types of career trajectories, for example:

- Boundaryless career: this concept, developed by Michael Arthur and Denise Rousseau, refers to transcending the boundaries of a 'job for life' with a single employer. Individuals who have a boundaryless career possess a higher propensity to learn and to reflect on their strengths and weaknesses than those who desire and pursue a traditional career path;[39]
- Protean career: developed by Douglas Hall in the 1970s (named after the Greek god Proteus who could change shape at will) describes a career orientation 'in which the person, not the organization, is in charge, where the person's core values are driving career decisions, and where the main success criteria are subjective (psychological success) versus objective (position, salary)'.[40]

Two other important thinkers in this field are Donald Super and Ed Schein. Donald Super, who researched vocations in the middle decades of the last century,[41] took a life-span approach to the analysis of careers based on the idea that one's self-concept changes over time. Super argued that organizations should offer employees opportunities to develop and use all their talents and that this is an important way of maximizing the value for the organization and the employee from the employment relationship.[42]

Schein developed the important and influential concept of 'career anchors' described as a guide for 'discovering your real values'. Career anchors reflect an individual's self-concept in terms of their self-perceived talents and abilities, basic values and evolved sense of motives and needs (as they pertain to the career). These factors manifest in Schein's eight career anchors: autonomy/independence; security/stability; technical/functional competence; general management competence; entrepreneurial creativity; service and dedication to a cause; pure challenge; and lifestyle. For example a person with a security/stability career anchor would be attracted towards a career that gave longer-term security, good benefits, job security, satisfactory income and secure pension and retirement provision. Schein noted even if anchors give us some stability, in a dynamic and unstable world we will 'have to become perpetual learners, more self-reliant, and more capable than ever in dealing with surprises of all sorts' (p. 88).[43]

In their own words 7.2

Charles Handy's 'empty raincoat' and Ed Schein's 'career anchors'

Charles Handy's *The empty raincoat: Making sense of the future* (1994) is a popular 'business philosophy' book that explores individuals' material, existential and spiritual needs.[44] It became a best seller in the 1990s. Handy explained the book's title as being named after a bronze sculpture in Park Minneapolis of an empty raincoat standing bolt upright but empty with no-one inside it: 'To me that empty raincoat is the symbol of our most pressing paradox. We were not destined to be empty raincoats, nameless numbers of a payroll, role occupants, the raw material of economics or sociology statistics in some government report. If that is to be its price, then economic progress is an empty promise. There must be more to life than to be a cog in someone else's great machine' (p. 2).

Ed Schein discovered career anchors inductively by, in his own words, simply 'Talking to adults and walking them through their history' and for each decision point asking them 'why did you do that?'. Schein found that the careers themselves were 'all over the map' but in describing, for example, what their 'safe harbour' was or reasons for moving out of a job because 'that wasn't me', the answers to the 'why?' question 'patterned very clearly'. The words people used were everyday intelligible phrases such as 'security' which Schein's model uses (rather than more abstract psychological terms), as in anchors such as 'autonomy/independence' or 'service and dedication to a cause'. His practical advice is to 'go over what you've done and figure out why you did that and look for the pattern in the whys'. One of the keys to effective career management is knowing what your priorities are (and as reflected in the anchors); by way of example he remarked that 'I know my priority is autonomy…the only work that I wanted to do was where I had complete control' which led Schein into a very successful career in academia.

Source: Handy, C. (1994). *The empty raincoat: Making sense of the future*. London; Hutchinson; Schein, E. (2105). Advice for young scholars: Find your career anchors. www.youtube.com/watch?v=iEMB5Ylw9LM

Reflective question 7.3

Building on Ed Schein's idea of 'the pattern of the whys' (see above), if you 'walk through' your personal life, educational or occupational history can you figure why you did what you did? Is there a pattern in your 'whys'? Are there any discernible 'safe harbours' or 'anchors' in the whys?

Talent development and talent management have become prominent topics in human resources and HRD research and practice in recent years as a result of a variety of economic and social factors, including increased international competition and internationalization of business, labour market factors and demographic changes, etc. A survey of CEOs by PwC found that 93 per cent of respondents recognized the need to change or were changing their strategies for attracting and retaining talent, and 63 per cent were concerned that the lack of key skills could threaten their business growth prospects. There is a clear need for talent management strategies if companies are to survive and thrive in volatile, uncertain, complex and ambiguous environments.

The CIPD defines talent management as a process of seeking to identify, attract, engage, develop, and retain individuals who are considered to be particularly valuable to an organization (that is, talented individuals) and who can add particular value to the organization's strategic ambitions. 'Talent development' is the learning and development part of this process; its role is to ensure that the organization can meet its current and future needs of employees with high-value individuals. There are a number of ways in which HRD can contribute to talent development, including formal programmes, developmental experiences (such as secondments), job-based developmental experiences (such as special projects, job enlargement, job enrichment) and informal development activities (for example, mentoring, networking, coaching, etc.) which build both intellectual and social capital.

Perspective from practice 7.3

Talent management at BlackRock

BlackRock is one of the world's leading asset management and investment corporations. At the time of writing it was the world's largest asset manager with over $7.4 trillion assets under its management. It manages huge swathes of pension funds as well as private wealth. It is described as being 'manically focused' on delivering high performance and its 14,000 or so employees are guided by its basic values which make it 'purpose-driven', 'performance-oriented' and 'principles-led' (see: www.blackrock.com/corporate). In 2020 the firm's CEO Larry Fink made headlines in his annual letter to shareholders in which he put the climate emergency front and centre by

(Continued)

acknowledging the risks that it poses and announcing that BlackRock will no longer invest in companies that 'generate more than 25% of their revenue from thermal coal production'.[45]

The company's talent management and talent development strategy is positioned as key driver of its mission which is 'to create a better financial future for our clients'.[46] The company deploys its talent strategies to balance the tensions of being scaled globally but relevant locally, fostering a collective culture whilst enabling individuals to thrive, and having policies that endure and yet are agile and open to revitalization. Talented employees are developed by giving them stretch assignments but also by having bosses who pay attention to mentoring, coaching and developing their direct report as cornerstones in the business talent development philosophy. Bosses themselves are developed purposively to be more effective coaches, delegators and drivers of high performance. The business's core principles and sense of purpose at Black-Rock create synergies and a virtuous cycle by acting as an attractive force for top talent. The case study of BlackRock shows how a leading financial management firm has sought to develop employees in ways that are consistent with a set of core values and principles. For more details on these consult the article by Ready and colleagues (see below).

Source: Ready, D. A., Hill, L. A., & Thomas, R. J. (2014). Building a game-changing talent strategy. *Harvard Business Review*, 92(1), 20.

Career development and HRD

Career development has been described as one-third of the 'holy trinity' of HRD (the others being training and development and organization development).[47] At the most basic level HRD's role is to ensure that an organization has programmes and activities and resources that will help employees to achieve their career goals but also to be able to master their own careers and promote the idea of lifelong learning. The general pattern is that career development has shifted from being primarily organizationally based to individually driven.[48] But regardless of where the locus of control for individual career development is, the fact remains that learning is central to the notion of careers, career management and career development (as Ed Schein has said, quoted above, we 'have to become perpetual learners').

HRD researchers Kimberly McDonald and Linda Hite argued that HRD can make a material difference to individuals' careers by attending to three important factors, 'fairness and equity', 'supervisor support' and 'work-life balance':

- Fairness and equity: career development has tended traditionally to be focused on higher echelon/high potential employees, however other employees, including hourly-paid employees, need as a basic right to be given the chance to think about actively managing and developing their careers. This is matter of workplace justice and fairness and equality of opportunity of access to a career development for all employees;

- Supervisor support: support from line managers and supervisors has a big influence on career development. HRD can help to educate and inform line managers and supervisors about career development issues, as well as equity, fairness and work-life balance so that they can play an active and constructive part in the process on the part of their direct reports;
- Work-life balance: conflicts between work and family life can have significant effects not only on immediate issues such as job satisfaction but also on longer term issues such as career management and career development, and these issues are amplified especially in relation to women's career development. HRD can contribute by building networks and by creating structures for learning/support that can alleviate problems with work/family conflicts and provide opportunities for networking/collaborative learning in support of career development.[49]

The educationalist Richard Bagnall, writing in the context of lifelong learning, also makes the pragmatic point that the amount of new knowledge that is being created and becoming available requires continuous learning if individuals are to maintain, let alone develop, their careers.[50] Careers are about changing through learning, and HRD as one of the drivers of learning in organizations is well-placed to be a 'broker' and 'enabler' of the lifelong learning opportunities and processes that employees will require if they are to maximize their full potential across the span of their careers during their working lives. One of the vital roles that HRD can play in career development and lifelong learning is to empower employees to be able to take charge of their own learning (for example, by making them more self-directed, developing meta-learning, etc.) and thereby helping them to create the futures that they truly desire.

Perspective from practice 7.4

Career guidance for human resources

Facilitating employees' career development is a vital part of HRD's professional responsibility. But what about HRD careers themselves? The CIPD describes HR as a diverse profession spanning a range of professional areas but which can be classified into two broad categories:

- HR generalists who perform a variety of activities in most of the areas of 'people practice';

(Continued)

- HR specialists who provide work in their area of expertise such as employee relations, people analytics, etc.

Some of the main areas of HRD in the HR profession, as described by the CIPD, are:

- Learning and development: 'L&D specialists identify learning needs across the organisation, creating a learning environment where people develop to their full potential';
- Organizational development and design: 'OD&D specialists shape organisational culture, performance and outcomes through systems thinking and behavioural science';
- Talent management: 'Talent management specialists maximize potential by identifying, engaging, developing, reviewing and retaining individuals who show the potential to be of greatest value.'[51]

The SHRM makes a similar distinction between generalist and specialist remits and it identifies several specialist roles: workforce planning and employment; employee reward; employee and labour relations; and HRD. The SHRM describes a typical entry-level/early career stage HRD position as a 'training or orientation/on-boarding/induction specialist' involving organizing, conducting and administrating off-job training sessions, on-the-job training programmes, evaluating training programmes and recording employees' participation in training and development programmes. The work could involve specific areas such as marketing and sales or health and safety programmes. Examples of job titles in this specialty area are 'trainer', 'employee development specialist or manager', 'leadership development specialist or manager', and 'organizational development (OD) specialist or manager'.[52]

Delve deeper 7.4

Professional bodies such as the Association for Talent Development (ATD), Chartered Institute for Personnel and Development (CIPD), and the Society for Human Resource Management (SHRM) offer information and guidance to help people move into HR and HR-related roles and manage their HR careers. Explore the latest professional frameworks, guidance, standards, qualification and membership routes by visiting the websites for ATD, CIPD and SHRM.

Leadership

One of the most concise and cogent definitions of leadership is provided by the prominent leadership educator Peter J. Northouse in his book *Leadership: Theory and practice*:

'leadership is a process whereby an individual influences a group of individuals to achieve a common goal'.[53] Northouse's definition has a number of significant implications:

- Being a process means that it's a transactional, mutual, reciprocal and on-going process that takes place between leaders and followers;
- Leadership occurs in groups ranging from leader-follower dyads, to teams, departments and entire corporations and nations;
- Leaders, and those whom they lead, have common goals based on a shared vision.

The UK's CIPD describes leadership as the ability to influence people by demonstrating positive personal attributes and behaviours that, when demonstrated skilfully, have the power to bring about positive outcomes for individuals, teams, organizations and wider communities.

Also, leadership and management are recognized widely as being fundamentally different. The 'In their own words' feature below offers some views on this from a number of the pioneers of leadership studies, the American leadership and management scholars Bernard Bass, Warren Bennis, John Kotter and Gary Yukl.

In their own words 7.3

Bass, Bennis, Kotter, and Yukl on leadership and management

Managers and management, and leaders and leadership are amongst the most widely used and widely misused terms in business. Here are some soundbites from leading figures in leadership research on what defines 'leadership' and the relationship between management and leadership. Warren Bennis (1925–2014), referred to by *Forbes* magazine as the 'dean of leadership gurus', said that 'managers do things right; leaders do the right thing'. Gary Yukl defined leadership as 'the process of influencing others to understand and agree about what needs to be done and how to do it, and the process of facilitating individual and collective efforts to accomplish shared objectives'.[54] Bernard Bass (1925–2007), one of the founders of the field of leadership studies, said that managers must be able to lead, and leaders must be able to manage, therefore the term manager may be seen as a role label whilst leader is a role function. Harvard Business School's John Kotter argued that managing is to do with planning, organizing and controlling, whereas leading is more to do with visioning, networking and building relationships.

Alongside the positive views of leadership there are a number of more critical perspectives, including those which argue that:

- Leadership involves power and influence in the relationships between leaders and followers, and without power and influence there can be no leadership, but power and influence create scope for the 'darker side' of leadership to emerge;
- Leadership does not exclude unethical practices whereby leaders (or followers) are involved in manipulative relationships or coercive processes to achieve personal or divisive ends.

In spite of the fact that many types of leadership are framed in terms of positive attributes and behaviours (for example, with optimistic labels for the different 'types' such as 'authentic', 'inclusive', 'transformational', 'servant', etc.), leadership is not unequivocally positive. Leadership has a 'dark side' as explored in Dennis Tourish's book *The Dark Side of Transformational Leadership,* and it goes without saying that leadership can be damaging and destructive ('destructive leadership' is a sub-field of leadership studies[55]). Leadership's more destructive manifestations range from abusive supervision to hubristic and narcissistic leadership to tyranny and despotism. Human history (for example, Adolf Hitler, Josef Stalin, etc.) and corporate life (for example, Lay and Skilling at Enron, Bernie Ebbers at WorldCom, Dick Fuld at Lehmans, etc.) are littered with examples of leaders who used power and influence for selfish, destructive and malign ends. The consequences of destructive leadership can be far-ranging and long-lasting, for example ten years on from the 2008 crash the UK economy was £300bn smaller than it would have been.[56] Part of HRD's critical role is critiquing the darker side issues of leaders and leadership learning and development, including the especially potent role that power and influence play in the leadership process.

Reflective question 7.4

The question of 'are leaders born or made?' is hotly debated. Who are the leaders that you admire and/or have influenced you significantly? Do you have a view on whether they were 'born' or 'made'? For further guidance follow the footnote for a link to Jonathan Doh's article that looked at this question closely.[57]

Leadership frameworks and leader power

An important question both for HRM and HRD if they're to influence leadership processes in organizations is 'are there any general patterns to the leader behaviours or leader competencies that organizations should seek to recruit for and develop in their workforce?'. There is a plethora of models and frameworks of leader competence and behaviours that provide some answers to this question. For example, in the USA, the SHRM has identified three domains of leader competencies (skills and abilities):

- Leading the organization: managing change; solving problems and making decisions; managing politics and influencing others; taking risks and innovating;
- Learning the self: demonstrating ethics and integrity; displaying drive and purpose; exhibiting leadership stature; increasing one's capacity to learn; managing yourself; increasing self-awareness; developing adaptability;
- Leading others: communicating effectively; developing others; valuing diversity and difference; building and maintaining relationships; managing effective teams and work groups.[58]

The SHRM's framework is generic but other sector- or organization-specific leadership competencies have been developed, for example, the UK's National Health Service's Leadership Framework seeks to develop leaders who are capable of demonstrating personal qualities, such as 'self-awareness', 'working with others' (for example, building and maintaining relationships), 'managing services' (for example, planning), 'improving services' (for example, encouraging improvement and innovation) and 'setting direction' (for example, taking decisions).[59]

Perspective from practice 7.5

Google's 'Project Oxygen'

In 2008 an internal team of researchers at Google embarked on 'Project Oxygen' which was a research project that aimed to find out how to build better team leaders at Google. Based on analyses of performance reviews, feedback surveys and nominations for top manager awards, they singled-out eight highly effective leader habits which, a decade on as the company grew in size and complexity, they expanded into ten so-called 'Oxygen' behaviours. At Google the 'best' team leaders:

- Are good coaches;
- Empower team members and don't micromanage;
- Create an inclusive and caring team environment;
- Are productive and results-oriented;
- Are good communicators, listeners and sharers;
- Support team members, career development and discuss their performance;
- Have a clear vision and strategy for the team;
- Have the right technical skills to be able to help and advise the team members;
- Collaborate more widely across Google;
- Are strong decision-makers.

The Google research found these behaviours to be associated with higher team performance (better satisfaction and performance) and lower turnover of team members.

(Continued)

Cautious about the possibility that happy employees simply rated their leaders higher (that is, causality was ambiguous or reversed), the researchers followed the relationship between the '10 Oxygen' behaviours and team outcomes such as satisfaction and performance and team turnover over time (good leadership appears to precede performance improvements) and accommodated personnel changes in the research (for example, when employees shifted to excellent leaders their performance improved). They found that there was more to the relationship than mere correlation; in Google's words they claimed to have found that high quality team leadership 'causes better employee outcomes'.

Source: https://rework.withgoogle.com/blog/the-evolution-of-project-oxygen/

'List' approaches, such as those above, can be helpful as an overall architecture for what good leadership looks like, however they've been criticized because they can sometimes focus too much attention on the individual at the expense of the context. This could be a problem because, as management and organization development researcher Joseph Raelin points out in the day-to-day practice of leading and leadership, the leader and the context are inseparable: 'you should never send a changed person back into an unchanged environment',[60] this is one reason why it's so important to take into account the person (the leader), the task and the environment as in John Adair's classic 'task-team-individual' model of action-centred leadership.

The discussion of the importance of context or environment highlights an important conceptual point as far as leading and learning are concerned: it's not only important to develop 'leaders' (that is individuals) but also to develop leadership (that is, a capacity within the organization itself):

- Leader development: expansion of a person's capacity to be effective in leadership roles and processes (setting direction, creating alignment, and maintaining commitment in groups who share common work and a common goal);
- Leadership development: the expansion of the organization's capacity to enact the basic leadership tasks needed for collective work (direction, alignment, commitment) which focuses on organizations and teams, and systems and learning as much as it does on individuals.[61]

Much of what is discussed in this section, even if it's under the label of leadership development, often refers to leader development. Leadership researcher David Day argued that much more is known about the practice of 'leader development' than is known about the practice of 'leadership development'.[62] Arguably, by developing leaders in an organization we also develop leadership across the organization as a whole. A related point is that although leader development usually applies to people who are seen as leaders by virtue of their job role, for example the CEO is the most senior leader, any employee at any level of the organization can demonstrate leadership and a leadership function. In terms of Peter Northouse's definition cited at the beginning of this section, leadership is the process whereby a person, who may not be formally designated as having a leader role, influences others in the pursuit of a common goal for example by shaping direction, critically questioning, etc. A leader's power can emanate from a variety of sources, as John French and Bertram Raven discovered over half a century ago:

- Positional power: reward power (the leader can grant rewards), coercive power (the leader can penalize) and legitimate power (the leader has the right to command);
- Personal power: expert power (the person has superior knowledge relevant to the task) and referent power (the person has relevant character traits such as charisma).[63]

The following perspective from practice illustrates a number of relevant points about the practicalities of the relationships between leaders, leadership and power.

Perspective from practice 7.6

Leading from the 'board' to the 'ward'

In a report by The King's Fund for the UK's National Health Service (NHS) it was recommended that leadership development in the NHS should extend 'from the board to the ward'. According to the report, one of the biggest failings in the NHS was its failure to engage clinicians, such as doctors, in the leadership of the organization and for leadership to be shared between clinicians (doctors, nurses and other health professionals, who may have personal power stemming from their expertise and experience) and managers (they have positional power). A related shortcoming was an adherence to outmoded 'heroic' models of leadership and the need to adapt to the idea that leadership is shared across the organization which requires a focus on developing team and organizational learning and development, and on followership as well as leadership. The researchers found that higher quality and better care results could be obtained through the sharing and re-distribution of leadership to nurses, doctors and other health professionals: 'Leadership development must not focus purely on technical competencies, but on the ability to create climates in which individuals can themselves act to improve services and care. Staff at all levels need to be given the skills to have the courage to challenge poor practice.'

A more desirable model of leadership flagged-up by the report was the shift from the old-fashioned heroic model of leadership to leadership that is shared, distributed and adaptive. It raised ethical and political issues with regard to changing the perceptions and practices of leadership in organizations (especially in organizations such as the UK's NHS, where decisions of clinical professionals can determine how the budget is spent and the impact on health outcomes for patients). It also has HRD implications in terms of who gets 'developed' as a leader and why.

Source: The King's Fund (2011). *The future of leadership and management in the NHS: No more heroes*. London: The King's Fund.

Leader and leadership development

As far as HRD is concerned, the following observation by leadership scholar David Day is significant: 'Leadership is something that all organizations care about. But what most interests them is not which leadership theory or model is "right" (which may never be settled definitively), but how to develop leaders and leadership as effectively and efficiently as possible.'[64] In so far as the practicalities of leader and leadership development are concerned, Day identifies the following key questions about the field's status and contribution:

- Is the substantial investment that's made in leader and leadership development worthwhile?;
- What difference does leader and leadership development make?;
- What leader and leadership development strategies work best?

Moreover, given that many critics have questioned the value of leader and leadership development, Day makes a plea for an evidence-based approach and for leader and leadership development to be designed and implemented in an integrated way so as to maximize the benefits for individuals, groups and organizations.[65]

If HRD is concerned with helping employees to become better leaders and building leadership capacity in organizations it assumes that leaders and leadership can be developed. It's been remarked in the past that 'managers are created, but leaders are born', therefore an important practical question for HRD and leadership development is whether leaders are 'born' (the ability to lead is an innate capacity) or 'made' (the ability to lead can be developed, see Reflective Question 7.4 above). Some people – influenced perhaps by the nineteenth-century Scottish historian/philosopher Thomas Carlyle, considered to be one of the first 'modern' writers on the subject and originator of the 'great man' [sic] theory of leadership – would respond that great leaders are 'born' with the necessary intellect, courage and inspiration, and that they emerge when the opportunity presents. If leadership were to be something that a person's born with – an innate talent with haves and have nots – it would negate somewhat the idea of leadership learning and development.

Reflective question 7.5

What would you say to a colleague who reads a lot of history and believes firmly in the widely used 'great *man*' [sic] theory of leadership,[66] who made this comment: 'People at the top of the leadership "bell curve" start out very good and tend to get even better as they go along. Then there are the people at the bottom of the curve, the 10–15 per cent who, no matter how hard they try, simply aren't ever going to be very good leaders.[67] The best thing is to focus all our leadership development efforts at the top end as they're the only ones who can get this organization to where it needs to be.'

Method	Description	Purpose
360 degree feedback	Multi-rater (peer, self, subordinates); perceptions of performance in leader/job relevant competencies/skills	Objective diagnosis/self-awareness; 'see themselves as others see them'
Experience/action based methods	Experiential learning (Kolb), action learning (Revans); problem/project-based; inquiry/dialogue; surfacing/sharing mental models	Learning by solving real problems in real time; builds skills of inquiry/dialogue
Assessment/development centres	Interviews; psychometric/reasoning tests; presentations, in-tray exercises, case study role-play; trained/qualified assessors	Identify individuals' capabilities, job and career potential, learning and development needs; fast-tracking; succession planning
Coaching	Collaborative solution-focused, results-orientated and systematic process	Enhancement of work performance, life experience, self-directed learning and personal growth
Mentoring	Relationship between older/experienced mentor and younger/inexperienced protégé; helping and developing the protégé's career	Psychosocial functions (role modelling, counselling, etc.); career development functions (sponsorship, exposure, etc.)
Outdoor development	Structured activities in outdoor context using 'artificial' tasks	Develop individuals' skills in areas such as team working, decision-making, problem solving, communication, etc.

Figure 7.5   Some of the more commonly used leader development methods

Leader and leadership development is big business. For example, according to research conducted on behalf of Deloitte, leadership development accounts for the largest proportion of HRD spending (35 per cent) and more than 60 per cent of organizations surveyed cited 'leadership gaps' as one of the main business challenges.[68] The consulting firm McKinsey reported in 2014 that US companies spend $14bn on leadership development.[69] Also, the popularity of leadership self-help books such as Steven Covey's best-selling *The 7 Habits of Highly Effective People* (2004) illustrates the level of interest that there is in this topic. The evidence suggests that leaders, aspiring leaders and organizations believe that leadership development is possible and is worth investing time and money in. But if leadership development is such a high priority for HRD spend, where are the efforts being allocated and what works best? Figure 7.5 gives a summary of the more commonly used leadership development methods.

A practical question for HRD practitioners is 'does leadership development work' and is there any association between leadership development and outcomes? One way to find an answer to this question is to look at the results of meta-analyses.

Research insight 7.2

Effectiveness of leader and leadership development

A comprehensive and detailed meta-analysis of the results from 355 studies of leadership training and development interventions found that:

- Leadership training can be effective in improving trainees' cognitive, skills-based and affective outcomes;
- Leadership training can lead to increases in learning and job performance of between 20 and 25 per cent.

It appears also that although both organizational and subordinate (that is, follower) outcomes increase as a result of leadership training, organizational outcome effects are larger than subordinate outcome effects suggesting an aggregating or 'trickle-up' effect. The meta-analysis also revealed that:

- Programmes developed on the basis of a needs analysis resulted in greater transfer of learning;
- Self-administered programmes were less effective than programmes that are professionally administered;
- Programmes using multiple methods of delivery are more effective than those using single methods of delivery;

- Feedback during a training session significantly bolsters the transfer and effectiveness of leadership training;
- On-site training is more effective than off-site training;
- Greater transfer of learning occurs after face-to-face than virtual leadership training.

Even though 'hard' leadership skills (such as problem-solving and data analytics) appear to be the easiest to learn and transfer, the 'softer' skills (such as inter- and intra-personal competencies) are likely to be as, if not more, important for achieving impact on the organization and followers.[70]

Source: Lacerenza, C. N., Reyes, D. L., Marlow, S. L., Joseph, D. L., & Salas, E. (2017). Leadership training design, delivery, and implementation: A meta-analysis. Journal of Applied Psychology, 102(12), 1686.

Other research suggests that the picture isn't quite as positive as suggested by these data. For example, an earlier meta-analysis by Doris Collins and Ed Holton found a somewhat mixed set of results where some leadership development programmes were 'tremendously effective' whilst 'others failed miserably'. They concluded that organizations can feel comfortable that leadership development can produce substantial positive results, but the programmes have to be the 'right development programs for the right people and at the right time'.[71]

Alongside debates about how effective leadership training and development can be, traditional training approaches to leader and leadership development (of the kind that figured in the meta-analysis discussed above) have been criticized because they focus too much on:

- Leader development and too little on developing leadership, that is leading-following processes, leadership relationships, and leadership structures in teams and organizations;
- Narrowly-defined sets of knowledge, skills and attitudes required by effective leaders, rather than broader issues around self-concept, identity, ethics, virtues, and leader character development.[72]

Joseph Raelin, who offers compelling arguments for 'rethinking' leadership and leadership development,[73] argued against putting leadership 'into' people by conducting leadership training in 'corporate offsites' and argued for putting leadership directly into the organization where it belongs. Raelin argues that the workplace offers as many, and probably many more, informal and work-based opportunities for learning as do the leadership classrooms of our business schools. This is essentially a situated learning perspective on leadership development in which learning takes place in the midst of action, based on the principles that:

- Learning arises not from the transfer of leader knowledge, skills and attitudes from teacher/expert to taught/novice but through the social relations embedded within the team as a community of practice;
- The context and the problems the workplace presents are debated critically and team members, as learners, create new knowledge by sharing mental models and reflecting together on the assumptions that guide their actions, and where appropriate, challenging these;
- Theory, as such, emerges as much from hands-on practice, and 'reflection-in-action' and 'reflection-on-action'[74] as it does from 'textbook' concepts and theory.

In the approach Raelin is suggesting – an 'action-based modality' – 'leaderful learning' becomes a meta-competence that transcends itself through learning-how-to-learn,[75] the primary source of which is learning via experience and reflecting-in-action and reflecting-on-action. But as we know, learning from experience is not automatic nor is it necessarily efficient or effective; it has to be the right experiences, at the right time, in the right circumstance and with the right people.[76] For example, Revans' method of action learning can be a highly effective approach for developing leaders and leadership (see Chapter 4). Case study research of leadership development based on action learning principles at organizations such as Boeing, US Department of Agriculture and Department of Commerce, found that action learning was a highly efficient and effective method because it focused firstly on a manageable set of key leadership skills (rather than generic sets of 20 or more) and secondly worked with the leaders' problem context and the development of actionable solutions to their real-world problems (rather than artificial case studies or abstract leadership puzzles).[77]

Delve deeper 7.5

For an 'academically robust account of the major theories and models of leadership' consult:

Northouse, P. G. (2016). *Leadership: Theory and practice*. Thousand Oaks: SAGE.

The Oxford University Press Handbook is a collection of 'comprehensive, state-of-the-science reviews and perspectives on the most pressing historical and contemporary leadership issues, with a particular focus on theory and research':

Day, D. (ed.) (2016). *Oxford handbook of leadership and organizations*. Oxford: Oxford University Press.

The SAGE Handbook is a collection of chapters from leading leadership scholars who've helped to 'define the territory' of leadership studies:

Bryman, A., Collinson, D., Grint, K., Jackson, B., & Uhl-Bien, M. (eds) (2011). *The SAGE handbook of leadership*. London: SAGE.

The Centre for Creative Leadership is a non-profit education institution. Its Handbook of Leadership Development offers practical guidance on how to design and implement leader and leadership development:

McCauley, C. D., & Van Velsor, E. (eds) (2004). *The Centre for Creative Leadership handbook of leadership development*. San Francisco: Jossey-Bass.

Find out more about current and emerging models and practices of leadership development by consulting the special issue of *Advances in Developing Human Resources* edited by Sasha Ardichvili and colleagues:

Ardichvili, S., Natt och Dag, K., & Manderscheid, S. (2016). Leadership development: Current and emerging models and practices. *Advances in Developing Human Resources*, *18*(3), 275–285.

For a study of the application of action learning to leadership development consult:

Skipton Leonard, H., & Lang, F. (2010). Leadership development via action learning. *Advances in Developing Human Resources*, *12*(2), 225–240.

Finally read more about developing leaders' 'emotional intelligence' in:

Sadri, G. (2012). Emotional intelligence and leadership development. *Public Personnel Management*, *41*(3), 535–548; Ovans, A. (2015). How emotional intelligence became a key leadership skill. *Harvard Business Review*, *28*, 3–6.

Conclusion: Character, practical intelligence and wisdom

The issue of what constitutes 'right behaviour' raises ethical questions for coaching, mentoring and leadership development, especially in the light of earlier comments made about the darker and more destructive aspects of leaders' behaviours. This includes the destructive power of hubris and narcissism and their relationships to power ('who wields it') and politics ('who gets to decide'). This has prompted some management and leadership researchers to explore the role of virtue ethics and moral character in shaping leadership and how to support the 'well-being' and 'flourishing' (in Aristotelian terms *eudaimonia*) of the organization and the community as a whole. For example, Mary Crossan and her colleagues describe an approach to the development of leader character in response partly to the fact that numerous corporate scandals, most famously Enron, have spotlighted the negative and dysfunctional effects that leaders of bad character have had not only on their organizations but on wider society. Lay and Skilling at Enron were jailed for their part in the corporate corruption and accounting fraud in America's seventh largest company that rocked the corporate world in 2001. Richard Fuld CEO of Lehman Brothers, the man at the centre of the storm in the financial crisis of 2008, was once referred to as 'the most hated man in America'.

Crossan and colleagues build on the Aristotelian notions of 'virtue' and the development of 'moral character' to propose a model for leader character based on the virtues of: wisdom; courage; humanity; justice; temperance and transcendence. Crossan and her colleagues examine critically the arguments both for and against whether character can be 'taught' and conclude that just as students can be taught to deal with complex situations in traditional areas of business education such as accounting, finance, strategy human resources, etc. then so can they be educated in the knowledge, skills and attitudes to deal with the complex moral judgements that pervade leadership and managerial work in general. They recommend instilling character development across all business school courses, as well as in business ethics-specific courses, and the principle can apply in HRD also. They suggest this can be done through the use of experiential methods (including role plays where students are put into character-stretching situations) combined with developing self-awareness (through guided reflection) and coaching and mentoring (where a more experienced and wiser person can help a less-experienced person to develop the requisite skills for 'doing the right thing').[78]

In the coaching and mentoring field, David Clutterbuck in *Coaching the Team at Work* described the essence of coaching and mentoring of leaders as using 'the wisdom of the coach to bring to consciousness the wisdom that those being coached hold within them' and as a way of helping newcomers to understand the collective wisdom of a team or organization. He further identifies three categories of wisdom: what he refers to as 'lean wisdom', which is context- and task-specific, 'broad wisdom' which is gleaned from reflections on life experience, and 'meta-wisdom' which brings together multiple, shifting perspectives into a deep and coherent insight.[79] Clutterbuck is alluding here to 'practical wisdom'. Coaching, mentoring and leader development are – and always have been, bearing in mind mentoring's Classical origins – ways of developing employees' practical wisdom.

Researchers have also explored this idea in relation to developing leaders' practical wisdom, as in Robert Sternberg's 'wisdom-intelligence-creativity' (WIC) model of leadership. In Sternberg's model the leaders' 'intelligence' aspect isn't IQ as such, it's a 'practical intelligence' (and linked to expertise, judgement, and prudence), which is the leader's 'ability to solve every-day problems by utilizing knowledge gained from experience in order to purposefully adapt to, shape, and select environments'. In Sternberg's model a two-way recursive process operates whereby agents (such as a leaders) change themselves to suit the environment (by 'adaptation') but also agents change the environment to suit themselves (by 'shaping') (and it can even mean selecting a new environment in which to work and make the best of one's talents).

The philosophy of practical wisdom can be traced back to Aristotle who argued that a person who, through learning and experience, has developed 'practical wisdom' (*phronesis*) is already predisposed to identify the 'right' purpose in a particular situation and is able to enact the 'right' response to accomplish that purpose. For example, a leader, although he or she might possess the virtue of courage for speaking out against injustices at work, may lack the necessary knowledge of the context and the experience to be able to act with courage to know the right time, right place and right way to speak-out.[80] Being able to act with practical wisdom demands both a virtuous character and the necessary practical intelligence, 'intuitive expertise' (that is in-depth knowledge developed in context) and wisdom to refine and carry out one's judgment with prudence. Because prudence, practical wisdom or phronesis (these terms all roughly approximate to each other) can be seen as the virtue that exercises control over the other virtues (for example, not just being courageous but knowing when and how to be courageous), it is a meta-virtue and perhaps the most important life skill that a leader can possess and the most important source of value that HRD can add to individuals and organizations through the processes of coaching, mentoring and leader and leadership development.

Chapter checkout

Use this list to check your understanding of the key points of this chapter.

1 **Coaching and mentoring**   Based on relationship of mutual respect, confidence, trust between mentor/mentee, coach/coachee; uses experience/expertise on part of the coach/mentor; have an agreed/defined purpose

2 **Coaching**   Collaborative solution-focused, results-orientated, systematic process; coach facilitates learning/personal growth by help, support, challenge, feedback

3 **Coaching functions and process**   Coaching can have both task and developmental functions; the process can be managed using the GROW model

4 **Coaching outcomes**   Positive effects on performance and skills, well-being, coping, and work attitudes, and goal-directed self-regulation; some research is limited by methodological shortcomings

5 **Mentoring**   Relationship between a more experienced mentor and a less experienced protégé for purposes and helping/developing protégé; career and psychosocial functions

6 **Mentoring outcomes**   Research suggests that mentoring is related to subjective indicators of career success and objective career success indicators, but more strongly to the former than the latter

7 **Criticisms of coaching and mentoring**   Availability and access for less-privileged groups; propagating cultural replication, overlooking roles of power and influence in the process

8 **Career development**   How work activities progress over course of a person's working life; HRD is an important enabler of career development and career management

9 **Talent management**   Identifies, engages, develops, and retains individuals who show the potential to be of greatest value to an organization

10 **Leader development**   Expanding person's capacity to be effective in leadership roles and processes

11 **Leadership development**   Expansion of organization's capacity to enact the basic leadership tasks needed for collective work

12 **Leadership development outcomes**   Effective if based on accurate needs analysis, be professionally administered, use multiple delivery methods, give feedback, focus on 'soft' as well as 'hard' leadership skills

13 **Criticisms of leader development**   Overly-focused on leader development at expense of leadership development; focus on narrow set of knowledge and skills, overlooking or exacerbating issues of power and influence

14 **Practical wisdom**   Developing practical wisdom; identify the 'right' purpose in a particular situation and is able to enact the 'right' response to accomplish that purpose; wisdom as a 'meta-virtue'

SKILLS DEVELOPMENT 7
GETTING THE RECIPE 'RIGHT' FOR LEADER AND LEADERSHIP DEVELOPMENT

For this exercise imagine that you're the HQ-based HRD adviser in a large grocery retailing organization. You have 3000 large stores distributed all over the country. Each store has a non-food manager (who has assistant managers for electrical and clothing), a food manager (who has assistant managers for fresh food and ambient food) and a personnel manager (who has a personnel assistant) who each report to the store manager, and the store manager reports to a regional manager, and all graduate trainees spend six months of their two-year programme in stores. The organization would like to introduce a 'Fit for the Future Development Program' which seeks to develop leaders and build leadership both within stores and across the business in general. You've been tasked by your boss, the Chief HR officer to produce a 'menu' of possible learning and development methods that could be used to deliver the 'Fit for the Future Development Program'. Your list of potential methods should specify the advantages and disadvantages of the available methods and make recommendations for a programme that will equip leaders with the necessary skills to take the business forward.

PART II
MACRO-HRD

8
THE BIGGER PICTURE

Contents

On completion of this chapter you should be able to:

- Describe and explain some of the challenges that business and society face as a result of 'megatrends' such as climate change, demographics, digitization, globalization, etc.;
- Offer practical suggestions for how HRD can support individuals and organizations in responding to these grand challenges.

Introduction

We live in interesting and unequal times. In 2016 Donald Trump occupied the White House for four extraordinary years, in 2019 the UK left the EU, and in 2020 COVID-19 wreaked havoc on lives and livelihoods across the globe. The smartphone that most of us carry on our person has more computing power than the supercomputers of the early 1990s.[1] Life expectancies in India in the 1950s were around 38 years, they are now closer to 70 years[2], and across the globe most people can now expect to live to at least 60 years. It is estimated that by 2050 there will be 2 billion over-sixty year-olds (up from 900 million in 2015). As far as learning is concerned, over the past half century enrolment in tertiary level education has risen from around ten per cent to almost 40 per cent.[3] The champions of scientific rationalism, such as the eminent cognitive psychologist and best-selling popular science author Stephen Pinker, argue that life has been getting progressively better for most people and that there's been no better time in human history to be alive.[4]

Alongside these positive transformations we also witnessed the rise of a right-wing populism that pitted 'the people' against 'experts' and 'elites', societal values became equated with celebrity and financial values, and the average income of the richest 10 per cent of the population was nine times that of the poorest 10 per cent across the OECD countries.[5] In 2019 there were, according to the UNHCR, almost 80 million forcibly displaced persons worldwide, 40 per cent of whom were children, representing approximately one per cent of the world's population.[6] According to the United Nations, climate change will impact the least developed countries disproportionality in spite of the fact that they have contributed least to the climate crisis,[7] and the whole world faces an environmental calamity if it fails to act effectively on carbon emissions.

Megatrends

The consulting group PricewaterhouseCoopers (PwC) defines 'megatrends' as 'macroeconomic and geostrategic forces that are shaping the world. They are factual and often backed by verifiable data. By definition, they are big and include some of society's biggest challenges – and opportunities'.[8] Megatrends are part of HRD's macro-context. These megatrends are having substantial impacts in terms of both the quantity and quality of jobs and how and by whom these jobs will be carried out across all nations. There are a number of significant opportunities and threats associated with the 'big three' megatrends of globalization, digitization and demography as identified by the Organization for Economic Cooperation and Development (OECD):

- New technologies and new markets mean that jobs that used to be carried out in one place by one or a small number of people can be 'de-bundled' into smaller task units and the work carried more efficiently on global 'digital' assembly lines;
- As a consequence workers will have more say about who they work for, how much they work and where and when they work; this creates both opportunities and challenges for everyone but especially for under-represented groups;
- Growing fears about mass unemployment in the advanced economies as production and other services and activities are 'offshored' and processes are automated and digitized, but also the 'reshoring' of jobs back to advanced economies creates challenges for less developed nations;
- The economic and social costs are likely to be felt most by those who are low-skilled and performing routine tasks that can be automated thus further fuelling disparities and inequalities, with concomitant negative effects on wealth and health.

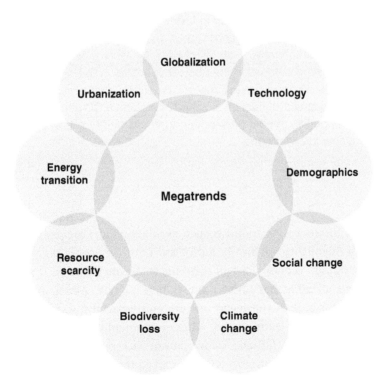

Figure 8.1 Megatrends

This is in a context in which economic and public health crises in one country can reverberate around a highly inter-connected globe with alarming rapidity, as was the case in the 2008 financial crisis and the 2020 pandemic. Other related megatrends and grand challenges that can be added to the OECD's list include climate change, loss of biodiversity, resource scarcity, energy transition, social change, and urbanization; see Figure 8.1.

Megatrends are sources of radical uncertainty. Take the megatrend of 'globalization' for example. Globalization is at the heart of the world economic order and has had many beneficial outcomes, for example economic development and increased living standards. However, uncertainty surrounds it and debates continue about whether globalization has been a force for good or bad. Some economists argue that globalization and free trade have fuelled growth, whilst others maintain that they've created and amplified inequalities.

In their own words 8.1

Nobel prize-winning economists Krugman and Stiglitz don't see eye-to-eye on globalization

Joseph Stiglitz (Nobel Prize in Economics 2001) argued that 'The rules of the game have been largely set by the advanced industrial countries' and that 'not surprisingly, they have shaped globalization to further their own interests'. The effect has been that 'they have not sought to create a fair set of rules, let alone a set of rules that would promote the well-being of those in the poorest countries of the world'. On the other hand, Paul Krugman (Nobel Prize in Economic Sciences 2008) argued that 'If we step back from a US perspective, step back actually from an OECD perspective, and take a ruthless cosmopolitan, global perspective, then this hyper-globalization thing has been an incredible force for good.'[9]

In spite of their differences, economists such as Stiglitz and Krugman agree that high levels of income inequality are clearly a problem both for economic as well as social reasons.[10] Even though economists will continue to debate the issue, it's clear that the megatrend of globalization has arrived and is here to stay. Along with other 'megatrends', it is a vital part of the bigger picture and especially so for HRD given the significant implications for learning and skills development in upskilling, reskilling and rectifying skill disparities within and across nations and societies. Barack Obama highlighted the importance of learning when he remarked that 'in a global economy, where the most valuable skill you can sell is your knowledge, a good education is no longer just a pathway to opportunity – it is a prerequisite'.[11]

Inequality
Unacceptable disparities exist across the globe in terms of living standards, health and economic well-being and opportunity.

Change
Technology and demographic change are immovable forces to which learning and development must adapt and respond.

Uncertainty
The future for the whole of humanity, as was highlighted vividly by the events of 2020, is volatile, uncertain, complex and ambiguous.

Figure 8.2 Some global 'certainties'

The same can be said of the other megatrends and their implications for learning, such as digitization (which has revolutionized accessibility to knowledge) and demographics (which has changed the structure and knowledge and skill requirements in the workforce). These and the other pressing global issues such as climate change, biodiversity loss, urbanization, etc. have created a macro-context in which inequality, change and uncertainty are endemic; see Figure 8.2.

Globalization

Globalization – the spread of products, technology, information, and jobs through the processes of free trade – has meant that people not only move more easily across international boundaries physically to work but also are able to work across international boundaries using technology. As a result nations, industries, institutions, organizations and people have become highly interdependent and intertwined. This has implications for the kinds of learning and development that employees and organizations require and also for how it takes place.

Challenges and opportunities for education, learning and development and HRD are presented by structural shifts in patterns of doing business and employment. For example, the OECD estimated that six out of ten adults lack basic IT skills, 14 per cent of jobs are at risk of automation and 32 per cent could be radically transformed as a result of technological developments. At the same time one in seven workers are self-employed, one in nine have a temporary contract, and participation in training by low-skilled adults is 40 per cent lower than for high-skilled adults.[12] In the UK the Commission for Employment and Skills has projected that by 2020 there will be an extra 1.5 million jobs in the service sector and 2 million more in 'white-collar' occupations and the majority of these will be in the IT sector.[13] The OECD's view is that governments and other institutions and professions who can influence learning and development at local, national and international levels will need to ensure that:

- workers are equipped with the right sorts of skills to add value in an increasingly technology-rich work environment;
- high quality pre-employment education and training is a right that is available for all;
- effective systems are in place for anticipating skills requirements and providing opportunities for workers to acquire those skills;
- systems of learning and development are as agile and anti-fragile as possible in order that they can respond quickly and effectively in the face of unknowns and in response to 'black swan' events.

Shifts towards sectors such as health care as the population ages and medical technology advances inexorably are a given. This shift will increase the requirement for softer skills to complement advanced technologies and automatization. At the same time demand for digital skills is surging. HRD can contribute to the challenges of globalization and technology by:

- Imparting the softer skills that complement AI and are indispensable in person-to-person interactions;
- Developing the creative skills to generate new and novel products and services;
- Empowering employees with the ultimate 'meta-skill' of learning how to learn.

Reflective question 8.1

To what extent have the megatrends discussed above and shown in Figure 8.1 affected you personally? Overall, have trends such as globalization, technology and demographics been a good or bad influence in your life so far? How have they affected your learning, education, and development in particular?

In the face of these challenges and opportunities, organizations and nations will require fit-for-purpose systems of lifelong learning, education and professional development in the form of learning ecosystems that are resilient and sustainable. The structural relationships are complex and intertwined; for example workers in advanced economies will need to upskill and re-skill as more and more routine jobs are off-shored; workers in developing economies run the risk of becoming trapped in low skill, low paid, low quality jobs with little prospect of any escape; and everyone will have to become more tech savvy and work for longer.

Using the head and heart at work

According to the OECD a significant part of global economic growth will be driven by creativity and innovation. This will require investment in the necessary skills, including 'soft skills' development.[14] Indeed the OECD and other organizations such as the CIPD have singled-out soft skills such as communication, leadership, team working and creativity, as potentially 'high value' skill sets since they're difficult to automate and copy and depend on human-to-human face-to-face interactions.

Research conducted on behalf of the CIPD into the need for soft skills in learning and development made a distinction between 'hard skills' (procedural, technical, scientific, domain specific) and 'soft skills' (people related, attitudinal, non-domain specific). Starting from the premise that there's 'much more to effective performance in the workplace than can be captured by cognitive intelligence, academic qualifications or hard technical skills alone' the report defined soft skills as:

'Experientially acquired self-, people- and task-related behaviours that complement the use of technical knowledge and skills in the workplace. They enable individuals to navigate successfully the requirements, challenges and opportunities of their job role in pursuit of personal, team or organisational goals.' (p. 20)

From a review of the policy-based literature the research identified three types of soft skills; see Figure 8.3.

Self-related soft skills
For example self-management skills
(such as self-related emotional intelligence),
learning how to learn, and moral skills
such as integrity

People-related soft skills
For example communication skills,
relating to others (such as other-related
emotional intelligence), leadership skills

Task-related soft skills
For example creativity, organizing skills,
problem solving skills and business related
skills (for example tacit knowledge of the
business and the practical intelligence to
navigate around it)

Figure 8.3 Three types of soft skill

(Continued)

One of the reasons cited for the importance of soft skills was that the majority of technical skills being taught in schools and universities are likely to be defunct by the time young people are ten years into their careers. Hence more durable and transferable softer skills and the generic skill of 'learning-how-to-learn' are likely to be vitally important in the longer-term. For example, soft skills are pivotal in enabling people to engage with others at work, whether face-to-face or virtually, and locally or globally. In days gone by the possession of technical skills offered protection in the job market, but now it's not a case of hard skills guaranteeing a job for life. Instead in a volatile, uncertain, complex and ambiguous business and social environment current and future generations of employees will need both hard and soft skills if they're to add value to themselves in terms of performance, career development and their personal well-being, as well as to their employing organizations and wider society.

Source: *Using the Head and Heart at Work* (2010). Wimbledon: CIPD.

Technology

Alongside, and inextricably intertwined with globalization, is the inexorable rise of technology as we enter the 'Fourth Industrial Revolution', 'Industry 4.0', or '4IR'.[15] For example, as far as learning and skills development are concerned one of the most dynamic areas of change is in the area of automatization. Skills and tasks, such as driving a vehicle, that could only until recently be performed by humans can now be performed by robots guided by artificial intelligence (AI). The rise of the 'gig economy' (where workers get paid on an ad hoc basis for the 'gigs' that they do such as delivering food) and 'platform economy' (where workers find work through online sourcing platforms and apps, such as Uber) has created demand for new ways of working and new types of knowledge and skill.[16] A report by the Wharton School at the University of Pennsylvania noted that whilst labour intensive jobs have already moved to emerging markets, new technologies may make even these occupations obsolete fuelling fears that robots could take away jobs in developing countries and further widening international disparities.[17] In the Fourth Industrial Revolution, boundaries between what is artificial and human-made and what is natural and real become blurred in a world powered by an 'internet of things'[18] (see Figure 8.4). The world is in the process of transitioning from an 'industrial era' to an 'information era' in which learning and the knowledge it creates and human creativity and the insights it reveals to us come into their own as one of the most important and sustainable sources of competitive advantage.

Machine learning (ML) is a technology (for example, in the form of complex, deep learning algorithms) that enable computer systems to be 'trained' and learn from data, examples and experience.[19] The OECD notes that advances in machine learning, data

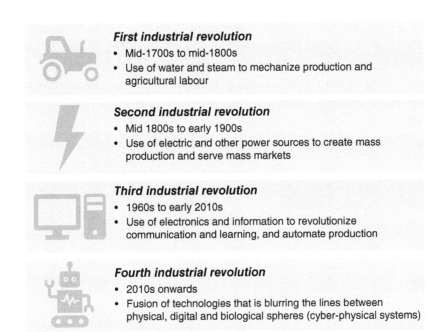

First industrial revolution
- Mid-1700s to mid-1800s
- Use of water and steam to mechanize production and agricultural labour

Second industrial revolution
- Mid 1800s to early 1900s
- Use of electric and other power sources to create mass production and serve mass markets

Third industrial revolution
- 1960s to early 2010s
- Use of electronics and information to revolutionize communication and learning, and automate production

Fourth industrial revolution
- 2010s onwards
- Fusion of technologies that is blurring the lines between physical, digital and biological spheres (cyber-physical systems)

Figure 8.4 Industrial revolutions in human history

analytics and AI are likely to create new jobs that haven't yet been imagined but nonetheless people are going to need to learn how to do these as yet unknown jobs.[20] HRD needs to have the foresight to anticipate and respond to these new skill requirements. These technological changes create opportunities for HRD for example by using big data to monitor performance and identifying performance gaps, designing 'chatbots' that automatically make training suggestions to employees, customization of training based on real-time performance data, and by chatbots and ML-based systems acting as virtual coaches or mentors.[21]

Delve deeper 8.1

Read more about this megatrend in The Fourth Industrial Revolution by world-renowned economist, Founder and Executive Chairman of the World Economic Forum (WEF), Klaus Schwab:

Schwab, K. (2017). *The fourth industrial revolution*. New York: Crown Business.

Read the about the HR implications of 4IR in:

World Economic Forum (2019). *HR4.0: Shaping people strategies in the fourth industrial revolution*. Geneva: WEF.

The opportunities and challenges that digitization offer for HRD are discussed in more depth in Chapter 11, 'Hybrid HRD'. Before we get too carried away with automation, AI and machine learning, we should note the comments of Leena Nair, Unilever's Chief HR Officer writing in 2019, who reminded us however, that 'the digital revolution is a human revolution', and that ultimately it's people who bring businesses to life and life to businesses.[22]

Reflective question 8.2

As a rough proportion, how much of your learning is 'screen-based'? Has this changed over your lifetime? Ask the same question of an older person, perhaps a 'baby boomer' (born between 1946 and 1964). Do you consider yourself a 'digital native', a 'digital convert' or a 'digital luddite'? Is digital learning the panacea that some have suggested it might be, is it simply one tool in the HRD toolkit, what can it do for HRD that a human can't and, on the other hand, what can a human do in HRD that a machine could never do?

Demographics

None of these megatrends exist in isolation. They are part of, and emerge out of, a complex interweaving of sociotechnical and environmental systems and sub-systems. For example, demographics interacts with and amplifies many of the challenges and opportunities associated with globalization and technology. As noted above, the OECD predicts that there'll be fewer births and longer life spans in all major regions of the world.[23] The implications for work, occupations and HRD are significant and manifest in different ways across the globe. In Japan the share of the working age population is anticipated to decline by 28 per cent. The decline in China's birth rate as a result of state policies allied to an increase in life expectancy means that there'll soon be 'too few workers to support an enormous and ageing population'.[24] In other countries working age population is predicted to balloon, for example in India by an estimated one-third. In many parts of the globe the retirement age is being pushed back (from 65 in 2012 to 67 in 2019 in Germany). A number of countries have adopted proactive policies towards older workers, for example by employers in Singapore offering 're-employment contracts' to eligible employees at 62 years of age whilst making it attractive for them to keep working albeit on a lower salary or in a different role. Many of these changes have significant implications for learning and development.[25]

The OECD notes that in countries with ageing workforces, the skills base of those who left full-time education years if not decades earlier are likely to be quickly out-moded and superseded by technological and cultural change, but people in these economies are required to stay in the workforce for longer as pension ages increase. A likely consequence will be labour shortages and the underuse of older people's talents and abilities. An imperative is created therefore for high quality systems of lifelong learning both in organizations and in the community to enable employees of all ages, especially those who are older, to up-skill and re-skill in order to stay employed or become reemployed and make a valid contribution to economic life whilst also attaining income, job satisfaction, personal fulfilment and well-being.

Older workers in ageing economics are going to have to not only learn new skills but also are going to have to work for longer whilst in the emerging markets, the gap between the supply of and demand for higher level skills is going to have to be filled. The educationalist Richard Bagnall, writing in the context of lifelong learning, argued that lifelong learning has four 'liberatory' outcomes. These outcomes reflect also the potential that HRD in organizations has to enhance inclusion and promote equity and fairness:

- Cognitive enlightenment giving liberation from ignorance;
- Individual empowerment giving liberation from dependence;
- Transformation of perspectives giving liberation from constraint;
- Individual personal development giving liberation from inadequacy.[26]

As neuroscience has shown, older workers have particular requirements as far as HRD is concerned but also have much to contribute based on their experience, expertise and wisdom (see Chapter 5). The CIPD noted a number of implications of demo-graphic changes,[27] for instance as older people eventually leave the workforce, they take with them knowledge and skills and experiences built up over a lifetime of learn-ing and working. On the other hand, it'll take time for their replacements to acquire knowledge, skills and expertise at the level of those that've left (given there's a 'ten-year rule of thumb' for the time that it takes to become an expert[28]). These two issues combined create the need to capture and pass on organizational knowledge, up-skill younger workers, and skill and re-skill older workers so that they can be employed meaningfully and for longer and also pass on their knowledge.[29] But as the CIPD notes, there are difficulties associated with these diversities and differences, for exam-ple older workers are less likely than younger colleagues to take part in or be offered training, and as we found in an earlier chapter there are brain-based differences in how older people learn. For good ethical and pragmatic reasons HRD needs to be made available for all workers at both ends of the age spectrum and at all points in between. As the need to re-skill older workers becomes more intense, lifelong learning has become a reality rather than a rhetoric.

Read about HRD-relevant megatrends in:

OECD (2017). *The future of work and skills*. OECD: Hamburg.

The CIPD has produced a number of reports on how various megatrends are affecting work and working lives, see:

www.cipd.co.uk/knowledge/work/trends/megatrends.

Find out more about the platform economy and its implications for working life in this report from the consulting group Deloitte:

www2.deloitte.com/content/dam/Deloitte/nl/Documents/humancapital/deloitte-nl-hc-reshaping-work-conference.pdf

Stakeholders

HRD, in the bigger picture, ought to be concerned with individual, societal and environmental well-being as well as with its traditional focus, organizational effectiveness. This is one reason why stakeholders (and not just shareholders) are important in HRD. HRD must be focused on creating value for its stakeholders. A stakeholder, broadly rather than narrowly defined, is a party (an individual or group of individuals) that has some vested interest in an organization and its operations. R Edward Freeman, a philosopher and business ethicist at the University of Virginia, in his pioneering work on stakeholder theory in the 1980s defined a stakeholder as 'any group or individual who can affect or is affected by the achievement of the organization's objectives'.[30] Freeman remarked in a TEDx talk that the only infinite resource that we have is in our minds ('our creative imagination') and that the '"juice" of business is our desire to create value for other people, to do something together no one of us can do alone'.[31] Regarding the important soft skill of creativity, the American poet Maya Angelou said that 'you can't use up creativity, the more you use it, the more you have' and Einstein is said to have remarked that 'imagination is more important than knowledge'.

'Stakeholder analysis' (SA) is a practical method for identifying, prioritizing and analysing the needs of different stakeholder groups.[32] These concepts and tools are useful because the axiom of maximizing shareholder value (MSV) has been challenged reflecting deeper problems with capitalism itself. In a critique of the assumptions on which much of modern business has been created, Freeman and colleagues have argued that we need to embrace a new set of assumptions about how value is conceptualized and created within the new, more resilient and sustainable vision of 'stakeholder capitalism'.

Discussions about stakeholders and capitalism necessarily entail, as Ed Freeman pointed out, consideration of 'value'. If HRD is about 'creating value' in and for organizations, fundamental questions arise about who benefits from the creation of this value?

Management and HRM has focused much of its attention traditionally on the needs of a dominant stakeholder group, which has customarily been the shareholders (and the senior managers in the organization), and this has influenced how HRM's and HRD's impact on performance has been 'operationalized' (that is, how the effect of what HRM and HRD 'do' is made measurable). The MSV model has dominated the global economy and management in general for many decades[33] and unsurprisingly, similar thinking has had a strong influence in HRM and HRD. This was part of a general, and undesirable trend towards equating societal value with financial value.[34] Taking a broader view encompasses other individuals/groups/entities who affect or are affected by HRD: employees (the group who receives HRD), HRD practitioners (the group that delivers HRD), managers (sponsors HRD), shareholders (gain financially from HRD), suppliers (provide/benefit from HRD), customers (benefit from HRD), the community/economy (impacted by HRD) and the natural environment (impacted indirectly by HRD).

But as critical HRD (CHRD) scholars Carole Elliot and Sharon Turnbull noted, a critical perspective in HRD does not assume that HRD's raison d'être consists solely to provide tools and methods principally designed to improve organizational performance. Instead it entails critical scrutiny of uncontested HRD philosophies and HRD practices that are taken for granted as being a 'good thing' (p. 2).[35] For example, the evaluation of HRD often focuses on the value that HRD creates in terms of return on investment (ROI) measured in monetary terms. This position privileges monetary value above other measures of worth.

Questions can, and arguably should, be asked about what constitutes 'value and worth', and whether what is of value and worth differs according to the perspective of different stakeholder groups. For example the value that HRD is perceived as having will be different for an employee (by helping them to do their job better or realize their personal and career potential), a senior leader (by helping the business achieve its strategic goals) or a shareholder (by adding value to the stock price of the firm). Unfortunately, a bias towards MSV has tended to undermine the importance of other stakeholders' perspectives across value and supply chains.

Encouragingly, in recent years the considerations of different stakeholder groups have begun to take a more prominent position in terms of what constitutes value and worth. For example, the USA Business Roundtable (a group of chief executives from America's top businesses, such as Amazon, Apple, Ford Motor Company, JP Morgan, Johnson & Johnson, etc.) published a statement that:

- Redefined the purpose of a corporation to promote an 'economy that serves all Americans';
- Moved away from shareholder primacy, includes commitment to all stakeholders.[36]

Conflicts are inevitable when the interests of a single group, typically capital market shareholders, are given priority. Stakeholder theory and the idea of multiple stakeholders is also captured in John Elkington's 'triple bottom-line (3BL) framework'; see Figure 8.5.[37]

Economic bottom line ('Profit')
- Impact (positive and negative) that an organization has on local, national and international economy
- Including wealth creation, tax revenue, innovation, employment, etc.

Environmental bottom line ('Planet')
- Impact (positive and negative) that an organization has on the natural environment
- Including reducing carbon footprint, effects on land-use, biodiversity, etc.

Social bottom line ('People')
- Impact (positive and negative) that an organization has on its stakeholders
- Including employees, suppliers, communities, and any other person affecting or being affected by the organization

Figure 8.5   Triple bottom line (3BL) framework[1]

[1]Kraaijenbrink, J. (2019). What the 3ps of the triple bottom line really mean. *Forbes*, 10 December. Available online: www.forbes.com/sites/jeroenkraaijenbrink/2019/12/10/what-the-3ps-of-the-triple-bottom-line-really-mean/ (accessed 27-01-21).

The 3BL model accommodates economic, social and environmental impacts, and acknowledges social and environmental as well as the economic embeddedness/responsibility of business and organizations' corporate social responsibility (CSR) obligations.

These issues and challenges relating to who are organizations' stakeholders have not gone unnoticed in HRD; indeed they have become more important in recent years as related issues such as ethics have moved more centre-stage in HRD. One of the earliest HRD studies that used stakeholder theory was by Thomas Garavan in the 1990s in which he identified various internal and external HRD stakeholder groups and their respective interests; for example, line managers (internal) and trade unions (external).[38] The question of who are HRD's internal and external stakeholders impacts directly on the issues of how HRD can add value for groups other than capital market stakeholders and the tensions between different groups of stakeholders. The question of HRD's purpose (see Chapter 1) highlighted tensions between HRD's 'performance purpose' (which might tend to privilege capital market stakeholders) and HRD's 'learning purpose' (which might tend to focus on the needs of individual employees). If we extend this discussion and take customers as an example of a group who are potential stakeholders in HRD, what can HRD do to add value for this group? One way in which HRD could add value is by enhancing the service quality offering that a business provides, and it could do so by enhancing employees' knowledge and skill in service quality and changing their attitudes towards service quality. HRD can therefore influence employees' ability to deliver customer satisfaction, which impacts on customer behaviour and loyalty, which then can affect company performance. In this example the effect of HRD on company performance is mediated through customer satisfaction. A positive effect on one stakeholder group (such as customers) has a positive effect on a different stakeholder group (shareholders). This example illustrates that the interests of different stakeholder groups are not necessarily mutually exclusive. Synergies can be created when an 'either/or mindset' in which there is a trade-off between learning and performance is replaced by a 'both/and' or 'paradox mindset' in which the tensions are used constructively. For example, unions exist to uphold the interests of employees and unions' views can be important in articulating what employees' needs are and how these might be addressed, and offer a counter-balance to a purely managerialist and shareholder perspective.[39]

Research insight 8.1

Embracing paradox to create synergies

Marianne Lewis and Wendy K Smith offer a guide for researching and managing paradoxes in business. They define a paradox as contradictory yet inter-related elements that exist simultaneously and persist over time. A well-known example in management is the paradox of exploration-versus-exploitation in organizational learning (see Chapter 12).[40] In HRD the relationship between learning and performance has been framed as a contradictory juxtaposition of opposites that requires either the privileging of learning or performance. But as Lewis and Smith point out, actors' responses to these relationships determine outcomes:

- Defensive reactions to paradoxes entail emphasizing one pole, for example (in HRD) 'performance', which fuels pressure from its opposite pole, for example 'learning'. This dynamic creates a 'vicious downward spiral' in which tensions are exacerbated;
- Embracing and accepting the tensions between, for example, learning and performance in the learning-performance paradox can catalyse divergent thinking and creative ways to reconcile tensions and fuel synergies that enable 'peak performance' thus creating a 'virtuous upward spiral'.

Lewis and Smith argue that paradox thinking (that is a 'both/and' rather than either/or' mind-set) is relevant especially in complex and dynamic environments and when organizations are seeking to satisfy multiple goals.

Source: Lewis, M. W., & Smith, W. K. (2014). Paradox as a metatheoretical perspective: Sharpening the focus and widening the scope. *The Journal of Applied Behavioral Science*, *50*(2), 127–149.

─Delve deeper 8.3─

Read about stakeholders, 'stakeholder capitalism', critiques of stakeholder theory, how to do a 'stakeholder analysis', and a model of 'stakeholder-based HRD' in:

Baek, P., & Kim, N. (2014). Exploring a theoretical foundation for HRD in society: Toward a model of stakeholder-based HRD. *Human Resource Development International*, 17(5), 499–513.

Freeman, R. E., Martin, K., & Parmar, B. (2007). Stakeholder capitalism. *Journal of Business Ethics*, 74(4), 303–314.

Stieb, J. A. (2009). Assessing Freeman's stakeholder theory. *Journal of Business Ethics*, 87(3), 401–414.

For practical guidance on how to conduct a stakeholder analysis consult:

Brugha, R., & Varvasovszky, Z. (2000). Stakeholder analysis: A review. *Health Policy and Planning*, 15(3), 239–246.

Power, politics and diversity

Power is the capacity of an individual or group of individuals to influence or exercise control over the actions, beliefs and behaviour of other individuals or groups in order to achieve their goals. In his book *Power: A New Social Analysis* (1938), the Nobel Prize winning philosopher Bertrand Russell (1872–1970) wrote that 'The fundamental concept in social science is Power, in the same sense in which Energy is the fundamental concept in physics' (p. xxiv).[41] Power can be positive in the sense of being creative and empowering but also negative in the sense of being constraining or antagonistic.[42]

Power follows on naturally from a discussion of stakeholders in HRD because different stakeholder groups have differing amounts of power and influence. And power in organizations is political because it's about 'who gets to decide'. Power is related to our assumptions about not only *what* is 'real' (and relevant) but also *who* gets to choose what is real and relevant. This decision has a profound influence as follows (which paraphrases Ed Schein):

- Power determines which members of a group decide what counts as 'relevant information' and how they interpret that information;
- Power influences how they determine when they, as the dominant group, have enough information to decide, whether or not to act, and what action they should take.[43]

The question as to what counts as relevant information and who gets to decide is pertinent to many of the most important aspects of HRD from the decision of who gets to participate in HRD and what form HRD takes right through to the evaluation of HRD's impact (and for example, what counts as 'impact'). As Malcolm Knowles and colleagues noted in the classic HRD text *The Adult Learner* (2015), when the learners' needs and the organizations' needs are congruent there is no tension between their interests, however, when an individual's learning needs are not congruent with the organization's performance requirements (operationalized, for example, in terms of profit) then tension may be created, and this 'inevitably results in some degree of organizational control' (p. 155). Knowles and colleagues highlight this as a justification for why HRD practices must try to balance the interests of not only employees and managers, but also other internal and external stakeholders as well.[44]

More generally, critical HRD researchers have argued that power and influence, and power dynamics, receive little attention in HRD.[45] Russ Vince, for example, suggested that there are a number of ways in which HRD research and practice can address the issues arising from power by acknowledging that:

- The practice of learning and development in organizations is beset with contradictions (for example, the performance and learning purposes of HRD) but this acknowledgement can be a spur to a process of critical reflection on the design and implementation of HRD;
- Learning and development interventions themselves sometimes de-problematize the issue of power when in fact in 'facilitating' another person's learning we may actually be, albeit unconsciously and unintentionally, exercising control and coercion over them;
- The learning environment offers opportunities to reinforce organizational identities (for example, learner versus instructor) but also to contest them constructively.

Vince also concludes that it's unrealistic to expect HRD to have a positive and sustainable effect on individuals and organizations without engaging critically with notions of power.[46] In a similar vein, Laura Bierema and Jamie Callahan argue that HRD has ignored power dynamics and power relations – as well as much wider issues such as patriarchy, sexism, diversity and racism – because, in their view, scrutinizing power is a risky enterprise for HRD which is inherently 'masculine rational'. They argue that the consequences are that HRD privileges 'performativity' and patriarchal power and helps in the 'commodifying' of workers. This transforms learning relationships into transactions of monetary value that are ultimately beholden to shareholders, thus putting HRD in a 'no-win' situation when, for example, it has to compromise personal ethics to achieve managerial expectations and overlook power relations. They propose critical HRD (CHRD) as a way to confront the fundamental question of 'whom do we [HRD] serve?' (p. 437).

Consequences of power asymmetries in the evaluation of HRD

In a qualitative study of understanding how power relations amongst stakeholders affects the evaluation process for a training programme in a Korean business organization, the researchers focused on a Manager Leadership Development Course (MLDC). The aims of the programme were to enable learners to develop key management knowledge and human relations/leadership skills and acquire problem-solving skills through action learning. It consisted of a one-week in-class session and four weeks of action learning. Three HRD practitioners were responsible for the evaluation. Data were collected by means of surveys completed by the learners and the instructors and interviews with representatives of five different stakeholder groups (HRD practitioners; one corporate manager; two instructors; one learner; and one colleague).

The researchers discovered that although the HRD practitioners' professional expertise was a source of their power, the power relationships within the organization were asymmetric in favour of the senior managers. Amongst the findings of this study was that despite the widely acknowledged criticisms of reaction-level evaluation measures (that is, end-of-course 'happiness sheets'; see Chapter 12), positive learners' reactions were used by the HRD practitioners as critical 'evidence' to uphold the power of their positions and efforts in the face of higher levels of senior manager power. Likewise, senior managers (who lacked training expertise) believed that positive reactions were a vital criterion for success. As a result positive reactions signalled successful functioning of the HRD, and 'the instructors also stated they sought positive feedback so that they could be rehired for the next programme' (p. 15). Learners' reactions were critical in maintaining a good relationship with the host organization and in justifying the programme. Even though the HRD practitioners were aware of the limitations of reaction level measures, reactions were nonetheless a 'politically powerful measure to advocate each stakeholder group's interests'. As the researchers noted, these findings raise important ethical issues in the evaluation of HRD, and the role that power has on the conduct of the process.

Source: Kim, H., & Cervero, R. M. (2007). How power relations structure the evaluation process for HRD programmes. *Human Resource Development International*, *10*(1), 5–20.

The issue of power and the asymmetries of power that exist in HRD as well as in organizations in general can be opened up to scrutiny when HRD researchers and practitioners come to the realization, as Kiran Trehan has pointed out, of how powerful managers are, yet how poorly 'traditional HRD' has prepared them for considering questions of power and influence and the responsibility that this entails.[47] Critics argue that only by politicizing HRD can prevailing relations of power be challenged and meaningful and lasting change be achieved. CHRD is an alternative which makes the claim that a negative effect of the 'dominant rationality' in HRD has been to marginalize those groups who, for structural and historical reasons, have had less power traditionally in a masculine hegemony.[48]

Writing from a critical perspective about the role of stakeholders in HRD, Sally Sambrook argued that particular groups of employees, 'particularly those marginalized by gender, age, education, ethnicity, disability and sexual orientation', have a particular stake in HRD in terms of seeking the right to learn, be involved in setting their learning agendas and having a right and responsibility to perform their roles effectively. She also points to the importance of managers' responsibility and commitment to these issues in terms of ensuring employees' right to learn regardless of age, disability, ethnicity, gender, sexual orientation, etc.[49]

It's clear therefore that HRD researchers and practitioners have a responsibility to examine critically the assumptions, beliefs and values that underlie their research and practice. The challenges that traditional masculine rationality poses for HRD have already been discussed, but in the same vein Laura Bierema and Maria Cseh asked the related question of 'to what extent is HRD based on feminist inquiry?', recognizing gender as a social construction in HRD research and practice. They identified the following as some of the critical issues that need to be addressed in taking HRD forward in ways that promote social change by reducing power asymmetries and supporting gender justice:

- Sexism and bias in research should be corrected by extending the populations to be studied beyond white, middle class college student samples (sometimes referred to as WEIRD samples),[50] and by legitimizing a wider range of research methodologies;
- Uncovering and discovering women's contributions to HRD research and women's role in the history of HRD and valuing women as a 'legitimate target of study' in HRD research thereby bringing women's voices into the knowledge creation and dissemination process;
- Recognizing power asymmetries in the workplace and in society more generally in terms of women's subordinate status as a product of 'unequal power distribution instead of deficiencies' and in recognition of the influence of power arrangements and masculine rational hegemonies on women's lives.

Julie Gedro remarked that 'LGBT issues remain controversial and complex' and represent 'perhaps one of the newer and the most misunderstood, and sometimes even feared, aspect of diversity'[51] (p. 365). As Gedro notes, from a pedagogical standpoint it's indisputable that the dynamics within any learning space need to be treated with care and skill 'so that students feel that the learning environment is safe and inclusive for all of them'. Building on this important emerging area of scholarship and practice Ann

Brooks and Kathleen Edwards, in a study of what LGBT allies do in the workplace, argue that HRD researchers and practitioners are also 'qualified uniquely' to take the lead in enabling organizations to act fairly for LGBT persons in terms of safety, inclusion and equity. They suggest this can be achieved in a number of ways, for example by education (such as in new employee orientation and diversity training), advocacy (by confronting bias and discriminatory behaviours), and organizational change (such as developing leader to champion change that addresses LGBT safety, inclusion and equity). They also argue for more research into issues around LGBT and learning in the workplace to develop better knowledge of the challenges that HRD faces and opportunities it has to foster meaningful change. All of which requires, as Brooks and Edwards note, ethical values and moral courage.

Delve deeper 8.4

Read about critical HRD, particularly in relation to gender and social justice, in:

Bierema, L., & Callahan, J. L. (2014). Transforming HRD: A framework for critical HRD practice. *Advances in Developing Human Resources, 16*(4), 429–444.

Byrd, M. Y. (2014). A social justice paradigm for HRD. In Chalofsky, N., Rocco, T., & Morris, M. L. (eds) *Handbook of human resource development.* Hoboken, NJ: Wiley, pp. 281–298.

Callahan, J. L., & Elliott, C. J. (2020). Gender hegemony and its impact on HRD research and practice. *Human Resource Development International, 23*(5), 469–472.

Environmental sustainability

Climate change is real, anthropogenic in origin, and threatens irreversible and dangerous impacts on the whole Earth system. The effects are being felt already in the most vulnerable ecosystems and human communities. The sudden and irreversible change in the Earth's climate to a new stable state that is non-munificent for human well-being is the greatest danger that humanity has faced. Business is a major cause but also can be a large part of the cure. It is estimated that greenhouse gas (GHG) emissions from a selection of global 500 companies approximate to those of the USA and the EU15 combined. Many of the managers, leaders and executives who run these organizations have business school degrees therefore it is plausible that management education and HRD are well-placed to influence how corporations respond to climate change. According to the Intergovernmental Panel on Climate Change (2014) mitigating severe, pervasive, and irreversible effects of climate change on people and ecosystems requires immediate, 'substantial and sustained reductions in greenhouse gas emissions' (p. 6). The Paris

Agreement, signed in April 2016, undertook 'to strengthen the global response to the threat of climate change by keeping a global temperature rise this century well below 2 degrees Celsius above pre-industrial levels'. Figure 8.6 (the Keeling curve) shows the change in CO_2 levels in the Earth's atmosphere. The symbolic threshold of 400 ppm was crossed in September 2016. Last time it was this high the world was several degrees hotter, sea levels were tens of metres higher, and horses and camels lived in the high Arctic.[52]

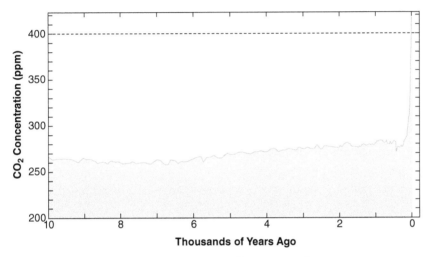

Figure 8.6 Keeling curve showing CO_2 concentration in Earth's atmosphere

An objective method for meeting obligations for greenhouse gas emissions reduction is through 'science based targets'. SBTs can be used to show companies how much and how quickly they need to reduce their greenhouse gas (GHG) emissions to prevent the worst effects of climate change. However, if SBTs are to be successful, employees in organizations have to learn about the climate science, accept them and behave in ways that are consistent with the science-based approach.[54] An emissions' reduction strategy is science-based if it is:

- Founded on relevant principles from physical and environmental science (sometimes referred to as Earth System Science);
- Aligned with the scale of GHG reductions necessary to keep global temperature increase below 2°C above pre-industrial levels.

Being 'science-based' in this context means that organizations should not set imprecise, arbitrary targets based simply on what is achievable or affordable, or to keep up with their peers, appease investors, grab a headline, or fit into a Tweet. Regrettably, an arbitrary, headline-grabbing target of 'halving our emissions by 2050[55]' is much more likely to be encountered rather than a much more precise statement such as Ericsson's '35 percent by 2022'.[56] There are good business reasons why managers should be motivated to adopt a science-based approach in emissions reduction strategies:

- Builds a business' resilience, sustainability and hence its competitiveness for a low-carbon economy in ways that go beyond mere costs savings and avoiding the risk of stranded assets;
- Drives innovations and transforms business practices in an informed way that prioritizes for the long-term;
- Enhances business' credibility and reputation with multiple stakeholders because it is based on the best scientific evidence;
- Offers lower-risk options for investors over the longer-term;
- Anticipates policy changes and future mandated adjustments proactively and may influence policy reciprocally.[57]

It is encouraging that 'green' issues have transitioned from being on the fringes of organizational discourse to being very much centre stage, and organizations are now required to demonstrate how they are becoming more environmentally responsible and responsive. In order to do so, managers will need a knowledge of the fundamentals of Earth system science (ESS), and HRD is well-placed to make this happen. Given this imperative, it is encouraging that a number of HRD scholars have taken a keen interest in environmental issues and sustainability.[58] For example, Claire Valentin proposed a framework for a 'green' HRD that transcends national boundaries operating at three levels;[59] see Figure 8.7.

David McGuire has argued that one way in which HRD can exercise leverage in this area is to 're-educate' (one of six Rs in his model for green HRD: the others are reduce, reuse, recycle, redesign, renew) so that employees are able to make sense of the science and the environmental consequences of their actions.[60] How might this be achieved? Research suggests that learning about climate change in ways that motivate meaningful changes in behaviour is more likely to be effective if the presentation of information is designed in such a way as to appeal both to learners' heads and hearts rather than their heads or their hearts. This is on the basis that human beings process information in two contrasting and complementary ways that reflect the operation of two systems of

Tactical green HRD

- Providing support for the organization in reducing waste, re-using and recycling
- Development of corporate social responsibility (CSR)
- Environmental education for employees

Strategic green HRD

- Promoting sustainability as part of the 'corporate glue'
- Unified sense of mission
- Culture of a transition to 'net zero'

Transformational green HRD

- Embedding sustainability into corporate HRD philosophy and practice
- Problematization and critical reflection on corporate assumptions and values as well as on ways of behaving
- Fostering organizational learning and change that is commensurate with reducing negative impacts on whole Earth system.

Figure 8.7 Valentin's Framework for green HRD (Valentin, 2015)

reasoning, a 'hot' intuitive/experiential system (System 1) and a 'cold' analytical/rational system (System 2). One of the problems associated with communicating the risk associated with climate change has been that spatial factors (its effects may be on other people far away) and temporal factors (the main effects will be on future generations) mean that people in developed countries here and now may not take the threats as seriously as they ought to, and consequently they fail to engage in climate change mitigation. Appealing to System 1 through the use of narratives, images and metaphors, as well as to System 2 through hard facts about temperature changes and sea level rises, is more likely to mobilize and motivate meaningful action.[61]

Delve deeper 8.5

Extend your knowledge of green and sustainability issues in HRD by consulting McGuire's call for a greater attention to environmental issues in HRD in his eight-point 'greenprint' for engaging organizations in meaningful and positive environmental change:

McGuire, D. (2010). Engaging organizations in environmental change: A greenprint for action. *Advances in Developing Human Resources, 12*(5), 508–523.

Read more about the psychology of developing employees' understanding of green issues by reading Sadler-Smith's discussion of how to mobilize intuitive and analytical cognition in making sense of global warming in:

(Continued)

Sadler-Smith, E. (2014). Making sense of global warming: Designing a human resource development response. *European Journal of Training and Development*, 38(5), 387–397.

Discover more about HRD's role in CSR more generally as well as environmental sustainability by consulting Jang and Ardichvili's content analysis of corporate social responsibility reports:

Jang, S., & Ardichvili, A. (2020). The role of HRD in CSR and sustainability: A content analysis of corporate responsibility reports. *European Journal of Training and Development*, 44(6/7), 559–573.

Finally, Scully-Ross offers a conceptual framework for understanding HRD's role in 'greening efforts' in the introduction to a special issue collection of articles on this topic in *Advances in Developing Human Resources*:

Scully-Russ, E. (2015). The contours of green human resource development. *Advances in Developing Human Resources*,17(4), 411–425.

Trust and HRD

At the heart of many of these 'big picture' issues is 'trust', for example trust between employees and senior leaders, trust between stakeholders, trust between organizations and their context, trust between voters and politicians, and trust that human ingenuity and cooperation will solve many of the challenges that megatrends pose to humanity. Trust comes from an old Norse word *traustr* meaning 'strong', and for a group living primate that relies heavily on cooperation such as *Homo sapiens*, the capacity to trust others is the 'glue' in social relations.[62] Trust researchers Reinhard Bachmann and Akbar Zaheer remind us 'trust is the beginning of everything'. In fact *'Vertrauenist der Anfang von allem'* was the Deutsche Bank slogan in the early 1990s but as Der Spiegel noted if 'everything starts with trust' then it can also be argued that 'lost trust is the beginning of the end'.[63] Denise Rousseau and colleagues argued that trust is important in organizational life for a number of reasons, including:

- Trust enables cooperative behaviour, reduces harmful conflicts and decreases transaction costs and, on the downside, lack or loss of trust can undermine risk taking, information sharing and access to resources;
- Trust promotes adaptive and flexible organizational forms such as networks and facilitates the rapid formulation of ad hoc work groups; on the downside lack of trust makes the establishment and effective functioning of such groups and relations difficult if not impossible to achieve.[64]

According to Rousseau and colleagues, trust entails a 'willingness to be vulnerable' and a 'willingness to rely' based on positive expectations of others, but as Bachman and Zaheer also remind us, trust (at least in financial institutions) was seriously undermined in the 2008 crash, and there's a well-known saying that 'trust takes years to build, seconds to break, and forever to repair'. Mark Saunders and colleagues found that employees' trust and distrust judgements are shaped to a large extent by managerial actions and policies, especially those relating to quality of communications and the fundamental issue of job security. When employees become distrustful, interventions (including organization development and HRD solutions) may be needed in order to rebuild trust.[65]

Trust is relevant to HRD for many of the same reasons as in management and organizations in general. However HRD researchers have highlighted a number of specific issues in relation to HRD and trust. For example, a lack of credibility in HRD can undermine senior managers' trust in HRD as a strategic partner, which may consign it to a diminished operational and tactical role in organizations. As Claire Gubbins and colleagues have noted, HRD has to achieve a fine balance between stakeholders, whose interests may at times diverge radically, in order to build trusting relationships with all parties. As noted earlier, this raises ethical and moral challenges for HRD practitioners.[66] In a business context where HRD is required to respond both to management and employee agendas, it's in everyone's interests that HRD reaches 'upwards' towards senior managers as their strategic partner but also reaches 'outwards' simultaneously as a 'learning partner' for all employees.[67] In a world context where the megatrends such as globalization, technology and demographics mean that the only certainty is uncertainty, it is vital that HRD plays its role in building a better future for all of its stakeholders.

Delve deeper 8.6

Read more about trust and HRD in:

Gubbins, C., Harney., B., van der Werff, L., and Rousseau, D. M. (2018). Enhancing the trustworthiness and credibility of HRD: Evidence-based management to the rescue? *Human Resource Development Quarterly*, 29(3), 193–202.

Gubbins, C., and MacCurtain, S. (2008). Understanding the dynamics of collective learning: The role of trust and social capital. *Advances in Developing Human Resources*, 10(4), 578–599.

Conclusion: Grand challenges

In 2013 President Barack Obama declared that 'grand challenges' were 'ambitious but achievable goals that harness science, technology and innovation to solve important national or global problems'.[68] Megatrends create grand challenges for HRD and can capture its imagination in terms of how it deploys its body of scientific, evidence-based, practical knowledge in responding positively to globalization, technology, demographics, climate change, etc. Through the processes of individual and organizational learning, and career, talent, leadership and organization development, HRD can be a source of productive solutions and positive change in response to many of the pressing problems faced by individuals, organizations, societies and humanity in general. In rising to the grand challenges, HRD should position itself, and be positioned as, a strategic partner; should marshal its skills, resources and reputation in pursuit of equity, fairness, inclusion and social justice; should think systemically and ecologically; should recognize the needs of all of its stakeholders; and should leverage learning and the knowledge that learning creates in the pursuit of the greater good.

In spite of all of its achievements, humanity remains essentially vulnerable in nature's grand scheme, but its ability to respond to challenges and exploit opportunities by learning, creating, inventing and innovating is one of humanity's main sources of resilience and sustainability. What can HRD add in the face of such scale and uncertainty? The broad definition of HRD offered by Gary and Laird McClean is both instructive and inspiring: 'HRD is any process or activity that, either initially or over the longer term, has the potential to develop adult's work based knowledge, expertise productivity and satisfaction, whether for group/team gain, or the benefit of an organization, community, nation or, ultimately, the whole of humanity.'[69] This definition speaks to why HRD matters in a volatile, uncertain, complex and ambiguous world. By responding to megatrends and grand challenges, HRD stands uniquely placed to be able to benefit not just individuals and organizations, but perhaps the whole of humanity.

Chapter checkout

Use this list to check your understanding of the key points of this chapter.

1 **Megatrends** Megatrends are macroeconomic and geostrategic forces that shape the world and to which individuals, organizations and societies must respond to survive and thrive; they're part of HRD's macro-context

2 **Globalization** Globalization is the spread of products, technology, information, and jobs through processes of free trade; people, capital and information move across international boundaries; there have been winners and losers from globalization

3 **Digitization** Technological advancements are resulting in more information- and service-related jobs, jobs that can be automated will decline; this creates skills shortages and changes in employment patterns

4 **Demographics** People have longer working lives; older people need new skills; younger people need learning and job opportunities commensurate with their abilities, education, motivations, skills and aspirations

8 **Stakeholders** Stakeholders are those who have some vested interest in an organization and its operations; traditionally shareholder interests have been privileged; in recent years the interests of a wider constituency of shareholders are acknowledged and accommodated

9 **Power** Power is important, and political, in HRD because it can influence which learning and development issues are important, what actions are taken and who gets to decide the questions and their answers

10 **Sustainability**   HRD can influence sustainability issues, including climate change, at the tactical, strategic and transformation levels; HRD's influence begins with the education of employees on the criticality of the climate emergency

11 **Diversity**   HRD has the potential to promote equity, fairness and human excellence by liberating all employees from ignorance, dependence, constraints and inadequacies

12 **Trust**   Trust enhances HRD's potential to be a strategic partner, building trust is essential for balancing potentially conflicting interests in HRD policy and practice

SKILLS DEVELOPMENT 8
GRAND CHALLENGES AND HRD'S RESPONSE

The world in which HRD operates presents practical and ethical 'grand challenges' as a result of 'megatrends' such as globalization, digitization, demographics, climate change, justice, equity and fairness, etc. Imagine that you've been called for interview for an entry level HRD post at an oil company which is undergoing radical transition from a vertically integrated oil and gas company (exploration, production, refining, distribution and trading) to an integrated energy company with rapidly developing interests in hydrogen, biofuels, solar and wind. The Executive Board, including the CEO, are predominantly Caucasian males with engineering backgrounds, mostly over the age of 45 years. The CEO has signed-up to a recent declaration by the 'Business Roundtable' (see above) which redefines the purpose of a corporation and undertakes to lead businesses for the benefits of all stakeholders and the planet. You have been asked to prepare a PowerPoint Presentation as part of the selection process; the chair of the selection panel will be the HR director. The presentation should last 15 minutes precisely and highlight the five main 'grand challenges' that the business faces and how HRD can help to address them. Prepare a PowerPoint (in accordance with the guidelines for best practice) entitled 'Preparing for an Uncertain Future: The Role of HRD'.

9

HRD AS A STRATEGIC PARTNER

Contents

On completion of this chapter you should be able to:

* Describe and explain the theory and practice of strategic HRD;
* Explain the relationships between strategic HRD and performance;
* Critically evaluate strategic HRD.

Introduction

It may seem slightly incongruous that the leading strategic management scholars John Kotter and Dan Cohen wrote in their widely acclaimed book *The Heart of Change* that 'The central issue is never strategy, structure, culture, or systems…the core of the matter is always about changing the behaviour of people.'[1] This chapter explores why. It begins by looking at strategy in general, it then focuses on strategy in HR and then on strategy in HRD in particular.

There's an old saying that 'a vision without a strategy is nothing more than a hallucination'. But what is a 'strategy'? A strategy is a longer-term plan for achieving a higher-level goal such as a 'vision' or 'mission'. For example, Bill Gates' vision when he set up Microsoft was simple and clear, it was to have 'a computer on every desk and in every home'[2]. Without a strategy this vision would have been only a vague aspiration.[3] One of the leading strategic management textbooks defines business strategy as 'the *direction* and *scope* of an organization over the *long-term*, which achieves *advantage* in a changing *environment* through its configuration of *resources and competencies* with the aim of fulfilling *stakeholder* expectations'.[4]

Organizations that achieve advantage in a fast-changing environment will survive and thrive, whilst those that don't will decline and eventually perish. To survive and thrive organizations need a strategy that acknowledges trends (including megatrends such as globalization, technology and demography) in the external environment. The Arcadia retail group in the UK – owner of famous high street brands such as Topshop – collapsed in 2020, many believe because its boss, Phillip Green, was (according to someone who worked with him) 'not strategic at all, there [was] no long-term plan'.[5] In particular Green was reluctant to engage with the megatrend of technology and its applications in online retailing. Arcadia ended up being outcompeted by the likes of e-retailers such as Boohoo and Asos.

What this and other examples of corporate failures demonstrate very clearly is that in a present that's volatile and complex and a future that's uncertain and ambiguous, organizations need at least three things to be able to survive and thrive:

* The 'managerial foresight' for imagining what the organization wants to be;

- The 'strategic competence' for developing and implementing a long-term plan for how the organization is going to get there;
- The right people with the right knowledge, skills and creative abilities ('human capital') to get the organization to where it wants to be; see Figure 9.1.

Figure 9.1   Managerial foresight ('where do you want to be?'), strategic competence ('how will you get there?') and human capital ('who will get you there?')

The right people with the right knowledge and skills and creative abilities are often claimed to be an organization's most important asset – a critical success factor for every organization in making the transition from an industrial to an information/knowledge economy.

Knowledge and skills, acquired through learning (formal and informal) and experience (incidental or planned), are a unique asset, or form of 'capital', which can help an organization to get from where it is now to where it wants to be. The idea of 'human capital', the roots of which can be traced back to Adam Smith (1723–1790) in his *Wealth of Nations*, is often associated with the work of Nobel Prize winning economist Gary Becker (1930–2014) and others of the so-called 'Chicago School'. In his 1964 book *Human Capital* Becker wrote that human capital is the knowledge, skills and experience possessed by individual employees that enables employees to achieve their goals individually and collectively; it can be developed by investing in education and training and has a rate of return that can be evaluated.[6] The implications for HRD are significant because:

- Human capital is a unique asset compared to other forms of capital (such as financial capital) because of human beings' exceptional capacities to learn and create knowledge, inventions and artefacts – everything from the wheel to the smartphone – that never existed before;
- It's very difficult to separate people from their knowledge and skills, especially their 'tacit' knowledge, which aren't 'owned' by their organization as such but can be secured through the employment relationship;

- Knowledge and skills can be developed by investing in HRD and managing HRD practices, processes and systems effectively.

As far as why strategy matters for HRD, and why HRD matters for strategy, are concerned, HRD has a vital role to play in getting an organization from where it is now to where it wants to be. HRD adds value to this strategic process by helping to ensure that the work-force possesses the right knowledge, skills and abilities, that they're kept up-to-date and that is has the capability to produce new knowledge. In the face of the bigger picture issues, HRD has the choice of whether to be a 'strategic partner' or a 'strategic passenger'.

- HRD as strategic passenger: engaging in the 'passive provision' of learning and development activities that are of marginal value and dubious benefit, that are out of touch with the new world of work and incapable of delivering demonstrable benefits for stakeholders, will consign HRD to the fringes of an organization;
- HRD as strategic partner: investing in and aligning value-adding HRD practices and processes with business strategy so as to deliver tangible benefits for the organization and its stakeholders will ensure that HRD has a place at the table as a strategic business partner that can yield significant returns in terms of performance, productivity and profitability.

One of the main goals and challenges of HRD research and practice is to identify which types of learning and development practices, processes and systems lead to superior performance and support the realization of organizational strategy whilst also enabling each individual to contribute meaningfully and realize their potential. These are some of the reasons why HRD matters to strategy and why strategy matters to HRD.

Theory and strategic HRD: Penrose's and Barney's contributions

By now it should be clear that there are compelling reasons why a strategic approach to HRD matters both for organizations and for HRD itself. The conceptual roots of this argument are traceable to theories in economics and strategic management, notably: Gary Becker's human capital theory (see above); Edith Penrose's *The Theory of the Growth of the Firm* (1959); and Jay Barney's 'Resource-Based View' of the firm (often shortened to RBV, and also known as Resource-Based Theory, RBT).

The American-British economist Edith Penrose (1914–1996) is amongst the most cited of economists, especially in the strategic management and corporate strategy literature. In *The Theory of the Growth of the Firm* (1959) she argued that existing personnel are a resource that cannot be substituted by personnel newly-hired from outside the firm 'because the experience they [existing personnel] gain from working within the firm and with each other enables them to provide services that are *uniquely valuable'* (p. 42, italics added).[7] The implications for learning and development from Penrose's ideas are profound:

- Working and learning within the firm develops firm-specific skills which don't necessarily transfer to other firms;
- Working and learning collaboratively in teams develops capabilities that are socially complex and causally ambiguous and are therefore difficult to disentangle and be replicated by competitors.

Learning is fundamental to Penrose's theory because 'learning drives the accumulation of resources'.[8] Penrose's work played a significant part in the development of RBV theory which is considered by many to be one of the most important strategic HRM theories.[9]

RBV was developed in the late 1980s and early 1990s and is most often associated with the work of Jay Barney, an American professor of strategic management[10] (although the idea was first mooted by the Danish economist Birger Wernerfelt in the early 1980s). RBV further underlines the importance of learning and knowledge in achieving sustainable competitive advantage (SCA) because:

- The knowledge and skills that employees co-create by working and learning together closely creates a highly firm-specific resource (as in Penrose's theory);
- This knowledge, which is often tacit in nature, is not only difficult to imitate and transfer between organizations, it's also hard – some would argue impossible – even for the knower herself to articulate.

In terms of the relationships between HRD activities (such as training), performance and human capital (of which knowledge and skills are the essence), human capital mediates the relationship between HRD activities and outcomes; see Figure 9.2.

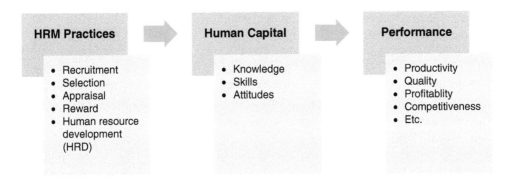

Figure 9.2 Human capital mediates between HRM/HRD practices and outcomes

As noted above, RBV is one of the building blocks of strategic management theory and the practice of business strategy.[11] It was a significant step forward in strategic management theory because it represented a shift and rebalancing in perspective from 'exogenous' (outside/external) factors which often have a macro-economic focus to 'endogenous' (inside/internal) factors as follows:

- Away from economic thinking, which focused mainly on external factors (such as industry position) and physical capital (such as buildings and machinery) as sources of competitive advantage;
- Towards internal (that is, endogenous) firm resources (for example, 'existing personnel' in Penrose's terms) as sources of competitive advantage: a firm's internal resources are revitalizing and renewing forces which are vital factors in creating a 'sustainable competitive advantage' (SCA).

The main principle of RBV is that sustainable competitive advantage (that is, one that is very hard or impossible to copy) derives from those resources and capabilities that a firm controls that are valuable (V), rare (R), inimitable (I), and non-substitutable (N).[12] These criteria are sometimes referred to by the acronym VRIN (see Figure 9.3).

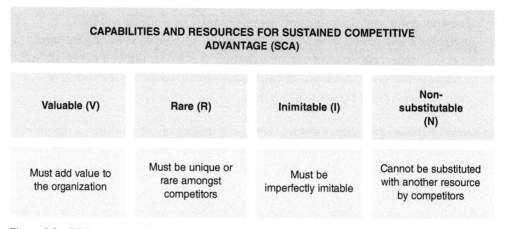

Figure 9.3 RBV's criteria (VRIN) for sustained competitive advantage (SCA)

VRIN is relevant to HRD because employees' knowledge, skills, attitudes and experiences are assets that are internal to the business, and developing them through the processes of learning (both formal and informal) can give a business sustainable competitive advantage. To emphasize: knowledge, skills and experiences are value-creating assets that are hard-to-copy and cannot – even in an age of robots, machine learning and AI – be easily substituted. This is particularly true in high-value, knowledge-intensive industries and especially when the knowledge that is the source of sustainable competitive advantage is tacit.

Edith Penrose, Gary Becker and Jay Barney

Here are some authoritative quotes from, and sources for, the works of Penrose, Becker and Barney which capture the essence of their arguments.

Penrose: 'Knowledge comes to people in two different ways. One kind can be formally taught, can be learned from other people or from the written word, and can if necessary, be formally expressed and transmitted to others. The other kind is also the result of learning, but learning in the form of personal experience...[and] experience itself can never be transmitted; it produces a change-frequently a subtle change-in individuals but cannot be separated from them.' Penrose, E. (1959/1995). *The theory of the growth of the firm*, 3rd edition. Oxford: Oxford University Press, p. 53.

Becker: 'Human capital refers to the knowledge, information, ideas, skills, and health of individuals. This is the "age of human capital" in the sense that human capital is by far the most important form of capital in modern economies. The economic successes of individuals, and also of whole economies, depends on how extensively and effectively people invest in themselves. Technology may be the driver of a modern economy, especially of its high-tech sector, but human capital is certainly the fuel. While all forms of capital are important, including machinery, factories, and financial capital, human capital is the most significant.' Becker, G. (2006). The age of human capital. In H. Lauder, P. Brown, J. Dillabough, & H. Halsey (eds), *Education, globalization and social change* (pp. 292–295). Oxford, UK: Oxford University Press, p. 293.

Barney: 'Research on the competitive implications of such firm resources as knowledge, learning, culture, teamwork, and human capital, among others, was given a significant boost by resource-based theory – a theory that indicated it was these kinds of resources that were most likely to be sources of sustained competitive advantage for firms.' Barney, J. B. (2001). Is the resource-based 'view' a useful perspective for strategic management research? Yes. *Academy of Management Review*, 26(1), 41–56, p. 45. You can listen to Jay Barney talking about why some firms outperform other firms from an RBV perspective in this short video clip: www.youtube.com/watch?v=-KN81_oYl1s

The effective development and configuration of employees' knowledge, skills and experience within the systems and structure of an organization make it difficult for managers in other organizations to simply copy or develop a 'blueprint' for a business and then proceed to hire-in people from outside to carry out functions laid-out in 'detailed "job descriptions"' (p. 42). An implication for HRD is that individual and organizational learning and development are uniquely placed to contribute to sustained competitive advantage by leveraging lower transferability of knowledge and skill and greater social complexity, and by enabling synergies between learning and development and other employment and human resources practices:

- Lower transferability: developing firm-specific knowledge and skills, including expertise and intuition, because these are (by definition) more tacit and hence less transferable than generic knowledge and skills;
- Greater social complexity: by investing in team building and organizational learning, because collective knowledge and skills are harder to imitate and less transferable (due to causal ambiguity and social complexity) than individuals' knowledge and skills;
- Synergy: integrating HRM and HRD activities into coherent, integrated 'bundles', creates synergistic effects in which the 'whole is greater than the sum of its parts'; this is because highly-integrated bundles of HR practices are much harder for competitors to disentangle and imitate, and are likely to be bound to the culture of the organization.[13]

RBV gives support to the view that securing, through HRM, and developing, through HRD, the right people in the right roles and managing them in the right way is instrumental in achieving and sustaining competitive advantage. This takes us back to the start of this chapter: the strategic question of *'who* will get you where you want to be?' is as important a question as *'where* do you want to be?' and *'how* will you get there?'.

This aspiration is more important than ever given the technological megatrends that we are witnessing and are subject to in the fourth industrial revolution (see Chapter 8).[14] For example, in knowledge-intensive businesses where human beings, with their unique capability for creating new knowledge (much of which is tacit), solving problems and inventing things (via insights), cannot be substituted for by machines in many of the most important tasks.[15] That said AI, machine learning, and robotics are revolutionizing workplaces and are part of the volatile external environment that HRD operates in and must therefore be prepared to respond to.

RBV has been described as a 'guiding paradigm' for strategic HRM research and practice. However, as you might expect, in challenging orthodoxies, RBV hasn't been without its critics. In the early 2000s Richard Priem and John Butler asked questions about whether or not RBV is actually a 'theory' that can be useful for building understanding in strategic management. They argued that considerable work is required before it can be considered such and therefore be useful.[16] More recently, RBV was criticized by Kaufman on the grounds that conventional models of the HR-performance link suffer from problems that lead to 'low explanatory power', 'mis-specified cause-and-effect relationships' (think back to the Google 'Project Oxygen' example in Chapter 7), a difficult-to-measure dependent variable (that is, 'competitive advantage' cannot be expressed in some common monetary unit), and that it tells managers to be 'strategic business partners' but does not provide any decision-making model or set of criteria to help them to work-out the 'answer' for how to be one.[17] Needless to say monetizing performance in the maximizing shareholder value (MSV) model is also littered with ethical, moral and related problems. You can read more about these fundamental and technical criticisms, and Barney's responses to them, in the 'Delve Deeper' below.

Reflective question 9.1

What would you say to a narrow-minded line manager who expressed the view that HRD should stick to what it's good at, that is reacting to employees' and line managers' requests for 'top quality' efficient and effective training that gives employees the knowledge and skills they need to do the job they're paid to do. This is the only 'need to have' for HRD; anything else is an unnecessary 'nice to have'.

Delve deeper 9.1

Read more about RBV and its criticisms in:

Priem, R. and Butler, J. E. (2001). Is the resource-based view a useful perspective for strategic management research? *Academy of Management Review*, 26(1), 22–40.

Barney, J. B. (2001). Is the resource-based view a useful perspective for strategic management research? Yes. *Academy of Management Review*, 26(1), 41–56.

Kraaijenbrink, J., Spender, J. C., & Groen, A. J. (2010). The resource-based view: A review and assessment of its critiques. *Journal of Management*, 36(1), 349–372.

Barney, J. B., Ketchen Jr, D. J., & Wright, M. (2011). The future of resource-based theory: Revitalization or decline? *Journal of Management*, 37(5), 1299–1315.

Kaufman, B. E. (2015). The RBV theory foundation of strategic HRM: Critical flaws, problems for research and practice, and an alternative economics paradigm. *Human Resource Management Journal*, 25(4), 516–540.

Barney, J. B., & Mackey, A. (2016). Text and metatext in the resource-based view. *Human Resource Management Journal*, 26(4), 369–378.

Dynamic capabilities and HRD

A complementary view of how learning and development contribute significantly to the creation of value for an organization and its stakeholders is through the development of an organization's 'capabilities'. Capabilities, or more accurately 'dynamic capabilities' are an organization's ability to 'integrate, build, and reconfigure internal and external competences to address rapidly changing environments'[18]. They're difficult to replicate and enable organizations to not only adapt to environmental changes (analogous to 'evolutionary fitness'[19]) but also shape the business environment itself. This idea speaks to the broader issue of the transformative power of learning and development as a consequence of the 'recursivity' of learning behaviour ('agency') and the learning context ('structure').[20] The interweaving of organizational structures (for example, its learning climate) and human agency (for example, employees' learning behaviours) are fundamental features of the interconnectedness and interdependence learning and the context in which learning takes place that are part of the learning ecosystem, see Figure 9.4.

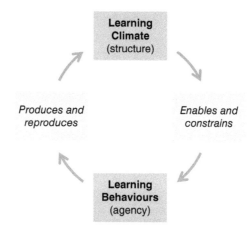

Figure 9.4 Recursive relationship between organizational structure (in this case learning climate) and human agency (in this case learning behaviours)

The originator of the dynamic capabilities concept, David Teece of the University of California Berkeley's Haas School distinguishes between:

- Ordinary capabilities: these are akin to 'best practices', typically start in one company and spread to the entire industry, for example, assembly line production, hence they are replicable;
- Dynamic capabilities: these are idiosyncratic and unique to each company and rooted in its history, culture and context; they're difficult to imitate and have been referred to as 'signature processes' or 'the ways things are done around here'.

Organizations develop dynamic capabilities by the processes of 'sensing' (identifying and assessing opportunities inside and outside the company), 'seizing' (mobilizing resources to capture value from these opportunities) and 'transforming' (continuous renewal).

Teece described dynamic capabilities as being about 'how to get the future right', and in this respect they resonate with the idea of 'foresight' discussed at the beginning of this chapter. He gives the example of Nokia which missed out on the smartphone revolution because it wasn't well equipped for sensing, whereas Apple was through the unique leadership style of Steve Jobs and by having its base in the San Francisco Bay area.[21] Learning is an intangible asset that is critical to business success[22] and through individual and organization learning processes, organizations are able to recognize and correct dysfunctional routines and collectively generate new, hard-to-replicate organizational knowledge. In Chapters 13 and 14 we'll explore the ways in which organizational learning processes help businesses to create what some people have referred to as 'memories of the future' in order to survive and thrive in volatile, uncertain, complex and ambiguous (VUCA) environments.

HRD researchers have recognized the importance of dynamic capabilities and the potential that a strategic approach to HRD (see below) has to contribute to the creation of new capabilities and the renewal and alteration of existing capabilities, based on the recognition that these are underpinned by organizational, as well as individual, learning processes.

Perspective from practice 9.1

Developing dynamic capabilities for competitive advantage

Outside the confines of academic theory and research, HR and leadership consultant Josh Bersin[23] writing in *Forbes* proposed a four-stage 'learning maturity' model for the evolution of learning and development that begins with ad hoc learning and culminates in an 'organizational learning capability':

- Step 1, Incidental and informal training: in the absence of formal training, managers and employees 'get by' through coaching each other to do their jobs better but this approach isn't scalable and depends on the capabilities and motivations of informal coaches. This would be typical of smaller firms and start-ups;
- Step 2, Training and development: a systematic approach based on needs analyses run by a professional training and development department, builds on and complements Step 1 processes;
- Step 3, Talent and performance improvement: based on the realization that learning is much more than training by building long-term career paths and continuous learning programmes integrated with HR and talent management processes;
- Step 4, Organizational capability: bringing together of formal and informal tools using combination of training, coaching, performance support and management that's unique to the organization to pursue 'capability development'. This 'level' of HRD evolution is similar to the concept of the learning organization that we'll meet in Chapter 14.

(Continued)

In Bersin's 'growth model' organizations need mastery of learning and development 'fundamentals' which are necessary but insufficient – they must be integrated with more strategic talent development practices in a culture of learning which recognizes the synergies between learning and working.

In a report by the consulting group McKinsey and Co it's suggested that one of the primary tasks of those who lead learning and development in organizations is to 'develop and shape a learning strategy based on the company's business strategy' and to develop and build capabilities across the company, on time, in a cost-effective manner. They define capabilities as the 'mind-sets, skills and expertise' that business needs most (for example in e-commerce these might be 'deep expertise in big data and predictive analytics') but note that 'Human capital requires ongoing investments in L&D to retain its value. When knowledge becomes outdated or forgotten – a much more rapid occurrence today than ever before – the value of human capital declines and needs to be supplemented by new learning and relevant work experiences.' This imperative for constant learning in a climate that is conducive to learning is vitally important for building resilience and sustainability during times of significant business and societal transformations in the face of the megatrends of globalization and digitization.

Sources: Bersin, J. (2013). How corporate learning drives competitive advantage. *Forbes*, 20 March; Brassey, J., Christensen, L. and van Dam, N. (2020). Components of a successful L&D strategy. McKinsey and Company

If, as the ancient Greek philosopher Heraclitus (circa 535-475BC) is reported to have said, 'change is the only constant', then developing an 'organizational learning capability' is a journey of 'becoming' and not a destination of 'being'. For example, 3M has been on an innovation journey for over a hundred years and by inventing and commercializing products such as Three-M-ite Abrasive cloth (1914), Scotch brand masking tape (1925), 3M sound recording tape (1947), Scotchgard Fabric Protector (1956), 3M Filtek Dental Restoratives (1964), Thinsulate Thermal Insulation (1979), and Post-It Notes (1980) to Light Redirecting Film for solar panels (2018) and its current portfolio of 60,000 3M products in use in homes, schools, hospitals and businesses.

The idea of 'change as the only constant' raises a conceptual and philosophical question of whether strategy is a fixed 'thing' or a dynamic and emergent 'process' that guides the development of the company's identity and purpose over time.[24] Process thinking, based in 'process philosophy', involves considering phenomena, such as strategy and learning, dynamically (that is, in terms of 'becoming' and movement, activity, events, change and temporal evolution) rather than statically (that is, in terms of 'being' and objects and things). Carole Elliott has asked whether HRD acknowledges 'human becomings' and that by viewing learning and developing employees 'from the perspective of human becomings, we can gain insights into HRD as a strategic process'.[25]

Delve deeper 9.2

Read more about process philosophy in learning and development in:

Chia, R. (1997). Process philosophy and management learning: Cultivating 'foresight' in management education. In Burgoyne, J., & Reynolds, M. (eds) *Management learning integrating perspectives in theory and practice*. London: Sage, pp. 71–88.

Elliott, C. (2000). Does HRD acknowledge human becomings? A view of the UK literature. *Human Resource Development Quarterly*, 11(2), 187–195.

Lee, M. (2001). A refusal to define HRD. *Human Resource Development International*, 4(3), 327–341.

For an accessible introduction to process philosophy read:

Rescher, N. (1996). *Process metaphysics: An introduction to process philosophy*. New York: SUNY Press.

Strategy and human resources

Personnel management – the 'managing of people in organizations' – has existed as an area of management practice for well over a century.[26] It began to be supplanted by human resource management (HRM) in the 1970s.[27] A further significant change came in the 1980s when strategic approaches to HRM rose to prominence in the USA. This gave birth to the field of 'strategic human resource management', SHRM. Two major contributions to the establishment of SHRM as a field of academic study – both published in 1984 – were *Strategic human resource management* by Fombrun, Tichy and Devanna and *Managing human assets* by Beer, Spector, Lawrence, Mills and Walton.

In terms of the definition of business strategy presented at the beginning of this chapter (which was from Johnson and colleagues' best-selling business strategy textbook), one of senior management's key tasks is setting strategic priorities and configuring resources in such a way as to create value that meets and exceeds stakeholder expectations. With this in mind, a strategic approach to HRM entails setting priorities, configuring human resources and taking people-related decisions in ways that link HR policies and practices with the business' strategic objectives. This fits well with academic and practitioner definitions of strategic HRM (SHRM):

- Strategic HRM scholar Wayne Cascio defined it as 'the choice, alignment, and integration of an organization's HRM system so [that] its human capital resources most effectively contribute to strategic business objectives';[28]
- The consulting group Ernst and Young (EY) defined it as 'framing and delivering strategic HR policies, practices and processes that support innovation and business

growth whilst simultaneously finding metrics and analytics that supply executives with the insights needed to gauge HR's impact on the business bottom line'.[29]

Arguably, the 'proof-of-concept' for SHRM depends on whether it actually leads to sustained competitive advantage.

If, for a moment, we step back in time and take a 'maximizing shareholder value' (MSV) view then the 'holy grail' of SHRM research can be seen as identifying and understanding the relationship between strategic human resource practices (that is, SHRM and including HRD) and organizational performance (as measured in tangibles such as 'financial performance'). On this basis, the two crucial questions are:

- Do HR practices have a positive impact on organizational performance?
- If so how is such impact achieved?[30]

In the 1990s the credibility and legitimacy of SHRM theory was given considerable impetus when various researchers[31] demonstrated positive relationships between SHRM practices and business performance in terms of measurable outcomes such as lower employee turnover, greater productivity, and financial benefits. Not only were these observed effects significant theoretically in that they were a 'proof-of-concept' for a shareholder value-based SHRM theory, they also had considerable practical relevance for the management of people (and profit) in organizations. SHRM offered a solution to the problem of ineffective utilization of human resources which had been seen as a major source of inefficiency in the management, leadership and organizations that had troubled US businesses during the 1970s.

Research insight 9.1

Overcoming the limitations of cross sectional studies

Many of the studies of the HRD performance link were cross-sectional and therefore suffered from significant limitations including conflating correlation with causation and causal ambiguity (for example, does a firm's adoption of SHRM practices lead to superior performance, or do firms with superior performance adopt SHRM practices?).[32] Subsequently additional evidence has accumulated in the form of longitudinal studies. For example, a meta-analysis of longitudinal studies by George Saridakis and colleagues found support for the hypotheses that:

- High performance work practices (HPWP) lead to better firm performance; they found that HPWPs 'adopted at time 1 will enhance organizational performances measured at time 2';
- HPWP systems have a stronger effect on firm performance compared to individual HRM practices, with a difference that was statistically significant suggesting that the

'relationship between HPWPs and firm performance is stronger when distinct but interrelated HRM systems are employed in organisations'.

HPWPs are designed to improve employees' knowledge, skills and ability (for example, by HRD and job design) and encourage and motivate employees to invest additional discretionary time and effort (for example, by performance related pay and empowerment). The researchers concluded that although longitudinal studies can be challenging to execute they are invaluable because they overcome the limitations of cross-sectional research that can often claim causation but actually only reveals association.

Source: Saridakis, G., Lai, Y., & Cooper, C. L. (2017). Exploring the relationship between HRM and firm performance: A meta-analysis of longitudinal studies. *Human Resource Management Review*, 27(1), 87–96.

Studies such as the above along with meta-analyses and systematic reviews have revealed consistent statistically significant relationships between SHRM (high performance work practices, HPWPs) and firm performance and that mutually-reinforcing 'bundles' of HPWPs appear to have a stronger impact on firm performance than do individual HRM practices alone.[33] A large body of empirical evidence legitimizes the claim that SHRM practices (including strategic approaches to learning and development) are one way in which organizations can differentiate themselves from competitors and thereby secure sustainable competitive advantage measured in financial terms.[34]

Turning to the role of HRD as part of a strategic approach to HRM, it's important to ensure that HR practices are both 'aligned vertically' with the business strategy and 'integrated horizontally' with each other. Hence, in differentiating an organization from the 'pack', a strategic approach to HRD should seek to align learning and development processes with business strategy and also integrate them with other HR practices.

- Horizontal integration between the various elements of the HR system (for example, recruitment and selection, performance appraisal, HRD and reward) gives consistency across HR practices. A consequence of this is that HR professionals need to have both generalist and specialist remits and competencies;[35]
- Vertical alignment between HR systems (including a horizontally-integrated HRM and HRD) and the business strategy and its context involves organizations not only using particular HR best practices but also developing HR practices that add value to the strategic priorities of the business and the context in which it is operating;[36] see Figure 9.5.

Any model of strategic HRD should emphasize vertical and horizontal linkages so that employees' knowledge and skills are developed in ways that support strategy. It is for these reasons that Thomas Garavan has defined strategic HRD (SHRD) as a 'coherent, vertically aligned and horizontally integrated set of learning and development activities'.[37]

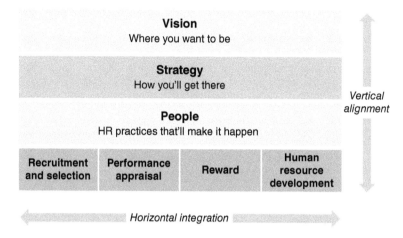

Figure 9.5 Horizontal integration and vertical alignment of HR and strategy

In practical terms, the Association for Talent Development (ATD) offers the following recommendations for making HRD a high-value strategic function:[38]

- Think of the HRD team as 'strategic enablers' not merely 'support staff';
- Understand the organization's goals, strategy and operations; be as knowledgeable about the business as about HRD;
- Align relevant aspects of HRD with the rest of the company, and don't live in an HRD or HR 'silo';
- Conceive, create, and champion learning and development solutions that enable the organization's strategy and drive behavioural change that directly drives results;
- Add value to the organization and be able to 'track-and-trace' it.

By doing so, HRD comes to be seen not as a mere support function, 'strategic passenger' or a cost rather than profit centre but as having 'earned a seat at the corporate strategic planning table' and hence a fully-fledged strategic partner.

Perspective from practice 9.2

Employee development at Johnson & Johnson

Johnson & Johnson ('J&J') is an American MNC headquartered in New Jersey with over 130,000 employees across 60 countries. As the largest and most broadly based healthcare company in the world Johnson & Johnson develops medical devices (for example, joint reconstruction, biomaterials, etc.), pharmaceutical (for example, immunological, cardiovascular, etc.), and consumer packaged goods (for example, brands such as Neutrogena, Band Aid, Listerine, Nicorette, etc.). In seeking to change 'the trajectory of health for humanity and help build prosperity around the world' its position on employee development is that investing in the knowledge and skills of employees:

- Is a 'key tool for the achievement of business goals';
- Helps to 'increase employee motivation and retention'.
- Serves local economies by 'injecting skills into local workforces and raising the quality of employability'.

Its 'Credo' is that 'There must be equal opportunity for employment, development and advancement for those qualified. We must provide highly capable leaders and their actions must be just and ethical.' Johnson & Johnson ensures that there are development opportunities for all employees irrespective of where they are on their career journey, fosters a 'learning culture' that 'shapes each person's unique career path' and empowers them to 'better contribute to achieving our business objectives' and deliver on the business's long-term strategies. Johnson & Johnson achieves this by:

- Professional development programmes and learning resources for all employees in the form of independent study courses, web-based courses, interviewing simulations, assessments, intensive workshops and action learning courses provided both on-the-job, off-the-job and via online learning (for example the SUMMIT integrated learning enrolment and management portal, and MyDevelopment framework based around a balanced portfolio 'Education, Exposure and Experience');
- Supporting employees' ownership of their personal learning, development and growth with 'shared accountability between an employee and his or her manager to ensure that opportunities for development are identified and pursued, and that the potential of the individual is maximized';
- Providing leadership development programmes (LDPs) that contribute to the mission of transforming 'the future of health for humanity' based on the precept that 'every employee at Johnson & Johnson is a leader' and the goal is to 'help employees realize this potential'.

The process is managed using 'robust performance management tools' in which employees discuss progress and plan their learning and development with the managers five times a year ('Five Conversations Framework').

Source: Johnson & Johnson: Position on Employee Development. www.jnj.com/about-jnj/policies-and-positions/our-position-on-employee-development (accessed 27-01-21).

This view underlines the distinction between being a strategic partner and a strategic passenger: if there's a lack of vertical alignment of HRD policy and practices with the business' strategic priorities and its vision, it reduces HRD's value-adding potential[39] Similarly, if horizontal integration between HRD and HRM practices does not take place, but instead HRD and HRM entrench in their separate silos, the benefits of HRM-HRD supportive fit and the potential synergies this could bring will be lost.[40] It is worth reiterating at this point the fundamental SHRM/SHRD principle that sustainable competitive advantage is delivered when strategy, HRM and HRD are vertically aligned and horizontally integrated thus creating a hard-to-replicate 'synergy factor'.[41]

Delve deeper 9.3

Read more about the processes that link HRM practices and organizational performance, longitudinal studies of, and the challenges of reverse causality in the SHRM-performance link in:

Chowhan, J. (2016). Unpacking the black box: Understanding the relationship between strategy, HRM practices, innovation and organizational performance. *Human Resource Management Journal, 26*(2), 112–133.

Jiang, K., Lepak, D. P., Hu, J., & Baer, J. C. (2012). How does human resource management influence organizational outcomes? A meta-analytic investigation of mediating mechanisms. *Academy of Management Journal, 55*(6), 1264–1294.

Jiang, K., & Messersmith, J. (2018). On the shoulders of giants: A meta-review of strategic human resource management. *The International Journal of Human Resource Management, 29*(1), 6–33.

Saridakis, G., Lai, Y., & Cooper, C. L. (2017). Exploring the relationship between HRM and firm performance: A meta-analysis of longitudinal studies. *Human Resource Management Review, 27*(1), 87–96.

Strategic human resource development (SHRD)

The move towards a strategic approach to the management of human resources has created opportunities not only for HRM but also HRD to be at the 'epicentre of change' in modern organizations.[42] In a world where technologies, product features, manufacturing processes, and distribution channels can be copied, the most important and sustainable source of competitive advantage is the ability to create new knowledge and learn faster than the competition. This places learning centre-stage as a key capability for organizations in volatile, uncertain, complex and ambiguous environments. However, learning processes, both individual and organizational, cannot be left to chance, and consequently they have to be planned, executed and managed in order to be efficient and effective. HRD adds value to organizations through its role as the key player in the enabling and management of individual and organization learning processes. The leverage that HRD exercises and the synergies it helps to create are amplified when these learning and development processes are strategically aligned and horizontally integrated.

─────Reflective question 9.2─────

From what you've learned about theories of learning, human capital, RBV and SHRM, what would be some general recommendations for how HRD should be configured at a micro-level (see Part I) if it is to be a strategic partner at the 'epicentre of change' and not just a passenger. Two examples might be: how can social and situated learning theories be used to help design HRD that builds a resource that is socially complex and causally ambiguous and hence difficult to imitate; how can HRD leverage managers' experiences so that they are able to ask insightful questions that help them stay ahead of the curve in times of change?

As noted above, early formulations of HRM as personnel management focused on employee administration and welfare activities. Similarly HRD was configured largely as piecemeal, largely reactive training interventions designed to create, maintain or enhance employees' job-relevant knowledge and skills. With the transition from HRM to SHRM there came a realization that HRD also needed to connect not only to business strategy but also to organizational knowledge and learning (see Chapters 13 and 14). The concept of SHRD is consistent with the principles of RBV and human capital theories, and these two foundational theories are reflected in SHRD's defining attributes:

> SHRD is a vertically-aligned and horizontally-integrated set of HRD practices. It is the outcome of a long-term planning processes which seeks to develops employees' knowledge, skills and experiences in anticipation of economic returns. SHRD is aligned with the vision/mission of the organization, acknowledges the needs of multiple stakeholders, is future-oriented, and differentiates the organization in ways that are hard-to-copy.[13]

Models of SHRD tend to be 'prescriptive'[14] rather than theoretical, which means that they specify *what* individuals or organizations should do in practice. Consequently prescriptive models tend to be concrete and specific and action-oriented, whereas explanatory models (or 'descriptive', theoretical models) aim to explain why certain phenomena, processes and outcomes are observed or likely to be observed (in terms of relationships between key variables, factors and conditions), consequently descriptive models tend to be more abstract and general.

'Seeing the wood for the trees' in the SHRD literature is a potential problem as there are many different SHRD models and there's a fair amount of overlap and duplication between them.[15] To simplify matters we'll look at one particular model of SHRD which was first proposed in the 1990s by Thomas Garavan and colleagues and has been described as 'seminal' in SHRD research.[16] The model is a prescriptive one and, as noted above, in common with prescriptive models in general it seeks to provide guidance for decision makers on how to configure systems and resources in such a way as to bring about a desired outcome.

The context of the 1990s in which the model was developed is relevant because:

- RBV had first appeared in the strategic management literature in 1984 with the publication of Birger Wernerfelt's original article entitled 'A resource-based view of the firm' in the *Strategic Management Journal* and subsequent work by Jay Barney and others;
- The SHRM literature was growing rapidly from virtually a 'zero base' in the early 1980s, for example, *Strategic human resource management* by Fombrun, Tichy and Devanna and *Managing human assets* by Beer, Spector, Lawrence, Mills and Walton; both were first published in 1984;
- In 1991 SHRD was new to the HRD and training and development (T&D) literature, and at the time the SHRD literature was virtually non-existent.[47]

Garavan critically evaluated the existing HRD literature which was concerned mainly with T&D and personnel management (over 60% of the references in Garavan's 1991 article were about, or in, training and/or personnel journals). He attributed the emergence of SHRD to five opportunities and challenges faced by organizations in the 1990s:

- Aligning employees' potential with the business' objectives;
- Developing a more flexible and adaptable employee skills base;
- Difficulties in recruiting skilled managers;
- Need for HR succession planning;
- Emphasis on performance management and evaluation.

Garavan's model is configured as a number of 'key characteristics' (nine in total, hence why it's referred to here as the 'Nine Characteristics Model of SHRD') derived from relevant HRM, SHRD and HRD literatures. The model has been discussed and reviewed extensively elsewhere,[48] and is presented usually in a simple 'list' format.[49] However, closer scrutiny suggests that different levels are implicit in the model – strategic, organizational and operational – and that these provide a useful simplifying and organizing framework which make the model easier to grasp, remember and use.

The model's 'strategic characteristics' give it vertical alignment with the organization at a macro-level whilst its 'operational characteristics' give the model horizontal integration with HRD, HRM and business operations at a micro-level. The model's 'organizational characteristics' are at the nexus ('meso-level') of strategic and the operational activities and form a bridge between the macro- and micro-levels; see Figure 9.6. The three levels and the nine characteristics are:

- Strategic characteristics (vertically aligned): environmental scanning; integration with organizational mission and goals (macro-level);

- Organizational characteristics (nexus of strategic and operational): recognition of culture; top management support (meso-level);
- Operational characteristics (horizontally integrated): HRD plans and policies; line manager commitment and involvement; expanded trainer role; existence of complementary HRM activities; emphasis on evaluation (micro-level).

Senior managers and the organizational culture – being at the nexus of the macro and micro levels – are the vital lynchpin in that they determine whether or not SHRD can rely on their engagement and support in enabling HRD activities to add value for stakeholders and assist with the realization of business strategy. Without senior manager support or indeed by not being implemented in the right context (that is, in an appropriate 'learning culture' or 'learning climate'), any attempts at trying to make HRD strategic are likely to be futile and result in failure, be a waste of the organization's resources and result in a loss of credibility for HRD.

As with the horizontal integration of HRM activities in SHRM, HRD should not only be integrated with HRM to achieve synergies but the individual HRD practices themselves should be integrated internally to form a coherent whole.[50] Amongst the strengths of the Nine Characteristics Model are that it is applicable across different contexts, accommodates multiple stakeholders, and consistent with the principles of human capital theory and RBV.[51]

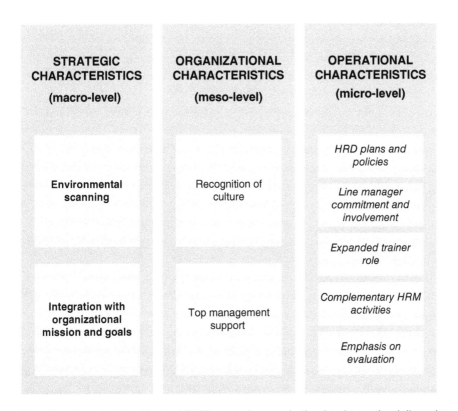

Figure 9.6 Nine Characteristics Model of SHRD, strategic, organizational and operational dimensions

---

┌─ Perspective from practice 9.3 ─────────────────────────────

Essential components of strategic learning and development

Volatility, uncertainty, complexity and ambiguity (VUCA) in the business environment, globalization, digitization, and an ageing workforce have created a 'perfect storm' for business organizations of all types and sizes across the globe. As a result, the 'shelf-life' of employees' knowledge and skills is becoming shorter and shorter and skilling, up-skilling and re-skilling of employees is more important than ever. The consulting group McKinsey recognize that HRD has a strategic role to play and in doing so it spans five areas of business and HRM practice:[52]

- Attracting and retaining talent: opportunities for learning and development are among the most important criteria for talented hires joining an organization, and lack of learning and development opportunities is one of the key reasons people cite for leaving;
- Developing people capabilities: to keep human capital up-to-date, relevant and value-adding requires on-going investment in HRD, and companies that do so see an 'impressive return';
- Creating a values-based culture: workforces are increasingly virtual, globally dispersed, and millennial. HRD can help to build a sense of community and a values-based culture – something that millennials appear to be particularly attracted to.
- Building an employer brand: brand is one of the most important but perhaps least tangible of a business' assets. Visible and proven commitment to and investment in HRD can help to boost an employer's brand and make them the employer of choice for potential high performers;
- Motivating and engaging employees: one of the most powerful ways to motivate and engage employees is to provide them with the opportunities to up-skill and re-skill, and to grow and develop both personally and professionally.

In its traditional role of 'maintenance' or as a 'passive provider' HRD was mainly focused on the design, delivery and evaluation of training programmes. However, in responding to rapidly and constantly changing external realities HRD moved beyond this narrow remit and aligned with strategy, built synergies with HRM and focused on creating value for all stakeholders, including employees, line managers, investors, customers and wider society.

Source: Brassey, J., Christensen, L., and van Dam, N. (2019). *The essential components of a successful L&D strategy*. McKinsey and Co.

Teece's concept of dynamic capabilities was discussed earlier with regard to its three core components of 'sensing', 'seizing' and 'transforming'. Thomas Garavan and colleagues have applied Teece's theory in proposing that HRD can be 'strategic' by developing dynamic capabilities in:

- Sensing, for example by developing employees' environmental scanning skills (as in for example front line workers being closely in touch with customers);
- Seizing, for example by developing employees' problem-solving skills (including their 'intuitive expertise', see below);
- Transforming, for example by building employees' resilience to change.[53]

As far as managers' thinking and deciding capabilities are concerned, researchers have pointed to the importance of different types of cognition (that is, analytical versus intuitive thinking) in relation to the development and execution of dynamic capabilities. For example, it's been proposed that organizations that incorporate intuition into their repertoire of sensing capabilities will be able to recognize and respond to opportunities and threats more effectively than organizations that rely exclusively on analytical thinking.[54] It's also been suggested that HRD can help to develop employees' intuitive thinking skills, and hence help to rebalance their repertoire of cognitive styles[55] and thereby enhance the dynamic capabilities of organizations. In terms of strategic cognition, intuitive thinking has a 'sensing' function whereas analytical thinking has a 'solving' function, and both are essential strategic capabilities.

Delve deeper 9.4

Read about SHRD and dynamic capabilities, the importance of intuition in dynamic capabilities and how to develop your own and employees' strategic intuition in:

Garavan, T., Shanahan, V., Carbery, R., & Watson, S. (2016). Strategic human resource development: Towards a conceptual framework to understand its contribution to dynamic capabilities. *Human Resource Development International*, 19(4), 289–306.

Hodgkinson, G. P., & Healey, M. P. (2011). Psychological foundations of dynamic capabilities: Reflexion and reflection in strategic management. *Strategic Management Journal*, 32(13), 1500–1516.

Sadler-Smith, E. (2010). *The intuitive mind: profiting from the power of your sixth sense*. Chichester: John Wiley and Sons.

The CIPD defined the purpose of a learning and development strategy as setting-out the 'workforce capabilities, skills and competencies the organisation needs, and how they can be developed to ensure a sustainable, successful organisation' based on an alignment between SHRD, SHRM and the overall business strategy.[56] To enable employees to acquire or update the knowledge and skills they need to perform satisfactorily in their current job role HRD doesn't necessarily have to consider the broader business strategy. HRD could perform quite adequately in an isolated tactical and operational role, passively providing training and development for employees by focusing on the here-and-now, micro-features of the HRD landscape, for example by assisting employees to get the right training to meet an annual performance appraisal objective. However, in the volatile, uncertain, complex and ambiguous business environments of our globalized, digitized and demographically dynamic world where change is the only constant, an isolated, tactical orientation is not an option for most organizations and not a viable position for HRD.

Here is an example of an organization's 'Learning and Development Ambition Statement':[57]

The organization will have in place and achieved a comprehensive electronic learning solutions and using the internet to maximize learning and a high quality leadership development programme. The learning and development offer will be aligned with internal crediting of continuing professional development (CPD). We will build the apprenticeship provision to ensure that there at least 50 new starters each year and establish evaluation models that monitor learning effectiveness, etc.

In the terms set out above is it 'strategic'? (Justify your reasoning.) What are the implications of such an approach?

This example illustrates the difference between an HRD strategy and SHRD. What is sometimes labelled as an HRD strategy may not necessarily be strategic in the terms outlined in this chapter. An HRD strategy is sometimes little more than a set of policies and practices which an organization adopts in order that employees have the requisite knowledge and skills needed to perform in their current and future job roles. A further consequence of a shift towards business partnering is that HRD roles and responsibilities have changed radically. For example, when learning is integrated more into the flow of work activities such as coaching, mentoring and on-job learning, assessing learning and development needs are best carried out by individuals who have understanding of the local context and the needs of specific employees (such as line managers) rather than by others (such as HRD practitioners) who are one step removed from the front line and who are likely to be better-positioned as advisors, innovators and change agents.

Criticisms of strategic approaches

Some of the criticisms of strategic approaches (including SHRM and SHRD) are summarized in Figure 9.7.[58] The situation has evolved such that some of the original architects and advocates of North American models of SHRM, such as Susan Jackson and Randall Schuler, which tended to focus on financial and related outcomes as metrics of success, have acknowledged that:

● There's more to 'performance' than the simple 'financial performance' metric which was the outcome measure in many of the SHRM-performance studies;

- Organizational success requires balancing the interests of a diverse range of stakeholders both internal and external to the organization.[59]

The internal stakeholders of HRM include employees, line managers, senior managers, executives and owners. The external stakeholders include customers, suppliers, host community, capital market stakeholders (for example, shareholders and banks), trade unions and employee organizations, governments, non-governmental organizations (including charities and environmental protection/pressure groups).

As has been noted the maximizing shareholder value (MSV) view has come under criticisms from several quarters. On this basis, SHRD theory and research might also be criticized for focusing on adding value for capital market stakeholders and measuring impacts in terms of financial metrics (such as ROI and benefit-to-cost ratios). In so doing it runs the risk of ignoring stakeholder groups other than shareholders and performance measures other than profit. In business generally, strong pressures have emerged for shifts towards a more balanced view of who or what counts as a stakeholder, and debates about profit-versus-purpose.[60] Multiple stakeholder and global stakeholder perspectives acknowledge not only non-financial as well as financial measures of stakeholder impact, they also recognize the impact that an organization's activities can have both in the short- and long-term on human and non-human entities such as the natural environment.

Claims to generalizability

- Debates about the generalizability of HRM and SHRM models beyond and between national and organizational contexts

Ethnocentricity

- The North American / European approach to HRM and SHRM promulgated as the 'best way'

Unitarist assumptions

- Uncritical assumption that what's good for employer is also good for employee and vice versa

Narrow view of stakeholders

- Focus on short-term performance and shareholder interest and overlooking a wider constituency of stakeholders

Positioning SHRM as panacea

- Elevation of strategic appraoch/SHRM/SHRD by some proponents to 'panacea' status

Treating HRM-performance link as 'black box'

- Lack of a solid understanding of detailed mechanisms through which the strategic/SHRM/SHRD-performance link works

Figure 9.7   Some criticisms of strategic approaches

There are encouraging signs that a broader view of who or what counts as a 'stakeholder' is emerging; for example the former CEO of Unilever, Paul Polman said 'We now have the opportunity to eradicate poverty and deal with the issue of climate change. What bigger opportunity do you want to see? Companies make up 60% of the global economy. If they don't play an active part, how can we solve [these crises]?.'[61] Recent developments, such as the Business Round Table (BRT) of leading CEOs, declarations for a broad constituency of stakeholders (customers, employees, suppliers, communities and shareholders), have seen sustainability and multiple stakeholder HRM practices move centre stage. The aim of a corporation is being re-envisaged in ways that acknowledge and accommodate the attainment of financial, social and ecological goals and the need for lasting positive impacts on customers, employees, suppliers, communities and shareholders without damaging the natural environment.[62]

As with the research into the SHRM-performance link, if there is causal ambiguity embedded in the HRD-performance link this raises questions about some of the conclusions that have been drawn from SHRD research. It's not clear if SHRD leads to better performance or whether better performing firms are able to invest in SHRD activities (which inevitably are more sophisticated and potentially costlier). It might be premature to assume that SHRD will inevitably result in performance gains in all circumstances and may therefore be prudent to temper some of the claims being made for SHRD. This criticism could apply to HRD in general and not just to SHRD.

Other methodological and theoretical questions have been asked, for example 'is SHRD culturally-biased?', SHRD is based on concepts and empirical data mainly from the US and Europe. There's undoubtedly a predominance of theory and research developed in US and Europe (especially Ireland and the UK) in SHRD. The debate about SHRD, not just HRD, needs to broaden out and consider its relevance and applicability in other countries.[63]

From a critical perspective it is fair to ask 'does SHRD adopt "managerialist" assumptions uncritically?', A tacit assumption in the 'strategic discourse' is that managers and employees will work together harmoniously and collaboratively to create value and pursue the business' strategic priorities unquestioningly. However, power asymmetries and the tensions that these may create are downplayed in many of the strategic HRM/HRD models and their assumptions. Is what's good for the organization and its 'bosses' necessarily also good for 'workers'?.[64] This raises issues, discussed in earlier chapters, about the neglect of power in HRD and SHRD discourse.[65] It is often assumed in strategic discourse that managers and employees will work collaboratively together to drive business success. However there may be naïve assumptions underpinning this with regard to alignment between the values, attitudes and motivations of employees and those of senior managers and the organization and its owners and shareholders. Employees are assumed to identify with the organization to the extent that they 'buy into' its mission and goals unquestioningly and engage in discretionary behaviour in exchange for job security, financial rewards and career and development opportunities.

However, the inequalities and the tensions that arise from this are downplayed within a unitary perspective and the idealization of the relationship between strategy and HRD.

Delve deeper 9.5

Read more about the criticisms of strategic approaches in:

Paauwe, J. & Boon, C. (2009). Strategic HRM: A critical review. In Collings, D.G. and Wood, G. (eds) *Human resource management: A critical approach*. London: Routledge, pp. 38–54.

For a critique of what HRD is doing and what it should be doing read:

Torraco, R. J., & Lundgren, H. (2019). What HRD is doing – What HRD should be doing: The case for transforming HRD. *Human Resource Development Review*, *19*(1), 39–65.

Read more about what it means to be a 'laggard' versus a 'leader' in HR business partnering in this report from Deloitte: *Business driven HR: Unlock the value of HR business partners.*

www2.deloitte.com/content/dam/Deloitte/nz/Documents/human-capital/unlockthevalueof hrbusinesspartners.pdf

Conclusion: Strategic alignment and strategic partnership

The HRD landscape has changed such that learning and development has become integrated into the everyday practices and 'flow' of work in ways that are commensurate with social, situated, experience-based and informal theories of learning. The digitization of learning has speeded-up and reinforced this process. Also HRD has become 'diffused and integrated' into a broad range of management, supervisory and leadership roles. It has become a delegated responsibility for a new generation of informed and digitally-savvy learners who are self-starters and self-motivators used to accessing information and acquiring knowledge from digital sources.[66] As more responsibility for learning and development is delegated and assumed by learners themselves and their managers, the question can be asked 'what is the role of HRD?' and how can this be proactively shaped to fit-for-purpose in a radically uncertain future?

One response to this question is that HRD's greatest potential to add value is by being a strategic business partner in ways that are consistent with theories and models of RBV, SHRM and SHRD. To be a strategic partner in the face of unprecedented levels of volatility, uncertainty, complexity and ambiguity in the business environment HRD needs to be positioned so as to be able to:

- Refute any criticism that it provides solutions that are peripheral to, and poorly aligned with, business strategy;

- Understand the organization's vision and strategy, have clarity on how an HRD strategy fits with this, and develop an HRD 'brand' that is commensurate with the business partner role;
- Identify the clients of and stakeholders in HRD's work and co-create with them meaningful contributions that add value and support sustained competitive advantage;
- Show how it can make a positive difference to the business's core capabilities and how it impacts across a multiplicity of stakeholders;
- Justify investment of the organization's resources in human capital development through the processes of HRD.

There's ample evidence for the positive impacts that HRD, when configured and implemented as a strategic partner, can have on realizing individual and organizational potential and performance. Investing in HRD is an investment in the resilience and longer-term sustainability of individuals and organizations. This confirms some of the basic tenets of human capital theory and RBV, namely that HRD is a powerful way to leverage organizational performance, contributes to longer-term productivity, quality and effectiveness of organizations, creates value for stakeholders and enables individuals to achieve their aspirations and maximize their potential. HRD that is strategically aligned simultaneously adds value for stakeholders and builds HRD's reputation and contribution, creating synergies that help organizations to survive and thrive.

Chapter checkout

Use this list to check your understanding of the key points of this chapter.

1. **Strategy** (1) Longer-term plan for achieving a higher-level goal (such as a vision or mission); (2) aim of creating stakeholder value and fulfilling stakeholder expectations
2. **Human capital** (1) knowledge, skills, attitudes and experience possessed by individual employees; (2) developed by investing in education and training; (3) has a rate of return that can be evaluated
3. **Resource-Based View of the firm** Sustainable competitive advantage (SCA) derives from resources and capabilities that a firm controls that are (1) valuable (V), (2) rare (R), (3) inimitable (I), and (4) non-substitutable (N)
4. **SHRM** Configuration of an organization's HRM purpose, policies, practices and plans so that its human capital resources and capabilities most effectively contribute to the organization's strategic objectives.
5. **SHRD** Coherent and vertically-aligned and horizontally-integrated set of HRD activities which: (1) are an outcome of strategic planning processes; (2) addresses overall goals of the organization; (3) acknowledges needs of stakeholders; (4) are future-oriented; (5) differentiate an organization from its competitors

6 **Nine Characteristics Model** A prescriptive model of SHRD at macro-(strategic), meso-(organizational), and micro-(operational) levels, for example environmental scanning, recognition of culture and line manager commitment

7 **HRD Strategy** The policies and practices which an organization adopts in order that employees have the requisite knowledge and skills needed to perform in their current and future job roles.

8 **Criticisms of SHRD** SHRD has been criticized on the grounds of: (1) undue focus on shareholder value; (2) culturally-biased; (3) causal ambiguity and reverse causality; (4) overlooks power, is managerialist and makes unitarist assumptions

SKILLS DEVELOPMENT 9

'JUST THE JOB'?

SHRD is only as good as the people you have in place to deliver on the organization's strategic priorities. Part-and-parcel of success in SHRD is recruiting and selecting HRD specialists who are committed to the ideal of aligning HRD with strategy, adding value to business for stakeholders, who are able to speak the language of business, and be the strategic partner doing business in ways that the twenty-first century demands.

Imagine that you're a newly hired HR manager who the CEO has brought in to revitalize the HRD function in what has been up until now a very traditional business, not least in terms of how its learning and development offering has been configured (that is, a traditional 'passive provider' training course model). There is a new post of 'HRD Advisor' to fill and her vision for the new role is very different from the way HRD has traditionally carried out. Here's the current job role which is due for a radical overhaul under your leadership and the direction of the CEO:

> The training and development officer is responsible for identifying staff
> training and development needs and for planning, organizing, overseeing
> appropriate training. In carrying out this role effectively you will: (1) Conduct
> job evaluation surveys; (2) Liaise with managers with regard to staff training
> and development needs; (3) Design, deliver and oversee the training of
> individual and groups of employees; (4) Engage external providers in delivery
> of specialist training courses; (5) Ensure that employees receive the statutory
> required training; (6) Evaluate trainees' and managers' levels of satisfaction
> with the training.

(Continued)

Your first major task in your new role is to re-write the job description to signal a significant shift of the emphasis away from T&D and towards SHRD in order to get someone on board with the necessary experience, knowledge and skills who's on the same page as the CEO and you. Write an email to your CEO with a draft of the job description which describes and explains the new SHRD job role as you see it to support you in helping to make HRD a 'strategic partner'.

10

THE HRD SYSTEM

Contents

Chapter check-in

On completion of this chapter you should be able to:

- Advise on how to design and develop learning and development strategies and plans to meet identified learning and development needs;
- Describe and explain systems and processes of: (1) smaller firms' HRD; (2) organization development (OD); (3) international HRD;
- Describe and explain the concept of a 'learning ecosystem'.

Introduction

As noted in Chapter 1, one of the pioneers of HRD, Richard Swanson, argued that HRD relies on three core theories in order to understand, explain and carry out its processes and roles. Swanson represented these three theories as the 'legs' of the HRD stool. The three core theories – which are in fact broad disciplinary areas rather than specific theories as such – were 'psychological', 'economic', and 'systems' theories. This chapter focuses on the latter, that is HRD from a 'systems' perspective.

In a review of the status of systems theory and thinking (ST&T) in HRD Robert Yawson concluded that HRD research and practice has tended to focus on 'hard systems thinking' based on a 'linear [that is, step-by-step] epistemology'. This approach has been used as the basis of generic systematic models such as the 'analysis, diagnosis, development, implementation, and evaluation' (ADDIE) model (closely related to the 'instructional systems design' or ISD model) and the numerous variations on this theme. The origins of the systematic (ADDIE) approach are in the USA government's Training Within Industry (TWI) project in World War II (WW2). The objective of the TWI projects was to support war equipment contractors in 'getting out greater quantities of higher quality products at lower cost, and in a way that both supervisors and workers like'.[1]

The principles of the ADDIE/systematic approach are summarized by Irwin Goldstein, author of the HRD classic textbook *Training in Organizations*, as follows:

- Workplace training is an intentional and systematic approach to employee learning and development;
- Training is conducted to meet a perceived need, and learning outcomes include changes in knowledge, skills and attitudes (KSAs);
- The resultant improvements are measured by the extent to which the learning that results from training leads to meaningful changes in individual and organizational performance.

The systematic approach to training (SAT), of which ADDIE is one variant, exists in various guises. This analyse, design, develop, implement, evaluate framework is a systematic process based essentially on a 'plan, do, check' logic; see Figure 10.1.

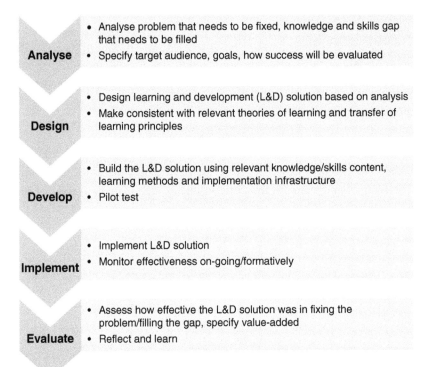

Analyse
- Analyse problem that needs to be fixed, knowledge and skills gap that needs to be filled
- Specify target audience, goals, how success will be evaluated

Design
- Design learning and development (L&D) solution based on analysis
- Make consistent with relevant theories of learning and transfer of learning principles

Develop
- Build the L&D solution using relevant knowledge/skills content, learning methods and implementation infrastructure
- Pilot test

Implement
- Implement L&D solution
- Monitor effectiveness on-going/formatively

Evaluate
- Assess how effective the L&D solution was in fixing the problem/filling the gap, specify value-added
- Reflect and learn

Figure 10.1   The ADDIE model

The systematic approach was developed as a way to improve training methods so as to produce measurable improvements in individual and organizational performance. One consequence of this is that it may lead to the perception of training as being the focal point of HRD.[2] As we know, from a number of the theories of learning discussed in Part 1 of this book, training is a method of formal learning and is only one element in the HRD 'mix'.

Following its development in the US military after WW2, the systematic approach was adopted by major US corporations such as Arthur Andersen, 3M and General Motors. W. Clayton Allen and Richard Swanson, in a retrospective on the use of systematic approaches in HRD, commented that the original ADDIE model (the precursor of subsequent systematic approaches) was suitable for a large homogenous HRD function, but proved less adequate for the more dynamic business organizations. Whilst Allen and Swanson note that 'although there are more glamorous HRD interventions – such as organization development and action learning – systemic training is at the core of HRD' (p. 428). The approach has stood the test of time and has helped organizations to create value-adding formal learning and development solutions.[3] Critics have argued that although systems thinking is a core foundation of HRD much of the theorizing in this area has been naïve, unitarist, apolitical, and overly-rationalist based on linear input–transformation–output system models which are incapable of handling the complexities that are inherent in modern forms of organizing.[4]

Delve deeper 10.1

Read Read more about the systematic approach in the Special Issue (SI) of the journal *Advances in Developing Human Resources* (*ADHR*) published in 2006 (Volume 8, Issue 4) edited by W. Clayton Allen and Richard A. Swanson.

Particular attention is given in this chapter to the early stages of the ADDIE process whilst Chapter 11 explores how HRD can use technology in combination with other modes of delivery to add value for its primary stakeholders. The final stage of the ADDIE approach, 'evaluation', is the main topic of Chapter 12.

Identifying and analysing learning and development needs

The initial steps of the systematic approach are vitally important because they lay the foundations for the subsequent stages by:

- Identifying the learning need: this stage determines whether or not a need actually exists, and whether the identified need can be 'fixed' using a learning and development solution (such as training, e-learning, coaching, etc.) or whether some other non-learning solution is required such as automation, changes to reward systems, etc. This stage is sometimes referred to as training needs identification (TNI) or learning needs identification (LNI);
- Analysing the learning need: in this stage the precise nature of the identified learning need is specified on the assumption that the required solution is learning-related. The intended outcomes are expressed typically in behavioural terms (for example, as 'learning objectives'). This stage delves deeper into the identified need and is sometimes referred to as training needs analysis (TNA) or learning needs analysis (LNA).

If these two stages are overlooked, neglected or carried out incompetently then any subsequent learning and development is unlikely to add value and more likely to be a waste of resources, and may have a negative impact on HRD's credibility and reputation. Learning needs can be identified and analysed at the individual, job and organizational levels; see Figure 10.2.

Learning needs identification and analysis at the individual level seeks to answer the question 'What are the learning and development needs of an individual employee?' Answers to this question could be found using tools and techniques such as performance appraisal (which applies to most job types and job levels) and 360 degree feedback (which may be especially useful in identifying learning needs for leadership development). In using performance appraisal caution may need to be exercised if managers are not able or aren't best-placed to make accurate or unbiased judgements. Ways around such potential biases include:

- Using standardized frameworks (such as competencies) to identify job-relevant knowledge and skills;
- Making appraisals more developmental rather than judgemental;
- Developing the skills of appraisers, for example by making them aware of implicit factors in the process such as unconscious biases related to factors such as stereotyping and liking/disliking.[5]

Appraisals are a source of information about individual learning needs and are typically carried out by the learner's line manager. A wider perspective can be gained from 360 degree feedback. This involves obtaining feedback on an employee's performance from multiple sources, for example from their line manager, peers, subordinates, internal customers and sometimes external customers as well. The process is highly structured, feedback is sought in the form of ratings across a range of competencies often through the use of formal instruments to ensure a consistency of approach. Both appraisals and 360 feedback should aim to identify not only the knowledge and skills that an employee needs to learn in order to realize her potential and ambitions but also how acquiring new knowledge and skills can add value to the organization's pursuit of its strategic objectives.

Individual-level needs analysis

- Uncover who needs training and determine what kind of training they need. Ensure it fits learners' needs. Also referred to as 'person analysis'

Job/task-level needs analysis

- Specify work, competency and teamwork requirements. Identify what is 'need to know' vs. 'nice to know'. Conduct hierarchical task analysis for procedural tasks/cognitive task analysis for knowledge-based jobs.

Organization-level needs analysis

- Examine strategic priorities and the culture, norms, resources, limitations, and support for training. Determine whether policies and procedures in place support training

Figure 10.2 The levels of needs analysis

Perspective from practice 10.1

'Personal development plans' (PDP) and 'continuing professional development' (CPD)

An outcome of learning needs identification and analysis at the individual level can be structured as a 'personal development plan' (PDP) and, for particular professional groups, can also be linked to 'continuing professional development' (CPD). Having a PDP is part of the process of becoming a 'reflective practitioner' and engaging in CPD is a vital aspect of most professional work and for membership of professional bodies

(Continued)

(such as CIPD) and a requirement for progression within professions such as health care, HR, etc.

In the UK's NHS people working in health care are encouraged to review their goals and achievements on a regular basis and maintain an up to date personal development plan. The NHS describes a PDP as an individualized systematic identification of personal learning, educational and professional development needs which specifies learning and development goals for the coming year and the timescale and resources required. A good PDP should be the product of careful thought and reflection preferably with a colleague or line manager, and specify:

- What is to be learned and what resources are needed;
- What are the timescales and when the review points will be;
- How the learner will know if outcomes have been achieved and what the supporting evidence will be.

A PDP, although it is a personal plan, should also make clear how individual learning and development connects and contributes to organizational objectives.

CPD helps employees to manage their learning and development throughout their career; it can open-up new opportunities, keep knowledge and skills up to date and ensure that employees have the knowledge and skills required to carry out their jobs legally and safely. The UK's CIPD uses a 'CPD Map' which is based on the 'CIPD Profession map' (consisting of several key areas of HR 'professional knowledge' such as 'Learning and Development', 'Organization Development and Design', 'Employee Engagement', etc.). The process begins with self-assessment to identify which grade of CIPD membership is appropriate and offers guidance for preparing for working at a higher level in the HR profession. Assessments on a rating scale from 'emerging' to 'exceeding' are made in relation to specific behaviours, for example at a senior practitioner level this might be 'Challenging and shaping strategic decisions with other leaders across the organization'. Tailored guidance and development actions that are specific to current role or to a new role or level that's being targeted are offered. The system offers a 'summary' assessment of where the individual is at (for example, 'seems like you're at the right level'), development actions (for example, 'identify external opportunities to discuss and share your organization's strategy', reading and research (books, etc.)) and suggested events. The system identifies the actions that need to be taken to advance to higher professional levels ('associate member', 'chartered member', or 'chartered fellow').

Sources: NHS Personal and Professional Development. Available online: www.healthcareers.nhs.uk/career-planning/developing-your-health-career/personal-and-professional-development (accessed 27-01-21); CIPD My CPD Map. Available online: https://mycpdmap.cipd.co.uk/ (accessed 27-01-21).

Learning needs identification and analysis at the job level aims to answer the question 'What are the learning needs of a specific job or the tasks that go to make up a job?' and overlaps with the individual level assessment discussed above. Organizational-level learning needs identification seeks to answer the question 'What are the learning needs for an organization at a particular time and under particular sets of circumstances?' and links to the topics of Organization Development (OD) (see below) and organizational learning (see Chapter 13). Potential sources of data for learning needs analyses include mining existing organizational data and intelligence, formal interviews and focus groups with stakeholders, informal 'water cooler' conversations with stakeholders, attending team and project meetings, surveys, data held in management information or learning management systems (LMS), competence frameworks and regulatory requirements for particular roles, and other business documents such as strategic plans, etc.[6]

—Delve deeper 10.2—

Read more about learning needs identification and analysis and the application of the systematic approach in:

Roberts, P. B. (2006). Analysis: The defining phase of systematic training. *Advances in Developing Human Resources*, 8(4), 476–491.

Robson, F. (2009). *Learning needs analysis. CIPD Toolkit*. London: CIPD.

Salas, E., Tannenbaum, S. I., Kraiger, K., & Smith-Jentsch, K. A. (2012). The science of training and development in organizations: What matters in practice. *Psychological Science in the Public Interest, 13*(2), 74–101.

HRD function and its stakeholders

The design and implementation of learning and development should be based on the application of relevant learning theories. The micro-aspects of the design of learning are covered in Chapters 2 through 7 of this book. The practical challenge is using these theories to inform the design and implementation of learning. In larger organizations the design and implementation of learning and development is the remit of the HRD function. It's the HRD function and the specialists within in it who are the learning and development 'experts' in organizations and their role is to manage learning processes in such a way as to enable individuals to realize their potential and also support the organization in achieving its strategic goals. Ultimately the HRD function exists in order to add value for its stakeholders. In this section we'll discuss the role and remit of the HRD function in organizations and explore in more depth who its main stakeholders are.

HRD function

In business the term 'function' refers to the activities carried out by an organization. Business functions are sometimes divided into 'core' functions (that is, the activities that are involved directly in the production of goods or the delivery of services, for example, primary care in a health service organization or manufacturing in the automobile industry) and 'support' functions (that is, ancillary activities that enable the organization to carry out its core activities). HRD, along with HR, is an example of a support function. It's not involved directly in the production of goods or delivery of services to the organizations' customers or clients but nonetheless its activities are required if the organization's core functions are to be fulfilled. HR and HRD have traditionally been categorized as an 'administrative' or 'management' function (other examples of support functions include marketing, logistics, finance, etc.).[7]

The HRD function (which may also be known as the 'Learning and Development (L&D) Function', 'Training and Development (T&D) Function', etc.) is the part of the organization that is responsible for the management of learning and development processes and systems within an organization. For example, in terms of systems, the HRD function could be responsible for learning management systems, e-learning systems, etc.; in terms of processes its responsibilities would likely include provision of workshops and training courses, designing and implementing management and leadership development, working with colleagues in other business functions, such as line managers, in the identification of employees' learning and development needs, etc. The HRD function is often located within the broader human resources (HR) function and may have an HRD (or L&D, T&D, etc.) Manager and HRD advisers who report in to the HRD manager and are responsible for the HRD function's operational activities.

Perspective from practice 10.2

A day in the life of an HRD specialist

The Samaritans is a charity based in the UK whose vision is that 'fewer people die by suicide'. The organization has over 200 local branches and over 20,000 trained volunteers who every year 'spend over one million hours answering calls for help via our unique 24-hour listening service, email, letter, face to face'. The CIPD offered 'Neil's story', a 'day in the life of Neil Barnett, Learning and Development Adviser at the Samaritans'. Neil described his overall role as 'producing learning solutions' that 'improve the service we provide to our users' (that is Samaritans' Volunteers). The key responsibilities of Neil's role include:

- Holding L&D project 'scoping meetings' with client managers who will use the L&D solution;
- Performing focus group meetings with representatives of the target audience;
- Developing learning solutions based on the evidence gathered from scoping and focus group meetings;
- If the solution is digital, working with external partners to provide digital learning solutions;
- Refining solutions by testing them out with pilot groups before they're delivered by trainers in the field, rolled out as an e-learning offering, etc.;

- Supporting and monitoring implementation of L&D solutions, for example to ensure compliance with organization's HR and HRD policies.

When asked what motivates him most in this work Neil commented that it is 'hugely satisfying' to know that the positive results from learning and development 'can lead to improving someone's emotional health and supporting them through tough times' and ultimately that 'a training course I created might help a Samaritans' service user come to a positive resolution, when they have been exploring suicidal thoughts, is incredibly rewarding'. These comments illustrate vividly the value that Neil's work can add for the Samaritans' stakeholders.

Source: CIPD (2021). A day in the life of an L&D specialist. Available online: www.cipd. co.uk/careers/career-options/learning-development-roles/day-in-learning-development (accessed 27-01-21).

Reflective question 10.1

To what extent does Neil's day-to-day activities align with the systematic approach discussed above, for example, plan, do, check cycle, the ADDIE method, systematic approach to training (SAT). Can you map his activities to each of the stages of one of these methods?

The purpose of the HRD function is to support the organization of which it is a part in the management of learning and development in order that individual employees can maximize their potential and so that the organization can achieve its strategic goals. Although the specifics are likely to vary across contexts, this is likely to involve (based on the CIPD's professional standards, for example) many if not all of the following activities:

- Designing, delivering and assessing learning solutions;
- Establishing learning and development needs at the individual, group and organizational levels;
- Applying learning theories to the selection of learning and development methods, and the design and delivery of learning solutions that meet identified learning needs;
- Engaging with managers in core and support business functions to enlist and engage their support for learning and development solutions of all types (on-job, off-job, coaching, mentoring, eLearning, etc);
- Evaluating the effectiveness of learning and development.

Management is essentially about asking questions, taking decisions and solving problems. Ed Salas and colleagues offered a list of questions that leaders, managers and practitioners might ask about the practice of learning and development in order to ensure that HRD solutions add value, summarized in Figure 10.3.

For HRD in general

- Have we invested sufficiently/wisely in learning-related infrastructure/resources/activities?
- How have we determined/prioritized most important learning needs?
- How clear are we about knowledge/skills/behaviours/competencies needed to survive and thrive?
- Where are the crucial knowledge/skills gaps?
- Have we diagnosed how conducive organizational culture is for learning?
- What are we doing to make our organization climate more conducive for learning?
- What do managers need to do to send the right signals about the importance of learning and development?
- How will we know that our overall efforts in learning and development have an impact and what evidence do we expect to see?

For specific HRD interventions

- What type of training needs analysis has been conducted to ensure we'll be developing the right knowledge/skills in the right way?
- What training strategy will be employed and how are we incorporating relevant learning theory into the design elements?
- How clear/measurable are the learning objectives?
- What are we doing to ensure we adequately engage, motivate, and challenge the learners?
- What are we going to do to ensure learners can apply new knowledge and skills?
- How will we prepare learners, remove obstacles, and reinforce/sustain learning?
- Is technology being used to enhance learning/job performance and not just 'look cool'?
- How will learning and development be evaluated, what will impact look like, and whose bottom line is value being added to?
- Would it make any difference if we didn't do this?

Figure 10.3   Key questions for and about HRD and other internal stakeholders (Salas et al., 2012)

In the HRD system the various individuals and groups involved have a requirement and responsibility to ask and provide the answers to these questions if they're to add value to the HRD system and receive value from learning and development activities and processes. Value creation is a two-way process of 'co-creation'. For example, learners have a requirement and responsibility to ask and provide answers to questions such as 'are you learning what you need to learn?'; similarly, line managers might ask 'what knowledge and skills does your team need to add value?' and senior managers might ask 'what are our learning and development priorities in taking this business forward?'.

As noted earlier, a stakeholder is an individual or group of individuals that has some vested interest in an organization and its operations. HRD's stakeholders are those individuals or groups who have some vested interest in learning and development processes in an organization and in how these processes are facilitated, enabled and managed by the HRD function. HRD stakeholders can be internal to the organization or external. Internal stakeholders include learners and HRD practitioners, as well as senior managers and line managers; these can also be described as HRD's 'primary stakeholders'. External stakeholders include providers and suppliers of learning and development solutions (these are sometimes referred to as 'value-chain stakeholders'), the organization's customers, its local community, and wider society. The idea of a stakeholder has also been extended to include the natural environment since it can be affected profoundly by business organizations' activities (for example, transitions to 'net zero', etc.). The roles of the various internal stakeholders in terms of 'ownership', 'participation' and 'feedback' are shown in Figure 10.4.

Role	Internal Stakeholders			
	Senior managers	**Line managers**	**Learners**	**HRD practitioners**
Ownership	Articulate a clear vision Value HRD's contribution to strategy Own the idea of learning as a source of competitive advantage	'Buy-in' to organizational goals and maximizing human potential Recognize HRD contribution to adding value	Engage in learning Commitment to continuous maintenance and / or improvement of job-related knowledge and skills	'Buy-in' to an HRD role that is proactive and transformative Share ownership with other stakeholders Outsource where necessary
Participation	Be a role model for line managers/learners Resource provision to support learning Participate as learners in manager and leader development	Identify learning needs Engage in coaching, mentoring, be a role model Create opportunities for learning Support transfer of learning	Self-direction and motivation Engagement in learning Apply new learnings in workplace Capture and share knowledge	Exhibit role flexibility: 'provider', 'internal consultant', 'change agent', etc. Integrate/align HRD activities vertically with strategy / horizontally with HRM
Feedback	Make it mandatory for learning and development to be evaluated Give feedback/listen to findings See learning as a means to shape strategy	Support evaluation Give feedback on HRD Listen to feedback from learners Act on feedback	Engage in evaluation Give formative feedback for continuous improvement of HRD	Elicit feedback and evaluation Be open to criticism Exhibit competence in evaluation techniques and methods

Figure 10.4 HRD's 'primary' stakeholders and their roles

Research insight 10.1

Stakeholder-based HRD (SBHRD)

Pyounggu Baek and Namhee Kim argued that one of the problems with traditional systematic approaches in HRD is that they tend to focus not only on one specific method, namely employee training, but also on a narrow group of stakeholder interests (for example when performance is measured in purely financial alignment with shareholder value), but that there is a need to embrace a variety of stakeholder interests.

(Continued)

Baek and Kim propose a framework for identifying and analysing the different interests of HRD's stakeholders. In their stakeholder-based HRD model (SBHRD) they argued that SBHRD:

- Reflects the true plurality of stakeholder interests and activities in HRD practice for instance by embracing formal/informal, tacit/explicit, on-job/off-job, planned/ incidental learning and development which goes beyond large-firm, systematic approach models of HRD;
- Can help HRD to earn legitimacy from a wider range of internal and external stakeholders, especially given that securing legitimacy for HRD's practices in organizations and wider society is essential to fulfilling its purpose. A failure to engage with stakeholders could end-up delegitimizing HRD;
- Identifies dichotomies, false dichotomies and 'binaries' such as learning versus performance paradigms, worker versus manager, individual versus organization, profit versus purpose and instead treats these as tensions in a paradox that can be productively debated and reconciled and resolved.

At a broader level, considering a wider range of stakeholders and their interests offers a more holistic, integrated, contextualized perspective. Ultimately SBHRD has a broad and encompassing vision which aligns with McLean and McLean's definition of HRD as 'Any process or activity that, either initially or over the long-term, has the potential to develop adult's work-based knowledge, expertise productivity and satisfaction, whether for personal or group/team gain or for the benefit of an organizational community, a nation or ultimately the whole of humanity' (see Chapter 1).

Source: Baek, P., & Kim, N. (2014). Exploring a theoretical foundation for HRD in society: Toward a model of stakeholder-based HRD. *Human Resource Development International*, *17*(5), 499–513.

Claire Gubbins and colleagues have noted that the 'Achilles heel of HRD' is the perception amongst some stakeholders, especially those that hold the purse strings, that its costs may outweigh its benefits. Their concept of evidence-based HRD (EBHRD) complements SBHRD in that EBHRD supports a process of decision-making in HRD (for example, which HRD solutions to use) that is grounded in the best available scientific evidence. EBHRD offers a means by which HRD practitioners can demonstrate their professional competence and enlist and enhance stakeholder support for HRD activity.[8] As noted in previous chapters, some of the best available scientific evidence is to be found in meta-analyses, experimental studies, longitudinal studies and systematic reviews.

The view that HRD's remit is solely to return value to shareholders has been superseded by the view that HRD has to engage with and has a responsibility to a wider group of stakeholders. This is aligned with more holistic perspectives such as 3BL (triple bottom line), CSR, and stakeholder capitalism in which the idea of purpose goes beyond but does not eschew financial performance and profit.[9] A significant question for HRD is how can it contribute to 'doing well by doing good'? This is an important ethical and pragmatic issue for HRD.

---Delve deeper 10.3---

Read more about stakeholders, SBHRD and EBHRD in:

Baek, P., & Kim, N. (2014). Exploring a theoretical foundation for HRD in society: Toward a model of stakeholder-based HRD. *Human Resource Development International, 17*(5), 499–513.

Beer, M., Boselie, P., & Brewster, C. (2015). Back to the future: Implications for the field of HRM of the multi-stakeholder perspective proposed 30 years ago. *Human Resource Management, 54*(3), 427–438.

Gubbins, C., Harney, B., van der Werff, L., & Rousseau, D. (2018). Enhancing the Trustworthiness and Credibility of HRD: Evidence-based Management to the Rescue? *Human Resource Development Quarterly, 29*(3), 193–202.

The HRD system in smaller firms

This chapter is about HRD systems, however small firms tend to lack formal HRD policies or systems. Some small firms may even pride themselves on their use of 'hands-on learning' which avoids the use of formalized and bureaucratic systems.[10] If this is a general phenomenon and if learning is occurring in smaller firms – as it surely must be – then it begs questions about how do smaller firms meet the learning and development needs of their employees and learn as organizations if they don't do so in a systematic and formalized way?

Small and medium-sized enterprises, also known as SMEs, are defined in various ways. For example, in terms of 'head count': in the UK and the EU a 'micro' company has less than ten employees; a 'small' company is one that has less than 50 employees; a 'medium-sized' company has less than 250 employees; a large company has more than 250 employees. In the UK according to the Federation for Small Businesses (FSB) at the start of 2020:[11]

- SMEs accounted for the vast majority of the business population (there were about 5.9 million of them);
- SMEs accounted for three-fifths of employment and around half of the turnover in the UK private sector;
- SMEs employed around 17 million people (62 per cent of the total);
- Around 20 per cent of all SMEs were in construction, 15 per cent in professional, scientific and technical and 9 per cent in retail.

It goes without saying that SMEs are a pillar of the UK economy, and the same is true in economies across the world. World Bank data show that SMEs represent about 90 per cent of business and more than 50 per cent of employment worldwide. As the global workforce grows over half a billion new jobs will be needed by 2030 and SMEs will be the major providers of new employment, especially in developing countries and hence contribute significantly to more inclusive globalization and growth.[12]

The practice of HRD in smaller firms, at least when thought of 'traditionally' (that is in terms of systematic approaches and training courses), is often significantly different to HRD in larger firms. Ronan Carbery summarized the differences as follows in that SMEs tend to have:

- No, or minimal, dedicated HRD function or significant HRD budget;
- Lower participation in government and formalized training schemes (including apprenticeships);
- Less formal training and management development;
- Different attitudes towards the value of formal HRD;
- Perception of HRD driven by attitude of owner/managers in absence of HRD specialists;
- Less structured approach to planning and delivery of learning;
- Recognition of, and greater reliance, on informal methods of learning.[13]

Figure 10.5 quantifies some of the differences between SMEs and larger firms based on the CIPD's *Learning and Skills at Work 2020* report.[14]

Learning in SMEs appears to be driven to a considerable extent by the characteristics, attitudes and values of SME owner-managers, pragmatic concerns of survival and growth and a need to solve immediate and pressing problems.[15] According to the OECD SMEs face barriers to their participation and contribution to economic growth as a result of deficiencies in physical resources, such as infrastructure and digitization, and access to 'strategic' human resource functions, such as learning and development. In the OECD view these key resources support SMEs' competitiveness and help them to

Learning and development (L&D)	SME	Large firms
Have specialist L&D function	11%	41%
No L&D function (part of operations/manager role)	36%	5%
L&D is part of generalist HR activity	22%	12%
Number of employees in L&D	7	118
L&D identifies learning needs	5%	27%
Senior directors identify learning needs	41%	17%
Not conducting evaluation of HRD	35%	26%
Delivering apprenticeships	15%	50%
L&D 'owns' learning budget	9%	31%

Figure 10.5 Differences in learning and development between SMEs and large firms

develop, grow and contribute to local and national economies. SMEs, unlike their large firm counterparts, often lack in-house knowledge and expertise in HRD and consequently are unable to devote scarce resources to accessing or developing the necessary expertise. Hence they may have to incur the costs of relying on external advisors in specialist areas such as HRD. The OECD identified significant consequences for SMEs including being held back from participation in the knowledge economy, difficulties in attracting and retaining highly qualified and ambitious employees and being behind the curve in the use of more sophisticated company-level learning strategies and technologies that promote learning.[16] The consequent knowledge and skill deficiencies are considered to impact negatively on many areas of small business activity.

These arguments, from the OECD and others, have created what has been referred to as a 'deficiency model' of HRD in SMEs based on the potentially flawed assumption that because 'not much formal HRD takes place' therefore learning does not take place.[17] Such an argument appears to be based on the view that informal learning solutions are inferior to planned interventions such as training courses. As we have discovered elsewhere in this book this is a questionable assumption. This 'deficiency' view of learning in SMEs overlooks the significant contribution that informal learning makes to the acquisition of job-relevant knowledge and skills. Small size is often interpreted as being a liability for learning; however, this need not be the case, smallness of size may offer the potential for SMEs to develop lean informal learning systems that are capable of agile responses to their learning needs.

Research insight 10.2

Employee training and employee learning in SMEs

SME researcher John Kitching conducted telephone interviews with 1005 employers and face-to-face interviews with a sample of 50 employers in UK SMEs. In the survey it was found that formal training activity was limited, for example only one in twenty reported having a training budget; however the face to face interviews revealed a slightly different picture. Only 26 out of the 50 reported external training (mostly short courses of a day or less duration) whereas workplace learning occurred 'most of the time' by means of a wide variety of practices including learning by doing, planned on-job learning guided by managers, co-workers, etc., unplanned interactions, learning from material artefacts, using computers to search for information. Methods such as these were preferred mainly for reasons of 'relevance' and 'convenience'. Kitching's conclusion was that the 'default position' for most small employers is to 'enable learning opportunities at the workplace unless there are strong reasons to do otherwise' (p. 54).

More recently, Idris Bochra and colleagues, in a survey of 15,000 owner-managers of SMEs in the UK, differentiated between off-job and on-job training and the combinations of both types of training and analysed their relationships with performance. They found

(Continued)

that on-job and off-job training are linked to performance and that the effect of combining the two types is stronger than the individual effects of each type. The researchers argued that combining on-job and off-job training is likely to be a more effective strategy to boost performance than is focusing on a single type of training. It seems that a combination of formal and informal learning creates a solution that works better than either formal (off-job) or informal (on-job) alone.

Sources: Bochra, I., Saridakis, G., and Johnstone, S. (2020). Training and performance in SMEs: Empirical evidence from large-scale data from the UK. *Journal of Small Business Management*. doi.org/10.1080/00472778.2020.1816431; Kitching, J. (2007). Regulating employment relations through workplace learning: A study of small employers. *Human Resource Management Journal*, *17*(1), 42–57.

HRD research has tended to focus on formal learning with a bias towards large organizations. As various researchers have noted the term 'HRD', which arose in academic circles in the USA several decades ago (see Chapter 1), is highly unlikely to be a term that owners and managers, let alone employees, in SMEs would recognize.[18] Research that is aligned with the deficiency model, as well as overlooking the power of informal learning, also erroneously assumes that SMEs are simply smaller versions of larger firms.[19] As Kitching has noted (see above), in the SME sector the term 'training' is seen to refer to something that employers 'provide' for their workforce whereas 'learning' as something that employees 'do' either with or without the support or intervention of their employer, and this informal learning occurs in the natural flow of working. The nature of SMEs themselves may mean that the amount of learning that actually takes place is under reported. As a result the informal and socially situated learning that occurs in SMEs in the everyday activities of running a business is often hidden from view in traditional HRD and training research.[20] For SMEs the synergies from the mix of both formal and informal learning seem to offer advantages over using either formal or informal learning.

Reflective question 10.2

Given what you have learned about theories of learning in previous chapters what advantages do social and situated learning, experience based modalities and informal and incidental learning offer SMEs? What are the disadvantages for SMEs of these approaches?

Ciara Nolan and Thomas Garavan noted any unwillingness to engage in formal HRD is an entirely rational and informed decision on the part of owner-managers who seek to embed learning within the day-to-day operations of the firm.[21] As such the concept of formal learning doesn't capture the richness of learning that takes place in successful small firms and which makes successful ones both resilient and sustainable cogs in the 'engine' of economic growth in nations across the globe. Indeed it may even be the case that in SMEs formalization of learning and development may be antithetical to the dynamism, agility and creativity that business venturing thrives on. If this is so we must be careful in our assessments of learning in SMEs and avoid conflating formalization and systematization with fitness-for-purpose and quality. The question arises however of at what point in the evolution or maturity of a small firm does an absence of formalization and systematization of HRD start to impact negatively on the efficiency and effectiveness of learning processes and become detrimental to outcomes?

―Delve deeper 10.4―

Read more about learning and development in SMEs in:

Nolan, C. T., & Garavan, T. N. (2016). Human resource development in SMEs: A systematic review of the literature. *International Journal of Management Reviews*, 18(1), 85–107.

HRD and organization development

Organization development (OD) is a method for integrated, systematic and system-wide interventions used in order to effect and embed meaningful change in organizational cultures and sub-cultures (which may be in varying degrees of alignment with each other). OD is defined as a planned and systematic change effort using the principles of organizational theory and behavioural science to help organizations become more robust, resilient and sustainable through the use of interventions based on values such as respect, inclusion, collaboration, authenticity, self-awareness, empowerment, democracy and social justice.[22] OD's roots can be traced to the work of Kurt Lewin (his model of change from the 1930s and '40s) and Richard Beckhard (who first coined the term 'OD' in the 1960s). OD was associated with the rise to prominence of the practice of 'T-groups' in the 1960s (that is, 'sensitivity training' or 'encounter groups'), the work of Wilfred Bion (the 'Tavistock school') and Eric Trist (sociotechnical systems theory) in the UK as well as later in W. Edwards Deming's work on continuous process improvement (1980s) and the TQM (Total Quality Management) movement.[23]

―In their own words 10.1―

Beckhard on the emergence of OD

Richard Beckhard (1918 to 1999) is often credited as the originator of the term OD; his classic work is *Organization Development: Strategies and Models* (1969). Beckhard's definition of OD is: 'Organization development is an effort (1) planned, (2) organization-wide, and (3) managed from the top, to (4) increase organization effectiveness and

(Continued)

health through (5) planned interventions in the organization's "processes", using behavioral-science knowledge.' Writing in 1969, he framed the emergence of the concept as a response to attempts in the first half of the twentieth century to 'cope with and shape [organizational] environments' through 'better "human engineering", to rationalize the way work was done; the way the workforce was utilized to increase output; and the productivity of goods and services produced'.[24] In the second half of the twentieth century there was a shift as a result of a 'considerably improved human condition' for 'working men [sic] to demand that the working environment meet some of their social needs in addition to needs for survival and security'. These observations may seem surprising now given that addressing employees' 'social needs' is taken for granted, but at the time management was still dominated by scientific management and 'Taylorism'.

Source: Grieves, J. (2000). Introduction: The origins of organizational development. *The Journal of Management Development, 19*(5), 345–447.

Organization development (OD) is closely related to HRD in a number of ways; for example they both have roots in similar areas, such as the behavioural sciences, and there are significant overlaps between them in terms of the solutions they employ and their goals. They also differ in a number of ways, for instance HRD's remit, as traditionally practised, is relatively narrow, formal learning is a key intervention and the focus is on performance as an outcome. For OD on the other hand formal training is simply one option amongst many solutions, but the main difference is that OD's 'canvas' is much larger and changes in organizational culture are at least as important as improvements in performance.[25] Traditional OD models have at their core the Lewinian three-stage model of 'unfreezing' (readiness), change (moving/adoption) and 'refreezing' (institutionalization). OD as traditionally practised is a systematic process and consists of the following general stages: 'entering and contracting' (Stage 1), 'diagnosing' (Stage 2), 'planning and implementing change' (Stage 3), and 'evaluating and institutionalizing change' (Stage 4) (although there are many variations on this theme), and various interventions are applied at different levels in the third stage; see Figure 10.6.[26]

The field of OD itself has gone through changes and an amount of 'soul searching' about its purpose, methods and the value that it adds. OD is a specialized skill that typically may reside in the HR function or be bought-in from external OD consultancies. The acquisition of OD skills by HR/HRD practitioners enables the HRD function to have greater strategic alignment of its activities and wider impact. OD exists in many different guises, for example external OD specialists working with HR colleagues to develop performance management systems, internal HR practitioners working in an OD role with colleagues in other functions to embed team working and empowerment in the organization, etc.[27] OD is related to organization design (reviewing and reshaping organization-wide systems and structures and the associated polices, practices and

Individual-level interventions

- Coaching, mentoring, multi-rater feedback, job redesign, conflict management, training, leader development, etc.

Team-level interventions

- Team building, process consultation, 'fishbowls', action learning, etc.

Process-level interventions

- Total Quality Management (TQM), 'lean', process improvement, benchmarking, Six Sigma, etc.

Organization-level interventions

- Culture change/transformation, stategic planning, reshaping/redesign, succession planning, organizational learning/learning organization, performance management, etc.

Transnational-level interventions

- Cultural change, transnational working, expatriate adjustment, etc.

Figure 10.6 Selection of OD interventions

processes) as 'Organization Development and Design'. From the perspective of the HR profession, the CIPD described OD as 'one of the most critical practices an organization needs to maintain performance within a rapidly changing environment'.

Perspective from practice 10.3

OD in the UK's National Health Service Leadership Academy (NHSLA)

The UK National Health Service's Leadership Academy (NHSLA) aims to 'develop better leaders, delivering better care' and offers Organization Development (OD) as one of a number of resources to help it achieve this goal. By developing its leaders the NHS will be able to lead change, deliver service improvements and better engage and motivate staff enabling them to deliver improved care for patients. The NHSLA commissioned the Institute for Employment Studies (IES) to better understand how to re-shape its development programme for people in Director-level roles across the service. This intervention is an example of OD aimed at senior leader development. The researchers found that the top three development needs were 'systems leadership' (that is, understand the changing health landscape, interpersonal skills for operating in complex cross-collaborative arrangements), 'leading without authority and through others' (as is necessary in cross-collaborative working) and 'resilience' (to be able to operate in a stressful, complex, ambiguous and dynamic environment). The research revealed a 'waning interest in big set-piece' generic leadership development

(Continued)

programmes and an increased appetite for bespoke whole-board development, place-based (for example, for large urban areas) and issue-based (for example, cross-sector participation) development interventions using short ('bite-sized') learning 'events', 'immersive'/experiential programmes and innovative methods such as 'mindfulness training' and the use of 'shadow boards'. The report concluded with a series of recommendations, including moving away from the generic set-piece programme, the use of modular 'pick-and-mix' provision, and positioning the NHSLA's development offerings as 'positive, stretching and challenging'.

Source: Institute for Employment Studies (2018). *Need for and provision of director-level leadership development: Research for NHS Leadership Academy*. Brighton: IES.

Reflective question 10.3

This book's definition of HRD practice is the 'management of individual and collective learning and development processes in organizations in such a way as to enable individual employees to achieve their full potential and organizations to achieve their strategic goals in ways that maximize stakeholder value, respect justice and fairness, and maintain the integrity of the natural environment'; other definitions are given in Chapter 1. OD is defined as 'a planned and systematic change effort using the principles of organizational theory and behavioural science to help organizations become more robust, resilient and sustainable through the use of OD interventions based on values such as respect, inclusion, collaboration, authenticity, self-awareness, empowerment, democracy and social justice'. On the basis of these definitions how are HRD and OD related (in terms of similarities and differences and overlap) and what is the distinct value-added of each field?

Delve deeper 10.5

Read more about OD in:

Burnes, B., & Cooke, B. (2012). The past, present and future of organization development: Taking the long view. *Human Relations*, 65(11), 1395–1429.

Burke, W. (2018). The rise and fall of the growth of organization development: What now? *Consulting Psychology Journal: Practice and Research*, 70(3), 186–206.

Read about the relationship between HRD and OD in:

Grieves, J., & Redman, T. (1999). Living in the shadow of OD: HRD and the search for identity. *Human Resource Development International*, 2(2), 81–102.

O'Toole, S. (2010). Training, L&D, OD, HRD – What's in a name? *Australian Journal of Adult Learning*, 50(2), 419–426.

Hamlin, B. and Stewart, J. (2011). What is HRD? A definitional review and synthesis of the HRD domain. *Journal of European Industrial Training*, 35(3), 199–220.

International HRD

The megatrend of globalization (see Chapter 8) has been an important factor in driving interest in international, comparative and cross-cultural HRD. The field of 'international HRD (IHRD)' has been defined as the 'formulation and practice of HRD systems, practices and policies at the global, societal and organization levels' which can be concerned with everything from how governments and international organizations develop global HRD systems and how organizations nurture international managers to 'how societies develop national HRD policies'.[28] However, the boundaries of this field are sometimes difficult to discern; for example, Thomas Garavan and Ronan Carberry noted that HRD researchers often refer to a number of constructs as being 'almost interchangeable with international HRD' including 'national HRD', 'comparative HRD' and 'cross-cultural HRD'. Garavan and colleagues in their introduction to an international handbook on the subject describe IHRD as 'fragmented', 'abstract', and 'elusive'. Valerie Anderson remarked that although there is a substantial body of literature devoted to international HRD (IHRD) a definition of the field remains elusive but nonetheless was able to identify four distinct areas of IHRD research and practice; see Figure 10.7.[29]

Pursuing the ambiguities around IHRD, Gary McLean and Laird McLean asked the question 'if we can't define HRD in one country how can we define it in an international context?' and observed in their review of the literature that:

- The most extensive literature on HRD has been created in UK and US contexts;
- US definitions appear to have influenced definitions around the world;
- Definitions of HRD vary between local companies and MNCs and in MNCs definitions appear to be influenced by their home country;
- Definitions appear to be influenced by local value systems, for example a 'performance orientation' in the US versus a 'community orientation' in Thailand;
- Levels of maturity of HRD in a particular context determine how it is defined.

IHRD is becoming increasingly relevant in a globalized world because of its focus on the learning and development of employees in MNCs, international organizations, global not-for-profit organizations and public sector organizations whose reach extends across national boundaries[30]. In their 21-chapter international handbook on the subject of IHRD Garavan and colleagues conclude by remarking that IHRD is a nascent but fact growing field which is ripe for future theorizing and research. An example of innovative thinking in IHRD is to be found in the model proposed by Thomas Garavan and colleagues in their 'ecosystems perspective' on IHRD.

National HRD	Internationalization of organizations and expatriate workers	Comparative and cross-cultural HRD	Global HRD
• Study of skill formation processes; workforce demographics; institutional relationships; workforce capability development; talent development and retention. Uses labour market theories, human capital, institutional, cultural, stakeholder theories, etc. • E.g. McLean and McLean's (2001) and Wang and McLean's (2007) studies of dilemma of defining national and international HRD	• Study of expatriate effectiveness; career development; individual and organizational performance in international contexts; business integration across national boundaries. Uses theories of career management and development, psychological contract, knowledge based views, human capital, etc. • E.g. Zhang's (2013) study of expatriate development for cross cultural adjustment; Stalker and Mavin's (2011) study of learning and development experiences of self-initiated expatriate women in the UAE	• Study of intercultural competencies; cross-cultural leadership; diversity and inclusion; learning effectiveness/organization development (OD) international contexts. Uses cultural theories, resource-based view (RBV), social capital and social network theories, institutional and labour market theories, etc. • E.g. Ardichvili and Kuchinke's (2002) study of leadership styles and cultural values among managers and subordinates across four countries in the former Soviet Union	• Study of organizational performance; learning, change and development in international contexts. Uses social network, structuration and stakeholder theories; knowledge-based view of the firm. • E.g. Gubbins and Garavan's (2009) study of understanding the role of HRD in MNCs and the significance of social capital and networking

Figure 10.7 Four dimensions of IHRD from Anderson (2015)[1]

[1]See: Anderson, V. (2015). International HRD and offshore outsourcing: A conceptual review and research agenda. *Human Resource Development Review*, 14(3): 259–278; McLean, G. N., & McLean, L. (2001). If we can't define HRD in one country, how can we define it in an international context? *Human Resource Development International*, 4(3): 313–326; Wang, X., & McLean, G. N. (2007). The dilemma of defining international human resource development. *Human Resource Development Review*, 6(1): 96–108; Stalker, B., & Mavin, S. (2011). Learning and development experiences of self-initiated expatriate women in the United Arab Emirates. *Human Resource Development International*, 14(3): 273–290; Zhang, Y. (2013). Expatriate development for cross-cultural adjustment: Effects of cultural distance and cultural intelligence. *Human Resource Development Review*, 12(2): 177–199; Ardichvili, A., & Kuchinke, K. P. (2002). Leadership styles and cultural values among managers and subordinates: A comparative study of four countries of the former Soviet Union, Germany, and the US. *Human Resource Development International*, 5(1): 99–117; Gubbins, C., & Garavan, T. N. (2009). Understanding the HRD role in MNCs: The imperatives of social capital and networking. *Human Resource Development Review*, 8(2): 245–275.

Research insight 10.3

An ecosystem perspective on international HRD

HRD 'ecosystems' exist at multiple levels of analysis from the individual/organizational (micro-) to the meso- and macro-levels and have distinct dynamics and processes that operate to produce HRD policies and practices. In their analysis (a 'meta-synthesis') of IHRD ecosystems Garavan and colleagues distinguished between content and process dimensions of the ecosystem:

- Ecosystem content: in the content dimension they distinguish between micro- (e.g. employees and workers, firm), meso- (e.g. suppliers, customers, educational institutions, consultants, etc.) and macro- (e.g. culture, institutions, governments, etc.) levels;
- Ecosystem processes: they note that the evidence for the process dimensions is more tentative but is likely to include emergence (with no actor in overall control), boundaries (that are open but distinctly defined), diversity (in the types of organizations, demographic characteristics of employees, etc.), coherence (e.g. the extent to which actors network with each other and coalesce around important practices and strategies, the density of and alignment within these relationships, etc.), and resilience (as a result of attention and attraction).

Their ecosystem model includes interactions, feedback and non-linear dynamics (for example systems grow and flourish where feedback is positive, best practices emerge, and the system becomes adaptable). Vicarious learning is also identified as an important process whereby actors learn from each other, for example through observing HRD in other organizations (Garavan et al., 2019). This novel approach is helpful in that it can show how affecting one part of the system can have knock-on effects because the parts of the system are interconnected, and that effects can be system-wide, complex, and 'emergent'.

Source: Garavan, T. N., McCarthy, A., & Carbery, R. (2019). An ecosystems perspective on international human resource development: A meta-synthesis of the literature. *Human Resource Development Review*, *18*(2), 248–288.

Delve deeper 10.6

Read more about international HRD research in:

Garavan, T. N., & Carbery, R. (2012). A review of international HRD: Incorporating a global HRD construct. *European Journal of Training and Development*, *36*(2/3), 129–157.

For extensive and authoritative reflections on the nature and scope of IHRD consult:

Garavan, T., McCarthy, A., & Carbery, R. (eds) (2017). International HRD: context, processes and people–introduction. In Garavan, T., McCarthy, A., & Carbery, R. (eds) *Handbook of international human resource development*. Cheltenham: Edward Elgar Publishing.

The learning 'ecosystem'

The 'ecosystem' concept is a potentially powerful metaphor that has attracted attention in recent years for describing and analysing systems and processes in organizations. A learning ecosystem consists of the systems and sub-systems that support the acquisition, sharing and application of knowledge and skills that enable individual employees to release their full potential, organizations to achieve their strategic goals and in which stakeholders (particularly HRD primary stakeholders) receive and create and value through mutual dependencies. An ecosystem of HRD view complements other holistic perspectives on learning in and by organizations such as strategic HRD (SHRD) (Chapter 9), organizational learning (Chapter 13) and learning organizations (Chapter 14).

The ecosystem approach utilizes 'systems thinking' which seeks to understand how elements in a system influence one another as part of an integrated whole through their linkages and interactions. As noted above systems thinking has a long heritage in HRD (as in Swanson's 'three-legged stool', see above) and in organizational learning theory and the learning organization concept (see Chapter 14). In HRD Swanson argued that a systems view 'captures the complex and dynamic interactions of environments, organizations, work processes and group/individual variables operating at any point in time and over time' (p. 305). In organizational learning theory, Peter Senge argued that a system (by definition) can only be understood by contemplating the whole rather than any individual part, and 'systems thinking' makes the patterns that are the functioning of the system clearer.

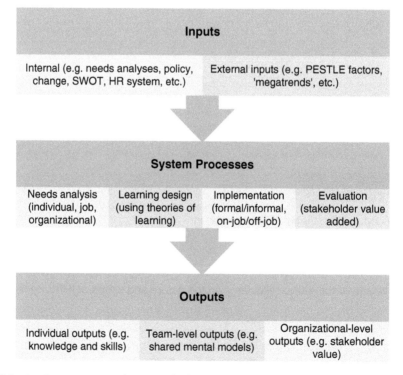

Figure 10.8 Inputs, processes and outputs of a learning system

To understand any system necessitates the study of 'system relationships that exist between the various parts that work in concert to determine the behaviour of the [whole] system'.[31] A simple framework for thinking about HRD systemically, that is in terms of inputs, processes and outputs, its actors, entities and contexts is shown in Figure 10.8.

However, this input–process–output model (IPO), whilst useful as a static picture, cannot capture the HRD system's complexities (the interweaving of the system's parts and processes) and dynamics (how the system as a whole changes over time or as a result of shocks to the system). This is because ecosystems are 'prototypical examples' of complex adaptive systems in which patterns at higher levels emerge from interactions at lower levels that simple linear models (such as that in Figure 10.8) cannot capture.[32] A 'complex adaptive system' (CAS) is as the name suggests not just 'complicated', it is complex, and has three characteristics:

- It has a number of heterogeneous agents who have the freedom to act and take decisions. In the case of HRD this would include its stakeholders, particularly its primary stakeholders since they add and receive most value from learning and development;
- Agents interact with one another in ways that are not always predictable, are non-linear, and one agent's action changes the context for other agents. In HRD, changes in consumer demand as a result of demographic factors might create requirements for employees to develop radically new skill sets in order to create and sustain competitive advantage in a volatile market place;
- Interactions and autonomous ('unowned') processes may lead to the emergence of global properties whereby the 'whole becomes greater than the sum of its parts' and may even take on a life of its own, with the implication that the whole cannot be understood by looking only at the individual parts.[33]

An example from nature of a complex adaptive system is an ant colony ecosystem:[34] the colony cannot be understood by looking at the behaviour of individual ants because they work and interact locally in very specific ways (for example, 'workers', 'soldiers', etc.). The ant colony system works extraordinarily well but can only be understood by looking at the whole; other examples of similarly complex systems include the stock market, the immune system and 'just about any collection of humans…for example a healthcare system'.[35] Complexity draws on ideas from physics in the work of scientists such as Ilya Prigogine and Fritjof Capra[36] who said, 'as we penetrate into matter, nature does not show us any isolated building blocks, but rather appears as a complex web of relations between the various parts of a unified whole'. Complex organizational systems have changed as a result of information flows and feedback processes within the system and have the potential to be non-linear and self-organizing with emergent properties and may give rise to unintended consequences (both positive and negative).

A systems view is much more suited to capturing complexity than are linear models (such as ADDIE, see above). The systems view and the complex adaptive systems perspective has wider implications as HRD researcher Alexandre Ardichvili has noted: complex adaptive systems are capable of self-renewal and improvement 'but could also regress to the edge of chaos and instability if the elements of the system are put out of balance' by reckless or unsustainable use (for example, anthropogenic global warming).[37]

Ecological thinking and the ecosystem metaphor can help HRD researchers and practitioners to think systemically, that is think holistically, about the totality of the system of learning processes in organizations (rather than merely 'systematically', that is 'methodically' and linearly about its individual parts). A learning ecosystem is an interconnected 'ensemble' of:

- Internal/primary and external stakeholders with a wide variety of motivations, needs, etc. which may or may not be commensurable (for example, learning versus performance);
- Tangible and intangible knowledge and skill assets and content (for example, tacit and explicit knowledge);
- Learning resources and technological infrastructure (for example, the internal and external digital learning infrastructure);
- Organizational culture and learning climate (for example, some organizational climates are likely to be more conducive, that is 'safer', for learning than others);
- Internal environment and external environments within and between which processes of interaction and exchange operate (for example, interactions between internal and external stakeholders, national higher/vocational education policies, market changes, megatrends such as globalization, etc.).

Learning ecosystems will vary between different types of organizations (large versus small, public versus private, etc.) and also have different levels of maturity. They are more than technology-based learning systems or learning management systems (LMS).

Perspective from practice 10.4

Learning ecosystems

The idea of a 'learning ecosystem' appears to have been innovated in the e-learning field and has been championed by learning and development consultants and e-learning developers (for example, most of the literature on this topic is on technical issues relating to e-learning ecosystem design). Practitioners working in this field have described a learning ecosystem as an environment in which there are complex interactions between a range of stakeholders, the use of performance tools such as simple 'job aids', social networks such as communities of practice, processes for continuous improvement, formal learning such as workshops and webinars, technology platforms such as LMS, and work-based learning such as action learning projects.[38] In terms of learning delivery, the ecosystem metaphor has been applied to the relationship between technology and content, for example managing delivery through a learning management system which enables relevant and digestible content to be delivered at the right place and at the right time to the right audience.[39] Other practitioners have suggested a 'garden' metaphor in which there are:

- 'Pathways': for example, the delivery system provides learners with choices about what and how they learn;
- 'Gardeners': for example the employees' manager is the key to an effective learning experience;
- 'Hothouses': for example, there are 'spaces' both real and virtual that allow learners to acquire new knowledge and skills and practise them;
- 'Streams': for example, learning isn't a one-off event divorced from day-to-day activities, instead learning takes place 'in the flow of work';
- 'Foundations': for example, learners have access to an extensive and fluid knowledge base inside and outside the organization and are able to access knowledge at the right time in the right place.[40]

In the learning ecosystem literature the focus has tended to be on the technological infrastructure and resources that support and enable learning (that is, the delivery sub-system). However, to be truly systemic the ecosystem view must go beyond the delivery sub-system because thinking ecologically goes deeper and broader than mere delivery; it involves mapping the interactions between the elements of the learning ecosystem, that is its stakeholders (internal and external), the resources that they deploy (including but not confined to learning technology), and context and culture in which interactions take place. Considering HRD as part of the organization's 'sociotechnical system' is important because the 'design and performance of any organizational system can only be understood and improved if both "social" and "technical" aspects are brought together and treated as interdependent parts of a complex system'[41] (see also, Harold J. Leavitt's 'diamond model' of people, task, structure and technology). The HRD ecosystem is made up of a set of interacting sub-systems including stakeholders who have specific goals, motivations, needs, etc., have particular sets of policies, processes and procedures (for example, learning needs analysis), where there is an infrastructure supported by technology embedded in an organizational culture and in which impact is measured in terms of different metrics for different groups of stakeholders; see Figure 10.8. The HRD ecosystem interacts with other ecosystems (such as HRM), and there are open exchanges between it and the wider organization and environmental systems.

Ecological thinking in HRD requires a multi-stakeholder perspective. One approach to modelling the HRD ecosystem, and the wider organizational learning ecosystem (the two are inseparable), is to combine the ideas of 'stakeholders' and 'value creation' and the notion of the 'co-creation' of value. The co-creation paradigm is to be found in the work of, amongst others, the management scholars C. K. Prahalad and Venkat Ramaswamy,

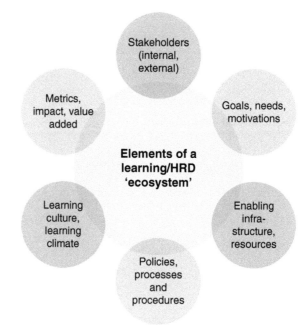

Figure 10.9   Elements of a learning/HRD ecosystem

who argued that the idea of 'co creation' is a dynamic perspective that sees the interactions of employees, managers, customers, suppliers, etc. as a mechanism or 'forum' for organizational learning, expanded capabilities, organizational resilience and sustained competitive advantage.[42] Producing a model of such a learning ecosystem begins with the identification of the multiple stakeholders (their motivations, resources and the outcomes they seek) and the value creation processes which operate between them.[43]

The HRD system and its processes seek to add value for the system's disparate stakeholders, both internal and external, and in a learning ecosystem relationships are bi-directional and reciprocal. For example, as far as its primary (internal) stakeholders are concerned, HRD creates value for learners by assisting them acquiring the knowledge and skills required to perform well in their job and develop their careers thereby helping them in realizing their potential, whilst learners create value for the organization by applying their newly acquired knowledge and skills. Likewise, HRD adds value for line managers by developing the knowledge and skills of the team she or he manages, whilst managers add value for HRD by articulating employees' learning needs and engaging with HRD to support the transfer of learning. HRD adds value for senior managers by assisting the organization in its pursuit of its strategic objectives, senior managers add value for HRD by incorporating learning and development into the realization of the company's vision and by legitimizing HRD's efforts in adding value to the overall company goals as a strategic partner.

This type of analysis suggests that in a learning ecosystem the process of value creation is two-way (bi-directional), that is different stakeholder groups receive and contribute value through their interactions. These interactions extend through the value chain and beyond organizations' boundaries, for example to customers, suppliers, communities and ultimately the natural environment.[44] In this approach to modelling the HRD ecosystem value creation is maximized through cooperation and exchanges between multiple stakeholders who have different needs and motivations and both give and receive value.[45] Modelling such a system also requires the enabling and constraining mechanisms to be identified (for example, learning climate) and the macro-forces in the external environment which drive change (for example, the megatrends of globalization, technology, demographics and climate change).

Delve deeper 10.7

Read more about learning ecosystems and the co-creation of value in:

Hecht, M., & Crowley, K. (2020). Unpacking the learning ecosystems framework: Lessons from the adaptive management of biological ecosystems. *Journal of the Learning Sciences*, 29(2), 264–284.

Garavan, T. N., McCarthy, A., & Carbery, R. (2019). An ecosystems perspective on international human resource development: A meta-synthesis of the literature. *Human Resource Development Review*, 18(2), 248–288.

Leavy, B. (2014). Venkat Ramaswamy – how value co-creation with stakeholders is transformative for producers, consumers and society. *Strategy and Leadership*, 42(1), 9–16.

Conclusion: Agile HRD

A challenge for HRD practice is the design and configuration of learning systems in ways that are commensurate with, responsive to and enabling of modern forms of organizing. According to organizational researcher Katherine Kellogg and colleagues such organizations are quite different from traditional forms of organization in that they are temporary and team-based, decisional authority is decentralized, accountabilities are shifting and distributed, relations are horizontal, and divisions of labour are dynamic and blurred, boundaries are fuzzy and permeable, work processes entail improvisation and flexibility, and participation and performance criteria are emergent, multiple and shared.[46] In modern organizations learning processes need to be configured and managed in ways that support the development of team mental models, horizontal integration of HRD with HRM and its vertical alignment with strategy, in which stakeholders share responsibility for learning and where the boundaries between working and learning are fuzzy and flexible. The ultimate goal of any learning system that is aligned with modern forms of organizing should be to facilitate the acquisition of knowledge and skills that transfer to the workplace, add value for stakeholders, have demonstrable impact, future-proof the organization and maximize the potential of the people who are the organization's most important asset. At the core of a learning eco-system are the individual and organizational learning systems and processes that create, maintain and expand organizational stability, resilience and sustainability. In becoming more 'ecological' and systemic in its approach HRD will need new processes, structures and tools which embrace 'hybrid methods', 'organizational learning', and 'knowledge management' (see Chapters 11, 13 and 14). A learning ecosystem will be an 'agile', 'people-led system' that enables the stakeholders who make up the 'extended enter-prise' to survive and thrive and realize meaningful and mutually beneficial goals.[47] Last words go to the great Austrian management thinker Peter Drucker (1909–2005) who described himself as a 'social ecologist' and reminded us that 'in an ecology, the "whole" has to be seen and understood and the "parts" exist only in contemplation of the whole'.[48] Likewise with HRD: in order to understand, appreciate and influence learning in and by organizations, learning must be seen holistically because the indi-vidual parts only exist meaningfully in relation to the whole.

Chapter checkout

Use this list to check your understanding of the key points of this chapter.

1   **Systematic approach**   HRD uses systematic approaches in order to meet perceived needs, and learning outcomes include changes in knowledge, skills and attitudes (KSAs) that lead to meaningful changes in individual and organizational performance

2   **ADDIE model**   Analyse, diagnose, design, implement, evaluate is a systematic model, the generic form of which is 'plan, do, check'; also systematic approach to training (SAT)

3   **Identification of learning needs**   Determines if need exists, whether learning and development is the solution; training needs identification (TNI)/learning needs identification (LNI)

4   **Analysis of learning needs**   Expressed typically in behavioural outcome terms; training needs analysis (TNA)/learning needs analysis (LNA)

5   **Levels of analysis**   Analysis is conducted at the individual, job and organizational levels

6   **HRD function**   HRD is an organizational support function responsible for the management of learning processes in organizations to meet the needs of its stakeholders

7   **HRD stakeholders**   Individuals/groups who have vested interest in learning and development processes; can be internal (for example, line managers) or external (for example, suppliers)

8   **HRD in SMEs**   SMEs have a less structured approach to planning and delivery of learning and greater recognition of/ reliance on informal methods of learning

9   **Organization development**   OD is a method for integrated, systematic and system-wide interventions in order to improve and effect meaningful change in organizational cultures and sub-cultures

10 **International HRD** International HRD is the formulation and practice of HRD systems, practices and policies at the global, societal and organization levels; encompasses learning and development issues associated with national HRD, cross-cultural HRD, expatriates, MNCs and global HRD

11 **Learning ecosystem** Interconnected system of stakeholders, knowledge and skill assets, learning resources and technological infrastructure, organizational culture and learning climate with open flows to wider internal/external environment

SKILLS DEVELOPMENT 10
PERSONAL DEVELOPMENT PLANNING

In this exercise you will have the opportunity to apply a systematic approach in developing a Personal Development Plan (PDP). Developing a PDP is a systematic process and there are a number of different models of how to do so, but in the main they involve a number of sequential steps such as 'identify', 'plan', 'act', 'record', and 'review'; see Figure 10.10.

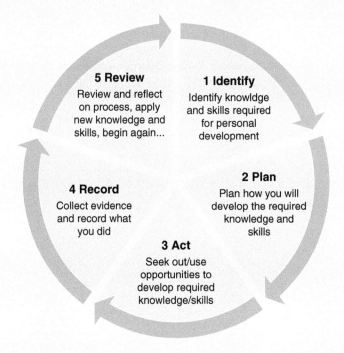

Figure 10.10 Personal development planning (PDP) process

(Continued)

Follow these five systematic steps (the illustrative example is for a presentation but you could also choose an area in which you'd like/need to develop):

- Step 1 Identify: Find an area in which you want to learn and improve, identify your strengths and weaknesses and the areas in which you'd like and/or need to develop; if necessary use benchmarks, role models, occupational standards, profession maps, etc, as a guide, for example 'improve presentation skills';
- Plan how you will improve on any gaps in your knowledge and skills, what your objectives should be, and write them down in such a way that you'll be able to show that you've achieved them, for example 'specific', 'measurable', 'achievable', 'relevant', and 'time bound' (SMART), for example, 'present to audiences competently (measured in terms of poise, articulation, volume, posture, eye contact, confidence, time keeping, etc.)';
- Seek out and use opportunities to access the knowledge, skills, experience that you need to achieve your objectives, for example looking at guides and examples, identifying and observing a role model give a presentation, etc.;
- Document what you've learnt and record your achievements in a journal, portfolio, etc., for example recording the actions that you took, videoing your presentation, getting and recording feedback, etc.;
- Review, reflect (and celebrate) your achievements, apply and practise your newly gained knowledge and skills and look for new areas in which to develop.[49]

Read more about how to develop a PDP at Open University (no date). Develop your career: Personal development plan (PDP). Available online: https://help.open.ac.uk/pdp

11
HYBRID HRD

Contents

On completion of this chapter you should be able to:

- Explain the advantages and disadvantages of digital learning;
- Explain what blended learning is and how it can be applied in HRD;
- Use your knowledge and understanding of hybrid methods to advise on the design and delivery of HRD.

Introduction

The consulting firm Deloitte in its 'Global Human Capital Trends Report' *Rewriting the Rules for the Digital Age* highlighted that, as a result of far-reaching and profound changes in social and technological landscapes, employees now and increasingly will have:

- The prospect of much longer and much more varied ('portfolio') careers;
- A working environment in which the 'half-life' of skills is falling rapidly;
- Access to technologies the power of which is increasing exponentially.

One inescapable and inevitable implication of these drivers of change (so-called 'megatrends', see Chapter 8) is that in order to attract and retain the best talent organizations must now be 'agile' in their HRD offering and re-think radically how they deliver 'always-on',[1] 'on-demand' and 'just-in-time' learning and development opportunities for cohorts of employees who increasingly will be 'digital natives'. A 'hybrid HRD' that is 'agile', 'always-on' and 'available on-demand' has significant implications for the expansion of HRD's role in terms of creating content, curating content and conveying content. The curation of content is an important quality control function for HRD given the vast amount of learning material that is available, the quality of which can be variable. The three-Cs of digital learning for HRD are:

- Creating content: creating content that ranges from 100 per cent new and 'bespoke' to the customization of 'off-the-shelf' content to meet employees' learning needs;
- Curating content: collecting, collating, and categorizing learning content from already-available sources in text, audio, visual and multiple media into an 'always-on' resource;
- Conveying content: conveying learning content from where it's held (whether that be in the head of an expert or as captured content in the cloud) to where it's required (that is, by learners).

There is a trade-off between these three Cs, for example between 'creation' which can take time ('sluggish creation') and 'curation' of ready-made content ('swift creation');[2] see Figure 11.1.

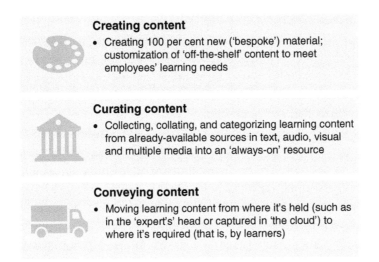

Creating content
- Creating 100 per cent new ('bespoke') material; customization of 'off-the-shelf' content to meet employees' learning needs

Curating content
- Collecting, collating, and categorizing learning content from already-available sources in text, audio, visual and multiple media into an 'always-on' resource

Conveying content
- Moving learning content from where it's held (such as in the 'expert's' head or captured in 'the cloud') to where it's required (that is, by learners)

Figure 11.1   The 'three Cs' of digital learning

Technology creates the possibility for HRD to be delivered not only in traditional classrooms (conveyed face-to-face, delivered synchronously, happening in real-time), but also in virtual classrooms (conveyed remotely, delivered synchronously, for example in a webinar) and via self-paced e-learning (online content, accessed asynchronously, with communication via discussion boards, email, etc.). These are some of the practical reasons why hybridizing HRD methods are important in a world that is changing dramatically both technologically and demographically.

If evidence were needed for how technology has the potential to rapidly and radically transform how people work and learn we need look no further than the consequences of the 2020 pandemic. During the spring of 2020 schools, colleges and universities transitioned – in some cases literally 'overnight' – in an unplanned shift from face-to-face to online learning. Online teaching and the digitization of delivery became a necessity not an option across the globe, so much so that it has been described as being a 'panacea' for learning during the pandemic. At the time of writing it seems likely that this will be a significant and permanent change in how both students and employees learn. The events of 2020 accelerated an underlying trend in the shift from instructor-led classroom training to technology-based, self-paced learning delivered via laptops, tablets, and smartphones. This was an area into which schools, colleges, higher education institutions and business organizations had been venturing for some time. Moreover, these technologies are used increasingly for a wider range of learning and development-related activities such as assessment, coaching, mentoring, etc. as well as didactic instruction (as in a lecture delivered online) and the delivery of content (as in on-demand learning materials). However, the shift also exposed and amplified inequalities. Students from the poorest families and in the poorest parts of the world who cannot afford or do not have access to technology have been left behind. This led to an estimated 850 million children and young people being denied access to education as a result of the closure of schools and colleges in 2020, further widening 'deep educational inequalities'.[5]

Over and above issues of learning technologies and the hybridization of methods, HRD methods in general also matter for political, reputational and marketing reasons: methods are the most 'client-facing' aspect of HRD practice. Getting the balance right adds value, increases the likelihood of an investment in HRD and a return on investment, and enhances the professional credibility and esteem of HRD practice. An important element of HRD practice in the digital age therefore is the ability to create, curate and convey content so as to address employees' learning needs, at the right time, in the right way and in the right place. In principle, and in practice, this means using learning technologies to their best effects, by blending HRD methods using multiple channels of delivery. However, in terms of the bigger picture, it's worth bearing in mind Steve Jobs' remarks about technology as a means to an end, not as an end in itself: 'Technology is nothing. What's important is that you have a faith in people, that they're basically good and smart, and if you give them tools, they'll do wonderful things with them.' Topics covered in this chapter are part of the 'design', 'develop' and 'implement' stages of the ADDIE model. We will look in particular at how HRD can use technology in combination with other modes of delivery to add value for its primary stakeholders (learners, HRD practitioners and managers).

Historical background of technology-based learning

The use of technology as a medium to facilitate learning has a long history in HRD ranging from the teaching machines first developed by behaviourists in the 1950s (a YouTube video exists of B. F. Skinner himself extolling the virtue of 'machine teaching'[6]) to the current digital learning landscape that includes massive open online courses (MOOC), webinars, podcasts, apps, etc. Terminology has changed since the earliest applications of computers to learning in the 1970s, for example from computer-assisted instruction (CAI), computer-aided learning (CAL), and computer-based training (CBT), to e-learning to digital learning. Digital learning is one of the fastest-moving fields of HRD practice. Technologies and terminologies change frequently, so much so that any attempt to capture digital learning in a chapter of a book such as this is likely to be a hostage to fortune and become quickly out-of-date. But what's in no doubt is that:

- Digital learning is here to stay and is an increasingly important part of the HRD landscape (for example the 2019 ATD State of the Industry Report reported that the use of technology for real-time virtual and self-paced delivery 'grew at a rapid pace');[7]
- For digital learning to be successful it must be driven theoretically (based on theories of learning) and take into account both the learners (for example,

familiarity with digital) and the context in which learning will take place (for example, availability of digital).

Some of the main landmarks and staging posts in the digital learning landscape and timeline are shown in Figure 11.2.

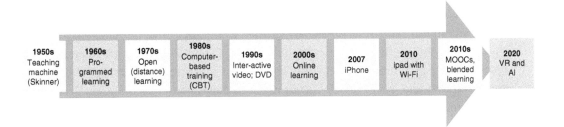

Figure 11.2 Timeline of learning technologies

The origins of technology based learning (TBL) can be traced to Skinner's applications of behaviourism (see above) and the principles and practice of instructional systems design (ISD) pioneered by American psychologists such as Robert M. Gagné and Leslie J. Briggs in the 1960s. Instructional design theory manifested in a variety of ways, for example as 'self-teach' text books which are still part of the self-directed learning and distance learning landscape. One of the most significant applications of technology-based learning in national HRD policy took place in the 1960s when the Labour Government in the 'white heat of technological change'[8] established the Open University (OU) in 1969. The OU is a distance learning university and it was founded on the leading learning technology of its day (self-instructional texts and videos) based on Instructional Systems Design (ISD) theory[9] and programmed learning principles. The OU was founded by Labour Prime Minister Harold Wilson as a means for widening access and participation in higher education (its motto is 'Learn and Live').

Industry followed suit in the application of learning technology: in the 1980s large companies such as British Gas and British Telecom, shortly after their privatizations by the Thatcher government, invested significantly in distance, open and technology-based learning. For these organizations distance and technology-based learning was an efficient means of proving flexible, consistent-message, company-wide 'just-in-time' (JIT) learning which obviated the need for employees to travel to a central training location which made better use of employees' time and reduced costs of travel, downtime, accommodation, etc. The approach typically involved the use of print-based learning materials blended with other supplementary materials such as video cassette (VHS) tapes that were mailed-out to employees in work locations including depots and overseas and offshore sites, and the use of primitive electronic page-turning CBT. Early attempts at synchronous distance learning (referred to as 'telematics') were also used to broadcast training sessions simultaneously to remote and/or inaccessible locations (for example, British Gas used this technology to broadcast learning to its offshore exploration and production platforms in the Irish Sea and North Sea).

Digital learning

As computers became cheaper, available more widely and more compact, CBT became more widespread, and the 1980s saw further technological developments with the invention of 'interactive laser discs' (looking like a CD but about the size of an LP vinyl record). They presented sound, video and text in an interactive design. The learner could respond and get feedback and be directed down particular branches depending on learning performance and diagnostic feedback. Next on the scene were DVDs in the 1990s. Since then the technology has moved on at a frantic pace with the advent of 'multimedia' and 'e-learning' (defined as 'instruction delivered on a digital device that is intended to support learning'[10]) and most recently 'digital learning'. The rate of progress in the sophistication and functionality of computer-mediated learning (of which CBT, e-learning and digital learning are various incarnations) has been rapid, driven by developments in mobile and digital technologies. 'E-learning' or 'digital learning' is distinctive in terms of 'message' (the learning content to be delivered), 'media' (how the

Message
Material to be stored/ transmitted in electronic form via intranets, internet, cloud-based systems etc.; contains content that's relevant to the learning needs and objectives of target audience

Media
Uses media elements such as text, sound and still and moving images to deliver content via instructional strategies such as examples, practice and feedback that enable learner interaction

Mode
Can be instructor-led or self-directed, and synchronous or asynchronous, and individualized and adaptive (i.e. customized to the user on basis of preferences, styles and performance)

Figure 11.3 Features of e-learning/digital learning

learning will be presented) and 'mode' (how the learning will be implemented);[11] see Figure 11.3.

The design of e-learning is a specialized instructional design task that addresses important issues of appearance, functionality and usability since these impact on learners' motivation, the learning processes themselves and the credibility of the content. Human-computer interaction research has helped to inform the design of such materials by taking into account relevant psychological factors such as cognitive load, learning styles, etc.[12] A simple example for a very basic format and appearance of e-learning is shown in Figure 11.4.

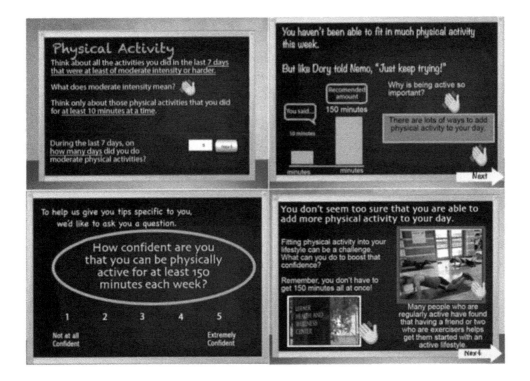

Figure 11.4 Example of simple screen design

The current landscape includes online learning from a wide variety of providers including Google's 'Digital Garage' building 'new skills for a digital world', LinkedIn Learning which provides over 16,000 online learning course for 'in-demand skills', Coursera which collaborates with over 200 universities and companies to provide online learning, etc. Courses and resources are widely and sometimes freely available to learners, enabling them to create their own unique learning platform on their computer, smartphone or tablet. For example, Digital Garage offers online courses which it lauds as 'approved by industry experts, top entrepreneurs and some of the world's leading employers' and offering learners 'up-to-date, real-world, skills that help you reach your goal'. The courses are created by Google itself and other providers, including higher education establishments linked to Coursera, the world-wide online learning platform founded in 2012 by two Stanford professors. Coursera offers massive open online courses (MOOCs) in a wide variety of subjects.

Reflective question 11.1

It's been said that, like money, technology is a 'good servant but a bad master'.[13] In your view, and from your experiences of digital learning, do you agree that digital learning can be a 'good servant' (that is, as a 'means to an end') but a 'bad master' (that is, when it's used as an 'end in itself')? What have been your experiences of digital learning – what worked well for you, and what worked less well, and why?

The world of digital learning is a complex and ever-evolving network of products, providers and promises. In order to help practitioners find a route through the morass of materials, the CIPD Research Report entitled *The Future of Technology and Learning* offered some general guidelines for choosing the right technology to address the needs of learners whilst avoiding the 'hype' of the latest in digital innovation:

- Digital learning needs to be more than a mere content delivery or information system that ends-up being simply 'electronic page turning';
- Digital learning technology should have instructional features that are capable of delivering effective learning experiences;
- Digital learning should apply relevant theories of learning and transfer of training theory to the design of digital content;
- Digital learning should facilitate knowledge and skill acquisition through practice, feedback and interactivity;
- The use of digital technology should be purpose-driven (focused on the learning needs that it seeks to address) rather than tech-driven;
- HRD practitioners need to be cognisant of potential barriers to the successful implementation of digital learning technologies.

The CIPD report concluded that 'blended learning' (see below) has the potential to create the 'best outcomes'. Digital learning should, therefore, be used for the things that it does best (high quality sound and video, connectivity, currency, etc.). For digital learning to be effective in HRD it needs to be supplemented with social interaction and follow-up, human contact and support in transferring the learning to the job, and opportunities for practice and application in the workplace of knowledge and skills that have been acquired digitally.[14] So doing closes the loop between instructional design and transfer of learning.

─Research insight 11.1─

Effectiveness of digital learning

One of the most important questions for digital learning theory and practice is whether it's more effective than conventional face-to-face instruction. Robert Bernard and colleagues[15] conducted a meta-analysis of the results from over 200 studies comparing the effects of e-learning and face-to-face instruction on learners' achievement, attitude and retention. There was a wide diversity in the findings indicating that in some studies e-learning was more much effective whilst in others it was not as good. The overall pattern seemed to be that the differences between e-learning and face-to-face were minimal. However, some variability was observed when the differences between synchronous and asynchronous delivery were considered, and not surprisingly e-learning was better asynchronous delivery whilst face-to-face was associated with better synchronous delivery. These findings suggested that a blended approach, that is one that plays to the strengths of different approaches, is to be recommended and hence for e-learning to be effective:

- Instructional design factors (including principles derived from theories of learning) should take precedence over technical and media issues in the design of e-learning;
- e-learning should be designed in such a way as to promote interactivity between the learner and the materials;
- e-learning should enable communication and interchange between learners and instructors and between groups of learners.

Source: Bernard, R. M., Abrami, P. C., Lou, Y., Borokhovski, E., Wade, A., Wozney, L., Wallet, P. A., Fiset, M., & Huang, B. (2004). How does distance education compare with classroom instruction? A meta-analysis of the empirical literature. *Review of Educational Research, 74*(3), 379–439.

The CIPD research recommends that technology should be used in HRD in a way that addresses learners' needs, appreciates individual differences in 'digital literacy', and is in alignment with business goals.[16]

One conclusion that can be drawn safely about the relationship between the medium and the message is that it's not the conveying medium as such that facilitates learning (for example, smartphone, laptop, pod cast, virtual reality, etc.), it's the message and the way in which the learning content has been created and curated which makes the biggest difference between success and failure. Learners need to be provided with the right content in the right format not the wrong content in the right format, or right content in the wrong format, or even worse wrong content in wrong format.[17] It bears reiterating that the driving force behind digital learning should be instructional design principles that draw on established theories from the psychology and neuroscience of cognition and learning. As educational and instructional psychologists Ruth Colvin Clark and Richard E. Mayer remind us, cognitive theory shows that:[18]

- Information is processed both visually and verbally, therefore where possible content should be presented in a dual mode, for example as sounds, text and images, and visual and verbal cues (such as typography, colour, animation, etc.) should be used to direct attention to the most important aspects of the content;
- People have differences in their styles of processing (also known as 'cognitive styles', 'thinking styles' or 'learning styles', see Chapter 4), for example some people are 'big-picture conscious' whilst others are 'detail focused', therefore e-learning should enable learners to see both the big picture and fine details, and in this regard cognitive maps and advance organizers serve as important guiding and orientating functions;
- Working memory capacity is limited, therefore essential information should be presented in manageable amounts ('bite-sized' chunks) to enable processing, and extraneous materials should be used judiciously with a focus on 'need-to-knows' rather than 'nice-to-knows' in order to avoid cognitive overload;
- Information is encoded and stored more effectively when it's actively ('generatively') processed (for example, by creating diagrams from the reading of textual content),[19] therefore e-learning materials should engage users actively rather than passively presenting them with information; it should also link new knowledge to existing knowledge (that is, digital learning should be consistent with Ausubel's theory of meaningful learning, see Chapter 2).[20]

In summary, digital learning should be based on relevant and up-to-date learning theories (including emerging insights from neuroscience), draw on the best available evidence for what works in practice, and have an eye to future developments in technology. HRD needs to look backwards to what's been shown to work over many years and look forward to the emergence and potential learning applications of new technologies. There's little doubt that there has been a significant and permanent change in how learning happens, the 'genie' of HRD that's 'always-on', 'on-demand' and 'just-in-time' is out of the bottle. This can be seen as part of a wider social context in which employees can access content for entertainment or edification purposes at the click of a mouse or TV remote control, and this is often free-of-charge and of high production standards. Employees may come to expect access to HRD opportunities that are equally seamless, slick and free.

However, digital HRD also faces challenges. The CIPD's 2016 *Preparing for the Future of Learning* Report found that around only a quarter of HR managers believe their HRD teams have the right skills to exploit technology for business advantage and the potential uses of learning technologies.[21] As the learning experts in organizations it's important that the HRD profession's levels of knowledge and skill keep pace with the technology.

The future is more likely to be a blended[22] or hybrid – rather than purely digital – integrated and intertwined 'learning ecosystem'.

―Reflective question 11.2―

What would you say to a designer of digital learning materials (who's very well-versed in the cognitivist principles for instructional design, as in the work of researchers such as Clark and Mayer cited above) who claims that the only theories that are relevant for the design of digital HRD are cognitivist learning theories? Which other theories of learning are relevant to the design and implementation of digital HRD?

―Delve deeper 11.1―

Find out more about the practical issues in designing digital learning in:

Bean, C. (2014). *The accidental instructional designer: Learning design for the digital age*. Alexandra VA: ASTD Press.

Clark, R. C., & Mayer, R. E. (2016). *E-learning and the science of instruction: Proven guidelines for consumers and designers of multimedia learning*. John Wiley & Sons.

Haythornthwaite, C., Andrews, R., Fransman, J., & Meyers, E. M. (eds) (2016). *The SAGE handbook of e-learning research*. Thousand Oaks: SAGE.

If you're interested in the history of technology-based learning then you might like to read:

Siemens, G., Gašević, D., & Dawson, S. (2015). *Preparing for the digital university: A review of the history and current state of distance, blended, and online learning*. Athabasca: Athabasca University.

Explore some of the critiques of digital learning in:

Beinicke, A., & Kyndt, E. (2019). Evidence-based actions for maximising training effectiveness in corporate E-learning and classroom training. *Studies in Continuing Education, 42*(2), 1–21.

Derouin, R. E., Fritzsche, B. A., & Salas, E. (2005). E-learning in organizations. *Journal of Management, 31*(6), 920–940.

Blended learning

The range of methods available to HRD practitioners has expanded significantly and continues to do so. Developments in theory, practice and technology, within a dynamic and uncertain work and social context, open-up exciting new possibilities for HRD. Designing, developing and implementing HRD in this context entails a carefully crafted combination of formal and informal learning using the full range of delivery methods and platforms in ways that optimize efficiency and effectiveness.

The term 'blended learning' has been around for over a decade, having developed out of distance leading and technology-based learning.[23] In its simplest and most basic form, blended learning incarnation involves combining an online mode of delivery with face-to-face methods. The reasons for the increased interest in blended approaches echo the reasons why distance- and technology-based approaches to learning were developed: seeking improved learning effectiveness, increasing access for learners, increasing the cost-effectiveness of learning, increased geographical reach, increased flexibility, etc. The blended approach offers a trade-off between purely face to face delivery and pure online, it seeks to get the 'best of both worlds'.[24] Instructional scientist Charles R. Graham, described blended learning (BL) environments as combining face-to-face instruction with technology-mediated (computer-mediated) instruction (TML) as a means for increasing learning effectiveness, increasing learning convenience and access, and increasing learning cost-effectiveness. There are, however, inevitable trade-offs between these different motivations and goals.[25]

Up until relatively recently the different modes of learning delivery (face to face and online) were considered to be separate, however they have recently begun to overlap increasingly as a result of the fact that:

- Digital can now do much of what was previously possible only with face-to-face, such as hosting group seminars and live online classes in virtual classrooms;
- Face-to-face can now take advantage of the connectivity that digital provides, for example by scaling its delivery to reach larger numbers of people who are more geographically dispersed.

One of the main factors in this change is related to the challenge of how to enable 'synchronous' delivery (that is, the capability for events, such as interactions with instructors, fellow learners, coaches, mentors, etc.) to occur simultaneously and at a distance. Mentoring for example, has traditionally been 'face-to-face' (mentor and mentee being in the same place at the same time). However, digital and communication technologies now make e-mentoring a reality and have the advantages of flexibility in scheduling, location, downtime and other costs. However, research into e-mentoring in the UK's NHS found that there were also some drawbacks, including the need for fast and reliable internet access, basic IT literacy, establishing a rapport may not be as easy in face to face, diminishing of non-verbal cues, privacy and confidentially may be compromised, and boundaries may become too blurred (for example, the mentor might end-up being 'too available').[26]

As technology evolves and becomes common place, learners' communication and learning styles, preference and expectations are likely to change in line with broader societal and demographic changes. For example, Generation Z learners (people born between mid-1990s and 2012) – described as a 'truly digital native generation' – are now entering higher education and the workforce. Even though this group are tech-savy they are nonetheless likely to benefit from being guided on how to make best use of digital learning by being shown how to assess the reliability, relevance and rigour of online content (and hence become more demanding and discerning consumers) and how to connect purely online content into their real-life experiences.[27]

Perspective from practice 11.1

Blended learning at L'Oréal

L'Oréal is one of the world's biggest cosmetics companies. Its 'colour specialist' training is, at the time of writing, branded as the most popular hair colouring course in the UK. It runs as an intensive 13-week mainly face-to-face programme including a three-day assessment. L'Oréal saw the potential of improving the course by blending e-learning modules with face-to-face delivery with the twin aim of enhancing the transfer of learning and enabling learners to complete more of the training in their own salon. The solution was developed by 'Leo' a commercial provider of blended and e-learning solutions. Two of the main challenges were to design and implement an e-learning resource that could be used alongside face-to-face which:

- Would be 'instinctive' to use by learners who weren't all that used to using digital technology for learning;
- Could be chunked into 'micro-learnings' that could be used flexibly, for example in 15-minute breaks between appointments.

The blended learning solution was developed to be delivered on a mobile or tablet device and used alongside tutoring in practical skills in the workplace of a busy salon. The e-learning was interactive, with regular knowledge assessments along the way and the opportunity for learners to annotate and upload images of real case studies to explain their decision-making.

The uploaded content could then be viewed and commented on by assessors remotely who were also able to give quick feedback to the learners on their decisions. The screen layout and design was lean, colourful and minimalistic with aspirational photographs to motivate learners who weren't familiar with the technology and to relate the learning directly to the aesthetic aspects of a hairdressers' task (see https://leolearning.com/case-studies/blended-learning-loreal-professionnel-elearning for a fuller description and screenshots).

A variant of the blended learning model that has gained some traction in higher education is the so-called 'flipped classroom'. In a traditional educational model (that is the traditional classroom) learners are 'given' content in the classwork and get the opportunity to practice or delve deeper in the 'homework'; the flipped classroom reverses this.[28]

The learners engage with the main knowledge 'content' of the class remotely/online (the classwork becomes the homework to be completed before class, and with the opportunity to delve deeper should the learner wish to do so) and the face-to-face (classroom) element is used for active and interactive learning, instructor-learner and learner-learner engagement, skills development with feedback, in-depth discussions of topics of interest, and social interaction.

Advantages and disadvantages of technology-based methods

One of the main benefits that print-based distance learning, stand-alone computer-based training and online methods brought to the repertoire of HRD methods was that they enabled the delivery of learning to be at a time, place and pace that suited learners' circumstances without the need for the instructor's presence (the instructor was 'present' vicariously in the materials that he or she had 'authored').

One of the advantages of distance learning was that it enabled asynchronous delivery: the person delivering the learning (the author of the print- or computer-based materials) was not in the same place at the same time as the learner. This freed-up the 'instruction' because the learning could take place virtually at any place and any time making it 'always-on', 'on-demand', and 'just-in-time' (JIT). A further breakthrough came with the combining of digital and communications technologies. This meant that the person delivering the learning can be anywhere in the world and deliver material synchronously to learners who also can be literally almost anywhere. Similarly, it is possible for the designer of digital materials to interact with learners in real time. Hence face to face and online could overlap in their time and place of delivery; they both can be delivered synchronously and asynchronously as well as distributed globally. Blended modes of delivery combine synchronous and asynchronous delivery:

- Synchronous online delivery, for example webinars (live online sessions), online discussions, 'group chat', etc.;
- Asynchronous online delivery, for example message boards, emails, recorded feedback, etc.

The other major change has been in terms of the quality and interactivity of the materials; digital learning now has the potential to be responsive and interactive.[29] Machine learning and artificial intelligence are proving to be increasingly viable in terms of responsiveness to the learner and levels of interactivity which attempt to mimic human beings. Blended learning brings together the advantages of synchronous learning (that is, instructor presence, flexibility of interaction, immediate feedback, social interaction, motivation) and asynchronous learning (that is, independence, self-pacing, flexibility of delivery, etc.).[30]

Research insight 11.2

Benefits of and barriers to blended learning

HRD researchers in Taiwan explored the use of blended learning for workplace learning and development. They found that the benefits of blended learning included:

- Richer instructional content using multiple modes of delivery;
- Appropriateness of learning content that could be tailored to learners' needs;
- Cost effectiveness, scalability and speed of delivery and distribution (although it's worth noting that some researchers have disputed the reduced costs arguments).[31]

They also found that amongst the barriers to the effective use of blended learning were:

- The time taken to develop quality blended learning materials;
- Instructor skills for developing materials and readiness of stakeholders to accept blended learning;
- Lack of understanding on the part of management of the potential benefits and appreciation of the need for management support in implementing and facilitating transfer of learning to the job.

Kim and colleagues' study of the current and future state of blended learning in workplace learning concluded that the two key barriers to its use for HRD are:

- HRD practitioners need professional development in how to make best use of blended learning especially on newly emerging technologies (such as VR and AI) and how they can be integrated into blended learning solutions;
- Lack of support and commitment from management for blended learning; they suggest that instructional design and organizational theories and best-practice case studies should be used to inform senior managers on the benefits of blended learning and to obtain support and commitment from management for the use of blended learning.

For blended learning (BL) to be used effectively sufficient infrastructure (technological and administrative) and support (technical and pedagogical) need to be in put in place to assist HRD practitioners in expanding and transitioning their role. Without this its benefits may not be fully realized.

(Continued)

Sources: Kim, K. J., Bonk, C. J., & Teng, Y. T. (2009). The present state and future trends of blended learning in workplace learning settings across five countries. *Asia Pacific Education Review*, *10*(3), 299–308; Teng, Y. T., Bonk, C. J., & Kim, K. J. (2009). The trend of blended learning in Taiwan: Perceptions of HRD practitioners and implications for emerging competencies. *Human Resource Development International*, *12*(1), 69–84.

Delve deeper 11.2

Read more about blended learning in:

Bonk, C. J., & Graham, C. R. (2012). *The handbook of blended learning: Global perspectives, local designs*. San Francisco: John Wiley & Sons; Stein, J., & Graham, C. R. (2020). *Essentials for blended learning: A standards-based guide*. New York: Routledge.

Learn more about the practical issues in introducing digital learning by consulting the Accenture consultancy report *Digital and Blended Learning as a way to Improve Employment and Entrepreneur Outcomes*:

www.accenture.com/_acnmedia/pdf-5/accenture-digital-learning-report_short-version.pdf

---

'70:20:10'

A convenient way of capturing the balance between informal and formal, incidental and planned, face-to-face and technology-mediated, individual- and group-based methods is the so-called '70:20:10' framework. 70:20:10 is a concept that is used to convey quickly and easily to people who are not learning and development specialists the idea that:

- A large majority of learning, '70 per cent', happens simply 'by working', through the things an employee encounters in their day-to-day experiences, for example in problem-solving, decision making, etc. none of which are configured deliberately as 'learnings' let alone as HRD; in 70:20:10 this is labelled as 'informal';
- A substantial minority of learning, '20 per cent', occurs 'by working together', such as team working, collaborating, communicating, giving and receiving feedback, getting coached or mentored, etc.; in 70:20:10 this is labelled as 'facilitative';
- A minority of learning, '10 per cent', occurs as a result of formal learning interventions such as a training course; in 70:20:10 this is labelled as 'formal'.

70:20:10 appears to be popular and widely adopted in practice. Its basis is more pragmatic than theoretical, nonetheless the concept is consistent with several of the theories of learning covered in Part 1 of this book. Its origins can be found in the work of leadership development practitioners such as Cynthia McCauley, Morgan McCall and others at the Centre for Creative Leadership (*Using Experience to Develop Leadership Talent*, 2014). It was popularized by learning and development consultant Charles Jennings (see below). 70:20:10 is not a model (theoretical or otherwise) and it's far from being a precise formula. The proponents of 70:20:10 would prefer that it is thought of as a 'framework', a 'rule-of-thumb', and as a 'metaphor' for how learning in the workplace can be configured. Some of the techniques that can be used in implementing 70:20:10 are shown in Figure 11.5.

70% Learning from Experience

For example, learning-by-doing, problem solving, managing projects, taking decisions, giving presentations, chairing meetings, reflecting, de-briefing, etc.

20% Learning from Others

For example, mentoring/being mentored, coaching/being coached, networking, observation/role modelling, dialogue, action learning, community of practice, etc.

10% Formal Learning

For example, induction, training courses, on-going education, self-development, online learning, etc.

Figure 11.5 Techniques for implementing 70:20:10

The CIPD described 70:20:10 as having 'a significant impact on the L&D [learning and development] profession' (p. 19).[32] As far as the learning needs of younger people in the workforce are concerned, the CIPD also noted that a 70:20:10 approach can be especially useful to build the employees' capabilities in the early stages of their careers/working lives because it develops both technical capability/hard skills and general working/softer skills such as confidence, communication and commercial acumen. On the broader topic of workforce demographics and learning and development, the co-existence of older members of the workforce with their lifetime of experience/ wisdom alongside millennial (born 1980s to mid-1990s)/Generation Z (born mid-1990s on) 'digital natives' creates opportunities for mentoring (from older to younger) and reverse mentoring (from younger to older) thus leveraging the experience and expertise of both groups,[33] all of which are important elements in an integrated learning ecosystem.

In their own words 11.1

Charles Jennings on 70:20:10

In HRD practice and consulting '70:20:10' is often associated with the work of Charles Jennings (https://702010institute.com/) as well as with that of other innovators and providers. Jennings is an HRD consultant who's been associated with the 70:20:10 framework for more than two decades and is co-founder, with Vivian Heijnen, of the '70:20:10 Institute'. In his book *70:20:10 Towards 100% Performance*, Jennings draws on the work of Lave and Wenger (see 'situated learning theory', Chapter 3), research reported in the *Economic Development Review* in 1998 which claimed that 'as much as 70% of all workplace learning may be informal'[34] and the writings of American economists Josef Stiglitz (b. 1943) and Kenneth Arrow (1921–2017).

Jennings is keen to remind us that 70:20:10 is not a 'rule', it's a 'practical metaphor' and the numbers aren't precise, and no one would ever try to get the balance exact, they're simply a convenient 'reference model'. He claims that the most effective and efficient learning and development configuration for adding value both for the employee and the business is by using a large proportion of learning-by-working (this is sometimes referred to as 'learning in the flow of work' – a term coined by Josh Bersin),[35] a considerably smaller proportion from working with others and a smaller proportion still from formal learning interventions. The model recognizes that people learn differently in different contexts depending on a wide range of individual (for example, learning preferences) and organizational (for example, organizational culture) factors.

Source: Jennings, C. (2018). New roles for L&D: The reality of 70:20:10. *Training Zone*, 15 November. www.trainingzone.co.uk/develop/talent/new-roles-for-ld-the-reality-of-702010 (accessed 27-01-21).

Reflective question 11.3

In the 70:20:10 framework there's the temptation to equate 'quantity' with 'quality', that is because '70%' of learning is as a result of 'experiences' this is the most important way to learn. But is this necessarily the case? Perhaps there are infrequent but significant learning experiences and perhaps one-off incidents can be impactful and even transformational? How does this resonate with your experiences of learning? If quantity does not necessarily equate to quality does it question the 'validity' of 70:20:10 as a useful framework?

Criticisms of 70:20:10

Although the 70:20:10 idea has been embraced enthusiastically by its proponents and followers, it appears to be backed-up more by common sense, anecdote and experience rather than an extensive body of empirical evidence notwithstanding Jennings' claims that economists cottoned-on to it decades ago. It's clear that the '70 per cent rule' cannot be a 'fact' and as such is open to misinterpretation and misuse. As HRD researcher Alan Clardy notes in his critique of 70:20:10,[36] 'the "fact" of the 70 per cent rule is far from a fact at all', instead it can be criticized as an over-simplified view which could be used to abandon unjustifiably the '10 per cent'. It's worth bearing in mind that in Chapter 6 we discovered that well-designed and well-executed formal training can not only add significant value to an organization's 'bottom line' it also creates other less tangible value-added for HRD's stakeholders. Taking 70:20:10 to the extreme and playing down or dismissing completely the value of formal learning and development, such as employee training, runs the risk of 'throwing the baby out with the bathwater'.[37] Another danger, Clardy notes, is that 70:20:10 can be used to reinforce distinctions and create barriers between structured, formal, unstructured and informal learning experiences which instead need to be integrated holistically into an overall learning and development system (the learning ecosystem) which integrates the three principal elements of learning by working, learning from others, and formal learning.[38]

Research insight 11.3

Implementing 70:20:10 effectively

A qualitative study by Australian researchers Samantha Johnson, Deborah Blackman and Fiona Buick explored the implementation of 70:20:10 in public sector organizations in Australia. Given that 70:20:10 combines three types of learning, they argued that if properly implemented 70:20:10 could guide HRD practitioners in the design of programmes that overcome transfer problems through structured experiences and social learning processes. They looked closely into if and how current implementation of 70:20:10 facilitates the transfer of learning and if and how it helped to build managers' capabilities. They found that the application of the 70:20:10 framework was beset by a number of problems, including:

- An 'overconfident assumption' that unstructured experiential learning automatically results in the development of job relevant capabilities (this finding resonates with comments made in Chapter 4 about the perils of experiential learning being 'left to chance');
- A narrow interpretation of social learning (coaching, mentoring and networking) and overlooking processes such as modelling (see Bandura's social cognitive learning theory, Chapter 3);

(Continued)

- Expectations that managerial behaviour would automatically change following formal training and development activities without the need to actively support the process;
- Lack of recognition of the requirement for a planned and integrated relationship between all three aspects of the framework.

They concluded that the 70:20:10 framework has 'potential to better guide the achievement of capability development through improved learning transfer in the public sector' but its potential will not be realized if its implementation guidelines fail to focus both on the different types of learning required and 'how to integrate them in a meaningful way' (p. 397). The key to successful 70:20:10 implementation appears to be giving experiential learning a structure in order to enhance its value, connecting experiential learning directly to formal learning through social processes such as line manager involvement, support and feedback, and also creating synergies between the 70 and the 20 and the 10 so that they reinforce each other.

Source: Johnson, S. J., Blackman, D. A., & Buick, F. (2018). The 70: 20: 10 framework and the transfer of learning. *Human Resource Development Quarterly*, 29(4), 383–402.

Conclusion: The means to an end

It goes without saying that we live in a world where, to paraphrase the Ancient Greek philosopher Heraclitus, 'change is the only constant', a world where, how and why people do the jobs that they do are radically different than they were only a decade or so ago. The pace of change, driven by demography, technology and economics, is relentless. In its most recent state of the industry survey the ASTD estimated that e-learning had amassed a 40 per cent share of formal training in organizations and this appears set to grow. Events of 2020 where remote working and remote learning were the norm only served to accelerate this trend.[39]

As a result of the 'megatrends'[40] of technology, demography and globalization (see Chapter 8), the vision of learning and development opportunities that can be delivered at the click of a mouse across a diversity of mobile platforms has arrived. In so doing technology gives HRD the possibility to add value in ways that were previously inconceivable or unimaginable. The advent of digital technologies, the quality and quantity of available learning 'content' and its ready accessibility have meant that for employees and HRD practitioners one of the biggest challenges is making sense of and using the abundance of learning content which, if it's not managed properly, can easily become an impenetrable jungle and source of confusion. Not surprisingly, these innovations in learning delivery have been scrutinized critically as well as embraced enthusiastically. As critically reflective HR researchers and practitioners it's important to be aware of and engage with the problems as well as the potential of the use of technology in HRD. For example the CIPD, in noting that making digital learning available to unprepared and unsupported employees is unlikely to be effective, highlighted the following challenges to 'digitizing' HRD successfully:

- Being aware of the limits of existing technology infrastructure as well as HR's digital expertise;
- Allocating and managing of employee time spent on digital learning that has the potential to be always-on at work and at home;
- Sourcing credible, high-quality content that meets employees' and organizations' needs and expectations;
- Recognizing individual differences in predispositions towards digital learning, for example generational differences between 'digital natives' and baby boomers.[41]

We should also bear in mind that cutting-edge learning technologies can be unavailable or prohibitively expensive for some groups, such as micro-businesses, or organizations in developing nations, poorer and disadvantaged groups of people, remote locations out of internet reach, etc. We should also bear in mind that different organizations can be at different stages of development in their use of digital learning technologies with early adopters far ahead of the pack whilst others lag behind for a variety of reasons. Also we should not conflate new with better.[42] Some of the most effective learning technologies (for example, a marker pen and a whiteboard) are ideally suited for their intended purpose and their purpose is as valid today as it has ever been. The key to the successful use of technology in HRD is to be grounded in what learners need, not what the tech industry can provide or wants to sell; this means delivering the right digital content in the format that's right for the learners and right for the business.[43]

A 'hybrid' is something of mixed origin or composition that's made by combining the benefits of formerly separate tools or technologies. Examples include: hybrid cars that combine petrol or diesel power with electric motor, and hybrid bicycles that combine the features of a road bike and a mountain bike. Each is designed as a means to an end. A hybrid car allows both fuels to be used as and when appropriate to suit the driver's purpose; a hybrid bike can go on- and off-road to suit the rider's intentions. A hybrid is not the same as a blend. A blended approach to personal transportation would involve using an electric car for some journeys and a petrol or diesel car for others, or by having a road bike and a mountain bike and using them as necessary. 'Hybridized HRD' in which its key elements are combined seamlessly into an entity that is both novel and useful, is likely to become the norm as learners (increasingly 'digital natives') and the social and technological landscape changes and methods become more and more integrated into a complete learning platform. A fast, interconnected, integrated learning ecosystem that can achieve depth of coverage and a global reach with which employees are increasingly able and willing to engage is fast becoming a reality.

The learning ecosystem of contemporary organizations, and in society more generally, is complex and inter-connected. The elements in the mix include digital and face-to-face, created resources and curated resources, learning at the workplace, at home, and in transit, etc. Hybrid approaches, which are the backbone of the learning ecosystem, leverage the strengths of internal and external provision, formal and informal delivery, team and individual development, face-to-face and digital methods, curated and created resources, on-job and off-job learning, etc. The brave new world of hybrid HRD as depicted by Deloitte is one in which:

- Employees aren't told what to learn by managers, they get to decide based on their learning needs and career goals;
- Corporate HRD no longer 'owns' learning and development, corporate HRD curates developments and creates a learning experience that adds value for clients and stakeholders;
- Employees have the opportunity and choice to learn at any time and in any place to suit their needs;
- Learning technology is no longer merely a catalogue of e-learning courses, instead technology enables an always-on, collaborative and curated stream of learning experiences and opportunities.

The learning ecosystem is an integrated whole comprised of people and processes, tools and technologies and, as with any highly complex and integrated system, if the system is truly integrated the whole will be greater than the sum of the parts.[44] This aspiration should be configured first-and-foremost on the basis of robust learning theory and rigorous empirical evidence which deploys the full inventory of learning methods effectively and efficiently; which avoids the scramble to get what is new for fear of missing out and in so doing overlooks the value of what is old; and which enables learning and development to be managed in such a way that individual employees' potential is maximized, and tangible value is added for stakeholders. 'Hybrid HRD' is, ultimately, a means to an end not an end in itself.

Chapter checkout

Use this list to check your understanding of the key points of this chapter.

1 **Drivers for hybrid HRD**   Drive towards technology in HRD as a result of longer working lives, portfolio careers, increased rate of skill obsolescence and technological advances and globalization

2 **HRD roles**   HRD's role has a vital role to play in the new learning landscape in creating, curating and conveying credible digital content

3 **Learning technology history**   Use of technology in learning stretches back to the 1950s teaching machines, through programmed learning, CBT, e-learning and present day hybrid digital solutions

4 **Computer-mediated (digital) learning** Stores/transmits learning in electronic form via intranets, internets, cloud-based systems, uses various media elements, employs instructional strategies, can be synchronous/asynchronous and generic/adaptive

5 **Blended learning** Combining online mode of delivery with face-to-face methods

6 **Advantages of digital/blended** Seeks improved learning effectiveness, increasing access for learners, and increasing the cost-effectiveness of learning; fits with preferences/expectation of newer generation of employees

7 **Drawbacks of/barriers to blended/digital** Time taken to develop quality content; instructor skills for developing materials; readiness of stakeholders to accept blended learning; managers' lack of understanding of benefits/need for support for implementation/ facilitating transfer

8 **70:20:10** Metaphor for a configuration of HRD delivery which emphasizes importance of learning through/in-the-flow of working; informal (70), facilitative (20), formal (10); unjustly diminishes the role of formal

9 **Learning capital and learning ecosystems** Efficient and effective learning ecosystem hybridizes modes of delivery based on theory and evidence

SKILLS DEVELOPMENT 11
MAKING THE CASE FOR HYBRID HRD IN BARISTA TRAINING

'Presto' is a chain of artisan coffee shops located in city centres and serves a young and discerning client base. Its barista training has traditionally been a one week face-to-face course held at the company's HQ in the capital city. The course is accredited and leads to a recognized 'Professional Barista' vocational qualification. The content and format of the course includes classroom-based and workshop-based learning in the knowledge and skill requirements for becoming a professional barista. The course covers topics such as raw materials, best brewing practices, setting-up, operating and maintaining equipment, customer service standards and expectations, providing excellent customer service, and health, safety and food hygiene requirements. Written and practical assessments take place on the final day of the course. The practical assessments take place in the training centre's simulated coffee shop with other members of the class role-playing customers. The cost of running the course of is £2500 per trainee (including instructor and materials costs) but this doesn't factor-in the costs of trainee downtime (which could be calculated at the rate of £10 hour for five days).

Presto has made a long-term, strategic commitment to hybridizing its approach to training and developing the company's employees. As noted, the existing HRD

(Continued)

offering is mainly face-to-face workshops, and this has proven to be successful and popular; however HRD needs to be made more agile and more cost-effective.

Your task in this exercise is to write a business case for hybridizing HRD in Presto. In your proposal you should:

- Identify the external and internal drivers for hybridizing HRD in Presto;
- Specify the potential benefits and beneficiaries of hybridizing HRD in Presto;
- Identify the main components of a proposed hybrid HRD model for Presto;
- Specify the potential risks and challenges of hybridizing HRD;
- Identify how the new hybrid model will be evaluated.

For inspiration and guidance you might like to look at: http://ccbaristatraining.com/training/city-guilds-2/

12

DOES HRD COST OR PAY?

Contents

On completion of this chapter you should be able to:

- Define evaluation and explain the purposes of evaluating HRD;
- Describe, apply and critically appraise frameworks for the evaluation of HRD;
- Advise on the design and implementation of the evaluation of HRD.

Introduction

Benjamin Franklin (1706–1790), one of the 'founders' of the United States of America, is reputed to have said that 'an investment in knowledge pays the best interest'. For some people the view that HRD 'pays' rather than 'costs' is self-evident, on the other hand the view that it 'costs' rather than 'pays' is a potential 'Achilles heel' for HRD.[1] Those stakeholders who hold the purse strings and have their eyes fixed firmly on the financial bottom line are likely to need convincing about the value that HRD adds to an organization, its return-on-investment (ROI) and whether the benefits it brings outweigh the costs incurred. This is a good commercial reason why evaluation matters especially to particular groups of stakeholders such as senior managers, owners and shareholders, but it's by no means the only reason nor are these groups the only stakeholders involved.

Evaluating anything that incurs costs and has potential benefits involves coming to a judgement about its value or worth based on an objective appraisal of the available evidence. This could be anything from evaluating a meal in a restaurant (in which case the question would be 'did it meet your expectations and was it good value for money?') to evaluating the investment you've made in your higher education ('how was the experience for you, what did you learn, could you apply the learning, and was it worth the costs you incurred?'). If HRD seeks to 'enable individual employees to achieve their full potential and organizations to achieve their strategic goals', then its value or worth depends on its contribution to both the fulfilment of individuals' potential and to the realization of an organization's goals based on an objective appraisal of the available evidence. Additionally, if HRD's accountability and credibility depends on demonstrable value-added to the 'bottom line', questions arise about 'to who's bottom line' is value being added and 'for what purpose?'.

Evaluation is one of the most technically, professionally, ethically and politically challenging aspects of HRD practice.[2] The situation is complicated by the fact that the reputation and practice of evaluation in HRD suffers when all that gets evaluated are trainees' feelings about formal learning in end of training course 'happiness sheets'. Selling stakeholders short on evaluation does little to contribute to improving either HRD practice or HRD's professional reputation. As Richard Torraco and Henriette Lundgren observed, when managers are dubious about the value that HRD can add they'll make decisions about learning and development primarily based on costs, and ultimately this could lead to a narrow view of how and where HRD can add value, under-investment in HRD and be detrimental to learning. Therefore it's important that HRD can demonstrate clearly the value it adds to the things that are difficult, as well as those that are easy, to measure.

Reflective question 12.1

What would you say to a senior manager who expressed the view that the only type of HRD impact that matters is impact that's measurable and that makes a difference to the financial 'bottom line'?

Evaluation defined

As always, history matters and the evaluation of HRD is no exception to this rule. Evaluation has been part of the 'science of training and development in organizations' for well over half a century. The World War II US 'Training Within Industry' (TWI) service (1940–1945), which was a 'major influence' on the development of modern HRD, described evaluation as an appraisal of the 'suitability of content, effectiveness of techniques and methods, and checking the results against the problem which was identified of the objective which was to be met'. This TWI view has stood the test of time quite well, as has that of one of the most influential figures in the training field, the industrial psychologist Irwin L. Goldstein of the University of Maryland (1937–2013). In the classic training textbook *Training in Organizations* Irwin Goldstein and J. Kevin Ford defined evaluation as: 'The systematic collection of descriptive and judgmental information necessary to make effective decisions related to the selection, adoption, value and modification of various instructional activities'. If we substitute 'formal and informal learning in organizations' for various 'instructional activities' (a more narrow and dated term) we have a broader, workable definition of evaluation.

That said, evaluating HRD is part of a larger and more integrated process than a simple reading of Goldstein's definition would suggest. Evaluation is concerned not only with HRD's effects on the relevant outcomes (whether the HRD 'worked' or not at the end of a process or causal chain) but also with whether or not the organization was right to try to solve the perceived problem through HRD in the first place (whether HRD was the 'right solution'). This ties-in both with systematic models of the HRD process such as ADDIE and SAT (see Chapter 10), and the original TWI focal concepts of 'problem, objectives, content and methods' (see above). Whether HRD has an impact runs backwards from the end of the process (the effect it had on important outcomes) to its beginning with the identification and analysis of the learning needs and all the stages in between. Evaluation must permeate HRD processes and systems if HRD is to be effective, see Figure 12.1.

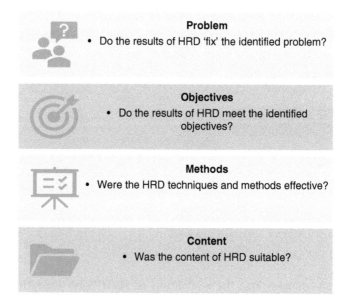

Figure 12.1 The role of evaluation in the HRD process

The fact that within the HRD system the various stages are inter-dependent highlights the fact that an inaccurate learning needs identification and analysis creates a shaky foundation for the subsequent stages. These issues translate into three straightforward and very familiar 'plan-do-check' questions:

- Did the organization need the HRD that was provided in the first place (plan)?
- Did the HRD work in practice (do)?
- Did the HRD add value for individuals and the organization (check)?

If this process works effectively then evaluation supports continuous improvement and contributes to, as well as assessing, the added value for stakeholders.[8,9]

─Delve deeper 12.1─

Read about the wider context of evaluation in:

Torraco, R. J. (2016). Early history of the fields of practice of training and development and organization development. *Advances in Developing Human Resources, 18*(4), 439–453.

Nickols, F. W. (2005). Why a stakeholder approach to evaluating training. *Advances in Developing Human Resources, 7*(1), 121–134.

Gubbins, C., Harney, B., van der Werff, L., & Rousseau, D. (2018). Enhancing the Trustworthiness and Credibility of HRD: Evidence-based Management to the Rescue? *Human Resource Development Quarterly, 29*(3), 193–202.

Purposes of evaluating HRD

The evaluation of HRD has several purposes ranging from the purely technical (for example, 'did the HRD achieve its aims?'), through political (for example, 'how might these findings about HRD be interpreted in this organization at this time?') to a 'promoting purpose' (for example, how can this information be used to market learning and development in the organization and presenting the 'HRD brand' to internal potential clients?); see Figure 12.2.

Pragmatic purpose
- Informs / provides feedback for stakeholders on how effective HRD has been
- Information used for continuous improvement purposes in context
- Results likely to be of limited generalizability

Research purpose
- Understanding processes of learning and development; why some methods more effective than others; informed by and informs theories of learning and instructional design
- More generalizable beyond specific organization / context to HRD field more widely; contributes to and advances HRD knowledge; builds evidence-based HRD practice

Professional-political purpose
- Evaluation in specific occupational, organizational and societal context
- Questions purpose and meaning of who is evaluation being conducted for and why; what results will be used for; what the degree of objectivity and subjectivity involved is; what counts as valid knowledge; what are the ethical issues?

Figure 12.2   Three purposes of evaluating HRD

Given that evaluation ultimately is about finding out – that is learning – if, how and why HRD worked or didn't work, evaluating HRD is an opportunity to find out if and how well individual and collective learning and development processes are being managed and if they're enabling individual employees to maximize their potential and organizations to achieve their strategic goals. Evaluation creates learnings about HRD as well as providing evidence of HRD's effects;[10] see Figure 12.3.

For evaluation to be a genuine source of learning, HRD practitioners and line managers must be willing to ask penetrating questions that may challenge established HRD orthodoxy, policy and practice, and also be prepared that the answers they get might not be the answers that they wanted or will like. Evaluation can help us to become 'reflective practitioners' capable of 'reflecting-in-action' and 'reflecting-on-action'.[11,12]

Asking

- Developing a spirit of curiosity which acts as a catalyst for learning through inquiry ranging from the broad and diagnostic (interpretative) to mundane factual questions

Challenging

- Values, beliefs and assumptions are the taken-for-granted behaviours and dispositions that may have been developed over long periods of time. For organizational learning to occur these assumptions need to be questioned openly and collectively

Reflecting

- Enabling HRD practitioners to reflect upon what happened and why it happened in the way that it did. Reflection can be during the process (to learn lessons for here-and-now improvements, a kind of 'formative' inquiry) or after the process (to learn lessons for future use, a kind of 'summative' inquiry)

Dialoguing

- Sustained collective inquiry into shared meanings to understand wholes and uncover assumptions and mental model by asking for reasons that underpin statements or answers thus making errors, biases and distortions more visible

Figure 12.3 Evaluation-as-learning

Delve deeper 12.2

Read more about Donald Schön's (1930–1997) concepts of 'reflection-in-action' and 'reflection-on-action' in the epistemology of HRD practice and the application of Schön's ideas in:

Schön, D.A. (1984). *The reflective practitioner: How professionals think in action*. New York: Basic Books.

Dirkx, J. M. (2008). The epistemology of practice: An argument for practice-based research in HRD. *Human Resource Development Review*, 7(3), 263–269.

Sadler-Smith, E., & Smith, P. J. (2006). Technical rationality and professional artistry in HRD practice. *Human Resource Development International*, 9(2), 271–281.

Related to the purposes of evaluation is the important practical question of 'how to evaluate HRD?'. The most common approach (explored in detail in the next section) involves evaluating at different 'levels' of outcome ranging from how individuals felt about their experience of learning and development (their reaction to it), through what they learned and how this transferred to their work, to its impact on organizational outcomes. The most widely-used of these levels of evaluation frameworks have four and five levels of outcome. The most well-known is the 'four-level' framework developed by Donald L. Kirkpatrick in the 1950s. The framework is a simple and logical 'taxonomy' (in other words a classification) or hierarchy of learning and development outcomes that range from the 'reaction' level (the lowest) to the 'results' level (the highest).

Kirkpatrick's framework isn't a research 'model' designed to generate testable hypotheses, nor it is a formal 'theory'; it's a simple, methodical framework for action. In Kirkpatrick's own words it's 'a systematic way of doing something' and a 'helpful guide' to HRD practitioners and managers 'who are more interested in practical ideas than scholarly research'.[13] Subsequently other HRD researchers and practitioners,[14] most notably Jack J. Phillips, extended Kirkpatrick's framework by adding a fifth level, 'return on investment' (ROI). Figure 12.4 gives an overview of the labels that Kirkpatrick and Phillips used for these different levels from the lowest to the highest.

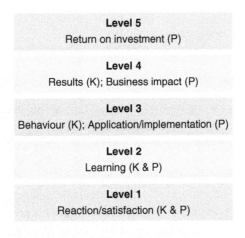

Figure 12.4   Levels-of-outcomes for the evaluation of HRD (lower to higher; K refers to Kirkpatrick's terminology, P refers to Phillips)

In the following sections we'll look at how to evaluate learning and development using these two 'levels-of-outcome' approaches (historically Kirkpatrick is first, and then Phillips), and also consider some critiques of and alternatives to levels-of-outcome frameworks.

Kirkpatrick's four-level framework

Donald L Kirkpatrick's four-level framework for the evaluation of learning and development, 'Techniques for Evaluating Training Programs', first appeared in the *Journal of the*

American Society of Training Directors, 1956. The Kirkpatrick framework's widespread and enduring popularity is attributable to its simplicity and practicability as a tool for helping HRD practitioners and managers to think about training evaluation criteria in a methodical and systematic way and put evaluation into action. Kirkpatrick based the framework on four straightforward questions:

- What were the learners' feelings about a given learning and development intervention (Level 1, 'reaction');
- What did they actually learn (Level 2, 'learning');
- Did the learning transfer to their job (Level 3, 'behaviour');
- What was the impact of the learning on the business (Level 4, 'results')?

These are the four-levels of evaluation. Research in the US shows consistently that around 80 per cent of organizations use reaction level evaluations, 30 per cent learning, 20 per cent behaviour and less than 10 per cent evaluate at the results level.[15]

---In their own words 12.1---

Kirkpatrick on how to evaluate training

In his classic 1956 article 'How to start an objective evaluation of your training program' Kirkpatrick set the scene as follows:

> Most training men [sic] agree that it is important to evaluate training programs. They also feel that the evaluation should be done by objective means.
> However, the typical training man uses evaluation sheets or comment sheets as the sole measure of the effectiveness of his programs. He realizes he should do more, but he just doesn't know how to begin an objective evaluation.

What is striking, more than half a century on, is that Kirkpatrick puts his finger on a perennial problem and significant shortcoming in the evaluation of learning and development: the use of 'evaluation or comment sheets' – sometimes referred to disparagingly as 'happiness sheets' – as the main, but sometimes the only, method for evaluating outcomes. Another interesting aside is that Kirkpatrick is clear in this 1956 article that he attributes the 'four-level' idea to the work of Raymond Katzell[16] (1919–2003). Katzell – described by Kirkpatrick as a 'well-known authority in this field' – was a member of the psychology faculty at New York University from 1943 to his retirement in 1983. His 1952 manuscript 'Can we evaluate training?' appears to have been lost to history.[17]

The four-step (or 'four level') approach is a 'hierarchy' of learning outcomes. It is clear and simple and offers a useful framework that's based on Kirkpatrick's practical experience rather than on theory.[18]

Reaction (level 1) evaluation

In Kirkpatrick's own words the reaction level refers to 'how well the trainees liked a particular training program'.[19] The reaction level (or 'Level 1') is most easily understood when applied to formal learning, for example, a training course. Trainees' reactions to a training course can be evaluated in terms of:

- Content and objectives, for example what the learners thought about its job relevance, the clarity and difficulty of the teaching, and the engagement, curiosity, interest, and motivation it stirred in them, etc.;
- Methods, for example how efficient and effective the methods were, etc.;
- Resources and environment, for example quality of the materials used and the physical space in which learning took place, etc.;
- Professional competence and effectiveness of the trainer/instructor or the designer of the materials.

Reaction level evaluation is, by definition, subjective; its focus is the learners' opinions and feelings. These are relevant because how employees feel about learning builds interest, motivation and commitment to further learning. It's self-evident that reactions don't necessarily relate to learning outcomes (and research supports this[20]) or to job performance since it's entirely possible to enjoy a learning experience and not learn very much or be able to apply it.[21] The most important relationships and causal mechanisms are between the three levels (that is 'learning', 'behaviour' and 'results') above the reaction level;[22] see Figure 12.5.

Figure 12.5 Relationships between levels in the Kirkpatrick model (the dashed line indicates a weak or tenuous relationship in causal chain to results level)

Kirkpatrick described the reaction level as 'basically a measure of customer satisfaction'. Kirkpatrick Partners (the commercial organization that's taken his work forward) recommend that in composing questions to assess learners' reactions (known as 'reaction level items' in a survey) attention should be focused on asking participants directly about their experiences of the training in relation to their needs, for example: 'I am clear about what is expected of me as a result of this training' or 'What were the three most important things you learned from this session?'.[23] From a commercial consulting perspective Kirkpatrick argued that a 'positive reaction' keeps the trainer 'in business'.[24]

Perspective from practice 12.1

Doing a reaction level evaluation

Reaction level data is gathered typically using questionnaires with questions (or 'items') designed using a Likert-scale format for example, on a five-point scale from 'very satisfied' to 'very dissatisfied' or a three-point scale for example, 'too much/long/fast' to 'too little/short/slow'. Goldstein and Ford[25] suggested the following guidelines for evaluation at the reaction level:

- Base reaction questionnaires on the content and objectives derived from the training needs identification and analysis phase;
- Design the questionnaire so that responses can be easily quantified, analysed, tabulated and compared;
- Provide for participant anonymity in questionnaire responses and space for issues that are not covered by standardized closed questions;
- Pre-test the questionnaire and modify as appropriate.

What methods such as these offer in terms of ease and accuracy of measurement they lose in terms of depth of meaning. In order to drill down into learners' reactions it's necessary to use open questions supplemented by one-to-one or focus group interviews. Also, timing can be important. Delayed reactions away from the training situation give learners the opportunity to give a more considered and objective view on its relevance and potential application in the workplace. On the other hand, delayed evaluation is administratively more difficult and response rates and engagement are likely to be lower.

Delve deeper 12.3

Read more about the updated and re-branded 'The New World Kirkpatrick Model' (NWKM) at the Kirkpatrick website[26] and in:

Moreau, K. A. (2017). Has the new Kirkpatrick generation built a better hammer for our evaluation toolbox? *Medical Teacher*, *39*(9), 999–1001.

Not all HRD researchers are sympathetic towards evaluating at the reaction level. Goldstein and Ford argue that while most analysts realize the limitations of this approach, there are still far too many efforts of this type,[27] and as noted above most data back up this critique. Some have suggested that reaction should be 'removed from evaluation models as a primary outcome of training'.[28] Nonetheless, reaction remains the most popular, if perhaps the least useful, measure of HRD impact.

Learning (level 2) evaluation

Learning level evaluation ('Level 2') focuses on whether the intended learning outcomes (also known as the 'learning objectives') have been met in terms of knowledge and/or skill acquisition, and attitude formation and change. Because each of these types of outcomes represent different categories of learning, whether they've been achieved has to be evaluated in different ways. Learning level evaluation can be:

- Formative (during the event): learners become aware of their progress towards pre-defined outcomes and HRD practitioners can become alerted, in the moment, about how effective the learning methods are;
- Summative (after the event): find out if the learning objectives were achieved.

Learning level evaluation should also consider taking into account unplanned as well as planned learning outcomes since some of the most valuable learning can be unplanned and incidental.[29] Learning level evaluation is important because it's the first substantive step (see Figure 12.5) in the causal chain through behaviour towards results (given that reaction level doesn't necessarily correlate with learning).

Knowledge outcomes

Knowledge outcomes differ substantially in terms of their level of complexity and levels of cognitive (intellectual) challenge for the learner. In 1956 the educational psychologist Benjamin S. Bloom (1913–1999) published a handbook of learning outcomes for the cognitive domain: *Taxonomy of Educational Objectives Handbook I Cognitive Domain*. Bloom also produced taxonomies for the psychomotor (manual and physical skills) and affective (feelings and emotions) domains. The cognitive domain in Bloom's original framework consisted of six categories from lower-order thinking processes and outcomes (that is 'knowledge' and 'comprehension') to higher-order (that is, synthesis and evaluation). The taxonomy was later revised by David Krathwohl in 2002[30] using verbs rather than nouns to capture the cognitive processes involved, for example 'remembering' rather than 'knowledge' and with 'synthesis' replaced by 'creating' and placed at the top of the hierarchy; see Figure 12.6.

Each of these various levels of outcome require different forms of evaluation, for example:

- 'Remembering' (that is, knowledge): this is the lowest level of cognitive learning; and to evaluate it the learner could be required to simply recall a piece of verbal information such as 'define the term "human resource development (HRD)"';
- 'Creating' (or 'synthesis' in Bloom's original taxonomy): the highest level of cognitive learning, and to evaluate it the learner could be required to integrate her knowledge and understanding of the field of HRD into a novel and coherent whole and apply it to 'devise an HRD strategy which helps the organization to meet its strategic goals'.

Remembering (knowledge)

- Retrieving relevant knowledge from long-term memory
- Defining; describing; labelling; listing; memorizing; naming; recognizing; recalling; repeating; stating; telling

Understanding (comprehension)

- Determining meaning of data, information, knowledge
- Classifying; comparing; discussing; explaining; giving examples; inferring; interpreting; outlining; paraphrasing; recognizing; summarizing

Applying (application)

- Carrying out a procedure or using knowledge in given situation
- Applying; computing; demonstrating; executing; implementing; operating; predicting; showing; solving; using

Analysing (analysis)

- Breaking something down into its parts and understanding the overall structure and how the parts relate to each other
- Analysing; attributing; comparing; contrasting; differentiating; discriminating; distinguishing; identifying; inferring; organizing; questioning; separating; sub-dividing

Evaluating (evaluation)

- Coming to a logical judgement based on knowledge, understanding and evidence
- Appraising; arguing; assessing; checking; critiquing; deciding; defending; judging; justifying; prioritizing; rating; selecting; supporting; weighing

Creating (synthesis)

- Putting different elements together to form coherent whole, that may be novel (creating)
- Authoring; constructing; creating; designing; developing; formulating; generating; making; planning; producing

Figure 12.6   Cognitive processes for the knowledge domain and indicative behaviours e.g. 'defining' (Bloom's original domain names in brackets; nouns rather than verbs)

The assessment that's being used to check if learning has taken place should match the pre-defined learning objectives which will themselves have been derived from a learning needs identification and analysis (see Chapter 10). For example, if a needs analysis had revealed the need for selection interviewers to be able to 'conduct interviews in ways which minimize unconscious biases' then:

- The knowledge objective could be 'by the end of this workshop learners should be able to list potential sources of unconscious biases in interviews';
- The evaluation of this knowledge outcome could be to 'design an interview schedule that minimizes the potential for unconscious biases to arise';

Ultimate proof would be if in subsequent interviews unconscious biases were reduced or eliminated (this would be at Level 3).

Assessment at the learning level is likely to involve a mix of various forms of knowledge tests and immediate post-training of the knowledge acquired. Bloom's taxonomy is used widely in HRD and education to specify systematically the various levels of learning outcome[31] and can be applied to various HRD methods, including e-learning. Building from the lower-levels to higher-levels is important. Doing so provides a cognitive 'scaffolding' for the higher levels of learning.[32]

Research insight 12.1

E-learning versus classroom learning for knowledge acquisition

This study investigated differences in training success across corporate e-learning and classroom training in terms of subjective and objective training success measures. The research was conducted in a German manufacturer of laboratory equipment. Participants were randomly assigned to two groups, e-learning (N = 41) or classroom training (N =45). Success was assessed using an online questionnaire at two points in time, immediately and then six to eight weeks later. Subjective success was measured using the Questionnaire for Professional Training Evaluation (Q4TE) which assesses at the four Kirkpatrick levels. Objective success was measured using a performance test of declarative and procedural knowledge (knowledge of 'what' and 'how' respectively). It was found that:

- With regard to subjective success, trainees in classroom training scored higher compared with e-learning trainees;
- This effect disappeared six to eight weeks after training;
- Satisfaction (reaction) scored highest, followed by knowledge, utility, application to practice, and organizational results;
- Immediately after training the declarative knowledge (knowledge of 'what') scores were similar for both groups of trainees, whereas procedural knowledge (knowledge of 'how') scores were higher for trainees in classroom training;
- Six to eight weeks later, declarative knowledge scores were higher for e-learners whilst there were no differences in procedural knowledge between the two groups.

E-learners gained over the longer term on declarative knowledge and caught up on procedural knowledge. The researchers concluded that e-learning is as effective as classroom training for procedural knowledge and more effective than classroom training for declarative knowledge. A practical implication is that declarative knowledge may be better delivered by e-learning rather than classroom settings.

Source: Beinicke, A., & Bipp, T. (2018). Evaluating training outcomes in corporate e-learning and classroom training. Vocations and Learning, 11(3), 501–528.

Skills outcomes

Skills are the abilities or proficiencies acquired through training or practice to carry out a specific behaviour or task.[33] They can be divided into two broad categories:

- Manual and psychomotor skills, for example 'operate a barista coffee machine';
- Social and interpersonal skills, for example 'greet customer politely'.

Sometimes it's not always straightforward to pigeon-hole a job-related skill since human behaviour, especially in the workplace, is likely to contain a mix of different types of skill as well as knowledge (for example, brewing a good cup of coffee requires knowledge about coffee and brewing) and attitudes (for example, giving good customer service depends on a genuine, caring attitude to customers). Likewise, interviewing skills are likely to have cognitive elements (such as knowing what an unconscious bias is) and social skills of applying knowledge such as this in an interpersonal encounter (such as a selection interview). Skills' tests assess performance and must therefore be practical in order to establish satisfactorily whether a learner can carry out a procedure proficiently, operate a piece of machinery safely, etc. One way of doing this is by an experienced person, such as a manager, expert or formal assessor, judging whether a piece of finished work is of acceptable quality (work sampling) or observing or questioning the learner to test their performance against a predetermined set of criteria.

'Performance testing' allows participants to demonstrate what they have learned in the training situation prior to applying it in their jobs (this is the next level, 'behaviour level', see below). In the example of interviewing skills and unconscious biases the skill outcomes (building on the knowledge outcomes discussed in the previous section) could be as follows:

- The skills objective could be 'by the end of this workshop learners should be able to conduct interviews in ways that minimize the influences of unconscious biases';
- The evaluation of skill learning could be to 'participate in an interview role play in which the learner conducts an interview in which the potential for unconscious biases are minimized'.

The issues of fidelity (degree of similarity of the training to the work situation), cost (of training and getting it wrong) and risk (to those involved) are important factors in skills assessment.

Simulations are a practical, and sometimes the only, way of assessing certain types of skills learning, for example where the costs of learning or being assessed in a 'live' situation are expensive and/or high-risk (for example, the emergency shut-down of a nuclear power station, landing a passenger aircraft, performing a surgical procedure for the first time, etc.). Simulations have a number of advantages:[34]

- Fidelity: they can mirror the work situation closely and allow learners to demonstrate skills in a safe context;

- Reproducibility: allow aspects of the job to be represented and reproduced multiple times thus enabling as much practice as appropriate;
- Cost-effectiveness: for certain skills simulators are the most cost-effective (both in terms of financial and other costs) way to develop and test skills (for example, in flight simulator training for aircraft pilots it simply wouldn't be cost effective to train and assess pilots in a real aircraft even if it were safe to do so);
- Safety: in many job roles such as firefighters, pilots, emergency medicine, etc. there is risk injury to life and property if learners don't get the chance to practise and be assessed in a simulated job situation.

The use of simulation in medical education is well-established. Teaching novice medics how to carry out demanding and risky procedures using simulations can deliver better results than traditional methods and the patterns of errors in simulated tasks are often similar to those found in actual practice.[35] The use of virtual reality (VR) simulators opens up new possibilities in medical training for developing surgeons' psychomotor skills, especially in novel areas such as laparoscopic procedures.

Research insight 12.2

Evaluating VR simulator training in laparoscopic surgery skills

Australian medical researchers evaluated the effectiveness of virtual reality (VR) training in improving the medical skills of gynaecological students. VR for surgical training uses simulation solutions to improve productivity and increase patient safety by helping doctors acquire, retain, and enhance their skills helping them improve patient outcomes.[36] A group of final year medical students, junior doctor trainees and senior doctors undertook standard gynaecological procedures both before and after VR training. The VR training involved a number of instructional sessions on the VR equipment over a two-month period mimicking the laparoscopic skills required to perform laparoscopic gynaecological procedures. The procedures were performed repeatedly up to 14 times In the training. VR skills performance was assessed and after the VR training participants undertook a second skills assessment on a live animal model (approved by the University's animal ethics committee). In the skills learning assessment (Kirkpatrick Level 2; learning; skills) the procedures were video-recorded and rated using a combination of surgical scores based on operative time and penalties for surgical errors (videos were edited so that the scorer was blind to the identity and seniority of the operator) which were then correlated with VR scores. The researchers found that junior doctors and medical students, who were not familiar with the procedures:

- Scored poorly on the pretraining scores;
- Showed significant improvement in their post VR live animal exercise scores.

(Continued)

They concluded that as the junior doctors have only limited opportunity to improve their surgical skills and medical students have no opportunity to do so, repeated sessions of VR training appear to significantly reduce surgical operating time and improve error scores in these groups. However, the benefits seem to apply only to those who have limited or no existing practical experience. The senior doctors showed better surgical skills on the initial surgical exercises on the animal model[37] since they were already competent with these procedures and their post training scores on the animal model showed no improvement. Moreover, senior doctors were reluctant to undertake repeated VR training.

Source: Hart, R., Doherty, D. A., Karthigasu, K., & Garry, R. (2006). The value of virtual reality–simulator training in the development of laparoscopic surgical skills. *Journal of Minimally Invasive Gynaecology, 13*(2), 126–133.

Simulations can also be used as complement to, rather than replacement for, traditional training and assessment methods and they needn't be high tech as in the case of piloting an aircraft or carrying out surgical procedures. Role play is a low-tech simulation that can be used to assess interpersonal skills learning. For non-safety critical tasks involving skills, such as selection interviewing, selling, etc., role plays are an efficient and effective simulation and assessment tool. Designing a role play involves specifying clearly the objectives (for example, selling a product), environment (for example, in a store), and the role (for example, salesperson). Role plays should build from simple to complex skills, focus on key skills, take account of psychological factors such as stress and fatigue amongst participants, and give clear and precise feedback on the behaviours being observed and assessed.

Attitudinal outcomes

The eminent social psychologist Gordon Allport (1897–1967) defined an attitude as a mental state of readiness, organized through experience which exerts a directive or dynamic influence on an individual's response to objects and situations. In simpler terms attitude is 'the affect [the underlying feeling] for or against an object' and has three components;[38] see Figure 12.7.

Evaluating attitudinal learning/change is important because attitude formation and change affect workplace behaviours. In the case of sales training an employee's attitudes towards customers, such as a positive and caring attitude, can have a significant impact on customers' buying behaviour and brand loyalty. A positive attitude towards an object (for example, a customer) predisposes an individual to behave in a positive way towards the object. One way in which attitudinal change can be mobilized is through persuasion using techniques such as role plays and simulations. Consistent with social

Cognitive (thoughts)
- Ideas and propositions that express relationships between situations and attitudinal objects, for example 'people spend too much time on their smart phones'

Affective (feelings)
- Emotional or feeling aspect that accompanies an idea, for example a feeling of frustration that 'people don't spend more time on things other than their smart phones'

Conative (behaviours)
- Predisposition or readiness to act towards an object or situation in a consistent way, for example, 'spend less time on one's smartphones'

Figure 12.7 Components of attitudes

learning theory (see Chapter 3), the effectiveness of persuasion through role play or simulation depends on the:

- Source of the message, for example, the credibility of a role model;
- Nature of the message, for example, whether it is perceived as balanced and unbiased;
- Recipients' underlying values and beliefs.

An unintended side-effect of attempts at attitudinal change can be a 'boomerang effect' when a message of low persuasiveness in comparison to the perceived threat to one's personal freedom induces a retrenchment of the attitude in the assertion of individuality and resistance to change.

Perspective from practice 12.2

Using big data in the evaluation of training

Learning management systems (LMS) can capture and process large amounts of data regarding employees' use of digital learning platforms and materials. By developing metrics based on time spent on learning, test results, questions and feedback data can be extracted from e-learning platforms to discover which modules are used most,

(Continued)

how they are being used, etc. Knowledge and skill tests can be used to assess which topics incur most errors and misunderstandings. Data derived from assessing individual performance, tracking progress, learning styles and learning history can be used to discover and provide the best 'personalized e-learning' approach by choosing paths and setting goals that are most suited to the individual. Using cloud technology, businesses can also share data across multiple sites in real time to give a bigger picture of how well training is being received and how well it is working as part of the LMS. By helping to make learning more personalized and responsive the application of big data in evaluating the effectiveness of learning can add value to the experience for learners and their organizations and improve engagement and performance.

Source: Kostusev, D. (2019). How to use big data to improve corporate training. *Forbes Magazine*[39]

Behaviour (level 3) evaluation

Behaviour level evaluation ('Level 3') assesses HRD's contribution to changes in workplace behaviour and improvements in job performance as a result of learning. The focus of behaviour-level evaluation (the third level in Kirkpatrick's framework) is on:

- Transfer: if any learning that occurred transferred from the learning situation to the job context;
- Application: if changes in workplace behaviours as a result of learning led to enhanced job performance.

In the causal chain shown earlier (Figure 12.5) transfer of learning and application make the link between Kirkpatrick level 2 and Kirkpatrick level 3. If knowledge, skills or attitudes transfer from the learning situation to the job situation the question then arises of how changes in job performance may be assessed (for a discussion of 'transfer of learning' see Chapter 6).

Methods that can be used to evaluate changes in workplace behaviour as a result of learning include post-training interviews with learners and their managers, observation and assessment of learners' performance in the workplace, and over the longer-term annual performance appraisal and assessment of employees' productivity (with the proviso that learning may be only one of a number of factors that may have produced the observed effects). Changes in job performance attributable to learning can be identified by asking (in surveys or interviews) learners and line managers about:

- Application, for example whether learners have actually used the newly acquired knowledge, skills or attitudes in the job situation;
- Utility, for example how useful the knowledge, skills or attitudes acquired have been in the job;

- Difficulty, for example what difficulties learners might have had in applying the new knowledge, skills or attitudes;
- Individual behaviour, for example whether learners have been able to perform the relevant tasks to the required standard;
- Wider effects, for example how the learning has contributed to learners' job performance/performance of their team.

Even though an individual may change their behaviour as a result of learning and development this may not translate into enhanced performance in the workplace. This can be because of a number of factors including the transfer climate within the organization not being conducive to applying learning in the workplace (see 'Learning Transfer System Inventory', Chapter 6) and extraneous influences that an individual, or even the organization itself, may not have control over (for example, macroeconomic factors). It's been argued that because there are so many variables that can affect organizational performance over-and-above the effectiveness of HRD that the evaluation of employee performance (i.e. behaviour, Level 3) may be the most direct and meaningful assessment of HRD's effectiveness.[10] The Kirkpatrick Foundation (www.kirkpatrickpartners.com/) offers some practical suggestions on how to evaluate at Level 3.

Perspective from practice 12.3

The 'success case method'

An alternative approach which doesn't neatly fit into the four levels was developed by Robert Brinkerhoff in his Success Case Method (SCM)[41]. The method uses 'critical incidents', or contrasting instances, of learning being applied successfully and unsuccessfully to the job. In this method individuals from 'successful' and 'unsuccessful' groups (that is, those who were able, and those who were unable, to use the learning productively) are interviewed:

- Successful group: a small number of those trainees who've been the most successful in using their learning to improve job performance. Interviews with this group identify the impact that the training had and the 'training system factors' (for example, timing, opportunity, support, etc.) that contributed to success;
- Unsuccessful group: a small number of those trainees who, for various reasons, haven't been able to apply their learning. Interviews with this group identify the factors that prevented them from being successful in applying their learning to the job.[42]

A case doesn't count as a success if there isn't adequate evidence that it was learning that helped to improve performance. The method is qualitatively-oriented and aims to produce in-depth credible and verifiable 'stories' (in other words, case studies) of

(Continued)

documented incidents of learning success stories that can be disseminated to a variety of audiences in the organization.[43] The SCM can serve professional and political purposes as well as having a proving and improving function. In practice the SCM approach bridges Kirkpatrick Level 3 (behaviour) and Level 4 (results).

Sources: Brinkerhoff, R. O. (2005). The success case method: A strategic evaluation approach to increasing the value and effect of training. *Advances in Developing Human Resources*, 7(1), 86–101; Lee, C., Jeon, D., Kim, W., & Lee, J. (2017). Evaluating training for new government officials: A case study using the success case method. *Public Personnel Management*, 46(4), 419–444.

Results (level 4) evaluation

Results level evaluation (Level 4) is concerned with assessing the effects that HRD has on organizational-level outcomes such as productivity, costs, turnover, absenteeism, job satisfaction, organizational commitment, etc. As such it's a switch in focus and level of analysis from individual learners and their job performance (that is, their behaviour, Level 3) to the organization of which they're a part. Return-on-investment (ROI) and benefit-cost analyses become increasingly important at the results level. This, at least in the Kirkpatrick framework, is the final link in the causal chain from the learning and development 'input' to the organizational results 'output'; see Figure 12.5.

Research insight 12.3

Meta-analysis of effectiveness of training in organizations at the four levels

In a major study of the relationship between specified training design and evaluation features, researchers in the United States used meta-analytic procedures to investigate the effectiveness of training in organizations. Specifically they sought an answer to the following question: will the magnitude of the effectiveness of training decrease from the learning level to the results level (for example, as a result of the influence of factors extraneous to training)? They looked at the published training and development literature from 1960 to 2000 using 162 sources. The overall 'effect size' (d, or 'standardized difference') for organizational training was 0.60 to 0.63 which is classified typically as 'large' (a d of 0.4 would be 'medium', and 0.2 'small') and better than and comparable to the effect sizes for some other organizational interventions, such as appraisal or goal-setting, on productivity. They also investigated studies that reported multiple evaluation criteria (i.e. at various combinations of the four levels) and found that for all comparisons of learning (level 2) evaluations with higher-level criteria (i.e. behaviour and results levels, 3 and 4) there was a progressive decrease in effect sizes from learning to behaviour and results. This finding is consistent with problems of learning transfer, lack of opportunity to perform newly learned behaviours and skill loss. They found that the effects of learning at the behaviour and results levels is likely to be related to environmental 'favourability of the post-training environment for the performance of the learned skills'. Favourability is the 'extent to which the transfer or work environment is supportive of the application of new skills and behaviours learned or acquired in training' (p. 242).

Sources: Arthur Jr, W., Bennett Jr, W., Edens, P. S., & Bell, S. T. (2003). Effectiveness of training in organizations: A meta-analysis of design and evaluation features. *Journal of Applied Psychology*, *88*(2), 234–245.

Thomas Garavan and colleagues conducted a moderated meta-analysis of the training and organizational performance relationship using data from 119 studies. They found that:

- Investment in training is associated with increased organizational performance (a one standard deviation increase in training expenditure was related to a 0.25 standard deviation increase in performance) and that this relationship was stronger (i.e. built-up) over time;
- Country contextual factors moderated the training and organizational performance relationship (for example, organizations located in low labour cost economies can potentially derive significantly greater benefits from training investment).

They concluded that HRD plays an important role in a 'context characterised by globalisation, increased scarcity of talent and changing generational expectations of work' (p. 21).[44]

We know from transfer of training theory that newly acquired knowledge, skills and attitudes cannot manifest as changes in behaviour if learners don't have the opportunity to apply them to their jobs in the workplace. If they can't apply them to their jobs then the training won't impact the organization. Therefore the organizational context and the suitability of the post-training environment for application of new learning plays a vital role in enabling the transfer of knowledge, skills and attitudes from the learning environment both to job behaviour and then onwards and upwards to organizational results.

The HRD–firm performance link is part of a complex chain of antecedent and contextual factors, inputs, processes and outputs, therefore to expect simple linear cause-and-effect relationships in complex organizational systems may be over-optimistic. One implication of this complexity is that there's a broad spectrum of HRD outcomes (in areas such as quality, business process, resources, stakeholder perception, and HR) that need to be taken into account, some of which are more measurable, but not necessarily more or less important, than others.

A challenge that becomes more significant as we move along the evaluation causal chain from learning to results is that, in the absence of rigorously executed experimentally-designed evaluations (which are often unwieldy, impractical and unrealistic beyond closely-controlled settings, such as labs), isolating the effects that a particular learning and development intervention has had on outcomes is challenging. The task is made more complex when the timing of the impact (for example, 'near transfer', short-term results versus 'far transfer', longer-term transfer[45]) and scope of effects (for example, unanticipated generalization of the learning to new situations) are factored in. Evaluation at the results level involves analytical skills and professional judgement based not only on high levels of technical knowledge but also experience and expertise.

Ethical and professional questions arise at all four levels, but especially so at the higher levels given their potential professional and political significance. Questions are also raised about who should undertake evaluations, when and for what purpose. The issue of who conducts evaluation also raises important ethical questions around issues such as:

- Confidentiality about one's own or others' behaviour and performance;
- Gaining informed consent in the collection of evaluation data;
- Transparency about the uses to which such data may be put;
- Pressure (for example amongst those who have vested interest) to produce positive results.[46]

Kirkpatrick described the results level evaluation as 'the most important and most difficult part of the process'[47] (p. 64); it's difficult because, according to the Kirkpatrick method, it involves seeking answers to questions such as: 'How much did productivity increase?', 'How much did quality improve?', 'What reduction did we get?', 'What has been the result?', 'How much tangible benefit have we received' and finally 'What is the return on investment for all the money we spend on training?'. Nonetheless, Kirkpatrick offers some clear guidelines for how to conduct a successful results level evaluation. The four levels can, and perhaps arguably should, be used 'upside down': that is, starting HRD projects by specifying measurable results-level indicators and back-tracking through what changes in behaviour are required and what learning needs to take place to bring this about: starting with the end in mind and ensuring that evaluation permeates the entire HRD process and system.[48]

Reflective question 12.2

For practical and ethical reasons, there are trade-offs between using evaluators who are internal to the organization (for example, managers, line managers or human resources practitioners) versus external agents (for example, academics or consultants). What are the pros and cons of using internal versus external evaluators to evaluate HRD? What ethical and professional issues are likely to be involved and need to be managed?[49]

Return-on-investment (ROI, level 5) evaluation

Jack J. Phillips of the ROI Institute expanded the 'levels-of-outcome' approach to include a fifth level, 'return-on-investment' (ROI), the 'investment' in question being investment in training. It's important to note that ROI is covered in other evaluation frameworks. For example, Kirkpatrick himself refers to it in his book *Evaluating Training Programs: The Four Levels*. The Phillips ROI method seeks explicitly to go beyond results evaluation (level 4, and the level Phillips calls 'business impact') to ROI (Level 5) evaluation by:

- Attempting to 'isolate' the effects of the training programme;
- Converting the results of HRD (Level 4) to monetary value;
- Comparing the monetary value to the 'fully loaded costs of the program'.[50]

Phillips stresses the importance of this final step: if more money is spent on an HRD project than is generated through the organizational-level benefits of the programme then you can end-up with a negative ROI. This is unlikely to impress those stakeholders whose sole focus is the financial bottom line. The stages in the Phillips' method (the 'Phillips' ROI Methodology') are summarized in Figure 12.8

An important element of Phillips' method is the 'isolating the effects of training' stage. The purpose of trying to do so is to answer the often-asked question 'how much of any observed improvement post-training was due to the training?'. Whilst observed improvements may be due to training they could also be down to other factors, for example introduction of new equipment or procedures, new bonus payment structure, changes in market conditions, etc. A credible evaluation plan must include techniques for

1 Plan Evaluation

- Developing evaluation plan and baseline data (e.g. customer satisfaction)

2 Collect Data

- Collecting data at Levels 1 (reaction) to 4 (business impact)

3 Analyse Data

- Tabulating programme costs; convert Level 4 data to monetary value

4 Calculate ROI

- Calculating return on investment (ROI) or benefit-cost ratio (BCR)

5 Report Findings

- Generating evaluation report and disseminating to stakeholders

Figure 12.8 Stages in the Phillips' ROI Methodology

isolating the effects of training. One of the commonest approaches for doing this is the use of trainees and/or managers' estimates of 'how much of a performance improvement is related to [the] training [provided]'.[51] Phillips suggests that the effects of training can be isolated and estimated through the use of at least one, and preferably more than one, of the methods (including trainee/manager estimates) shown in Figure 12.9.[52]

Training and control group

- One group receives training whilst other group doesn't
- Performance of two groups is compared post-training
- Difference is an estimate of the effect of training

Trend lines

- Project values of key output variables (for example sales, complaints, etc.) if training hadn't been undertaken then compare with actual data
- Difference is an estimate of the impact of training (more sophisticated versions use mathematical forecasting)

Participants' estimates

- Trainees estimate amount of post-training improvement in performance is related to training
- Trainees' supervisors/managers estimate amount of post-training improvement in performance is related to training
- Correction factor for accuracy of estimates is proposed and applied to participants', supervisors' and managers' estimates of the effects of training; for example a correction factor of 1.0 would mean that there was total confidence in the accuracy, a correction factor of 0.5 would mean there's 50% confidence in the accuracy of the estimation

Figure 12.9 Methods for isolating effects of training in Phillips' ROI method

These 'isolation factors' taken together can be used to provide a portfolio of estimates for the effects of training. Phillips also attempts to take into account other less tangible benefits of training that can be measured but cannot easily be converted to monetary value (for example, job satisfaction, organizational commitment, work climate, customer complaints, employee stress, etc.). These are difficult to quantify but Phillips urges HRD practitioners to gather estimates from various stakeholders, including learners, supervisors and senior managers in order to seek convergence on an agreeable estimate for the less tangible aspects of performance that might be attributable to HRD.

Perspective from practice 12.4

Safety training at a city centre hotel

A large city centre hotel introduced an accident reduction and equipment maintenance programme for ten supervisors and management staff. The programme was delivered over two days by an external training provider. There was an end-of-course assessment of knowledge, a practical assessment and a pre and post-course safety attitude survey as well. Trainees completed a standard reaction questionnaire. All participants passed the end of course knowledge and practical tests and there was a significant improvement in attitudes towards safety. Accident and maintenance reporting records (for example, reporting near misses, risk assessment forms, equipment repairs, etc.) were monitored for one month after the course. Two noticeable changes in performance post-training were reduction in accidents (by 15 per cent in the month after training) and fewer equipment repairs (eight fewer in the month after the training saving €1000). The costs of the training were calculated as follows:

Cost of training (€3080) = trainee salaries (€1600) + food (€700) + trainer costs (€780)

The intended outcome of a reduction in accidents (by 15 per cent) wasn't able to be attributed reliably to the training but the fewer equipment repairs were. Managers estimated that 80% of this improvement was down to the training. Eight fewer repairs per month extrapolated over the year gave a total projected saving of €1000 × 12 months × 80 per cent (€9600) which meant:

Benefit to cost ratio = €9600 : €3080 = 3.12 :1
ROI = (€9600-€3080)/€3080 = €6520/€3080 = 2.12%

Every euro spent on the training was anticipated to return €3.12 in benefits over the first year after the training. Other intangible benefits included increased feelings of safety, increased alertness, increased confidence about safe working, and longer equipment life span.

Adapted from: *Case studies form the Skills Net Project: Measuring the impact of training and development in the workplace*. Dublin: Skills Net Ltd.

The quantifiable 'cash' returns from learning and development and the relationship between costs and benefits can be expressed in a number of different ways; alternative approaches are outlined in Figure 12.10.

Phillips and Phillips in their 2005 ASTD book *ROI at Work: Best Practice Case Studies from the Real World* offer a number of case studies of ROI in action and you should consult their work for detailed illustrations of how to conduct a Phillips-type ROI analysis.[53] Phillips doesn't recommend that all programmes should be evaluated at the ROI level. Level 5 evaluations should be reserved only for those programmes that are:

- Longer term: have a life cycle of 12–18 months and are in the upper 20 per cent of training budget and therefore require clear justification of expenditure;
- Higher profile: have a large or high profile target audience and where the programme is highly visible, sensitive, change-oriented and potentially controversial;
- Strategically significant: are strategically important in meeting organization's goals and in which senior management have an interest.

Method	Calculation	Example	Meaning
Benefit-cost ratio	Monetary benefits of HRD project/ Costs of HRD project	The ABC company has measured the impact of its latest marketing training project over the past three years as £600,000 in increased sales. The project cost £120,000 to implement over that same period. BCR = £600,000/£120,000 = 5.0	At ABC for every £1 spent on the marketing training project £5 in benefits were returned
Cost-benefit ratio	Costs of HRD project/ Monetary benefits of HRD project	The XYZ company has measured the impact of its latest marketing training project over the past three years as £600,000 in increased sales. The project cost £120,000 to implement over that same period. CBR = £120,000/£600,000 = 0.2	At XYZ every £1 accrued in benefits from the marketing training project cost the company 20p
Payback period	Costs of HRD project/Annual savings	The ABC's marketing training project had a shelf life of three years. Over that time it accrued £600,000 in increased sales and cost £120,000 to implement over that time. Payback period = £120,000/(£600,000/3) = £120,000/£200,000 = 0.6	The marketing training project at the ABC company broke even after 0.6 years (i.e. 7.2 months)
Return on investment	Monetary benefits of HRD project minus costs of HRD project/ Costs of HRD project	The overall financial benefit from the ABC company's marketing training project was £600,000 in increased sales. The costs over the three year period over which the project ran were £120,000. ROI = (£600,000-£120,000)/(£120,000) = 4.0	For every £1 invested in the ABC company's marketing training project there was a return of £4 in net benefits

Figure 12.10 Some metrics for quantifying relationships between benefits and costs of HRD

HRD that is 'politically or professionally, significant', in the sense of fulfilling evaluation's political and professional purpose, can be added to this list. Evaluations at Levels 4 (Kirkpatrick Results) and 5 (Phillips ROI) have particular implications for power relations and power dynamics between the HR/HRD function and other parts of the organization, and are related to the use of the evaluation of learning and development as a political or 'bargaining' tool.[54] Research by the ATD suggests that in the USA around 16 per cent of organizations evaluate at Level 5.[55]

Reflective question 12.3

What would you say to a traditional 'sage-on-the-stage' trainer who was a highly skilled performer able to both educate and entertain groups of trainees, who always got 'rave reviews' from his classes and who expressed the view that the only 'need to have' as far delivering training goes is that the learners were 'happy at the end of the day' and that 'any other type of impact was just a 'nice-to-have' bonus'?

──── Delve deeper 12.4 ────

Read more about evaluation in:

Passmore, J., & Velez, M. J. (2015). Training evaluation. In Kraiger, K., Passmore, J., Rebelo dos Santos, N., & Malvezzi, S. (eds) *The Wiley Blackwell handbook of the psychology of training, development, and performance improvement*. Chichester: John Wiley and Sons, pp. 136–153.

Wang, G. G., Dou, Z., & Li, N. (2002). A systems approach to measuring return on investment for HRD interventions. *Human Resource Development Quarterly, 13*(2), 203–224.

Saks, A. M., & Burke, L. A. (2012). An investigation into the relationship between training evaluation and the transfer of training. *International Journal of Training and Development, 16*(2), 118–127.

Tamkin, P., Yarnall, J., & Kerrin, M. (2002). *Kirkpatrick and Beyond: A review of models of training evaluation*. Brighton: Institute for Employment Studies.

Wang, G. G., & Wilcox, D. (2006). Training evaluation: Knowing more than is practiced. *Advances in Developing Human Resources, 8*(4), 528–539.

Criticisms of, and alternatives to, levels-of-outcome models

Whilst the attempts to quantify ROI are vitally important in a 'performance paradigm' HRD, the approaches and even the rationale for ROI are by no means uncontentious. Robert Brinkerhoff (see 'Success Case Method' above) has gone as far as to argue that attempting to isolate the effects of training 'flies in the face' of what we know about how intertwined learning and performance improvement are and their inseparability in the complex system of a business organization. Brinkerhoff argues that any attempts to try to partial-out training's effects are likely not only to be 'ineffectual' but could also:

- be detrimental to HRD as a partnership and shared responsibility between human resources, line managers, senior managers and other stakeholders;
- end-up damaging the reputation of the learning and development (HRD/HR) function if evaluation comes across as 'self-serving' and 'defensive'.[56]

Brinkerhoff goes further in his criticisms by questioning the value and purpose of the concept of ROI itself (he challenges the view 'that training is capable of any independent ROI in the first place'), an unquestioning 'buy-in' to an HRD performance paradigm, and instrumental-izing learning.[57] An implication of this latter point is that instrumentalizing learning could imply that it doesn't have any intrinsic value ('learning for its own sake') and that its only value lies in the effects that it produces (see discussions of learning versus performance paradigms of HRD, and questions about maximizing shareholder value). A balanced state of affairs, as noted in previous chapters, is that HRD should have both a learning and a performance purpose. HRD evaluation should also focus on the value added for different groups of stakeholders, whereas critics might argue that the focus on ROI tends to privilege senior managers', owners' and shareholders' interests.

Evidence versus proof in results-level evaluation

Kirkpatrick's approach emphasizes 'weight of evidence' rather than 'scientific proof' of the effects of HRD. It offers practical guidelines for evaluating at the results level including using a control group and measuring intended outcomes pre- and post-training, repeating measurements at appropriate times, and allowing time for results to materialize. It seeks to create a 'compelling chain of evidence'[58] using both quantitative and qualitative data that connect the four levels to business outcomes. However, Kirkpatrick also remarks pointedly that 'I almost laugh when I hear people say that training professionals should be able to show benefits in terms of ROI [and] the same thought occurs to me when they expect trainers to relate training programmes directly to profits. Just think of all the factors that affect profits. And you can add to the list when you consider all the things that affect ROI' (p. 67); he concluded with the strong recommendation 'most important, be satisfied with *evidence* because *proof* is almost impossible to get' (p. 70, emphases added).

Several HRD researchers have drawn attention to the shortcomings of levels-of-outcomes approaches to evaluation.[59] For example, Ed Holton criticized Kirkpatrick's four-level evaluation model on the basis of its:

- Labelling: it's a taxonomy not a model and therefore the Kirkpatrick and Phillips approaches should be labelled as taxonomies (or hierarchies) of training (or learning) outcomes rather than as researchable 'models' as such;
- Mechanisms: The mechanisms are unclear, and proponents of levels-of-evaluation models are vague about the mechanisms behind the proposed causal linkages and this can lead to unjustified inferences about causal relationships that haven't been demonstrated empirically;
- Utility: they're not useful as guides for HRD decisions (for example, what methods to use) since their causalities are only implied not verified therefore they're of limited utility for taking practical decisions for how to implement effective HRD.[60]

Holton concludes that Kirkpatrick's four-level model doesn't meet the necessary criteria for a model (or indeed) a theory; instead it's a pragmatic framework for action.

Brinkerhoff's 'Success Case Method' (SCM, see above) criticized 'the venerable Kirkpatrick (1976) model' on the grounds that it didn't include evaluation beyond the 'training alone' view and lacked a focus on the 'larger performance environment'.[61] Brinkerhoff argues that the use of control groups and other techniques for 'analysing variance and partialling out causal factors' in evaluating HRD training are not only unwieldy, they also require time, resources, and expertise that's well beyond the scope of the typical HRD practitioner or workplace setting.

Which side of the evaluation debate we choose to be on depends on our personal positioning and purpose. For HRD researchers who are interested in identifying and understanding mechanisms and processes Holton's criticisms and his theoretical model offer scope for scientific exploration of learning and transfer mechanisms. On the other hand busy line managers and training practitioners who simply want to get the job of evaluation done might be satisfied with the pragmatism of a Kirkpatrick- or Phillips-type approach. Evaluators who incline towards qualitative methods may find that Brinkerhoff's approach of story-telling and case studies can help to capture the contextual factors that can enable or constrain learning and development's impact on individual and organizational learning, behaviour and performance.

Other criticisms focus on the organizational politics of HRD and criticisms that HRD is 'performative' (that is, it enables a shift away from human values towards efficiency and performance), it commodifies workers, is beholden to shareholders, ignores power relations, and is 'saturated with sexism, racism and managerialism'[62] (p. 68). The work of Stanford psychologist Professor Carol Dweck on the 'growth mindset'[63] is also relevant in that when organizations embrace a growth mindset employees are likely to be more satisfied, committed, empowered, collaborating and innovative. HRD is one of the principal means through which an organizational growth mindset can be nurtured and realized even though the outcomes may be hard to quantify in simple ROI terms.

Delve deeper 12.5

Read more about these issues in:

Bierema, L. L. (2009). Critiquing human resource development's dominant masculine rationality and evaluating its impact. *Human Resource Development Review*, 8(1), 68–96.

Dweck, C. S. (2017). *Mindset: Changing the way you think to fulfil your potential*. London: Robinson.

Reio, T. G., Rocco, T. S., Smith, D. H., & Chang, E. (2017). A critique of Kirkpatrick's evaluation model. *New Horizons in Adult Education and Human Resource Development*, 29(2), 35–53.

Torraco, R. J., & Lundgren, H. (2020). What HRD is doing – What HRD should be doing: The case for transforming HRD. *Human Resource Development Review*, 19(1), 39–65.

Conclusion: Whose 'bottom line'?

This chapter began with the assertion that evaluation is about the 'worth or value' of HRD for employees and their organizations. At the end of this journey we might pause to consider what are the values and purposes towards which HRD is directed ultimately? At the beginning of the twenty-first century the notions of 'worth' and 'value' are being reinterpreted and rediscovered and this adds new dimensions and complexities to questions about the meaning and purpose of learning in the workplace. HRD researcher Neal Chalofsky[64] has developed a construct of 'meaningful work' which is re-interpreted here as an expression of person, purpose and potential:

- Person: the sense of personhood and bringing one's whole self – intellect, emotion and essence – to the workplace;
- Purpose: the sense of purpose in one's life and having a positive belief system and a growth mindset for attaining meaning and purpose;
- Potential: the acknowledgement of one's potential for lifelong learning and continuous growth and the capacity to seek challenges and aspire to achieve.

These 'three Ps' align with an 'HRD learning paradigm' but they need not be antithetical to the HRD performance paradigm and related ideas such as ROI either. For HRD it needn't be a question of 'either purpose or profit', or 'either learning or performance'. Evaluation exposes and surfaces this debate. HRD should embrace the tensions and challenges of both purpose and profit and both learning and performance. They are paradoxical, but the productive challenge that any paradox presents is the reconciliation of the tensions between the paradox's focal elements.[65] The tensions in this HRD paradox are more likely to be reconciled and resolved in organizations where work is more than mere occupation, where employees can feel both challenged and nurtured, and where there are increased opportunities for employees to use their strengths, talents and capabilities to their fullest extent.

Chapter checkout

Use this list to check your understanding of the key points of this chapter.

1 **Evaluation**   Critical appraisal of HRD's value or worth is based on its contribution to both the fulfilment of individuals' potential and the realization of an organization's goals based on objective assessment of the available evidence
2 **Process**   Evaluation permeates the HRD process from learning needs identification and analysis, through delivery and implementation to its effects on outcomes
3 **Purposes**   Amongst the main purposes of HRD are a pragmatic purpose, research purpose and professional/political purpose
4 **Kirkpatrick framework**   The four levels of the Kirkpatrick framework are 'reaction' (Level 1), 'learning' (Level 2), 'behaviour' (Level 3) and 'results' (Level 4)
5 **Reactions**   Lowest level or first step in Kirkpatrick's four levels; refers to how well the trainees liked / responded to a training programme

6 **Learning** Learning outcomes can be assessed in terms of knowledge (Bloom's taxonomy; declarative or procedural), skills (intellectual, psychomotor) and attitudes (thoughts, feelings, behaviours)

7 **Behaviour** Requires transfer of learning to workplace context and application to the job

8 **Results** Effects that HRD has on tangible and intangible organizational-level outcomes such as productivity, costs, turnover, absenteeism, job satisfaction, organizational commitment, etc.

9 **ROI** Phillips added a fifth level as means to quantify the return-on-investment (ROI) or benefit-cost ratio of HRD

10 **Criticisms and alternatives** Levels-of-outcomes frameworks low explanatory/ predictive power, adherence to performance paradigm; alternatives include qualitative methods/case studies/learning paradigm/success case method (SCM)

SKILLS DEVELOPMENT 12
DESIGNING AN EVALUATION

Many of the readers of this book are likely to be students of human resource-related subjects on degree-level and professional development courses in colleges and universities. Such programmes have a practical focus and are designed as preparation for professional practice in areas such as HR, occupational and organizational psychology, consulting as well as general management roles. Your task in this skills development activity is to design an evaluation which answers the question of 'what was the worth and value of this programme of study?'. You might choose to design an evaluation using a traditional levels-type framework (such as Kirkpatrick or Phillips) or a more qualitative type approach such as that of Brinkerhoff. Whichever approach you choose your design for the evaluation should specify: (1) the questions that the evaluation seeks to answer; (2) how relevant data will be collected and analysed; (3) how the results of the analysis will be presented and used.

13

THE ONLY SUSTAINABLE SOURCE OF COMPETITIVE ADVANTAGE

Contents

On completion of this chapter you should be able to:

- Define organizational learning;
- Explain theories of organizational learning;
- Critically appraise theories of organizational learning;
- Use your knowledge and understanding of organizational learning to advise on the design and delivery of HRD.

Introduction

The renowned strategic management thinker, practitioner and author Arie de Geus (1930–2019), Former Head of Group Planning at Royal Dutch Shell, wrote in his widely acclaimed book *The Living Company* that 'The ability to learn faster than your competitors may be the only sustainable competitive advantage.'[1] This chapter explores why. It's a basic principle of HRD that learning – acquiring new knowledge and skills – is a capability that every employee needs in order to perform effectively in their job, develop personally and professionally, and contribute to the business. Similarly, organizations need to be able to learn how to do the things they do in better ways (for example, by becoming more 'efficient') and also learn how to do different, new and better things (and therefore becoming more 'effective'). Organizations that learn will become adept at:

- Identifying and remedying shortcomings in the ways they currently do things;
- Anticipating and forestalling challenges and threats from the external environment;
- Foreseeing the future and embracing opportunities by changing and innovating.

As a consequence, organizations that learn collectively and adapt continuously are more likely to survive and thrive as their business environment changes. On the other hand, organizations that fail to learn are more likely to go the way of so many companies and fail to survive, living for a few decades at most. Organizational learning has been described as a 'habit for survival'[2] that all organizations need in the volatile, uncertain, complex and ambiguous business environments of the twenty-first century.

Organizational learning is a process that involves changes in an organization's knowledge about itself and its environment. It differs from individual learning (organizational learning isn't the sum of individual learnings) and 'the learning organization' (see Chapter 14). A selection of definitions of organizational learning from some of the leading scholars in this field is given in Figure 13.1.

Individual learning theories are concerned with the learning of individuals *in* organizations whereas organizational learning is concerned with learning *by* organizations.

Herbert Simon (1969)

- '...the growing insights and successful re-structuring of organisational problems by individuals reflected in the structural elements and outcomes of the organisation itself' (p. 26)

James March and Johan Olsen (1975)

- 'Organisations and the people in them learning from their experience. They act, observe the consequences of their action, make inferences about those consequences, and draw implications for future action. The process is adaptively rational.' (p. 168)

Chris Argyris and Donald Schön (1977)

- '...when individuals, acting from their own images and mental maps, detect a match or mismatch of outcomes to expectation which confirms or disconfirms organisational theory-in-use' (p. 116)

Marlene Fiol and Marjorie Lyles (1985)

- 'Organisational learning means the process of improving actions through better knowledge and understanding.' (p. 803)

Barbara Levitt and James March (1988)

- 'Organisations are seen as learning by encoding inferences from history into routines that guide behaviour. The generic term 'routines' includes the forms, rules, procedures, conventions, strategies and technologies around which organisations are constructed and through which they operate.' (p. 320)

Peter Senge (1990)

- 'The expansion of an organisation's capacity to create its own future and the results it truly desires' (p. 14)

SD Noam Cook and Dvora Yanow (1993)

- 'The capacity of an organization to learn how to do what it does, where what it learns is possessed not only by individual members of the organization but by the aggregate itself' (p. 360)

George Huber (1996)

- 'An organisation learns when, through its processing of information, it increased the probability that its future actions will lead to improved performance' (p. 822)

Figure 13.1   Selected leading scholars' definitions of organizational learning

Organizations need both individual and organizational learning but the question arises immediately of how can an organization as an inanimate thing learn? In exploring these issues we'll look at theories of organizational learning, how organizational learning manifests in practice, and the benefits it can bring to organizations. But we also need to be wary of the claims made on behalf of the proponents of organizational learning. Being critical requires that we understand the theories behind organizational learning and also appreciate and are able to objectively assess the empirical evidence for the claims that are being made for learning as the only sustainable source of competitive advantage.

Forward-thinking organizations have come to the realization that they need to be able to harness the learning power that individuals have and channel it into the collective learning that will solve the problems and create the solutions that organizations need if they are to survive and thrive in the volatile, uncertain, complex, ambiguous and globalized world of the twenty-first century. HRD, as the function in organizations with in-depth knowledge and understanding of learning processes is best-placed to work with internal and external stakeholders to co-create the collective learning capabilities that organizations require. These are some of the reasons why organizational learning matters in HRD, and why HRD matters for organizational learning.

Reflective question 13.1

To survive and thrive in VUCA environments in a globalized world, organizations need to learn how to be both more efficient and more effective. Can you define each of the terms 'efficiency' and 'effectiveness' using only the three words 'better', 'do' and 'things'? Why do you think *both* efficiency *and* effectiveness are important rather than *either* one *or* the other? In a VUCA world do you think a 'both/and' (i.e. paradox) mindset is better than an 'either/or' mindset? Why?

Learning and corporate longevity

A remarkable fact, revealed in research commissioned by the energy company Royal Dutch Shell in the 1990s was that the average life span of a company is less than 40 years, and since then corporate longevity has shortened considerably. There are very few companies that live for more than a hundred years. Some of us can just about remember 'Blockbuster' (a high-street VHS tape video rental store), the 'Blackberry Messenger' (a messaging and mobile phone device) and 'Pan American World Airlines' (Pan Am, once the official 'flag carrier' for the USA), all of whom have now departed the corporate scene. On the other hand, the long-term corporate survivors learned to adapt and are still household names, for example Johnson & Johnson (established in 1886 as a manufacturer of antiseptic surgical dressings), HarperCollins (established 1817 founded by the merger of two even older family businesses), Du Pont (established 1802 as a gunpowder manufacturer), Stella Artois (established 1366, in fact some of the oldest businesses in the world are breweries) and Nintendo (established 1889 as a playing cards and toy company long before Super Mario was thought of).[4]

Organizational learning is the key to long-term business sustainability. But why? The Shell research mentioned above was the feature article of *Harvard Business Review* in

March–April 1997 in which Arie de Geus explained how firms that 'die' prematurely do so from 'collective learning disabilities'. By this de Geus meant that such firms failed to adapt as the world around them changed. In this 'survival-of-the-fittest' business world the long-term corporate survivors identified by the research had three stand-out features:

- Sensitivity to their business environment;
- Strong 'learning cultures';
- Tolerance of new, and often radically different, ways of doing things.

Take the Finnish-Swedish packaging company Stora Enso which de Geus offered as an example of a corporation that survived and thrived by adapting to its environment. Stora was founded in the thirteenth century as the Swedish copper mining company Stora Kopparberg (meaning 'great copper mountain'); it survived the Middle Ages, the Reformation, the wars of the 1600s, the Industrial Revolution, and two world wars. Its business shifted from copper to forestry, to iron smelting, to hydropower and eventually to paper, wood pulp and packaging. It became Stora Enso in 1998 when it merged with the Finnish forestry products company Enso Oyj. Its revenues in 2019 (i.e. pre-pandemic) were over £10bn.

Nintendo began life in Japan over 130 years ago as a handmade playing card and toy company; it has been producing video games for over 40 years and has sold over 4.7 billion video games and 750 million hardware units. The company website describes it core values, the 'Nintendo DNA', as having three components:

- Uniqueness: Nintendo seeks to constantly redefine entertainment;
- Flexibility: the entertainment market is always changing so Nintendo always aims to deliver innovative products;
- Sincerity: Nintendo aims to be humble which means learning from experiences in order to improve and evolve.[5]

These three components – uniqueness, flexibility and sincerity – are the core of an organizational learning culture at Nintendo. The longevity of corporate survivors and thrivers, like Stora and Nintendo has been attributed, metaphorically, to a 'gene' for learning and renewal that's integral to their corporate 'DNA'. The ability to respond to the environment, learn faster than the competition and therefore stay ahead of the curve gives such businesses a capacity for agility and adaptability.

Successful businesses that survive and thrive, like Stora and Nintendo, create an organizational learning system in which employees at every level in the organization seek and create and then share and apply new knowledge and skills. Organizations that learn collectively have crafted the culture and habits of questioning and challenging current ways of doing things. This enables them to identify new purposes that support and renew the organization's long term vision and create value for stakeholders.[6]

In order to make the 'learning organization' a reality we need theories of how organizations learn in order to describe and explain the phenomenon of organizational
learning and also to make recommendations and take actions. Two concepts that are
fundamental to organizational learning theory are: 'mental models', which is based
on a cognitive perspective, and 'routines', which is based on a behavioural theory of
the firm. These two perspectives offer different but related answers to the question
'how can an organization learn?'.

Mental models

A model is a simplified representation of a more complex entity that is constructed for
some purpose. Mental models are 'small-scale representations of reality'. We use them
to make sense of the world and decide how to behave and act. Mental models are
important because individual learning involves changing one's personal mental models
whilst organizational learning involves changing an organization's shared (collective)
mental models. Mental models, as an individual's representation of reality are:

- Action-based: they play a pivotal role in how we think, decide and problem solve;
- Subjective: they can be highly subjective and differ substantially between individuals.

A reason why mental models are so important in organizational learning is that continuous adaptation and growth depends on how well organizations challenge and where necessary change their shared mental models of *what* the organization does and *why* it does it. For example Stora (see above) challenged and changed its mental model of Stora as a copper mining company to Stora as a paper and packaging company. 3M (originally short for the Minnesota Mining and Manufacturing Company) has transformed itself from a company founded in 1902 that mined for corundum (a mineral used for making sandpaper and grinding wheels) to becoming one of the world's most respected and innovative science, technology and manufacturing companies. 3M describes its 100-year journey as evolving from 'mining rocks' to 'rocking innovation'[8].

The concept of mental models originated in cognitive psychology. It was first suggested by the Scottish experimental psychologist Kenneth Craik (1914–1945) in 1943 to refer to 'small scale models of reality'. The idea was developed further by the cognitive scientist Philip Johnson-Laird (b.1936) of Princeton University. A mental model is an internal representation which, if only in some abstract or metaphorical sense, correspondences to the external reality that it represents.[9] As simplified representations of how the world is and how it works, mental models enable us to reason about and explain events as well as anticipate the future (for example, by simulating in our 'minds' eye').[10] According to Arie de Geus surviving and thriving requires businesses to develop collective perceptions (shared mental models) and processes (organizational learning) to create 'memories of the future' that simulate 'mental time paths' to alternative near and distant futures.[11]

We all use mental models in our regular thinking processes as a way to simplify complex cognitive tasks (such as understanding cause-and-effect relationships) and reduce cognitive load. They can be thought of as 'tools for thinking'. For example, the relationship between 'supply and demand' is a simple model of how the economy works and it's a model that we use in many areas of our personal lives such as purchasing decisions.[12]

As tools for thinking mental models help us to take decisions and solve problems. But different people can sometimes think, decide and problem solve about the same issues on the basis of quite different mental models, as illustrated in the ancient Indian parable of the blind men and the elephant (who all had different subjective experiences of the elephant, for example the one who felt the leg thought it was a tree, whereas the one who felt the trunk thought it was a snake). In business, for example, imagine if one person or team works on the basis of the mental model that 'good today is better than great tomorrow' (their mental model is 'expediency') but a different person or team in the same organization works on the basis of 'never let good get in the way of great' (their mental model is 'perfection'); in coming together the two would likely be at odds with each other.[13] Why? Because they don't share the same mental model. But how could they develop a shared mental model? A good starting point would be to 'dialogue'.

Research insight 13.1

Dialoguing to create shared mental models for strategic innovation

This research, based on Hamel and Prahalad's concept of 'strategic innovation', argues that there are two types of innovation: (1) market driven, incremental innovation that results in new products or services, changes in market positioning, new marketing tactics, etc.; (2) market driving, fundamental strategic innovation that results in new competencies and new business models that break the rules and transform not only organizations, but entire industries. IBM, Apple, Microsoft, Amazon and IKEA are examples of organizations who've innovated in ways that are market *driving* rather than market *driven*. From a cognitive perspective, fundamental innovation that is market driving requires the mental model that managers have of their industry to undergo radical transformation in order that they see things in new ways that are 'unconstrained by history' (p. 338). Jacobs and Heracleous' research sought to find out how mental models can undergo the kind of radical shifts that change both organization and industries. They found from action research in a Swiss bank that the requisite shift in mental models can be enabled through 'reflective dialogue' entailing:

- A reflective form of conversation that allows participants to 'critically review and inquire into the underlying assumptions of individual and collective mental models';
- The emergence of a 'collective language' through which new mental models can take shape.

They concluded that fundamental strategic innovation cannot be deliberately 'designed', but it can be 'designed for' through the facilitation of reflective dialogue that enables the sharing and radical re-framing of managers' mental models of their organization and the industry in which it operates, and out of which market driving strategic innovations might emerge.

Source: Jacobs, C. D., & Heracleous, L. (2005). Answers for questions to come: Reflective dialogue as an enabler for strategic innovation. *Journal of Organizational Change Management, 18*(4), 338–352.

Incidentally, the terms 'mental model' and 'schema' tend to be used interchangeably in management (they're also related to 'dominant logics', 'causal maps', 'cognitive maps', 'frames', 'mental building blocks', 'mental templates', etc.). But they can all be thought of as 'cognitive patterns' that are mental representations of some aspect of experience or reality (such as the law of supply and demand) that are structured to facilitate their use in reasoning, problem-solving and decision making (such as buying a house). To complicate things further, there are also different types of schemas, and this difference is important, especially when it comes to social behaviour and social judgement:

- Schemas that are representations of events, for example how to conduct oneself in an employment interview, are referred to as scripts and as such they can be 'recipes' for action;
- There are also person schemas, self-schemas, and social schemas, for example a cultural stereotype is an example of a person schema.

Schemas are a basis for mental shortcuts (or heuristics) and have both advantages and disadvantages. We often use person schemas routinely to make judgement and predictions, but these can sometimes be biased and prejudiced about people and their behaviour. Schemas can expedite decision making (by giving us recipes for action) but in so doing they can also skew reasoning and judgement negatively and give rise to prejudice and discrimination.

Perspective from practice 13.2

Don't mix-up your mental models

The US financial institution Self-Help Credit Union (SHCU) provides responsible financial services, lending to small businesses and non-profits, developing real estate and promoting fair financial practices. SHCU focuses its work on those who may be underserved by conventional lenders, including people of colour, women, rural residents and low-wealth families and communities. But the industry mental model of what constitutes a financial practice did not resonate strongly with SHCU's potential clients. SHCU found that more of its potential clients used its services when it opened a branch in a strip mall that didn't conform to the mental model of a typical financial organization such as a bank. The branch was used more when it was designed to look like a check-casher with fluorescent lighting and linoleum floors rather than when it had a traditional bank-branch design, with plush carpets and leather chairs. The conventional mental model of what a bank should be like (plants, carpets and sofas) and how clients might be judged or expected to behave conflicted with the SHCU's clients' mental model of what an institution kitted-out to help them financially should look like. As this article in *Forbes* notes: 'we all have mental models and use them all of the time, but when it comes to designing customer experiences it's important to distinguish between the company mental model and the customer mental model. Doing so helps businesses deliver customer experiences that add value for stakeholders.'

Source: Swinscoe, A. (2014). Are Your Mental Models Getting in the Way of Improving Your Customer Experience? *Forbes Magazine*. Available online: www.forbes.com/sites/adrianswinscoe/2014/12/22/are-your-mental-models-getting-in-the-way-of-improving-your-customer-experience/#1e2ff930dd7c (accessed 27-01-21).

A key idea, given that this chapter is about organizational, rather than individual, learning is that mental models can be shared; they're referred to as 'shared mental models' or sometimes 'team mental models'. For example, top management teams' shared mental models in the grocery retailing industry is the jointly-understood mental representation of the competitive space they operate in (see below).[14] As we shall see, in the case of grocery retailing it appears not to have been just within-company but was shared almost as an industry-wide mental model, except for the innovative new entrants who had a very different and industry-disrupting mental model.

An axiom of organizational learning theory is that performance will improve if a group of people, such as teams or even entire organizations, have shared mental models. Organizational learning involves, amongst other things, building a shared vision, and as we'll discover in the next chapter for organizations to learn and to become a 'learning organization' there must be a clearly articulated shared vision of where the business is headed.

Assimilation and accommodation

Another way to think about mental models is as 'index cards' that are part of the brain's 'filing system'. As such they serve as templates against which new information can be compared and made sense of. Based on the work of the child and developmental Swiss psychologist Jean Piaget (1896–1980), new information encountered in the environment can relate to information in our current mental models in two contrasting ways both of which are important for learning; see Figure 13.2.

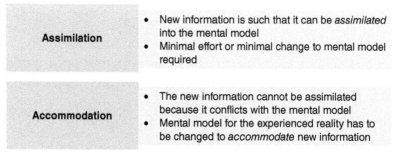

Figure 13.2 Assimilation, accommodation and mental models

In 'assimilation' actors' extant mental models undergo little or no modification, whereas when 'accommodation' takes place actors' mental models either are changed radically or a new mental model is developed. New mental models may be developed through direct experiences that do three things:

- Challenge: question, contest and challenge existing mental models;

- Critique: force the learner to critically reflect on the assumptions underlying existing mental models;
- Change: modify existing mental models incrementally or radically.[15]

Through the processes of challenging, critiquing and changing, organizations can collectively create ways of 'doing things better' and 'doing better things' (see Reflective Question 13.1).

Reflective question 13.2

By way of illustration of the concepts of accommodation and assimilation, ask yourself what's your mental model of a car? You might say it has a petrol or diesel driven engine, four wheels, doors, seats, steering wheel, etc. So clearly a motorbike doesn't qualify. What about a car with an electric engine? No, but with a small tweak to the model (an engine that's fuelled by petrol, diesel or electricity), the electric car can be assimilated into the mental representation of a car. What about a car with three wheels? Can this be assimilated? No. Therefore the model has to be changed more radically for 'three-wheelers' to be accommodated. So an electric three-wheeler also would then fit. What about if in the future inventors manage to cross a car with a drone? The mental model for this vehicle would be radically different from the accepted image of a car. We'd need a new mental model of what a car is, what it can do, and how it should or could be used. In fact the label 'car' would no longer suffice.

Perspective from practice 13.3

Mental models of grocery retailing in the UK

The grocery retailing business in the UK (supermarkets) is ruthlessly competitive. Consumers are faced with an enormous range of competitively-priced products and seductive special offers. As a result of transformations in the industry, executives in UK grocery retailing had to change their mental model of the industry's competitive space quite radically (and literally). The 'big four' UK supermarkets (Tesco, Sainsbury, Asda and Morrisons) faced significant losses of market share to the new entrant 'deep discounters' (the German companies, Aldi and Lidl). For example, in 2017 Tesco's market share of 28 per cent was 1.7 down whereas Aldi's market share of 6.8 per cent was up by 17.6 per cent (Source: Kantar World Panel).

Since the early 1990s the supermarket industry's mental model of what a store should be like was 'bigger is better', based on assumptions about economies of scale, increased consumer choice, efficiency savings, less complicated logistics, etc. More generally, the mental model that bigger is better can be traced back to Henry Ford and

(Continued)

the concept of 'minimum efficient scale' which suggests that operations smaller than a certain size cannot be cost-effective and therefore are commercially unviable.[16] The UK big four battled it out in what was dubbed a 'space race' to build ever-bigger aircraft hangar-sized mega-supermarkets on the edges of towns and cities and 'brown field' locations. The assumption was that shoppers would make a big weekly shop so as to pile-high their cupboards and freezers with bulk-bought bargains. The result was a single-minded focus on scaling-up. But quite suddenly shoppers' habits appeared to change quite radically. They started to make more frequent but smaller shopping trips, they became promiscuous and flitted between stores for specialized products and the best prices, and moved rapidly to online shopping. It dawned on the major players that size was no longer the thing that mattered most.

Tesco is the biggest player and it tried all sorts of tactics to get people to come into its stores and bolster its business, for example by adding restaurants (the 'Giraffe' brand) to its portfolio and higher-standard coffee shops ('Harris and Hoole' brand) both to fill space and draw-in customers. The big four were frantically trying to assimilate the new harsh realities about consumer behaviour into their 'big store' mental model, but to no avail: the world had moved on. In the end the big four's mindset of grocery retailing based on the mental model of minimum efficient scale, had no choice but to change: out went the building of mega-stores (some, including Tesco's £22m Chatteris store on the outskirts of Cambridge, were 'mothballed') and in came high-street convenience stores and a big push to online as new mental models of consumer behaviour and choice and competition took hold. In terms of organizational learning theory, the industry's shared mental model had to be changed to accommodate the harsh reality of the radically different competitive space they found themselves in.

Source: *The Guardian*, 'Supermarkets sense that size may no longer be key to conquering universe'. www.theguardian.com/business/2013/mar/17/supermarkets-realise-size-no-longer-key-to-universe (accessed 27-02-2020).

According to organizational learning theory, organizations have no option but to learn in order to survive and thrive, and the lessons can be very painful, but ultimately the process can be creative, transformative and opportunity-generating for organizations that are open to adaptation.

The upsides and downsides of mental models

Mental models influence individual and organizational learning processes both positively (by enabling new ways of thinking) and negatively (by constraining new ways of thinking);[17] see Figure 13.3.

Mental models as 'enablers' of learning

- *Perceptions of Patterns*
  Mental models influence what we pay attention to; people are more likely to attend to things that fit with their current mental models; serve as patterns
- *Speed of Processing*
  New learnings are likely to be assimilated more efficiently if they fit with existing mental models and more slowly if they need to be accommodated or if entirely new mental models need to be developed
- *Organizing of Information*
  Mental models are useful advance organizing devices because people learn more efficiently and effectively when they know what's coming and when new information can be related to information that's already in long-term memory

Mental models as 'constrainers' of learning

- *Distortion*
  Strongly-held mental models can result in new information being distorted in order to fit the current model (be assimilated) rather than changing the model to fit the facts (i.e. be accommodated)
- *Stereotyping*
  Stereotypes, including cultural stereotypes, can be deeply 'embrained' in mental models; stereotypes lead to biases and prejudices in reasoning, problem solving and decision making
- *Stickiness*
  Mental models can be very 'sticky'; changing them takes skilful intervention and careful management; mental model change isn't likely to happen overnight

Figure 13.3   How mental models can enable and constrain learning

On the down-side, mental models can be sources of bias because they direct attention selectively towards particular information in the environment, such as that which is readily and easily available. This can lead to selected information being used in decision making whilst other potentially relevant information gets overlooked or ignored (this is sometimes referred to as the 'availability bias' and is a type of heuristic). In this sense, mental models are a 'double-edged sword': the fact that they are pattern-based means they can improve the efficiency of individual, team and organizational thinking, deciding and problem-solving (through pattern matching processes), but they can also screen-out information if it doesn't happen to fit with an individual's, team's or organization's preferred or established ways of seeing, or ideas about, the world.

When groups fail to correct errors the shortcomings in their mental models can become magnified as a result of sticking to old, outmoded ways of doing things. A failure to challenge shared mental models and to learn collectively can be linked to the negative phenomenon of 'groupthink'. When this happens a shared mental model can become highly dysfunctional. The concept of groupthink was first discovered by psychologist Irving Janis in the early 1970s and it applies to decision-making and problem-solving processes in groups (hence groupthink is more than simple conformity). Groupthink happens when a group of people make irrational decisions on the basis of an urge to conform or as a result of an intolerance of dissent.[18] Groupthink has been blamed by some for the NASA space shuttle Challenger disaster in 1986 when groupthink amongst NASA managers over-rode the expert opinions of the Morton-Thiokol engineers responsible for the solid rocket combustion system that was the source of the failure. Cass Sunstein and Reid Hastie in their book *Wiser: Getting beyond Groupthink to Make Groups Smarter* (2015) suggest that some of the problems of groupthink can be fixed by:

- Voicing: Overcoming 'self-silencing' behaviours by using methods that solicit individual input without undue influence from others in the group;
- Questioning: Stimulating critical thinking by asking questions that challenge existing mental models;
- Listening: Focusing on expertise, and listening to those with experience and who are 'in the know';
- Reframing: Use 'perspective shifting' or reframing techniques, for example asking what would cause a proposed solution to fail, doing 'pre-mortems' on how a solution might go wrong (rather than post-mortems of actual failures) and by nominating individuals to be devil's advocates to challenge proposed solutions.[19]

Delve deeper 13.1

It's been claimed that 'mental model' is an 'ambiguous concept'. Laura Rook's article synthesizes, analyses and evaluates definitions of the concept:

Rook, L. (2013). Mental models: A robust definition. *The Learning Organization, 20*(1), 38–47.

Extend your knowledge of team (shared) mental models by reading Susan Mohammed and colleagues' 15-year review of the research:

Mohammed, S., Ferzandi, L., & Hamilton, K. (2010). Metaphor no more: A 15-year review of the team mental model construct. *Journal of Management, 36*(4), 876–910.

Routines

Routines, or organizational routines, are a basic component of organizations and their behaviour. In the same way that mental models are a building block of the cognitive theory of organizational learning, so routines are a building block of a behavioural theory of organizational learning. One of the best-known definitions of a routine is 'a regular and predictable behaviour pattern of a firm'.[20] Routines can be thought of as part of the organizational 'infrastructure'. They function as repositories, or stores, of organizational knowledge and capability. Organizations store knowledge *in* routines and apply knowledge *through* routines. The knowledge contained in routines may be hard to articulate because the people involved may not always be able to say how they do what they do because they may be based on tacit knowledge acquired through implicit learning processes.

Organizational learning takes place when an organization develops new knowledge and skills that enable it to change its existing routines. Hence, organizations change why, what and how they do things by changing their routines. Examples of organizational routines include the activities on a manufacturing assembly line, the processing of a customer complaint, and the landing of an aircraft. These examples have in common the fact that they are, in the words of organizational learning researcher Brian Pentland, 'recognizable', 'repetitive', 'interdependent patterns of action' that involve 'multiple actors'.[21]

The fact that routines are repetitive imply stability, but through the processes of learning, change and innovation, organizational routines are periodically subject to change both incrementally and radically. On the other hand routines that are highly embedded (as 'core rigidities'[22]) may create barriers to learning, change and innovation, hence it may be necessary to 'unlearn' entrenched routines before new routines can take their place. Discarding old patterns of working makes room for new ones after the processes of 'destabilization' and 'discarding'.[23] Also, Chris Argyris, whose work we'll meet in a later section, discovered that organizations sometimes develop 'defensive routines' that by-pass mistakes, ignore the by-passing of mistakes, make the by-passing of mistakes undiscussable, and make the undiscussability of the by-passing of mistakes undiscussable. Defensive routines protect old structures and embedded ways of doing things.[24]

Reflective question 13.3

What would you say to an organizational learning sceptic who is of the view that the very idea of 'organizational learning' is an oxymoron.[25] They take this view because they think that learning can only take place at the individual level, and if there is such a thing as 'organizational leaning' then 'it's the sum of all the learnings that are inside employees' heads, nothing more or less than that, and to talk of an organization having any kind of "brain", "cognitive system", or "organizational memory" is clearly nonsensical!'.

A behavioural theory of organizational learning

Organizations accomplish much of what they do – such as manufacturing goods and providing services – by means of their routines. A fundamental assumption in organizational learning is that learning to 'do things better' and learning to 'do better things' by changing routines or discarding them in favour of new ones will improve performance, making it more efficient and effective respectively.[26] Even though, as was noted above, the concept of organizational learning came to prominence in the 1990s, the earliest mentions of it in management and organization research were in the 1960s in Richard Cyert (1921–1998) and James G. March's (1928–2018) 'behavioural theory of the firm'. Cyert and March are considered by many to have produced one of 'the foundational works' in organizational learning theory.[27]

Another leading organizational learning scholar, George Huber of the University of Texas, also defined organizational learning in behavioural terms: 'an entity learns if, through processing of information, the range of its potential behaviours is changed' (p. 89) and he itemized some of the processes by which this change occurs:

- Drawing on knowledge that's already available to the organization;
- Learning from the experiences that the organization goes through;
- Learning by observing other entities or organizations;
- Grafting onto itself components that possess requisite knowledge;
- Noticing or searching for relevant information in the organization or its environment.[28]

In Cyert and March's model of decision-making, firms learn from experience and adapt to their environments through organizational learning processes. In addition to routines, this theory also emphasized the process of 'problemistic search', by which Cyert and March mean searching that's induced by problems and the need to find a fix or solution.[29] In the 1990s March developed his ideas further by proposing an 'exploration/exploitation' model of organization learning in which he argued that organizations have to find the right balance between:

- Exploitation: activities such as adaptation, efficiency, refinement, routinization, implementation and execution;
- Exploration: activities such as risk taking, experimentation, 'play', flexibility, discovery and innovation.

Exploitation activities can improve short-term outcomes, but the danger is that these may come at the expense of longer-term survival. This is because adaptation to the current environment (using only 'exploiting' behaviours) becomes a liability if the environment is changing, and when change takes place, as it inevitably does, 'exploring' behaviours are required. However, there are risks associated with exploration since the payoffs of experimenting and innovating are less certain and further into the future, hence there are risks. Focusing solely on exploration at the expense of exploitation can lock organizations into a vicious cycle in which failed experimentation leads to further search and change which may lead to further failure, leading to more search and change, and so on.[30] The nature of exploration and exploitation means that they can pull in different directions and create tensions because:

- What's good in the short-term is not always good in the long-term especially in turbulent business environments (this is why learning has been described as a 'habit for survival');

- What's good for one part of the organization or group of stakeholders is not always good for another part or a different group of stakeholders (different parts of the organization may move at different speeds);
- What's good for the organization is not always good for the larger social or ecological system of which it is a part (for example, exploitation of fossil fuels at the expense of exploration of alternative sources of power).[31]

March's theory illustrates that organizational learning can be a paradox.[32] But perhaps it's not a case of 'either exploration or exploitation' but 'both exploration and exploitation'. In other words, in order to be both 'steady and stable' and 'agile and adaptable' organizations need to learn how to reconcile tensions and balance exploration and exploitation. For example, Royal Dutch Shell in its 2021 energy transition strategy will continue to extract fossil fuels whilst investing in alternative energies; the company will seek to reduce emissions from its fossil fuel operations (i.e. the production of oil and gas) by increasing energy efficiency and capturing or offsetting any remaining emissions. These tensions between the different types of firm's behaviours parallels similar tensions that we find in cognitive theories of organizational learning which proposes different 'types' of organizational learning which may appear to be related yet contradictory (see below, 'single- and double-loop learning').

Perspective from practice 13.4

Learning to transition to a low carbon future

March's observations are prescient for current debates in business and society more generally in areas such as multiple stakeholder perspectives (what's good for shareholders is not always good for other stakeholders, including the environment) and environmental sustainability (what's good for a traditional oil and gas company is by no means good for the environment). Choices between explorations for how transition from an 'oil and gas company' to an 'energy company' versus exploitations of current ways of working to return short-term value to shareholders are fundamental tensions that organizations such as BP and Royal Dutch Shell are having to manage given anxieties about the effects of greenhouse gas (GHG) emissions on the stability of the Earth's climate. Both companies have arrived at the strategic position that they need to be part of an 'energy transition' towards a low carbon future given that, in the words of BP's chairman Helge Lund, the world's energy consumption is 'on an unsustainable path'.[33] How they do that is one of the trickiest balancing acts that any organization or industry has ever been faced with. The problem was anticipated in the 1990s by Arie de Geus, the former Head of Group Planning at Shell and author of *The Living Company*, when he commented in a BBC television programme

(Continued)

that a fundamental question for companies such as Shell is 'is there life after oil?', to which the answer is 'only if you do something other than oil'. One way in which Royal Dutch Shell learned as an organization about possible alternative futures was through the method of scenario planning. Scenario planning is a tried-and-tested and highly effective tool for organizational learning innovated by Shell in the 1980s. In a recent incarnation Shell's 'New Lens Scenario' is a scenario-based approach to learning about possible alternative futures through an in-depth analysis of how complex economic, social and political forces might play out over the twenty-first century. Scenario planning is an organizational learning tool which enables organizations to surface, share and challenge their mental models, 'story' the future, and create mental time paths to alternative near and distant futures (thereby creating 'memories of the future'). Learning organization scholar Michael Marquardt describes this approach as 'anticipatory learning', that is learning from anticipating various futures which is a more 'generative' and 'creative' type of learning than is simple 'adaptive' learning which is 'more a coping form of learning'.

Sources: Bentham, J. (2014). The scenario approach to possible futures for oil and natural gas. *Energy Policy, 64*, 87–92; De Geus, A. (1997). *The living company: Habits for survival in a turbulent business environment*. Boston, MA: Harvard Business School Press; Marquardt, M. (2011). *Building the Learning Organization* (3rd edition). Boston, MA: Hachette Book Group.

Levels of learning

The concepts of exploitation and exploration suggest that there can be different types of organizational learning. One way to think about these types is as 'lower' and 'higher' levels of organizational learning. Whether a particular 'level' of learning is appropriate or effective depends on the context that the organization is operating in. There is also an assumption that higher levels of learning are 'better' than lower levels in that they lead to more favourable outcomes under dynamic and uncertain market conditions.

'Lower-level' learning works well under conditions of stability and certainty, in contexts that are well understood, and within a given system of assumptions and rules. These lower levels of learning are likely to result in efficiency gains in the short term and should not be construed as unconditionally bad. In such situations learning by assimilation into the prevailing mental model is likely to be appropriate. But in volatile and uncertain environments, in contexts that are poorly understood, and in the face of change they're likely to be ineffective at least and dysfunctional at worst. In cognitive organizational learning theory (see below) 'single-loop' learning is a type of lower-level learning.

By contrast, in conditions of instability and uncertainty and in less well understood contexts, the problems that a firm encounters (in terms of organizational learning theory these are the errors it detects and must correct) and the solutions it must find entail questioning and adjusting assumptions and underlying rules. Organizations have to enquire into 'what lies beneath?'. This requires 'higher-level learning'. In such situations learning by accommodating new information into a significantly adjusted, or even new, mental model will be required. This may entail the 'unlearning' of extant routines and unravelling prior beliefs, assumptions and values. In organizational learning theory 'double-loop learning' is a type of higher-level learning. Marlene Fiol and Marjorie Lyles, in their seminal paper from the 1980s distinguished between:

- Lower-level learning: occurs through repetition and where contexts are well-understood, it is routine and involves incremental change, has behavioural outcomes, institutionalizes formal rules and adjustments to processes and systems;
- Higher-level learning: occurs through insights (which are often arrived at 'intuitively'), is non-routine and non-incremental, it develops new structures and rules to deal with ambiguity and lack of control, occurs mostly at the upper levels of the organization, creates new mission and direction.[34]

Lower-level learnings involve minor changes in direction, whereas higher-level learnings are associated with significant shifts in direction. An implication of this is that organizations must monitor their internal and external environments constantly if they're to notice when things aren't going as planned, that is when there are 'errors'. The idea of errors (and their correction) links to a definition of organizational learning as: the process by which members of an organization detect errors and anomalies and correct them by restructuring the organizational 'theory in use'. This definition of learning is from the work of Chris Argyris and Donald Schön. Their work is highly significant because it's one of the foundations of organizational learning theory from the cognitivist perspective, and it is to their work that we now turn our attention.

Reflective question 13.4

In the 'parable of the boiled frog', as told by organizational learning researcher Peter M. Senge, if you place a frog in a pan of boiling water it'll immediately jump out. However, if you place a frog in a pan of room temperature water it'll say put. If you turn on the gas and very gradually turn-up the heat the frog will happily sit there until it boils to death. Why do you think the frog got boiled in this fictitious parable? What has it got to do with organizational learning?[35]

In their own words 13.1

James G. March on organizational learning

Read more about Professor James G. March's (1928–2018) seminal ideas in his 'classic' article from *Organization Science* in which he considers the relationship between the 'exploration of new possibilities' and the 'exploitation of old certainties'. March argues that adaptive processes that refine exploitation more than exploration are 'likely to become effective in the short run but self-destructive in the long run' (p. 71). With Dan Levinthal, March also argued that when exploration drives out exploitation 'organizations are turned into frenzies of experimentation, change, and innovation' which can also lead to failure. March was the originator of foundational ideas such as 'standard operating procedures', 'exploration' and 'exploitation', and 'organizational learning'. In the words of Professor Nils Brunsson of the University of Upsala, March's 'significance for the field of organization studies cannot be overestimated'. The Stanford University website contains an article and interview with Jim March: www.gsb.stanford.edu/newsroom/school-news/james-g-march-professor-business-education-humanities-dies-90

Sources: Brunsson, N. (2019). In memoriam: James G. March. *Organization Studies, 40*(2), 291–295; Levinthal, D. A., & March, J. G. (1993). The myopia of learning. *Strategic Management Journal, 14*(S2), 95–112; Gioia, D., et al. (2020). A Special 'Provocations and Provocateurs' Section Honouring Jim March. *Journal of Management Inquiry, 29*(2), 119–127; March, J. G. (1991). Exploration and exploitation in organizational learning. *Organization Science, 2*(1), 71–87.

Delve deeper 13.2

There are a number of 'classic' (that is 'old' but still highly relevant) articles on organizational learning that students of HRD might like to read:

Cangelosi, V. E., & Dill, W. R. (1965). Organizational learning: Observations toward a theory. *Administrative Science Quarterly, 10*(2), 175–203.

De Geus, A. P. (1988). Planning as learning. *Harvard Business Review, 66*(2), 70–74.

Easterby-Smith, M. (1997). Disciplines of organizational learning: Contributions and critiques. *Human Relations, 50*(9), 1085–1113.

Fiol, C. M., & Lyles, M. A. (1985). Organizational learning. *Academy of Management Review, 10*(4), 803–813.

Huber, G. P. (1991). Organizational learning: The contributing processes and the literatures. *Organization Science, 2*(1), 88–115.

For a concise and up to date summary of the current state of the field consult this review article:

Basten, D., & Haamann, T. (2018). Approaches for organizational learning: A literature review. *SAGE Open, 8*(3), 2158244018794224.

A cognitive theory of organizational learning

In this section we'll begin by exploring a cognitive theory of organization learning first proposed by two highly influential scholars in this field: Chris Argyris (1923–2013) and Donald Schön (1930–1997). Argyris and Schön described the organizational learning process as follows:

- Learning in an organization occurs when individuals in an organization experience a problem and inquire into it on behalf of their organization;
- Problems (also referred to as 'errors') are when there's a mismatch between the expected results of an action and the actual results of that action;
- Individuals respond by reasoning about the causes and processes that have brought about the mismatch between experienced results and expected results.

The learning that occurs as a result of this process of inquiry and problem-solving results in members of the organization modifying their mental models, changing their 'theory-in-use', and modifying their behaviour to bring action and results back into line. By theory-in-use Argyris and Schon mean the 'theories' (that is, assumptions, beliefs about cause-and-effect relationships, etc. rather than a formal scientific theory) that are implicit in managers' ways of behaving (in the examples of 'expediency' and 'perfection' in the 'mental models' section above). In order for the learning that results from this process of inquiry and problem-solving to become 'organizational' it must be:

- Embedded: new knowledge must be 'embedded' in the shared mental models of the members of the organization;
- Encoded: new knowledge must be 'encoded' into the routines, processes, procedures that make up the organizational memory.[36]

One of the key ideas in Argyris and Schön's theory is the distinction between 'single-loop learning' and 'double-loop learning'. This is based on the concept of 'error detection and correction'. It's important to note that 'error' here has a quite specific meaning; it does not mean 'mistake', instead it refers to any mismatch between our intentions and what actually happens. For example, if a fast food outlet doesn't meet its sales target that's an error, if a department doesn't balance the books at the end of the financial year that's an error, and if a company fails to implement its strategy that's also an error. Learning occurs when knowledge is arrived at which results in a mismatch being turned into a match and this new knowledge is 'institutionalized' (described by Mary Crossan and colleagues as 'embedding learning that has occurred by individuals and groups' into the organization's systems and processes, including routines and procedures).[37] Turning a mismatch into a match can happen in two ways.

The first way is by the process of 'single-loop learning'. To explain this Argyris used the analogy of a central heating system that is controlled by a thermostat set to, let's say for the sake of argument, 17°C:

- The intention (goal) is to keep the house's temperature at 17°C;
- The function of a thermostat is to detect mismatch between the actual temperature in the house (which could be higher or lower than 17°C) and the desired temperature of 17°C;
- If the actual temperature in the house deviates from 17°C this is an error (a mismatch);
- The system is designed to take corrective action to resolve the mismatch;
- The heating is turned on or off automatically to raise or lower the temperature in the house to 17°C.

The intention (goal) is to maintain the house at a temperature of 17°C based on the assumption that keeping a house at a certain temperature (i.e. 17°C) is a desirable state of affairs; this desirable state of affairs is based on a set of assumptions (for example, about the occupants) and those assumptions are satisfied through the action of turning the source of heat (the radiators) on or off.

In a business context single-loop learning occurs when an organization deals with mismatches or discontinuities (errors) between intentions (goals) and outcomes (results) without changing the underlying assumptions, values and beliefs that guide its actions. For example, a shortfall (error) in sales (results) in a retail outlet might be corrected by making price reductions (correction). If the correction has the desired effect of restoring sales to required levels single-loop learning has occurred. The organization now knows how to correct this error and could do so again if required (for example, having weekly 'special offers' might be part of the organization's systems and procedures). But what if making a change such as a price reduction has no effect, i.e. the mismatch (shortfall in sales) persists? We'll come back to this in our discussion of double-loop learning.

Single-loop learning enables modifications to existing products and services, incremental changes to routines and procedures, and small-scale experiments with rapid feedback. It's appropriate for routine, programmable, repetitive tasks and problems under conditions of stability, predictability and certainty, in Argyris' words 'it helps get the everyday job done'; see Figure 13.4. Single-loop learning can be thought of as being about 'doing things better' (that is, improving organizational efficiency).

Double-loop learning occurs when an organization responds to mismatches between its intentions or goals and the observed outcomes or results by inquiring into, reflecting on, and modifying in appropriate ways, the underlying assumptions that guide its behaviour. To return to the analogy of the heating system: in the single-loop learning system the focus was on the action of maintaining the room's temperature at 17°C.

Under double-loop learning conditions the question might arise of whether a particular set temperature is the appropriate way to deal with the discontinuity which then may lead to alternatives being explored such as suggesting to the occupants that they wear thicker clothes, re-design the house, or even suggesting not living in a house but some other form of dwelling that would ensure their comfort. Double-loop learning involves searching for and developing alternative ways of doing things and integrating and institutionalizing them into the organization.

In the case of a retail outlet with sales figures that fail to meet set targets, if any small-scale corrections that it introduces (for example, price reductions, two-for-price of one offers, etc.) don't correct the mismatch between intentions and outcomes then it might be worthwhile seriously considering the underlying assumptions (sometimes called the 'governing variables') that are guiding its behaviour. Looking into what lies beneath could invoke radical change in strategic direction, perhaps because consumers, markets and entire industries may be undergoing significant change. In the same way that single-loop learning can be thought of as learning how to do things better (improving organizational efficiency), double-loop learning could be thought of as learning to do better things (improving organizational effectiveness).

In the process of double-loop learning, organizations' fundamental beliefs, values and assumptions (the things that make up its mental model of how the world works) are reviewed, revised, and reframed. This is not always as easy as it sounds (in fact it can be a very difficult thing to do) since the assumptions that guide behaviour may be obscured, forgotten, unknown and may even exist as tacit and implicit knowledge and hence be difficult to discuss or even be undiscussable (see Figure 13.4). Stakeholders may also have vested interests in old ways of doing things.

One inference that can be drawn from this is that double-loop learning is always and unequivocally 'better' than single-loop learning. However, as we found with exploration and exploitation, this isn't necessarily the case and whether single- or double-loop is appropriate depends on the organization's context and operating environment.

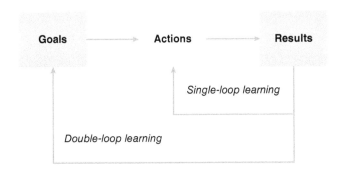

Figure 13.4 Single- and double-loop learning

For example, there are risks associated with double-loop learning. In the case of the Chernobyl nuclear disaster the engineers departed radically from existing routines and standard operating procedures (SOPs) in 'experimenting' with a new online refuelling system in what could be interpreted as an exercise in double-loop learning that failed to pay-off.[38] As with March's idea of exploitation versus exploration, one of the delicate balancing acts that managers have to perform is handling the trade-off between being 'steady and stable' or 'agile and adaptable'. It's also worth noting that scholars have suggested a third level of learning, 'triple-loop learning'; its exact meaning is contentious but for our purposes we can take it to be 'learning-about-learning', 'learning how to learn', or 'meta-learning' at the organizational level.[39]

In their own words 13.2

An interview with Chris Argyris

Chris Argyris (1923–2013) was the James Bryant Conant Professor Emeritus of Education and Organizational Behaviour at Harvard University. In an interview with Kurtzman, Argyris argues that companies fail because they have created cultures that inhibit their ability to learn. Argyris' observations are especially relevant to HRD because, as he argued in the late 1990s, management is increasingly the art of managing knowledge, which means that it's the people in the organization and the knowledge that they create and carry around in their heads that have to be led and managed effectively. HRD has a vital role in creating the conditions and managing the learning processes that enable people to create and share knowledge that adds value for stakeholders.

Source: Kurtzman, J. (1998) An interview with Chris Argyris. *Business + Strategy*. www.strategy-business.com/article/9887?gko=36773 (accessed 27-02- 2020).

Research insight 13.2

Organizational learning employee flexibility and job performance

Research shows that the link between learning and performance isn't always a simple one; other variables may have a vital role to play, such as employee flexibility. In a study of the relationships between organizational learning capability (OLC), employee flexibility and performance in the turbulent context of higher education, it was found that organizational learning does have a positive influence on employees' (that is academics') performance, but that this is mediated through employee flexibility (the employees' adaptability to turbulent context). OLC is a composite construct consisting of 'experimentation', 'risk-taking', 'interaction', 'dialogue' and 'participative decision-making'; it was measured using a 14-item self-report scale. Flexibility was measured using a 15-item scale, and performance was assessed in terms of in-role behaviours (including employees' performance of duties, responsibilities, and tasks) and assessed by managers as informant for the dependent variable (performance). The results showed that there is a relationship between organizational learning and performance, but it is mediated through employee flexibility. The observation that employee flexibility mediates the relationship between organizational learning and performance suggests that employee flexibility is a mechanism through which organizational learning produces changes in performance, as shown by the standardized path coefficients (β) in Figure 13.5.

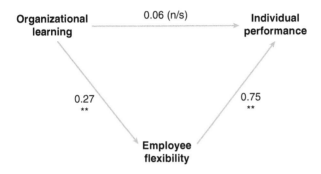

Notes: n/s, not significant; **p < 0.01

Figure 13.5   Employee flexibility mediated the relationship between learning and performance

The authors concluded that their research confirms empirically the idea that one of the consequences of learning, in terms of employees' performance at work, is an improvement in their flexibility. The idea of flexibility resonates with the concepts of routines and single- and double-loop learning in organizational learning theories. Flexibility can be thought of as an aspect of organizational culture, and as we shall see in the next chapter, organizational culture is an important factor in the creation of a learning organization.

Source: Camps, J., Oltra, V., Aldás-Manzano, J., Buenaventura-Vera, G., & Torres-Carballo, F. (2016). Individual performance in turbulent environments: The role of organizational learning capability and employee flexibility. *Human Resource Management*, 55(3), 363–383.

Delve deeper 13.3

Read more about organizational learning in:

Argote, L. (2011). Organizational learning research: Past, present and future. *Management Learning*, 42(4), 439–446.

(Continued)

Basten, D., & Haamann, T. (2018). Approaches for organizational learning: A literature review. *SAGE Open*, 8(3), 2158244018794224.

Popova-Nowak, I. V., & Cseh, M. (2015). The meaning of organizational learning: A meta-paradigm perspective. *Human Resource Development Review*, 14(3), 299–331.

Dierkes, M., Antal, A. B., Child, J., & Nonaka, I. (eds) (2003). *Handbook of organizational learning and knowledge*. Oxford: Oxford University Press.

Read a thoughtful appreciation of Arie de Geus' enormous contribution to the field of organizational learning in:

Robinson, G. (2020). An appreciation of Arie de Geus' contribution to the learning organization. *The Learning Organization*, 27(5), 429–440.

Conclusion: A 'coming of age'?

Amongst the criticisms of the organizational learning theories presented here is that March's theory over-emphasizes the behavioural aspects of learning (for example, in the importance accorded to routines) whereas Argyris and Schon's theory over-emphasizes the cognitive aspects of learning (for example, in the importance that's given to mental models). An implication of these criticisms is that organizational learning theories could be used to make some unwarranted assumptions or incorrect inferences, such as:

- Organizational learning is simply about adaptation to environmental turbulence by changing an organization's routines;
- Organizational learning is the sum of individual cognitive learnings;
- Individual learning can be used as an analogue or a metaphor for organizational learning;
- Organizational learning processes mirror the cognitive learning processes of individuals.

A purely behavioural or cognitive view does not give sufficient emphasis to the significance of social processes or the role that organizational culture plays in learning processes in organizations. Earlier chapters explored the importance of theories of social learning and learning as a phenomenon that is 'situated' in groups known as 'communities of practice'. Studying organizational learning through the lenses of social and situated processes also sheds light on the role that organizational culture plays and how it influences learning and the links between individual, group and organizational learning.

It's undeniable that surviving and thriving in environments that are volatile, uncertain, complex and ambiguous depends on individual and organizational learning. In this chapter we've seen how the concepts of routines, mental models, exploration/exploitation and single- and double-loop learning help us to understand the processes by which organizations' mental models, systems and processes can resist or respond to the demands for change. However the pragmatic question for HR and other management practitioners is how can learning processes and systems in organizations be enabled and managed to give the organization an 'increased capacity for effective action'? A practical way for businesses to create the conditions for organizational learning to occur is by becoming a learning organization. Perhaps the grand challenges that HRD currently faces in response to volatility, uncertainty, complexity and ambiguity mean that the idea of 'the learning organization' has truly 'come of age'? If as Arie de Geus claimed 'learning is the only sustainable source of competitive advantage', then learning and development in organizations is at the focal point of organizational resilience and sustainability. The next chapter considers the question of whether in the volatile, uncertain, complex and ambiguous, information-laden age of the twenty-first century the idea of organizational learning has truly come of age. If it has then the question arises of how an organization can become an entity that learns continuously and thereby increases its capacity for effective action.

Chapter checkout

Use this list to check your understanding of the key points of this chapter.

1. **Corporate Longevity**   Long-term corporate survivors have sensitivity to their environments, strong learning cultures, and tolerance of new and often radically different ways of doing things
2. **Mental Models**   A mental model is an internal representation which has correspondences to an external reality; play significant role in reasoning, judgement and decision making; can be highly subjective/differ substantially between individuals
3. **Routines**   Behavioural theories of organizational learning; rules, procedures, conventions and technologies around which organizations are configured; beliefs, frameworks, paradigms, codes, cultures and knowledge that are 'substrates' of routines
4. **Organizational Learning**   Not sum of all individual learnings in an organization; different types/levels; lower and higher levels; utility of different types depends on context (e.g. efficiency vs. effectiveness)
5. **Single-Loop Learning**   Organization deals with mismatches (errors) between intentions (goals) and outcomes (results) without changing the underlying assumptions, values and beliefs that guide its actions
6. **Double-Loop Learning**   Organization responds to mismatches between intentions/goals and observed outcomes/results by acknowledging/inquiring into/ reflecting on, and modifying in appropriate ways, the underlying assumptions which guide its behaviour
7. **Source of competitive advantage, etc.**   In VUCA environments learning is sustainable source of competitive advantage, organizational resilience and agility, and long-term sustainability

SKILLS DEVELOPMENT 13
SINGLE- AND DOUBLE-LOOP LEARNING IN ACTION

'Burger Shack' is a fast food chain. It has hundreds of restaurants across high streets, shopping malls, airports, etc. It employs 25,000 staff and annual revenue is of the order of several hundreds of millions of pounds. Burger Shack's core product range is beef burgers, also chicken- and fish-based products, as well as various vegetarian options. Core to Burger Shack's mission and strategy are exceptional standards of freshness and quality. Food is freshly prepared in store and has a maximum shelf life of four hours. It carries out extensive market research on product range, pricing and packaging of its products and researches reaction amongst its current customers to product range, prices and packaging. It's prepared to alter its product range, pricing and packaging in response to the results. It has franchisees also who are dedicated to keeping up these core standards and feedback confirms that restaurant staff are committed to and delivering on these core values.

However, Burger Shack has experienced a steady decline in its share price and sales and profits. Its share price reached a high of £30 three years ago, but now stands at £15. Burger sales are falling: there has been a same-store sales steady decline month-on-month for the past twelve months. The CEO and board are under pressure from major institutional shareholders to deliver acceptable shareholder value or face serious consequences.

In response to these challenges Burger Shack's senior sales and marketing team at the company headquarters Burger House had a series of high level meetings in order to come up with some solutions to try to reverse these worrying trends. Creativity was the theme of these meetings which were facilitated by a well-known creativity consultant. One solution they brainstormed, which was novel at the time, was to try to introduce local variations to suit the ethnic diversity in many major cities giving the business an offering more suited to disparate cultural and religious beliefs. This increased the through traffic of customers from various ethnic groups in large cities, but it was not enough to have any major impact on the overall downward trend in sales and profits.

They then called in a marketing consultancy group to help them sort the problems out. Their analysis was that in the economic recession people didn't have much spare cash to spend on fast food therefore prices needed to be lowered. Also a new low-cost competitor, Trendy's Burger Bar, opened up in a number of high streets with the backing of a group of major venture capitalists. This presented a major threat.

To compete with this challenge and appeal to as wide a demographic range as possible and hence better compete with Trendy's Burger Bar, Burger Shack added a multi-tiered value menu with items priced at £1. Unfortunately this had very little effect on key business metrics. Moreover, Trendy's went out of business and the venture capitalists who were less experienced compared to Burger Shack lost money on the venture.

The board got to hear about 'organizational learning' via an executive MBA course one of its managers had recently completed. Apparently the basis for learning was 'dialogue'. In response Burger Shack started to involve staff in a 'dialogical process'. In this project a series of staff 'huddles' were held at hundreds of their restaurants across the country. These were essentially brainstorming sessions in which staff were rewarded for coming up with as many fast food ideas as possible. These ideas were then taken away to Burger House to be sorted, prioritized and the best ones implemented.

Various novel changes were suggested and adopted, including: free range eggs in the breakfast menu; healthier sweet potato fries; low fat products; declaring the calorific value of all of the products; changing packaging to appeal to a different demographic; changing the packing so that its recycling credentials were to the fore; making burgers bigger; giving away mobile phone credits as a free gift; a loyalty card, etc.

These innovative ideas had little or no effect in spite of the fact that the high street is changing, eating establishments and coffee bars are springing-up everywhere to meet surges in demand, and eating out is now a major high street pastime for the population. The proportion of income spent on high street eating is actually rising per capita, but in the face of this Burger Shack is undergoing a significant and unsustainable decline. In terms of organizational learning theory what error is Burger Shack attempting to correct, how successful have they been in correcting error and, if you were called in as a consultant to help them fix the error, what would you suggest they ought to do? Explain your reasoning in terms of relevant organizational learning theories.

14

KNOWLEDGE AND THE NEW LEARNING ORGANIZATION

Contents

> **Chapter check-in**
>
> On completion of this chapter you should be able to:
>
> * Distinguish between different types of organizational knowledge;
> * Describe, explain and critically appraise a model of knowledge creation;
> * Describe and explain the characteristics of a learning organization;
> * Critically evaluate the idea of 'learning organizations' and the potential for a 'new learning organization';
> * Use your knowledge of organizational knowledge and the learning organization to advise on the design and delivery of HRD.

Introduction

The Elizabethan philosopher and statesman Sir Francis Bacon (1561–1626) is reputed to have remarked that 'knowledge is power'. If this is true, and if knowledge is created through learning, then learning is one of the most significant sources of power. The fact that we live in a knowledge economy – which according to the Organisation for Economic Co-operation and Development (OECD) is the 'most advanced practice of production' – places learning at the forefront of human progress, fulfilment and well-being. Shortly after coming to office in 2009 President Barack Obama said in his Address to the Joint Session of Congress that in a globalized economy ' ... the most valuable skill you can sell is your knowledge'. Learning is not only a pathway to opportunity, it is a prerequisite for success in the knowledge economy.[1]

'Knowledge intensive' firms make up a significant proportion of businesses in many advanced economies (for example, it's estimated that 39% of UK businesses are knowledge-intensive).[2] In the 'knowledge-based view' of the firm, knowledge is the most important factor of production for sustained competitive advantage.[3] The capability to create and utilize knowledge[4] provides organizations with 'bundles' of assets that are valuable, rare, inimitable and non-substitutable. Knowledge-based industries are built around insight, invention and innovation and their value lies not in physical capital but in the intangibles of brands, software, designs patents and, above all, the ideas and intellectual capital that are the individual and collective products of an educated, skilled and creative work-force.[5] In the information age the mantra that 'people are our most important asset' has come of age and the most successful companies are likely to be those that:

* Create new knowledge through the processes of learning in anticipation of an uncertain and unknown future.
* Interpret, integrate and institutionalize the newly-created knowledge widely throughout the organization.
* Use the knowledge to develop new products and services, move into new technologies and markets, etc.[6,7]

An important part of HRD's role in the knowledge economy is in enabling organizations' most important asset – its people – to create and utilize new knowledge that adds value for stakeholders. The HR profession recognizes the importance of learning and knowledge, for example the SHRM literature offers practical recommendations for how HR can contribute to organizational knowledge management:[8]

- Organizational incentive schemes must be re-aligned to recognize and reward knowledge creation and sharing;
- Creating an internal knowledge market in which individuals can exchange knowledge;
- Knowledge maps of where knowledge resides so that expertise in the organization can be located effectively and efficiently;
- Refreshing and replenishing stocks of knowledge through HRD and new hires;
- Protecting knowledge with strategic importance from planned and unplanned deletion and destruction, for example in downsizing, M&A, knowledge theft, and using measures such as background checks and NDAs as preventative measures.

According to the UK's Chartered Institute of Personnel and Development (CIPD), learning and development (L&D) has a key role to play as facilitator of the creation and management of organizational knowledge.[9] However, the CIPD's own research, whilst acknowledging that knowledge management is a key driver of organizational growth and development, recognized that knowledge management is over-focused on processes, systems and technologies and not enough on the people-related issues.[10,11] In order to understand how HRD can support the people-related aspects of knowledge creation and organizational learning we need to comprehend what is meant by 'organizational knowledge', have a theory of knowledge creation, and hence be able to advise on designing the systems and structures that can create value-adding organizational knowledge assets. Ultimately, we need to understand how to create 'learning organizations'.

Organizational knowledge

In order to understand organizational knowledge it's important to appreciate the differences between 'data', 'information', and 'knowledge' and the different forms that knowledge can take. One of the most important contributions to knowledge management was Thomas Davenport and Laurence Prusak's seminal book *Working Knowledge*. In it they set out clearly the differences between data, information and knowledge,[12] summarized in Figure 14.1.

Davenport and Prusak argued that there's a chain of events whereby information derives from data, and knowledge derives from information, but this process doesn't happen automatically. They underlined the importance of HR issues in knowledge management in their claim that humans must do 'virtually all the work' in transforming

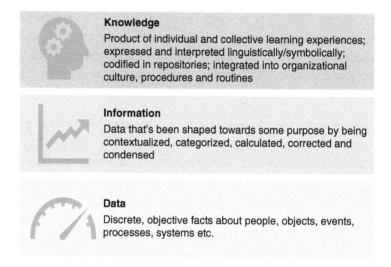

Knowledge
Product of individual and collective learning experiences; expressed and interpreted linguistically/symbolically; codified in repositories; integrated into organizational culture, procedures and routines

Information
Data that's been shaped towards some purpose by being contextualized, categorized, calculated, corrected and condensed

Data
Discrete, objective facts about people, objects, events, processes, systems etc.

Figure 14.1   Data, information and knowledge

data into knowledge through knowledge-creating activities (p. 6). This view highlights the important role – even in a big data, machine learning and AI age – that people play in the creation and management of knowledge and reinforces the view that our most valuable intelligence isn't artificial. Moreover, in terms of how people produce knowledge it's important to recognize that 'knowledge creation' is both a cognitive and social learning process: knowledge is a product of individual experiences and cognitions (for example, individuals' insights and intuitions) and collective reflections and interpretations (when individual's insights and intuitions are interpreted collectively and shared mental models are created). It is through the processes of organizational learning that knowledge becomes integrated and institutionalized into organizational values and beliefs, procedures and routines, and this gives organizations an increased capacity for effective action.

Research insight 14.1

The four 'I's of organizational knowledge creation and learning

Mary Crossan and her colleagues modelled how the process of surfacing and sharing mental models works in terms of a 'four-I' organizational learning framework. The four 'I's in their model are 'intuiting', 'interpreting', 'integrating' and 'institutionalizing'. These four processes operate across individual, group and organizational levels and therefore link individual cognition to organizational culture. The model places considerable emphasis on 'intuition' (as a preconscious pattern recognition process that 'senses possibilities') at the beginning of the process. The model is based on the principle that an individual's personal intuitive insights (which are personal, subjective and tacit, often manifesting as 'gut feelings' or 'hunches') need to be externalized and 'interpreted' by others if they are to be useful and acted upon (that is, they need to be surfaced and shared). Individuals' 'intuitive insights' once they have been surfaced, shared and interpreted also need to be integrated into the organization's processes and systems if they are to be useful. They are then ultimately institutionalized in the organization's culture; see Figure 14.2.

Intuiting (individual level)

- 'Preconscious recognition' of pattern and/or possibilities inherent in a persons' 'stream of experiences' (an 'intuitive insight'); affects individuals' cognitions, behaviours and interactions with others

Interpreting (individual level to group level)

- Externalizing and explaining, both to one's self and to others through words and actions, the 'intuitive insight' which is the core of a new idea

Integrating (group level to organizational level)

- Developing shared understanding among individuals through dialogue and adjusting ways of working through coordinated joint actions; reflects shared understanding (shared mental model)

Institutionalizing (organization level)

- Integration of individual intuitions are initially ad hoc but eventually become formalized in revised organizational routines, processes, systems and strategies which reflect revised mental models that are embedded into the organization's culture (its way of 'doing things')

Figure 14.2   The levels and processes in the four-I model of organizational learning

Crossan and colleagues proposed that a organizational learning framework shows how a learning organization – an entity that's distinct from any one individual – can come into being through the interactions between processes (the four 'I's) operating at multiple levels (individual, group, organizational).

Source: Crossan, M., Lane, H.W., & White, R.E. (1999) An organizational learning framework: From intuition to institution. Academy of Management Review, 24(3): 522–537.

Reflective question 14.1

What would you say to the claim that learning and the knowledge it creates is the most potent form of power? If, as the great German sociologist Max Weber (1864–1920) claimed, power is the ability to realize your own will, how have learning and knowledge given you the ability to realize your own will in your personal, professional or educational life?

Types of knowledge

Having distinguished between data, information and knowledge, it's also important to recognize that there's more than one type of knowledge. In simple terms, knowledge can be either formal/explicit/rational or informal/tacit/intuitive:

- Formal versus informal (for example, a written down set of rules versus a taken-for-granted way of doing things);
- Rational (for example, solving a maths problem) versus intuitive (for example, 'sensing' when something isn't quite right or knowing what to do without knowing why);
- Tacit (knowledge that can't be put into words) versus explicit (knowledge that can be put into words).

These three aspects are inter-related, for example intuitive knowledge is often tacit and informal. They are simply 'qualitatively' different ways of knowing in that rational isn't 'better' than intuitive, they're just different and used in different circumstances. For example, in some organizational processes such as decision-making, problem-solving, creativity and innovation, intuitive knowledge ('going with your gut') can be as important as rational knowledge ('weighing up the pros and cons'). From a practical perspective, and particularly for passing-on knowledge, tacit knowledge presents challenges because it can be difficult even for the knower to understand how they do what they do (for example, riding a bike). It is difficult to express in words. It's hard to say how one avoids falling off a bike, but we can do it all the same. Hence this knowledge is hard to capture and codify (for example, imagine trying to write down instructions for how to learn to ride a bike).[13] These comments don't just apply to psychomotor skills and procedural knowledge, other more complex cognitive and social skills are also tacit (for example, doctors often accomplish medical diagnoses tacitly and intuitively).

In their own words 14.1

Michael Polanyi on knowing more than we can tell

Without doubt the most famous saying in knowledge management is by the physical chemist-come-philosopher Michael Polanyi (1891–1976) in his 1966 book *The Tacit Dimension*: 'We can know more than we can tell' (p. 4).[14] This seemingly innocuous and much quoted phrase has sparked significant interest and has stimulated considerable debate ever since. Here's what Polanyi said: '...we can know more than we can tell. This fact seems obvious enough; but it is not easy to say exactly what it means. Take an example. We know a person's face, and can recognize it from among a thousand, indeed among a million. Yet we cannot tell how we recognize a face we know' (p. 4). In terms of learning, Polanyi was referring to knowledge that can't be spoken (the word 'tacit' comes from the Latin *tacere* meaning 'be silent') but which can be demonstrated and imitated, and therefore learned by another person.[15] Polanyi's work is essentially philosophical, but it contains an important pragmatic point, captured in the idiosyncratic term 'indwelling'. By indwelling Polanyi was referring to the 'tools' that we use to do our work, be they linguistic (for example, the manager's negotiating skills) or physical tools (for example, the surgeon's scalpel) and the way in which we interiorize the tools we use and 'make ourselves dwell within them', hence 'indwelling' (p. 148). The idea of learning and practice as being closely related resonates with situated learning theory (see Chapter 3).

The fundamental differences between tacit and explicit knowledge are as follows:

- Tacit: hard to articulate, personal, difficult to share and context dependent, examples include intuition, 'know how', 'rules of thumb' and 'practical intelligence' and it can be acquired (that is, learned) through talk, modelling practice, and more planned methods such as apprenticeships, coaching and mentoring;
- Explicit: easier to articulate, impersonal, easier to share and context-free, examples include information, 'know what' (declarative knowledge), procedures (including routines), and theoretical knowledge, and it can be captured and acquired through codification and documentation in hard or soft formats.[16]

One of the best illustrations of the concept of tacit knowledge is to be found in a milestone paper in the journal *Organization Science* by Scott Cook and John Seely Brown. They used the easy-to-understand but compelling example of riding a bicycle. It is self-evident that anyone who can ride a bike has knowledge of bike riding, but they cannot put this knowledge into words, in paraphrasing Polanyi: they 'know more about bike riding than they can tell about bike riding'. They also linked the tacit/explicit distinction to the individual and group levels of analysis to show how different types of knowledge manifest at different levels in a two-by-two format:

- Individual/explicit, for example 'concepts', 'theories', etc.;
- Individual/tacit, for example 'skills', 'know how', 'intuition', etc.;
- Group/explicit, for example 'stories', 'anecdotes', etc.;
- Group/tacit, for example culture, genres, etc.

As far as HRD and the acquisition of the different types of knowledge are concerned another important distinction is between 'implicit learning' and 'explicit learning'.[17] We're very familiar with explicit learning processes from our experiences of formal education. Implicit learning on the other hand is a process of knowledge and skill acquisition that takes place:

- Largely independently of conscious attempts to learn;
- Without awareness of how learning took place;
- In the absence of explicit knowledge about what knowledge or skill was acquired (for example, by implicitly learning desirable behaviours from simply 'being around' an admired and respected role model).

Like intuition and rationality, implicit and explicit learning are 'qualitatively' different, that is they have different strengths and weaknesses, and each has different applications and a different job to do. Finally, tacit and explicit knowledge may be thought of as learning 'outcomes', whereas explicit and implicit learning can be thought of as 'processes'.

Research insight 14.2

Intuitive knowledge in medical diagnoses, friend or foe and can it be learned?

In a focus group study of 28 hospital specialists' diagnostic reasoning processes it was found that all participants agreed that intuition plays an important role in their medical diagnoses and many agreed that intuition could guide them, however they were also cautious not to be misguided by their gut feelings. For example, one participant commented that 'We all have this, if we first meet a patient, those first couple of seconds that you see somebody, you get a feeling of whether the situation is serious or not, alarming or not' (p. 3). It was found that the precondition for relying on intuition in medical diagnosis was learning through on-the-job experience and everyone agreed that 'intuitive hunches must be followed by analytical reasoning'. The researchers also commented that physicians' learning and development has an important role to play in honing their intuitive expertise. This could be by helping them to be more self-reflective in the diagnostic phase (for example by developing critical thinking skills), getting feedback from experienced colleagues (for example through coaching), and learning how to use intuitive and analytical processes jointly (for example, through better understanding of their own thinking styles or 'metacognition'). This resonates with other research with police officers which found that when something 'doesn't feel right' (intuitively and instinctively) officers 'go and find out why' (analytically and rationally).

Sources: den Brink Van, N., Holbrechts, B., Brand, P. L. P., Stolper, E. C. F., & Van, P. R. (2019). Role of intuitive knowledge in the diagnostic reasoning of hospital specialists: a focus group study. *BMJ Open*, 9(1), e022724–e022724; Akinci, C., & Sadler-Smith, E. (2020). 'If something doesn't look right, go find out why': How intuitive decision making is accomplished in police first-response. *European Journal of Work and Organizational Psychology*, 29(1), 78–92.

——Delve deeper 14.1——

Read about tacit knowledge/explicit knowledge in:

Cook, S. D., and Brown, J. S. (1999). Bridging epistemologies: The generative dance
    between organizational knowledge and organizational knowing. *Organization Science*,
    10(4), 381–400.

Miller, K. D. (2008). Simon and Polanyi on rationality and knowledge. *Organization Studies*,
    29(7), 933–955.

Hadjimichael, D., & Tsoukas, H. (2019). Toward a better understanding of tacit knowledge
    in organizations: Taking stock and moving forward. *Academy of Management Annals*,
    13(2), 672–703.

Knowledge creation and management

The question for an applied field such as HRD is how these different types of knowledge are created and how can the process of knowledge creation be facilitated in order that the knowledge assets created add value for organizations. There are many different frameworks and models for the management of knowledge creation processes in organizations and researchers have identified at least 160 of these in the research and practice literatures.[18] Amongst this array of models and frameworks the Japanese organizational theorist, Ikujiro Nonaka (b. 1935) stands out in terms of academic citations and practical influence.[19] His work will be the main focus of this section. Nonaka's model of knowledge creation consists of four 'modes' for knowledge creation ('socialization', 'externalization', 'combination', and 'internalization', with the acronym SECI) based on four permutations of tacit and explicit knowledge.

Nonaka is one of the most influential thinkers about knowledge. His theory is also important because it depicts organizations not as static information processing machines but as dynamic entities that create knowledge and in so doing change their environments. For example, the knowledge creation process at Apple that led to the innovation of the iPhone changed the business environment fundamentally, in the words of Apple CEO Tim Cook it became a 'category definer' and in so doing Apple redefined radically the market it was operating in.[20]

The core of Nonaka's model of knowledge creation is the distinction between tacit and explicit knowledge. One of the reasons that Nonaka places so much emphasis on tacit knowledge can be traced to cultural differences between Japan and the West. Nonaka claimed that traditional Western management viewed knowledge mainly as explicit and rational, expressible in words and numbers, and codifiable and transferable in the form of data, formulae, standard operating procedures, organizational routines, etc. Nonaka argued that Japanese culture and Japanese companies had a very different view of knowledge: they recognized that explicit knowledge is the tip of a knowledge 'iceberg', that knowledge is primarily tacit, it's not easily visible or expressible, is highly personal, hard to formalize, and difficult to communicate to others except through the use of figurative language, metaphors, stories and analogies. For Nonaka knowledge is essentially rooted in actions, experiences, ideas, values, beliefs and emotions. He includes insights, intuitions and 'hunches' in this category of knowing.

In their own words 14.2

Ikujiro Nonaka on the philosophical background to SECI

Nonaka's theory is in many ways philosophical. In an interview with Kristine Marin Kawamura published in 2016 Nonaka showed the breadth and depth of the intellectual roots of the four stages of his SECI model by referring to a plethora of deep thinkers ranging from Aristotle to Mao Zedong. He commented on the problems that a Western way of thinking creates for understanding knowledge: 'In the modern world we are influenced by Western thinking, which originates in Plato, and its prejudiced view that only the purified, objective, and explicit may be considered "knowledge".' He made a plea that we 'free ourselves' from this limited viewpoint and 'restore the balance between the competing dichotomies of subjectivity and objectivity, belief and rationality, body and mind, and art and science' (p. 641). You can listen to Professor Nonaka discuss knowledge creation, practical wisdom and other interesting and important topics at: www.youtube.com/watch?v=Ynulo288a4M

Source: Kawamura, K. M. (2016). Kristine Marin Kawamura, PhD interviews Ikujiro Nonaka, PhD. *Cross Cultural & Strategic Management*, 23(4), 637–656.

In Nonaka's theory tacit knowledge can include both technical elements (informal, hard-to-pin-down know-how, crafts and skills and intuitive expertise) and cognitive elements (images of reality encapsulated in mental models, schemata, paradigms).[21] The cornerstones of Nonaka's thinking are the beliefs that:

- Tacit and explicit knowledge are complementary, and even symbiotic, in knowledge creation;
- Tacit knowledge can be converted to explicit knowledge and back again via 'knowledge conversion';
- The dynamic relationship between tacit and explicit knowledge is a social process between individuals.

A prime motivation in Nonaka's theory is knowledge creation both as a route to innovation and as a philosophy for the rejuvenation or re-creation of a company, and even to an extent of the re-defining of entire markets, in a continuous process of personal and organizational self-renewal. Innovations that are based on employees' tacit knowledge is difficult to formalize and codify and therefore much harder to imitate than those based on explicit knowledge.[22]

Nonaka elaborated his ideas subsequently with colleagues, most notably with Hirotaka Takeuchi in their influential book *The Knowledge Creating Company* (1995).[23]

The Nonaka–Takeuchi model is based on the relationships and transitions between tacit and explicit knowledge and the conversion of tacit knowledge to explicit knowledge and back to tacit knowledge again. The model can be represented as a simple two-by-two framework which gives four 'basic patterns' or 'modes' for knowledge creation ('socialization', 'externalization', 'combination', and 'internalization', with the acronym SECI) which are arranged into a knowledge creation 'spiral'. Nonaka and Takeuchi add a further element to the model which acknowledges the role that 'place' (which can be a cognitive or physical space, which they refer to as *ba* in Japanese) plays in knowledge creation (not discussed here). The SECI model (minus *ba*) is shown in Figure 14.3.

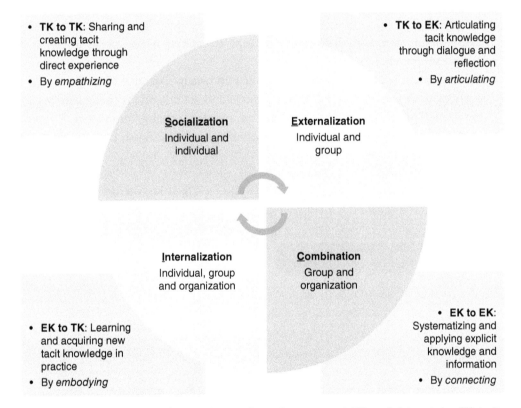

Figure 14.3   The SECI model of knowledge creation and management (EK, explicit knowledge; TK, tacit knowledge)

The importance of social processes of knowledge conversion is especially important in business environments where innovation cycles are fast, where the codification of knowledge can have limited effectiveness because once knowledge has been made explicit and codified it may have become outdated or redundant. In such situations the individuals themselves (such as researchers or knowledge workers) become a living 'repository' for fast-changing knowledge and expertise.[24] This is typical of knowledge intensive industries, and the challenge for such organizations is to retain the loyalty of their knowledge workers so as to secure the knowledge assets that they embody and have the potential to create continuously. Possible HRD solutions for the creation and management of the different models of knowledge production include:

- Socialization (tacit to tacit): sharing and creating tacit knowledge through direct experiences and spending time together in physical proximity; an atmosphere of caring and trust rather than through written or verbal instructions;
- Externalization (tacit to explicit): articulating individual tacit knowledge and skills in a form that can be understood by others, for example as metaphors, analogies, stories and visuals through methods such as verbal coaching, demonstration, etc.;
- Combination (explicit to explicit): capture, collation and categorization of explicit knowledge and skills into more complex forms of explicit knowledge and skills in hard and soft formats in data bases, meetings, etc. so that it gets spread amongst organization members;
- Internalization (explicit to tacit): the explicit knowledge becomes the organization's tacit knowledge and is embodied in action and practices; manifests in methods of strategizing, decision making, problem-solving, innovating, continuous improvement; and is passed on in the onboarding and on-going training of employees.

Through these processes the cycle is complete and new tacit knowledge is created and the process can begin again in a knowledge and skill creation 'spiral'.

Perspective from practice 14.1

Learning and innovation in Japanese businesses

Nonaka's collaborator, Hirotaka Takeuchi, highlighted a number of case studies in support of the view that to be at the cutting edge in a knowledge economy a company must an innovative 'knowledge creator'. For example, the convenience stores Seven Eleven Japan (SEJ) use dialogue deliberately to question existing ways of working and help managers to make sense of their experiences by having regular face to face meetings at which operational 'field counsellors' and headquarters staff (including the CEO) share tacit knowledge on better ways to provide services. HQ-based managers get out into the field and visit distribution centres and share knowledge in conversation, some employees are even given the task of wandering around stores in order to socialize with customers and deliberately gather new insights, and employees are encouraged to articulate their intuitions and insights and test them out, etc. These interchanges are configured as dynamic conversational contexts in which new shared meanings are created, on the other hand simple data-dump meetings or meetings where most attendees remain silent are not contexts for organizational learning.

Source: Takeuchi, H. and Shibata, T. (2006). *Japan, Moving Toward a More Advanced Knowledge Economy*. Washington: World Bank.

Nonaka's model connects to the practice of learning and development in several ways, for example learners need exposure to tacit knowledge in situ so that they can observe and model right behaviours with the right person in the right context. Also, opportunities need to be made available for experts to articulate their tacit knowledge through analogies, models, metaphors and stories. Systems should be put in place that enable knowledge from diverse sources (bottom-up and top-down) to be identified, captured, connected, combined, shared and accessed.

Criticisms of Nonaka's SECI model

The SECI model can be seen as a product of the Japanese national and organizational cultural contexts[25] with its high collectivism, high uncertainty avoidance and large power distance. Takeuchi traces the emphases placed on tacit knowledge to Japanese Zen Buddhist and Samurai martial traditions: 'Managers in Japan learn with their *bodies*, not just with their *minds*...Learning from direct experience stands in stark contrast to "systems thinking" which focuses on learning with the mind.'[26]

Knowledge management researchers such as Teece (see 'dynamic capabilities', Chapter 9) have questioned whether the SECI process is transferable to North American and European contexts. For example, knowledge-sharing and team-based learning may be linked to employees' strong identification with and commitment and loyalty to the firm and to social reciprocity which, in turn, are rooted deeply in Japanese cultural values but which may be less strong, or even alien, in other national and organizational cultures.[27]

Other critics have argued that tacit knowledge is not something that can be converted into explicit knowledge because of the highly personal character and 'ineffability' (not being capable of being expressed in words) of tacit knowledge. Organizational theorist Hari Tsoukas argued that the model is flawed because it overlooks the ineffable, situationally-embedded and embodied nature of tacit knowledge. Cook and Brown argue that it's not possible for tacit knowledge to become explicit under any circumstances because it is so deeply embedded in cognition or physical abilities.[28,29] We shouldn't underestimate the challenges and complexities of trying to make the ineffable effable (i.e. trying to make tacit knowledge into explicit knowledge) and be wary of simple formulas for how to do so.

Reflective question 14.2

Lewis E. Platt (1941–2005) who rose from being an entry level engineer to be CEO of Hewlett Packard in the 1990s (and famous for 'the HP way'), is reputed to have said: 'If only HP knew what HP knows, we would be three times more productive'.[30] How can cognitive, social, and situated learning theories and action-based modalities such as experiential and action learning help organizations capture the knowledge it already has ('to know

(Continued)

what it knows') and create the new knowledge that it needs? Make a list of five HRD 'recommendations' based on your knowledge of theories of learning, for example 'Use action learning sets to surface and share mental models.'

Delve deeper 14.2

Read more about the theory and operationalization of the SECI model in:

Farnese, M. L., Barbieri, B., Chirumbolo, A., & Patriotta, G. (2019). Managing knowledge in organizations: Nonaka's SECI model operationalization. *Frontiers in Psychology, 10,* 2730.

Hong, J. F. (2012). Glocalizing Nonaka's knowledge creation model: Issues and challenges. *Management Learning, 43*(2), 199–215.

Kawamura, K. M. (2016). Kristine Marin Kawamura, PhD interviews Ikujiro Nonaka, PhD. *Cross Cultural & Strategic Management, 23*(4), 637–656.

The learning organization

The concept of the learning organization is a body of 'actionable knowledge' that developed out of the theories of organizational learning developed by Argyris, March, Schon and others in the 1960s and 1970s. The idea of an 'organization that can learn' was appealing at the time (the 1980s and 1990s) because it offered a way for managers to respond to uncertainty and volatility in the business environment and was part of a growing interest in issues such as 'business processes', 'total quality', 'organizational 'excellence', etc. One of the earliest mentions of the term learning organization was by ex-McKinsey, world-renowned management consultants Tom Peters and Robert H. Waterman in their 1982, three million-selling best-seller *In Search of Excellence*. Peters completed his doctorate in organizational behaviour at Stanford in 1977 and was influenced by Jim March and Herbert Simon (both at Stanford). Peters and Waterman's interest in learning can be seen as part of a more general response in the USA to the competitive challenge and threats to US businesses and the economy from overseas, and principally from Japan. In *In Search of Excellence* Peters and Waterman argued that:

- Evolution is continuously at work in the market place;
- Adaptation is crucial;
- Few big businesses manage to adapt effectively;
- Those that do so, do it by means of 'intentionally seeded evolution'.

By 'intentionally seeded evolution' Peters and Waterman were referring to learning, and an important part of their argument was that excellent companies (the subject of their book) 'are *learning organizations*' who don't wait around for the marketplace to eventually 'do them in' (p. 110). Instead excellent companies develop approaches deliberately to stave-off becoming out-competed and out-dated: they experiment more, permit small failures, keep things small scale, stay close to customers and markets, encourage internal competition, and maintain an environment that's rich in information and knowledge that's cross fertilized across functional, hierarchical and geographical boundaries and use this knowledge to deliberately 'seed' new ideas.

Research insight 14.3

Differences between organizational learning and learning organization

Mark Easterby-Smith and Marjorie Lyles[31] argued that 'organizational learning' research (see Chapter 13) is the study of collective learning processes within organizations and is conducted largely from an academic point of view. The 'learning organization' on the other hand is an entity or an ideal type of organization which has the capacity to learn and hence survive and thrive. Similarly, Erik Tsang identified the differences between organizational learning and the learning organization as follows:

- Organizational learning: process and theory of learning by organizations; takes a descriptive approach; asks 'how do organizations learn?'; is the province of academics; uses systematic data collection and analysis; and is concerned with theory building;
- Learning organization: process and practice of learning by organizations; takes a prescriptive approach; asks 'how should organizations learn?'; is the province of consultants and practitioners; uses consulting experience, case study and action research; and is concerned with improving performance.

Easterby-Smith and Lyles also distinguish between 'organizational knowledge' (theoretical, the study of knowledge within organizations) and 'knowledge management' (technical, concerned with creating ways of disseminating knowledge to enhance performance).

Sources: Easterby-Smith, M. and Lyles, M. (2011). Introduction: Watersheds of organizational learning and knowledge management. In Easterby-Smith, M. and Lyles, M. (eds) (2012). *The Blackwell handbook of organizational learning and knowledge management*. Oxford: Blackwell, pp. 1–16; Tsang, E. W. (1997). Organizational learning and the learning organization: A dichotomy between descriptive and prescriptive research. *Human Relations*, 50(1), 73–89.

In the 1990s the idea of the learning organization was taken up enthusiastically, so much so that the 'holy grail' for many large organizations was to become a learning organization. The concept became popularized in Peter M. Senge's highly successful book *The Fifth Discipline: The Art and Practice of the Learning Organization* (1990).

The Fifth Discipline sold over two-and-a-half million copies and is still in print three decades on from its original date of publication. The term 'learning organization' also appeared a few years earlier in Bob Garrett's *The learning organization* (1987) and also in Mike Pedler, John Burgoyne and Tom Boydell's book *The Learning Company* (1988). The originator of the concept of 'action learning' (see Chapter 4), Reg Revans, wrote about 'the enterprise as a learning system' in 1982.

In HRD, the informal and incidental learning researchers Karen Watkins and Victoria Marsick focused on the idea of developing – or to use their phrase 'sculpting' – the learning organization. Marsick and Watkins developed a diagnostic tool for organizations, the 'Dimensions of the Learning Organization Questionnaire' (DLOQ), as did Michael Marquardt in his 2011 book *Building the Learning Organization* (selected as 'Book of the Year' by the Academy of HRD). Clearly the learning organization mattered to organizations and HRD in the 1990s.

There are many definitions of 'the learning organization'. Some of these appear tautological (amounting to little more than saying that 'a learning organization is an organization which learns') whilst others are based on the 'characteristics' or 'dimensions' of a learning organization (for example, there are 11 characteristics in Pedler and colleagues' model, 5 in Senge's, and 7 in Marsick and Watkins); see Figure 14.4.

Senge (1990)

- Organizations where people continually expand their capacity to create the results they truly desire, where new and expansive patterns of thinking are nurtured, where collective aspiration is set free and where people are continually learning how to learn together.

Pedler, Burgoyne and Boydell (1997)

- A learning organization facilities the learning of all its members and continuously transforms itself.

Marquardt (1996)

- A learning organization learns powerfully and collectively and is continually transforming itself, to better collect, manage and use knowledge for corporate success. It empowers people within and outside the company to learn as they work.

Marsick and Watkins (1999)

- The learning organization is a living breathing organism that creates the space that enables people and the system to learn, to grow and to endure.

Figure 14.4 A selection of definitions of the learning organization

Many organizations have claimed to be learning organizations but some of these confuse and conflate the quality and quantity of individual learning and development with being a learning organization. Critics have argued that the idea of the learning organization was a management fashion whose time has passed and that it's been replaced by newer ideas such as 'knowledge management'.[32] Which begs the question:

is the learning organization concept still relevant today? Two of the pioneers of the concept, Mike Pedler and John Burgoyne, argue that the learning organization idea is 'quite definitely alive', for example:

- The subject has its own academic journal, *The Learning Organization*;
- Organizational learning is widely accepted as an underlying assumption of business management (it's now a 'taken-for-granted');
- The need for learning in today's volatile, uncertain, complex and ambiguous environments is now even more central to organizations than it was in the 1990s. [33]

Pedler and Burgoyne quoted a comment from an HRD practitioner in response to the question of whether the learning organization is alive or dead: 'I work in L&D [learning and development] and I believe the learning organization is our day-to-day business.'

The learning organization and the theory that it's based on, organizational learning, have emerged as a 'mainstream concept' [34] in business and management. David Garvin and his colleagues from Harvard Business School writing in the early 2000s acknowledged that the concept of the learning organization is not a new one, but in the face of intensifying competition, advances in technology and shifts in customer preferences, it's as relevant as ever because 'each company must become a learning organization'. [35] More recently still, *Forbes* magazine argued that companies should embrace the idea of becoming a learning organization because it enables continuous improvement, increased collaboration and business sustainability and longevity. [36] The idea is also endorsed by management and HR professional bodies. In the UK, the Chartered Institute of Personnel and Development (CIPD) promoted the idea of the 'new learning organization' in which a culture of learning is established where learning is not only a 'daily habit' but also a 'strategic pillar'. [37] In the US, the Society for Human Resource Management (SHRM) endorses the creation of a 'learning culture' in which people not only want to learn and apply what they've learned but also feel 'compelled to share their knowledge with others'. [38]

In their own words 14.3

Bob Garratt and Peter Senge on the learning organization

One of the earliest discussions of 'the learning organization' was in the 1987 book *The Learning Organization* by the UK management consultant Bob Garratt. Garrett described how some people argued against it at the time on the grounds that it was 'like playing with fire'. For the sceptics, not only was it dangerous and futile because organizations couldn't learn, but also by making organizational learning processes transparent it would upset the existing power balances and so could actually destroy

(Continued)

organizations, and more particularly could damage the interests of the most power-ful groups, such as managers, executives and owners.[39] Garrett focused on the role that directors and boards play in learning and likened their role to that of a 'business brain': 'the vision and courage of those giving the tone from the top is crucial to the success of any learning organization' (p. 134). The 'directors' dilemma' in a learning organization – reflecting the tension between single- and double-loop learning in organization learning theory – was 'how do we balance seeing the way ahead whilst also keeping the organization under prudent control?'. Garratt reflected on both the history and relevance of an influential idea from the 1990s in the second decade of the twenty-first century: 'Organizational ideas seem to move in twenty year cycles. The learning organization concept continues. I reprise, there is good and bad learn-ing in all organizations. The aspiration of a learning organization is to always keep learning "good"' (p. 134).

Peter M. Senge, author of *The Fifth Discipline* in an interview for *The Learning Organization* journal spoke about the importance of motivation: 'real learning is always motivated by the aspirations or intentions of the learner (or learners within the organi-zational context)' and of reflection in that 'if the learning does not turn out as expected the learner has to think "huh, that didn't quite work, I want to do it differently"' and this trial-and-error process requires action, success or mistake, followed by reflection (p. 10). Senge talks about the importance for individuals and organizations of a deep and persistent commitment to learning in this short video clip from MIT: www.youtube.com/watch?v=OpiqnCAQ6S8.

Sources: Garratt, B. (2019). Personal paradoxes in learning to design 'the learning organization'. In Örtenblad, A. (ed.) *The Oxford handbook of the learning organization*. Oxford: Oxford University Press, pp. 119–136; Reese, S. (2020). Taking the learning organization mainstream and beyond the organizational level: An interview with Peter Senge. *Learning Organization*, 27(1), 6–16.

Senge's five disciplines of a learning organization

A landmark publication in this field is *The fifth discipline* (1990) by Peter M. Senge. Senge, an MIT researcher, was heavily influenced by 'system dynamics' and the work of Jay W. Forrester in particular. *The fifth discipline* is the most famous book about the learning organization and its main idea was that 'the organizations that will truly excel in the future will be the organizations that discover how to tap people's com-mitment and capacity to learn at all levels in an organization' and that these will be the antithesis of 'traditional, authoritarian controlling organizations' (pp. 4–5). *The fifth discipline* sold over two million copies and was recognized by *Harvard Business*

Review as 'one of the seminal management books of the last 75 years'.[40] The importance of the idea of the learning organization was summed up by internationally renowned management academic, author and researcher Henry Mintzberg and his colleagues in their book *Strategy Safari* as one of the 'biggest breakthroughs' in management thinking of recent decades.

One of the central ideas of Senge's model is that learning starts with turning the metaphorical 'mirror' inwards on the organization to unearth its internal pictures of the world (mental models) in a process of reflection. A further idea that resonates with organizational learning theory is that:

- A learning organization has an 'adaptive' capacity (where adaptive learning is analogous to single-loop learning);
- A learning organization also has 'generative' capacity (where 'generative learning' is analogous to double-loop learning).

Senge's model is essentially pragmatic in that becoming a 'learning organization' requires mastery of certain basic 'disciplines', of which there are five. Students of HR and related subjects are sometimes perplexed by the seemingly obscure title of Senge's book (*The fifth discipline*) even though its sub-title is *The art and practice of the learning organization*. By 'discipline' Senge is referring to principles or a 'developmental path for acquiring certain skills or competencies' (p. 10) that must be studied and 'mastered' in order to be put into practice. Moreover, the disciplines may never be fully acquired, instead the learning occurs in the on-going 'mastering' of them and as one learns more

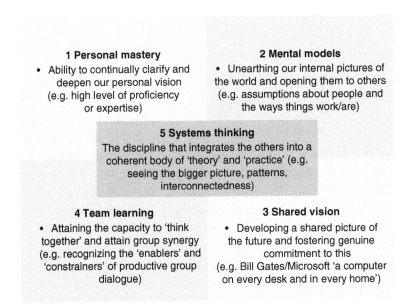

Figure 14.5 Senge's five disciplines of a learning organization

one becomes more aware of one's ignorance. The five 'disciplines' (also referred to as 'component technologies') for a learning organization are shown in Figure 14.5.

According to Senge, the learning organization is not a destination ever to be arrived at; it's more like a state of being which unfolds continuously as one's understanding of oneself, one's organization, the world and one's place in the world develops. There are spiritual, and specifically Buddhist, undercurrents in these ideas: 'everything that exists in the physical world exists in a web of interconnectedness, and it's always continually in flux' but somehow we don't see this because we tend to see 'things' not processes and therefore 'perceive things as being more or less fixed'.[41] These powerful and profound ideas manifested explicitly in one of Senge's co-authored works *Presence* (2004): 'The Buddhist approach rests on rigorous disciplines of cultivation that start with paying attention to our present way of living' (p. 230).[42] The fifth of the five disciplines is 'systems thinking' which serves to integrate the others into a coherent body of personal (as opposed to academic) theory and practice. The idea also resonates with the concept of a learning ecosystem.

Delve deeper 14.3

Read more about Senge's model in:

Bui, H., & Baruch, Y. (2010). Creating learning organizations: A systems perspective. *The Learning Organization, 17*(3), 208–227.

Hsu, S. W., & Lamb, P. (2020). Still in search of learning organization?: Towards a radical account of The Fifth Discipline: The Art and Practice of the Learning Organization. *The Learning Organization, 27*(1), 31–41.

Marsick and Watkins' dimensions of a learning organization

Adult education and HRD researchers Victoria Marsick and Karen Watkins, originators of theories of informal and incidental learning in the workplace (see Chapter 6), presented their learning organization model originally in the 1993 book *Sculpting the Learning Organization*. They described the learning organization as an 'integrative vision' for HRD and argue that simply adopting someone else's solution will not work because learning organizations grow organically, and different organizations will create different configurations. They adopt the metaphor of 'sculpting': the sculptor of the learning organization shapes structures that nurture learning, chips away at existing systems, attitudes, and practices which thwart learning. They operationalize their model of the learning organization in terms of seven 'action imperatives' or dimensions; see Figure 14.6. This is an example of a learning organization 'blueprint' or prescriptive model.

1 Create continuous learning opportunities

- Learning is designed into work so that people can learn on the job; opportunities are provided for ongoing education and growth.

2 Promote inquiry and dialogue

- People gain productive reasoning skills to express their views and the capacity to listen and inquire into the views of others; the culture is changed to support questioning, feedback, and experimentation.

3 Encourage collaboration and team learning

- Work is designed to use groups to access different modes of thinking; groups are expected to learn together and work together; collaboration is valued by the culture and rewarded.

4 Create systems to capture and share learning

- Both high- and low-technology systems to share learning are created and integrated with work; access is provided; systems are maintained.

5 Empower people toward a collective vision

- People are involved in setting, owning, and implementing a joint vision; responsibility is distributed close to decision making so that people are motivated to learn towards what they are held accountable to do.

6 Connect the organization to its environment

- People are helped to see the effect of their work on the entire enterprise; people scan the environment and use information to adjust work practices; the organization is linked to its communities.

7 Provide strategic leadership for learning

- Leaders model, champion, and support learning; leadership uses learning strategically for business results.

Figure 14.6 Marsick and Watkins' dimensions of a learning organization

From an HRD perspective, Marsick and Watkins' model offers a good fit with the concepts of strategic HRM (SHRM) and strategic HRD (SHRD, see Chapter 9) because it focuses on aligning people around a common vision for the organization, sensing and interpreting changes in the organization's external and internal environments, and generating new knowledge which is used to develop products and services that add value for the organization's stakeholders and deliver on its vision.[33] Whether organizational learning is effective or not is influenced by a variety of contextual factors including organizational culture and climate. For example, cultures which are flexible and de-centralized with flatter hierarchies, team-based working and open communication channels are more likely to create a positive atmosphere in which employees are empowered to learn and where learning is recognized and rewarded. On the other hand some organizational cultures, for example those which are highly bureaucratic, authoritarian, hierarchical, coercive, inflexible and psychologically unsafe, may be simply unsuited to organizational learning and becoming a learning organization.[44] Needless to say, managers have a vital role to play in the process since their commitment and support is vital in bringing about success or failure of the cultural change that might be necessary to create the context and conditions for organizational learning to take place.[45] Marsick and Watkins' diagnostic tool, the *Dimensions of Learning Organization Questionnaire* (DLOQ) can be used both for research purposes and in planning learning interventions in organizations.

Research insight 14.4

The impact of learning organization dimensions on performance

HRD researchers in the USA set out to assess the relationships between the seven dimensions of the DLOQ (the independent variables) and knowledge performance and financial performance (the dependent variables) measured 'perceptually' (i.e. self-reported) in a questionnaire and also objectively:

- The 'perceptual measures' of knowledge performance included customer satisfaction, new products and services developed, etc., and perceptual measures of financial performance including return on investment, productivity, etc.;
- The four objective organizational outcome variables were return on equity (ROE), return on assets (ROA), Tobin's q and market value added (MVA).

Ellinger and colleagues used a mail-based survey to gather data from a sample of four hundred mid-level managers in US manufacturing firms. The results indicated that there was a statistically significant association between the seven dimensions of the learning organization:

- The perceptual measures of financial performance and knowledge performance: the strength of the relationship was such that 25 per cent of the variance in firm performance can be accounted for by the seven dimensions ($p < 0.01$);
- The four financial performance indicators: more than 10 per cent of the variance in financial performance could be explained by the seven dimensions of the learning organization ($p < 0.05$).

This and other more recent research using the same instrument and same research design offer encouraging support for the normative assertions and prescriptions that are to be found in the learning organization literature (that is, becoming a learning organization is a desirable goal). The more recent research by Kim and colleagues reported the influence that each individual dimension has on performance. It found that all the dimensions had statistically significant effects ($p < 0.001$) and that empowering people towards a collective vision and strategic leadership for learning had the strongest effects. The effect of learning performance on financial performance was not direct, instead it was mediated through knowledge performance. As was the case with SHRM and SHRD, the cross-sectional nature of this research is a limitation and reverse causality (for example, higher performers have the slack and resources to engage in learning organization behaviours) cannot be ruled out.

Sources: Ellinger, A. D., Ellinger, A. E., Yang, B., and Howton, S. W. (2002). The relationship between the learning organization concept and firms' financial performance: An empirical assessment. *Human Resource Development Quarterly, 13*(1), 5–22; Kim, K., Watkins, K. E., and Lu, Z. L. (2017). The impact of a learning organization on performance. *European Journal of Training and Development, 41*(2): 177–193.

Reflective question 14.3

Compare Senge's 'five disciplines' and Marsick and Watkins' 'seven dimensions' of a learning organization. Do you see any similarities and differences? For example Senge's 'Shared vision (3)' appears to be roughly equivalent to Marsick and Watkins' 'Empower people toward a collective vision (5)'. Do you think it is possible to design a learning organization model that integrates Senge's disciplines and Marsick and Watkins' dimensions?

In a comparison of the various learning organization models Anders Örtenblad constructed a four-fold 'typology' of the learning organization based on the research literature and on practitioners' views. The four key aspects of the learning organization concept that he identified were:

- Organizational learning occurs at different levels/in different modes;
- Organizational learning takes place in the social setting of the workplace;
- A learning culture/climate is vital to encourage/reward learning;
- Organizational structures need to be flexible enough to accommodate learning.[46]

Örtenblad's research distilled a small number of key attributes from the plethora of models. The model with the 'best fit' to his typology was Marsick and Watkins' 'seven dimensions' model.

Criticisms of the learning organization

Because organizational learning is a social and situated activity it is inevitably 'power-laden',[47] and one of the main criticisms of the learning organization is that it is often presented as an 'ideal state' that overlooks problems of hierarchy, power and privilege. Also, it can be seen as serving managerial and shareholder agendas rather than the agendas of employees in general or a wider group of stakeholders. Several of its assumptions obscure issues of power and power asymmetries and make certain assumptions about employees' behaviour by presuming that they'll engage in organizational learn-ing by sharing the new knowledge and skills that their learnings create.[48,49] Critical management scholar Alessia Contu and colleagues questioned the assumption that learning is unconditionally 'good' (which they argue it is not necessarily; their article was called 'Against learning'[50]):

- Empowerment has limits that are defined and proscribed by those who hold power (that is senior managers and business owners);
- Learning can occur only within the limits proscribed by powerful others (such as managers and owners);
- Learning may actually exacerbate power asymmetries by giving senior managers access to newly generated knowledge.

In the end learning may end up maintaining patterns of subordination and be used to support 'exploitative practices' (p. 945). For example, learning and the new knowledge it creates may be being used exclusively to maximize shareholder value and thereby overlook or obscure the interests of other stakeholders.

Motivation and self-direction, and cultural specificity are also problematic issues. HRD scholar Rob Poell argued that the learning organization, as an 'ideal' type of organization, assumes that all workers will be able and willing to find their own learn-ing pathway and be able to chart a route through it by being self-motivated self-developers. The question of what to do if workers are not motivated, able or willing to learn continuously, to innovate and double-loop learn on an on-going basis, to be responsible for their own development and share their knowledge (which could be a personal source of competitive advantage in the internal labour market) is sometimes glossed over in the learning organization literature.[51]

Pedler and Burgoyne, who were amongst the earliest proponents of the idea of a 'learning company', argued that the culture of performance management that has per-vaded HR and organizations in the private and public sectors (short-term focus on cost reduction, narrowly defined metrics and increasing shareholder value) may have weak-ened the longer-term learning organization ethos and accounted for its demise in recent years. On the other hand, the stranglehold that metric-driven performance management and maximizing shareholder value has can be weakened if stakeholders are defined more broadly, and this could create space for the learning organization to breathe again.

As far as issues of national culture and context are concerned, Mak and Hong have noted that the 'traditional' (first wave) learning organization models were developed mostly in the West. The assumption that they can be directly applied in non-Western contexts and cultures (for example, in countries that have a different level of economic development) could be false, and the idea itself may in fact be resisted by employees in different cultures. 'Differentiated prescriptions' are required[52] and an alternative approach might be a set of general principles, rather than specific characteristics, that create the conditions for learning to take place and for knowledge to flow from between individual, group and organizational levels. For example, a set of principles that create the conditions for intuiting, interpreting, integrating and institutionalizing processes (see Crossan and colleagues' four-I model referred above) which enables 'feed-forward' (learning) and 'feed-back' (reflection) between the individual, group and organizational levels.

Russ Vince notes that there is a tension always when we put the words learning and organization together (Karl Weick and Frances Westley referred to 'organization learning' itself as an 'oxymoron', that is two apparently contradictory terms being used in conjunction[53]), therefore we can't simplistically expect to create environments that enable learning if we don't also recognize ways in which these same environments might constrain learning. According to Vince, within the paradox that is the learning organization there are two contradictory dynamics: 'The ability to create "learning-*in-action*", to mobilise ongoing transformations of capability and practice, is often accompanied by "learning *inaction*", which reflects emotional and political limits to learning that are characteristic of an organisation'.[54] In spite of these criticisms, as an entity that facilitates the learning of all its members and continuously transforms itself,[55] a new learning organization that seeks to meet the challenges of the twenty-first century is worth striving for.[56]

Delve deeper 14.4

Read about criticisms of the learning organization in:

Örtenblad, A. (2018). What does 'learning organization' mean? *The Learning Organization.* 25(3), 150–158.

Pedler, M., & Burgoyne, J. G. (2017). Is the learning organisation still alive? *Learning Organization*, 24(2), 119–126.

Shin, H., Picken, J., & Dess, G. (2017). Revisiting the learning organization. *Organizational Dynamics*, 1(46), 46–56.

Tsang, E. W. (2017). How the concept of organizational unlearning contributes to studies of learning organizations: A personal reflection. *Learning Organization*, 24(1), 39–48.

Conclusion: Now's the time?

Has the 'learning organization' finally come of age such that now is the time for the 'New Learning Organization'? As noted earlier, two of the pioneers of the learning organization in the UK, Mike Pedler and John Burgoyne, have been critical and have asked the question 'is the learning organization still alive?'. They offered a balanced argument for both sides of the debate, but one of the conclusions that they arrived at was that the learning organization needs now to be brought up-to-date and aligned to current conditions and contexts as well as to related topics such as 'organizational knowledge', 'knowledge management', 'dynamic capabilities', etc. Elsewhere Pedler has argued that the 'first wave' of the learning organization that was innovated in the 1990s hasn't achieved what was hoped for, but he wonders whether the time is right for a revival.[57] A number of alternatives and re-incarnations of the learning organization have been suggested.

In their proposal for 'second wave' learning organizations Pedler and his colleague Shih-wei Hsu offer a radical approach which departs from 30-year old 'first wave' assumptions. They argue that ancient and traditional forms of wisdom such as the Buddhist and Taoist principles of how to live a 'good life' might offer a more sustainable set of assumptions. In this view organizational learning would have a 'critical impulse' and be governed by principles that restrict our desires for material goods, is mindful of our relationships with the environment, and is cognisant of the intended and unintended consequences, both positive and negative, of our actions. They suggest that a second wave of learning organizations could seek to develop organizational purposes, processes, products and services in line with these principles, contrary to concerns for survival and competitive advantage that were features of the first wave. They cite the Mondragon Cooperatives in Spain as an exemplar. It's notable that these ideas resonate with the principles that Senge has expounded in his thinking and subsequent work with Buddhist inspired scholars and practitioners such as Francisco Varela and Otto Scharmer who is noted for his *Theory U* (2007) subtitled 'Learning from the future as it emerges'.

The HR profession has also recognized the need for the learning organization idea to evolve and become aligned with the twenty-first century context. Research undertaken on behalf of the CIPD identified a number of characteristics of a future-focused 'New Learning Organization': a 'learning ecosystem' that enables people, teams and the organization to learn in ways that are linked to common goals based on an agile, digitally enabled infrastructure that enables a fluid exchange of knowledge.[58] The extent to which these new initiatives are fundamentally different from the first wave learning organization remains to be seen. But putting things into perspective, the Chief Executive of the CIPD, Peter Cheese, commented that Senge's compelling vision of the learning organization 'has been elusive' perhaps because it 'was simply ahead of its time' and speculated that the climate for the re-emergence of the new learning organization has arrived.

In the 30 years that have passed since the inception of the learning organization concept, the business environment, the world of work, and employee learning and development have undergone transformational changes. In this context the challenge for the learning organization – and HRD has a vital role in its realization – is to evolve in ways that meet the needs of and delivers value for all of its stakeholders. The idea of the fluid exchange of knowledge is a recurring theme in discussions of the new learning organization. Organizations in which knowledge is exchanged efficiently and effectively:

- Encourage employees to offer new ideas and ask critical questions;
- Enable the widespread sharing of information from multiple internal and external sources;
- Have a psychologically safe climate which encourages experimentation and idea generation;
- Involve employees in collaborative decision making;

- Use technology to enable organizational knowledge creation and sharing.[59]

In Chapter 8 it was argued that HRD can be a strategic partner by ensuring that employees have the necessary knowledge, skills and creative abilities to get the organization from where it is now to where it wants to be. Hence, one of the most important HR and HRD challenges for organizations is attracting, motivating, developing and, above all, retaining the loyalty and commitment of knowledge workers.[60] In the information age[61] many, if not most, jobs contain a significant knowledge element and the knowledge content of many forms of work is increasing. New opportunities and challenges are arising for HRD as a result of innovations in big data, machine learning (ML) and artificial intelligence (AI). Important issues are raised regarding the respective roles of humans and computers, job replacement by computers, and how to keep humans in the loop if or when artificial intelligence becomes capable of taking better decisions than human intelligence. The coming together in the 'fourth industrial revolution' of the internet, robotics and AI creates challenges and opportunities that aren't likely to be addressed by framing the issue as '*either* people *or* machines', a more productive way forward is more likely to be found in framing the issue as '*both* people *and* machines'. Throughout history combining the complementary capabilities of humans and machines has produced superior results.[62] The best of both worlds will be achieved by engaging humans in the things that machines can't and are unlikely ever to be able to do, that is: intuition, insight, invention, innovation, empathy and emotion, and above all, wisdom.

The great American pragmatist philosopher, John Dewey (1859–1952), defined human 'habits' in terms of an on-going process of adaptation involving conscious, self-aware, self-critical, proactive and creative attempts to survive and thrive in their environment. Habits help us to navigate the world successfully. For Dewey, wisdom has a special place, as a 'meta-habit', that consciously and constantly adjusts and adapts the other habits in a world that is both uncertain and unpredictable as well as complex and dynamic.[63] Wisdom is exercised through good judgement. Wisdom, or more accurately 'practical wisdom', is an intellectual virtue that guides decision-making and actions to serve the common good and enhance individual and societal well-being, flourishing and thriving.[64] The eminent American psychologist Robert Sternberg described wisdom as the application of intelligence and creativity toward the achievement of a common good through a balance of intra-personal, inter-personal and extra-personal interests in order to adapt to and shape existing environments and, if necessary, select new environments.[65]

But the wisdom to do these things can't be extracted from data by a machine to be distilled into an algorithm, reduced to a recipe or set out as formal rules for effective action; on the other hand humans as social beings can become wiser through their socially constructed learnings from their own and others' experiences, through processes such as intuiting, articulating and connecting, as part of a collective endeavour towards the realization of a shared vision. The role of HRD is to help employees to flourish at work,[66] actualize their full potential, and contribute meaningfully and with a purpose beyond profit that maximizes stakeholder value, respects justice and fairness, and maintains the integrity of the natural environment and in so doing both *actualizes* and *transcends* the self.[67]

Chapter checkout

Use this list to check your understanding of the key points of this chapter.

1 **Organizational knowledge** Product of individual and collective learning experiences; expressed and interpreted linguistically/symbolically; codified in repositories; integrated into organizational culture, procedures and routines

2 **Types of knowledge** Knowledge can be either formal/explicit/rational or informal/tacit/intuitive

3 **Model of knowledge creation** Nonaka's model of knowledge creation consists of four tacit/explicit permutations: 'socialization', 'externalization', 'combination', and 'internalization' (SECI)

4 **The learning organization (LO)** Organization that facilitates learning of all its members and continuously transforms itself

5 **Models of learning organization** Peter Senge's 'five disciplines of a learning organization'; Marsick and Watkins' seven dimensions

6 **Criticisms of LO** Managerialist, prescriptive, de-problematizing power, Western-centric

7 **The new learning organization** Time is right for a less prescriptive, principles-based, more sustainable and multi-stakeholder 'new learning organization' model for the twenty-first century; the wisdom and practical intelligence to navigate VUCA environments

---

SKILLS DEVELOPMENT 14

GAINING SUPPORT FOR THE 'LEARNING ORGANIZATION' THROUGH THE APPOINTMENT OF A CHIEF LEARNING OFFICER (CLO)

The world has changed radically since the first wave of the learning organization in the 1990s: we live in a digitized and globalized world where technology has raced ahead and shows no sign of slowing down. On top of this there are expectations that businesses take a multi-stakeholder perspective and HRD is hybrid and multi-channel. Volatility, uncertainty, complexity and ambiguity (VUCA) are the norm and resilience and sustainability are the main challenges faced by organizations. One way of rising to this challenge is by becoming a learning organization under the leadership of a Chief Learning Officer (CLO).

For this exercise imagine that you are a Chief HR Officer (CHRO) who would like to create a new board-level role of Chief Learning Officer (CLO). The CLO will be an HRD specialist who has the remit of turning the organization into a new learning organization (NLO). To create the CLO role you have to sell the NLO and CLO ideas to the CEO and the other board members. By way of background, Lundberg and Westerman argue in *Harvard Business Review*,[66] a CLO isn't someone who's simply responsible for training and development, instead they have a much more all-embracing and powerful role in which they reshape and transform the company's capabilities and its organizational culture to enable continuous learning that delivers value for stakeholders.

Your task in this exercise is to create a Briefing Note that communicates clearly and concisely the benefits to the organization of: (1) becoming a new learning organization; (2) creating a new Board-level CLO role to facilitate this process of becoming. A successful Briefing Note will convince the CEO and other Board members that becoming a learning organization is a worthwhile ambition and that the CLO role is worth investing in.

REFERENCES

Preface

1   See Senge, P. M. (1990). *The fifth discipline*. London: Century.
2   Rodrigo, C. G. (2020). *Micro and macro: The economic divide*. International Monetary Fund. Available online: www.imf.org/external/pubs/ft/fandd/basics/bigsmall.htm (accessed 07-02-21).
3   CIPD (2020) *The new profession map, specialist knowledge: Learning and development*. London: CIPD. Available online: www.cipd.co.uk (accessed 07-02-21).
4   Sadler-Smith, E. (2006). *Learning and development for managers: Perspectives from research and practice*. Oxford: Blackwell.

Chapter 1

1   Jacobs, R. L. (1990). Human resource development as an interdisciplinary body of knowledge. *Human Resource Development Quarterly*, 1(1): 65–71, p. 66.
2   Wang, X., & McLean, G. N. (2007). The dilemma of defining international human resource development. *Human Resource Development Review*, 6(1): 96–108.
3   *Oxford Dictionary of English*, 2005: 256.
4   Davies, B., Diemand-Yauman, C., and van Dam, N. (2019). Competitive advantage with a human dimension: From lifelong learning to lifelong employability. *McKinsey Quarterly*, February. Available online: www.mckinsey.com/featured-insights/future-of-work/competitive-advantage-with-a-human-dimension-from-lifelong-learning-to-lifelong-employability (accessed 24-12-20).
5   Myers, C. A. (1963). Education, manpower and economic growth. In *Academy of Management Proceedings* 1: 69–70. Briarcliff Manor, NY 10510: Academy of Management. Available online https://journals.aom.org/doi/pdf/10.5465/ambpp.1963.5068061 (accessed 24-12-20).
6   Storberg, J. (2002). The evolution of capital theory: A critique of a theory of social capital and implications for HRD. *Human Resource Development Review*, 1(4): 468–499.
7   Goldin, C. (2016). Human capital. In Diebolt, C. and Haupert, M. (eds) *Handbook of cliometrics*. Berlin: Springer. Available online: https://scholar.harvard.edu/files/goldin/files/human_capital_handbook_of_cliometrics_0.pdf (accessed 24-12-20).
8   Blackler, F. (1995). Knowledge, knowledge work and organizations: An overview and interpretation. *Organization Studies*, 16(6): 1021–1046.
9   Anderson, V., Garavan, T. and Sadler-Smith, E. (2014) Corporate social responsibility, sustainability, ethics and international human resource development, *Human Resource Development International*, 17: 497–498, p. 498.
10 McGuire, D., Cross, C. and O'Donnell, D. (2005) Why humanistic approaches in HRD won't work, *Human Resource Development Quarterly*, 16: 131–137.
11 This information is from re:Work which is a project by Google and others to help share and push forward the practice and research of data-driven HR with the aim of designing work so that it makes employees 'happier, healthier, and more productive' by putting 'employees first, trust [ing] and treat [ing] them like owners'. The re:Work website is a curated platform of practices, research, and ideas from Google and others.
12 https://rework.withgoogle.com/subjects/learning-development/ https://rework.withgoogle.com/guides/learning-development-employee-to-employee/steps/introduction/
13 Swanson, R. A. (2001). Human resource development and its underlying theory. *Human Resource Development International*, 4(3): 299–312.

14 For a discussion of the tensions between HRD and adult education (AE) in the US see: Hatcher, T., & Bowles, T. (2006). Bridging the gap between human resource development and adult education: Part one, assumptions, definitions, and critiques. *New Horizons in Adult Education and Human Resource Development*, 20(2): 5–23.

15 Bates, R. A., Hatcher, T., Holton, E. F., III, & Chalofsky, N. (2001). Redefining human resource development: An integration of the learning, performance, and spirituality of work perspectives. In Aliaga, O. A.(ed.) *Academy of Human Resource Development 2001 Conference proceedings* (pp. 205–212). Academy of Human Resource Development, Tulsa, Oklahoma.

16 Tranfield, D., Huff, A., & Van Aken, J. E. (2006). Management as a design science mindful of art and surprise. *Journal of Management Inquiry*, 15(4): 413–424, p. 413.

17 Simon, H. A. (1996). *The sciences of the artificial*. Cambridge, MA: MIT Press, p. 4.

18 Kim, J. (2018). 6 attributes of an academic discipline. *Inside Higher Ed*. Available online: www.insidehighered.com/blogs/technology-and-learning/6-attributes-academic-discipline (accessed 24-12-20).

19 Barney, J. B. (2002). Strategic management: From informed conversation to academic discipline. *Academy of Management Perspectives*, 16(2): 53–57.

20 Kuchinke, K. P. (2001). Why HRD is not an academic discipline. *Human Resource Development International*, 4(3): 291–294.

21 Woodall, J. (2005). Theoretical frameworks for comparing HRD in an international context. *Human Resource Development International*, 8(4): 399–402.

22 Leonard Nadler Obituary, *New York Times*, 24–25 October 2017. Available online: www.legacy.com/obituaries/nytimes/obituary.aspx?pid=187041191 (accessed 24-12-20).

23 Association for Talent Development (no date). *Talent Development Glossary Terms*. Available online: www.td.org/glossary-terms (accessed 24-12-20).

24 Van de Ven, A. H. (1989). Nothing is quite so practical as a good theory. *Academy of Management Review*, 14: 486–489.

25 Brockbank, W., Ulrich, D., & Beatty, R. W. (1999). HR professional development: Creating the future creators at the University of Michigan Business School. *Human Resource Management*, 38(2): 111–118.

26 Gioia, D. A., & Pitre, E. (1990). Multiparadigm perspectives on theory building. *Academy of Management Review*, 15(4): 584–602.

27 Piazza, A., & Abrahamson, E. (2020). Fads and fashions in management practices: Taking stock and looking forward. *International Journal of Management Reviews*. doi.org/10.1111/ijmr.12225

28 Swanson, R. A. (2001). Human resource development and its underlying theory. *Human Resource Development International*, 4(3): 299–312.

29 Swanson, R. A. (1995). Human resource development: Performance is the key. *Human Resource Development Quarterly*, 6(2): 207–213.

30 Kuchinke, K. P. (2001). Why HRD is not an academic discipline. *Human Resource Development International*, 4(3): 291–294.

31 Sadler-Smith, E. (2006). *Learning and development for managers: Perspectives from research and practice*. Oxford: Blackwell.

32 Corley, K. G., & Gioia, D. A. (2011). Building theory about theory building: what constitutes a theoretical contribution? *Academy of Management Review*, 36(1), 12–32.

33 Gray, D. E. (2014) *Doing research in the real world*. London: SAGE; Saunders, M., Lewis, P., & Thornhill, A. (2012). *Research methods for business students*. Harlow: Pearson.

34 Gray, D.E. (2014) Doing research in the real world. London: SAGE; Saunders, M., Lewis, P., & Thornhill, A. (2012). *Research methods for business students*. Harlow: Pearson.

35 Gray, D.E. (2014) *Doing research in the real world*. London: SAGE; Saunders, M., Lewis, P., & Thornhill, A. (2012). *Research methods for business students*. Harlow: Pearson.

36 McGoldrick, J., Stewart, J., & Watson, S. (2004). Philosophy and theory in HRD. In Lee, M., Stewart, J. and Woodall, J. (eds) *New frontiers in HRD*. Abingdon: Routledge, pp. 27–40.

37 Gubbins, C., and Rousseau, D. M. (2015). Embracing translational HRD research for evidence-based management: Let's talk about how to bridge the research–practice gap. *Human Resource Development Quarterly*, 26(2): 109–125.

38 Crane, A., & Matten, D. (2004). *Business ethics: Managing corporate citizenship and sustainability in the age of globalization*. Oxford: Oxford University Press.

39 Stewart, J. (2007). The future of HRD research: Strengths, weaknesses, opportunities, threats and actions. *Human Resource Development International*, 10(1): 93–97.

40 Hatcher, T. (2002/2010). *Ethics and HRD: A new approach to leading responsible organizations*. Cambridge, MA.: Basic Books.

41 Krefting, L. A. (2003). Ethics and HRD: A new approach to leading responsible organizations. Academy of Management Review, 28(3): 512–512.

42 Holton III, E. F. (2002). Theoretical assumptions underlying the performance paradigm of human resource development. *Human Resource Development International*, 5(2): 199–215.

43 Hamlin, B., & Stewart, J. (2011). What is HRD? A definitional review and synthesis of the HRD domain. *Journal of European Industrial Training*, 35(3): 199–220.

44 Holton III, E. F. (2002). Theoretical assumptions underlying the performance paradigm of human resource development. *Human Resource Development International*, 5(2): 199–215.

45 Holton III, E. F. (2002). Theoretical assumptions underlying the performance paradigm of human resource development. Human Resource Development International, 5(2): 199–215.

46 Adler, P. S., Forbes, L. C., & Willmott, H. (2007). Critical management studies. *The Academy of Management Annals*, 1(1): 119–179, p. 119

47 Antonacopoulou, E. (1999). Individuals' responses to change: the relationship between learning and knowledge. *Creativity and Innovation Management*, 8(2): 130–139.

48 Callahan, J. L. (2007). Gazing into the crystal ball: Critical HRD as a future of research in the field. *Human Resource Development International*, 10(1), 77–82; Sambrook, S. (2009). Critical HRD: a concept analysis. *Personnel Review*, 38(1): 61–73.

49 Fenwick, T. J. (2004). Toward a critical HRD in theory and practice. *Adult Education Quarterly*, 54(3): 193–209.

50 Baek, P., & Kim, N. (2017). The subjective perceptions of critical HRD scholars on the current state and the future of CHRD. *Human Resource Development Quarterly*, 28(2): 135–161.

51 Elliott, C. (2000). Does HRD acknowledge human becomings? A view of the UK literature. *Human Resource Development Quarterly*, 11(2): 187–195, p. 188.

52 Hamlin, B., & Stewart, J. (2011). What is HRD? A definitional review and synthesis of the HRD domain. *Journal of European Industrial Training*, 35(3): 199–220.

53 Chalofsky, N., & Cavallaro, L. (2013). A good living versus a good life: Meaning, purpose, and HRD. *Advances in Developing Human Resources*, 15(4), 331–340.

54 White, A. 2020. How to make beautiful PowerPoint presentations. *Shutterstock Blog*. www.shutterstock.com/blog/tips-on-how-to-make-effective-beautiful-powerpoint-presentations (accessed 24-12-20).

Chapter 2

1 Locke, E. A., & Latham, G. P. (1990). *A theory of goal setting & task performance*. Englewood Cliffs, NJ: Prentice-Hall, Inc.

2 Knowles, M., Holton, E., & Swanson, R. (2015). *The adult learner*. London: Routledge, p. 9.

3 Swanson, R. A. (2001). Human resource development and its underlying theory. *Human Resource Development International*, 4(3): 299–312.

4 Sadler-Smith, E. (2014). HRD research and design science: Recasting interventions as artefacts. *Human Resource Development International*, 17(2): 129–144.

5 Lewin, K. (1945). The research centre for group dynamics at Massachusetts Institute of Technology. *Sociometry*, 8(2): 126–136.

6   Ghoshal, S. (2005). Bad management theories are destroying good management practices. *Academy of Management Learning & Education*, 4(1): 75–91.

7   CIPD Learning in the flow of work. Available online: www.cipd.co.uk/knowledge/strategy/development/learning-factsheet (accessed 27-12-20).

8   Gubbins, C., Harney., B., van der Werff, L., & Rousseau, D. M. (2018). Enhancing the trustworthiness and credibility of HRD: Evidence-based management to the rescue? *Human Resource Development Quarterly*, 29(3): 193–202.

9   Gigerenzer, G. (2020). How to explain behaviour. *Topics in Cognitive Science*, 12: 1363–1381, p. 1364.

10 Gigerenzer, G. (2020). How to explain behaviour. *Topics in Cognitive Science*, 12: 1363–1381, p. 1364.

11 McLeod, S. (2018). B.F. Skinner -operant conditioning. *Simply Psychology*. Available online: www.simplypsychology.org/operant-conditioning.html (accessed 27-12-20).

12 Conole, G., Dyke, M., Oliver, M., & Seale, J. (2004). Mapping pedagogy and tools for effective learning design. *Computers & Education*, 43(1–2): 17–33.

13 Reimann, A. (2018). Behaviourist learning theory. *The TESOL encyclopaedia of English language teaching*, 1-6. Available online: https://onlinelibrary.wiley.com/doi/abs/10.1002/9781118784235.eelt0155 (accessed 27-12-20).

14 Pinker, S. (1997). *How the mind works*. London: Allen Lane.

15 Gigerenzer, G. (2020). How to explain behaviour. *Topics in Cognitive Science*, 12: 1363–1381, p. 1366.

16 CIPD's 'Behavioural Science' webpage on understanding how to apply behavioural science to HR and L&D in the workplace. Available online: www.cipd.co.uk/knowledge/culture/behaviour#15763 (accessed 13-01-21).

17 Association for Psychological Science. Remembering the father of cognitive psychology. Available online: www.psychologicalscience.org/observer/remembering-the-father-of-cognitive-psychology (accessed 27-12-20).

18 Galotti, K. M. (2017). *Cognitive psychology in and out of the laboratory*. London: SAGE.

19 Galotti, K. M. (2017). *Cognitive psychology in and out of the laboratory*. London: SAGE.

20 Kauffeld, S., & Lehmann-Willenbrock, N. (2010). Sales training: Effects of spaced practice on training transfer. *Journal of European Industrial Training*, 34(1): 23–37; Russ-Eft, D. (2002). A typology of training design and work environment factors affecting workplace learning and transfer. *Human Resource Development Review*, 1(1): 45–65.

21 Cowan, N. (2014). Working memory underpins cognitive development, learning, and education. *Educational Psychology Review*, 26(2): 197–223.

22 Cowan, N. (2015). George Miller's magical number of immediate memory in retrospect: Observations on the faltering progression of science. *Psychological Review*, 122(3): 536–541.

23 McLeod, S. (2010) Long-term memory. *Simply Psychology*. Available online: www.simplypsychology.org/long-term-memory.html (accessed 13-01-21).

24 For practical guidance on design strategies for eLearning that teaches to the different types of LTM see: https://elearningindustry.com/enhancing-long-term-memory-7-strategies-elearning-professionals (accessed 27-12-20).

25 McLeod, S. (2010) Long-term memory. *Simply Psychology*. Available online: www.simplypsychology.org/long-term-memory.html (accessed 13-01-21).

26 Reber, A. S. (1993). *Implicit learning and tacit knowledge: An essay on the cognitive unconscious. Oxford psychology series, No. 19*. Oxford: Oxford University Press.

27 Mayer, R. E., & Moreno, R. (2003). Nine ways to reduce cognitive load in multimedia learning. *Educational Psychologist*, 38(1): 43–52.

28 Foer, J. (2011). *Moonwalking with Einstein*. London: Penguin.

29 For a comprehensive and sometimes irreverent list of business acronyms go to: www.businessballs.com/glossaries-and-terminology/acronyms-finder/#banjo

30 Sweller, J., & Chandler, P. (1994). Why some material is difficult to learn. *Cognition and Instruction*, 12(3): 185–233, p. 226

31 Ausubel, D. P. (1968). *The psychology of meaningful verbal learning*. New York: Grune & Stratton.

32 Smith, P. J., & Sadler-Smith, E. (2006). *Learning in organizations: Complexities and diversities*. Taylor & Francis.

33 Latham, G. P. (2004). The motivational benefits of goal-setting. *Academy of Management Perspectives*, 18(4): 126–129.

34 Robbins, P., & Aydede, M. (eds) (2008). *The Cambridge handbook of situated cognition*. Cambridge University Press.

35 Roth, W. M., & Jornet, A. (2013). Situated cognition. *Wiley Interdisciplinary Reviews: Cognitive Science*, 4(5): 463–478, p. 464.

36 Hutchins, E. (1995) *Cognition in the wild*. Cambridge, MA: MIT Press.

37 For an introduction to Andy Clark and David Chalmers' notion of the 'extended mind' see: www.nyu.edu/gsas/dept/philo/courses/concepts/clark.html (accessed 27-12-20).

38 Andersen, E. (2016). Learning to learn. *Harvard Business Review*, March. Available online: https://hbr.org/2016/03/learning-to-learn (accessed 27-12-20).

39 Werner, J. M., & DeSimone, R. L. (2009). *Human resource development*. Mason, OH: South Western Cengage Learning.

40 Coultis, S. (no date). *Water Bear Learning: How to create effective job aids*. Available online: https://waterbearlearning.com/create-effective-training-job-aids/#:~:text=A%20job%20aid%20is%20any,instructional%20lists (accessed 13-01-21).

Chapter 3

1 Blackler, F. (1995). Knowledge, knowledge work and organizations: An overview and interpretation. *Organization Studies*, 16(6): 1021–1046.

2 Wragg Sykes, R. (2020). *Kindred neanderthal life, love, death and art*. London: Bloomsbury.

3 Bandura, A. (1969). Social-learning theory of identificatory processes. In Goslin, D. (ed.) *Handbook of socialization theory and research*. Chicago: Rand McNally & Company. pp. 213–262, p. 214

4 Bandura, A. (1969). Social-learning theory of identificatory processes. In Goslin, D. (ed.) *Handbook of socialization theory and research*. Chicago: Rand McNally & Company. pp. 213–262.

5 Bandura, A. (2008). Observational learning. In *The international encyclopaedia of communication*. Wiley online library.

6 Cherry, K. (2019). How social learning theory works. *Very well mind*. Available online: www.verywellmind.com/social-learning-theory-2795074 (accessed 03-01-21).

7 Condry, J. (2017). *The psychology of television*. Abingdon: Routledge.

8 Lowry, P. B., Zhang, J., Wang, C., & Siponen, M. (2016). Why do adults engage in cyberbullying on social media? An integration of online disinhibition and deindividuation effects with the social structure and social learning model. *Information Systems Research*, 27(4): 962–986.

9 Bandura, A. (1978). Social learning theory of aggression. *Journal of Communication*, 28(3): 12–29, p. 14.

10 Bandura, A. (1983). Temporal dynamics and decomposition of reciprocal determinism. *Psychological Review*, 90(2): 166–170.

11 Based on the schoolroom example from www.verywellmind.com/what-is-reciprocal-determinism-2795907

12 Rizzolatti, G., Fogassi, L., & Gallese, V. (2001). Neurophysiological mechanisms underlying the understanding and imitation of action. *Nature Reviews Neuroscience*, 2(9): 661–670.

13 Warhurst, R. (2011). Role modelling in manager development: Learning that which cannot be taught. *Journal of European Industrial Training*, 35(9): 874–891, p. 888.

14 Bandura, A. (1986). *Social foundations of thought and action: A social cognitive theory*. Englewood Cliffs, NJ: Prentice Hall, p. 391.

15 Wood, R., & Bandura, A. (1989). Social cognitive theory of organizational management. *Academy of Management Review*, 14(3): 361–384.

16 Gardner, A. K., Diesen, D. L., Hogg, D., & Huerta, S. (2016). The impact of goal setting and goal orientation on performance during a clerkship surgical skills training program. *The American Journal of Surgery*, 211(2): 321–325; Zimmerman, B. J., Schunk, D. H., & DiBenedetto, M. K. (2017). The role of self-efficacy and related beliefs in self-regulation of learning and performance. In Elliot, A. J. and Dweck, C. (eds) *Handbook of competence and motivation: Theory and application*. New York: The Guilford Press, pp. 313–333.

17 Bakker, A., & Schaufeli, W. B. (2015) Work engagement. In *Wiley encyclopaedia of management*. Available online: https://onlinelibrary.wiley.com/doi/abs/10.1002/9781118785317.weom110009 (accessed 03-01-21).

18 Weinberg, F. J. (2019). How and when is role modelling effective? The influence of mentee professional identity on mentoring dynamics and personal learning outcomes. *Group & Organization Management*, 44(2): 425–477, p. 430.

19 CIPD. *Member-to-member mentoring*. CIPD available online: www.cipd.co.uk/learn/volunteer/mentoring/member-to-member (accessed 03-01-21).

20 Moorley, C., & Chinn, T. (2016). Developing nursing leadership in social media. *Journal of Advanced Nursing*, 72(3): 514–520.

21 Fox, S. (1997). Situated learning theory versus traditional cognitive learning theory: Why management education should not ignore management learning. *Systems Practice*, 10(6): 727–747, p. 727.

22 Vygotsky, L. S. (1997). *The collected works of L.S. Vygotsky. Volume 4: The development of the higher mental functions*. New York: Springer. Available online: https://link.springer.com/content/pdf/bfm%3A978-1-4615-5939-9%2F1.pdf (accessed 13-01-21).

23 Lave, J. (1991). Situating learning in communities of practice. Perspectives on socially shared cognition. In Resnick, L. B., Levine, J. M., & Teasley, S. D. (eds). *Perspectives on socially shared cognition*. Washington, DC, US: American Psychological Association: 63–82; Wenger, E. (1998). *Communities of practice: Learning, meaning, and identity*. Cambridge: Cambridge University Press.

24 Bolisani, E., & Scarso, E. (2014). The place of communities of practice in knowledge management studies: A critical review. *Journal of Knowledge Management*, 18(2): 366–381.

25 Lave, J. (1991). Situating learning in communities of practice. Perspectives on socially shared cognition. In Resnick, L. B., Levine, J. M., & Teasley, S. D. (eds). *Perspectives on socially shared cognition*. Washington, DC, American Psychological Association, pp. 63–82.

26 Jeon, S., Kim, Y. G., and Koh, J. (2011). An integrative model for knowledge sharing in communities-of-practice. *Journal of Knowledge Management*, 15(2): 251–269.

27 Lave, J. (1991). Situating learning in communities of practice. Perspectives on socially shared cognition. In Resnick, L. B., Levine, J. M., & Teasley, S. D. (eds). *Perspectives on socially shared cognition*. Washington, DC, US: American Psychological Association: 63–82, p. 81.

28 Wenger, E. (no date) Communities of practice: A brief introduction. Available online: https://wenger-trayner.com/introduction-to-communities-of-practice/ (accessed 27-01-20).

29 DeFillippi, R. & Ornstein, S. (2005). Psychological perspectives underlying theories of organizational learning. In Easterby-Smith, M. and Lyles, M. (eds) *Handbook of organizational learning and knowledge management*. Oxford: Blackwell Publishing, pp. 19–37.

30 Brown, J. S., & Duguid, P. (1991). Organizational learning and communities-of-practice: Toward a unified view of working, learning, and innovation. *Organization Science*, 2(1): 40–57.

31   Orr, J. E. (1996). *Talking about machines: An ethnography of a modern job*. Ithaca, NY: Cornell University Press.

32   Lave, J. (1991). Situating learning in communities of practice. Perspectives on socially shared cognition. In Resnick, L. B., Levine, J. M., & Teasley, S. D. (eds). *Perspectives on socially shared cognition*. Washington, DC, US: American Psychological Association: 63–82.

33   Garavan, T. N., Carbery, R., & Murphy, E. (2007). Managing intentionally created communities of practice for knowledge sourcing across organisational boundaries: Insights on the role of the CoP manager. *The Learning Organization: An International Journal*, 14(1): 34–49.

34   Jeon, S., Kim, Y. G., & Koh, J. (2011). An integrative model for knowledge sharing in communities-of-practice. *Journal of Knowledge Management*, 15(2): 251–269.

35   Garavan, T. N., Carbery, R., & Murphy, E. (2007). Managing intentionally created communities of practice for knowledge sourcing across organisational boundaries: Insights on the role of the CoP manager. *The Learning Organization: An International Journal*, 14(1): 34–49.

36   Wang, C. Y. (2014). *Apprenticeships in China: Experiences, lessons and challenges*. National Institute for Education Sciences. OECD. Available online: www.oecd.org/els/emp/C_WANG-Apprenticeships%20in%20China%20Update.pdf (accessed 28-12-20).

37   Elbaum, B. (1989). Why apprenticeship persisted in Britain but not in the United States. *The Journal of Economic History*, 49(2): 337–349.

38   Oxford Dictionary definition.

39   Becker, H. (1972). A school is a lousy place to learn anything. *American Behavioral Scientist*, 16: 85–105. Cited in Lave, J. (1991). Situating learning in communities of practice. Perspectives on socially shared cognition. In Resnick, L. B., Levine, J. M., & Teasley, S. D. (eds). *Perspectives on socially shared cognition*. Washington, DC, US: American Psychological Association: 63–82.

40   Fuller, A., & Unwin, L. (2016). Applying an apprenticeship approach to HRD: Why the concepts of occupation, identity and the organisation of workplace learning still matter. In Sparrow, P., Shipton, H., Budhwar, P., & Brown, A. (eds.) *Human resource management, innovation and performance* (pp. 66–79). London: Palgrave Macmillan.

41   Polanyi, M. (1962). *Personal knowledge. Towards a post-critical philosophy*. Corrected edition. The University of Chicago Press (first published in 1958): 53. Cited in Neuweg, G. H. (2004). *Tacit knowing and implicit learning. European perspectives on learning at work: The acquisition of work process knowledge*. Cedefob Reference Series Luxemburg: Office for Official Publications for the European Communities.

42   Fuller, A., & Unwin, L. (1998). Reconceptualising apprenticeship: Exploring the relationship between work and learning. *Journal of Vocational Education & Training*, 50(2): 153–173.

43   Torff, B., & Sternberg, R.J. (1998). Changing mind, changing world: Practical intelligence and tacit knowledge in adult learning. In Smith, M. C., & Pouchot, T. (eds) *Adult learning and development*. New York: Lawrence Erlbaum Associates: 109–126, p. 121.

44   Wenger, E., McDermott, R. A., & Snyder, W. (2002). *Cultivating communities of practice: A guide to managing knowledge*. Cambridge, MA: Harvard Business Press.

45   Roberts, J. (2006). Limits to communities of practice. *Journal of Management Studies*, 43(3): 623–639.

46   Wenger, E., McDermott, R. A., & Snyder, W. (2002). *Cultivating communities of practice: A guide to managing knowledge*. Cambridge, MA.: Harvard Business Press.

47   Tomasello, M. (2014). The ultra-social animal. *European Journal of Social Psychology*, 44(3): 187–194.

48   Lave, J. (1991). Situating learning in communities of practice. Perspectives on socially shared cognition. In Resnick, L. B., Levine, J. M., & Teasley, S. D. (eds). (1991). *Perspectives*

on socially shared cognition. Washington, DC, US: American Psychological Association: 63–82; p. 66

49 van Schaik, C. P., & Burkart, J. M. (2011). Social learning and evolution: The cultural intelligence hypothesis. *Philosophical Transactions of the Royal Society B: Biological Sciences,* 366(1567): 1008–1016.

Chapter 4

1 Kolb, D. A. (1984/2014). *Experiential learning: Experience as the source of learning and development.* Upper Saddle River, NJ: Pearson, p. 67.

2 Revans, R. (1998). *The ABC of action learning.* Aldershot: Gower, p. 103.

3 Knowles, M. S., Holton III, E. F., & Swanson, R. A. (2015). *The adult learner: The definitive classic in adult education and human resource development.* Abingdon: Oxford, p. 175.

4 Cherry, K. (2020). Biography of John Dewey, *Very well mind.* Available online: www.verywellmind.com/john-dewey-biography-1859-1952-2795515 (accessed 29-12-20).

5 Dewey, J. (1938) *Experience and education. Chapter 6. The meaning of purpose.* Available online: https://archive.org/stream/ExperienceAndEducation-JohnDewey/dewey-edu-experience_djvu.txt. Emphasis added (accessed 13-01-21).

6 Illeris, K. (2007). *How we learn: Learning and non-learning in school and beyond.* Abingdon: Routledge.

7 Boud, D., Cohen, R., & Walker, D. (1993). *Using experience for learning.* Open University Press: Buckingham, p. 8. In Beard, C., & Wilson, J. P. (2018). *Experiential learning: A practical guide for training, coaching and education.* Kogan Page Publishers.

8 Centre for Creative Leadership (no date) *The 70:20:10 rule for leadership development.* Available online: www.ccl.org/articles/leading-effectively-articles/70-20-10-rule/ (accessed 13-01-21).

9 Kolb, D. A. (1984/2014). *Experiential learning: Experience as the source of learning and development.* Upper Saddle River, NJ: Pearson, p. 15.

10 The full video which was posted in 2012 and lasts for 2′40′ was accessed at www.youtube.com/watch?v=1ZeAdN4FB5A on 07-07-20.

11 A gerund is the,-ing' form of a verb that is used like a noun, e.g. 'everyone enjoys Nigella's *cooking'*.

12 The term 'processual' is linked to the concept of 'process philosophy', see: Rescher, N. (1996). *Process metaphysics.* New York: SUNY Press. Moreover, John Dewey is considered by some scholars to be a 'processist' as well as a pragmatist.

13 Kolb, A. & Kolb, D. (2018). Eight important things to know about the experiential learning cycle. *Australian Educational Leader,* 40(3): 8–14.

14 Kransdorff, A. (1999). Applying experiential learning to work. *Knowledge Management Review,* 9: 12–15.

15 Klein, G. (2007). Performing a project premortem. *Harvard Business Review,* 85(9): 18–19. For a succinct summary see Wild, S. (2019). How mastering time travel makes for better decisions. *Change Board.* Available online: www.changeboard.com/article-details/17089/how-mastering-time-travel-makes-for-better-decisions-gary-klein-s-pre-mortem-planning/ (accessed 29-12-20).

16 Cunliffe, A. L., & Easterby-Smith, M. (2004). From reflection to practical reflexivity: Experiential learning as lived experience. In Reynolds, M. & Vince, R. (eds) *Organizing reflection.* Abingdon: Ashgate, pp. 30–46.

17 Reynolds, M. (2009). Wild frontiers – reflections on experiential learning. *Management Learning,* 40(4): 387–392.

18 Reynolds, M., & Vince, R. (eds) (2007). *Handbook of experiential learning and management education*. Oxford: Oxford University Press.

19 Kolb's original labels for the styles are in brackets (e.g. 'diverger') whereas the term 'imagining' style is a more recent term for the experiencing (concrete experience, CE)-thinking (abstract conceptualization, AC) style, see: https://learningfromexperience.com/themes/kolb-learning-style-inventory-lsi/

20 *Sources:* Kolb, D. A., Boyatzis, R. E., & Mainemelis, C. (2001). Experiential learning theory: Previous research and new directions. *Perspectives on Thinking, Learning and Cognitive Styles*, 1(8): 227–247; Knoll, A. R., Otani, H., Skeel, R. L., & Van Horn, K. R. (2017). Learning style, judgements of learning, and learning of verbal and visual information. *British Journal of Psychology*, 108(3): 544–563; Sadler-Smith, E., & J. Smith, P. (2004). Strategies for accommodating individuals' styles and preferences in flexible learning programmes. *British Journal of Educational Technology*, 35(4): 395–412.

21 Kolb, D. A., Boyatzis, R. E., & Mainemelis, C. (2001). Experiential learning theory: Previous research and new directions. *Perspectives on Thinking, Learning and Cognitive Styles*, 1(8): 227–247.

22 *Honey and Mumford Learning Styles Questionnaire* (no date) Pearson: Talent Lens. Available oinline: www.talentlens.co.uk/product/learning-style-questionnaire/ (accessed 29-12-20).

23 https://infokf.kornferry.com/US-PS-Talent-NUR-2015-12-Catalog-lead-nurtures-N-America-LANG-EN-X1Y3_CATALOG_US_LTSITE_LP_LSI32.html (accessed 29-12-20).

24 Knoll, A. R., Otani, H., Skeel, R. L., & Van Horn, K. R. (2017). Learning style, judgements of learning, and learning of verbal and visual information. *British Journal of Psychology*, 108(3): 544–563.

25 Riding, R. J. and Sadler-Smith, E. (1992). Type of instructional material, cognitive style and learning performance. *Educational Studies*, 18(3): 323–340; Sadler-Smith, E. (1992). *Individual Differences and the Design of Instructional Materials*. Unpublished PhD Thesis. School of Education, University of Birmingham.

26 Nadler, J., Thompson, L., & Boven, L. V. (2003). Learning negotiation skills: Four models of knowledge creation and transfer. *Management Science*, 49(4): 529–540.

27 Woodall, J., & Winstanley, D. (1998). *Management development: Strategy and practice*. Abingdon: Blackwell Business, p. 154.

28 Vince, R. (1998). Behind and beyond Kolb's learning cycle. *Journal of Management Education*, 22(3): 304–319.

29 Kolb, D. A. (2007).*The Kolb learning style inventory*. Boston, MA: Hay Resources Direct; Manolis, C., Burns, D. J., Assudani, R., & Chinta, R. (2013). Assessing experiential learning styles: A methodological reconstruction and validation of the Kolb Learning Style Inventory. *Learning and Individual Differences*, 23: 44–52.

30 Clancy, A., & Vince, R. (2019). 'If I want to feel my feelings, I'll see a bloody Shrink': Learning from the shadow side of experiential learning. *Journal of Management Education*, 43(2): 174–184.

31 Morris, T. H. (2019). Experiential learning – a systematic review and revision of Kolb's model. *Interactive Learning Environments*, 1–14. Available online: https://doi.org/10.1080/10494820.2019.1570279 (accessed 13-01-21).

32 Morris, T. H. (2019). Experiential learning – a systematic review and revision of Kolb's model. *Interactive Learning Environments*, 1–14. Available online: https://doi.org/10.1080/10494820.2019.1570279 (accessed 13-01-21).

33 Brook, C., & Pedler, M. (2020). Action learning in academic management education: A state of the field review. *The International Journal of Management Education*, 18(3). Available online https://doi.org/10.1016/j.ijme.2020.100415 (accessed 13-01-21); Pedler, M., Burgoyne, J., & Brook, C. (2005). What has action learning learned to become? *Action Learning: Research & Practice*, 2(1): 49–68.

34 Marquardt, M. (2007). Action learning. In Silberman, M. (ed.) *The handbook of experiential learning*. San Francisco: John Wiley & Sons, pp. 94–110.

35 Raelin, J. A. (2009). Action learning and related modalities. In Armstrong, S. & Fukami, C. (eds) *The SAGE handbook of management learning, education and development*. Thousand Oaks: SAGE, pp. 419–438.

36 Revans, R. W. (1982). What is action learning? *Journal of Management Development*, 1(3): 64–75.

37 Revans, R. W. (1982). *The origins and growth of action learning*. Bromley: Chartwell-Bratt.

38 Raelin, J. A. (2009). Action learning and related modalities. In Armstrong, S. & Fukami, C. (eds) *The SAGE handbook of management learning, education and development*. Thousand Oaks: SAGE, pp. 419–438.

39 Raelin, J. A. (2009). Action learning and related modalities. In Armstrong, S. & Fukami, C. (eds) *The SAGE handbook of management learning, education and development*. Thousand Oaks: SAGE, pp. 419–438.

40 Knowles, M. S., Holton III, E. F., & Swanson, R. A. (2015). *The adult learner: The definitive classic in adult education and human resource development*. Abingdon: Oxford, pp. 38–39.

41 Kaufman, D. M. (2003). Applying educational theory in practice. *BMJ*, 326(7382): 213–216.

42 Holton, E. F., Swanson, R. A., & Naquin, S. S. (2001). Andragogy in practice: Clarifying the andragogical model of adult learning. *Performance Improvement Quarterly*, 14(1): 118–143.

43 Gitterman, A. (2004). Interactive andragogy: Principles, methods, and skills. *Journal of Teaching in Social Work*, 24(3–4): 95–112.

44 Werner, J. M., & DeSimone, R. L. (2011). *Human resource development*. Mason, OH.: Cengage Learning., pp. 85–87.

45 Dewey, J. (1902). *Child and the curriculum*. Chicago, IL: University of Chicago Press; Dewey, J. (1933). *How we think*. Boston, MA: D.C. Heath & Co Publishers. Both in Dewey, J. (1998). *The essential Dewey: Pragmatism, education, democracy* (Vol. 1). Indiana University Press.

46 Petkus Jr, E. (2000). A theoretical and practical framework for service-learning in marketing: Kolb's experiential learning cycle. *Journal of Marketing Education*, 22(1): 64–70.

Chapter 5

1   Powell, T. C. (2011). Neurostrategy. *Strategic Management Journal*, 32(13): 1484–1499.

2   The Royal Society (2011) *Brain waves module 2: Neuroscience: Implications for education and lifelong learning*. London: The Royal Society

3   Blakemore, S. J., & Frith, U. (2005). *The learning brain: Lessons for education*. Oxford: Blackwell Publishing.

4   Fox, A. (2011). Leading with the brain. *HR Magazine*. Available online: www.shrm.org/hr-today/news/hr-magazine/pages/0611fox.aspx (accessed 26-01-21).

5   CIPD (2020). *Learning theories for the workplace*. London CIPD. Available online: www.cipd.co.uk/knowledge/strategy/development/learning-psychology-factsheet (accessed 26-01-21).

6   Caveat emptor is Latin for 'let the buyer beware'; it's used in property and other aspects of law but has generally come to mean exercise caution when buying, or buying into, something.

7   Lim, D. H., Chai, D. S., Park, S., & Doo, M. Y. (2019). Neuro-scientism, the neuroscience of learning. *European Journal of Training and Development*, 43(7–8): 619–642.

8   Blakemore, S. J., Winston, J., & Frith, U. (2004). Social cognitive neuroscience: Where are we heading? *Trends in Cognitive Sciences*, 8(5): 216–222.

9   The Royal Society (2011) *Brain waves module 2: Neuroscience: Implications for education and lifelong learning*. London: The Royal Society.

10 Ariely, D., & Berns, G. S. (2010). Neuromarketing: The hope and hype of neuroimaging in business. *Nature reviews neuroscience*, 11(4): 284–292; Hill, A. (2015) Heads of

business need neuroscience. *Financial Times*, 6 April. Available online: www.ft.com/content/11812676-d79a-11e4-94b1-00144feab7de (accessed 26-01-21).

11 Herculano-Houzel, S. (2009). The human brain in numbers: A linearly scaled-up primate brain. *Frontiers in Human Neuroscience*, 3, 31. Available online: www.ncbi.nlm.nih.gov/pmc/articles/PMC2776484/ (accessed 22-04-20).

12 Carter, R. (1998). *Mapping the mind*. Berkley: University of California Press.

13 Jenkins, T. A., Nguyen, J. C., Polglaze, K. E., & Bertrand, P. P. (2016). Influence of tryptophan and serotonin on mood and cognition with a possible role of the gut-brain axis. *Nutrients*, 8(1): 56.

14 NHS (no date) *Schizophrenia: Causes*. Available online : www.nhs.uk/conditions/schizophrenia/causes/#:~:text=Research%20suggests%20schizophrenia%20may%20be,of%20the%20cause%20of%20schizophrenia (accessed 26-01-21).

15 Lumen (no date) *Boundless psychology: Neurons*. Available online: https://courses.lumenlearning.com/boundless-psychology/chapter/neurons/ (accessed 22-04-20).

16 Ornstein, D. (2018). MIT scientists discover fundamental rule of brain plasticity. *MIT News*. Available online: http://news.mit.edu/2018/mit-scientists-discover-fundamental-rule-of-brain-plasticity-0622 (accessed 21-04-20).

17 Owens, M. T., & Tanner, K. D. (2017). Teaching as brain changing: Exploring connections between neuroscience and innovative teaching. *CBE Life Sciences Education*, 16(2), fe2. Available online: www.ncbi.nlm.nih.gov/pmc/articles/PMC5459260/ (accessed 26-01-21).

18 Davis, C. (2018). Stephen Hawking quotes. *Daily Express*. Available online: Stephen Hawking quotes: HERE is the scientist's most ICONIC quote (accessed 26-01-21).

19 Men, W. , Falk, D., Sun, T., Chen, W., Li, J., Yin, D., Zang, L., & Fan, M. (2014). The corpus callosum of Albert Einstein's brain: Another clue to his high intelligence? *Brain*, 137 (4): e268. Available online: https://academic.oup.com/brain/article/137/4/e268/365419 (accessed 26-01-21).

20 Gewin, V. (2005). A golden age of brain exploration. *PLoS Biology* 3(1): e24. Available online: https://doi.org/10.1371/journal.pbio.0030024 (accessed 13-01-21).

21 Lumen (no date) *Boundless psychology: Brain imaging techniques*. Available online: https://courses.lumenlearning.com/boundless-psychology/chapter/brain-imaging-techniques/ (accessed 26-01-21).

22 Becker, W. J., Cropanzano, R., & Sanfey, A. G. (2011). Organizational neuroscience: Taking organizational theory inside the neural black box. *Journal of Management*, 37(4): 933–961.

23 Kolb, B., Gibb, R., & Robinson, T. E. (2003). Brain plasticity and behaviour. *Current Directions in Psychological Science*, 12(1): 1–5.

24 Cherry, K. (2020). How experience changes brain plasticity. *Very Well Mind*. Available online: www.verywellmind.com/what-is-brain-plasticity-2794886 (accessed 21-04-20).

25 Heid, M. (2018). Does thinking burn calories? *Time*, 19 September. Available online: https://time.com/5400025/does-thinking-burn-calories/ (accessed 13-01-21).

26 Fox, R. (2015). Sat nav has made 'the Knowledge' redundant. *Financial Times*. Available online: www.ft.com/content/63d0d9dc-818e-11e5-8095-ed1a37d1e096 (accessed 13-01-21).

27 Transport for London (no date) Learn the knowledge of London. Available online: https://tfl.gov.uk/info-for/taxis-and-private-hire/licensing/learn-the-knowledge-of-london (accessed 26-01-21).

28 *BBC News* (2000). Taxi drivers' brains grown on the job. Available online: http://news.bbc.co.uk/1/hi/677048.stm (accessed 26-01-21).

29 CIPD (2014). *Fresh thinking in learning and development*. Part 1 of 3 Neuroscience and learning. CIPD: London, p. 7.

30 Blakemore, S. J., & Frith, U. (2005). *The learning brain: Lessons for education*. Oxford: Blackwell Publishing.

31 Blume, H. (1998). Neurodiversity. *The Atlantic*, September. Available online www. theatlantic.com/magazine/archive/1998/09/neurodiversity/305909/ (accessed 26-01-21).

32 Baron-Cohen, S. (2017). Editorial perspective: Neurodiversity–a revolutionary concept for autism and psychiatry. *Journal of Child Psychology and Psychiatry*, 58(6): 744–747.

33 Keneally, C. (2020). Does autism hold the key to what makes humans special? *The New York Times*. Available online: www.nytimes.com/2020/12/08/books/review/pattern-seekers-simon-baron-cohen-autism.html (accessed 26-01-21).

34 Bailin, A. (2019). Clearing up some misconceptions about neurodiversity. *Scientific American*. Available online: https://blogs.scientificamerican.com/observations/clearing-up-some-misconceptions-about-neurodiversity/ (accessed 26-01-21)

35 Pisano, G. (2017). Neurodiversity as competitive advantage. *Harvard Business Review*, May-June. Available online: https://hbr.org/2017/05/neurodiversity-as-a-competitive-advantage (accessed 13-01-21).

36 Microsoft accessibility blog (2018) Individuals with autism can bring untapped talent to every business. Available online: https://blogs.microsoft.com/accessibility/autismawareness2018/ (accessed 26-01-21)

37 www.peoplemanagement.co.uk/experts/legal/managing-neurodiversity-in-the-workplace

38 ACAS (no date) Neurodiversity in the workplace. Available online: https://archive.acas.org.uk/neurodiversity (accessed 26-01-21).

39 Rao, B., & Polepeddi, J. (2019). Neurodiverse workforce: Inclusive employment as an HR strategy. *Strategic HR Review*, 18(5): 204–209.

40 Richards, J., Sang, K., Marks, A., & Gill, S. (2019). 'I've found it extremely draining.' Emotional labour and the lived experience of line managing neurodiversity. *Personnel Review*, 48(7): 1903–1923.

41 Silberman, S (2015). *Neuro-tribes*. London: Penguin Random House.

42 Armstrong, T. (2011). *The power of neurodiversity: Unleashing the advantages of your differently wired brain*. Boston: Da Capo Lifelong Books.

43 Panksepp, J., Knutson, B., & Pruitt, D. L. (1998). Toward a neuroscience of emotion. In: Mascolo, M. F., & Griffin S. (eds) *What develops in emotional development?. Emotions, personality, and psychotherapy*. Springer, Boston, MA. https://doi.org/10.1007/978-1-4899-1939-7_3 (accessed 26-01-21).

44 Vuilleumier, P. (2005). How brains beware: Neural mechanisms of emotional attention. *Trends in Cognitive Sciences*, 9(12): 585–594.

45 Kensinger, E., & Corkin, S. (2003). Effect of negative emotional content on working memory and long-term memory. *Emotion*, 3(4): 378–393.

46 Hamilton, D. M. (2015). Calming your brain during conflict. *Harvard Business Review*, December. Available online: https://hbr.org/2015/12/calming-your-brain-during-conflict (accessed 26-01-21).

47 Lumen (no date). Boundless psychology: Structure and function of the brain. Available online: https://courses.lumenlearning.com/boundless-psychology/chapter/structure-and-function-of-the-brain/ (accessed 26-01-21).

48 Slovic, P., & Peters, E. (2006). Risk perception and affect. *Current Directions in Psychological Science*, 15(6): 322–325.

49 Tyng, C. M., Amin, H. U., Saad, M. N., & Malik, A. S. (2017). The influences of emotion on learning and memory. *Frontiers in Psychology*, 8: 1454. Available online: www.frontiersin.org/articles/10.3389/fpsyg.2017.01454/full (accessed 26-01-21).

50 Vogel, S., & Schwabe, L. (2016). Learning and memory under stress: Implications for the classroom. *npj Science of Learning*, 1(1): 1–10.

51 Oudeyer, P. Y., Gottlieb, J., & Lopes, M. (2016). Intrinsic motivation, curiosity, and learning: Theory and applications in educational technologies. *Progress in Brain Research*, 229: 257–284.

52 Ohman, A., Flykt, A., & Esteves, F. (2001). Emotion drives attention: Detecting the snake in the grass. *Journal of Experimental Psychology: General*, 130(3): 466–478.

53 Immordino-Yang, M., & Damasio, A. (2007). We feel, therefore we learn: The relevance of affective and social neuroscience to education. *Mind, Brain, and Education*, 1(1): 3–10.

54 Carlén, M. (2017). What constitutes the prefrontal cortex? *Science*, 358(6362): 478–482; Nature Research (no date) Prefrontal cortex. Available online: www.nature.com/subjects/prefrontal-cortex (accessed 26-01-21).

55 Pinsker, J. (2015). Corporations' newest productivity hack: Meditation. *The Atlantic*, 10 March. Available online: www.theatlantic.com/business/archive/2015/03/corporations-newest-productivity-hack-meditation/387286/ (accessed 26-01-21).

56 Sadler-Smith, E., & Shefy, E. (2007). Developing intuitive awareness in management education. *Academy of Management Learning & Education*, 6(2): 186–205.

57 www.businessinsider.com/ceos-who-meditate-2012-5?op=1&r=US&IR=T

58 Jonathan Passmore explains 'how to do mindfulness in coaching' in three short articles in the professional publication *The Coaching Psychologist*. Passmore, J. (2017). Mindfulness in coaching: A model for coaching practice. *The Coaching Psychologist*, 13(1): 27–30; Passmore, J. (2018). Mindfulness in coaching: Choosing our attitude. *The Coaching Psychologist*, 14(1): 48–49; Passmore, J. (2018). Mindfulness in coaching: Being the observer. *The Coaching Psychologist*, 14(2): 105–107.

59 Mindfulness All-Party Parliamentary Group (2015). *Mindful Nation UK*. London: The Mindfulness Initiative.

60 www.un.org/en/development/desa/population/publications/pdf/ageing/WorldPopulationAgeing2019-Highlights.pdf

61 Wang, J. (2018). HRD scholarship: Trends, reality, and opportunities. *Human Resource Development Review*, 17(3): 227–233.

62 Jarrett, C. (2017). *Significant loss of neurons is a normal part of aging and other brain cell myths*. British Psychological Society: Research Digest. Available online: https://digest.bps.org.uk/2017/12/01/significant-loss-of-neurons-is-a-normal-part-of-ageing-and-other-brain-cell-myths/ (accessed 13-01-21); Eichenbaum, H. (2017). Prefrontal–hippocampal interactions in episodic memory. *Nature Reviews Neuroscience*, 18(9): 547–558.

63 Beier, M. E., Teachout, M. S., & Cox, C. B. (2012). The training and development of an aging workforce. In Hedge J. W., & Borman, W. C. (eds) *The Oxford handbook of work and aging*. Oxford: Oxford University Press (pp. 436–453).

64 Brugman, G. M. (2006). Wisdom and aging. In Birren, J., & Schaie, K. W. (eds) *Handbook of the psychology of aging*. New York: Academic Press (pp. 445–476).

65 Swartz, A. (2011). Wisdom, the body, and adult learning: Insights from neuroscience. *New Directions for Adult and Continuing Education*, 131(1): 15–24.

66 Cozolino, L. (2006). *The neuroscience of human relationships*. New York: W.W. Norton; Damasio, A. (2010). *Self comes to mind: Constructing the conscious brain*. New York: Pantheon.

67 Goldberg, E. (2006). *The wisdom paradox: How your mind can grow stronger as your brain grows older*. London: Penguin.

68 CIPD (2014). *Neuroscience in action: Applying insights to L&D practice*. London: CIPD. Available online: www.cipd.co.uk/Images/neuroscience-action_2014-applying-insight-LD-practice_tcm18-9714.pdf (accessed 26-01-21).

69 Cheese, P., & Hills, J. (2016). Understanding the human at work–how neurosciences are influencing HR practices. *Strategic HR Review*. 15(4): 150–156.

Chapter 6

1 SHRM (2021). *Developing employees*. Available online: www.shrm.org/resourcesandtools/tools-and-samples/toolkits/pages/developingemployees.aspx (accessed 27-01-21).

2   CIPD (2020). *Learning Methods*. Available online: www.cipd.co.uk/knowledge/
     fundamentals/people/development/learning-methods-factsheet (accessed 27-01-21).

3   Cerasoli, C. P., Alliger, G. M., Donsbach, J. S., Mathieu, J. E., Tannenbaum, S. I., & Orvis,
     K. A. (2018). Antecedents and outcomes of informal learning behaviours: A meta-analysis.
     Journal of Business and Psychology, 33(2): 203–230.

4   Salas, E., & Cannon-Bowers, J. A. (2001). The science of training: A decade of progress.
     Annual Review of Psychology, 52: 471–499.

5   Calculated by projecting the average training budget to a weighted universe of
     127,095 companies, with more than 100 employees. See: https://trainingmag.com/
     trgmag-article/2018-training-industry-report/#:~:text=Spending%20on%20outside%20
     products%20and,13%20percent%20to%20%2447%20billion.

6   The Balance (2020). *FY 2018 Federal Budget*. Available online: www.thebalance.com/
     fy-2018-trump-federal-budget-request-4158794. (accessed 30-12-20).

7   UK Commission for Employment and Skills (no date) *Employer Investment in Training*.
     Available online: https://assets.publishing.service.gov.uk/government/uploads/system/
     uploads/attachment_data/file/306433/ukcess13-employer-investment-in-training.pdf
     (accessed 27-01-21).

8   HM Treasury (2018). Policy Paper Budget 2018. www.gov.uk/government/publications/
     budget-2018-documents/budget-2018 (accessed 30-12-20).

9   Blume, B. D., Ford, J. K., Baldwin, T. T., & Huang, J. L. (2010). Transfer of training: A
     meta-analytic review. *Journal of Management*, 36(4): 1065–1105, p. 1065.

10 Crocetti, E. (2016). Systematic reviews with meta-analysis: Why, when, and how?
     Emerging Adulthood, 4(1): 3–18.

11 McGuire, D., & Gubbins, C. (2010). The slow death of formal learning: A polemic. *Human
     Resource Development Review*, 9(3): 249–265.

12 Meyer, S. (2014) Why workplace learning fails, and why it's time to ban the fire hose.
     Forbes, 1 July. Available online: https://www.forbes.com/sites/stevemeyer/2014/07/01/why-
     workplace-learning-fails-and-why-its-time-to-ban-the-fire-hose/ (accessed 13-01-2021).

13 Blume, B. D., Ford, J. K., Baldwin, T. T., & Huang, J. L. (2010). Transfer of training: A
     meta-analytic review. *Journal of Management*, 36(4): 1065–1105.

14 Matthews, P. (2018). Near and far transfer of learning. *Training Journal*, 26 March. Available
     online: www.trainingjournal.com/blog/near-and-far-transfer-learning (accessed 30-12-20).

15 Blume, B. D., Ford, J. K., Baldwin, T. T., & Huang, J. L. (2010). Transfer of training: A
     meta-analytic review. *Journal of Management*, 36(4): 1065–1105.

16 Robinson, D. G., & Robinson, J. C. (1995). Performance consulting: Moving beyond
     training. Berrett-Koehler Publishers; Michalak, D. P (1981). The neglected half of training.
     Training and Development Journal, 35: 22–28.

17 Baldwin, T. T., & Ford, J. K. (1988). Transfer of training: A review and directions for future
     research. *Personnel Psychology*, 41(1): 63–105.

18 This is the so-called DIF (difficulty, frequency, importance) analysis. In its full form there
     are 18 different permutations. For how to apply the method in automotive training see:
     www.automotiveip.co.uk/wp-content/uploads/sites/7/2016/04/SSD1388-AIP-Guidance-
     Doc-2-of-4-Analysis-Phase-v1.pdf

19 Thorndike, E. L., & Woodworth, R. S. (1901) The influence of improvement in one
     mental function upon the efficiency of other functions. *Psychological Review*, 8: 247–261.

20 Ausubel, D. P. (1963). *The psychology of meaningful verbal learning*. New York: Grune and Stratton.

21 Goldstein, I. L., & Ford, J. K. (2002). *Training in organizations*. Belmont, CA: Wadsworth
     Thompson Learning, p. 131.

22 Perkins, D. N., & Salomon, G. (1992). Transfer of learning. *International encyclopaedia of
     education*, 2: 6452–6457.

23 Matthews, P. (2018). Near and far transfer of learning. *Training Journal*, 26 March.
     Available online: www.trainingjournal.com/blog/near-and-far-transfer-learning (accessed
     30-12-20).

24   Matthews, P. (2018). Near and far transfer of learning. *Training Journal*, 26 March. Available online: www.trainingjournal.com/blog/near-and-far-transfer-learning (accessed 30-12-20).

25   Lateef, F. (2010). Simulation-based learning: Just like the real thing. *Journal of Emergencies, Trauma, and Shock*, 3(4): 348–352, p. 348.

26   Landman, A., van Oorschot, P., van Paassen, M., Groen, E. L., Bronkhorst, A. W., & Mulder, M. (2018). Training pilots for unexpected events: A simulator study on the advantage of unpredictable and variable scenarios. *Human Factors*, 60(6): 793–805.

27   Klein, G., Moon, B., & Hoffman, R. R. (2006). Making sense of sensemaking 2: A macro-cognitive model. *IEEE Intelligent Systems*, 21(5): 88–92.

28   Mayer, R. E. (1999). Designing instruction for constructivist learning. *Instructional-design theories and models: A new paradigm of instructional theory*, 2: 141–159.

29   Rouillier, J. Z., & Goldstein, I. L. (1993). Determinants of the climate for transfer of training. *Human Resource Development Quarterly*, 4: 377–390.

30   Blume, B. D., Ford, J. K., Baldwin, T. T., & Huang, J. L. (2010). Transfer of training: A meta-analytic review. *Journal of Management*, 36(4): 1065–1105.

31   Ellingson, J. E., & Noe, R. A. (eds) (2017). *Autonomous learning in the workplace*. New York, NY: Taylor & Francis.

32   Burke, L. A., & Baldwin, T. T. (1999). Workforce training transfer: A study of the effect of relapse prevention training and transfer climate. *Human Resource Management*, 38(3): 227–242.

33   Ford, J. K., Baldwin, T. T., & Prasad, J. (2018). Transfer of training: The known and the unknown. *Annual Review of Organizational Psychology and Organizational Behaviour*, 5: 201–225.

34   Billett, S. (2004). Learning through work: Workplace participatory practices. In Fuller, A., Munro, A., & Rainbird, H. (eds) *Workplace learning in context* (pp. 125–141). New York, NY: Routledge.

35   Watkins, K. E., & Marsick, V. J. (1992). Towards a theory of informal and incidental learning in organizations. *International Journal of Lifelong Education*, 11(4): 287–300.

36   Marsick, V. J., & Watkins, K. (2015). *Informal and incidental learning in the workplace*. Abingdon: Routledge.

37   Cross, J. (2007). *Informal learning: Rediscovering the natural pathways that inspire innovation and performance*. San Francisco, CA: Pfeiffer.

38   Fuller, A. , Ashton, D. N., Felstead, A., Unwin, L., Walters, S., & Quinn, M. (2003). *The impact of informal learning at work on business productivity*. London: Department for Trade and Industry.

39   Noe, R. A., Tews, M. J., & Marand, A. D. (2013). Individual differences and informal learning in the workplace. *Journal of Vocational Behaviour*, 83(3): 327–335.

40   Eraut, M. (2004). Informal learning in the workplace. *Studies in Continuing Education*, 26(2): 247–273, p. 247.

41   Billett, S. (1995). Workplace learning: Its potential and limitations. *Education and Training*, 37(4): 20–27.

42   Poell, R. (2014). Workplace learning. In Chalofsky, N., Rocco, T., & Morris, M. L. (eds) *Handbook of human resource development*. San Francisco: Jossey-Bass, pp. 215–227.

43   Raelin, J. A. (2004). Don't bother putting leadership into people. *Academy of Management Executive*, 18(3): 131–135

44   Poell, R. (2014). Workplace learning. In Chalofsky, N., Rocco, T., & Morris, M. L. (eds) *Handbook of human resource development*. San Francisco: Jossey-Bass, pp. 215–227.

45   Cerasoli, C. P., Alliger, G. M., Donsbach, J. S., Mathieu, J. E., Tannenbaum, S. I., & Orvis, K.A. (2018). Antecedents and outcomes of informal learning behaviours: A meta-analysis. *Journal of Business Psychology*, 33: 203–230.

46   Noe, R. A., Tews, M. J., & Marand, A. D. (2013). Individual differences and informal learning in the workplace. *Journal of Vocational Behaviour*, 83(3): 327–335.

47   Marsick, V. J., & Watkins, K. E. (1990). *Informal and incidental learning in the workplace*. London: Routledge.

48 Mezirow, J. (1991). *Transformative dimensions in adult learning*. San Francisco: Jossey-Bass.

49 Noe, R. A., Tews, M. J., & Marand, A. D. (2013). Individual differences and informal learning in the workplace. *Journal of Vocational Behaviour*, 83(3): 327–335.

50 For more on the process of induction and why it is 'iterative' see: Sadler-Smith, E., & Wray, T. (2020). Abductive reasoning, creativity and the logic of intuition. In Dorfler, V. & Stierand, M. (eds) *Handbook of research methods on creativity*. Cheltenham: Edward Elgar Publishing, pp.111–125.

51 Oh, J. W., Huh, B., & Kim, M. R. (2019). Effect of learning contracts in clinical paediatric nursing education on students' outcomes: A research article. *Nurse Education Today*, 83: 104–191.

52 Boak, G. (1998). *A complete guide to learning contracts*. Aldershot: Gower Publishing.

53 Berson, J. (2018). A new paradigm for corporate training: Learning in the flow of work. Available online: https://joshbersin.com/2018/06/a-new-paradigm-for-corporate-training-learning-in-the-flow-of-work/#_ftnref1 (accessed 27-01-21).

54 Eraut, M. (2004). Informal learning in the workplace. *Studies in Continuing Education*, 26(2): 247–273.

55 Edmondson, A. (1999). Psychological safety and learning behaviour in work teams. *Administrative Science Quarterly*, 44(2): 350–383.

56 Nikolova, I., Van Ruysseveldt, J., Van Dam, K., & De Witte, H. (2016). Learning climate and workplace learning: Does work restructuring make a difference? *Journal of Personnel Psychology*, 15(2): 66–75; Nikolova, I., Van Ruysseveldt, J., De Witte, H., & Van Dam, K. (2014). Learning climate scale: Construction, reliability and initial validity evidence. *Journal of Vocational Behaviour*, 85(3): 258–265.

57 Cangialosi, N., Odoardi, C. & Battistelli, A. (2020) Learning climate and innovative work behaviour, the mediating role of the learning potential of the workplace. *Vocations and Learning*, 13: 263–280.

58 Jamu, J. T., Lowi-Jones, H., & Mitchell, C. (2016). Just in time? Using QR codes for multi-professional learning in clinical practice. *Nurse Education in Practice*, 19: 107–112.

59 Cerasoli, C. P., Alliger, G. M., Donsbach, J. S., Mathieu, J. E., Tannenbaum, S. I., & Orvis, K. A. (2018). Antecedents and outcomes of informal learning behaviours: A meta-analysis. *Journal of Business and Psychology*, 33(2): 203–230.

Chapter 7

1 Westfall, C. (2019). Leadership development is a $36bn industry: Here's why most programs don't work. *Forbes*, 20 June. Available online: www.forbes.com/sites/chriswestfall/2019/06/20/leadership-development-why-most-programs-dont-work/#4eb6002361de (accessed 27-01-21).

2 Coaching Federation (2016). *ICF Coaching Study*. Available online: https://coachfederation.org/app/uploads/2017/12/2016GCS_FactSheet.pdf (accessed 27-01-21).

3 Gutner, S. (2009). Finding anchors in the storm. *The Wall Street Journal*, 27 January. Available online: www.wsj.com/articles/SB123301451869117603 (accessed 27-01-21).

4 Jones, M. (2017). Why can't companies get mentorship programs right? *The Atlantic*, 2 June. Available online: www.theatlantic.com/business/archive/2017/06/corporate-mentorship-programs/528927/

5 Institute of Coaching (no date). *Benefits of coaching*. Available online: https://instituteofcoaching.org/coaching-overview/coaching-benefits (accessed 27-01-21).

6 Symonds, M. (2011). Executive coaching – another set of clothes for the Emperor. *Forbes*, 21 January. Available online: www.forbes.com/sites/mattsymonds/2011/01/21/executive-coaching-another-set-of-clothes-for-the-emperor/#740cdcfa118b (accessed 27-01-21).

7 Faragher, J. (no date). How to choose the right coach or mentor. Available online: http://new.coachingnetwork.org.uk/find-a-coach-mentor/the-right-coach-mentor/

(accessed 27-01-21). Faragher, J. (2012). The benefits of embedding coaching into your organization. *Personnel Today*, 7 December. Available online: www.personneltoday. com/hr/the-benefits-of-embedding-coaching-into-your-organisation/ (accessed 27-01-21).

8   Cowlett, M. (2011). Coaching and mentoring: Doing more with less training budget. *HR Magazine*, 18 May. Available online: www.hrmagazine.co.uk/article-details/coaching-and-mentoring-doing-more-with-less-training-budget (accessed 27-01-21).

9   Coaching and Mentoring Network (no date). How to choose the right coach or mentor. Available online: http://new.coachingnetwork.org.uk/find-a-coach-mentor/the-right-coach-mentor/ (accessed 27-01-21).

10 Gray, D. E., Ekinci, Y., & Goregaokar, H. (2011). Coaching SME managers: Business development or personal therapy? A mixed methods study. *The International Journal of Human Resource Management*, 22(04): 863–882, p. 863.

11 Hawkins, P. (2008). The coaching profession: Some of the key challenges. *Coaching: An International Journal of Theory, Research and Practice*, 1(1): 28–38.

12 Boersma, M. (2016). Coaching, no longer the preserve of executive. *Financial Times*, 26 February. Available online: www.ft.com/content/60d6ae0a-d0b2-11e5-92a1-c5e23ef99c77 (accessed 27-01-21).

13 Boersma, M. (2016). Coaching, no longer the preserve of executive. *Financial Times*, 26 February. Available online: www.ft.com/content/60d6ae0a-d0b2-11e5-92a1-c5e23ef99c77 (accessed 27-01-21).

14 Coaching Federation (2016). *ICF Coaching Study*. Available online: https://coachfederation.org/app/uploads/2017/12/2016GCS_FactSheet.pdf (accessed 27-01-21).

15 CIPD (2015). *Learning and development: Annual survey report.* London: CIPD. Available online: www.cipd.co.uk/Images/learning-development_2015_tcm18-11298.pdf. This version of the survey ran up until 2015 (accessed 27-01-21).

16 Grant, A. M. (2003). The impact of life coaching on goal-attainment, metacognition and mental health. *Social Behaviour and Personality*, 31: 253–264, p. 254; Gray, D. E. (2006). Executive coaching: Towards a dynamic alliance of psychotherapy and transformative learning processes. *Management Learning*, 37(4): 475–497.

17 Merrick, L. (no date). *How coaching and mentoring can drive success in your organizations* (White paper). London: Chronus Corporation.

18 The Alexander Partnership (2019). Executive coaching at Alexander. Available online: www.thealexanderpartnership.com/about-us/ (accessed 27-01-21).

19 Performance Consultants (2019). The GROW model. Available online: www.performanceconsultants.com/grow-model (accessed 27-01-21).

20 Grant, A. M. (2014). The efficacy of executive coaching in times of organisational change. *Journal of Change Management*, 14(2): 258–280.

21 Francis, S., & Zarecky, A. (2016). Working with strengths in coaching. In Bachkirova, T., Spence, G., & Drake, D. (eds) *The SAGE handbook of coaching*, pp. 363–380. London: SAGE, p. 363.

22 Bibb, S. (2017). *The strengths book*. London: LID Publishing Limited.

23 Hawkins, P. (2008). The coaching profession: Some of the key challenges. *Coaching: An International Journal of Theory, Research and Practice*, 1(1): 28–38.

24 Performance Consultants (2019). Evaluating extraordinary coaching results at EasyJet. Available online: www.performanceconsultants.com/leadership-coaching-easyjet-case-study (accessed 27-01-21); Alexander Partnership (2019). Alexander: Executive coaching. Available online: www.thealexanderpartnership.com/project/alexander-executive-coaching/ (accessed 27-01-21).

25 Gray, D. E. (2006). Executive coaching: Towards a dynamic alliance of psychotherapy and transformative learning processes. *Management Learning*, 37(4): 475–497. The late David E Gray was Professor of Leadership and Organisational Behaviour at the University of Greenwich and prior to that a professor at Surrey Business School, University of Surrey, UK. He is sadly missed by colleagues and friends.

26 House of Commons Library (2015). A short history of apprenticeships in England: From medieval craft guilds to the twenty-first century. Available online: https://commonslibrary. parliament.uk/economy-business/work-incomes/a-short-history-of-apprenticeships-in-england-from-medieval-craft-guilds-to-the-twenty-first-century/ (accessed 27-01-21).

27 Harvard TH Chan School of Public Health (no date). Who mentored you: Oprah Winfrey. Available online: https://sites.sph.harvard.edu/wmy/celebrities/oprah-winfrey/ (accessed 27-01-21).

28 Kram, K. E. (1983). Phases of the mentor relationship. *Academy of Management Journal*, 26(4): 608–625.

29 Chandler, D. E. (2011). The maven of mentoring speaks: Kathy E. Kram reflects on her career and the field. *Journal of Management Inquiry*, 20(1): 24–33.

30 ABC (no date). How to be a mentor on best practice. *ABC Radio*. Available online: https://radio.abc.net.au/programitem/pgQ7eMqgL7?play=true (accessed 27-01-21).

31 Coaching and Mentoring Network (2015). David Clutterbuck shares his thoughts about the future of coaching and mentoring. Available online: https://new.coachingnetwork. org.uk/video/david-clutterbuck-shares-his-thoughts-about-the-future-of-coaching-mentoring/ (accessed 27-01-21).

32 Clutterbuck, D. (2020). *Challenging times for coaches*. David Clutterbuck Partnership. Available online at https://www.linkedin.com/posts/prof-david-clutterbuck-84aa6b_challenging-times-for-coaches-activity-6746795146160939008-UYGU/ (accessed 29-12-20).

33 Allen, T. D., Eby, L. T., Poteet, M. L., Lentz, E., & Lima, L. (2004). Career benefits associated with mentoring for protégés: A meta-analysis. *Journal of Applied Psychology*, 89(1): 127–136.

34 Jones, M. (2017). Why can't companies get mentorship programs right? *The Atlantic*, 2 June. Available online: www.theatlantic.com/business/archive/2017/06/corporate-mentorship-programs/528927/ (accessed 13-01-21).

35 Murrell, A. J., Forte-Trammell, S., & Bing, D. (2008). *Intelligent mentoring: How IBM creates value through people, knowledge, and relationships*. London: Pearson Education.

36 McDonald, K. S., & Hite, L. M. (2005). Ethical issues in mentoring: The role of HRD. *Advances in Developing Human Resources*, 7(4): 569–582.

37 McDonald, K. S., & Hite, L. M. (2005). Ethical issues in mentoring: The role of HRD. *Advances in Developing Human Resources*, 7(4): 569–582, p. 573.

38 Arthur, M. B., & Rousseau, D. M. (1996). Introduction: The boundaryless career as a new employment principle. In M. B. Arthur & D. M. Rousseau (eds) *The boundaryless career: A new employment principle for a new organizational era*. New York, NY: Oxford University Press, pp. 3–20.

39 Arthur, M. B., and Rousseau, D. M. (1996). Introduction: The boundaryless career as a new employment principle. In M. B. Arthur & D. M. Rousseau (eds) *The boundaryless career: A new employment principle for a new organizational era*. New York, NY: Oxford University Press, pp. 3–20.

40 Hall, D. T. (2004). The protean career: A quarter-century journey. *Journal of Vocational Behaviour*, 65(1): 1–13, p. 4.

41 Super, D. E. (1969). Vocational development theory: Persons, positions, and processes. *The Counselling Psychologist*, 1(1): 2–9.

42 Werner, J. M., & DeSimone, R. L. (2011). *Human resource development*. Mason, OH: Cengage Learning, p. 385; Super, D. E. (1980). A life-span, life-space approach to career development. *Journal of Vocational Behaviour*, 16(3): 282–298.

43 Schein, E. H. (1996). Career anchors revisited: Implications for career development in the 21st century. *Academy of Management Perspectives*, 10(4): 80–88.

44 Pinnington, A. (2001). Charles Handy: The exemplary guru. *Philosophy of Management*, 1(3): 47–55.

45 Pettifor, A. (2020). BlackRock get praise for coal divestment. *The Guardian*, 16 January. Available online: www.theguardian.com/commentisfree/2020/jan/16/blackrock-coal-divestment-regulation-fund-manager (accessed 27-01-21).

46 BlackRock (2021). What we stand for. Available online: www.blackrock.com/institutions/en-axj/mission-and-principles (accessed 27-01-21).

47 Bierema, L., & Callahan, J. L. (2014). Transforming HRD: A framework for critical HRD practice. *Advances in Developing Human Resources*, 16(4): 429–444.

48 McDonald, K. S., & Hite, L. M. (2005). Reviving the relevance of career development in human resource development. *Human Resource Development Review*, 4(4): 418–439.

49 McDonald, K. S., & Hite, L. M. (2005). Reviving the relevance of career development in human resource development. *Human Resource Development Review*, 4(4): 418–439.

50 Bagnall, R. (2001). Locating lifelong learning and education in contemporary currents of thought and culture. In Aspin, D., Chapman, J., Hatton, M., & Sawano, Y. (eds) *International handbook of lifelong learning* (pp. 35–52). Dordrecht: Springer.

51 CIPD (2021). Career option in the people profession. Available online: www.cipd.co.uk/careers/career-options? (accessed 27-01-21).

52 SHRM (2021). Career in HRM. Available online: www.shrm.org/membership/student-resources/pages/careersinhrm.aspx. (accessed 27-01-21).

53 Northouse, P. (2016). *Leadership: Theory and practice*. Thousand Oaks: SAGE, p. 7.

54 Ardichvili, A., Natt och Dag, K., & Manderscheid, S. (2016). Leadership development: Current and emerging models and practices. *Advances in Developing Human Resources*, 18(3): 275–285.

55 See the special issue of *The Leadership Quarterly* in 2007: Tierney, P., & Tepper, B. J. (2007). Introduction to The Leadership Quarterly special issue: Destructive leadership. *The Leadership Quarterly*, 3(18): 171–173.

56 Cribb, J. & Johnson, P. (2018). 10 years on – have we recovered from the financial crisis? Institute for Fiscal Studies. Available online: www.ifs.org.uk/publications/13302 (accessed 27-01-21).

57 Doh, J. P. (2003). Can leadership be taught? Perspectives from management educators. *Academy of Management Learning & Education*, 2(1): 54–67.

58 SHRM (2018). Leadership competencies. Available online: www.shrm.org/resourcesandtools/hr-topics/behavioral-competencies/leadership-and-navigation/pages/leadershipcompetencies.aspx (accessed 27-01-21).

59 NHS Leadership Academy (2011), Clinical leadership competency framework. Warwick: NHS. Available online: www.leadershipacademy.nhs.uk/wp-content/uploads/2012/11/NHSLeadership-Leadership-Framework-Clinical-Leadership-Competency-Framework-CLCF.pdf (accessed 27-01-21)

60 Raelin, J. A. (2004). Don't bother putting leadership into people. *Academy of Management Executive*, 18(3): 131–135.

61 The Centre for Creative Leadership. Available online: www.ccl.org/

62 Raven, B. H. (1992). A power/interaction model of interpersonal influence: French and Raven thirty years later. *Journal of Social Behavior and Personality*, 7(2): 217–244.

63 Raven, B. H., & Bertram, H. (2004). Power, Six Bases of. *Encyclopaedia of Leadership*. Thousand Oaks: SAGE.

64 Day, D. V. (2000). Leadership development: A review in context. *The Leadership Quarterly*, 11(4): 581–613.

65 Day, D. V. (2021). Leadership development. In Bryman, A., Collinson, D., Grint, K., Jackson, B., & Uhl-Bien, M. (eds) *The SAGE handbook of leadership*. London: SAGE.

66 For a critical review of the great man theory see: Mouton, N. (2019). A literary perspective on the limits of leadership: Tolstoy's critique of the great man theory. *Leadership*, 15(1): 81–102.

67 Andersen, E. (2012). Are leaders born or made. *Forbes*, 21 November. Available online: www.forbes.com/sites/erikaandersen/2012/11/21/are-leaders-born-or-made/#45a241b48d56 (accessed 27-01-21).

68 Deloitte (2016). Learning and leadership. Available online: www2.deloitte.com/us/en/pages/human-capital/solutions/employee-development-methods-for-hr.html (accessed 27-01-21).

69 Gurdjian, P., Halbeisen, T., & Lane, K. (2014). Why leadership-development programs fail. *McKinsey Quarterly*, 1(1): 121–126.

70 Lacerenza, C. N., Reyes, D. L., Marlow, S. L., Joseph, D. L., & Salas, E. (2017). Leadership training design, delivery, and implementation: A meta-analysis. *Journal of Applied Psychology*, 102(12): 1686–1718.

71 Collins, D. B., & Holton III, E. F. (2004). The effectiveness of managerial leadership development programs: A meta-analysis of studies from 1982 to 2001. *Human Resource Development Quarterly*, 15(2): 217–248.

72 DeRue, D. S., & Myers, C. G. (2014). Leadership development: A review and agenda for future research. In Day, D. V. (ed.) *The Oxford handbook of leadership and organizations* (pp. 832–855). Oxford: Oxford University Press.

73 Raelin, J. A. (2015). Rethinking leadership. *MIT Sloan Management Review*, 56(4): 95–96.

74 Schon, D. A. (1987). *Educating the reflective practitioner*. San Francisco: Jossey-Bass.

75 Raelin, J. A. 2004). Don't bother putting leadership into people. *Academy of Management Executive*, 18(3): 131–135.

76 McCall, M. W. (2004). Leadership development through experience. *The Academy of Management Executive*, 18(3): 127–130.

77 Skipton Leonard, H., & Lang, F. (2010). Leadership development via action learning. *Advances in Developing Human Resources*, 12(2): 225–240.

78 Crossan, M., Mazutis, D., Seijts, G., & Gandz, J. (2013). Developing leadership character in business programs. *Academy of Management Learning & Education*, 12(2): 285–305.

79 Clutterbuck, D. (2020). An eclectic perspective on coaching supervision. In Lucas, M. (ed.) *101 Coaching supervision techniques, approaches, enquiries and experiments*. London: Routledge.

80 Moberg, D. (2008). Mentoring and practical wisdom: Are mentors wiser or just more politically skilled? *Journal of Business Ethics*, 83(4): 835–843.

Chapter 8

1 McBride, S. (2019). These three computing technologies will beat Moore's law. *Forbes*, 23 April. Available online: www.forbes.com/sites/stephenmcbride1/2019/04/23/these-3-computing-technologies-will-beat-moores-law/?sh=5505164a37b0 (accessed 27-01-21).

2 James, K. S. (2011). India's demographic change: Opportunities and challenges. *Science* (July): 576–580

3 The World Bank (2020). School enrolment, tertiary (gross %). Available online: https://data.worldbank.org/indicator/SE.TER.ENRR (accessed 27-01-21).

4 Pinker, S. (2018), *Enlightenment now*. London: Allen Lane.

5 OECD (2017). Inequality. Available online: www.oecd.org/social/inequality.htm (accessed 27-01-21).

6 UNHCR (2019). Figures at a glance. Available online: www.unhcr.org/uk/figures-at-a-glance.html (accessed 13-01-21).

7 www.un.org/press/en/2019/gaef3516.doc.htm (accessed 27-01-21).

8 PwC (2016). Five megatrends. Available online: www.pwc.com/gx/en/government-public-services/assets/five-megatrends-implications.pdf (accessed 27-02-21).

9 Horner, R., Schindler, S., Haberly, D., & Aoyama, Y. (2018). Globalisation, uneven development and the North–South 'big switch'. *Cambridge Journal of Regions, Economy and Society*, 11(1): 17–33.

10 Yueh, L. (2013). Krugman vs Stiglitz on what's holding back the recovery. *BBC News*, 21 November. Available online: www.bbc.co.uk/news/business-25035267 (accessed 27-01-21).

11 The White House (2009). Remarks of President Obama, 24 February. Available online: https://obamawhitehouse.archives.gov/the-press-office/remarks-president-barack-obama-address-joint-session-congress (accessed 27-01-21)

12 OECD (2019). The future of work. Available online: www.oecd.org/employment/Employment-Outlook-2019-Highlight-EN.pdf (accessed 27-01-21).

13 CIPD (2015). *Avoiding the demographic crunch*. London: CIPD. Available online: www.cipd. co.uk/Images/avoiding-the-demographic-crunch-labour-supply-and-ageing-workforce_ tcm18-10235.pdf (accessed 27-01-21).

14 OECD (2016). Science, technology and innovation outlook. Available online: www.oecd. org/sti/Megatrends%20affecting%20science,%20technology%20and%20innovation.pdf (accessed 27-01-21).

15 PwC (no date). The Fourth Industrial Revolution: Are you ready? Available online: www. pwc.com/us/en/library/4ir-ready.html (accessed 29-01-21).

16 Deloitte (2016). The rise of the platform economy. Available online: www2.deloitte. com/content/dam/Deloitte/nl/Documents/humancapital/deloitte-nl-hc-reshaping-work-conference.pdf (accessed 27-01-21).

17 Wharton School (2017). How to mange the top five global economic challenges. Available online: https://knowledge.wharton.upenn.edu/article/what-are-the-top-five-challenges-for-international-organizations/(accessed 27-01-21).

18 World Economic Forum (2016). the fourth industrial revolution. Available online: www. weforum.org/agenda/2016/01/the-fourth-industrial-revolution-what-it-means-and-how-to-respond/ (accessed 27-01-21).

19 The Royal Society (no date). Can machines really learn? Available online: https:// royalsociety.org/topics-policy/projects/machine-learning/what-is-machine-learning-infographic/ (accessed 27-01-21).

20 OECD (2016). Science, technology and innovation outlook. Available online: www.oecd. org/sti/Megatrends%20affecting%20science,%20technology%20and%20innovation.pdf (accessed 13-01-21).

21 Insight (2019). Using AI in learning and development. Available online: www.insight. com/en_US/content-and-resources/2019/10252019-using-artificial-intelligence-for-learning-and-development.html (accessed 27-01-21).

22 World Economic Forum (2019). *HR4.0: Shaping people strategies in the fourth industrial revolution*. Geneva: WEF, p. 5.

23 OECD (2016). Science, technology and innovation outlook. Available online: www. oecd.org/sti/Megatrends%20affecting%20science,%20technology%20and%20 innovation.pdf (accessed 13-01-21).

24 Myers, S. L. , Wu, J., & Fu, C. (2020). China's looming crisis – a shrinking population. *New York Times*, 17 January. Available online: www.nytimes.com/interactive/2019/01/17/ world/asia/china-population-crisis.html (accessed 27-01-21).

25 Eisenberg, R. (2018). How these three countries embrace older workers. *Forbes*, 10 May. Available online: www.forbes.com/sites/nextavenue/2018/05/10/how-these-3-countries-embrace-older-workers/?sh=37d3546d1bd4 (accessed 27-01-21).

26 Bagnall, R. (2001). Locating lifelong learning and education in contemporary currents of thought and culture. In Aspin, D., Chapman, J., Hatton, M., & Sawano, Y. (eds) *International handbook of lifelong learning* (pp. 35–52). Dordrecht: Springer.

27 CIPD (2015). *Avoiding the demographic crunch*. London: CIPD. Available online: www.cipd. co.uk/Images/avoiding-the-demographic-crunch-labour-supply-and-ageing-workforce_ tcm18-10235.pdf (accessed 27-01-21).

28 Ericsson, K. A., Prietula, M. J., & Cokely, E. T. (2007). The making of an expert. *Harvard Business Review*, 85(7/8): 114–121.

29 CIPD (2015). *Avoiding the demographic crunch*. London: CIPD. Available online: www.cipd. co.uk/Images/avoiding-the-demographic-crunch-labour-supply-and-ageing-workforce_ tcm18-10235.pdf (accessed 27-01-21).

30 Freeman, R. E. (1984). *Strategic management: A stakeholder approach*. Boston, MA: Pitman, p. 46.

31 Freeman R. E. (n.d.). Business is about purpose. Available online: www.youtube.com/ watch?v=7dugfwJthBY&feature=emb_title (accessed 13-01-21).

32 Brugha, R., & Varvasovszky, Z. (2000). Stakeholder analysis: A review. *Health Policy and Planning*, 15(3): 239–246

33 CIPD (2018). *Creating and capturing value at work: Who benefits?* London: CIPD.

34 BBC (2021). The Reith Lectures: Mark Carney, How we get what we value. 4 December.

35 Elliott, C., & Turnbull, S. (eds) (2004). *Critical thinking in human resource development.* Abingdon: Routledge.

36 Business Roundtable (2019). Purpose of a corporation. Available online: www.businessroundtable.org/business-roundtable-redefines-the-purpose-of-a-corporation-to-promote-an-economy-that-serves-all-americans (accessed 27-01-21).

37 Elkington, J. (1998). Accounting for the triple bottom line. *Measuring Business Excellence* 2(3): 18–22; Elkington, J. (2018). 25 years ago I coined the phrase 'triple bottom line.' Here's why it's time to rethink it. *Harvard Business Review*, 25: 2–5.

38 Garavan, T. N. (1995). Stakeholders and strategic human resource development. *Journal of European Industrial Training*, 19(10): 11–16.

39 Colakoglu, S., Lepak, D. P., & Hong, Y. (2006). Measuring HRM effectiveness: Considering multiple stakeholders in a global context. *Human Resource Management Review*, 16(2): 209–218.

40 March, J. G. (1991). Exploration and exploitation in organizational learning. *Organization Science*, 2(1): 71–87.

41 Russell, B. (1938/2004). *Power: A New Social Analysis.* Abingdon: Routledge.

42 Clegg, S., Courpasson, D., & Phillips, N. (2006). *Power and organizations.* London: SAGE.

43 Schein, E. (1992). *Organisational Culture and Leadership.* San Francisco: Jossey-Bass.

44 Knowles, M. S., Holton, E. F., & Swanson, R. A. (1998). *The adult learner: The definitive classic in adult education and human resource development* (5th ed.). Houston, TX: Gulf.

45 Bierema, L., & Callahan, J. L. (2014). Transforming HRD: A framework for critical HRD practice. *Advances in Developing Human Resources*, 16(4): 429–444.

46 Vince, R. (2014). What do HRD scholars and practitioners need to know about power, emotion, and HRD? *Human Resource Development Quarterly*, 25(4): 409–420.

47 Trehan, K. (2004). Who is not sleeping with whom? What's not being talked about in HRD?. *Journal of European Industrial Training*, 28(1): 23–38.

48 Bierema, L., & Callahan, J. L. (2014). Transforming HRD: A framework for critical HRD practice. *Advances in Developing Human Resources*, 16(4): 429–444.

49 Sambrook, S. (2014). Critical HRD. In Chalofsky, N., Rocco, T., & Morris, M. L. (eds) *Handbook of human resource development.* Hoboken, NJ: Wiley, pp. 145–163.

50 Sometimes referred to as WEIRD samples, that is white, educated, industrialized, rich and democratic. See: Henrich, J., Heine, S. J., & Norenzayan, A. (2010). The weirdest people in the world? *Behavioral and Brain Sciences*, 33(2–3): 61–83.

51 Gedro, J. (2010). Understanding, designing, and teaching LGBT issues. *Advances in Developing Human Resources*, 12(3): 352–366.

52 National Geographic (2016). Climate milestone: Earth's CO_2 level passes 400ppm. Available online: www.nationalgeographic.org/article/climate-milestone-earths-co2-level-passes-400-ppm/ (accessed 14-01-21).

53 Based on Donald Trump's claims about climate change.

54 See Science-Based Targets (2020). https://sciencebasedtargets.org/https://sciencebasedtargets.org/

55 IATA (2021). Halving emission by 2050. Available online: www.iata.org/en/pressroom/pr/2009-12-08-01/. (accessed 27-01-21).

56 See: www.ericsson.com/en/about-us/sustainability-and-corporate-responsibility/environment/science-based-targets; www.theguardian.com/sustainable-business/blog/counting-carbon-emissions-targets-science (accessed 15-04-20).

57 See Science-Based Targets (2020). https://sciencebasedtargets.org/

58 Garavan, T. N., & McGuire, D. (2010). Human resource development and society: Human resource development's role in embedding corporate social responsibility, sustainability, and ethics in organizations. *Advances in Developing Human Resources*, 12(5): 487–507.

59 Valentin, C. (2015). Greening HRD: Conceptualizing the triple bottom line for HRD practice, teaching, and research. *Advances in Developing Human Resources*, 17(4): 426–441.

60 McGuire, D. (2014). *Human resource development.* London: SAGE.

61 Sadler-Smith, E. (2014). Making sense of global warming: Designing a human resource development response. *European Journal of Training and Development,* 38(5): 387–397.

62 Engelmann, J. M., & Herrmann, E. (2016). Chimpanzees trust their friends. *Current Biology,* 26(2): 252–256; Lehmann, J., Korstjens, A. H., & Dunbar, R. I. M. (2007). Group size, grooming and social cohesion in primates. *Animal Behaviour,* 74(6): 1617–1629.

63 Bachmann, R., & Zaheer, A. (eds) (2013). *Handbook of advances in trust research.* Edward Elgar Publishing; see: www.spiegel.de/international/business/deutsche-bank-reputation-at-stake-amid-a-multitude-of-scandals-a-873544.html

64 Rousseau, D. M., Sitkin, S. B., Burt, R. S., & Camerer, C. (1998). Not so different after all: A cross-discipline view of trust. *Academy of Management Review,* 23(3): 393–404.

65 Saunders, M. N., Dietz, G., & Thornhill, A. (2014). Trust and distrust: Polar opposites, or independent but co-existing? *Human Relations,* 67(6): 639–665.

66 Gubbins, C., Harney., B., van der Werff, L., and Rousseau, D. M. (2018). Enhancing the trustworthiness and credibility of HRD: Evidence-based management to the rescue? *Human Resource Development Quarterly,* 29(3): 193–202.

67 Gubbins, C., & Garavan, T. (2016). Social capital effects on the career and development outcomes of HR professionals. *Human Resource Management,* 55(2): 241–260.

68 Available online: https://obamawhitehouse.archives.gov/administration/eop/ostp/grand-challenges (accessed 31-01-21).

69 McLean, G. N., & McLean, L. (2001). If we can't define HRD in one country, how can we define it in an international context? *Human Resource Development International,* 4(3): 313–326, p. 322.

Chapter 9

1 Kotter, J. P., & Cohen, D. S. (2012). *The heart of change: Real-life stories of how people change their organizations.* Boston, MA: Harvard Business Press, p. xii.

2 Bae, H. (2015). Bill Gates 40th anniversary email. Available online: https://money.cnn.com/2015/04/05/technology/bill-gates-email-microsoft-40-anniversary/index.html (accessed 25-10-19).

3 Read more about how Gates' vision at Microsoft was implemented in the words of its former COO Robert J. Herbold and how the company managed to balance creativity and discipline at: Herbold, R. J. (2002). Inside Microsoft: Balancing creativity and discipline. *Harvard Business Review.* https://hbr.org/2002/01/inside-microsoft-balancing-creativity-and-discipline

4 Scholes, K., Johnson, G., & Whittington, R. (2002). *Exploring corporate strategy.* Harlow: Financial Times Prentice Hall, p. 4 (original italics).

5 Eley, J. (2020). The rise and fall of Phillip Green's Arcadia retail empire. *Financial Times,* 30 November. Available online: www.ft.com/content/cd2e9b8a-c9b6-4a2f-8810-cb749ea37421 (accessed 27-01-21).

6 Pirie, M. (2014). Gary Becker was right: Part Five, Human Capital. Adam Smith Institute. www.adamsmith.org/blog/uncategorized/gary-becker-was-right-part-five-human-capital; Becker, G. (1994). *Human Capital: A Theoretical and Empirical Analysis with Special Reference to Education,* Third Edition. Chicago: University of Chicago Press. Published by National Bureau of Economic Research. www.nber.org/books/beck94-1 (accessed 19-10-19).

7 Penrose, E. (1959/2009). *The Theory of the Growth of the Firm.* Oxford: Oxford University Press.

8 Thompson, S., & Wright, M. (2005). Edith Penrose's contribution to economics and strategy: An overview. *Managerial and Decision Economics,* 26(2): 57–66, p. 63.

9 Jiang, K., & Messersmith, J. (2018). On the shoulders of giants: A meta-review of strategic human resource management. *The International Journal of Human Resource Management,* 29(1): 6–33.

10 Barney, J. B. (1986). Strategic factor markets: Expectations, luck and business strategy. *Management Science*, 42: 1231–1241; Wernerfelt, B. (1995). The resource-based view of the firm: Ten years after. *Strategic Management Journal*, 16(3): 171–174.

11 Barney, J., Wright, M., & Ketchen Jr, D. J. (2001). The resource-based view of the firm: Ten years after 1991. *Journal of Management*, 27(6): 625–641; Rugman, A. M., & Verbeke, A. (2002). Edith Penrose's contribution to the resource-based view of strategic management. *Strategic Management Journal*, 23(8): 769–780; Kor, Y. Y., & Mahoney, J. T. (2004). Edith Penrose's (1959) contributions to the resource-based view of strategic management. *Journal of Management Studies*, 41(1): 183–191.

12 Barney, J., Wright, M., & Ketchen Jr, D. J. (2001). The resource-based view of the firm: Ten years after 1991. *Journal of Management*, 27(6): 625–641.

13 Delery, J. E., & Roumpi, D. (2017). Strategic human resource management, human capital and competitive advantage: Is the field going in circles? *Human Resource Management Journal*, 27(1): 1–21.

14 World Economic Forum (no date). Fourth Industrial Revolution. Available online: www.weforum.org/focus/fourth-industrial-revolution (accessed 27-01-21).

15 Wright, P. M., Dunford, B. B., & Snell, S. A. (2001). Human resources and the resource based view of the firm. *Journal of Management*, 27(6): 701–721.

16 Priem, R. L., & Butler, J. E. (2001). Is the resource-based 'view' a useful perspective for strategic management research? *Academy of Management Review*, 26(1): 22–40.

17 Kaufman, B. E. (2015). The RBV theory foundation of strategic HRM: Critical flaws, problems for research and practice, and an alternative economics paradigm. *Human Resource Management Journal*, 25(4): 516–540.

18 Teece, D. J., Pisano, G., & Shuen, A. (1997). Dynamic capabilities and strategic management. *Strategic Management Journal*, 18(7): 509–533.

19 Teece, D. J. (2007). Explicating dynamic capabilities: The nature and microfoundations of (sustainable) enterprise performance. *Strategic Management Journal*, 28(13): 1319–1350, p. 1321.

20 See: Giddens, A. (1984).*The constitution of society: Outline of the theory of structuration.* Berkeley: University of California Press.

21 Kleiner, A. (2013). The dynamic capabilities of David Teece. *Strategy + Business*. Available online: www.strategy-business.com/article/00225?gko=32b8d (accessed 27-01-21).

22 Teece, D. J. (2007). Explicating dynamic capabilities: The nature and microfoundations of (sustainable) enterprise performance. *Strategic Management Journal*, 28(13): 1319–1350.

23 See Josh Bersin https://joshbersin.com/

24 Langley, A. (2007). Process thinking in strategic organization. *Strategic Organization*, 5(3): 271–282; Montgomery, C. A. (2008). Putting leadership back into strategy. *Harvard Business Review*, 86(1): 54–60.

25 Elliott, C. (2000). Does HRD acknowledge human becomings? A view of the UK literature. *Human Resource Development Quarterly*, 11(2): 187–195, p. 188.

26 Wright, P. M., Snell, S. A., & Dyer, L. (2005). New models of strategic HRM in a global context. *The International Journal of Human Resource Management*, 16(6): 875–881.

27 Schuler, R. S., & Jackson, S. E. (2005). A quarter-century review of human resource management in the US: The growth in importance of the international perspective. *Management Revue*, 16(1): 11–35.

28 Cascio, W. F. (2015). Strategic HRM: Too important for an insular approach. *Human Resource Management*, 54(3): 423–426, p. 423.

29 Ernst and Young (2016). The call for a more strategic HR: How its leaders are stepping up to the plate. Available online: https://hbr.org/sponsored/2016/04/the-call-for-a-more-strategic-hr (accessed 14-10-19).

30 Armstrong, M., & Baron, A. (2002). *Strategic HRM: The key to improved business performance.* Wimbledon: CIPD Publishing, p. 105

31 For example: Arthur, J. B. (1994). Effects of human resource systems on manufacturing performance and turnover. *Academy of Management Journal*, 37(3): 670–687; Huselid, M. A., Jackson, S. E., & Schuler, R. S. (1997). Technical and strategic human resources management effectiveness as determinants of firm performance. *Academy of Management Journal*, 40(1): 171–188.

32 Lervik, J. E., Hennestad, B. W., Amdam, R. P., Lunnan, R., & Nilsen, S. M. (2005). Implementing human resource development best practices: Replication or re-creation? *Human Resource Development International*, 8(3): 345–360.

33 Saridakis, G., Lai, Y., & Cooper, C. L. (2017). Exploring the relationship between HRM and firm performance: A meta-analysis of longitudinal studies. *Human Resource Management Review*, 27(1): 87–96.

34 Jiang, K., & Messersmith, J. (2018). On the shoulders of giants: A meta-review of strategic human resource management. *The International Journal of Human Resource Management*, 29(1): 6–33; Saridakis, G., Lai, Y., & Cooper, C. L. (2017). Exploring the relationship between HRM and firm performance: A meta-analysis of longitudinal studies. *Human Resource Management Review*, 27(1): 87–96.

35 Schuler, R. S., & Jackson, S. E. (2005). A quarter-century review of human resource management in the US: The growth in importance of the international perspective. *Management Revue*, 16(1): 11–35.

36 Schuler, R. S., & Jackson, S. E. (2005). A quarter-century review of human resource management in the US: The growth in importance of the international perspective. *Management Revue*, 16(1): 11–35.

37 Garavan, T. N. (2007). A strategic perspective on human resource development. *Advances in Developing Human Resources*, 9(1): 11–30, p. 25.

38 Hawkins, M. (2015). Make L&D strategic to the business-and prove its value. *Association for Talent Development*. www.td.org/insights/make-l-d-strategic-to-the-businessand-prove-its-value

39 Wognum, A. A. M. (2001). Vertical integration of HRD policy within companies. *Human Resource Development International*, 4(3): 407–421.

40 Heneman III, H. G., & Milanowski, A. T. (2011). Assessing human resource practices alignment: A case study. *Human Resource Management*, 50(1): 45–64.

41 Cascio, W. F., & Boudreau, J. W. (2012). *Short introduction to strategic human resource management*. Cambridge: Cambridge University Press.

42 Society for Human Resource Management (n.d.). *Managing organizational change*. www.shrm.org/resourcesandtools/tools-and-samples/toolkits/pages/managingorganizationalchange.aspx (accessed 01-11-19).

43 Sadler-Smith, E. (2006). *Learning and development for managers*. Oxford: Blackwell.

44 Bailey, C., Mankin, D., Kelliher, C., & Garavan, T. (2018). *Strategic human resource management*. Oxford: Oxford University Press.

45 Mitsakis, F. (2019). Modify the redefined: Strategic human resource development maturity at a crossroads. *Human Resource Development Review*, 18(4): 470–506.

46 McGuire, D. (2014). *Human resource development*. London: SAGE, p. 143.

47 Garavan, T. N. (2007). A strategic perspective on human resource development. *Advances in Developing Human Resources*, 9(1): 11–30.

48 Garavan, T., Shanahan, V., Carbery, R., & Watson, S. (2016). Strategic human resource development: Towards a conceptual framework to understand its contribution to dynamic capabilities. *Human Resource Development International*, 19(4): 289–306; McCracken, M., & Wallace, M. (2000). Towards a redefinition of strategic HRD. *Journal of European Industrial Training*, 24(5): 281–290.

49 Garavan, T. N. (1991). Strategic human resource development. *Journal of European Industrial Training*, 15(1), 17–30.

50 Garavan, T. N. (2007). A strategic perspective on human resource development. *Advances in Developing Human Resources*, 9(1): 11–30.

51 Garavan, T. N. (2007). A strategic perspective on human resource development. *Advances in Developing Human Resources*, 9(1), 11–30.

52 McKinsey and Co. (2019). The essential components of a successful L&D strategy. www.mckinsey.com/business-functions/organization/our-insights/the-essential-components-of-a-successful-l-and-d-strategy (accessed 23-10-19).

53 Garavan, T., Shanahan, V., Carbery, R., & Watson, S. (2016). Strategic human resource development: Towards a conceptual framework to understand its contribution to dynamic capabilities. *Human Resource Development International*, 19(4): 289–306.

54 Hodgkinson, G. P., & Healey, M. P. (2011). Psychological foundations of dynamic capabilities: Reflexion and reflection in strategic management. *Strategic Management Journal*, 32(13): 1500–1516.

55 Sadler-Smith, E. (2010). *The intuitive mind: Profiting from the power of your sixth sense*. Chichester: John Wiley and Sons.

56 CIPD (2020). *Learning and Development Strategy Factsheet*. London: CIPD. www.cipd.co.uk/knowledge/strategy/development/factsheet

57 *Learning and Development Strategy 2014-2019*. Nottinghamshire Health Care NHS Trust.

58 Boselie, P., & Brewster, C. (2015). The search for panaceas in strategic Human Resource Management: A wrong turn for HRM research? *Handbook of Research on Management Ideas and Panaceas: Adaptation and Context*, 130; Farndale, E., & Paauwe, J. (2018). SHRM and context: why firms want to be as different as legitimately possible. *Journal of Organizational Effectiveness*, 5(3): 202–210; Guest, D., & King, Z. (2004). Power, innovation and problem-solving: The personnel managers' three steps to heaven? *Journal of Management Studies*, 41(3): 401–423.

59 Jackson, S. E., Kim, A., & Schuler, R. S. (2018). HRM practice and scholarship in North America. In Brewster, C., Mayrhofer, W., & Farndale, E. (eds) *Handbook of research on comparative human resource management*. Cheltenham: Edward Elgar Publishing.

60 Colakoglu, S., Lepak, D. P., & Hong, Y. (2006). Measuring HRM effectiveness: Considering multiple stakeholders in a global context. *Human Resource Management Review*, 16(2): 209–218.

61 Burn-Callander, R. (2015). Unilever boss Paul Polman slams capitalist obsession with profit. *Daily Telegraph*, 28 January. Available online: www.telegraph.co.uk/ finance/newsbysector/epic/ulvr/11372550/Unilever-boss-Paul-Polman-slams-capitalist-obsession-with-profit.html (accessed 01-11-19).

62 Järlström, M., Saru, E., & Vanhala, S. (2018). Sustainable human resource management with salience of stakeholders: A top management perspective. *Journal of Business Ethics*, 152(3): 703–724.

63 McGuire, D. (2014). *Human resource development*. London: SAGE.

64 Hamlin, R. & Jim Stewart, J. (2011). What is HRD? A definitional review and synthesis of the HRD domain. *Journal of European Industrial Training*, 35 (3): 199–220; Lee, M. M. (1997). Strategic human resource development: A conceptual exploration. In *Academy of human resource development conference proceedings* (pp. 92–99). Baton Rouge, LA: Academy of HRD.

65 Garavan, T. N., Barnicle, B., & Heraty, N. (1993). The training and development function: Its search for power and influence in organizations. *Journal of European Industrial Training*, 17(7): 22–32.

66 Torraco, R. J., & Lundgren, H. (2020). What HRD is doing – What HRD should be doing: The case for transforming HRD. *Human Resource Development Review*, 19(1): 39–65.

Chapter 10

1 Dooley, C. R. (2001). The training within industry report 1940–1945. *Advances in Developing Human Resources*, 3(2): 127–289.

2 Baek, P., & Kim, N. (2014). Exploring a theoretical foundation for HRD in society: Toward a model of stakeholder-based HRD. *Human Resource Development International*, 17(5): 499–513.

3 Allen, W. C., & Swanson, R. A. (2006). Systematic training – Straightforward and effective. *Advances in Developing Human Resources*, 8(4): 427–429.

4 Iles, P., & Yolles, M. (2003). Complexity, HRD and organisation development: Towards a viable systems approach to learning, development and change. In Lee, M. (ed.) *HRD in a complex world*. London: Routledge, pp. 25–41.

5 Wilson, K. Y. (2010). An analysis of bias in supervisor narrative comments in performance appraisal. *Human Relations*, 63(12): 1903–1933.

6 CIPD Learning Needs Fact Sheet. Available online: www.cipd.co.uk/knowledge/fundamentals/people/development/learning-needs-factsheet (accessed 13-01-21).

7 Eurostat Statistics Explained (no date). Glossary: Business functions. Available online: https://ec.europa.eu/eurostat/statistics-explained/index.php/Glossary:Business_functions (accessed 13-01-21).

8 Gubbins, C., Harney, B., van der Werff, L., & Rousseau, D. (2018). Enhancing the trustworthiness and credibility of HRD: Evidence-based management to the rescue? *Human Resource Development Quarterly*, 29(3): 193–202.

9 Beer, M., Boselie, P., & Brewster, C. (2015). Back to the future: Implications for the field of HRM of the multistakeholder perspective proposed 30 years ago. *Human Resource Management*, 54(3): 427–438.

10 Cardon, M. S., & Stevens, C. E. (2004). Managing human resources in small organizations: What do we know? *Human Resource Management Review*, 14(3): 295–323.

11 Federation of Small Businesses (2019). UK Small Business Statistics. Available online: www.fsb.org.uk/uk-small-business-statistics.html (accessed 27-01-21).

12 World Bank (no date). Small and Medium Enterprises (SMEs) Finance. Available online: www.worldbank.org/en/topic/smefinance (accessed 27-01-21).

13 Carbery, R. (2015). Introduction to HRD. In Carbery, R. and Cross, C. (eds) *Human resource development: A concise introduction*. London: Palgrave, pp. 1–25.

14 CIPD (2020). *Learning and skills at work 2020*. London: Chartered Institute of Personnel and Development.

15 Hill, R., & Stewart, J. (2000). Human resource development in small organizations. *Journal of European Industrial Training*, 24: 105–117.

16 www.oecd.org/industry/C-MIN-2017-8-EN.pdf

17 Nolan, C. T., & Garavan, T. N. (2016). Problematizing HRD in SMEs: A 'critical' exploration of context, informality, and empirical realities. *Human Resource Development Quarterly*, 27(3): 407–442.

18 Short, H. (2019). Learning in SMEs. *Human Resource Development International*, 22(5): 413–419.

19 Nolan, C. T., & Garavan, T. N. (2016). Problematizing HRD in SMEs: A 'critical' exploration of context, informality, and empirical realities. *Human Resource Development Quarterly*, 27(3): 407–442.

20 Short, H. (2019) Learning in SMEs. *Human Resource Development International*, 22(5): 413–419.

21 Nolan, C. T., & Garavan, T. N. (2015). HRD in smaller firms: Current issues, insights and future directions in research and practice. In Chalofsky, N., Rocco, T., & Morris, M. L. (eds) *Handbook of human resource development*. Hoboken, NJ: John Wiley and Sons, pp. 526–546.

22 Organization Development Network, www.odnetwork.org/

23 McLean, G. (2005). *Organization development: Principles, processes, performance*. San Francisco: Berrett-Koehler Publishers, p. 25.

24 Gallos, J. V. (ed.) (2006). *Organization development: A Jossey-Bass reader*. San Francisco: Jossey-Bass/Wiley.

25 DeMars, S. K. (2006). Organization development: Principles, process, performance (Book review). *Performance Improvement*, 45(8): 41–43.

26 McLean, G. (2005). *Organization development: Principles, processes, performance.* San Francisco: Berrett-Koehler Publishers; Cummings, T. G., & Worley, C. G. (2014). *Organization development and change.* Boston, MA: Cengage Learning.

27 Armstrong, C. (2015). Organization development. In Carbery, R., & Cross, C. (eds) *Human resource development: A concise introduction.* London: Palgrave, pp. 103–116.

28 Metcalfe, B. D., & Rees, C. J. (2005). Theorizing advances in international human resource development. *Human Resource Development International,* 8(4): 449–465, p. 455.

29 Anderson, V. (2015). International HRD and offshore outsourcing: A conceptual review and research agenda. *Human Resource Development Review,* 14(3): 259–278.

30 Garavan, T., McCarthy, A., & Carbery, R. (eds) (2017). International HRD: Context, processes and people–introduction. In Garavan, T., McCarthy, A., & Carbery, R. (eds) *Handbook of international human resource development.* Cheltenham: Edward Elgar Publishing

31 Yawson, R. M. (2013). Systems theory and thinking as a foundational theory in human resource development – A myth or reality? *Human Resource Development Review,* 12(1): 53–85.

32 Levin, S. A. (1998) Ecosystems and the biosphere as complex adaptive systems. *Ecosystems,* 1: 431–436, p, 431.

33 Levin, S. A. (1998) Ecosystems and the biosphere as complex adaptive systems. *Ecosystems,* 1: 431–436.

34 Bonabeau, E. (1998). Social insect colonies as complex adaptive systems. *Ecosystems,* 1(5): 437–443.

35 Plsek, P. E., & Greenhalgh, T. (2001). The challenge of complexity in health care. *British Medical Journal,* 323(7313): 625–628.

36 Capra, F. (1982). The new visions of reality: Parallels between modern physics and eastern mysticism. *India International Centre Quarterly,* 9(1): 13–21.

37 Ardichvili, A. (2012). Sustainability or limitless expansion: Paradigm shift in HRD practice and teaching. *European Journal of Training and Development,* 36(9): 873–887.

38 https://learnnovators.com/blog/6-steps-to-creating-learning-ecosystems-and-why-you-should-bother/

39 e4j (no date). *The learning ecosystem.* Available online: www.ej4.com (accessed 13-01-21); Learnnovators (2016). *6 steps to creating learning ecosystems (and why you should bother).* Available online: https://learnnovators.com/blog/6-steps-to-creating-learning-ecosystems-and-why-you-should-bother/ (accessed 13-01-21).

40 Sprout Labs (no date). A learning ecosystem model. Available online: www.sproutlabs.com.au/blog/a-learning-ecosystem-model/ (accessed 27-01-21).

41 Leeds University Business School (no date). Sociotechnical systems theory. Available online: https://business.leeds.ac.uk/research-stc/doc/socio-technical-systems-theory (accessed 13-01-21).

42 Leavy, B. (2014). Venkat Ramaswamy. How value co-creation with stakeholders is transformative for producers, consumers and society. *Strategy and Leadership,* 42(1): 9–16.

43 Pera, R., Occhiocupo, N., & Clarke, J. (2016). Motives and resources for value co-creation in a multi-stakeholder ecosystem: A managerial perspective. *Journal of Business Research,* 69(10): 4033–4041.

44 Gyrd-Jones, R. I., & Kornum, N. (2013). Managing the co-created brand: Value and cultural complementarity in online and offline multi-stakeholder ecosystems. *Journal of Business Research,* 66(9): 1484–1493; Pera, R., Occhiocupo, N., & Clarke, J. (2016). Motives and resources for value co-creation in a multi-stakeholder ecosystem: A managerial perspective. *Journal of Business Research,* 69(10): 4033–4041.

45 Pera, R., Occhiocupo, N., & Clarke, J. (2016). Motives and resources for value co-creation in a multi-stakeholder ecosystem: A managerial perspective. *Journal of Business Research,* 69(10): 4033–4041.

46 Kellogg, K. C., Orlikowski, W. J., & Yates, J. (2006). Life in the trading zone: Structuring coordination across boundaries in post-bureaucratic organizations. *Organization Science,* 17(1): 22–44.

47 CIPD (2017). Driving the new learning organization. Available online: www.cipd.co.uk/knowledge/strategy/development/learning-organisation-report (accessed 27-01-21).

48 Drucker, P. F. (2011). *The Daily Drucker,* 31 March. Abingdon: Routledge.

49 These guidelines from the *British Medical Journal* offer clear and simple guidance for developing PDPs in the health professions; however the guidelines are generic and could be used by other professional groups, managers, students, etc. Available online: www.bmj.com/content/363/bmj.k4725 (accessed 13-01-21).

Chapter 11

1 Deloitte (2017). *Rewriting the rules for the digital age*. Deloitte University Press.

2 CIPD (2016). Future L&D. Available at: https://www.cipd.co.uk/podcasts/future-ld (accessed 29-01-21).

3 Open University (no date). Take your teaching online. Week 1, Synchronous and asynchronous modes of teaching. Available online: www.open.edu/openlearn/ocw/mod/oucontent/view.php?id=77528&section=1 (accessed 13-01-21).

4 Dhawan, S. (2020). Online learning: A panacea in the time of COVID-19 crisis. *Journal of Educational Technology Systems*, 49(1): 5–22.

5 *Nature* (2020). Online learning cannot just be for those who can afford its technology. *Nature*, 23 September. Available online: www.nature.com/articles/d41586-020-02709-3 (accessed 13-01-21).

6 Skinner, B. F. (2011). Teaching machine and programmed learning. Available online: www.youtube.com/watch?v=jTH3ob1IRFo (accessed 27-01-21).

7 Association for Talent Development (2019). State of the Industry Report. Available online: www.td.org/research-reports/2019-state-of-the-industry (accessed 27-01-21).

8 Fielding, S. (2013). Harold Wilson's white heat speech. *The Guardian*, 20 September. Available online: www.theguardian.com/science/political-science/2013/sep/20/harold-wilson-white-heat-speech (accessed 13-01-21).

9 Reigeluth, C. M. (ed.) (2013). *Instructional-design theories and models: A new paradigm of instructional theory*. Abingdon: Routledge.

10 Clark, R. C., & Mayer, R. E. (2016). *E-learning and the science of instruction: Proven guidelines for consumers and designers of multimedia learning*. John Wiley & Sons.

11 Clark, R. C., & Mayer, R. E. (2016). *E-learning and the science of instruction: Proven guidelines for consumers and designers of multimedia learning*. John Wiley & Sons.

12 Hollender, N., Hofmann, C., Deneke, M., & Schmitz, B. (2010). Integrating cognitive load theory and concepts of human–computer interaction. *Computers in Human Behaviour*, 26(6): 1278–1288.

13 The original saying 'money is a good servant but a bad master' is attributed to the English Elizabethan philosopher and statesman Francis Bacon (1561–1626).

14 CIPD (2017). *The future of technology and learning. CIPD Research Report*. London: CIPD.

15 Bernard, R. M., Abrami, P. C., Lou, Y., Borokhovski, E., Wade, A., Wozney, L., Walet, P. A., Fiset, M., & Huang, B. (2004). How does distance education compare with classroom instruction? A meta-analysis of the empirical literature. *Review of Educational Research*, 74(3): 379–439.

16 CIPD (2017). *The future of technology and learning. CIPD Research Report*. London: CIPD.

17 McKay, F. (2017). Digital in L&D -friend or foe? *People Management*, 31 March. Available online: www.peoplemanagement.co.uk/voices/comment/digital-learning-friend-foe# (accessed 27-01-21).

18 Clark, R. C., & Mayer, R. E. (2016). *E-learning and the science of instruction: Proven guidelines for consumers and designers of multimedia learning*. San Francisco, CA: John Wiley & Sons.

19 Mayer, R. E. (2014). *The Cambridge handbook of multimedia learning*. Cambridge; Cambridge University Press

20 Ausubel, D. P. (1963). *The Psychology of Meaningful Verbal Learning*. New York: Gruene and Stratton.

21 McKay, F. (2017). Digital in L&D -friend or foe? *People Management*, 31 March. Available online: www.peoplemanagement.co.uk/voices/comment/digital-learning-friend-foe# (accessed 27-01-21).

22 Kimiloglu, H., Ozturan, M., & Kutlu, B. (2017). Perceptions about and attitude toward the usage of e-learning in corporate training. *Computers in Human Behavior*, 72: 339–349.

23 Hockly, N. (2018). Blended learning. *Elt Journal*, 72(1): 97–101.

24 Dziuban, C., Graham, C. R., Moskal, P. D., Norberg, A., & Sicilia, N. (2018). Blended learning: The new normal and emerging technologies. *International Journal of Educational Technology in Higher Education*, 15(1): 1–16.

25 Graham, C. R. (2009). Blended learning models. In *Encyclopaedia of Information Science and Technology, Second Edition* (pp. 375–382). IGI Global.

26 Griffiths, M., & Miller, H. (2005). E-mentoring: Does it have a place in medicine? *Postgraduate Medical Journal*, 81: 389–390; Macaffee, D. (2008). E-mentoring: Its pros and cons. *British Medical Journal*, 336. Avalable online: www.bmj.com/content/336/7634/s7 (accessed 27-01-21).

27 Chicca, J., & Shellenbarger, T. (2018). Connecting with Generation Z: Approaches in nursing education. *Teaching and Learning in Nursing*, 13(3): 180–184.

28 Advance HE (no date). Flipped learning. Available online: www.advance-he.ac.uk/knowledge-hub/flipped-learning (accessed 27-01-21).

29 Graham, C. R. (2006). Blended learning systems. In Bonk, C. J. and Graham, C. R. (eds) *The handbook of blended learning: Global perspectives, local designs*. San Francisco: John Wiley and Sons, pp. 3–21.

30 Open University (no date). Blended learning. Available online: www.open.edu/openlearn/ocw/mod/oucontent/view.php?id=77528&section=2 (accessed 27-01-21).

31 Horn, M. and Staker, H. (2012). How much does blended learning cost? Available online: https://thejournal.com/articles/2012/04/05/how-much-does-blended-learning-cost.aspx (accessed 27-01-21).

32 CIPD (2015). *Developing the next generation*. Wimbledon: CIPD.

33 Chaudhuri, S., & Ghosh, R. (2012). Reverse mentoring: A social exchange tool for keeping the boomers engaged and millennials committed. *Human Resource Development Review*, 11(1): 55–76.

34 Leslie, B., Aring, M. K., & Brand, B. (1998). Informal learning: The new frontier of employee & organizational development. *Economic Development Review*, 15(4): 12.

35 Bersin, J. (2018). A new paradigm for corporate training: Learning in the flow of work. Available online: https://joshbersin.com/2018/06/a-new-paradigm-for-corporate-training-learning-in-the-flow-of-work/ (accessed 11-08-21).

36 Clardy, A. (2018). 70-20-10 and the dominance of informal learning: A fact in search of evidence. *Human Resource Development Review*, 17(2): 153–178.

37 This is an old saying that means to discard something valuable (metaphorically speaking, 'the baby') with other things that are undesirable/not valuable ('the dirty bathwater').

38 Johnson, S. J., Blackman, D. A., & Buick, F. (2018). The 70: 20: 10 framework and the transfer of learning. *Human Resource Development Quarterly*, 29(4): 383–402.

39 The final ASTD (now the ATD) state of the industry survey was conducted in 2014. There's little reason to suppose that the proportion of learning that's delivered electronically has done anything but increased significantly; https://onlinelibrary.wiley.com/doi/pdf/10.1111/dsji.12095?casa_token=1g2bP5tYAVAAAAAA:qIK6sPGtIF3cVXVSuiX6Exdgaz4eCGV-bHkNG5aNcwW6LxeFj53BAl6ZZv93LPQF233CH-d6WYHhCt-H

40 Cascio, W. F. (2019). Training trends: Macro, micro, and policy issues. *Human Resource Management Review*, 29(2): 284–297.

41 www.cipd.co.uk/knowledge/fundamentals/people/development/digital-learning-factsheet#6957

42 Rosenbusch, K. (2020). Technology intervention: Rethinking the role of education and faculty in the transformative digital environment. *Advances in Developing Human Resources*, 22(1): 87–101.

43 Faraghaer, J. (2018). Why fresh approaches to L&D are presenting new problems. *People Management*, 25 October.

44 Benedicks, R. (2018). Learning ecosystems. Available online: https://trainingindustry.com/articles/strategy-alignment-and-planning/learning-ecosystems-what-are-they-and-what-can-they-do-for-you/ (accessed 13-01-21); Learnovators (2016) Six steps to creating learning ecosystems. Available online: https://learnnovators.com/blog/6-steps-to-creating-learning-ecosystems-and-why-you-should-bother/ (accessed 13-01-21); Sprout Labs (no date). A learning ecosystem model. Available online: www.sproutlabs.com.au/blog/a-learning-ecosystem-model/ (accessed 27-01-21).

Chapter 12

1 Gubbins, C., Harney, B., van der Werff, L., & Rousseau, D. (2018). Enhancing the trustworthiness and credibility of HRD: Evidence-based management to the rescue? *Human Resource Development Quarterly*, 29(3): 193–202.

2 Proper evaluation is an activity often 'more honoured in the breach than the observance', *Hamlet* Act 1, scene 4, 7–16, meaning a good intention which is more often broken than observed.

3 Torraco, R. J., & Lundgren, H. (2020). What HRD is doing – What HRD should be doing: The case for transforming HRD. *Human Resource Development Review*, 19(1): 39–65.

4 Salas, E., Tannenbaum, S. I., Kraiger, K., & Smith-Jentsch, K. A. (2012). The science of training and development in organizations: What matters in practice. *Psychological Science in the Public Interest*, 13(2): 74–101.

5 Torraco, R. J. (2016). Early history of the fields of practice of training and development and organization development. *Advances in Developing Human Resources*, 18(4): 439–453, p. 440.

6 Dinero, D. (2005). *Training within industry: The foundation of lean*. London: CRC Press, p. 88.

7 Goldstein, I., & Ford, J. K. (2002). *Training in organizations*. Belmont: Wadsworth, p. 177.

8 Nickols, F. W. (2005). Why a stakeholder approach to evaluating training. *Advances in Developing Human Resources*, 7(1): 121–134.

9 Thomas, N. G. (1995). Stakeholders and strategic human resource development. *Journal of European Industrial Training*, 19(10): 11–16.

10 Preskill, H., & Martineau, J. (2004). Learning from evaluation: A conversation with Hallie Preskill. *Leadership in Action*, 23(6): 9–12.

11 Ruona, W. E., & Gilley, J. W. (2009). Practitioners in applied professions: A model applied to human resource development. *Advances in Developing Human Resources*, 11(4): 438–453.

12 Tseng, C. C., & McLean, G. N. (2008). Strategic HRD practices as key factors in organizational learning. *Training*, 32(6): 418–432.

13 Kirkpatrick, D. L. (1996). Invited reaction: Reaction to Holton article. *Human Resource Development Quarterly*, 7(1): 23–25, pp. 23–24.

14 For a review of other evaluation taxonomies see Sadler-Smith, E. (2006). *Learning and development for managers*. Oxford: Blackwell.

15 Van Buren, M. E., & Erskine, W. (2002). *The 2002 ASTD state of the industry report*. Alexandria, VA: American Society of Training and Development; for a more recent survey see: www.td.org/insights/l-ds-struggle-with-learning-evaluation

16 Association for Psychological Science (2003). In appreciation: Raymond A Katzell. Available online: www.psychologicalscience.org/observer/in-appreciation-raymond-a-katzell (accessed 27-01-21).

17 Work-Learning research (2018). Donald Kirkpatrick was not the originator of the four-level evaluation model of learning evaluation. Available online: www.worklearning.com/2018/01/30/donald-kirkpatrick-was-not-the-originator-of-the-four-level-model-of-learning-evaluation/ (accessed 27-01-21).

18 Holton III, E. F., & Naquin, S. (2005). A critical analysis of HRD evaluation models from a decision-making perspective. *Human Resource Development Quarterly*, 16(2): 257–280.

19 Kirkpatrick, D. L. (1979). Techniques for evaluating training programs. *Training and Development Journal*, 33(6): 78–92, p. 78.

20 Alliger, G. M., Tannenbaum, S. I., Bennett Jr, W., Traver, H., & Shotland, A. (1997). A meta-analysis of the relations among training criteria. *Personnel Psychology*, 50(2): 341–358.

21 Goldstein, I., & Ford, J. K. (2002). *Training in organizations*. Belmont: Wadsworth.

22 Alliger, G. M., & Janak, E. A. (1989). Kirkpatrick's levels of training criteria: Thirty years later. *Personnel Psychology*, 42(2): 331–342.

23 Kirkpatrick, J. (no date). The new world level 1 reaction sheets, Available online: www.kirkpatrickpartners.com/ (accessed 27-01-21).

24 Kirkpatrick, D. L. (2006). Seven keys to unlock the four levels of evaluation. *Performance Improvement*, 45(7): 5–8.

25 Goldstein, I., & Ford, J. K. (2002). *Training in organizations*. Belmont: Wadsworth.

26 Kirkpatrick Partners (no date). The Kirkpatrick methodology – a brief history, and The new world Kirkpatrick model. Available online: www.kirkpatrickpartners.com/Our-Philosophy/The-New-World-Kirkpatrick-Model (accessed 13-01-21).

27 Goldstein, I., & Ford, J. K. (2002). *Training in organizations*. Belmont: Wadsworth.

28 Holton III, E. F. (1996). The flawed four-level evaluation model. *Human Resource Development Quarterly*, 7(1): 5–21.

29 Watkins, K. E., Marsick, V. J., & Fernández de Álava, M. (2014). Evaluating informal learning in the workplace. In T. Halttunen, M. Koivisto, & S. Billett (eds) *Promoting, assessing, recognizing, & certifying lifelong learning: International perspectives and practices*. Berlin, Germany: Springer-Verlag, p. 71

30 Krathwohl, D. R. (2002). A revision of Bloom's taxonomy: An overview. *Theory into Practice*, 41(4): 212–218.

31 McCarthy, A., & Garavan, T. N. (2008). Team learning and metacognition: A neglected area of HRD research and practice. *Advances in Developing Human Resources*, 10(4): 509–524.

32 Johnston, J. (2016) E-learning with Bloom's taxonomy. Available online: www.youtube.com/watch?v=XJWFQI4TV5E (accessed 27-01-21).

33 American Psychological Association (no date). APA dictionary of psychology, 'skill'. Available online: https://dictionary.apa.org/skill (accessed 27-01-21).

34 Phillips, P., Phillips, J. J., Stone, R., & Burkett, H. (2006). *The ROI Fieldbook*. Abingdon: Routledge.

35 Brown, M., Syrysko, P., Sharples, S., Shaw, D., Jeune, I. L., Fioratou, E., & Blakey, J. (2013). Developing a simulator to help junior doctors deal with night shifts. In Andersen, M. (ed) *Contemporary ergonomics and human factors*, pp. 289–296. Routledge in association with GSE Research.

36 Mentice (no date). Improve patient outcomes. Available online: www.mentice.com/ (accessed 27-01-21).

37 DeMasi, S. C., Katsuta, E., & Takabe, K. (2016). Live animals for preclinical medical student surgical training. *Edorium Journal of Surgery*, 3(2): 24–31.

38 Gagné, R. M. (1985). *Conditions of learning and theory of instruction*. New York: Holt, Rinehart and Winston, pp. 221–222.

39 Kostusev, D. (2019). How to use big data to improve corporate training. *Forbes*, 22 February. Available online: www.forbes.com/sites/forbesbusinessdevelopmentcouncil/2019/02/22/how-to-use-big-data-to-improve-corporate-training/#346111476e8c (accessed 27-01-21).

40 Burrow, J., & Berardinelli, P. (2003). Systematic performance improvement – refining the space between learning and results. *The Journal of Workplace Learning*, 15(1): 6–13.

41 Brinkerhoff, R. O. (2006). Increasing impact of training investments: An evaluation strategy for building organizational learning capability. *Industrial and Commercial Training*, 38(6): 302–307.

42 Brinkerhoff, R. (2003). *The success case method: Find out quickly what's working and what's not*. San Francisco: Berrett-Koehler Publishers; Brinkerhoff, R. O. (2005). The success case method: A strategic evaluation approach to increasing the value and effect of training. *Advances in Developing Human Resources*, 7(1): 86–101; Brinkerhoff, R. O. (2006). *Telling training's story*. San Francisco, CA: Berrett Koehler Publishing.

43 Brinkerhoff, R. O. (2005). The success case method: A strategic evaluation approach to increasing the value and effect of training. *Advances in Developing Human Resources*, 7(1): 86–101.

44 Garavan, T., McCarthy, A., Lai, Y., Murphy, K., Sheehan, M., & Carbery, R. (2020). Training and organisational performance: A meta-analysis of temporal, institutional, and organisational context moderators. *Human Resource Management Journal*, 31(1): 93–119.

45 Holton, E. F., & Baldwin, T. T. (2000). Making transfer happen: An action perspective on learning transfer systems. *Advances in Developing Human Resources*, 8(2): 1–6, p.4

46 Werner, J. M., & DeSimone, R. L. (2011). *Human resource development*. Mason, OH: Cengage Learning. pp. 218–219.

47 Kirkpatrick, D. L. and Kirkpatrick, J. D. (2006). *Evaluating training programs: The four levels*. San Francisco: Berrett-Koehler.

48 Matthews, P. (2013). Training evaluation in this new world. *Training Journal*, 21 August. Available online: www.trainingjournal.com/blog/training-evaluation-new-world (accessed 27-01-21).

49 Internal (e.g. HRD practitioners) advantages include: Insider knowledge; more efficient in design/executing evaluation; quicker and easier access to information/stakeholders; costs kept in-house. On the down side: less able to bring as much objectivity to the process as an outsider; vested interests; conflicts of interest. External (e.g. consultants, academics) advantages include: may be able to be more objective and detached; have less at stake; be able to bring a fresh pair of eyes; external perspective; state of the art technical skills. On the down side: likely to have a steeper learning curve with respect to understanding organization-specific issues and concerns.

50 Phillips, J. J. (2003). *Return on investment*. Burlington, MA: Butterworth Heinemann, p. 242.

51 Kirkpatrick, D. L., & Kirkpatrick, J. D. (2006). *Evaluating training programs: The four levels*. San Francisco: Berrett-Koehler, p. 334.

52 Phillips, J. J. (2003). *Return on investment*. Burlington, MA: Butterworth Heinemann, p. 47.

53 Phillips, J. J., & Phillips, P. P. (2005). *ROI at work: Best practice case studies from the real world*. Alexandria, VA: ASTD.

54 Kim, H., & Cervero, R. M. (2007). How power relations structure the evaluation process for HRD programmes. *Human Resource Development International*, 10(1): 5–20.

55 www.td.org/insights/l-ds-struggle-with-learning-evaluation

56 Brinkerhoff, R. O. (2005). The success case method: A strategic evaluation approach to increasing the value and effect of training. *Advances in Developing Human Resources*, 7(1): 86–101; Brinkerhoff, R. O. (2006). Telling training's story. San Francisco, CA: Berrett-Koehler Publisher, p. 25.

57 Brinkerhoff, R. O. (1997). Invited reaction: Response to parsons. *Human Resource Development Quarterly*, 8(1): 15.

58 Kirkpatrick Partners (no date). Kirkpatrick foundational principles. Available online: www.kirkpatrickpartners.com/Our-Philosophy/Kirkpatrick-Foundational-Principles (accessed 27-01-21).

59 Bates, R. (2004). A critical analysis of evaluation practice: The Kirkpatrick model and the principle of beneficence. *Evaluation and program planning*, 27(3): 341–347; Reio, T. G., Rocco, T. S., Smith, D. H., & Chang, E. (2017). A critique of Kirkpatrick's evaluation model. *New Horizons in Adult Education and Human Resource Development*, 29(2): 35–53.

60 Holton III, E. F. (2005). Holton's evaluation model: New evidence and construct elaborations. *Advances in Developing Human Resources*, 7(1): 37–54, p. 37.

61 Brinkerhoff, R. O. (2005). The success case method: A strategic evaluation approach to increasing the value and effect of training. *Advances in Developing Human Resources*, 7(1): 86–101, p. 90.

62 Bierema, L. L. (2009). Critiquing human resource development's dominant masculine rationality and evaluating its impact. *Human Resource Development Review*, 8(1): 68–96.

63 Dweck, C. (2016). What having a 'growth mindset' actually means. *Harvard Business Review*, 13: 213–226.

64 Chalofsky, N. (2003). An emerging construct for meaningful work. *Human Resource Development International*, 6(1): 69–83.

65 Lewis, M. W., & Smith, W. K. (2014). Paradox as a metatheoretical perspective: Sharpening the focus and widening the scope. *The Journal of Applied Behavioral Science*, 50(2): 127–149.

Chapter 13

1 De Geus, A. (1988). Planning as learning. *Harvard Business Review*, March–April: 70–74; Robinson, G. (2020). An appreciation of Arie de Geus' contribution to the learning organization. *The Learning Organization*, 27(5): 429–440.

2 De Geus, A. (1997). *The living company: Habits for survival in a turbulent business environment*. Boston, MA: Harvard Business School Press.

3 Popper, M., & Lipshitz, R. (2000). Organizational learning: Mechanisms, culture, and feasibility. *Management Learning*, 31(2): 181–196.

4 Holiday, R. (2017). The 25 businesses will surprise you with how old they are. *Observer*, 23 August. Available online: https://observer.com/2017/08/these-25-businesses-will-surprise-you-with-how-old-they-are-fiskars-zildjian-harpercollins-craigslist-nintendo-kikkoman/ (accessed 27-01-21).

5 Nintendo Job Portal. www.nintendo.co.uk/Corporate/Career/About-Nintendo/About-Nintendo-825979.html (accessed 27-01-21).

6 Wolfe, D. (2019). Does your organization have an effective learning culture? Strategies to consider. *Forbes Magazine*, 10 July. Available online: www.forbes.com/sites/forbeshumanresourcescouncil/2019/07/10/does-your-organization-have-an-effective-learning-culture-key-strategies-to-consider/#3c1a4f9b3ada (accessed 13-01-21); Pathgather (2018). What is a learning ecosystem? Available online: www.pathgather.com/what-is-a-learning-ecosystem/ (accessed 27-01-21).

7 CIPD (2017). *Driving the New Learning Organization*. London: CIPD. www.cipd.co.uk/Images/driving-the-new-learning-organisation_2017-how-to-unlock-the-potential-of-Land-d_tcm18-21557.pdf (accessed 27-02-20). Also podcast script available at: www.cipd.co.uk/podcasts/new-learning-organisation (accessed 27-02-20).

8 3M history (no date). www.3m.com/3M/en_US/company-us/about-3m/history/ (accessed 27-01-21).

9 *Oxford dictionary of psychology*. Oxford: Oxford University Press, p. 440.

10 The mental models global laboratory. Available online: www.modeltheory.org/about/what-are-mental-models/#1567056429041-e8d98f8d-83e2 (accessed 27-01-21).

11 De Geus, A. (1997). *The living company: Habits for survival in a turbulent business environment*. Boston, MA: Harvard Business School Press.

12 The website of the best-selling author James Clear has a list of commonly used mental models from many different areas of life. Available online: https://jamesclear.com/ (accessed 13-01-21).

13 Harmon, S. (2020). Mental models and metaphors. *Forbes*, 11 June. Available online www.forbes.com/sites/harmoncullinan/2020/06/11/mental-models-and-metaphors-how-to-stay-on-the-same-page-when-youre-not-in-the-same-place/ (accessed 27-01-21).

14 Mohammed, S., Klimoski, R., & Rentsch, J. R. (2000). The measurement of team mental models: We have no shared schema. *Organizational Research Methods*, 3(2): 123–165.

15 Johnson, H. H. (2008). Mental models and transformative learning: The key to leadership development?. *Human Resource Development Quarterly*, 19(1): 85–89.

16 Pil, F. K., & Holweg, M. (2003). Exploring scale: The advantages of thinking small. *MIT Sloan Management Review*, 44(2): 33–39.

17 Cherry, K. (2019). The role of a schema in psychology. Available online: www.verywellmind.com/what-is-a-schema-2795873 (accessed 26-02-20).

18 *Psychology Today* (no date). Groupthink. Available online: www.psychologytoday.com/gb/basics/groupthink (accessed 27-01-21).

19 Reese, S. R. (2020). Wiser: Getting beyond groupthink to make groups smarter. *The Learning Organization*, 27(2): 181–184.

20 Nelson, R. R., & Winter, S. G. (1982). The Schumpeterian trade-off revisited. *The American Economic Review*, 72(1): 114–132.

21 Brian Pentland explaining the basic features of organizational routines. www.youtube.com/watch?v=UAA0kw1zZoA; Feldman, M. S., & Pentland, B. T. (2003). Reconceptualizing organizational routines as a source of flexibility and change. *Administrative Science Quarterly*, 48(1): 94–118.

22 Sadler-Smith, E., Spicer, D. P., & Chaston, I. (2001). Learning orientations and growth in smaller firms. *Long Range Planning*, 34(2): 139–158.

23 Fiol, M., & O'Connor, E. (2017). Unlearning established organizational routines – Part I. *Learning Organization*, 24(1): 13–29, p. 16.

24 Argyris, C. (1992). Overcoming organizational defences. *The Journal for Quality and Participation*, 15(2): 26.

25 Weick, K. E., & Wesley, F. (1996). Organizational learning: affirming an oxymoron. In Clegg, S. R., Hardy, C., & Nord, W. R. (eds) *Handbook of organizational studies*. London: SAGE.

26 Fiol, C. M., & Lyles, M. A. (1985). Organizational learning. *Academy of Management Review*, 10(4): 803–813.

27 Easterby-Smith, M., & Lyles, M. (2005). Introduction. In Easterby-Smith, M. & Lyles, M. (eds) *The Blackwell handbook of organizational learning and knowledge management*. Oxford: Blackwell, p. 9.

28 Huber, G. P. (1991). Organizational learning: The contributing processes and the literatures. *Organization Science*, 2(1): 88–115.

29 Levitt, B., & March, J. G. (1988). Organizational learning. *Annual Review of Sociology*, 14(1): 319–338.

30 Uotila, J., Maula, M., Keil, T., & Zahra, S. A. (2009). Exploration, exploitation, and financial performance: Analysis of S&P 500 corporations. *Strategic Management Journal*, 30(2): 221–231.

31 March, J. G. (1991). Exploration and exploitation in organizational learning. *Organization Science*, 2(1): 71–87.

32 For more on organizational learning and the learning organization as a paradox, see: Vince, R. (2018). The learning organization as paradox: Being for the learning organization also means being against it. *The Learning Organization*, 25(4): 273–280.

33 Crooks, E. (2019). The week in energy: Big Oil faces the energy transition. *Financial Times*, 25 May. Available online: www.ft.com/content/4523afd8-7e73-11e9-81d2-f785092ab560 (accessed 27-01-21).

34 Fiol, C. M., & Lyles, M. A. (1985). Organizational learning. *Academy of Management Review*, 10(4): 803–813.

35 Senge, P. M. (1990). *The fifth discipline: The art and practice of the learning organization*. London: Century.

36 Schön, D., & Argyris, C. (1996). *Organizational learning II: Theory, method and practice*. Reading: Addison Wesley, p. 16.

37 Crossan, M. M., Lane, H. W., & White, R. E. (1999). An organizational learning framework: From intuition to institution. *Academy of Management Review*, 24(3): 522–537, p. 525.

38 Easterby-Smith, M., Araujo, L., & Burgoyne, J. (eds) (1999). *Organizational learning and the learning organization: Developments in theory and practice*. London: SAGE, p. 4.

39 Tosey, P., Visser, M., & Saunders, M. N. (2012). The origins and conceptualizations of 'triple-loop' learning: A critical review. *Management Learning*, 43(3): 291–307.

Chapter 14

1 https://obamawhitehouse.archives.gov/the-press-office/remarks-president-barack-obama-address-joint-session-congress

2   OECD (no date). *The knowledge economy*. Available online: www.oecd.org/naec/the-knowledge-economy.pdf (accessed 27-01-21).

3   Grant, R.M. (2002). The knowledge-based view of the firm. In Choo, C. W., & Bontis, N. (eds) *The strategic management of intellectual capital and organizational knowledge*. Oxford: Oxford University Press, pp. 133–148.

4   Zheng, W., Yang, B., & McLean, G. N. (2010). Linking organizational culture, structure, strategy, and organizational effectiveness: Mediating role of knowledge management. *Journal of Business Research*, 63(7): 763–771, p. 764.

5   *Daily Telegraph* (2019). Making sense of the knowledge economy. Daily Telegraph, 23 May. Available online: www.telegraph.co.uk/business/tips-for-the-future/the-knowledge-economy/ (accessed 26-02-20).

6   Nonaka, I. (1991). The knowledge-creating company. *Harvard Business Review*, November–December: 96–104.

7   De Geus, A. (2002). *The living company*. Cambridge, MA: Harvard Business Press.

8   Desouza, K. C., & Awazu, Y. (2003). Knowledge management. *HR Magazine*. Available online: www.shrm.org/hr-today/news/hr-magazine/pages/1103desouza.aspx (accessed 27-01-21).

9   CIPD (2020). The new profession map. Available online: https://peopleprofession.cipd.org/Images/full-standards-download-v2_tcm29-50113.pdf (accessed 27-01-21).

10 McGurk, J., & Baron, A. (2012). Knowledge management-time to focus on purpose and motivation. *Strategic HR Review*, 11(6): 316–321.

11 von Krogh, G., Ichijo, K., & Nonaka, I. (2000). *Enabling knowledge creation: How to unlock the mystery of tacit knowledge and release the power of innovation*. Oxford: Oxford University Press.

12 Davenport, T. H., & Prusak, L. (1998). *Working knowledge: How organizations manage what they know*. Cambridge, MA: Harvard Business Press.

13 Malhotra, Y. (ed.) (2000). *Knowledge management and virtual organizations*. IGI Global; Quintas, P., Lefrere, P., & Jones, G. (1997). Knowledge management: A strategic agenda. *Long Range Planning*, 30(3): 385–391.

14 Polanyi, M. (1966). *The tacit dimension*. Chicago: The University of Chicago Press.

15 Nye, M. J. (2002). HYLE biographies: Michael Polanyi (1891–1976). *International Journal for Philosophy of Chemistry*, 8(2): 123–127.

16 Goffin, K., Koners, U., Baxter, D., & Van der Hoven, C. (2010). Managing lessons learned and tacit knowledge in new product development. *Research-Technology Management*, 53(4): 39–51.

17 Reber, A. S. (1993). *Implicit learning and tacit knowledge: An essay on the cognitive unconscious*. New York: Oxford University Press.

18 Heisig, P. (2009). Harmonisation of knowledge management-comparing 160 KM frameworks around the globe. *Journal of Knowledge Management*, 13: 4–31.

19 Wang, P., Zhu, F. W., Song, H. Y., Hou, J. H., & Zhang, J. L. (2018). Visualizing the academic discipline of knowledge management. *Sustainability*, 10(3): 1–28.

20 Safian, R. (2018). Why Apple is the world's most innovative company. *Fast Company Magazine*, 21 February. Available online: www.fastcompany.com/40525409/why-apple-is-the-worlds-most-innovative-company (accessed 27-01-21).

21 Nonaka, I., Toyama, R., Byosiere, Ph. (2001). A theory of organizational knowledge creation: Understanding the dynamic process of creating knowledge. In Dierkes, M., Antal, A.B., Child, J., & Nonaka, I. (eds) *Handbook of organizational learning and knowledge*, pp. 487–491. Oxford: Oxford University Press. Oxford.

22 Takeuchi , H., & Shibata, T. (eds) (2006) *Japan, moving towards a more advanced knowledge economy*. Washington: World Bank, p. 84.

23 Teece, D. (2008). Foreword: From the management of R and D to knowledge. In: Nonaka, I, Toyama, R. & Hirata, T. (eds) *Managing flow: A process theory of the knowledge-based firm*. New York: Palgrave Macmillan, pp. ix–xvii.

24 Leonard, D., & Sensiper, S. (1998). The role of tacit knowledge in group innovation. *California Management Review*, 40(3): 112–132.

25 Glisby, M., & Holden, N. (2003). Contextual constraints in knowledge management theory: The cultural embeddedness of Nonaka's knowledge-creating company. *Knowledge and Process Management*, 10(1): 29–36.

26 Takeuchi, H. (2006). *Japan, moving towards a more advanced knowledge economy*. Washington: World Bank. The 'systems thinking' to which Takeuchi is referring is Peter Senge's fifth discipline, see Senge, P. M. (1990). *The fifth discipline*. New York: Doubleday.

27 Hong, J. F. (2012). Glocalizing Nonaka's knowledge creation model: Issues and challenges. *Management Learning*, 43(2): 199–215.

28 Cook, S. D., & Brown, J. S. (1999). Bridging epistemologies: The generative dance between organizational knowledge and organizational knowing. *Organization Science*, 10(4): 381–400.

29 Tsoukas, H. (2005). What do we really understand about tacit knowledge? In Easterby-Smith, M. and Lyles, M. (eds) *The Blackwell handbook of organizational learning and knowledge management*. Oxford: Blackwell, pp. 410–427; Tsoukas, H., & Vladimirou, E. (2001). What is organizational knowledge? *Journal of Management Studies*, 38(7): 973–993.

30 Sieloff, C. G. (1999). 'If only HP knew what HP knows': The roots of knowledge management at Hewlett-Packard. *Journal of Knowledge Management*, 3(1): 47–53.

31 Easterby-Smith, M. and Lyles, M. (2005) Introduction. In Easterby-Smith, M. & Lyles, M. (eds) *The Blackwell handbook of organizational learning and knowledge management*, Oxford: Blackwell, p. 4.

32 Calhoun, M., Starbuck, W. H., & Abrahamson, E. (2011). Fads, fashions and the fluidity of knowledge: Peter Senge's The Learning Organization'. In Easterby-Smith, M. and Lyles, M. (eds) *The Blackwell handbook of organizational learning and knowledge management*, 2nd edition. Oxford: Blackwell, pp. 225–248.

33 Pedler, M., & Burgoyne, J. G. (2017). Is the learning organisation still alive? *Learning Organization*, 24(2): 119–126.

34 Calhoun, M., Starbuck, W. H., & Abrahamson, E. (2011). Fads, fashions and the fluidity of knowledge: Peter Senge's The Learning Organization'. In Easterby-Smith, M. and Lyles, M. (eds) *The Blackwell handbook of organizational learning and knowledge management*, 2nd edition. Oxford: Blackwell, pp. 225–248.

35 Garvin, D. A., Edmondson, A. C., & Gino, F. (2008). Is yours a learning organization? *Harvard Business Review*, 86(3): 109–116.

36 Gibbs, R. (2020). Four positive effects of fostering a learning organization. *Forbes*, 5 June. Available online: www.forbes.com/sites/forbescoachescouncil/2020/06/05/four-positive-effects-of-fostering-a-learning-organization/#59e3e73b2b09 (accessed 27-01-21).

37 CIPD (2017). Driving the new learning organization. London: CIPD. Available online: www.cipd.co.uk/Images/driving-the-new-learning-organisation_2017-how-to-unlock-the-potential-of-Land-d_tcm18-21557.pdf (accessed 27-01-21)

38 Grossman, R. J. (2015). How to create a learning culture. *HR Magazine*, 1 May. Available online: www.shrm.org/hr-today/news/hr-magazine/pages/0515-learning-culture.aspx (accessed 27-01-21).

39 Garratt, B. (1997). *The learning organization*. London: HarperCollins.

40 Senge, P. M. (no date). Faculty pages, MIT. https://mitsloan.mit.edu/faculty/directory/peter-m-senge

41 Schuyler, K. G. (2017). Peter Senge: 'Everything that we do is about shifting the capability for collective action…'. Available online: https://link.springer.com/referenceworkentry/10.1007%2F978-3-319-49820-1_100-1 (accessed 27-01-21).

42 Senge, P., Scharmer, C. O., Jaworski, J., & Flowers, B. S. (2004). *Presence: Human purpose and the field of the purpose*. Cambridge, MA: The Society for Organizational Learning.

43 Yang, B., Watkins, K. E., & Marsick, V. J. (2004). The construct of the learning organization: Dimensions, measurement, and validation. *Human Resource Development Quarterly*, 15(1): 31–55.

44 Örtenblad, A. (2015). Towards increased relevance: Context-adapted models of the learning organization. *The Learning Organization*, 22(3): 163–181; Schein, E. H. (1999). Empowerment, coercive persuasion and organizational learning: Do they connect? *Learning Organization*, 6(4): 163–172.

45   Popper, M., & Lipshitz, R. (2000). Organizational learning: Mechanisms, culture, and feasibility. *Management Learning*, 31(2): 181–196.

46   Örtenblad, A. (2002). A typology of the idea of learning organization. *Management Learning*, 33(2): 213–230.

47   Pedler, M., & Hsu, S. W. (2019). Regenerating the learning organisation: Towards an alternative paradigm.*The Learning Organization*, 26(1): 97–112.

48   Coopey, J. (1995). The learning organization, power, politics and ideology introduction. *Management Learning*, 26(2): 193–213.

49   Contu, A., Grey, C., & Örtenblad, A. (2003). Against learning. *Human Relations*, 56(8): 931–952.

50   Contu, A., Grey, C., & Örtenblad, A. (2003). Against learning. *Human Relations*, 56(8): 931–952.

51   Poell, R. (1999). The learning organisation: A critical evaluation. In Wilson, J. P. (ed.) *Human resource development: Learning and training for individuals and organisations*. London: Kogan Page.

52   Mak, C., & Hong, J. (2020). Creating learning organization 2.0: A contextualized and multi-stakeholder approach. *The Learning Organization*, 27(3): 235–248.

53   Weick, K. E., & Wesley, F. (1996) 'Organizational learning: affirming an oxymoron'. In Clegg, S. R., Hardy, C., & Nord, W. R. (eds) *Handbook of organizational studies*. London: SAGE.

54   Vince, R. (2018). The learning organization as paradox: Being for the learning organization also means being against it. *The Learning Organization*, 25(4): 273–280.

55   Pedler, M., Burgoyne, J.G., & Boydell, T. (1991). *The learning company*. Maidenhead: McGraw Hill.

56   Hong, J., & Mak, C. (2019). The empire strikes back: How learning organization scholars can learn from the critiques. *The Oxford handbook of the learning organization*. Oxford: Oxford University Press, pp. 356–367.

57   Pedler, M., & Hsu, S. W. (2019). Regenerating the learning organisation: Towards an alternative paradigm.*The Learning Organization*, 26(1): 97–112.

58   CIPD (2017). Driving the new learning organization. London: CIPD. Available online: www.cipd.co.uk/Images/driving-the-new-learning-organisation_2017-how-to-unlock-the-potential-of-Land-d_tcm18-21557.pdf (accessed 27-01-21).

59   Shin, H., Picken, J., & Dess, G. (2017). Revisiting the learning organization. *Organizational Dynamics*, 1(46): 46–56.

60   Horwitz, F. M., Heng, C. T., & Quazi, H. A. (2003). Finders, keepers? Attracting, motivating and retaining knowledge workers. *Human Resource Management Journal*, 13(4): 23–44.

61   Spender, J. C., & Grant, R. M. (1996). Knowledge and the firm: Overview. *Strategic Management Journal*, 17(S2): 5–9.

62   Tian, X. (2017). Big data and knowledge management: A case of déjà vu or back to the future? *Journal of Knowledge Management*, 21(1): 113–131.

63   Statler, M. (2014). Developing wisdom in a business school? Critical reflections on pedagogical practice. *Management Learning*, 45(4): 397–417.

64   Statler, M., & Küpers, W. (eds) (2019). *Leadership and wisdom: Lessons from folklore*. Abingdon: Routledge, p. 13.

65   Sternberg, R. J. (2003). *Wisdom, intelligence, and creativity synthesized*. Cambridge, England: Cambridge University Press.

66   Zigarmi, D., Roberts, T. P., & Shuck, B. (2018). Motivation and internal frames of reference: Do we have the wisdom to help employees flourish at work? *Advances in Developing Human Resources*, 20(2): 127–132.

67   Koltko-Rivera, M. E. (2006). Rediscovering the later version of Maslow's hierarchy of needs: Self-transcendence and opportunities for theory, research, and unification. *Review of General Psychology*, 10(4): 302–317.

68   Lundberg, A, & Westerman, G. (2020). The transformer CLO. *Harvard Business Review*, January–February. Available online: https://hbr.org/2020/01/the-transformer-clo (accessed 27-01-21).

INDEX

Note: Page numbers in *italics* refer to figures.